THE
Art Lover's Almanac

Serious Trivia for the Novice
and the Connoisseur

Helen D. Hum

JOSSEY-BASS
A Wiley Imprint
www.josseybass.com

Published by Jossey-Bass
A Wiley Imprint
989 Market Street, San Francisco, CA 94103-1741   www.josseybass.com

The clip art in this book is from Art Explosion by Nova Development Corporation.

Jossey-Bass books and products are available through most bookstores. To contact Jossey-Bass directly, call our Customer Care Department within the U.S. at (800) 956-7739, outside the U.S. at (317) 572-3993 or fax (317) 572-4002.

Jossey-Bass also publishes its books in a variety of electronic formats. Some content that appears in print may not be available in electronic books.

Library of Congress Cataloging-in-Publication Data
Hume, Helen D., 1933–
   The art lover's almanac : serious trivia for the novice and the connoisseur / Helen D. Hume.
      p. cm.
   Includes index.
      ISBN 0-7879-6714-9 (pbk.)
      1. Art—Encyclopedias.   I. Title.
      N31.H86 2003
      703—dc21   2003013856

Printed in the United States of America
FIRST EDITION
PB Printing 10 9 8 7 6 5 4 3 2 1

Dedication

To my friends and family
Each and every one is of vast importance to me

To Margaret and Joe,
Hope you enjoy reading and
sharing information about art.
Fondly,
Helen Hume

Acknowledgments

Years of travel, teaching art and art history, reading, researching, and of course conversation with friends, family, fellow artists, and professional colleagues have contributed to the scope of this book. At numerous National Art Education Conferences in the United States, museum professionals have introduced us to their own collections and I shall forever be indebted to the St. Louis Art Museum's educational staff for enabling me to talk and write about art. It is a joy to pass on the information I have gleaned from so many different people and places.

For their input in the fields in which they are experts, I want to thank Sylvia and Ron Tapley, Betty Anderson, Peter Trueblood, LuWayne Younghans, Pat Palmer, Susan Hume, John Baker, Susan Rodriguez, John Dunivent, Shirley and Farrel Schell, Dr. Thomas Pfizenmeier, Wayne Younger, Lydia Ash, Jim Crow, Karin Breuer, prints and drawings curator at the San Francisco Fine Arts Museums, and Juliana Yuan, professor of Asian art at the University of Missouri, St. Louis.

My grateful appreciation to the librarians in the St. Louis Art Museum: Clare Vasquez, Cheryl Vogler, and Stephanie Sigala, who have been so completely supportive, and the entire Educational Staff, including former director Dr. Elizabeth Vallance. Tim Willman and Mary Frechette of the St. Louis Library Fine Arts Room have enthusiastically joined in the chase to provide information.

My everlasting gratitude to the professionals who have contributed so much to the development of the book. For their confidence, friendship, and encouragement, I especially want to thank Connie Kallback, Win Huppuch, Susan Kolwicz, and Debbie Yost. For the great care with which they shepherded the manuscript through the production process, my appreciation to editors Sharon L. Gonzalez, Gloria Fuzia, Mary Hogan Hearle, Mariann Hutlak, Diane Turso, and Carolyn Uno; to designer Anne Ricigliano; and to other staff members at Jossey-Bass: Leslie Iura, Sachie Jones, Elisa Rassen, Pam Berkman, and Steven Thompson.

Introduction

Art lovers come in all ages, cultures, and educational backgrounds. They don't necessarily agree on what art is, but they know what they like! This *Art Lover's Almanac* gives an overview of where to find art, who makes it, and how to enjoy it. It includes quotations, definitions, locations, illustrations, precautions, and suggestions.

The definition of *fine art,* perhaps, is that it serves no purpose other than to be appreciated. This does not, however, include the practical applications of such "art objects" as buildings, woven objects, or pottery.

In common with most readers, I enjoy a book with a good plot, but when reading books on art, I often find myself going to the backs of the books to get information in the concise format seen here. The book is divided into chapters about specific areas of art such as painting, drawing, sculpture, or about specific interests such as architecture or collecting.

As an artist, educator, art historian, and tourist, one of my great pleasures in the world of art has been going to galleries and museums whenever and wherever I have the opportunity.

The lists are the result of many conversations with artists, collectors, dealers, museum professionals, fellow art educators, and friends who also travel widely. I've tried to share the things that I find to be profound, interesting, useful, and fun.

About the Author

An artist and art educator, Helen D. Hume has studied and taught art history, sculpture, photography, painting, and graphic arts in the United States, Europe, and South America. Currently teaching art methods at Fontbonne University in St. Louis, Hume continues as an exhibiting artist in individual and group shows. An active member of the St. Louis Artists' Guild for more than 25 years, she was honored as Missouri's Higher Art Educator of the Year in 2001, as well as in Marquis's *Who's Who of American Women*. She has written for art education publications and has been a contributing writer and researcher for the St. Louis Art Museum's Educational Resource Center. She has written five other books, including two art history books for art educators.

Contents

CHAPTER 3.   ART FROM MANY CULTURES   157

CHAPTER 9. SCULPTURE 539

CHAPTER 10. ARCHITECTURE 605

THE
Art Lover's Almanac

CHAPTER 1

About Art

"Art still has truth, take refuge there."
—MATTHEW ARNOLD, 1822–1888, English poet and critic

75 ART TERMS TO KNOW

These art terms are some of the words you read in art reviews, or hear at art openings. If you truly want to be comfortable in art circles, these are the ones you'll need to know. They will help you chat away with confidence through any art opening. Terms related to specialties such as sculpture, painting, architecture, or drawing are in those sections later in the book.

Abstract. An artwork that is not realistic, though it is often based on an actual subject. The technique of abstraction came into vogue in the 20th century and is still among the most controversial art forms.

Academic art. Art that follows prescribed rules; not experimental. Art training in an Academy formerly led to realistic, conservative artwork. Since the early 20th century, however, even artists with formal training sometimes see rules as made to be broken.

Acrylic. A water-based paint developed in the 1950s that may be applied thinly like watercolor or thickly like oil paint, and will adhere to almost any surface. It is sometimes used as an underpainting for oil paint. Many contemporary paintings are painted in acrylic.

Aesthetic. Aesthetics is the philosophy of what is considered beautiful in art based on social, visual, and contemporary standards. Each society or culture may have a different idea of what is aesthetically pleasing, depending on its customs or visual standards.

Appropriation art. A scene or subject "borrowed" from another, generally famous, artwork but changed slightly so as not to be considered a copy or forgery.

Archaic art. Art in its most ancient form, usually Greek sculpture or vases from 620 to 500 B.C.

Art brut. Literally "crude art," created by untutored artists such as criminals or the insane who feel driven to express themselves through art. Also known as Outsider Art.

Avant garde. Anything that is at the forefront of new expressions or developments in art.

Balance. Gives stability (equilibrium) to a composition; can be either symmetrical (the same on either side of an imaginary middle dividing line) or asymmetrical (unequal objects yet of equal weight).

Bas-relief. Also called low-relief, this is one-sided sculpture that projects slightly from a background.

Camp. Artwork deliberately created to be amusing because of its affected characteristics, or out-of-date, exaggerated subject matter. The work of Gilbert and George, English artists who typically feature themselves dressed in suits as the subjects of their gigantic photographs, would be considered camp.

Caricature. Character studies that usually exaggerate one or more features, often in a comic-like expression. Made famous by Al Hirschfeld and often seen in celebrity restaurants in large cities.

Cartoon. A full-scale drawing for wall painting or tapestries was sometimes created by masters such as Michelangelo, Leonardo, or Rubens, and is often exhibited in museums. The modern "cartoon" is a comic strip or caricature.

Ceramic. Any object made of clay that is dried, then placed in a kiln (furnace) or pit and made permanent through "firing" (baking) with an extremely high temperature.

Classical. Refers to works of "unadorned beauty." The term is frequently applied to work that originated in ancient Greece and Rome.

Cloisonné. An Asian technique for fusing ground glass to a metal surface that has had patterns applied with thin metal strips. It is used to decorate vases, jewelry, and small ornamental objects.

Collage. A grouping of different textures, objects, and materials glued on a supporting base. Artists such as Robert Rauschenberg and Richard Chamberlain, as well as folk artists, have brought it to a high art form.

Composition. Renaissance masters arranged forms, lines, and colors within geometric formats such as triangles or rectangles to create pleasing compositions. While not all *elements* and *principles* of art (see definitions below) are present in every composition, this use of space, repetition, movement, color, and line creates harmony and leads the viewer's eye through a painting or sculpture.

Conceptual art. The idea is as important as the reality, and might often have been *only* in writing. The 1970s movement of conceptual art was an art of ideas that might be written about, but from which an artwork may or may not have been completed. Even though at times there was no art as such, dealers sold documentation of the idea (photographs, videos, sets of instructions, drawings, diagrams, and maps) to collectors.

Conté. A greaseless, hard chalk available in black, gray, white, bistre (brown), and sanguine (red) that was used in drawing by many of the old masters.

Contour. An outline drawing of a form or object. Matisse and Picasso were masters of the contour line, with their assured practiced line drawings.

Contrapposto. Classical Greek and Roman art was noted for the realistic posture of its sculpture that featured contrapposto, an S-curve or shift of the hip caused by placing the weight on one foot.

Copy. A faithful rendition of an original work of art, often done with permission inside a museum. These works are usually done by unidentified artists, sometimes students of the master painter, and after a few hundred years, are usually labeled as "School of (the master artist's name)."

Design. Artists and designers arrange their compositions by emphasizing one or more of the elements—line, form, color, value, texture, and space—in their artwork.

Diptych. Two painted or carved panels that are usually hinged together. They are most commonly seen as altarpieces in a church, and have been most popular since the Crusades. Travelers have sometimes carried small portable diptych or triptych (three-panel) altarpieces.

Donor. A client or patron of an artist who donates the work to an institution. In Gothic and early Renaissance altarpieces, the donor and family were often included in the painting.

Earthworks. A deliberate moving of earth and change in natural topography designed by artists. Andy Goldsworthy of England and American Robert Smithson (*Spiral Jetty*) are two of many artists who have made an impact through their "Land Art."

Eclecticism. Incorporating stylistic ideas from a variety of periods and cultures in an artwork.

Element. Reference to artistic design considerations such as color, line, texture, shape or form, and space.

Elongated. A form of stylization in which the human figure is vertically distorted deliberately for dramatic effect, as in the "International Style" of the Limburg Brothers in the 15th century, or in the work of El Greco and Alberto Giacometti.

Emphasis. A design principle that gives dominance to a particular area through color, size, or repetition.

Environmental art. Also called Land Art or Earth Art, this is usually created in outdoor spaces such as a sculpture park or garden. An *environment* is usually a gallery display of objects, light, or sound grouped together to create a work of art.

Etching. In this process, a design is scratched on a metal plate that has been covered in a thin coat of a dark waxy substance. The plate is then placed in acid, and the scratched areas are made deeper (etched) by the action of the acid, while the waxed areas remain untouched.

Focal point. The largest, lightest, darkest, or most important part of a composition.

Foreshortening. In drawing the human figure, a portion that is projected toward the artist (such as a foot, hand, or knee) must be drawn to appear much larger (foreshortened) than the parts that are farther away in order to create an illusion of depth.

Forgery. An artwork created in the manner of a specific artist or culture with the deliberate intent to defraud.

Found object. Ordinary objects used to create art by combining, as in a sculptural assemblage.

Fresco. The technique of painting into freshly laid plaster. The most famous frescoes are Michelangelo's paintings on the ceiling of the Sistine Chapel in the Vatican.

Genre. A form of realistic painting of people that depicts ordinary events of the day, not religious, historical, or mythological.

Gilt. A thin coat of gold leaf applied to the surface of a painting, frame, or architecture.

Glaze. A mineral coating that becomes glass-like when fired and makes ceramics waterproof. It is also used to create a luminous effect in oil or watercolor paintings by building up transparent layers of color.

Golden section. A proportion in a rectangular painting of a ratio of roughly 8 to 13 (inches or centimeters) that was considered by Renaissance masters to express perfect visual harmony.

Happening. A (usually one-time) spontaneous performance, under the direction of an artist, that combines the visual arts and a theatrical event. It is somewhat related to contemporary "body art."

Horizon line. The distant view where sky meets water or land at the artist's eye level.

Illustration. An artwork developed to accompany a story, advertisement, or written text.

Installation. An arrangement of objects in a gallery or elsewhere that in itself constitutes a work of art.

Intaglio printing. A method in which damp paper is pressed into the inked etched or engraved lines of a metal printing plate.

Kinetic art. Artwork that involves real or apparent movement, such as sculptures by Alexander Calder or self-destructing sculptures by Jean Tinguely. Op art, in which images appear to move because of an optical illusion, might also be considered kinetic art.

Kitsch. Artwork, often mass-produced, that goes beyond good taste. An example would be Michelangelo's *Pieta* (Mary holding her son) with a clock in her stomach.

Landscape. A scenery painting. A cityscape and seascape are also considered landscape.

Lithograph. This printmaking method discovered in 1798 has allowed artists great artistic freedom ever since. Although it originally was drawn on a special stone, today's technology allows for offset printing and photo-lithography.

Lost-wax. Also known as a *cire perdue* (French). This is a method of creating a replica of a wax sculpture by covering the model with a material similar to plaster, then heating the mold to melt the wax inside. Molten metal (usually bronze) is then poured into the cavity to create an exact metal replica of the wax model.

Medium. Refers to the actual material used in creating an artwork, such as watercolor, oil, or pastel.

Mobile/stabile. Terms coined in 1932 by Marcel Duchamp to describe work created by Alexander Calder. The mobile is a hanging, movable sculpture. The stabile rests on the ground, but may also have moving parts.

Modeling. In sculpture, the process of physically working the clay or wax into a form. In painting, the process of varying the colors to give a three-dimensional quality.

Mosaic. A design or picture created by imbedding small stones or pieces of glass in cement. Often used in vaulted ceilings, walls, and floors in churches and private homes.

Mural. A very large continuous painting made to fill an entire wall or even a room.

Naturalism. Reality-based painting.

Non-objective. An abstract artwork not based on anything in reality.

Odalisque. A term used in the 19th century to describe a painted nude or semi-nude reclining woman. The term is taken from the word for a Turkish harem slave.

Oil paint. A paint consisting of powdered pigment held together with oil. Jan van Eyck is credited with discovering almost 500 years ago that ground pigment mixed with linseed oil allowed the artist greater freedom in painting. Larger paintings were possible because canvas isn't as heavy as panels or plaster. New effects such as transparency and opacity in the same painting gave a glowing richness to paintings. Unlike water-based paints, oil colors remain unchanged when they have dried, and do not fade over time.

Outsider art. Artwork that is created by people who are not part of the normal "art world" and are usually untrained or self-taught. They express their feelings in a variety of art forms such as sculpture, carvings, paintings, and drawings. These may be folk artists or even people who have spent their lives in an institution.

Pastel. A type of painting created with pigment held together with a binder and pressed into stick form. Comes in dry or oil-based sticks that allow the artist to achieve many different effects.

Perspective. Refers to the depth created in a painting that gives it a three-dimensional quality. The lines of the work lead to a vanishing point that may be on or beyond the canvas. Aerial or atmospheric perspective, shown through haziness or changes in color, also gives the effect of distance.

Polychrome. Many-colored.

Polyptych. A painting that consists of four or more panels hinged together.

Principles of art. The application of the elements of design through repetition, balance, emphasis, contrast, rhythm, and proportion.

Public art. Artwork that is commissioned by a public or private enterprise to be displayed in a viewing area that can be seen by the public.

Ready-made. A found object, such as the urinal that Dada artist Marcel Duchamp signed with his name and declared to be a work of art. Duchamp also put his signature on a new snow shovel and called it *In Advance of a Broken Arm.*

Realism. An artist's effort to portray a subject as accurately as possible.

Romanticism. A type of painting that idealizes an image, often with Surrealistic or imaginative composition.

Still life. Also known by the French as *nature morte,* a composition featuring inanimate objects, such as food, dead animals, or flowers.

Stylize. Taking creative license to abstract a recognizable image or form, leaving it simpler, yet recognizable.

Texture. The tactile quality of an artwork's surface. It can be *actual* texture or *implied* (by pattern or brushstrokes).

Tone. The overall quality of color in a painting, such as a prevailing green tone, achieved through color, value, and intensity.

Value. Differences in the lightness or darkness of a hue, one of the elements of design.

"(Art is) . . . a product of the untalented,
sold by the unprincipled to the utterly bewildered."
—AL CAPP, 1909–1979, creator of *Li'l Abner* comic strip,
commenting on abstract art, 1963

PRONUNCIATION GUIDE

Although pronunciations vary according to the country (for example, no outsider can ever pronounce van Gogh like the Dutch), these are generally accepted English pronunciations. The syllables are run together, with the accent on the highlighted syllable.

ARTISTS

Albers, Josef—*al* burrs, josef

Bosch, Hieronymus—bosh, her *on* ee mus

Botticelli, Sandro—bot tee *chel* lee, *san* dro

Boucher, François—boo *shay*, frahn *swah*

Braque, Georges—brock, zhorzh

Brueghel, Pieter—*Broy* ghel, peter

Caravaggio, Michelangelo—car a *vod* jo, mike el an jel o

Cézanne, Paul—say *zan*, paul

Chagall, Marc—shah *gall*, mark

Chardin, Jean Baptiste—shar *dan*, zhon bahteese

Chirico, Giorgio de—*Kee ree* co, Georg gee-O dee

Dali, Salvador—*dah* lee, sal va dor

Daumier, Honoré—*dough* mee eh, *on* o ray

David, Jacques-Louis—dah *veed*, zhock loo ee

Degas, Edgar—day *gah*, ed gar

Delacroix, Eugène—della crwah, *U*-gen

Dufy, Raoul—doo *fee*, rah ool

Dürer, Albrecht—*dure* er, al brekt

Eyck, Jan van—ike, yon van

Fragonard, Jean Honoré—frag o nar, zhan on o ray

Gauguin, Paul—go *ganh*, Paul

Gericault, Jean-Louis—*zhay* ree co, zhon loo ee

Giorgeone—geor gee *oh* nay

Giotto di Bondone—*jot* toe dee bon *doe* nee

Gogh, Vincent van—go, vin cent van

Goya, Francisco de—*goy* ah, frahn *cees* co day

Greco, El—*greck* o, ell

Gris, Juan—greece, whahn

Grünewald, Mathis—*grewn* vahlt, mah tis

Holbein, Hans—*hole* byne, hahns

Ingres—*ann* g'r

Klee, Paul—clay, Paul

Kokoschka, Oskar—ko *kosh* ka, oh-scar

Kollwitz, Käthe—*call* vits, ka ty

Leonardo da Vinci—lay o *nar* doe da vin chee

Leyster, Judith—*lie* ster

Manet, Édouard—mah *nay*, aid wahr

Mantegna, Andrea—mon *tane* ya, an *dray* a

Martini, Simoné—mar *tee* nee, see mon ee

Masaccio—ma *sotch* o

Matisse, Henri—mah *teess*, on ree

Medici, Giuliano de—*may* de chee, jool *yah* no de

Medici—*may* dee chee

Michelangelo (Buonarroti)—mee kel *an* jel o bwoe na *rot* tee

Millet, Jean François—mill *ay*, zhahn frahn swah

Mondrian, Piet—moan dree *ahn*, peet

Monet, Claude—mo *nay*, clowd

Picasso, Pablo—pea *kass* o, pab lo

Pollaiuolo, Antonio—paul eye woe lo, an *tone* ee o

Poussin, Nicolas—poos *an*, neek o lahs

Raphael—rafe ee ul

Redon, Odilon—r'dawn, o dee lawn

Renoir, Pierre-Auguste—ren *wahr*, pee air oh *goost*

Rivera, Diego—ree *vay* ra, dee ay go

Rouault, Georges—roo *oh*, zhorzh

Rousseau, Henri—roo *sew*, on ree

Ruisdael, Jakob van—ryes *doll*, yah cob

Seurat, Georges—sir ah, zhorgh

Toulouse-Lautrec, Henri de—too *looze* low trek, on ree de

van Gogh, Vincent—van go, vin cent

Velazquez, Diego—vay *las* kez, dee *ay* go

Vermeer, Jan—ver *mare*, yahn

Warhol, Andy—*wohr* hohl

Watteau, Jean-Antoine—wah *toe*, zhon on twon

TECHNIQUES

casein—cay seen
chine collé—sheen cole ay
gesso—*jess* o
gouache—gwahsh
intaglio—in *towl* yo

MISCELLANEOUS

Art Nouveau—ar *nu* vo
Bauhaus—*bough* house
Beaux-Art—*bows* ar
Champs Élysees—shahns ay lee *zay*
chiaroscuro—key *are* o skoo ro
cloisonné—cloy zon *nay*
douanier—dwahn yay
en plein air—ahn plen er
fauve—fove
genre—*jahn* reh
magi—may-jigh
Notre Dame—no-trah dahm
objet d'art—obe *zhay* dar
putti—*put* ti
Savonarola—sav on a roll a
sfumato—sphoo *mah* toe
triptych—trip tick
trompe l'oeil—trome *p'loil*
Uffizi—you *feet* zee

TITLES OF PAINTINGS

Der Blaue Reiter—dehr blah way right er
Grand Jatte, La—grahnd *jhot*
Guernica—*gware* nee ka
Icarus—*ik* are us
La Primavera—lah pree ma *vay* ra
Lascaux—lass *ko*

Las Meninas—lahs men *yeen* yahss

Les Demoiselles d'Avignon—lay dem wah zel *dahv* een yone

Mona Lisa—moan a *lees* a

Montefeltro, Federigo da—mon te *fell* tro, fay day *ree* go dah

Mont Sainte-Victoire—mawn sant veek twah

Moulin Rouge—moo lan roozh

Pieta—pea eh *tah*

Sabine—*say* byne

WHAT DID IT SELL FOR?

A work of art should never be judged solely by its cost, but it is still big news when a painting sells for a huge amount of money. The art market has its ups and downs, as has the popularity and consequently the value of work by particular artists. But, some would argue, value is in the eye of the beholder. The artworks listed here are mostly oil paintings, which, more often than not, command the biggest prices. All were sold at auction. While some went to museums, most were sold to private collectors. Some of the titles are English translations, and dates are given where available.

Artist	Year Sold	Auction Price	Title and Date
Artist Unknown	1999	$277,500	*Bust of a God* (Osiris), 380–342 B.C.
Bacon, Francis	1994	$353,500	*Self Portrait-Diptych*, 1977
Bacon, Francis	2001	$8,600,000	*Studies of the Human Body*, (triptych), 1979
Bartolommeo, Fra	1996	$22,500,000	*Rest on the Flight into Egypt with Saint John the Baptist*, 1509
Baselitz, Georg	2001	$1,106,000	*The Shepherd*, 1966
Basquiat, Jean-Michel	2001	$1,200,000	*Baby-Boom*, 1982
Beckmann, Max	1994	$1,496,350	*Quapi auf Blau mit Butchy*, 1943
Bellows, George	1995	$2,862,500	*Easter Snow*, 1915
Bellows, George	1999	$27,500,000	*Polo Crowd*, 1910
Botero, Fernando	1996	$670,000	*La Casa de las Gamelas*, 1973

Artist	Year Sold	Auction Price	Title and Date
Boucher, François	1994	$291,970	*Une Dame à sa Toilette,* c. 1738
Brancusi, Constantin	1998	$6,600,000	*Sleeping Muse* (bronze, cast), 1920s
Calder, Alexander	1994	$1,817,500	*Constellation,* 1960
Calder, Alexander	2000	$4,100,000	*Stegosaurus,* 1973
Calder, Alexander	2001	$1,760,000	*Janey Waney,* 1969
Canaletto	2000	$11,150,000	*The Campo Santi Giovanni è Paolo, Venice,* c. 1730
Carracci, Annibale	1994	$2,202,500	*Boy Drinking,* c. 1580
Carracci, Annibale	2000	$5,300,000	*The Lamentation,* c. 1582
Cassatt, Mary	1996	$3,700,000	*In the Box,* c. 1880
Cézanne, Paul	1994	$28,602,500	*Nature Morte: les Grosses Pommes,* c. 1890–1894
Cézanne, Paul	1996	$11,002,500	*La Côte du Galet, à Pontoise,* c. 1879–1881
Cézanne, Paul,	1997	$50,000,000	*Still Life, Flowered Curtain and Fruit,* 1900
Cézanne, Paul	2000	$8,500,000	*La Côte du Galet, à Pontoise,* c. 1879–1881
Cézanne, Paul	2001	$38,500,000	*La Montagne St. Victoire,* 1888
Close, Chuck	1999	$1,200,000	*Cindy II,* 1988
Dali, Salvador	1995	$3,522,500	*Swans Reflection of the Elephants,* 1937
Degas, Edgar	1995	$4,950,000	*Woman in the Tub,* 1884
Degas, Edgar	1996	$11,882,500	*Young Dancer at 14* (bronze), 1878–1881
Disney, Walt	1995	$29,900	Celluloid from *Cinderella,* 1950
Dubuffet, Jean	2001	$3,000,000	*L'automobile Fleur de l'Industrie,* 1961
Duchamp, Marcel	1999	$1,760,000	*Fountain* (a "readymade" urinal, signed), c. 1917
Francis, Sam	2001	$1,100,000	*Yellow,* 1953–1955
Gauguin, Paul	1989	$24,200,000	*Mata Mua—in Olden Times,* 1892

Artist	Year Sold	Auction Price	Title and Date
Gauguin, Paul	1995	$7,898,890	*Tahitiennes près d'un Ruisseau*, 1893
Gauguin, Paul	1996	$2,000,000	*Huttes sous les Arbres*, 1887
Giacometti, Alberto	2000	$14,300,000	*Grande femme debout I*, 1962
Gogh, Vincent van	1987	$53,900,000	*Irises*, c. 1889/1890
Gogh, Vincent van	1990	$82,500,000	*Portrait du Dr. Gachet*, 1890
Gogh, Vincent van	1990	$26,400,000	*Autoportrait*, 1888
Gogh, Vincent van	1993	$57,000,000	*Wheat Field with Cypresses*, 1889
Gogh, Vincent van	1998	$71,502,500	*Self Portrait Without Beard*, 1889
Greco, El	1995	$2,312,500	*Christ on the Cross in a Landscape with Horseman*, late 16th century
Hassam, Childe	1998	$7,922,500	*Afternoon on the Avenue*, 1917
Hicks, Edward	1994	$486,500	*Peaceable Kingdom of the Branch*, c. 1830
Hirst, Damien,	2000	$750,000	*In Love-Out of Love*, 1998
Homer, Winslow	1998	$30,000,000	*Lost on the Grand Banks*, 1885
Johns, Jasper	1988	$17,500,000	*False Start*, 1959
Johns, Jasper	1988	$7,040,000	*White Flag*, 1955–1958
Johns, Jasper	1989	$11,000,000	*Two Flags*, 1973
Johns, Jasper	1997	$8,300,000	*Corpse and Mirror*, 1974
Johns, Jasper	2001	$3,800,000	*Alphabet*, 1959
Johns, Jasper	2001	$3,700,000	*Montez Singing*, 1989
Kahlo, Frida	1995	$3,192,500	*Autoretrato con Chango y Loro*, 1942
Kandinsky, Wassily	1998	$19,000,000	*Composition V*, 1911
Kelly, Ellsworth	2001	$1,430,000	*Red White Blue*, 1968
Klimt, Gustave	1994	$11,662,500	*Dame mit Facher*, c. 1917–1918
Kooning, Willem de	1989	$18,800,000	*Interchange*, 1949
Kooning, Willem de	1996	$15,622,500	*Woman*, 1949

Artist	Year Sold	Auction Price	Title and Date
Koons, Jeff	2000	$369,000	*Red Butt (Distance)*, 1991
Koons, Jeff	2000	$1,800,000	*Pink Panther*, 1988
Koons, Jeff	2001	$5,600,000	*Michael Jackson and Bubbles*, 1988
Lawrence, Jacob	1992	$62,500	*Northbound*, 1962
Léger, Fernand	2001	$16,726,000	*Le Moteur*, 1918
Lichtenstein, Roy	1989	$5,500,000	*Torpedo . . . Los*, 1963
Lichtenstein, Roy	1995	$1,600,000	*Emeralds*, 1961
Lichtenstein, Roy	1996	$3,600,000	*Tex!*, 1962
Lichtenstein, Roy	2001	$1,800,000	*Swimming Figure with Mirror*, 1977
Manet, Édouard	1989	$26,000,000	*La Rue Mosnier aux Drapeaux*, 1878
Manet, Édouard	1990	$16,500,000	*Le Banc, le Jardin de Versailles*, 1881
Manet, Édouard	1996	$2,650,000	*Portrait of Mlle. Suze*, 1880
Mapplethorpe, Robert	1994	$63,250	*Calla Lily* (photograph), 1987
Matisse, Henri	1994	$13,752,500	*La Vis* (gouache & cut paper), 1951
Matisse, Henri	1995	$14,852,500	*Hindoue*, 1923
Matisse, Henri	1999	$9,200,000	*Nu Couche I (Aurore)*, c. 1912
Matisse, Henri	2000	$14,000,000	*La Serpentine* (bronze), 1909
Matisse, Henri	2001	$4,200,000	*Anemones Au Miroir Noir*, 1918–1919
Matisse, Henri	2001	$7,596,000	*Deux Négresses* (sculpture), 1907–1908
Miro, Joan	2001	$5,600,000	*Nocturne*, 1941
Miro, Joan	2001	$8,916,000	*Danseuse Espagnole*, 1927
Miro, Joan	2001	$12,656,000	*Portrait de Mme K*, 1924
Modigliani, Amedeo	1995	$5,942,500	*Portrait de Jeanne Hebuterne*, 1919
Mondrian, Piet	1994	$5,612,500	*Composition No. 8*, 1939–1942
Mondrian, Piet	1998	$40,000,000	*Victory Boogie Woogie*, 1944

Artist	Year Sold	Auction Price	Title and Date
Monet, Claude	1989	$14,300,000	*Le Parlement, Coucher de Soleil*, 1904
Monet, Claude	1996	$6,500,000	*Les Meules, Giverny, Effet du Matin*, c. 1889
Monet, Claude	1996	$4,600,000	*Nympheas*, 1908
Monet, Claude	1999	$22,500,000	*Water Lilies*, 1906
Monet, Claude	2000	$24,200,000	*The Door in the Sun* (Rouen Cathedral), 1894
Munch, Edvard	1996	$7,702,500	*Girls on a Bridge*, c. 1902
O'Keeffe, Georgia	1987	$1,300,000	*At the Rodeo*, 1929
O'Keeffe, Georgia	1989	$1,500,000	*Dark Iris No. 2*, 1927
O'Keeffe, Georgia	2001	$6,166,000	*Calla Lilies with Red Anemone*, 1928
Picasso, Pablo	2000	$9,900,000	*Compotier et Guitare*, 1932
Picasso, Pablo	1989	$51,300,000	*Pierrette's Wedding*, n.d.
Picasso, Pablo	1989	$47,850,000	*Yo Picasso*, 1901
Picasso, Pablo	1995	$29,152,500	*Angel Fernandez De Soto*, 1903
Picasso, Pablo	1999	$45,100,000	*Nude on a Black Armchair*, 1932
Picasso, Pablo	1999	$49,500,000	*Woman Seated in a Garden*, 1938
Picasso, Pablo	2000	$55,000,000	*Femme aux Bras Croisés*, 1901–1902
Picasso, Pablo	2001	$6,826,000	*Buste de Femme à la Chemise*, 1922
Pissarro, Camille	2001	$6,600,000	*La Rue Saint-Lazare*, 1893
Pollock, Jackson	1989	$10,500,000	*Number 8*, 1950
Pollock, Jackson	2001	$8,000,000	*Black and White/Number 6*, 1951
Pontormo, Jacopo da	1990	$35,200,000	*Portrait of Cosimo de Medici*, 1518–1519
Prendergast, Maurice	1995	$1,432,500	*On the Shore*, after 1907
Rembrandt van Rijn	1995	$5,529,230	*Cupid Blowing a Soap Bubble*, 1634
Rembrandt van Rijn	1998	$9,077,500	*Portrait of a Bearded Man in a Red Coat*, 1633
Rembrandt van Rijn	2000	$28,675,830	*Portrait of a Lady, Aged 63*, 1632

Artist	Year Sold	Auction Price	Title and Date
Remington, Frederic	1993	$1,212,500	*Coming Through the Rye* (bronze), 1902
Renoir, Pierre-Auguste	2000	$1,700,000	*Women in a Garden,* 1872–1873
Renoir, Pierre-Auguste	1990	$78,100,000	*Au Moulin de la Galette,* 1876
Renoir, Pierre-Auguste	2000	$13,200,000	*La Liseuse,* 1875
Richter, Gerhard	2001	$5,400,000	*Drei Kerzen* (candles), 1982
Rivera, Diego	1995	$3,082,500	*Ball in Tehuantepec,* 1928
Rothko, Mark	1997	$5,900,000	*No. 14 1960,* 1960
Rothko, Mark	2000	$14,300,000	*Yellow over Purple No. 2,* 1956
Rothko, Mark	2000	$11,000,000	*No. 2, (Blue, Red and Green),* 1953
Rubens, Peter Paul	1995	$882,500	*Portrait of the Young Anthony Van Dyck,* 1615
Rubens, Peter Paul	1989	$5,000,000	*A Forest at Dawn with a Deer Hunt,* c. 1635
Sargent, John Singer	1994	$7,592,500	*Spanish Dancer,* c. 1880
Sargent, John Singer	1996	$11,112,500	*Cashmere,* 1908
Schiele, Egon	2001	$9,900,000	*Suburban House with Washing,* 1917
Schnabel, Julian	1999	$321,500	*Maria Callas No. 4,* 1982
Seurat, Georges	1990	$1,992,030	*Casseur Arias de Pierres,* 1882
Seurat, Georges	1999	$35,200,000	*Landscape, Island of La Grande Jatte,* 1884
Signac, Paul	1994	$897,496	*La Place aux Herbes,* 1908
Smith, David	1995	$1,982,500	*Three Circles and Planes* (sculpture), c. 1957
Van Dyck, Anthony	1989	$1,333,000	*Portrait of Mary Princess Royal,* n.d.
Warhol, Andy	1996	$376,500	*Soup Can,* 1962
Warhol, Andy	1999	$772,500	*Last Supper,* 1986
Warhol, Andy	1998	$17,500,000	*Orange Marilyn,* 1964
Warhol, Andy	2000	$1,870,000	*Flowers,* 1964
Warhol, Andy	2001	$2,100,000	*Holly,* 1966

THE PRICE OF PASSION

Why would anyone spend six-, seven-, and even eight-figure sums on a work of art? These quotes give insight into the passion that drives members of this exclusive club.

"Buy to enrich your life, not your bank account. . . . Buy what makes your heart beat faster."
—Dr. George Goldner, collector and Curator of Prints and Drawings, Metropolitan Museum of Art

"My philosophy has always been to buy the best or nothing." —Tsukasa Shishima, collector, Japan

"I love the challenge of developing my eye for new objects in an area that no one else is paying attention to."
—James Goode, collector, New York

"My first rule is that I want to collect only living art. . . . I want to be impressed with the art and I want to know the artist." —Donald Hess, collector, California

"I would never have started collecting to enjoy my treasures all alone. Thinking and reflecting, I find, function better when one exchanges ideas with others."
—Harald Falckenberg, collector, Hamburg, Germany

"The cornerstone of great art for me is a work that makes one person exclaim, 'That's fabulous!' and another ask, 'How can you have that hanging in your house?'"
—Gordon Sondland, collector, Seattle

"If collectors don't make one mistake out of every 10 purchases, they're buying too cautiously."
—Paul Sachs, Curator, Fogg Art Museum

"Ultimately a gallery is only as good as the artists it represents; thus it must constantly prove itself useful to them."
—Janelle Reiring, art dealer, Metro Pictures

"In essence, the gallery world functions as a collective museum of modern art in a way The Museum of Modern Art can't function any more."
—Arnold Grimcher, art dealer

"Our big collectors today are corporations, which sounds beautiful in principle. But I believe the best large collections of the past were all built by one person's eye."
—Tibor de Nagy, art dealer

"Good art dealers don't sell art; they allow people to acquire it."
—Andre Emmerich, art dealer

"At Vassar I had seen a fine collection of work by Calder and art at the apartment of one of my professors, Miss Barber. It taught me that you didn't have to be either immensely wealthy or terribly powerful to collect art. Intelligence and taste are the critical factors in collecting."
—Holly Solomon, art dealer

"Collecting young artists requires a sense of adventure and a knack for being in the right place at the right time."
—Mary Boone, art dealer

"My definition of a collector is someone who has to borrow money to buy things and then has to put them in storage because he has no room."

—Jack Lenor Larsen, American textile designer and collector of sculpture and fine crafts

"Take care of the luxuries and the necessities will take care of themselves."   —Frank Lloyd Wright, 20th-century architect

TOP TIPS FOR ART COLLECTORS

When you purchase a work of art, consider whether you are purchasing for enjoyment or investment. In either case, most advisors suggest purchasing only what you love, as you may never realize more than your investment in an artwork.

GETTING STARTED

- Look at artwork wherever you can: people's homes, museums, magazines, books, and galleries.
- Looking at artwork on the Internet is a quick, easy way to educate yourself and determine what art appeals to you. Most major museums and galleries,

auction houses, and many artists maintain an up-to-date Web site. While you would not likely make major purchases online, looking at artwork helps you determine what is genuinely of interest to you.

- Know your limitations: financial, space, availability to travel, time.
- Work out a budget and buy the best you can afford.
- Collect the work of an artist before it begins to appreciate. Another reason to buy only what you love is that it might not appreciate!
- Look for classic art that looks like new—art that has been in private hands and has not been on the market repeatedly.
- Look at the work several times before making a decision.
- Consider focusing on one aspect of a medium. In photography, for example, consider photographs of a particular time period, or architectural prints.
- Learn about variations within one art medium: paintings, prints, photographs, posters, sculpture.
- Learn to distinguish between reproductions and originals. When you can't tell the difference yourself, ask an artist or dealer.
- When going to a commercial gallery exhibition, get a general overview of everything there. If you find yourself drawn to one work in particular, ask the dealer for information about the artist.
- Avoid purchasing at auction until you feel comfortable that you know what you want—and what you're really getting. The enthusiasm at an auction house can be contagious.
- Online purchases are risky, but many galleries that maintain a Web site exhibit paintings from their collection online. You may still wish to see the actual item, using the Internet simply as a way of narrowing down your options.
- If collecting is an endeavor that you share with your significant other, agree that either one of you will have veto power for a certain percentage of your selections (one out of five, for example). Another option is to decide in advance that both of you must agree on every purchase.

DEPENDABLE PLACES TO BUY ART

✧ Commercial art gallery or artists' cooperative

✧ Directly from the artist at a fair or special exhibition where the artists appear with their work

✧ Auctions at reputable art houses where catalogs are available for prior inspection of work

✧ Established art and antique fairs

✧ The artist's studio (Major artists have their personal dealers, and the price will include the dealer's fee, even when you are visiting in their studio.)

GETTING SERIOUS

Once you are serious about collecting art, keep the following tips in mind to avoid some potential pitfalls.

- Educate yourself through reading, traveling, visiting commercial galleries, going to museums, attending auctions to observe, and taking gallery tours and lecture series offered by museums.

- Purchase books and catalogs that relate to your special interest.

- Select work you love. Research has shown that if making money is your only motivation for buying art, you would be better off investing in the stock market or real estate.

- Buy only the best. This means that you are already spending top dollar, but if growth is your purpose, second-rate artwork isn't going to fill the bill. "The best" of an artist's work will appreciate more than second-rate work by the same artist.

- Narrow your collection to a manageable ideal—for example, choose one subject, one time period, one person, one medium, or two- or three-dimensional works.

- Decide in advance whether the work will be bought to display or to be stored and brought out to look at from time to time.

- Look at the proportion of the work. It is easier to find a place to hang large horizontal works than large vertical artworks.

- Read about collectors and collecting from sources such as *Forbes, Art News, Arts and Antiques* and *The Wall Street Journal* or *The New York Times.*

- Buy from an established, reputable dealer who will stand behind the work he or she sells. Get provenance (the history of previous ownership), a certificate of authenticity and condition, and a money-back guarantee in writing to protect yourself if the work isn't what the dealer claims it is. By law you will have to return the work to the rightful owner if it is discovered to have been stolen.

- Talk with other collectors, dealers, or museum curators who are knowledgeable about the medium or period you want to collect.

- If buying at auction, inspect the work as closely as possible.

- Consider hiring an art consultant, such as an appraiser, dealer, or curator. This person may have contacts that will allow you to get the rare or unusual. Carefully check references. Pay either by the time spent or 10 percent of the cost of the transaction.

- Be wary of anyone pushing one particular dealer or artist.

- Learn how to distinguish excellent from poor condition.

- Keep careful records of purchases. If your collection becomes large enough, you may need the advice of a professional curator.

IMPORTANT QUESTIONS TO ASK

- ✧ When in the artist's career was this work created?
- ✧ Is it a recognizable example of the artist's work from his or her best period?
- ✧ Is it similar to other work done about the same time?
- ✧ Is work by the artist in any major museums or collections?
- ✧ Is there an expert on this particular artist who will authenticate it?
- ✧ Do you think the artwork is powerful enough to endure the test of time?
- ✧ Was the artwork signed by the painter or was the signature added later? Work prior to the 18th century was often left unsigned. Ultraviolet light may reveal that someone else signed the artist's name long after the artist was dead.
- ✧ Does the seller have a clear title to the work?

ALSO CONSIDER:

- Where you want the artwork to go when you die. Some major collectors often make their purchases specifically for a museum, working closely with the curators to fill "holes" in the museum's collection.
- Do you hope to share your selections with the public on a regular basis? Many collectors offer views of the collection in their homes or a private "museum" on a regular schedule.

WHAT TO EYE

- Condition, condition, condition.
- In a photograph, find if it is a vintage print (printed at approximately the same time the negative was exposed) or a later print from the original negative.
- In a print, look for a signature in pencil, and evidence of fading. Try to find out when the print was made, as some very old plates continue to be printed.
- If buying an old painting, look at the back for holes or repairs. If the front appears to be old but the back is newer, the painting may have been *lined* by attaching it to new linen. Most old paintings will show age through a fine crazing (crackling) on the surface. The painting may have been repeatedly varnished, obscuring the original appearance, or may have been sufficiently damaged to need professional restoration.

AUCTION KNOWLEDGE

Art auctions are no longer only for the privileged few who attend by invitation. Modern communication allows people to "attend" an auction almost anyplace in the world through the telephone and Internet.

FAMILIAR TERMS

- **Auction house.** A reputable house with its own curatorial and research staff.
- **Buyer's premium.** The fee charged by the auction house above and

beyond the bid price. Generally, the fee is from 15 percent to 20 percent and is less on Internet than live sales.

- **Catalog.** The book containing description and provenance of the works for sale at a particular auction. The catalogs sell for as much as fifty dollars but may be free of charge to dealers and regular collectors. It is possible to become a subscriber to catalogs of specific areas of interest from some of the major auction houses.

- **Conditions of sale.** An explanation of buyer's premium, taxes, warranty (if any), shipping, or anything else pertaining to this particular sale.

- **Live auction.** Sometimes now called a "bricks and mortar sale," this is a traditional-style auction held in an auction or sales room.

- **Lot number.** Either a single item or a grouping of items offered for a single sale.

- **Paddle.** When you register at a live auction you are issued a bidding-paddle that you raise to signal a bid. At least one large auction house receives payment for a bidding paddle.

- **Reserve price.** The minimum sale price set by the seller. If the reserve is not met, the seller can withdraw the item.

- **Seller's fee.** A percentage deducted from the price the seller receives.

- **Telephone bid.** An official representative of the auction house accepts pre-arranged telephone bidding during a live auction.

- **Virtual gallery.** An online gallery representing artists and dealers.

GOING LIVE

Take time before the actual auction to visit the auction rooms and identify by lot number those items that are of interest to you. At first you may simply want to go as a spectator; it is an exciting opportunity to learn auction protocol. Because copies and forgeries are usually undetectable by the novice, be cautious about purchasing anything at auction until you have done your homework, or work with a knowledgeable advisor.

- Purchase the catalog if one is available.

- Take notes of lots that are of particular interest to you.

- Carefully inspect items on which you may bid, noting condition that will not be visible from a distance.

- Educate yourself about a piece that you intend to bid on. You can find out recent auction prices for specific artists through catalogs in your local library. (This mostly applies to paintings costing more than $10,000.) Current information about auction prices is usually available on the Internet simply by typing in the name of the artist and the artwork.

- Major auction houses such as Sotheby's, Christie's, and Phillips maintain a Web site with photos of some of the work that will be auctioned and estimates of what these might sell for.

- Know the value of items on which you will bid. Write down your absolute top limit and decide if you are willing to make one or two bids beyond it, if necessary.

- Frequently, dealers will be bidding on the object you want. Don't be deterred. You may still be able to get it by being persistent.

- Stay late. Sometimes, after the crowd has thinned, you may be able to obtain something for less than expected.

INTERNET BUYING

The great promise of Internet auctions has been somewhat disappointing in reality; the larger auction houses have discontinued online sales. The Internet continues to cater to the purchaser of less-expensive fine art items such as prints, art pottery, photographs, paintings by lesser-known artists, antiques, glass, and jewelry. An obvious disadvantage of buying online is that you can't inspect potential purchases, but looking at galleries' and artists' Web sites is an education in itself.

Information You Can Usually Get on the Internet

- A photograph of the item for bid
- Description, dimensions, medium, title, artist, condition
- Bidding information to date: beginning bids, bid increments, number of bids, and current high bid, and the amount of time left in the auction
- Type of payment, length of waiting time for delivery, additional costs, sales tax, shipping costs, handling fee
- Rating of the seller by previous clients, phone number
- Written experiences of some attendees, which often includes photos of the pre-sale exhibit

PRECAUTIONS

- Look at the pictures and read the description carefully as to size, medium, condition, and provenance.

- Because you may see only the front and a detail of the artwork, ask if there is a label on the back. Some artists who have not signed their originals may place a label on the back to certify the artwork's authenticity.

- Ask that a signature be checked with ultraviolet light to determine if it was added later. Ultraviolet light may reveal changes and retouching on the surface, or damage in a three-dimensional object. In addition, glue used for repair may be visible under this kind of light.

- Check databases for feedback about the seller from other consumers. (This could include FTC and Better Business Bureau Web sites.)

- Determine who will pay for shipping, insurance, and commissions.

- Pay by credit card or money order. You can telephone your credit card number to the dealer if you don't want to give it out online.

- If you telephone the seller, ask for specific information such as where the item was obtained, how it was authenticated, and if you may have the item appraised before the sale is considered final.

Note: Adventures at the Auction by Leslie Hindman (Clarkson Potter, New York, 2001) is written by a professional appraiser who has worked for one of the major auction firms, and contains great tips for buying at live or Internet auctions.

*"Ah, good taste! What a dreadful thing! Taste
is the enemy of creativeness."*
—PABLO PICASSO, 1881–1973, Spanish-born Cubist painter

DISPLAYING YOUR ARTWORK

Museums have curators and restoration specialists to ensure that artwork is well cared for. You don't! Poor framing and exposure to a host of indoor elements can cause deterioration over time. How you frame your picture and where you hang it is, in a sense, an art in itself. Here are some generally accepted guidelines.

CHOOSING FRAMES

- The frame should be historically accurate—that is, it should appear to be from the same general era as the artwork.
- A concave frame will create interesting shadows that draw the eye inward toward the artwork.
- Contemporary frames frequently are flat on front and deep on the sides, forming a box to enhance the print.
- Work on paper can be held between two pieces of glass several inches larger than the artwork that allow the wall color behind the picture to be the "mat." This is especially effective with deckle edges (the fringed-type edge found on high quality or handmade paper).
- Another option is to place the artwork on top of, rather than under, a contrasting mat so all four edges of the paper are visible. Contemporary artwork (watercolors, drawings, and prints) created on heavy paper is sometimes "floated" on a white background to allow the beautiful deckle edges to show. The artwork is usually supported at the top with Japanese rice paper hinges, allowing the lower portion of the paper to float free.

FRAMING PAINTINGS, PRINTS, AND DRAWINGS

- Ideally, a work of art should remain as if it had just come from the artist's hand. Anything framed for longer than twenty years should be removed from its frame and inspected for changes around the edges, since many changes in framing materials occur over time. Hanging wires should be inspected and perhaps changed, as they may become weak, and could allow the artwork to fall and be damaged.
- Oil paintings are never matted in matboard, but occasionally have a linen-covered wooden border inside the frame, though this is rarely done nowadays.

- Oil paintings should never be put behind glass, even though museums sometimes do so in order to prevent people from touching them.
- Pastel drawings should be protected only by glass, as Plexiglass can develop static that could damage a powdery surface.
- Use archival (museum quality, 100 percent cotton or rag-board) materials for mats and backing. Avoid gummed or masking tape.
- A hinged mat (a double mat with the open, top mat attached with paper hinges to the lower mat on which the artwork is mounted) allows the work's edges to be inspected. Hinging materials should also be archival.
- Mats for works on paper generally should be at least 3 to 3½ inches wide, and may be much larger.
- Mats should be the same on three sides and may be slightly larger on the bottom than the top for visual stability.
- Neutral color mats generally call attention to the artwork.
- Brown corrugated cardboard should never be used as a backing because the acid in it will ultimately damage the artwork. Archival board is available at frame shops.
- The artwork should never touch glass, because it could be damaged as changes in temperature cause condensation on the glass.
- UV-blocking glass or Plexiglass will protect delicate works from sun damage. Laminated glass with a plastic UV-blocking core is now available.

HANGING ARTWORK

Hanging a piece of artwork is an art in itself.
- A large work of art may need an entire wall. Placement will be dictated by its size and shape.
- A single artwork might be hung above a chest and balanced with a lamp, vase, or sculpture.
- Hang art above a seating area a few inches below eye level—as most people will be seated when looking at it—but high enough so that someone leaning back will not hit it.
- To highlight a special work, consider having a spotlight installed, remembering that works on paper are vulnerable to fading.

- If you intend to move artwork around often, prop it on a shelf with a ledge, or have an adjustable system that allows you to hang artwork from a molding near the ceiling.
- Small works may be placed on table-top easels.
- If you prop work on a mantle piece, put push-pins in front to keep it from slipping.

For a grouping:
- Consider having similar frames for a grouping.
- It is effective to hang like items together (photographs with photographs, watercolors with watercolors, drawings with drawings, etc.).
- Leave several inches between each work of art. (A good rule of thumb is to leave space equal to the width of the mat.)
- Small paintings are sometimes more effective when hung one above the other, or seen above a table as part of a composition.
- The only place it is really effective to hang pictures in a stair-step (angled) grouping is above stair-steps.

KEEPING YOUR ARTWORK SAFE

- Works on paper such as watercolors, lithographs, drawings, etchings, and photographs are fragile and should be kept away from direct sunlight. Museums maintain quality by placing a collection of works on paper in low-light and rotating the collection every few months.
- Works on paper not being exhibited can be stored in portfolios or metal drawers. Keep acid-free paper between unframed stacked artworks to protect them.
- Avoid hanging delicate works in a house near the ocean, or have humidity control, as humidity can damage works on paper. As much as possible, maintain the work in a "museum" atmosphere: temperature at 68 to 72 degrees, 50 percent humidity.
- Document your collection. Take quality photographs or videos of your artwork and keep pertinent information in a safe place off-site. Note title, name of artist, date of artwork, medium, size, description, price, place of purchase, and provenance (anything you know about previous ownership).

- Computer software is now available that allows you to store a photograph of the artwork and information.
- Insure your artwork, in the event of fire or theft.
- Have artwork appraisals updated regularly.

SPECIAL ART EXHIBITIONS AND FAIRS WORLDWIDE

Small annual art fairs exist in many places, but this list concentrates on large, established fairs that attract people and gallery owners from all over the world. Most of these exhibitions have a theme, whether it is contemporary art, old masters, studio crafts, sculpture, or works on paper. You can find specific information about them on the Internet or in art magazines. Biennial and triennial exhibitions usually include work of internationally known artists and feature cutting-edge work.

Melbourne, Australia	Melbourne Art Fair
South Brisbane, Australia	Asia-Pacific Triennial of Contemporary Art
Sydney, Australia	Biennale of Sydney
Sao Paulo, Brazil	Bienal de Sao Paulo
Shanghai, China	Shanghai Biennial
Havana, Cuba	Cuba, Biennial Exhibition
London, England	Asian Art in London
	British Art Fair
	Grosvenor House Art & Antiques Fair
	Contemporary Art Fair
	International Art and Design Fair
	Olympia Fine Arts & Antiques Fair
	Original Print Fair
	Watercolors & Drawings Fair
Lyon, France	Biennale d'Art Contemporain de Lyon
Paris, France	FIAC, International Fair of Modern and Contemporary Art in Europe
	Paris Photo Fair
Berlin, Germany	Biennial Exhibition
	Art Forum Berlin
	The International Fair for Contemporary Art
Cologne, Germany	Art Cologne Internationale Kunstmarkt
Munich, Germany	Munich Art Fair, established 1955

Bologna, Italy	Bologna Art Fair
Venice, Italy	Venice Biennale Exhibition
Kwangju, Korea	Kwangju Biennial Exhibition
Maastricht, Netherlands	International Fine Art and Antiques Fair
Auckland, New Zealand	Auckland Biennial Exhibition
Moss, Norway	Nordic Festival of Contemporary Art
Barcelona, Spain	Barcelona Triennial
Madrid, Spain	International Contemporary Art Fair
Basel, Switzerland	Cultura, The World Art & Antiques Fair
Istanbul, Turkey	Biennial Exhibition
Ljublana, Yugoslavia	Graphic Biennale

UNITED STATES

Scottsdale, Arizona	Indian Artists of America Show
Los Angeles, California	Los Angeles Art Show (FADA)
San Diego, California	InSITE, San Diego/Tijuana
San Francisco, California	International Art Exposition
	American Crafts Council (ACC) Crafts Markets, San Francisco
	San Francisco Arts of Pacific Asia
	San Francisco International Art Exposition
	Tribal, Folk & Textile Arts Show
Miami, Florida	Art Miami
Palm Beach, Florida	Art Palm Beach, International Modern and Contemporary Art Fair
	International Art & Antiques Fair
Chicago, Illinois	Art Fair Chicago
	SOFA (Sculpture, Objects & Functional Art)
	International Antiques & Fine Art Fair
Baltimore, Maryland	American Craft Council (ACC) Craft Show
Santa Fe, New Mexico	SITE Santa Fe, Biennial Exhibition
	Indian Market
New York City	Artexpo (Biennial)
	"Armory Fair," Contemporary Art
	Asian Art Fair
	International 20th-Century Arts Fair
	International Fine Arts & Antiques Dealers Fair
	New York Ceramics Fair

	Outsider Art Fair, Museum of American Folk Art
	SOFA (Sculpture, Objects & Functional Art)
	The Art Show, Art Dealers Association of America (ADAA)
	Whitney Biennale
Charlotte, North Carolina	Mint Museum of Craft & Design
Washington DC	Renwick Gallery

GALLERIES OF INTEREST WORLDWIDE

Most major cities have famous museums, such as the Louvre in Paris and the Metropolitan Museum of Art in New York, that every art lover *must* see when traveling. But these cities often have many wonderful commercial galleries as well that are usually not in the tour books. Some galleries have been in one family for generations, while others come and go. Here are a few of the not-so-famous but well-worth-the-trip galleries in major cities. You'll find that taking the time to look them up and visit them will be time well spent.

NETHERLANDS

Cramer Gallery, The Hague
Galerie Delaive BV, Amsterdam
Noortman, Old Masters and Impressionists, Amsterdam

LONDON

Annely Juda
Colnaghi
Connaught Brown
Fabien Boulakia
Fine Art Society
Frost and Reed
Gagosian Gallery
Hirschl Contemporary Art
Lefevre Gallery
Marlborough Fine Arts

Michael Richardson
    Contemporary Art
New Art Centre Sculpture Park
    & Gallery
Peter Nahum
Richard Green
Rossi and Rossi
Saatchi Gallery
Waddington Galleries

PARIS

Enrico Navarra
Galerie Adrien Maeght
Galerie Lelong

Galerie Schmit
Robert Bowman

UNITED STATES

Chicago

Alan Koppel Gallery
Carl Hammer Gallery
Donald Young Gallery
Jean Albano Gallery
Maya Polsky

Perimeter
Peter Bartlow Gallery
Portals
Richard Gray
Worthington Gallery

Los Angeles

Andrew Dierken
Forum Gallery
Gagosian
Galerie Michael

Jack Rutberg Fine Arts
L. A. Louver, Venice
Leslie Sacks Fine Art
Steven Cohen Gallery

New York City

Adelson Galleries
Allan Stone
Artemis, Greenberg Van Doren
D. C. Moore Gallery
Dickenson Roundell, Inc.
Forum Gallery
Gagosian
Galerie St. Etienne
Hirschl & Adler Galleries Inc
Joan T. Washburn Gallery

Knoedler & Company
Marlborough
Matthew Marks Gallery
PaceWildenstein
Paula Cooper
Peter Blum
Richard Gray Gallery
Robert Miller Gallery
Sonnabend
Tibor de Nagy Gallery

Philadelphia

> Locks Gallery

San Francisco

> Galerie Paule Anglim
> Hackett-Freedman Gallery
> John Berggruen Gallery
> Martin Lawrence Galleries

> Meyerovich Contemporary
> Gallery
> Rena Bransten
> Robert Koch Gallery

Santa Fe

> Nedra Matteucci Galleries

SCANDALS AND HEADLINES IN ART

Groundbreaking ideas and subjects may thrust an artist to the forefront of the art world, particularly if the artist's work is considered "scandalous" in the artist's particular culture. The very lives of artists and the inner workings of the art world are subject to scandals. The romantic idea of the "Bohemian" life, unsavory friends, poverty, and unscrupulous dealers contribute to the legends. Here are a few of the headline-makers.

PATENTLY BOGUS!

Nicholas Turner, the Getty Museum's former curator of European drawings and a scholar with an impeccable reputation, resigned from the Getty Museum in Malibu in 2001 when his research regarding several forgeries in the Getty collection was disputed. "Some of the drawings were so patently bogus that they began to annoy me to look at them," says Nicholas Turner.

FRAUD LAWSUITS ROCK ART WORLD, SHOW WEAK LINK

In 2001, Sotheby's and Christie's agreed to pay $512 million to settle a class-action antitrust lawsuit. Plaintiffs alleged that commission fees had been secretly agreed to by these two venerable auction houses.

MYSTIC LAMB IN CRYPT?

A panel from Jan van Eyck's masterpiece *Adoration of the Mystic Lamb*, in Ghent, Belgium, vanished in 1934. The common theory at the time was that it was taken for ransom by a local banker, who died without divulging where he put it. A recent theory that it may be in the royal crypt may result in reopening the investigation (and the crypt).

KEMPER O'KEEFFES FAKE?

Georgia O'Keeffe's *Canyon Suite* of 28 water colors (so called because she was said to have painted them when she was an art teacher in Canyon, Texas) are considered forgeries by O'Keeffe scholars. The series was sold for $5 million to the Kemper Museum of Contemporary Art in Kansas City, Missouri. The Kemper's money was refunded by a New York art-dealer.

"SICK STUFF"

This was the term used by New York Mayor Rudolph Giuliani when he cut off city funding to the Brooklyn Museum of Art because of a controversial exhibition of Englishman Charles Saatchi's collection. At the heart of the controversy was the *Holy Virgin Mary*, a painting that included paintings of body parts and elephant dung. On the basis of the First Amendment, a court decision restored funding.

ANDREW WYETH'S SECRET OBSESSION

Between 1970 and 1985, Andrew Wyeth created some 246 portraits of a "mystery woman"—neighbor Helga Tesdorf. The series came to be known as the Helga Paintings. These works came to light when 240 of them were sold to a collector. Even Wyeth's wife, Betsy, had not been told of their existence.

"THE GOLD TRAIN"

A train full of treasures captured from Hungarian Jews by the Nazis was intercepted by American forces in May, 1945. A large group of paintings was given to Austria, while other items simply suffered "mysterious disappearance."

THE EIGHT REVOLT

William Glackens, Maurice Prendergast, John Sloan, George Luks, Ernest Lawson, Everett Shinn, and their leaders, Robert Henri and Arthur B. Davies, rebelled against the National Academy by choosing subject matter from the slums of New York. In 1908, Academic leaders showed their strong disapproval of subject matter by the rebel art group, "The Eight," by dubbing it The Ashcan School!

GAUGUIN SENTENCED TO PRISON

Paul Gauguin, who exhibited with the Impressionists, moved to Tahiti when he was 41. He took a 13-year old wife (13 was considered a marriageable age in that culture), and was the despair of the local priests with his habit of inviting young girls to pose for him. In 1891, he was sentenced to three months in jail, which he never served. The local Catholic priest, reporting to France, wrote, "The only noteworthy event here has been the sudden death (at 55) of a contemptible individual named Gauguin, a reputed artist but an enemy of God and everything that is decent."

"KEEP THIS OBJECT LIKE A TREASURE"

"On Sunday night, at half past eleven, a painter named Vincent van Gogh, a native of Holland, appeared at the maison de tolérance No. 1, asked for a girl called Rachel, and handed her his ear with these words: 'Keep this object like a treasure.' Then he disappeared. The police, informed of these events, which could only be the work of an unfortunate madman, looked the next morning for this individual, whom they found in bed with scarcely a sign of life." (Source: Arles newspaper, 1889, as quoted in *The World of Van Gogh*, Time-Life Books, New York, 1969).

"DEGRADATION OF ART"

In 1880, Thomas Eakins was dismissed from the Pennsylvania Academy of Art over his teaching methods. In his battle against prudery in art, he insisted that if young women were to be trained as artists, they must be allowed to "face the absolute nude" in his life-drawing classes. He had further shocked the public with his painting *The Gross Clinic* (1875), which showed Dr. Gross, scalpel in bloody hand, turning away from his patient to lecture to a class. This painting was considered a "degradation of Art."

HARNETT ARRESTED BY TREASURY AGENTS

Still Life—Five Dollar Bill. This picture led to the arrest of artist William Harnett by Treasury agents in 1887. His trompe l'oeil (fool the eye) painting of this currency was so realistic that it was thought it was actual counterfeit money glued on to the canvas. Expressions such as "By Jove," " 'S'help me," and "Gee Whittikers" were used by people viewing his "photo realistic" paintings.

BIZARRE OUTDOOR PICNIC

Édouard Manet's 1863 painting *Luncheon in the Grass* left its viewers scandalized. The strange scene showed two fully dressed men enjoying a luncheon repast with a nude young lady whose clothes were nearby. The shame of Manet's *Olympia* (a reclining nude) done in the same year followed him throughout his career. Words such as "female Gorilla" or "vulgar virgin" were used to describe its model.

POOR PLUNDER FROM A BLEEDING LAND

From 1801 to 1806, while he was a diplomat in Greece, Thomas Bruce (the 7th Earl of Elgin) "rescued" 56 pieces of the bas-relief frieze and 34 other Parthenon sculptures from the occupying Turks. These were sold in 1816 to the British Museum, unleashing both praise and criticism. Further injury was inflicted in the 1930s when the museum "cleaned" the marbles, removing the honey-colored patina. Controversy continues to this day about the legality of taking national treasures from a country occupied by a foreign government, and the Greeks continue to press for a return of the *Elgin Marbles*.

GOYA'S MYSTERY WOMAN

Sometime around 1800, Francisco Goya painted two versions, *The Clothed Maja* and *The Naked Maid*, of the notorious Duchess of Alba, his mistress. Never mind that experts are certain these are not portraits of the Duchess of Alba, nor do they believe that she was ever his mistress. Tradition, rumor, and gossip have kept this scandal alive for two hundred years.

COPIES, FAKES, AND FORGERIES

Copies and forgeries have existed as long as there has been a market for art. Some copies were completed in the studio of a master painter, sometimes even touched up and signed by him for family members or favored students in order to help them sell their work. In Asia, copying the work of a master has always been considered a tribute to the master, and some artists today continue to (legally) imitate the painting style of masters from a thousand years ago. The difference between a copy and a forgery is that one is created with the intent to defraud while the other might have been created as a valid way of learning how a master painted. Egyptian mummies have been forged (new bones in old cloth), and "ancient" Egyptian artifacts of all types continue to be made today. Modern science has assisted in detecting forgeries, but even the experts can be fooled.

TERMS YOU SHOULD KNOW

Appropriationism. Many famous artists have "appropriated" a composition from another artist, often titling it after the master's work, but painting it in a style uniquely their own. Pablo Picasso did several interpretations of Velazquez's work; Roy Lichtenstein "quoted" several masters; photographer Sherrie Levine has become known for her reproductions of well-known photographs by others that have then become *her* originals.

Copy. An artwork that is faithfully reproduced in the same medium (but not always the same size) by an art student or gifted artist. Copying the old masters was considered a valid way to learn how to paint, and these may actually have been copied from the original (with a museum's permission). Museum labels often say "From the school of . . ." or "Attributed to . . ." or have an artist's name with a question mark after it.

Some artists made many copies of their own successful paintings, which were then also "originals." Gilbert Stuart painted almost 70 copies of his *Athenaeum Portrait of George Washington*. Today one may order "custom copies," painted in oil on canvas, made to size by such artists as members of the conservation department at the State Russian Museum in St. Petersburg, or from galleries in Asia with artists under contract. Generally these are copies of paintings in the public domain.

Fake. A work of art, such as a pre-Columbian artifact made to resemble the original.

Forgery. An imitation of an existing artwork by an established artist that is copied by an unknown artist and deliberately passed off as the original. Forgeries are created by simply copying in the same medium.

Original print. This means that a "plate" was involved in the printing process, and it was printed either by the artist or under the supervision of the artist. An original print (lithograph, etching, lino-cut, wood-cut, mono-print, monotype, silk screen/serigraph) is traditionally signed and numbered by the artist in pencil (because ink can fade). Theoretically, the plate is defaced, never to be printed again.

Pastiche. Portions of several different paintings in the recognizable style of one artist are combined in one painting by a forger.

Photographic reproduction. A mechanical reproduction of an original work of art (for example, those used in posters or reproductions) may be purchased by mail or in an art museum. If you purchase a *print* of an oil or watercolor (non-printing techniques), even though signed in pencil, this is a mechanical reproduction of an artwork, done in a different medium. Sometimes these are signed with a number such as 100/1000. The larger the number of the edition, the less likely that the artist was personally involved in the printing process. With this said, some contemporary artists are authorizing large (1,000) photo-copied editions of their work to be created, which does allow collectors to purchase "original" work from a famous artist at a low price.

Prints. An unscrupulous practice of printing a new edition on a different paper surface, using the artist's original plate (not defaced) sometimes hundreds of years later. Works by artists such as Rembrandt, Dürer, and Mantegna were reprinted after their deaths from their original plates. Some "Dali" prints that were reportedly never even seen by Dali were printed on blank sheets he had signed prior to a later printing.

Sculpture. Normally an edition of twelve to fifteen bronzes is cast from the original sculpture in wax or clay. In France, twelve sculptures from one original is the legal limit, even if the master's original molds are used. The *sur-moulage* method involves having a new mold made from an existing bronze sculpture. This is a generation away from the original clay, plaster, or wax model and consequently loses some of the "hand of the artist." In a few cases, such as with the work of Dégas and Daumier, the original wax sculptures were not cast in bronze until after the artists' deaths, but are still considered *originals* rather than copies.

SOME MASTER FORGERS

While most forgers are anonymous, a few, known as "master" forgers have made a name of their own because of their skills. Here is a sampling.

Chasseriau, Th., *Mona Lisa.* During the time that the *Mona Lisa* was missing after being stolen from the Louvre in 1911, it is certain that copies were made by this French forger.

de Hory, Elmyr. This 20th-century Hungarian forger copied Modigliani, Monet, Derain, Dufy, and others. He produced approximately 1,000 fakes, many of which are in museum collections. Examples are Matisse's *Seated Woman* and *Woman at Table, Hands Against Chin,* Modigliani's *Portrait of a Woman,* and *Portrait of Lunia Czechowska.* De Hory was so good that others forged *his* work!

Dossena, Alceo. This Italian-born artist, known as the "King of Forgers," was expert in painting in the manner of Donatello, Mino da Fiesole, Simone Martini, Giovanni Pisano, and Vecchietta during the late 18th and early 19th centuries. An example, *Diana the Huntress* (an "Etruscan" statue), is in the St. Louis Art Museum collection. He might have been an unwitting forger, with unscrupulous dealers selling his copies as genuine.

Drewe, John, and his accomplice, **John Myatt.** These two 20th-century English forgers faked work by Nicolas de Stäel, Ben Nicholson, Graham Sutherland, Marc Chagall, Jean Dubuffet, and Alberto Giacometti.

Durig, Ernest. A Swiss-born forger of the 19th century, Durig passed many of his drawings off as those of Auguste Rodin, whose work he admired.

Hain, Guy. Despite the outstanding quality of the forgeries by this contemporary French mastermind, they are still illegal. He has flooded the market with thousands of sculptures for an alleged total of 98 artists whose work he has copied illegally. Almost a quarter of them are Rodins, some created from Rodin's molds. An independent art evaluation expert says

"Hain produced almost industrial quantities of sculptures" during his fifteen years of activity.

Hebborn, Eric. A contemporary English forger who was murdered in Rome in 1996, Hebborn made more than 1,000 drawings and "studies" by many different masters. He purchased old books to use paper of the period and created his own inks using authentic ingredients. He even wrote an autobiography explaining how he made some "authentic" sketches that are in large museum collections.

Schuffenecker, Claude-Emile. A French contemporary of van Gogh and Gauguin, Schuffenecker was also an artist in his own right. After van Gogh paintings became fashionable in the 1920s, his "van Gogh-style" paintings were sold as genuine.

Smith, William and **Charles Eaton.** These English partners specialized in casting "Medieval" works of art such as medallions and statuary. An example is *Pair of Bishops,* c. 1850.

Stein, David. Stein, who was born in France and was active in the 1970s, counterfeited Picasso, Chagall, and Matisse. Others whose work he imitated were Cocteau, Bonnard, Derain, van Dongen, and Marie Laurencin. His wife (and partner) has written a book about their forgeries.

The Spanish Forger. An anonymous painter who may have been French, the Spanish Forger was active in Paris in the late 19th and early 20th centuries. He created five full-sized illuminated Medieval manuscripts and miniatures.

Van Meegeren, Hans. The Dutch Van Meegeren, one of the most notorious forgers of the 20th century, has works currently in the collection of Amsterdam's Rijksmuseum such as Vermeer's *The Magdalen Washing Christ's Feet, Woman Playing the Cittern,* and *Woman Reading a Letter,* Frans Hal's *Malle Babbe*, and Terborch's *A Man.* The Courtauld Institute has his Baburen forgery entitled *The Procuress,* and Rotterdam's Museum Boymans-van Beuningen has his forgery of Vermeer's *The Supper at Emmaus.* Van Meegeren's copy of Vermeer's *The Woman Taken in Adultery* was sold to the infamous Nazi Hermann Goering. Other known copies were *Portrait of a Burgher* (in the manner of Terborch) and *The Letter* (in the manner of Vermeer).

*"Fine Art is that in which the hand, the head, and
the heart of man go together."*

—JOHN RUSKIN, 1819–1900, British writer and critic

ANONYMOUS COPIES AND FORGERIES

As well as the famous forgers named, there were also many "anonymous" forgers, possibly students or family members, many of whom copied the master's work as a way of learning a technique. Museums display such work, created in approximately the same time period as work by the master, and label it as "Attributed to _____," "School of _____" or (for example) "Rembrandt??"

And, of course, the marketplace is filled with forgeries of sculpture and cultural or ancient artifacts. While you can assume that museum curators have done scholarly research and labeled their works honestly, it isn't quite so safe to assume that anything you see for sale in a gallery is what it purports to be. Just know the reputation of the gallery owner before making any substantial purchase.

> **Kouros.** A Grecian Kouros (stiffly standing male figure), purchased by the Getty in 1985 for between $9 and 12 million, is considered by some experts to have been made in Rome in 1980. The verdict is still out on this one, as other experts still maintain its authenticity. The museum now displays it with a label: "Circa 530 BC or modern forgery."

> **Terracotta Warrior.** This "Etruscan" (c. 9th century B.C.) artifact originally in the Metropolitan Museum's Collection was made in 1961 in Italy.

ARTISTS FREQUENTLY COPIED

> **Blakelock, Ralph Albert.** Sometimes his name was signed on paintings he had not done—by an unscrupulous dealer or (to produce income) by his daughter, Marian.

> **Chagall, Dali, Miro,** and **Picasso.** Popular artists such as these were easily imitated, and forged prints by these artists continue to be sold by the hundreds as originals.

Corot, Jean Baptiste. One wit says, ". . . of the 700 authentic works painted by Jean Baptiste Corot, 8,000 of them are in the United States."

Harnett, William. Harnett specialized in trompe l'oeil still lifes. A total of 79 forged or misattributed "Harnett" paintings were done by at least 35 different artists. Moreover, many paintings by John F. Peto, a contemporary of Harnett and also a well-recognized trompe l'oeil painter, had Harnett's signature added by forgers because Harnett's work sold for more money than Peto's.

Homer, Winslow. Over 500 pictures attributed to Homer were not done by him.

Miró, Joan. According to the man who was given authority by the Joan Miró family to authenticate his work, several hundred fake Miró paintings and several thousand forged Miró prints and lithographs exist.

Remington, Frederic. Although a Yale graduate, Remington painted the "Wild West" during the late 19th century. If a painting of his bears a signature accompanied by a tiny drawing of a bucking mule, it was probably added by a Chicago forger.

Russell, Charles M. Like Remington, Russell was a famous 19th-century painter of the American West. There are 107 counterfeit Russell oils on record. One way to identify a fake is if it is signed "Chas. M. Russell."

Ryder, Albert Pinkham. An American who worked in the late 19th and early 20th centuries, Ryder specialized in dark, Romantic paintings of the sea. He painted approximately 165 oils, but 1,000 fake "Ryders" exist.

Sargent, John Singer. At least 100 fakes have been verified as not having been painted by this famous late 19th-century American portrait artist.

Warhol, Andy. Many prints by this 20th-century Pop artist were made without his knowledge from his silk screens by people visiting his studio. Occasionally they signed them with his name (poorly), whereas Warhol didn't always bother to sign his work or sometimes had his mother, whose handwriting he loved, sign for him.

Whistler, James Abbott McNeill. Whistler was a 19th-century American painter whose most famous work was *Arrangement in Grey and Black: The*

Artist's Mother. One *Whistler's Mother* was painted as a joke, with Whistler's knowledge, by his friend, Harper Pennington. It was later assumed, even by heirs of Whistler, to be genuine.

Zurbarán, Francisco. This Spanish 17th-century painter specialized in somber paintings of monks and religious subjects. An almost identical copy of an original Zurbarán *Still Life* from the Norton Simon Museum was created hundreds of years later.

ART AND THE FORTUNES OF CRIME, LOVE, AND WAR

From ancient Egyptian tomb robbers to the 19th-century traveler who stole part of the *Sphinx's* Beard, art crime is as old as art itself. Possession of the artwork and monetary gains have not always been the motivator. For example, art that belonged in one country was moved to another through the "fortunes of war" or intermarriage between royal families and changing boundaries.

Depending on how you look at it, perhaps some of the greatest thieves (in addition to Hitler's Great Acquisitor Hermann Goering and Napoleon, who had his own "Removal Man") were German archaeologist Heinrich von Schliemann and England's Lord Elgin. Von Schliemann discovered and excavated the treasure of Troy *(Priam's Treasure)*, which was taken to Germany. It vanished from Germany at the end of World War II, and only in 1991 was it announced that the gold was in Russia. Lord Elgin "saved" the friezes of Athen's Parthenon from the Turks in 1801, later selling them to the British Museum.

Since 1998, work that was looted during World War II has been gradually returned to rightful owners or their heirs. Much of the work was purchased in good faith by dealers, collectors, and museums, but was later discovered to have been stolen. An attempt to halt rampant art theft has resulted in the establishment of the following agencies: (Information from some of these agencies is readily available on the Internet.)

✧ Association of American Museums (AAM) and the Association of Art Museum Directors are in the process of creating uniform guidelines for posting Holocaust-era acquisitions on the Internet.

✧ Art Loss Register, New York and London, was founded in 1991 as a database of stolen art and antiques.

✧ Art Recovery Team, an agency formed in 2001 by the U.S. Customs Service, is dedicated to increasing public awareness. It posts stolen images on its Web site, www.customs.gov.

✧ Art Theft Units are maintained by the New York Police Department and the Los Angeles Police Department.

✧ Art Theft/World's Most Wanted Art/Art Recovery Project is on the Internet and contains interesting information about art crime.

✧ European Commission on Looted Art (ECLA) was established as a response to the international conference on World War II-era looted cultural assets.

✧ International Foundation for Art Research (IFAR) maintains a database to help avoid forgery, theft, and misattribution.

✧ Interpol is an international police organization located in Lyon, France, which also tracks art thefts from 17 countries.

✧ Museum Security Network. A mailing list "offers information about cultural property incidents such as art theft, looting of art in wartime, fire, forgery, etc."

✧ National Stolen Art File (NSAF), maintained by the FBI since the early 1980s, is available only to law-enforcement agencies for thefts of paintings, prints, and sculpture with a minimum value of $2,000.

✧ The Art Dealers' Association puts out theft-alert notices to its members.

✧ World Jewish Congress Art Recovery Commission, New York, has identified 1,700 artworks in museums worldwide that are of questionable provenance.

✧ Internet Project Restitution, a new Russian Web site, is posting some looted art treasures at www.lostart.ru.

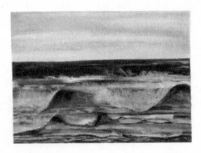

Art Crime: A Tale of Four Horses

The four famous bronze horses on the balcony of St. Mark's Church in Venice are reproductions of what may be the most traveled horses in history. (The originals are in the church museum.) They demonstrate admirably the fortunes of war, as you'll discover from the following timeline.

c. 330 B.C.	The four bronze horses on the balcony of the Church of St. Mark, Venice, are said to be the work of the Greek sculptor Praxiteles.
A.D. 54–68	They were taken by Nero to Rome and placed atop a triumphal arch.
A.D. 200	The horses were brought to Venice.
A.D. 320	The horses were taken to Constantinople (Istanbul) by Emperor Constantine.
1204	The Italians took the horses from Constantinople as trophies from the Fourth Crusade and brought them back to Venice.
1797	Napoleon conquered Italy and took the horses to Paris.
1815	The horses were returned to Venice by the French at the fall of the French Empire. Copies of the horses may be seen in Paris on an arch in the Tuileries Gardens.
1941	The horses were taken to Rome during World War II and returned to Venice after the war.

"Sir, when their backsides look good enough to slap, there's nothing more to do."

—PETER PAUL RUBENS, 1577–1640, Flemish painter, commenting on when he considers a work complete

GREAT ART THEFTS

Here are just a few notable art thefts that have occurred in recent years. (Values given represent what the work was worth at the time of the theft, not what the artwork might be worth in the current market.) If a "Year Recovered" is not noted, further information was not available.

Year Stolen	Year Recovered	
1876	1901	Thomas Gainsborough's *Duchess of Devonshire* was stolen by a thief to trade for his brother's release from prison.
1911	1913	Leonardo da Vinci's *Mona Lisa* was taken from the Louvre by an Italian, who claimed to resent Napoleon's "taking" it from Italy. (It was actually originally sold to a French citizen.) It was missing for two years.
1914	1988	Nine objects were stolen from the Musée des Beaux Arts et d'Archéologie, Bésançon, France. One was *Hypnos*, god of sleep, a 1st-century Roman Bronze. It was returned to Bésançon by the St. Louis Art Museum in 1988 when it was discovered it had been stolen.
1921	1922	Eight Cézanne paintings were stolen in Aix-en-Provence, France, and reportedly found after ransom was paid.
1930s	1970	Art and archaeological treasures, including the remains of an entire Roman temple, Etruscan vases, and Renaissance gold and silver were discovered hidden in a barn near Rome.
1940	1999	Gustav Klimt's *Fulfillment*, painted in 1910, was appropriated by the Nazis, returned 59 years later.
1941	1999	Fernand Léger's *Woman in Red and Green* was taken from a Paris gallery by the Nazis. It was returned to the collector's family.
c. 1943	2000	Giorgio Vasari's *Marriage Feast of Cana* was returned to the Fine Arts Museum in Budapest by the Montreal Museum of Fine Arts, which had purchased it from a pawnshop in 1961.
1944	1945	A 1944 inventory of artwork in Hitler's personal art gallery at Linz, Austria, listed Brueghel's *The Harvesters*, Rembrandt's *Hendrikje Stoffels*, Jan Vermeer's *Artist's Studio*, and Watteau's

The Dance. These artworks had formerly belonged to private collections in the occupied countries and Germany. Both Hitler and Goering planned postwar museums, and their acquisitions were stored in the castle of Neuschwanstein and a salt mine near Alt Ausee (where van Eyck's *Altarpiece* was one of thousands of stolen treasures).

1945	2000	Jacopo de'Barbari's *Portrait of Christ,* stolen by American troops at the end of World War II, was offered to the Weimar Museum (who had title to it) for $100,000. The framer who "discovered" it attempted to sell it, but was arrested.
1961	1965	Goya's *The Duke of Wellington* was stolen from the National Gallery in London by an unemployed truck driver who insisted that a sum equal to the painting's price ($392,000) be donated to the needy.
1966	1966	Two young men took a Picasso *Demoiselles d'Avignon* watercolor study from the Philadelphia Museum of Art. Unable to sell the painting because it was thought to be a fake by a potential buyer, they demanded maximum publicity or they would burn the painting.
1966	1966	Coreggio's *Madonna and Child with St. John,* stolen from The Art Institute of Chicago, was found (following a tip) in a trash-can, wrapped in stained brown paper.
1967	1967	Eight famous paintings were taken from the Dulwich Art Gallery in England and recovered after only a few days. They included Rembrandt's *A Girl at a Window, Portrait of Titus,* and *Portrait of Jacob de Ghyn,* Rubens's *St. Barbara, Three Nymphs with Cornucopia,* and *Three Graces,* Elsheimer's *Susannah and the Elders,* and Gerrit Dou's *Lady at the Virginals.*
1968	1968	Rembrandt's *Portrait of a Young Man* was stolen from the George Eastman House in Rochester, New York, and recovered nine months later.
1970	1972	Five French oil paintings stolen from the Ohara Art Museum in Kurashiki, Japan, were recovered two years later.
1971	1973	Rembrandt's *The Flight Into Egypt* was stolen from the Municipal Museum of Tours, France, and recovered two years later.

Year Stolen	Year Recovered	
1972		Eighteen paintings, including Rembrandt's *Landscape with Cottage* and Rubens's *Head of a Young Man,* were taken from the Montreal Museum of Fine Arts.
1971	1972	Vermeer's *The Letter* was stolen by a thief who demanded that $4.8 million ransom be paid to assist Bengali refugees. The painting was recovered.
1972		Paintings including *Judgment of Cambyses* by Rubens and several other paintings were stolen from a moving van en route from Detroit to New York.
1973		Two Rembrandts were taken from the Taft Museum, Cincinnati, Ohio.
1972	1972	Rembrandt's *St. Bartholomew,* Picasso's *Mother and Child,* and Gauguin's *Head of a Woman* and *Brooding Woman* were stolen, and recovered from the Worcester, Massachusetts Art Museum.
1973	1973	Eighteen 14th- and 15th-century religious panels stolen from Ravenna's Fine Arts Academy were hurled in a sack out a car window during a police chase. Police stopped to recover the artwork, lost the thieves.
1974	1974	A Winslow Homer painting, taken from the Malden, Massachusetts Public Library, was recovered shortly thereafter.
1974	1974	The (then) "World's biggest art theft" ($20.4 million), Vermeer's *A Woman Writing a Letter* ($7.2 million), Franz Hals' *The Lute Player,* Goya's *Woman in a Mantilla,* and other artworks were stolen from a private estate in Ireland. A wealthy young woman was the daring leader who led the group of thieves to take 19 paintings. Her ransom note asked for $1.5 million and the transfer of IRA prisoners from England to prison in Ireland.
1975	1975	Thirty-six paintings worth $13.2 million, including those of van Gogh, Cézanne, Gauguin, Renoir, and Corot, were stolen from Milan's Municipal Gallery of Modern Art. They were recovered two months later in an empty apartment.
1975	1976	Raphael's *The Mute Girl,* a *Flagellation of Christ,* and *The Madonna of Senigalia* were taken from Urbino's Ducal Palace, but later found in a hotel room and the thieves arrested.

1977		Nineteen paintings were stolen from the Pitti Palace, including Rubens' *Three Graces,* and several paintings that dated back to the Medici collection. Sixteen of the nineteen were recovered.
1977		Several Grandma Moses paintings were taken from her childhood home.
1978	1978	Twenty-two paintings, including a Dégas and Renoir, were stolen from the Hamburg Art Gallery. The thief, a fish dealer, who intended to sell them back to the museum, was caught when recognized by a museum employee (and, one presumes, a customer of his).
1978	1999	Rembrandt's *Portrait of a Rabbi,* Aert van der Neer's *River Scene at Night*, and Anthonie de Lorme's *Interior of the Church of Saint Lawrence, Rotterdam* were stolen from the M. H. De Young Memorial Museum, San Francisco. All three paintings were left in a box 22 years later at a free, walk-in weekly appraisal session at the William Doyle Galleries in New York.
1978	1980	Ten paintings, including Gauguin's *Portrait of Madelaine Bernard,* Sisley's *Lane of Poplars Near Moret,* and *The Yellow Scarf,* and paintings by Daubigny, Sisley, Courbet, and Signac were stolen from a truck as they were being returned from an exhibition to museums around France.
1978	1978	An employee stole four silver candlesticks from the Brooklyn Museum, later recovered by New York City's Art Crime Squad.
1978	1978	Six sculptures stolen and recovered from the St. Louis Art Museum included: 18th-century German bronzes, *Hope* and *Prudence,* a 17th-century wood carving of *St. Sebastian,* Remington's *Bronco Buster,* and three Rodin sculptures. Two of the three thieves were mysteriously shot within a few days of the theft.
1978	1979	Three Cézannes were stolen from the Art Institute of Chicago: *Madame Cézanne in Yellow Armchair, Still Life of Apples,* and *Landscape of House by a River.* All three were recovered several months later from the home of a museum shipping clerk.
1980		*The Tree of Life,* part of Judy Chicago's *The Birth Project,* was stolen.

Year Stolen	Year Recovered	
1980		Nineteen paintings including Picasso's *Young Boy on a Horse* and Renoir's *The Bust of a Child* and *A Large Woman Bathing* were stolen from a Monte Carlo private collection.
1980	1980	$750,000 worth of Andrew Wyeth paintings stolen from his collection were recovered soon afterward.
1980		Sixteen paintings, including three Renoirs, were stolen from the Buenos Aires Museum (total value of theft, $24 million).
1983	1983	$35 million worth of old-master paintings were stolen from the Budapest Museum of Fine Arts. Included were Raphael's *Mary with the Christ Child, Young John the Baptist* (called the *Esterhazy Madonna*), a *Portrait of a Young Man,* (attributed to Raphael), and a Tintorreto painting. They were recovered in 1983 in a monastery near Athens, Greece.
1985	1990	Nine paintings including Caravaggio's *Nativity of Christ,* Vermeer's *Lady Writing a Letter with Her Maid,* and Monet's *Impression, Soleil Levant* were stolen by five gunmen from the Musée Marmottan, Paris, and not recovered for five years.
1985	1989	One hundred forty Pre-Columbian treasures, including Mayan, Aztec, Mixtec, and Zapotec items, were stolen from the National Museum of Anthropology, Mexico City. One hundred eleven were recovered.
1986		Countless artifacts were looted from the Sipan tomb in Peru.
1986	1986	A Picasso painting was stolen from the National Gallery of Victoria, Australia, by "Australian Cultural Terrorists" who demanded an increase in the national arts budget and the awarding of an annual prize to young artists.
1986		Three hundred paintings were taken from the Bennington Museum, Vermont. Most of them were recovered.
1987		Three Picassos on paper, four Wifredo Lam artworks, 20 prints and two originals by Luis Caballero were stolen from a gallery in Coral Gables, Florida.
1987		Five hundred etchings and lithographs of Raphael Soyer's work from the 1920s to his death in 1987 (worth several hundred thousand dollars) were taken from his home.
1988		*Trading at Westport Landing* by Thomas Hart Benton was stolen from a collector.

1988	1988	Artworks by Joan Miró and Henri de Toulouse-Lautrec were taken from the Fundacion Miró Museum in Barcelona. All work was recovered, and the eight thieves arrested.
1988	1988	Two Picasso sculptures taken from a gallery were recovered: a diver found one in the Amite River near McComb, Mississippi, where the sculpture had been thrown from a bridge, and the other from a pawnshop where the thief received $50.00 for it.
1988		Édouard Manet's *Bouquet of Peonies* was stolen from the Heckscher Museum in Huntington, New York.
1988	1988	Van Gogh's *Carnations,* Cézanne's *Bottle with Apples,* and Johan Jongkind's *House of Maitre Billaud in Nevers* were taken from Amsterdam's Municipal Museum. These artworks, valued at $52 million, were recovered within two weeks.
1988	1988	Artwork worth $10 million was stolen from a New York gallery specializing in work by old masters. Included were two paintings by Fra Angelico, a Tintoretto, Carracci, Castiglione, Veronese, and other French, Dutch, and Italian master paintings and drawings. All were recovered through a middleman who contacted insurance companies.
1988	1988	Eighty-one items of Asian artwork taken from the Walters Art Gallery in Baltimore were recovered in the basement of a museum guard's home. These included snuff bottles, figurines, incense burners, and a "Peach Bloom" vase.
1989	1989	Three van Gogh's, *The Potato Eaters* (valued at $39.9 million), *Dried Sunflowers,* and *Weavers Interior,* were taken for ransom from the Kroller Mueller Museum in Otterlo, Netherlands. The thieves were caught and the paintings recovered.
1989		Two Velasquez paintings worth $2.3 million, and a Carreno de Miranda worth $820,000 were stolen from the Royal Palace in Madrid.
1989		Four paintings were stolen from a Boston gallery owner. The thieves asked the owner which paintings they should take, and he suggested well-known pieces that would be easy to trace, including two paintings by Grandma Moses.
1989		A Yuan Dynasty vase was stolen from the Museum of Fine Arts, Boston.

Year Stolen	Year Recovered	
1989	1989	Sixty-five Russian icons were stolen from a Houston gallery. The thief, who was caught, was a Russian citizen carrying false American documents.
1989	1990	Matisse's *View Over Collioure Port, Woman in Brittany, Devilacqua* and five other paintings were stolen from an apartment in Nice, France, and recovered within eleven days. They were in the back seat of the thief's car when he was pulled over for a routine check.
1989	1989	Renaissance paintings worth $4 million were stolen from a gallery in Zurich. All three thieves were arrested by the FBI.
1990		A van Gogh painting, *Wheat Field with Shocks* (worth $1.8 million) was stolen from a customs warehouse in Zurich.
1990		Two hundred sixty-eight ancient objects were stolen from the Museum of Ancient Corinth, Greece.
1990		Thirteen paintings worth $200 million, including Vermeer's *The Concert*, were stolen from the Isabella Stewart Gardner Museum, Boston.
1991	1991	Twenty van Gogh paintings were stolen from Amsterdam's National Museum, but quickly recovered. Several were seriously damaged.
1994	1994	Edvard Munch's *The Scream* was stolen from the Oslo National Gallery during the Lillehamer Olympics. It was returned after negotiations with an influential art dealer who brokered the return of the painting.
1992	1999	Rubens's *Unidentified Man Wearing a Ruff* was stolen from a private Belgian owner by swindlers and recovered by the FBI from a private American collector who did not know it was stolen at the time of purchase. The painting was returned to its Belgian owner.
1998	1998	Vincent van Gogh's *The Gardener* and *L'Arlesienne* and Cézanne's *Cabonon de Jourdan* were stolen from the National Gallery of Modern Art, Rome. A security guard was among the eight Italians arrested.
1998		A Corot, *The Chemin de Sèvres*, was stolen from the Louvre.
c. 1943	1999	Two hundred fifty art objects, including three Frans Hals paintings, were returned by Austrian State Museum collections to the heirs of the Rothschild banking family.

c. 1943	1999	Matisse's *Odalisque* was returned to its Jewish owners by the Seattle Art Museum, which had purchased it in good faith from a dealer.
1941	2001	Cezanne's *The Sea at l'Estaque* was returned to its heirs by the Rau Collection in Paris.
1941	2001	A 17th-century Flemish still life was returned to heirs by the National Gallery of the United States.
2000		The first major theft of the millennium occurred on January 1, 2000 when Cézanne's *Auvers-sur-Oise* was stolen from the Ashmolean Museum, Oxford, England.
2001		Rembrandt's *Self-Portrait* (1630) and Renoir's *The Conversation* and *The Young Parisian Girl* were stolen for ransom from the Stockholm Museum. One Renoir has been recovered, and the thieves are in jail.
2001	2002	Chagall's *Study for Over Vitebsk* (1914), painted while Chagall lived in Russia, was taken from the Jewish Museum in New York. It was found in a postal facility in Topeka, Kansas.
2003		Cellini's *Saliera* (the "Mona Lisa of sculptures") was stolen from Vienna's Art History Museum (Kunsthistoriches), despite high-tech motion sensors and round-the-clock guards.

25 BOOKS FOR THE ART LOVER

Literally thousands of art books have been written about specific artists, exhibitions, movements, techniques, and cultures. Following are a few that would make good resources for an art lover's or collector's personal library.

Archer, Michael, *Art Since 1960,* Thames and Hudson, London, 1997

Arnasan, H. H. and Marla F. Prather, *History of Modern Art,* Fourth edition, Harry N. Abrams Inc., New York, 1998

Art: A World History, DK Publishing, New York, Dorling Kindersley, London, 1998, 2002

Bearden, Romare and Harry Henderson, *A History of African American Artists from 1792 to the Present,* Pantheon Books, New York, 1993

Beckett, Sister Wendy, *Sister Wendy's 1000 Masterpieces,* DK Publishing, New York, 1999

Belton, Robert, *The World of Art from Aboriginal to American Pop, Renaissance Masters to Post Modernism,* Watson-Guptil, New York, 2002

Cerrito, Joan (editor), *Contemporary Artists,* St. James Press, Detroit, Michigan, 1996

Chilvers, Ian, *Oxford Dictionary of Twentieth Century Art,* Oxford University Press, Oxford, England, 1999

Chilvers, Ian, Harold Osborne, and Dennis Farr, *The Oxford Dictionary of Art,* Oxford University Press, Oxford, England, 2001

Clarke, Michael, *Oxford Concise Dictionary of Art Terms,* Oxford University Press, Oxford, England, 2001

Collings, Matthew, *This is Modern Art,* Watson Guptill, New York, 2000

Gombrich, Ernst Hans, *The Story of Art,* Phaidon Press Ltd., London, 1995

Hodge, Nicola and Libby Anson, *The A–Z of Art, The World's Greatest and Most Popular Artists and Their Works,* Carlton Books, London, 2001

Hoving, Thomas, *Art for Dummies,* IDG Books Worldwide, Inc., New York, 1999

Janson, H. W., *History of Art,* Sixth edition, Harry N. Abrams, New York, 2001

Jeffrey, Ian, *The Photography Book,* Phaidon Press Ltd., London, 1997

Lucie-Smith, Edward, *Art Today,* Phaidon Press Ltd., London, 1995

Reimschneider, Burkhard and Uta Grosenick (editors), *Art at the Turn of the Millennium,* Taschen, Cologne, Germany, 2000

Reimschneider, Burkhard and Uta Grosenick, editors, *Art Now,* Taschen, Cologne, Germany, 2001

Richter, Klaus, *Art from Impressionism to the Internet,* Prestel, Munich, New York, 2001

Rush, Michael, *New Media in Late 20th-Century Art,* Thames & Hudson, New York, 1999

Skokstad, Marilyn, *Art History,* Harry N. Abrams, Inc., New York, 2002

Steele, James, *Architecture Today,* Phaidon Press Ltd., London, 1997

The Art Book, Phaidon Press, Ltd., London, 1994

The Twentieth Century Art Book, Phaidon Press Ltd., London, 1996

25 GREAT ART MAGAZINES

Art magazines can be as varied in focus as art itself. Before selecting one for subscription, go to the library or buy a single issue to see if it offers what interests you. These magazines were selected because they are well established and have a large circulation.

Magazine	Publisher	Location
African Arts	African Studies Center	Los Angeles
American Art	Rizzoli International	New York
American Artist	BPI Communications, Inc.	New York
American Craft	American Craft Council	New York
American Indian Art Magazine	American Indian Art	Scottsdale, Arizona
American Photo	Hachette Filipacchi Magazines, Inc.	New York
Aperture	Aperture	New York
Apollo	Apollo Magazine Limited	London
Architectural Digest	Condé Nast Publications, Inc.	New York
Art & Antiques	Trans World Publishing, Inc.	Atlanta, Georgia
Art & Auction	Art & Auction	New York
Art in America	Brant Publications, Inc.	New York
Art Newspaper	Umberto Allemandi & Co. Publishing	London
Art on Paper	Fanning Publishing Co.	New York
Artforum	Artforum International Magazine	New York
Artist's Magazine	F & W Publications	Cincinnati, Ohio
ARTnews	Artnews Associates	New York
Arts of Asia	Arts of Asia	Hong Kong
Burlington Magazine	Burlington Magazine Publications	London
Canadian Art	Canadian Art Foundation	Toronto, Ontario, Canada
Canadian Forum	Canadian Forum	Ottawa, Ontario, Canada

Magazine	Publisher	Location
Fine Art Magazine	Sunstorm Arts Publishing Co., Inc.	Ronkonkoma, New York
Modern Painters	Universal House	London
New Art Examiner	New Art Examiner Press	Chicago
Southwest Art	Cowles Magazine, Inc.	Stamford, Connecticut

FILMS AND PLAYS ABOUT ART

Artists tend to lead interesting, often eccentric lives, which makes them great fodder for entertainment, whether in the form of film or plays. Here are a few recommendations for you to consider.

FILMS

Artist	Film	Release Date
Dali, Salvador	*Bunuel and King Solomon's Table*	2001
Basquiat, Jean-Michel	*Basquiat*	2001
Gainsborough, Thomas	*Kitty*	1945
Gauguin, Paul	*Gauguin the Savage*	1980
	The Moon and Sixpence	1942
	Wolf at the Door	1987
Gautier, Henri	*Savage Messiah*	1972
Gentileschi, Artemisia	*Artemisia*	1998
Gogh, Vincent van	*Vincent*	1987
Goya, Francisco	*The Naked Maja*	1959
	Goya in Bordeaux	2000
Greco, El	*El Greco*	1966
Kahlo, Frida	*Frida*	2002
Mapplethorpe, Robert	*Dirty Pictures*	2000
Michelangelo	*The Agony and the Ecstasy*	1965
Modigliani, Amedeo	*The Lovers of Montparnasse*	1957

Artist	Film	Release Date
O'Keeffe, Georgia, and Stieglitz, Alfred	*Stieglitz Loves O'Keeffe*	1996
	Til' the End of Time	2000
Picasso, Pablo	*The Adventures of Picasso*	1978
	The Mystery of Picasso (French)	1955
	The Picasso Summer	1969
	Surviving Picasso	1996
	Picasso at the Lapin Agile	1996
Pollock, Jackson	*Pollock*	2001
Rembrandt van Rijn	*Rembrandt*	1936
Rivera, Diego	*The Cradle Will Rock*	2000
Rothko, Mark	*The Rothko Conspiracy*	1983
Toulouse-Lautrec, Henride	*Moulin Rouge*	1953 and 2001
Warhol, Andy	*I Shot Andy Warhol*	1996
Art theft	*The Thomas Crowne Affair*	1968 and 1999

PLAYS ABOUT ARTISTS

Title	Subject	Premiere
Art	An all-white painting and a group of friends	1997
Basquiat	Basquiat, Warhol, and Schnabel	1996
The Cradle Will Rock	Diego Rivera	2000
Occupant	Sculptor Louise Nevelson	2002
Pandora's Bell (Japanese)	Discovery of an ancient art object	1999
Stanley	English painter Stanley Spencer	1996
Sunday in the Park with George	Georges Seurat	1984

OPERA ABOUT ART

The Moon and Sixpence	Gauguin	1957

BOOKS ABOUT ART AND ARTISTS

Browse the art section of your local bookstore or library, and you'll find dozens of nonfiction books about individual artists or "schools" of art—and those would just be a fraction of the published works on these subjects. In addition, you can also find a number of fiction works with art as a key element of the plot. Following are a few good fiction selections. If you love art, at least a few of these should appeal to you. (When a book is about a specific artist, that artist is noted in parentheses after the title.)

FICTION ABOUT ARCHITECTS

Author	Title	Publisher	Release Date
Begley, Louis	*As Max Saw It*	Knopf	1994
Boll, Heinrich	*Billiards at Half-Past Nine*	McGraw-Hill	1962
Colegate, Isabel	*The Summer of the Royal Visit*	Knopf	1992
Dickens, Charles	*Martin Chuzzlewit*	Knopf	1994
Ferber, Edna	*So Big*	Doubleday	1987
Gill, William	*Fortune's Child*	HarperCollins	1993
Greene, Graham	*A Burnt-out Case*	Viking	1961
Lively, Penelope	*City of the Mind*	Harcourt	1991
Rand, Ayn	*The Fountainhead*	Penguin Books	1943

FICTION ABOUT ART, GENERAL

Author	Title	Publisher	Release Date
Francis, Dick	*To the Hilt*	G. P. Putnam's Sons	1996
Francis, Dick	*Shattered*	G. P. Putnam's Sons	2000
Hoving, Thomas	*Discovery*	Simon & Schuster	1989
Koning, Hans	*Pursuit of a Woman on the Hinge of History*	Lumen Editions	1997
Malcolm, John	*Hung Over: a Tim Simpson Mystery*	St. Martin's Press	1994
McCarthy, Mary	*Cannibals and Missionaries*	Harcourt	1979

FICTION ABOUT ART CRITICS, DEALERS, AND COLLECTORS

Author	Title	Publisher	Release Date
Hoving, Thomas	*Discovery*	Simon & Schuster	1989
Krentz, Jayne Ann	*Grand Passion*	Pocket Books	1994
MacInnes, Helen	*Prelude to Terror*	Harcourt	1978
Morrow, James	*City of Truth*	St. Martin's Press	1992
Moynihan, Danny	*Boogie Woogie*	St. Martin's Press	2001
Schwartz, Gary	*Bets and Scams*	Marion Boyars	1996
Sipherd, Ray	*The Audubon Quartet*	St. Martin's Press	1998
West, Morris L.	*Masterclass*	St. Martin's Press	1991
Wharton, Edith	*False Dawn*	Old New York Publishers	1928
Woods, Stuart	*Imperfect Strangers*	HarperCollins	1995

FICTION ABOUT ART FORGERY

Author	Title	Publisher	Release Date
Banks, Oliver T.	*The Rembrandt Panel*	Little, Brown	c. 1980
Davies, Robertson	*The Lyre of Orpheus*	Viking	1989
Davies, Robertson	*What's Bred in the Bone*	Viking	1995
Fell, Doris E.	*Before Winter Comes*	Thorndike Press	1993
Hoving, Thomas	*Masterpiece*	Simon & Schuster	1986
Ramus, David	*The Gravity of Shadows*	HarperCollins	1998
Ramus, David	*Thief of Light*	HarperCollins	1995

FICTION ABOUT ART GALLERIES AND MUSEUMS

Author	Title	Publisher	Release Date
Brown, Rita Mae	*Venus Envy*	Bantam Books	1993

FICTION ABOUT ART OBJECTS

Author	Title	Publisher	Release Date
Archer, Jeffrey	*A Matter of Honor*	Simon & Schuster	1986
James, Henry	*The Spoils of Poynton* republished in	Houghton	1896
	The Complete Tales of Henry James	Lippincott	1962/1965
Johnson, Velda	*The Etruscan Smile*	Dodd Mead	1977

FICTION ABOUT PAINTERS AND PAINTINGS

Author	Title	Publisher	Release Date
Aiken, Conrad	*Conversation; or Pilgrim's Progress*	Duell, Sloan & Pearce	1940
Banks, Oliver T.	*The Caravaggio Obsession*	Little, Brown	1984
Cary, Joyce	*The Horse's Mouth*	Harper	1950
Chevalier, Tracy	*Girl With a Pearl Earring* (about Vermeer)	Dutton	2000
Clark, Mary Higgins	*A Cry in the Night*	Pocket Books	1993
Colwin, Laurie	*Family Happiness*	Knopf	1982
Durrell, Lawrence	*Clea*	Dutton	1961
Eden, Dorothy	*The Vines of Yarrabee*	Coward McCann	1969
Farmer, Philip Jose	*Riders of the Purple Wage* republished in the	Crown Publishers	1952/1964
	Classic Philip Jose Farmer	Crown Publishers	1984
Frayn, Michael	*Headlong*	Metropolitan Books	1999
Gallico, Paul	*The Snow Goose*	Doubleday	1959
Godwin, Gail	*Violet Clay*	Random House	1978
Graham, Winston	*The Walking Stick*	Collins	1967
Gray, F. du Plessix	*World Without End*	Simon & Schuster	c. 1981
Hemingway, Ernest	*Islands in the Stream*	Scribner	1970
Ishiguro, Kazuo	*An Artist of the Floating World*	Faber	1986
James, Henry	*The Europeans*	Oxford University Press	1985
Kipling, Rudyard	*The Light That Failed*	Doubleday	c. 1899
Krantz, Judith	*Mistral's Daughter*	Thorndike Press	c. 1982
Lofts, Nora	*The Day of the Butterfly*	Doubleday	c. 1979
Mackay, Shena	*The Artist's Widow*	Moyer Bell	1999
Mason, Richard L.	*The World of Suzie Wong*	World Publishing Co.	1957
Momaday, N. Scott	*The Ancient Child*	Doubleday	1989
Murdoch, Iris	*Nuns and Soldiers*	Viking Press	c. 1980
Nathan, Robert	*Portrait of Jennie*	Knopf	1939
Potok, Chaim	*My Name is Asher Lev*	Knopf	1972
Potok, Chaim	*The Gift of Asher Lev*	Knopf	1990
Roberts, Kenneth Lewis	*Northwest Passage*	Doubleday	1937

Author	Title	Publisher	Release Date
Sarton, May	*Joanna and Ulysses*	W.W. Norton & Co.	1963
Siddons, Ann R.	*Hill Towns*	HarperCollins	c. 1993
Sollers, Philippe	*Watteau in Venice*	Charles Scribner and Sons	1994
Stassinopoulos Huffington, Ariana	*Picasso: Creator and Destroyer*	Simon & Schuster	c. 1988
Stone, Irving	*Lust for Life* (van Gogh)	Doubleday	1954
Stone, Irving	*The Agony and the Ecstasy* (Michelangelo)	Doubleday	1961
Styron, William	*Set This House on Fire*	Random House	1960
Vreeland, Susan	*Girl in Hyacinth Blue* (Vermeer)	MacMurray and Beck	1999
Vreeland, Susan	*The Passion of Artemsia*	Penguin, Viking	2002
Weber, Katherine	*The Music Lesson* (Vermeer)	Crown	1999
Wharton, William	*Dad*	Knopf	1981
White, Patrick	*The Vivisector*	Cape	c. 1970
Whitney, Phyllis A.	*The Golden Unicorn*	Doubleday	1976

FICTION ABOUT SCULPTORS

Author	Title	Publisher	Release Date
Delbee, Anne	*Camille Claudel, une femme*	Mercury House	1992
Hawthorne, Nathaniel	*The Marble Faun*	New American Library	1987
Hesse, Hermann	*Narcissus and Goldmund*	Farrar, Straus & Giroux	1968
James, Henry	*Roderick Hudson*	Houghton Mifflin & Co.	1917
Piercy, Marge	*Summer People*	Summit Books	c. 1989
Walters, Minette	*The Sculptress*	St. Martin's Press	1993

"Any art communicates what you're in the mood to receive."
—LARRY RIVERS, 1923–2002, Abstract Expressionist painter

ARTISTS' BIRTHDAYS

J A N U A R Y

1 Bartolomé Esteban Murillo, 1618, Paul Revere, 1735, Alfred Stieglitz, 1864	**2** Ernst Barlach, 1870	**3** August Macke, 1887 Jack Levine, 1915	**4** Marsden Hartley, 1877	**5** Yves Tanguy, 1900	**6** Gustave Doré, 1832	**7** Albert Bierstadt, 1830
8	**9**	**10** Barbara Hepworth, 1903	**11** Alexander Stirling Calder, 1870	**12** John Singer Sargent, 1856 Jusepe Ribera, 1591	**13** Jan van Goyen, 1596	**14** Berthe Morisot, 1841 Henri Fantin-Latour, 1836
15	**16**	**17**	**18** Antoine Pevsner, 1886	**19** Paul Cézanne, 1839	**20**	**21**
22 Francis Picabia, 1879	**23** Édouard Manet, 1832	**24** Robert Motherwell, 1915	**25**	**26** Kees van Dongen, 1877	**27**	**28** Jackson Pollock, 1912 Claes Oldenburg, 1929
29 Barnett Newman, 1905 Peter Voulkos, 1924	**30** Bernardo Bellotto, 1720	**31** Max Pechstein, 1881				

F E B R U A R Y

1 Thomas Cole, 1801	**2**	**3** Norman Rockwell, 1894	**4** Fernand Léger, 1881 Manuel Alvarez Bravo, 1902	**5**	**6**	**7**
8 Franz Marc, 1880 John Ruskin, 1819	**9**	**10**	**11** William H.F. Talbot, 1800 Kazimir Malevich, 1878	**12** Max Beckmann, 1884 Eugene Atget, 1857	**13** Grant Wood, 1892	**14**
15 Charles François Daubigny, 1817	**16**	**17** Raphaelle Peale, 1774	**18** Louis Comfort Tiffany, 1848 Max Klinger, 1857	**19**	**20** Elie Nadelman, 1882 Ansel Adams, 1902	**21** Constantin Brancusi, 1876
22 Rembrandt Peale, 1778 Horace Pippin, 1888	**23** Tom Wesselmann, 1931	**24** Charles Le Brun, 1619 Winslow Homer, 1836	**25** Pierre A. Renoir, 1841	**26** Honoré Daumier, 1808	**27** Joaquin Sorolla, 1863 Marino Marini, 1901	**28**
29 Balthus, 1908						

M A R C H

1 Oscar Kokoschka, 1886 August Saint-Gaudens, 1848	**2**	**3** Arnold Newman, 1918	**4** Sir Henry Raeburn, 1756	**5** Giovanni Battista Tiepolo, 1696	**6** Michelangelo Buonarroti, 1475	**7** Piet Mondrian, 1872 Milton Avery, 1893
8 Anthony Caro, 1924	**9** David Smith, 1906	**10**	**11** Charles Lock Eastlake, Jr., 1836	**12**	**13** William Glackens, 1870 Alexei von Jawlensky, 1864	**14** Reginald Marsh, 1898 Diane Arbus, 1923
15	**16** Rosa Bonheur, 1822	**17** Kate Greenaway, 1846 François Girardon, 1628	**18** Adam Elsheimer, 1578	**19** Josef Albers, 1888, Georges de La Tour, 1593 Albert Pinkham Ryder, 1847	**20** George C. Bingham, 1811 Jean-Antoine Houdon, 1741	**21** Hans Hofmann, 1880
22 Anthony van Dyck, 1599 John Frederick Kensett, 1816	**23** Juan Gris, 1887	**24** John Smibert, 1688 William Morris, 1834, Edward Weston, 1886	**25** Gutzon Borglum, 1867	**26**	**27** Ludwig Mies van der Rohe, 1886 Edward Steichen, 1879	**28** Grace Hartigan, 1922
29	**30** Francisco de Goya, 1746 Vincent van Gogh, 1853	**31** William Morris Hunt, 1824 John La Farge, 1835				

A P R I L

1	**2** Max Ernst, 1891	**3** Henri van de Velde, 1863	**4** Grinling Gibbons, 1648 Edward Hicks, 1780	**5** Jean Honoré Fragonard, 1732	**6** Raphael, 1483, Gustave Moreau, 1826 René Lalique, 1860	**7** Gerrit Dou, 1613
8 Cornelis de Heem, 1631	**9** Eadweard Muybridge, 1830 Victor Vasarely, 1908	**10** Kenneth Noland, 1924	**11** Gustav Vigeland, 1869	**12** Robert Delaunay, 1885, Imogen Cunningham, 1883	**13** Thomas Jefferson, 1743 James Ensor, 1860	**14**
15 Leonardo da Vinci, 1452, Charles Willson Peale, 1841, Theodore Rousseau, 1812	**16** Elisabeth Vigee-Le Brun, 1755	**17**	**18** Max Weber, 1881 Ludwig Meidner, 1884	**19**	**20** Joan Miró, 1893 Daniel Chester French, 1850	**21**
22 Odilon Redon, 1840	**23** J.M.W. Turner, 1775	**24** Willem de Kooning, 1904 Bridget Reiley, 1931	**25** Karel Appel, 1921 Cy Twombly, 1928	**26** Eugène Delacroix, 1798 Dorothea Lange, 1895	**27** Samuel F.B. Morse, 1791	**28**
29	**30**					

M A Y

1	2	3	4	5	6	7
Benjamin Henry Latrobe, 1764 George Inness, 1825			Frederic Edwin Church, 1826		Ernst Kirchner, 1880	
8	**9**	**10**	**11**	**12**	**13**	**14**
Alphonse Legros, 1837					Joseph Stella, 1877 Georges Braque, 1882	
15	**16**	**17**	**18**	**19**	**20**	**21**
Jasper Johns, 1930			Walter Gropius, 1883	Jacob Jordaens, 1593 Gaston Lachaise, 1886	William Thornton, 1759	Albrecht Dürer, 1471 Henri Rousseau, 1844
22	**23**	**24**	**25**	**26**	**27**	**28**
Mary Cassatt, 1844 Marisol, 1930	Franz Kline, 1910	Emmanuel Leutze, 1816	Wil Barnet, 1911		Georges Rouault, 1871	
29	**30**	**31**				
	Alexander Archipenko, 1887	Ellsworth Kelly, 1923				

J U N E

1	2	3	4	5	6	7
Red Grooms, 1937		Raoul Dufy, 1877		Thomas Chippendale, 1718	Velasquez, 1599 John Trumbull, 1756	Paul Gauguin, 1848
8	**9**	**10**	**11**	**12**	**13**	**14**
Sir John Everett Millais, 1829 Frank Lloyd Wright, 1867	Pieter Saenredam, 1597	Gustave Courbet, 1819 André Derain, 1880	John Constable, 1776 Julia Margaret Cameron, 1815	Annie Albers, 1899	Christo, 1935	Margaret Bourke-White, 1906
15	**16**	**17**	**18**	**19**	**20**	**21**
	Jim Dine, 1935	Charles Eames, 1907	Robert W. Weir, 1803	Thomas Sully, 1783	Kurt Schwitters, 1887	Henry Tanner, 1859
22	**23**	**24**	**25**	**26**	**27**	**28**
	Carl Milles, 1875	Robert Henri, 1865	Sam Francis, 1923 Antonio Gaudi, 1852		Philip Guston, 1913	Peter Paul Rubens, 1577
29	**30**					
Robert Laurent, 1890						

J U L Y

1	2	3	4	5	6	7
	André Kertész, 1894	John Singleton Copley, 1738 Jean Dubuffet, 1901	William Rush, 1756	Jean Cocteau, 1889		Marc Chagall, 1887
8 Käthe Kollwitz, 1867	**9** David Hockney, 1937	**10** Camille Pissarro, 1830 J.M. Whistler, 1834, Georgio de Chirico, 1888	**11**	**12** Amedeo Modigliani, 1884 Andrew Wyeth, 1917	**13**	**14** Gustav Klimt, 1862
15 Rembrandt van Rijn, 1606	**16** Sir Joshua Reynolds, 1723 Charles Sheeler, 1883	**17** Camille Corot, 1796 Lyonel Feininger, 1871, Bérénice Abbott, 1898	**18** Gertrude Kasebier, 1852	**19** Edgar Dégas, 1834	**20** László Moholy-Nagy, 1895	**21**
22 Edward Hopper, 1882 Alexander Calder, 1898	**23**	**24** Alex Katz, 1927	**25** Thomas Eakins, 1844	**26** George Catlin, 1796 George Grosz, 1893	**27**	**28** Beatrix Potter, 1866 Marcel Duchamp, 1887
29 Hiram Powers, 1805 Eastman Johnson, 1824	**30** Giorgio Vasari, 1511 Henry Moore, 1898	**31** Erich Heckel, 1883				

A U G U S T

1	2	3	4	5	6	7
	John Sloan, 1871 Arthur Dove, 1880		John Twachtman, 1853	George Tooker, 1920 Naum Gabo, 1890		Emil Nolde, 1867
8 Andy Warhol, 1931	**9**	**10** William M. Harnett, 1848 Reuben Nakian, 1897	**11** Martin Johnson Heade, 1819	**12** George Bellows, 1882	**13** George Luks, 1867	**14**
15	**16**	**17** Larry Rivers, 1923	**18**	**19** Gustave Caillebotte, 1848 Bradley Walker Tomlin, 1899	**20** Eliel Saarinen, 1873 Eero Saarinen, 1910	**21** Asher Durand, 1796 Aubrey Beardsley, 1872
22 Jacques Lipchitz, 1891 Henri Cartier-Bresson, 1908	**23**	**24** George Stubbs, 1724 Alphonse Mucha, 1860	**25**	**26**	**27** Man Ray, 1890	**28** Morris Graves, 1910
29 J.A.D. Ingres, 1780	**30** Jacques Louis David, 1748 Theo van Doesburg, 1883	**31** Georg Jensen, 1866				

S E P T E M B E R

1	2	3	4	5	6	7
Yasuo Kuniyoshi, 1893	Romare Bearden, 1914	Louis Sullivan, 1856	Oskar Schlemmer, 1888		Horatio Greenough, 1805	Grandma Moses, 1860 Jacob Lawrence, 1917
8	**9**	**10** Sir John Soane, 1753	**11**	**12** Ben Shahn, 1898	**13** Robert Indiana, 1928	**14**
15 Antoine Louis Barye, 1795	**16** Jean Arp, 1887 Carl André, 1935	**17**	**18** Mark de Suvero, 1933	**19**	**20**	**21** Hans Hartung, 1904
22	**23** Paul Delvaux, 1897	**24**	**25** Francesco Borromini, 1599 Mark Rothko, 1903	**26** Theodore Gericault, 1791 Lewis W. Hine, 1874	**27**	**28** Caravaggio, 1573 Frederick William MacMonnies, 1863
29 François Boucher, 1703	**30**					

O C T O B E R

1	2	3	4	5	6	7
Claes Berchem, 1620 Larry Poons, 1937		Pierre Bonnard, 1867	**4** Giovanni Battista Piranesi, 1720, Jean François Millet, 1814, Frederick Remington, 1861		LeCorbusier, 1887	
8	**9** Frank Duveneck, 1848	**10** Antoine Watteau, 1684, Benjamin West, 1738, Alberto Giacometti, 1901	**11**	**12** Al Held, 1928	**13**	**14**
15 John Vanderlyn, 1775 Ralph Blakelock, 1847	**16**	**17** Childe Hassam, 1859	**18** Canaletto, 1697	**19** Umberto Boccioni, 1882	**20** Aelbert Cuyp, 1620 Sir Christopher Wren, 1632	**21** Katsushika Hokusai, 1760
22 Robert Rauschenberg, 1925	**23**	**24**	**25** Pablo Picasso, 1881 Arshile Gorky, 1904	**26**	**27** Roy Lichtenstein, 1923	**28** Andrea della Robbia, 1435 Francis Bacon, 1909
29	**30** Alfred Sisley, 1839	**31** Jan Vermeer, 1632, Meindert Hobbema, 1638 Richard Morris Hunt, 1827				

N O V E M B E R

1 Benvenuto Cellini, 1500 Antonio Canova, 1757	**2** Jean Baptiste Chardin, 1699	**3** Walker Evans, 1903	**4** Gerrit van Honthorst, 1590	**5** Philips Koninck, 1619, Washington Allston, 1779, Raymond Duchamp-Villon, 1876	**6**	**7** Francisco de Zurbarán, 1598
8 Charles Demuth, 1883	**9** Stanford White, 1853	**10** William Hogarth, 1697 Sir Jacob Epstein, 1880	**11** Paul Signac, 1863 Édouard Vuillard, 1868	**12** Auguste Rodin, 1840	**13**	**14** Claude Monet, 1840 John Steuart Curry, 1897
15 Georgia O'Keeffe, 1887 Wayne Thiebaud, 1920	**16**	**17** Agnolo Bronzino, 1503 Isamu Noguchi, 1904	**18** Louis Daguerre, 1787	**19**	**20** Paulus Potter, 1625	**21** René Magritte, 1898
22	**23** José Orozco, 1883	**24** Henri de Toulouse-Lautrec, 1864 Cass Gilbert, 1859	**25**	**26** George Segal, 1924	**27** Joséde Creeft, 1884	**28** William Blake, 1757 Morris Louis, 1912
29 James Rosenquist, 1933	**30** Andrea Palladio, 1508 Adriaen van de Velde, 1636					

D E C E M B E R

1	**2** Georges Seurat, 1859 Otto Dix, 1891	**3** Gilbert Stuart, 1755	**4** Wassily Kandinsky, 1866	**5** Walt Disney, 1901	**6** Frederic Bazille, 1841	**7** Gian Lorenzo Bernini, 1598 Stuart Davis, 1894
8 Aristide Maillol, 1861 Diego Rivera, 1886	**9** Roy deCarava, 1919	**10** Adriaen van Ostade, 1610	**11** Mark Tobey, 1890	**12** Edvard Munch, 1863 Helen Frankenthaler, 1928	**13**	**14**
15 David Teniers II, 1610, George Romney, 1734, Oscar Niemeier, 1907	**16**	**17** Paul Cadmus, 1904	**18** Willem van de Velde II, 1633 Paul Klee, 1879	**19**	**20** Pieter de Hooch, 1629	**21** Masaccio, 1401
22 Max Bill, 1908	**23** John Marin, 1870	**24** Joseph Cornell, 1903 Ad Reinhardt, 1913	**25** Paul Manship, 1885 Raphael Soyer, 1899	**26**	**27**	**28**
29	**30** W. Eugene Smith, 1918	**31** Henri Matisse, 1869				

CHAPTER 2

Art History and Appreciation

*"I like to make an image that's so simple you can't avoid it,
and so complicated you can't figure it out."*
—ALEX KATZ, 1927, American Pop Art painter

TIMELINES OF ART HISTORY

Art was not created independently of the other events of civilization, but rather reflects the influence of everything else that was happening in that particular culture. Long before art was recognized as a civilized pursuit, when it took on such "primitive" forms as cave painting, art was still an important part of human culture. It served as a tool for decorating functional items for everyday use, recording important events, bringing good fortune in the present or hereafter, and enhancing worship. It is important for us to recognize that objects and paintings that we see in museums belonged to some person or place where they may not even have been considered art.

ART AND CULTURE, 35,000–500 B.C.

Most of what we know about what the world was like at this time comes from objects found in tombs, ancient sculpture, and cave paintings and buried treasure. We can only speculate how people lived by examining the artifacts and architecture where they lived.

VISUAL ARTS AND ARCHITECTURE

35,000–20,000 B.C.	Old Stone Age, China
c. 35,000–10,000 B.C.	cave paintings, Pêche Merle, France
c. 25,000 B.C.	*Venus of Willendorf,* Austria
8,000–500 B.C.	rock paintings, Sahara Desert, Africa
c. 3100 B.C.	White Temple, Ur (Iraq)
c. 3000 B.C.	Narmer's Palette, Egypt
c. 2800–1550 B.C.	Stonehenge, England
2530 B.C.	Great Sphinx, Egypt
2528 B.C.	Pyramid of Cheops, Egypt
800–700 B.C.	Dipylon Vase, Greece
500 B.C.	Charioteer of Delphi, Greece

LITERATURE

c. 2150 B.C.	tale of *Gilgamesh,* Sumer
c. 1500–1300 B.C.	*Rigveda* stories, India
1100 B.C.	first Chinese dictionary
750–650 B.C.	Homer's *Iliad* and *Odyssey*
618 B.C.	woodblock printing, China
600–551 B.C.	Aesop's *Fables*

MUSIC

4000 B.C.	harps and flutes, Egypt
c. 3000 B.C.	bamboo pipes, China
800 B.C.	earliest music recorded, Sumer
c. 700 B.C.	seven-string lyre introduced, Greece

SCIENCE AND TECHNOLOGY

c. 12,000 B.C.	use of fire
c. 5000 B.C.	woven cloth, Sumer
c. 3150 B.C.	irrigation, China and Egypt
2155 B.C.	Chinese observed solar eclipse
1500 B.C	silk production, China

GOVERNMENT

3500–2000 B.C.	Sumerian culture, Middle East
3500–100 B.C.	Egyptian kingdoms
2500–1800 B.C.	Indus Valley culture, India
2300–1100 B.C.	Mycenaean culture, Greece
c, 1780 B.C.	Hammurabi's *Code of Law* stele
c. 1340 B.C.	Tutankhamen (King Tut) ruled, Egypt
850–150 B.C.	Olmec culture, Mexico
750–200 B.C.	Etruscan culture, Italy

WORLD EVENTS

1250 B.C.	Israelites leave Egypt
1185 B.C.	Trojan War
776 B.C.	first Olympics, Greece
c. 563–483 B.C.	life of Buddha (Gautama Siddhartha), India
551–479 B.C.	life of Confucius, Chinese philosopher

ART AND CULTURE, 500 B.C.–A.D. 500

Naturally, as we travel back to the more recent past, it is easier to learn about the events that shaped the times. This section includes key events that influenced modern history and culture as we know it.

VISUAL ARTS AND ARCHITECTURE

442–437 B.C.	Parthenon, Greece
400–330 B.C.	Praxiteles, Greek sculptor
300 B.C.–A.D. 400	Great Serpent Mound, present-day Ohio, United States
c. 214 B.C.	Great Wall of China
c. 140 B.C.	*Venus de Milo*, Greece
100 B.C.	Villa of the Mysteries, Pompeii
1st century A.D.	Pont du Gard, Roman aqueduct

LITERATURE

443 B.C.	Sophocles, *Antigone*
431 B.C.	Euripides, *Medea*
384–322 B.C.	Aristotle, *Metaphysics, Politics,* and *Rhetoric*
360 B.C.	Plato's *Republic*
C. 200 B.C.	*Bhagavad-Gita,* India
195 B.C.	Rosetta Stone, Egypt
19 B.C.	Virgil's *Aeneid*
C. A.D. 70–100	Gospels of *New Testament*

MUSIC

C. 500 B.C.	Greek choral music
C. 340 B.C.	Aristotle's Musical Theory
50 B.C.	oboe developed, Rome
A.D. 450	flutes, horns, tubas, drums, Peru
A.D. 500	Greek Melodos' hymns

SCIENCE

C. 300 B.C.	Deductive mathematics, Euclid
C. 140 B.C.	Trigonometry, Hipparchus
C. A.D. 80	magnetism discovered, China
A.D. 105	paper making, China

GOVERNMENT

332–30 B.C.	Ptolemaic period, Egypt—Alexander the Great, Cleopatra
C. 300 B.C.–A.D. 300	Colima, Jalisco, Nayarit cultures, Peru
A.D. 470	Mayan civilization, Mexico and Central America
A.D. 476	fall of Western Roman Empire

WORLD EVENTS

A.D. 1–30	life of Jesus
A.D. 43	founding of London
A.D. 79	Vesuvius erupts at Pompeii
A.D. 331	Constantine moves Roman Empire to Constantinople (Istanbul)
C. A.D. 323–1453	Byzantine Empire
A.D. 450–500	Mississippi Valley Culture

ART AND CULTURE, A.D. 500–1000

In the so-called "dark ages" or Middle Ages, an amazing number of wonderful buildings were erected, orchestras were formed, explorations took place, and Charlemagne, an illiterate, ordered manuscripts copied to further civilization.

VISUAL ARTS AND ARCHITECTURE

532–537	Hagia Sophia, Istanbul
535	earliest Chinese scroll landscape
595	Horyuji Temple, Japan
c. 655	*Sutton Hoo* burial ship treasure, England
691	Dome of the Rock, Jerusalem
700	Cave Temple at Ellora, India
900	Mosque of Cordoba, Spain

LITERATURE

550	*Hero and Leander,* Greek epic poem
600	book printing, China
640	Library at Alexandria, contained 300,000 scrolls
760	*The Book of Kells,* Ireland
800	Charlemagne has books copied
832	Utrecht Psalter, Reims school

MUSIC

619	orchestras formed, China
750	Gregorian church music, Germany, France, and England
980	Winchester Cathedral organ installed

SCIENCE AND TECHNOLOGY

595	decimal system, India
618	cast iron, China
851	crossbow used in France
980	canal locks invented, China

GOVERNMENT AND CULTURE

618–906	T'ang Dynasty, China
742–814	Charlemagne, First Holy Roman Emperor
800–1550	Kingdom of Mali, Africa

WORLD EVENTS

570–632	Life of Muhammad
1000	Leif Ericson arrived in North America

ART AND CULTURE, 1000–1500

It is much easier to relate to architecture and art from this time period because much of it is still standing or in museums. It has been the model for what has occurred in the thousand years since the first millennium. The great plague that decimated Europe in the 1300s was a major influence on Western art for the next several hundred years.

VISUAL ARTS AND ARCHITECTURE

700–1750	Anasazi pottery (Native American)
1067–1083	Bayeux Tapestry, France
1078–1300	Tower of London
1147	Abbot Suger's *Chalice*
1150	Mesa Verde Cliff Palace, present-day Colorado
1235	Notre Dame Cathedral, Paris

c. 1267–1337	Giotto, Arena Chapel paintings, Padua, Italy
14th century	Lion Court statuary and architecture, Alhambra Palace, Spain
1395–1441	Jan van Eyck, oil painting
1419	Florence Cathedral, Italy
1450–1500	Macchu Picchu, (Inca) Peru
1480	*Birth of Venus,* Botticelli

LITERATURE

1027–1123	Omar Khayyam, *Rubaiyat*
1340–1400	Chaucer, *Canterbury Tales*
1348–1353	Boccacio, *Decameron*
1454	Gutenberg's *Bible*

MUSIC

1100	secular music begins
1125	troubador musicians, France
1220	boys choir founded, Dresden
1322	Pope forbids use of counterpoint in Church music
1465	first printed music

SCIENCE AND TECHNOLOGY

c. 1150	gunpowder, China
1285	eye glasses, Friar Alessandro Spino, Italy
1450–1500	Sun Stone, Aztec calendar

GOVERNMENT AND CULTURE

1066	Norman Conquest of England
1200–1530	Inca culture, Peru

WORLD EVENTS

1040	Duncan of Scotland killed by Macbeth
1096–1099	First Christian Crusade, Middle East
1215	*Magna Carta* issued by King John of England
1348	Black Death, Europe
1431	Joan of Arc burned at stake
1492	Columbus sails to West Indies

"You are lost the instant you know what the result will be."
—JUAN GRIS, 1887–1927, Spanish Cubist painter

ART AND CULTURE, 1500–1750

Great civilizations (and consequently great works of art) emerged in this time period. Perhaps they had been occurring all along, and only became known to the Western world because of explorations. The art of African, Native American, Indian, Hispanic, and Asian cultures became increasingly appreciated as explorers brought examples to Europe and the Americas.

VISUAL ARTS AND ARCHITECTURE

c. 1500–1897	Benin culture, Africa
1503–1505	*Mona Lisa,* Leonardo da Vinci
1502	Bramante's *Tempietto*
1508–1512	Sistine Chapel, Michelangelo
1510–1511	School of Athens, Raphael
c. 1635	Taj Mahal, Agra, India
1642	*The Night Watch,* Rembrandt
1665–1667	San Carlo alle Quattro Fontane, Rome, Borromini
1675–1710	St. Paul's Cathedral, London
1700–1775	*Ukiyo-e* woodprints, Japan

LITERATURE

1605–1606	*Macbeth,* Shakespeare
1605–1615	*Don Quixote,* Cervantes
1611	*King James Bible*
1726	*Gulliver's Travels,* Jonathan Swift
1732	Benjamin Franklin's *Poor Richard's Almanack*

MUSIC

1644–1737	Antonio Stradavari, violin maker
1685–1750	Johann Sebastian Bach
1685–1759	George Frideric Handel
1709	piano introduced, Bartolomeo Christofori

SCIENCE

1503–1566	Nostradamus, astrologer
1609	Galileo's astronomical telescope
1667	first blood transfusion
1684	Isaac Newton's *Theory of Gravity*

GOVERNMENT AND CULTURE

1491–1547	Henry VIII, England
1533	Pizarro conquers Peru
1600	Kingdom of Asante, Africa
1620	*Mayflower Compact*

WORLD EVENTS

1519	Cortez brings horses to America
1534	Anglican Church founded
1588	Spanish Armada defeated
1607	Jamestown, Virginia, settled
1610	Santa Fe, New Mexico, founded
1636	Harvard University founded
1692	witches hanged in Massachusetts
1701	Captain Kidd hanged in London
1745	Pompeii and Herculaneum discovered

ART AND CULTURE, 1750–1875

The artwork, the scientific discoveries, and the governmental changes are familiar history to most Westerners. This period still predates the exponential changes of the 20th and 21st centuries.

VISUAL ARTS AND ARCHITECTURE

1748–1777	Strawberry Hill, England, Horace Walpole
1770–1782	Monticello, Thomas Jefferson
1782	*Watson and the Shark*, John Singleton Copley
1796	*George Washington*, Gilbert Stuart
1814	*The Grande Odalisque*, Ingres
1827	*Birds of America*, John James Audubon

1874	*The Opera*, Paris, Charles Garnier
1871	*The Artist's Mother*, James Abbot McNeill Whistler
1880	*Ballet Dancer*, Edgar Dégas

LITERATURE

1759	*Candide*, Voltaire
1776	*The Rights of Man*, Thomas Paine
1813	*Pride and Prejudice*, Jane Austen
1851–1852	*Uncle Tom's Cabin*, Harriet Beecher Stowe
1861	*Great Expectations*, Charles Dickens
1864	*War and Peace*, Leo Tolstoy

MUSIC

c. 1730	premiere of *Beggar's Opera*, John Gay
1756–1791	Wolfgang Amadeus Mozart
1770–1827	Ludwig van Beethoven
1813–1883	Richard Wagner

SCIENCE AND TECHNOLOGY

1752	kite experiments, Ben Franklin
1769	steam engine, James Watt
1822–1884	Gregor Mendel, founder of genetic science
1837	daguerrotype, Louis Daguerre
1844	telegraph, Samuel F. B. Morse
1859	*Origin of the Species*, Charles Darwin
1861	theory of germ fermentation, Louis Pasteur
1867	antiseptic surgery, Joseph Lister
1869	Periodic Table of Elements

GOVERNMENT AND CULTURE

1775–1783	American Revolutionary War
1784–1947	British rule in India
1789	French Revolution begins
1803	Louisiana Purchase, United States
1824	Simon Bolivar leads revolutions in Latin America

1857	Dred Scott decision upholds slavery
1861–1865	The Civil War, United States
1865	Lincoln assassinated
1869–1948	Mahatma Gandhi (India's Prime Minister)

WORLD EVENTS

1815	Napoléon's Battle at Waterloo
1821	first Cherokee written alphabet
1821–1859	Suez Canal, Egypt
1836	Davy Crockett killed at battle of The Alamo, San Antonio, Texas
1837	Queen Victoria crowned
1848–1920	women's suffrage movement
1849	California Gold Rush
1860	Pony Express mail, United States
1867	United States buys Alaska from Russia
1869	Union Pacific and Central Pacific form first transcontinental railroad, United States

ART AND CULTURE, 1875–1950

Consider the changes in the last 150 years. The world has gone from traveling by horse and buggy to reaching the moon and beyond. World events shape the arts and our attitudes toward them. Consider Germany's "degenerate art" by such artists as Franz Marc, Max Beckmann, Oskar Kokoschka, Paul Klee, and Piet Mondrian, among others. Their work was taken from German museums and mocked by being displayed alongside work by inmates of lunatic asylums. This same work, much of which was influenced by Bauhaus principles, is now appreciated as ground-breaking. Our attitudes about artworks that incorporate advertising motifs or borrow from other artists have also made an about-face, as artists such as Roy Lichtenstein or Picasso have "appropriated" art from other well-known artists.

VISUAL ARTS AND ARCHITECTURE

1891	Wainwright Building, skyscraper, St. Louis, Missouri, Louis Sullivan
1893	*The Scream,* Edvard Munch

1893	*The Banjo Lesson,* Henry O. Tanner
1899	Eiffel Tower, Paris, Gustave Eiffel
1907	*Demoiselles d'Avignon,* Picasso
1913	Armory Show, first European modernism exhibition in the United States
1919–1933	Bauhaus opened first in Weimar, moved to Dessau, then to Berlin, Germany
1926	*Reclining Figure,* Henry Moore
1926	*Black Iris,* Georgia O'Keeffe
1928–1930	Chrysler Building, New York City, William van Alen
1930	*American Gothic,* Grant Wood
1931	*The Persistence of Memory,* Salvador Dali
1936	Fallingwater, Frank Lloyd Wright

LITERATURE

1876	*Tom Sawyer,* Mark Twain
1902	*Hound of the Baskervilles,* Arthur Conan Doyle
1924	*Mein Kampf,* Adolph Hitler
1925	*The Great Gatsby,* F. Scott Fitzgerald
1926	*The Sun Also Rises,* Ernest Hemingway
1941	*Citizen Kane,* Orson Wells

FILM

1931	*It Happened One Night,* Oscar winner
1939	*Gone With the Wind,* Oscar winner
1943	*Casablanca,* Oscar winner

MUSIC

1890–1971	Louis Armstrong
1900–1990	Aaron Copland
1901	ragtime jazz, Scott Joplin
1912–1992	John Cage
1915–1959	Billie Holiday
1918–1990	Leonard Bernstein

SCIENCE AND TECHNOLOGY

1876	telephone, Alexander Graham Bell
1879	lightbulb, Thomas Edison
1885	dynamite, Alfred B. Nobel
1885	gas auto engine, Karl Benz
1895	motion pictures, Lumière brothers
1902	discovery of radium, Marie and Pierre Curie
1903	Wright Brothers' first flight at Kitty Hawk
1904	Yellow fever eradicated, Panama Canal Zone
1905	Einstein's theory of relativity
1906	test for syphilis developed, August von Wasserman
1910–1926	Thomas H. Morgan researches and introduces his theory of the gene
1916	first birth control clinic established, Margaret Sanger
1925	Scopes trial (evolution vs. creation), Tennessee
1928	penicillin discovered, Alexander Fleming
1936	jet engine built, Frank Whittle
1938	photocopier invented, Chester Carlson
1942	Enrico Fermi splits the atom
1943	electronic computer, Max Newman and T. H. Flowers
1947	Polaroid camera introduced, Edwin H. Land

GOVERNMENT

1912–1949	Republic of China
1913	income tax introduced, United States
1917	Russian Revolution
1920	prohibition of alcohol, United States
1920	19th Amendment passed, women get the vote, United States
1931	Japan invades Manchuria
1933	Hitler appointed German Chancellor
1936	Spanish Civil War
1945	atomic bomb dropped on Japan
1947	British rule ends in India
1948	Palestine partitioned to establish Israel
1949	People's Republic of China established

WORLD EVENTS

1885	AFL (American Federation of Labor) established
1886	Coca-Cola Company founded
1892	Ellis Island established as a port of entry for immigrants
1908	Model T Ford introduced
1912	*Titanic* sinks
1914–1918	World War I
1919–1929	Harlem Renaissance
1920	League of Nations founded
1927	Lindbergh flies solo across Atlantic
1929	Stock Market crash
1941–1945	World War II
1946	United Nations founded
1949	NATO founded

ART AND CULTURE, 1950–PRESENT

In the last half of the second millennium and early in the third millennium, new materials, new techniques, new technology, and new artists push the potential for discoveries in every field. More than ever, artists are aware of past break-throughs, of the necessity for an open mind, for using what artists already know. The computer and technology offer new tools that have only begun to be explored.

VISUAL ARTS AND ARCHITECTURE

1954	*Flag,* Jasper Johns
1955	*The Bed,* Robert Rauschenberg
1959	Guggenheim Museum, New York City, Frank L. Wright
1960	Geodesic dome, Buckminster Fuller
1962	*Marilyn Monroe,* Andy Warhol
1979	*The Dinner Party,* Judy Chicago
1983	Pont Neuf Bridge wrapped, Paris, Christo
1981	Portland Public Service Building, Michael Graves
1998	Guggenheim Museum, Balboa, Spain, Frank Gehry

LITERATURE

1951	*Catcher in the Rye,* J. D. Salinger
1952	*Invisible Man,* Ralph Ellison
1961	*Catch-22,* Joseph Heller
1961	*To Kill a Mockingbird,* Harper Lee
1962	*Silent Spring,* Rachel Carson
1971	*August 1914,* Alexander Solzhenitsyn
1983	*The Color Purple,* Alice Walker
1987	*The Bonfire of the Vanities,* Tom Wolfe
1988	*Satanic Verses,* Salman Rushdie
2000	*Harry Potter* series, J. K. Rowlings

FILM

1954	*On the Waterfront*
1964	*The Sound of Music*
1957	*The Bridge on the River Kwai*
1975	*One Flew Over the Cuckoo's Nest*
1977	*Star Wars*
1984	*Amadeus*
1991	*The Silence of the Lambs*
2000	*Star Wars Episode I: The Phantom Menace*
2001	*Harry Potter and the Sorcerer's Stone*
2002	*A Beautiful Mind*

MUSIC

1956	Elvis Presley records *Blue Suede Shoes*
1968	The Beatles record their *White Album*
1969	Woodstock (New York) Festival and Concert
1980	John Lennon shot
1991	U2's *Achtung Baby*
2001	George Harrison dies

SCIENCE

1953	measles vaccine, John F. Enders
1955	polio vaccine, Jonas Salk
1957	USSR launched Sputnik
1967	first human heart transplant, Dr. Christiaan Bernard

1967	DNA molecular stucture determined, J. D. Watson, F. H. C. Crick, and M. H. F. Wilkins
1969	American astronauts land on the moon
1978	first test-tube baby is born, England
1982	AIDS is diagnosed
1989	DNA fingerprinting completed
1990	Hubble Space telescope launched
1993	World Wide Web introduced
1995	American Space Shuttle docks with Russia's Mir
1997	Dolly the sheep is cloned
2000	human genome mapping completed
2001	space surveyor Athena rover launch to Mars

GOVERNMENT AND CULTURE

1952	Queen Elizabeth II crowned
1954	*Brown* v. *Topeka Board of Education,* ends segregation, United States
1957	European Common Market
1959	Alaska and Hawaii achieve U.S. statehood
1965–1968	Chinese Cultural Revolution
1973–1974	Watergate, Nixon resigns
1979	Fall of Shah of Iran
1981	Sandra Day O'Connor first woman Supreme Court Justice
1997	British rule ends in Hong Kong

WORLD EVENTS

1960	OPEC formed, with 13 member nations
1963	John F. Kennedy assassinated
1965–1973	Vietnam War
1966	National Organization of Women formed
1967	Six-Day War, resulting in Israeli occupation of the Gaza Strip, West Bank, and Golan Heights
1968	Martin Luther King, Jr., assassinated
1973	*Roe* v. *Wade* ruling legalizes abortion, United States
1989	Tiananmen Square uprising, China
1990	Berlin Wall came down
1991	Gulf War, Iraq
1991	Break-up of Soviet Union
1994	Channel tunnel ("Chunnel") between England and France opens
2000	worldwide millennium celebrations
2001	September 11, terrorist attacks; World Trade Center towers destroyed
2003	United States invades Iraq

LOOKING AT ART

To develop an "eye" for art, ask yourself some of these questions as you view artwork, whether in books or at galleries and museums.

- Why is this one work of art by a well-known artist considered a masterpiece, when a hundred others exist by the same artist? What distinguishes it? Color? Subject matter? Liveliness?

- Is there another artist whose work looks almost like this?

- What emotion might have the artist been feeling while creating this piece?

- What do *I* feel when I look at this work of art?

- How did the artist use repetition of color, shape, or line—almost to lead the viewer through the picture?

- Which of the elements dominate this artwork—line, shape, color, value, or texture?

- Squint through your eyelashes to see differences in value. Where are the darkest, the lightest, the brightest areas?

- Are the colors bright? muted? grayed? garish? pretty? soft? clashing?
- Are the shapes in the work geometric or amorphous?
- What about lines? Are they thick? thin? curvy? Is there variety? Are the edges fuzzy? soft? hard? blurry? blended?
- Close your eyes for a few moments. When you open them, what is the first thing that you notice? Why?

LOOKING AT CONTEMPORARY ART

As you view a contemporary artwork, consider the following:
- Note the sensory properties such as line, color, texture, value, form, and space (elements of art) and the formal properties such as repetition, rhythm, variety, center-of-interest, and balance (principles of art).
- What is the medium used by the artist? Is more than one medium used?
- Are there clues as to the mood or meaning? The title or informational plaque may give you an idea as to what the work is about.
- Do you think the artist needed any particular skill to create this artwork? Do you think the artist had other persons do the physical work based on his or her design?
- Could the artist be trying to comment on a social issue? What do you think is the meaning?

LOOKING AT PORTRAITS

Looking at portraits requires a different perspective. Prior to the invention of the camera, a portrait was the only way to forever "capture" family members, leaders of countries, ordinary people. Portraits taken since the advent of the camera still serve the purpose they have for thousands of years—to say "Here is someone special," and to immortalize the subject. Some elements of the work you should note when looking at a portrait include the following:
- Are there clues about the sitter's status through background, clothing, jewelry, objects seen nearby?
- Does the portrait display an *attitude,* such as calmness, arrogance, intelligence, or humor?
- Is there enough information about the subject that you could make up a story based on what is in the picture? Vermeer's *Girl with a Pearl Earring* inspired a novel.

- Do you think the artist has tried to flatter the sitter, or would you consider the portrait not too flattering, yet perhaps more revealing of the person's inner personality?
- If you're looking at an artist's self-portrait, do you think the artist painted what he or she perceived as the "inner" spirit?

THE AESTHETICS OF ART

According to the German philosopher Alexander Baumgarden, "Aesthetics is the science of the beautiful." Because a reaction to art is such a personal thing, there simply aren't absolute answers that would be valid for all time periods and cultures. Consider the following questions about art.

- Can advertising provide an example of good art? Could propaganda?
- Can an object found in nature be considered a work of art?
- Could a photograph in a newspaper be considered a work of art?
- Do you need to know the artist's intention to appreciate the artwork?
- If an artist *says* it is art, *is* it?
- What about copying? If you take someone else's idea and base your art on it, does this make it an original?
- Is something that is manufactured in quantity less a work of art than something that is one of a kind?
- If a well-known artist hires someone else to interpret his ideas, who is the real artist?
- Is there a way to tell what an artwork means?
- Might an artwork speak more to one segment of society than to another, yet still be art?
- Should we all agree on what is beautiful?
- Can a car be considered a work of art?
- What is the difference between an abstract painting made by an elephant or chimpanzee and one made by a human?
- What is the difference between art and craft?
- Can an object or artwork be considered ugly in one time period and beautiful in another?
- Who decides what an artwork is?

- Without an artist to create it, is there art?
- Do preferences in art have anything to do with masculinity or femininity?
- What might be masculine or feminine art?
- What is considered art in your own culture?
- Identify something that anyone *anywhere* can agree is art.

IDENTIFYING CLASSICISM AND ROMANTICISM IN ART

Art does not develop independent of the time in which it is created, but often reflects the philosophies of writers and scientists, the religious beliefs, and politics of its time and place. Throughout history, architecture, sculpture, and painting seem to go back and forth between periods of Classicism and Romanticism. The term *Classical* refers to Greek and Roman art, which was straightforward and realistic. It has come to mean the best or most simple of designs, whether applied to art, architecture, or clothing. *Romanticism* is flamboyant, imaginative, and emotional. In architecture, it is decorative; in clothing, it features such "frivolous" elements as ruffles; in art, it is energetic and characterized by swirling lines and shapes.

CHARACTERISTICS OF CLASSICAL ART

balanced	decorous	rational
calm	detached	serious
cleanly outlined	dignified	simple
conservative	elegant	symmetrical
controlled	formal	traditional
cool	intellectual	tranquil

CHARACTERISTICS OF ROMANTIC ART

asymmetrical	expressive	sad
blurred outlines	nature at center	spiritual
conveys a mood	mysterious	strong diagonals
dynamic	other worldly	swirling
emotional	personal to the artist	unrestrained

ROMANTIC PERIODS IN ART

Etruscan	750–200 B.C.
Early Christian	A.D. 40–400
Byzantine	323–1453
Migration/Late Roman	375–550
Medieval	c. 800–1250
Romanesque	1000–1150
Gothic	1100–1400
Baroque	1590–1750
Rococo	1700–1800
Romanticism	c. 1800–1850
Symbolism	1880s–1890s
Art Nouveau	c. 1880–1910
Fauvism	1905–1907
Dadaism	1916–1922
Expressionism	1905–1925
Futurism	1908–1918
Fantasy Art	1910–1932
Abstract Expressionism	c. 1940–1970

CLASSICAL PERIODS IN ART

Classical Greek Art	480–323 B.C.
Hellenistic Greek Art	323–30 B.C.
Roman Art	c. 750 B.C.–A.D. 476
Late Gothic art	c. 1250–1470
Early Renaissance	c. 1250–1470
Northern Renaissance	1350–1600
International Style	c. 1380–1416
High Renaissance	1450–1520
Mannerism	1525–1600
Neo-Classicism	1770–1820
Realism	c. 1850–1880
Impressionism	1870–1905
Art Nouveau	c. 1880–1910

Post-Impressionism	c. 1886–1920
Cubism	1907–1920
Bauhaus	c. 1919–1933
Realism	1920–1940s
Surrealism	1922–1940s
Op (Optical) Art	1960s
Hyperrealism	1965–1977
Light Art	1970s–present
Post-Modernism	1970s–present

ARTISTIC PERIODS AND ARTISTS OF THE WESTERN WORLD

Although this list is basically about Western Art History, it includes artists of many other cultures because they were an important influence on Western art. As Europeans (and later, Americans) traveled to the Middle East and Asia, they brought back art forms of those cultures. For example, the work of the French Impressionists was heavily influenced by the popularity in Europe at that time of Japanese prints. Picasso, Matisse, and other 20th-century painters demonstrate the influence in their artwork of African and Mexican art forms. Particularly today, with the ease of world travel, many artists choose not to live in their native countries, but migrate and reflect other cultures in their work.

Some artists' names will appear in more than one list because they were an integral part of several specific groups.

PREHISTORY

Prehistory simply means that there is no *written* history of the time. The Chinese, Egyptian, Indian, Mesopotamian, and Sumerian civilizations developed in great river valleys from 35,000 to 5000 B.C. The art that remains from these cultures is found on cave walls and in tombs and ancient structures. These were people like us in many ways, with daily occupations, religious beliefs, and concern about the after-life. The art that remains is based on realistic human and animal forms, although we can only speculate why they painted and sculpted such forms.

WESTERN ART

The historic period of Western art began in Egypt approximately 4000–2000 B.C., and moved from Egypt through Greece, to Southern Europe, then Northern Europe, and eventually to the Americas.

GREEK ART

Greek art evolved from stiff, rigid human forms to classical sculptures such as the *Discus Thrower,* and architecture such as that of the Parthenon. Throughout the centuries, Neo-Classical revivals based on Greek and Roman art continue to surface in painting, sculpture, and architecture.

ETRUSCAN, ROMAN, AND EARLY CHRISTIAN ART (C. 750 B.C.–A.D. 476)

The Etruscans (early Romans, really) were centered in what would be modern Tuscany, and were greatly influenced by Greek immigrants. Their art forms were vases that closely resembled those of the Greeks, sophisticated terra cotta funerary urns, sarcophagi (incorporating scenes of an ideal after-life), sophisticated bronzes (sculpture and everyday items), and fresco wall paintings.

Although the Roman Empire fell in A.D. 476, its influence was widespread, as Romans occupied Egypt and North Africa, Great Britain, and portions of Northern and Southern Europe. Because the Roman Empire endured for such a long time, and was so far-flung, Romans were particularly influential in the artwork, city design, and architecture throughout much of Europe, North Africa, and the Middle East.

BYZANTINE ART (A.D. 323–A.D. 1453)

The Byzantine Empire began with Roman Emperor Constantine's move to Byzantium (later called Constantinople, now Istanbul). Early Byzantine church decoration was notable for rich mosaics made of brilliantly colored pieces of glass.

ART OF THE MIDDLE AGES (C. A.D. 400–1000)

This period in art includes the time between classical antiquity and modern times. The fifth to tenth centuries were sometimes referred to as the "Dark

Ages." This time was primarily notable for manuscript illumination, grave goods (such as elaborately carved burial ships for northern kings), carved ivory book covers, and beautiful metalwork reliquaries (to house the relics of saints) and jewelry.

THE ROMANESQUE PERIOD (A.D. 1000–1150)

The Romanesque period reflected the Roman influence, particularly in the building of churches. The vaulted ceilings and long nave were reminiscent of the Roman marketplace. An intense period of church building commenced in approximately 1100, when masses of people made pilgrimages across Europe to Santiago de Compostelo in Spain.

GOTHIC ART (C. A.D. 1100–1400)

The glory of this period is seen in its beautiful churches, with their heaven-reaching spires and glowing stained glass windows. Although use of the barrel and groin vaults began in Romanesque times, it wasn't until the flying buttress (outside support) was perfected—during the Gothic period—that churches could rise to previously unheard-of heights.

PRE-RENAISSANCE ART AND ARTISTS (C. 1250–1470)

The primary patron of artists during this time, which was also known as the late Gothic period, was the Church. Religious artwork was used to decorate churches and instruct a population that was basically illiterate. It was in the late 13th century that artists' names became known. Because of the strong influence of the Church in Rome, the best-known artists of the Pre-Renaissance are from Italy.

Italy

Angelico, Fra, c. 1400–1455
Bellini, Jacopo, c. 1400–1470
Castagno, Andrea del, c. 1421–1457
Cimabue, c. 1240–1302
Duccio di Buoninsegna, 1255– c. 1319

Fabriano, Gentile, c. 1370–1427
Gaddi, Taddeo, c. 1300–1366
Giotto di Bondone, c. 1266–1337
Gozzoli, Benozo, c. 1420–1497
Lippi, Fra Filippo, c. 1406–1469
Lorenzetti, Ambrogio, active 1319–1348

Lorenzetti, Pietro, active
1320–1348
Martini, Simone, 1315–1344
Pisano, Nicola, d. 1278/84
Pollaiuolo, Antonio del,
1432–1498

Uccello, Paolo, 1397–1475
Veneziano, Domenico,
c. 1410–1461
Verrocchio, Andrea Del,
c. 1435–1488

"Art does not reproduce what we see. It makes us see."
—PAUL KLEE, 1879–1940, Swiss painter, Bauhaus professor

NORTHERN RENAISSANCE ART AND ARTISTS (1350–1600)

This artistic period is sometimes also considered late Gothic. During this time, artists traveled more and brought back innovations in style and technique; thus, an International Style evolved. Elongated, stylized figures, luxurious fabrics, and crowded scenes were typical. Paintings became more portable and affordable for the merchant class as well as for royalty and the aristocracy. Jan van Eyck is credited with introducing the use of oil as a painting medium during this period.

Netherlands (Flemish and Dutch)

Bosch, Hieronymus, c. 1450–
1516
Bouts, Dieric, d. 1475
Brueghel, Pieter, c. 1525–1569
Campin, Robert, 1375–1444
David, Gerard, c. 1450–1523
Eyck, Jan van, c. 1390–1441
Goes, Hugo van der,
c. 1440–1482

Heemskerck, Maerten van,
1498–1574
Limbourg brothers, Paul,
Herman, Jean, active
1380–1416
Massys, Quentin, 1466–1530
Memling, Hans, c. 1430–1494
Weyden, Rogier van der,
c. 1399–1464

Germany

Altdorfer, Albrecht, c. 1480–1538

Baldung, Hans, c. 1484–1545

Cranach, Lucas, 1472–1553

Dürer, Albrecht, 1471–1528

Elsheimer, Adam, 1578–1610

Grunewald, Mathis, c. 1470–1530

Holbein, Hans, the Younger, c. 1497–1543

Schongauer, Martin, c. 1450–1491

ITALIAN RENAISSANCE ART AND ARTISTS (1450-1520)

The Italian Renaissance is known as the age of Humanism. Renaissance literally means "rebirth," and was based on the "rebirth" of principles derived from the ancient Greeks and Romans. Renaissance philosophers, writers, scientists, and artists based their work on philosophy, science, and mathematics as they knew it. Leonardo da Vinci felt that even the human form might be based on geometric principles.

Alberti, Leon Battista, 1404–1472

Bellini, Gentile, c. 1429–1507

Bellini, Giovanni, c. 1431–1516

Botticelli, Sandro, 1444–1510

Bramante, Donato, 1444–1514

Brunelleschi, Filippo, 1377–1446

Correggio, Antoni Allegri, c. 1489–1534

del Sarto, Andrea, 1486–1530

di Cosimo, Piero, 1462–1521

Donatello (Donato di Niccolo), 1386–1466

Francesca, Piero Della, 1420–1492

Ghiberti, Lorenzo, 1378–1455

Ghirlandaio, Domenico, 1449–1494

Giorgione, Giorgio da Castelfranco, 1478–1510

Leonardo da Vinci, 1452–1519

Mantegna, Andrea, 1431–1506

Masaccio, Tommaso, c. 1401–1428

Michelangelo (Buonarroti), 1475–1564

Perugino, Pietro, c. 1450–1523

Raphael (Raffaello Sanzio), 1483–1520

Verrocchio, Andrea del, 1435–1488

MANNERISM (1525–1600)

During the period of Mannerism, artists chose to depart from the faithfulness to nature that characterized the Renaissance, and instead elongated and distorted the human figure, using harsh, vivid colors for emotional impact.

France

> Clouet, François, c. 1522–1572
> Clouet, Jean, c. 1486–1541
> Goujon, Jean, c. 1510–1568

Italy

> Anguissola, Sofonisba, c. 1532–1625
> Arcimboldo, Giuseppe, 1527–1593
> Bronzino, Agnolo, 1503–1572
> Cellini, Benvenuto, 1500–1571
> Fiorentino, Rosso, 1495–1540
> Giorgione, c. 1478–1510
> Palladio, Andrea, 1508–1580
>
> Parmigianino, 1503–1540
> Pontormo, 1494–1556
> Primaticcio, Francesco, 1504–1570
> Tintoretto, Jacopo, 1518–1594
> Titian (Tiziano Vecellio), c. 1485–1576
> Vasari, Giorgio, 1511–1574
> Veronese, Paolo, 1528–1588

Spain

> El Greco ("The Greek"; Domenikos Theotocopoulos), 1541–1614, born in Greece but considered a Spanish artist

BAROQUE ART (1590–1750)

Baroque art developed almost as a reaction to the discipline of Renaissance art, and was intended to appeal to the emotions of the viewer. It was everything the Renaissance was not, in painting, sculpture, and architecture. In place of geometrically developed composition, Baroque paintings were notable for swirling intensity, strong diagonals, brilliant coloration, dramatic contrasts, and an emotional intensity.

Flanders

Brueghel, Jan, 1568–1625
Jordaens, Jacob, 1593–1678
Rubens, Peter Paul, 1577–1640
Teniers, David, the Younger, 1610–1690
van Dyck, Anthony, 1599–1641

France

La Tour, Georges de, 1593–1652
Le Nain, Louis, 1593–1648
Lorrain, Claude, 1600–1682
Poussin, Nicolas, 1594–1665
Puget, Pierre, 1620–1694

Italy

Bernini, Gianlorenzo, 1598–1680
Caravaggio, Michelangelo da,
    1571–1610
Carracci, Annibale, 1560–1609
Gentileschi, Artemisia, c. 1565–1647

Netherlands

Avercamp, Hendrick, 1585–1634
Claesz, Pieter, 1590–1661
Cuyp, Aelbert, 1620–1691
Hals, Frans, 1580–1666
Heda, Willem Claez,
    1594–1680/2
Heem, Jan Davidsz De,
    1606–1683
Hobbema, Meindert, 1638–1709
Honthorst, Gerrit van,
    1590–1656

Hooch, Pieter de, 1629–1684
Ostade, Adriaen van, 1610–1685
Potter, Paulus, 1625–1654
Rembrandt Harmenz van Rijn,
    1606–1669
Ruisdael, Jacob van, 1628–1682
Saenredam, Pieter, 1597–1662
Steen, Jan, 1626–1679
Terbruggen, Hendrick,
    1588–1629
Vermeer, Jan, 1632–1675

Spain

> Murillo, Bartolomé, 1617–1690
> Ribera, José de (Jusepe), 1591–1652
> Velazquez, Diego, 1599–1660
> Zurbarán, Francisco de, 1598–1664

Switzerland

> Liotard, Jean Etienne, 1702–1789

ROCOCO ART (1700-1800)

Rococo Art applies to the furniture and interior design of the time of Louis XV of France. It featured designs based on naturalistic forms such as plants, rocks, shells, and flowers. The term is still in use today, meaning excessive ornamentation in the decorative arts.

England

> Hogarth, William, 1697–1764
> Lely, Peter, 1618–1680

France

> Boucher, François, 1703–1770
> Chardin, Jean-Battiste-Simone, 1699–1779
> Falconet, Etienne-Maurice, 1716–1791
> Fragonard, Jean-Honoré, 1732–1806
> La Tour, Maurice Quentin de, 1704–1788
> Watteau, Jean-Antoine, 1684–1721

Italy

> Bellotto, Bernardo, 1720–1780
> Canaletto, Giovanni Antonio Canal, 1697–1768
> Guardi, Francesco, 1712–1793
> Longhi, Pietro, 1702–1785
> Piazzetta, Giovanni Battista, 1683–1754
> Tiepolo, Giambattista, 1696–1770

COLONIAL ART (UNITED STATES, 1700s)

Many Colonial artists were self-taught or reflected the artistic traditions of the country from which they immigrated.

Feke, Robert, c. 1707–1752
Greenwood, John, 1727–1792
Hesselius, Gustave, 1682–1755
Smibert, John, 1688–1751

NEO-CLASSICISM (1770–1820)

This was a movement to recreate the ideals of Greece and Rome, and a reaction against the excesses of the Rococo style.

England

Raeburn, Sir Henry, 1756–1823
Reynolds, Sir Joshua, 1723–1792

France

Canova, Antonio, 1757–1822
Corot, Jean-Baptiste Camille, 1796–1875
David, Jacques Louis, 1748–1825
Greuze, Jean-Baptiste, 1725–1805
Ingres, Jean-Auguste Dominique, 1780–1867
Vigée-LeBrun, Elizabeth, 1755–1842

United States

Bulfinch, Charles, 1763–1844
Copley, John Singleton, 1738–1815
Earl, Ralph, 1751–1801
Greenough, Horatio, 1805–1852
Jefferson, Thomas, 1743–1826
Peale, Charles Willson, 1741–1827
Revere, Paul, 1735–1818
Rush, William, 1756–1833
Stuart, Gilbert, 1755–1828
Trumbull, John, 1756–1843
West, Benjamin, 1738–1820

ROMANTICISM (c. 1800–1850)

Romanticism was a reaction against Neo-Classicism, and was closely related to contemporary music and literature. Art of this period might tell a story or commemorate an historic event, emphasizing personal expression and imagination.

England

    Blake, William, 1757–1827
    Constable, John, 1776–1837
    Gainsborough, Thomas,
        1727–1788
    Romney, George, 1734–1802
    Turner, J. M. W., 1775–1851

France

    Delacroix, Eugène, 1798–1863
    Géricault, Théodore, 1791–1824
    Millet, François, 1814–1875
    Moreau, Gustave, 1826–1898

Germany

    Friedrich, Caspar David,
        1774–1840

Spain

    Goya, Francisco, 1746–1828

United States

    Allston, Washington, 1779–1843
    Audubon, John James,
        1785–1851
    Bingham, George Caleb,
        1811–1879
    Hicks, Edward, 1780–1849
    Leutz, Emanuel Gottlieb,
        1816–1868
    Peale, Raphaelle, 1774–1825
    Peale, Rembrandt, 1778–1860
    Peale, Titian Ramsey II,
        1779–1885
    Quidor, John, 1801–1881
    Sully, Thomas, 1783–1872

"You should keep on painting no matter how difficult it is, because this is all part of experience, and the more experience you can have, the better it is—unless it kills you, and then you know you have gone too far."
—ALICE NEEL, 1900–1984, American portrait painter

WESTERN PAINTERS (UNITED STATES, c. 1800-1900)

These painters captured many facets of frontier life, including wild life, Indian scenes, landscape, and army life.

Audubon, John James, 1785–1851
Bodmer, Karl, 1809–1893
Catlin, George, 1796–1872
Eastman, Seth, 1808–1875
Heade, Martin Johnson, 1819–1904
Johnson, Eastman, 1824–1906
King, Charles Bird, 1785–1862
Remington, Frederic, 1861–1909
Russell, Charles M., 1864–1926
Ryder, Albert Pinkham, 1847–1917

HUDSON RIVER SCHOOL (UNITED STATES, c. 1825-1875)

This was a group of painters whose work reflected their pride in the beauty and grandeur of the American landscape. The second-generation members of this "school" were sometimes called "luminist artists" because of their treatment of light.

Church, Frederick Edwin, 1826–1900
Cole, Thomas, 1801–1848
Cropsey, Jasper Francis, 1823–1900
Doughty, Thomas, 1793–1856
Durand, Asher, 1796–1886
Fisher, Alvan, 1792–1863
Inman, Henry, 1802–1846
Inness, George, 1825–1894
Morse, Samuel F. B., 1791–1872

ROCKY MOUNTAIN SCHOOL (UNITED STATES, c. 1860-1890)

The Rocky Mountain School of art refers to Western artists who painted views of the frontier and Rocky Mountains and whose work reflected pride in the American landscape.

Berninghaus, Oscar E., 1874–1952
Bierstadt, Albert, 1830–1902
Hill, Thomas, 1829–1908
Keith, William, 1839–1911
Moran, Thomas, 1837–1926
Wimar, Charles F., 1828–1862

BARBIZON SCHOOL (FRANCE, 1840s)

This group of landscape painters took its name from the village of Barbizon near Fontainebleau, where they settled and painted. They preferred to paint in their studios, as opposed to the Impressionists, who painted outdoors whenever possible.

Daubigny, Charles-François, 1817–1878
Diaz, Narcisse Virgile, 1807–1876
Dupré, Jules, 1811–1889
Millet, Jean-François, 1814–1875
Jacque, Charles-Emile, 1813–1894
Rousseau, Théodore, 1812–1867
Troyon, Constant, 1810–1865

PRE-RAPHAELITE BROTHERHOOD (ENGLAND, 1848–1910)

A group of young English painters adopted this name in the hopes of recapturing a simpler time (before Raphael/academic training). Their work reflected nature in minutely detailed landscapes and allegories.

Brown, Ford Madox, 1821–1893
Collinson, James, 1825–1881
Hunt, William Holman, 1827–1910
Millais, John Everett, 1829–1896
Rossetti, Dante Gabriel, 1828–1882
Rossetti, W. M., 1829–1919
Stephens, F. G., 1828–1907
Strudwick, John Melhuish, 1849–1937
Woolner, Thomas, 1825–1892

REALISM (c. 1850–1880)

Instead of lofty subjects such as mythology, history, or religion, Realistic painters preferred subjects of everyday, modern life.

France

Boudin, Eugène, 1824–1898
Corot, Jean-Baptiste, 1796–1875
Courbet, Gustave, 1819–1877
Daumier, Honoré, 1808–1879
Fantin-Latour, Henri, 1836–1904
Houdon, Jean-Antoine, 1741–1828, sculptor

Germany

Friedrich, Caspar David, 1774–1880

Japan

Hiroshige, Ando, 1797–1858
Hokusai, Katsushika, 1760–1849

Netherlands

Mauve, Antoine, 1838–1888

United States

Eakins, Thomas, 1844–1916
Homer, Winslow, 1836–1910

IMPRESSIONISM (1870–1905)

Although it occupied a very short time period in the history of art, this is one of the most popular art movements of all time. The very name of the group was used derisively by a critic to describe Monet's painting *Impression, Sunrise.* Although techniques and subjects varied within the Impressionist group, there was a common emphasis on an outdoor painting technique that shows the changing effects of light and color.

France

Dégas, Edgar, 1834–1917
Manet, Edouard, 1832–1883
Monet, Claude, 1840–1926
Morisot, Berthe, 1841–1895
Pissarro, Camille, 1830–1903
Renoir, Auguste, 1841–1919

Germany

Corinth, Lovis, 1858–1925
Liebermann, Max, 1847–1935

Spain

Sorolla y Bastida, Joaquin, 1863–1923

United States

Butler, Theodore E., 1861–1936
Cassatt, Mary, 1845–1926
Hassam, Childe, 1859–1935
Perry, Lilla Cabot, 1848–1933
Robinson, Theodore, 1852–1896

TROMPE L'OEIL PAINTERS (UNITED STATES, c. 1876–1900)

A term that literally means "deceiving the eye," a number of Americans were virtuosos of this technique through their extremely realistic paintings—so much so that William Harnett was arrested by Treasury agents for using counterfeit money in a painting.

Harnett, William Michael, 1848–1892
Peale, Raphaelle, 1774–1825
Peto, John Frederick, 1854–1907

SYMBOLISM (FRANCE, 1880s–1890s)

Symbolist painters, writers, and poets attempted to represent the mystical and occult in their art. Some of their favorite subjects were death, disease, and sin.

Gauguin, Paul, 1848–1903
Moreau, Gustave, 1826–1898
Puvis de Chavanne, Pierre, 1824–1898
Redon, Odilon, 1840–1916

ART NOUVEAU (c. 1880–1910)

This was an asymmetrical decorative style that featured sinuous forms based on objects found in nature. It was mostly used in applied design such as fabrics, stained glass windows, book design, posters, furniture, and architecture.

Austria

Klimt, Gustave, 1862–1918

Czech Republic

    Mucha, Alfonse, 1860–1939

England

    Beardsley, Aubrey, 1872–1898
    Waterhouse, John William,
      1849–1917

United States

    LaFarge, John, 1835–1910
    Tiffany, Louis Comfort,
      1848–1933

> *"I skirmish and battle with the sun. And what sun here!*
> *. . . One would have to paint with gold and gems."*
> —CLAUDE MONET, 1840–1926, French Impressionist painter

POST-IMPRESSIONISM (c.1886–1920)

Post-Impressionist artists continued the groundbreaking experiments in color and form of the Impressionists. Some also returned to the emotional strengths of earlier movements.

Australia

    Roberts, Tom, 1856–1931

France

    Bazille, Fred, 1841–1870
    Bonnard, Pierre, 1867–1947
    Caillebotte, Gustave, 1848–1894
    Cézanne, Paul, 1839–1906
    Gauguin, Paul, 1848–1903
    Matisse, Henri, 1869–1954
    Rodin, Auguste, 1840–1917
      (sculptor)
    Rousseau, Henri, 1844–1910
    Seurat, Georges, 1859–1891

France (continued)

    Signac, Paul, 1863–1935
    Sisley, Alfred, 1839–1899
    Toulouse-Lautrec, Henri de,
      1864–1901
    Utrillo, Maurice, 1883–1955
    Vuillard, Edward, 1868–1940

Netherlands

    van Gogh, Vincent, 1863–1890

Norway

    Munch, Edvard, 1863–1944

NABIS (FRANCE, 1890s)

The Nabis (Hebrew for "Prophet") adopted Gauguin's emotional use of color and distortion of line as a reaction against the naturalistic colors of the Impressionists.

Bernard, Émile, 1868–1941
Bonnard, Pierre, 1867–1947
Denis, Maurice, 1870–1943
Gauguin, Paul, 1848–1903

Maillol, Aristide, 1861–1944
Serusier, Paul, 1863–1927
Vuillard, Edward, 1868–1940

THE TEN (UNITED STATES, 1898–1919)

Most of this group of "American Impressionist" painters had studied in Europe and reflected the popularity of Impressionism in Paris. Their first exhibition, "Ten American Painters," was in 1898, and they continued to exhibit together for twenty years.

Benson, Frank W., 1862–1951
Chase, William Merrit,
   1849–1916 (a replacement for
   J. H. Twachtmann)
De Camp, Joseph R., 1858–1923
Dewing, Thomas W., 1851–1938
Hassam, Childe, 1859–1935

Metcalf, Willard L., 1853–1925
Reid, Robert, 1862–1929
Simmons, Edward, 1852–1931
Tarbell, Edmund C., 1862–1938
Twachtmann, John Henry,
   1853–1902
Weir, J. Alden, 1852–1919

TURN-OF-THE-CENTURY REALISTS (UNITED STATES, c. 1900)

This group of sculptors and painters represents a variety of personal styles and media, but most attempted to realistically portray what was of interest to them. Subjects varied from portraiture to landscape, and techniques ranged from sculpture to lithography and oil painting.

Paintings or Lithography

Currier and Ives, active
   1835–1907
Parrish, Maxfield, 1870–1966
Ryder, Albert Pinkham,
   1847–1917

Sargent, John Singer, 1856–1925
Tanner, Henry Ossawa,
   1859–1937
Whistler, James McNeill,
   1834–1903

Sculpture

French, Daniel Chester,
  1850–1931
Hosmer, Harriet, 1830–1908
Saint-Gaudens, Augustus,
  1848–1907

Ward, John Quincy Adams,
  1830–1910
Warner, Olin Levi,
  1844–1896

"A portrait is a painting with something a little wrong with the mouth."

—JOHN SINGER SARGENT, 1856–1925, American society
portrait painter

THE EIGHT (ALSO KNOWN AS "THE ASHCAN SCHOOL") (UNITED STATES, 1900-1920)

The Eight began as the "Philadelphia Realists" (where most of them had been newspaper artists), then moved to New York, and became the "New York Realists." Their true-to-life paintings of people standing on crowded sidewalks where one might see steps and ash cans, at the park, the theater, and entertainment spectacles earned them the epithet of "Ashcan School."

Davies, Arthur B., 1862–1928
Glackens, William, 1870–1938
Henri, Robert, 1865–1929
Lawson, Ernest, 1873–1939
Luks, George, 1866–1933

Prendergast, Maurice,
  1859–1924
Shinn, Everett, 1873–1958
Sloan, John, 1871–1951

PHOTO SECESSION (UNITED STATES, 1905-1917)

This movement was headed by photographer Alfred Stieglitz. Exhibitions in his Gallery 291 spearheaded the modern movement in the United States. Numerous modern European painters such as Henri Matisse, Henri de Toulouse-Lautrec, and Henri (Le Douanier) Rousseau, and sculptors Auguste Rodin and Constantin Brancusi were shown in the gallery. Modernist American painters were no longer concerned with total realism, but rather with expressing what they felt. Their work was simplified and showed less detail, and was highly individualized.

Dove, Arthur, 1880–1946
Hartley, Marsden, 1877–1943
Marin, John, 1870–1953
O'Keeffe, Georgia, 1887–1986
Steichen, Edward, 1879–1973
Stieglitz, Alfred, 1864–1946

FAUVISM (1905-1907)

The word *Fauve*, which translates as "wild beasts," comes from the public's reaction to this style of painting in which non-naturalistic, intense colors were used for emotional effect. These artists were influenced by Gauguin, van Gogh, and Cézanne.

Belgium

Dongen, Kees van, 1877–1968
Vlaminck, Maurice, 1876–1958

France

Braque, Georges, 1882–1963
Derain, André, 1880–1954
Dufy, Raoul, 1877–1953
Matisse, Henri, 1869–1954
Picabia, Francis, 1878–1953
Rouault, Georges, 1871–1958

Germany

Heckel, Erich, 1883–1970

"I would not cast off my illness, for there is much in my art that I owe to it."

—EDVARD MUNCH, 1863–1944, Norwegian Expressionist painter

EXPRESSIONISM (1905-1925)

Expressionism was less the painting of what is seen than what is felt by the artist. Exaggeration of color and shape in painting expressed the artist's emotions and reaction to the subject.

Austria

Kokoschka, Oscar, 1886–1980
Schiele, Egon, 1890–1918

Belgium

Ensor, James, 1860–1949
Permeke, Constant, 1886–1952

Denmark

Jorn, Asger, 1914–1973
Hammerskoi, Vilhelm,
1864–1916

France

Rouault, Georges, 1871–1958

Italy

Modigliani, Amadeo, 1884–1920

Norway

Munch, Edvard, 1863–1944

Russia

Jawlensky, Alexei von,
1864–1941
Kandinsky, Wassily, 1866–1944
Lissitsky, El, 1890–1941
Malevich, Kasimir, 1878–1935
Soutine, Chaim, 1894–1943

Switzerland

Klee, Paul, 1879–1940

DIE BRÜCKE (GERMANY, 1905-1913)

The founders of this style of painting considered it "a bridge" between the past and the future. It featured bright, unrealistic colors, similar to those of the Fauves.

Bleyl, Fritz, 1880–1966
Kirchner, Ernst, 1880–1938
Nolde, Emil, 1867–1956
Pechstein, Max, 1881–1955
Schmidt-Rottluff, Karl, 1884–1976

GERMAN EXPRESSIONISM (1910-1932)

This style emerged about the same time as French Fauvism, but featured even more distortion and exaggeration.

Baumeister, Willi, 1889–1955
Beckmann, Max, 1844–1950
Corinth, Lovis, 1858–1925
Dix, Otto, 1891–1969
Feininger, Lyonel, 1871–1956
Grosz, George, 1893–1959

Heckel, Erich, 1883–1970
Kollwitz, Käthe, 1867–1945
Meidner, Ludwig, 1884–1966
Modersohn-Becker, Paula, 1876–1907

THE BLAUE REITER GROUP (GERMANY, 1911)

This was considered the high point of German Expressionism. The name of the group (which means The Blue Rider) derived from a Kandinsky painting, and was used for a collection of writings and an exhibition. Their work was an attempt to show their spirituality through symbolism.

Kandinsky, Wassily, 1866–1944
Macke, August, 1887–1914
Marc, Franz, 1880–1916

CUBISM (1907-1920s)

Picasso, Braque, and Gris were the founders of Cubism, in which the appearance of a real subject is fragmented and reassembled to show different aspects. It was inspired by African art and Cézanne paintings done late in his career.

France

Archipenko, Alexander,
  1887–1964
Braque, Georges, 1882–1963
Delaunay, Robert, 1885–1941
Delaunay, Sonia, 1885–1979
Duchamp, Marcel, 1887–1968
Léger, Fernand, 1881–1955
Lipchitz, Jacques, 1891–1973
Villon, Jacques, 1875–1963

Spain

Gris, Juan, 1887–1927
Picasso, Pablo, 1881–1973

United States

Weber, Max, 1881–1961

FUTURISM (1908-1918)

Futurism was largely an Italian movement that attempted to show the violent speed and energy of a mechanized society in an industrialized world.

Italy

Balla, Giacomo, 1871–1958
Boccioni, Umberto, 1882–1916
Carra, Carlo, 1881–1966
Severini, Gino, 1883–1966

United States

Feininger, Lyonel, 1871–1956
Stella, Joseph, 1877–1946

RAYONISM (RUSSIA, 1911-1914)

Rayonist paintings were similar to Futurism, with slanting rays used to break up objects and background.

Goncharova, Natalia, 1881–1962
Larionov, Mikhail, 1881–1964

SYNCHROMISM (UNITED STATES, 1913-1918)

Synchromist paintings were filled with swirling, colorful shapes that were softly painted and modeled (shaded).

Macdonald-Wright, Stanton, 1890–1973
Morgan, Russell, 1886–1943

CONSTRUCTIVISM (RUSSIA, c. 1913–1922)

This largely Russian movement was based on a philosophy that artworks should reflect modern technology, with sculpture "constructed" using such industrial materials as plastic and glass.

Gabo, Naum, 1890–1977
Kandinsky, Wassily, 1866–1944
Lissitzky, El, 1890–1941
Malevich, Kasimir, 1878–1935
Pevsner, Anton, 1886–1962

Popova, Lyubov, 1889–1924
Rodchenko, Alexander, 1891–1956
Tatlin, Vladimir, 1885–1953

PRECISIONISM (UNITED STATES, 1915)

Precisionist painters were sometimes called Cubist-Realists or the Immaculates. Frequently based on photography, their paintings featured transformed cities, industrial landscape, and machinery. The flattened shapes with strong shadows that they favored were stripped of detail almost to the point of abstraction.

Demuth, Charles, 1883–1935
Sheeler, Charles, 1883–1965

DADA (1916–1922)

This movement began in France as a revolt against World War I. It fostered creativity by rebelling against traditional forms of logic, art, and culture. Dada is a nonsense word that means "hobbyhorse." Each artist associated with Dada had a unique method of working, which ranged from highly abstract amorphous (free-form) shapes to works such as Duchamp's "ready-mades" (items he had purchased and on which he signed his name, declaring them *art* because he *said* they were).

France

Arp, Jean, 1887–1966
Brancusi, Constantin, 1876–1957
Duchamp, Marcel, 1887–1968
Picabia, Francis, 1879–1953

Germany	*United States*
Grosz, George, 1893–1959	Man Ray, 1890–1977
Schwitters, Kurt, 1887–1948	

DE STIJL (NETHERLANDS, 1917)

These artists' work was based on the belief that art should reflect the mystery of the universe, and was primarily composed of geometric shapes and lines.

Doesburg, Theo van, 1883–1931
Mondrian, Piet, 1872–1944
Rietveld, Gerrit Thomas, 1888–1964
Vantongerloo, Georges, 1886–1965

BAUHAUS (GERMANY, c. 1919–1933)

The Bauhaus Center of Modern Design was founded in Weimar, Germany, to further the ideals of its founders that the craftsman-designer could be involved in industrial mass-production to create affordable art and architecture.

Bayer, Herbert, 1900–1985
Breuer, Marcel, 1902–1981
Gropius, Walter, 1883–1969
Kandinsky, Wassily, 1866–1944
Klee, Paul, 1879–1940
Mies van der Rohe, Ludwig, 1886–1969
Moholy-Nagy, Laszlo, 1895–1946

HARLEM RENAISSANCE (UNITED STATES, 1919–1929)

During the Harlem Renaissance African Americans in all the arts received recognition. Writers, musicians, painters, sculptors, dancers, and actors portrayed the African American experience in their art, with far-reaching results. Many of these young artists were recruited by the government to paint murals during the Great Depression.

Alston, Charles, 1907–1977
Bearden, Romare, 1914–1988
Biggers, John, 1924–2001
Douglas, Aaron, 1899–1979
Fuller, Meta Vaux Warrick,
   1877–1968
Gilliam, Sam, 1933
Hayden, Palmer, 1890–1973
Johnson, William H., 1901–1970

Jones, Lois Mailou, 1905–1998
Lawrence, Jacob, 1917–2000
Lewis, Samella, 1924
Motley, Archibald, Jr.,
   1891–1981
Savage, Augusta, 1892–1962
Tanner, Henry, 1859–1937
Woodruff, Hale, 1900–1980
Zee, James Van Der, 1886–1983

REALISM (1920-1940)

True to its name, artists who worked in this style simply presented naturalistic representations of what they saw. Frequently this included a visual commentary on what was happening in society and government.

France

   Utrillo, Maurice, 1883–1955

Italy

   Guttoso, Renato, 1912–1987

Mexico

   Orozco, José Clemente,
     1883–1949
   Rivera, Diego, 1886–1957
   Siqueiros, David A., 1896–1974
   Tamayo, Rufino, 1899–1991

United States

   Beaux, Cecelia, 1863–1942
   Bellows, George, 1882–1925
   Burchfield, Charles, 1893–1967
   Hopper, Edward, 1882–1967
   Kane, John, 1860–1932
   Marsh, Reginald, 1898–1954
   Moses, Anna Mary (Grandma),
     1860–1961
   Pippin, Horace, 1888–1946
   Rockwell, Norman, 1894–1978
   Shahn, Ben, 1898–1969

"It does not matter how badly you paint, so long as you don't paint badly like other people."
—GEORGE MOORE, 1873–1958, English philosopher,
Confessions of a Young Man, 1888

AMERICAN SCENE PAINTING AND REGIONALISM (1920s–1930s)

American Scene painters represented typically American landscapes, legends, and scenes of people at work. Paintings of the rural Midwest created during the 1920s and 1930s dominated this genre.

Bellows, George, 1882–1925
Benton, Thomas Hart,
   1889–1975
Curry, John Steuart, 1897–1946
Gwathmey, Robert, 1903–1988
Jones, Joe, 1909–1963

Soyer, Isaac, 1907–1981
Soyer, Moses, 1899–1974
Soyer, Raphael, 1899–1987
   (Moses' twin)
Wood, Grant, 1892–1942
Wyeth, Andrew, 1917

SURREALISM (1922–1940s)

Literally translated, *surrealism* means "above reality." The movement, which features unrealistic or fantastic images, began in France, inspired by the stream-of-consciousness writings of André Breton. Freud's theories of the unconscious were also popular at this same time period and influenced the movement.

Belgium

Delvaux, Paul, 1897–1994
Magritte, René, 1898–1967
Tanguy, Yves, 1900–1955

England

Carrington, Leonora, 1917

France

Dubuffet, Jean, 1901–1985
Ozenfant, Amédée, 1886–1966
Redon, Odilon, 1840–1916

Germany

Ernst, Max, 1891–1975

Italy

Chirico, Giorgio di, 1888–1978

Mexico

Kahlo, Frida, 1907–1954

Netherlands

Escher, Maurits C., 1898–1972

Russia

Chagall, Marc, 1887–1985
Tchelitchew, Pavel, 1898–1957

Spain

    Dali, Salvador, 1904–1988

    Miró, Joan, 1893–1983

Switzerland

    Giacommetti, Alberto,
      1901–1966

    Klee, Paul, 1879–1940

    Oppenheim, Meret, 1913–1985

    Seligman, Kurt, 1900–1962

United States

    Cornell, Joseph, 1903–1972

    Man Ray, 1890–1977

    Roy, Pierre, 1880–1950

    Tanning, Dorothea, 1910

    Tobey, Mark, 1890–1976

MAGIC REALISM (c. 1925–1943)

Magic Realism refers to a style of painting in which the images are so realistic that they appear almost *un*realistic.

Belgium

    Magritte, René, 1898–1967

United States

    Albright, Ivan Le Lorraine, 1897–1983

    Blume, Peter, 1906–1992

ART DECO (FRANCE, c. 1920s–1930s)

Art Deco referred to applied design that was primarily popular worldwide during the 1930s. The name is from the Exposition Internationale des Arts Décoratifs et Industriels Modernes that was held in Paris in 1925. The geometric forms and bright colors that characterized Art Deco were primarily applied to buildings, furniture, decorative objects, jewelry, advertising, typefaces, and bookbindings. Few painters or sculptors adapted these forms in their art, but the "streamlined" influence is seen in posters, statuary, transportation, and clothing. The term "Art Deco" could be applied to the art of many of the Modernist painters and sculptors such as Paul Manship (1885–1966).

MODERNISM (UNITED STATES, 1930s)

Artists of the Modernist period were departing from naturalism, and were painting abstracts of real objects, and developing individual, recognizable styles.

Davis, Stuart, 1894–1964
Demuth, Charles, 1883–1935
Diller, Burgoyne, 1906–1965
Dove, Arthur, 1880–1946
Evergood, Phillip, 1901–1973
Hartley, Marsden, 1877–1943

Kuhn, Walt, 1880–1949
Lachaise, Gaston, 1882–1935
Nadelman, Elie, 1882–1946
O'Keeffe, Georgia, 1887–1986
Steinberg, Saul, 1914–1999
Tooker, George, 1920

SOCIAL REALISM (UNITED STATES, EARLY 1930s–1940)

Social Realists used their art to comment on the plight of poor or oppressed Americans. In 1936 they formed an Artists' Congress for the purpose of fighting Facism, social inequities, and economic depression through their art.

Evergood, Phillip, 1901–1973
Hirsch, Stefan, 1899–1964
Hopper, Edward, 1882–1967

Lawrence, Jacob, 1917–2000
Shahn, Ben, 1898–1969

GROUP F.64 (UNITED STATES, 1930s)

This group of San Francisco photographers shared the belief that a photograph should not try to imitate a work of art by creating an abstract or romantic composition, but should simply be what it was—a black-and-white image of the finest possible clarity. They used the smallest possible lens opening on a view camera (F.64) to achieve supreme sharpness, hence their name.

Adams, Ansel, 1902–1984
Cunningham, Imogen,
    1883–1976
Edwards, John Paul, 1883–1958

Noskowiak, Sonya, 1900–1975
Swift, Henry, 1891–1960
Van Dyke, Willard, 1906–1986
Weston, Edward, 1886–1958

ARTS AND CRAFTS MOVEMENT (ENGLAND, 1930s)

England's Arts and Crafts Exhibition Society in 1888 was the basis for this return to the handmade decorative arts. Leaders were William Morris, a designer, and Walter Crane, a children's illustrator, painter, and teacher. The movement, which encouraged "hand industry in the machine age," spread eastward through Europe, and was primarily used to describe architecture, furniture, and interior design items such as wallpaper and textiles.

> Crane, Walter, 1845–1915
> Morris, William, 1834–1896

FEDERAL ARTS PROJECTS (UNITED STATES, 1933–1943)

During the Depression, the Federal Government formed a number of different agencies to aid 5,000 artists. Among these were PWAP (Public Works of Art Project), the WPA (Works Progress Administration), and the FSA (Farm Security Administration).

> Adams, Ansel, 1902–1984
> Evans, Walker, 1903–1975
> Lange, Dorothea, 1895–1965

THE BAUHAUS (CHICAGO, LATE 1930s)

When the Nazis closed the Bauhaus School in Dessau, Germany, in 1933, many Bauhaus artists were displaced and immigrated to the United States. They established a short-lived American Bauhaus in 1938.

> Albers, Josef, 1888–1976
> Feininger, Lyonel, 1871–1956
> Gropius, Walter, 1883–1969
> Hofmann, Hans, 1880–1966
> Maholy-Nagy, László, 1895–1946
> Mies van der Rohe, Ludwig, 1886–1969

ABSTRACT EXPRESSIONISM (c. 1940–1970)

Abstract Expressionists conveyed emotion through their artwork, whether or not they had a subject. Many of the artists, such as Jackson Pollock and Sam Francis, did not have a subject at all, while others such as Willem de Kooning and Larry Rivers had recognizable subjects that were created with large, loose brush strokes. Still others created huge wall paintings or murals that may have been quite realistic, and expressed their reaction to contemporary life. This movement, which was largely centered in New York, was sometimes called "action painting."

Australia

> Boyd, Arthur, 1920–1999
> Tjapaltjarri, Clifford Possum, 1932–2002

Denmark

> Kirkeby, Per, 1938

England

> Bacon, Francis, 1909–1992
> Hepworth, Barbara, 1903–1975 (sculptor)
> Moore, Henry, 1898–1986 (sculptor)
> Sutherland, Graham, 1903–1980

France

> Buffet, Bernard, 1928–1999
> Delaunay, Robert, 1885–1941
> Dubuffet, Jean, 1901–1985
> Soulages, Pierre, 1919

Germany

> Bill, Max, 1908–1995
> Richter, Gerhard, 1932
> Schlemmer, Oskar, 1888–1943

Italy

> Balla, Giacomo, 1871–1958
> Burri, Alberto, 1915–1995
> Modigliani, Amadeo, 1884–1920

Mexico

> Tamayo, Rufino, 1889–1991

Netherlands

> Appel, Karel, 1921
> Mondrian, Piet, 1872–1944

Romania

> Brancusi, Constantin, 1876–1957

Russia

DeStael, Nicolas, 1914–1955

Gontcharova, Natalia,
1881–1962

Kandinsky, Wassily, 1866–1944

Lissitsky, El, 1890–1941

Malevich, Kasimir, 1878–1935

Rodchenko, Aleksandr,
1891–1956

Tatlin, Vladimir, 1885–1953

Switzerland

Giacometti, Alberto, 1901–1966

United States

Avery, Milton, 1893–1965

Baziotes, William, 1912–1963

Calder, Alexander, 1898–1976

Cornell, Joseph, 1903–1972

de Kooning, Elaine 1920–1989

de Kooning, Willem, 1904–1997

Flavin, Dan, 1933–1996
(sculptor)

Francis, Sam, 1923–1994

United States (continued)

Gorky, Arshile, 1904–1948

Gottlieb, Adolph, 1903–1974

Graves, Morris, 1910–2001

Guston, Philip, 1913–1980

Hofman, Hans, 1880–1966

Katz, Alex, 1927

Kline, Franz, 1910–1962

Krasner, Lee, 1908–1984

LeWitt, Sol, 1928

Marden, Brice, 1938

Martin, Agnes, 1912

Motherwell, Robert, 1915–1991

Nevelson, Louise, 1900–1988

Newman, Barnett, 1905–1970

Pollock, Jackson, 1912–1956

Reinhardt, Ad, 1913–1967

Rivers, Larry, 1923–2002

Rothko, Mark, 1903–1970

Smith, David, 1906–1965

Stella, Frank, 1936

Still, Clyfford, 1904–1980

Thomas, Alma, 1891–1978

Tobey, Mark, 1890–1976

ART INFORMEL (EUROPE 1940s-1950s)

This movement developed at the same time as Abstract Expressionism in the United States. Art Informel painters applied paint thickly, using free brush-strokes, resulting in paintings that might or might not include a recognizable subject such as the human form.

France

> Balthus (Balthasar Klossowski de Rola), 1908–2001
> de Stael, Nicolas, 1914–1955
> Dubuffet, Jean, 1901–1985
> Klein, Yves, 1928–1962

Germany

> Hartung, Hans, 1904–1992

Italy

> Burri, Alberto, 1915–1995
> Fontana, Lucio, 1899–1968

Spain

> Tapies, Antoni, 1923

POP ART (1945-1965)

Pop artists avoided the emotional qualities of Expressionist paintings, instead choosing banal consumer products as themes for their paintings. They often directly copied advertising techniques, such as the Benday dot, or comic book styles.

England

> Blake, Peter, 1932
> Hamilton, Richard, 1922
> Paolozzi, Eduardo, 1924

Germany

> Polke, Sigmar, 1941

Italy

> Fontana, Lucio, 1899–1968
> Mazoni, Piero, 1933–1963

Switzerland

> Oppenheim, Meret, 1913–1985

United States

> Bengston, Billy Al, 1934
> Bontecou, Lee, 1931
> Diebenkorn, Richard, 1922–1993
> Dine, Jim, 1935
> Escobar, Marisol, 1930 (sculptor)
> Goode, Joe, 1937

Indiana, Robert, 1928
Johns, Jasper, 1930
Kitaj, R. B., 1932 (active in
    England)
Lichtenstein, Roy, 1923–1997
Oldenburg, Claes, 1929
    (sculptor)

Paschke, Ed, 1939
Ramos, Mel, 1935
Rauschenberg, Robert, 1925
Rosenquist, James, 1933
Ruscha, Edward, 1937
Warhol, Andy, 1930–1987
Wesselman, Tom, 1931

COBRA (SHORT FOR COPENHAGEN, BRUSSELS, AMSTERDAM, 1948–1951)

In this short-lived movement, a group of well-known Expressionist painters who met in Paris decided to paint purely from the unconscious, using fantastic imagery that resembled the art of children. Some of the artists sought to combine words and images, much as Pop artists also did.

Belgium

    Alechinsky, Pierre, 1927
    Corneille (Corneille Beverloo),
        1922
    Dotremont, Christian,
        1922–1979

Denmark

    Jorn, Asger, 1914–1973

England

    Gear, William, 1915–1997

France

    Atlan, Jean-Michel, 1913–1960
    Dubuffet, Jean, 1901–1985

Germany

    Baselitz, Georg, 1938

Japan

    Yoshihara, Jiro, 1905–1972

Mexico

    Tamayo, Rufino, 1899–1991

Netherlands

    Appel, Karel, 1921

United States

    de Kooning, Willem, 1904–1997

FUNK ART (UNITED STATES, 1950–1960s)

Funk Art originated in the San Francisco Bay area. Although painters founded the movement, sculptural techniques and assemblage soon dominated it. The most notable accomplishment of this movement was that taboo subjects and materials that previously would not have been considered suitable for art became acceptable forms of artistic expression.

> Arneson, Robert, 1930–1992
> DeForest, Roy, 1930

POST PAINTERLY ABSTRACTION (UNITED STATES, c. 1955–1964)

These artists avoided the appearance of brush strokes or subject matter in their methods of applying smooth, unmodeled (unshaded) pigment. The movement includes Hard-Edge painting, in which colors were not blended into one another, and Color-Field painting. Color-Field painters stained large unprimed canvas with acrylic paints (often by pouring diluted paint), avoiding strong contrasts or visible brushstrokes.

Hard-Edge Painting

> Held, Al, 1928
> Kelly, Ellsworth, 1923
> Noland, Kenneth, 1924
> Olitski, Jules, 1922
> Stella, Frank, 1936

Color-Field Painting

> Francis, Sam, 1923–1994
> Frankenthaler, Helen, 1928
> Liberman, Alexander, 1912–1999
> Louis, Morris, 1912–1962
> Newman, Barnett, 1905–1970
> Rothko, Mark, 1903–1970
> Still, Clyfford, 1904–1980

"A good portrait . . . has more than just accurate features.
It has some other thing."

—ALICE NEEL, 1900–1984, American portraitist

HAPPENINGS (UNITED STATES, LATE 1950s–PRESENT)

"Happenings" (performance art) were usually nonverbal spontaneous or (sometimes) carefully planned theatrical presentations that might involve the audience. Some of these events resulted in concrete artwork, while in others the performance was the art. Many of the artists listed here participated in performance art, then went on to produce paintings and sculpture.

Dine, Jim, 1935
Grooms, Red, 1937
Kaprow, Allan, 1927
Oldenburg, Claes, 1929
Whitman, Robert, 1935

MINIMALISM (1960s–PRESENT)

"Minimal Art" was a term that applied to a number of art movements, including Op Art, Color-Field Painting, Serial Imagery (related works in a series), Hard-Edge painting, and the shaped canvas (canvas that has escaped the normal rectangular format and is stretched to follow curves or points of the painting). It sometimes featured the use of high-tech materials such as neon, plastic, and metals. Essentially, Minimalist artworks were nondecorative, featured extreme simplicity, and were purposely devoid of any "artist's touch or expressive content." An example would be an all black painting.

Bell, Larry, 1939
Judd, Donald, 1928–1994
Lewitt, Sol, 1928
Marden, Brice, 1938

Martin, Agnes, 1912
Rothko, Mark, 1903–1970
Ryman, Robert, 1930
Serra, Richard, 1939

OP ART (1960s)

Op (optical) artists were painters who juxtaposed moiré patterns, geometric shapes, and vibrating colors of equal intensity to create optical illusions of movement.

England

    Riley, Bridget, 1931

France

    Vasarely, Victor, 1908–1997

Israel

    Agam, Yaacov, 1928

United States

    Anuszkiewicz, Richard, 1930
    Davis, Ron, 1937
    Poons, Larry, 1937

FLUXUS (1962–1970s)

This "Neo-Dada group," which originated in Germany through the influence of Joseph Beuys, briefly spread through Europe and to New York. It was closely related to Environmental art and performance, and based on "happenings" or "actions" as opposed to traditional art forms that produce a product such as a painting.

England

    Knowles, Alison, 1933

Germany

    Beuys, Joseph, 1921–1986
    Richter, Gerhard, 1932

United States

    Andersen, Eric, 1943
    Maciunas, George, 1931–1978
    Nauman, Bruce, 1941
    Ono, Yoko, 1933
    Paik, Nam Jun, 1932
    Watts, Robert, 1923–1988

EARTH ART (1968–PRESENT)

Earth Art (often called Environmental Art) began when artists used a "new" medium: unlikely materials to form installations in galleries. Examples are a heap of sand or a circle of rocks on a museum or gallery floor that might be shaped by chance or arranged by the artist. Ultimately, artists went to out-of-the-way places such as the Great Salt Lake in Utah or a desert in New Mexico to create their (often impermanent) artworks. Drawings, films, and photographs recorded the work in progress.

England

> Goldsworthy, Andy, 1956
> Long, Richard, 1945

Germany

> Baumgarten, Lothar, 1944
> Horn, Rebecca, 1944

Netherlands

> Dibbets, Jan, 1941

United States

> André, Carl, 1935
> Aycock, Alice, 1946
> Chin, Mel, 1951
> Christo (Javacheff), 1935

United States (continued)

> Christo, Jeanne-Claude
>   Guillebon, 1935
> Harrison, Newton, 1932
> Heizer, Michael, 1944
> Holt, Nancy, 1938
> Johanson, Patricia, 1940
> Keinholz, Ed, 1927–1994
> Keinholz, Nancy, 1943
> Kelly, Mary, 1941
> Lin, Maya, 1960
> Oppenheim, Dennis, 1938
> Pepper, Beverly, 1924
> Roloff, John, 1947
> Smithson, Robert, 1938–1973
> Turrell, James, 1943
> Warhol, Andy, 1928–1987

FEMINIST ART (LATE 1960s–PRESENT)

Feminism was a movement of women artists who sought to have their rightful place in the art world. No one style or idea dominated the movement, although some artists did use "female" materials such as fibers and clay to interpret their ideas. Some of the people in this list were obviously quite young when the movement began, but are now part of a Neo-Feminism movement. All see themselves as artists first, feminists second. (See the separate list of women artists on pages 137 to 143).

Canada

Rockburne, Dorothea, 1934

England

Emin, Tracey, 1963
Wilson, Jane, 1967
Wilson, Louise, 1967
(Jane's twin)

France

Messager, Annette, 1943

Germany

Kollwitz, Käthe, 1867–1945
Munter, Gabriele, 1877–1962

Mexico

Kahlo, Frida, 1907–1954

United States

Chicago, Judy, 1939
Fish, Janet, 1938
Flack, Audrey, 1931
Frank, Mary, 1933
Graves, Nancy, 1940–1995
Hamilton, Ann, 1956
Holzer, Jenny, 1950
Kruger, Barbara, 1945
Levine, Sherri, 1947
Neel, Alice, 1900–1984
Ringgold, Faith, 1930
Saar, Alison, 1956
Saar, Betye, 1926
Schapiro, Miriam, 1923
Sherman, Cindy, 1954
Smith, Kiki, 1954

PHOTOREALISM OR HYPERREALISM (UNITED STATES, 1965-1977)

Artists had as their subjects the everyday environment as seen through the eye of a camera. Photorealist artists tended to specialize, with some doing signs, others faces, and others still lifes.

Bechtle, Robert, 1932
Bell, Charles, 1935–1995
Close, Chuck, 1940
de Andrea, John, 1941
Eddy, Don, 1944

Estes, Richard, 1932
Flack, Audrey, 1931
Hanson, Duane, 1925–1996
Pearlstein, Philip, 1924

ARTE POVERA (c. 1969)

This largely Italian movement used junk objects in composition, a form of rebellion against materialism. It included Happenings, Land or Earth Art, and Installations.

England

Goldsworthy, Andy, 1956
Long, Richard, 1945

Germany

Beuys, Joseph, 1921–1986

Netherlands

Dibbets, Jan, 1941

United States

André, Carl, 1935
De Maria, Walter, 1935
Morris, Robert, 1931

INSTALLATION ART (1970-PRESENT)

Installation or Conceptual art allows the artist to create an artwork that can be photographed, moved, destroyed, or taken down and reassembled elsewhere. Installation art includes Video Art, Earth or Land Art, and Light Art (lasers, neon, holography). These installations sometimes also include conventional art such as sculpture, paintings, and photography.

England

Gilbert and George
    Gilbert Proesch, 1943
    George Passmore, 1942

Germany

Beuys, Joseph, 1921–1986
Haacke, Hans, 1936

Netherlands

Dibbets, Jan, 1941

United States

Borofsky, Jonathan, 1942
Holzer, Jenny, 1950
Kabakov, Ilya, 1933
Serra, Richard, 1939

VIDEO ART (c. 1970-PRESENT)

Each of the artists listed here is a video artist, but each has a different concept, and the only thing they have in common is the use of the video screen as the transmitter of their art. Many of the video installations cause the viewer to be involved as he or she moves and observes what is happening on the (sometimes room-sized) projections.

England

> Taylor-Wood, Sam, 1967
> Wearing, Gillian, 1963

Germany

> Froese, Dieter, 1937
> Trockel, Rosemary, 1952

Japan

> Mori, Mariko, 1967

Switzerland

> Rist, Pipilotti, 1962

United States

> Allen, Terry, 1943
> Barney, Matthew, 1967
> Finlay, Ian Hamilton, 1925
> Graham, Dan, 1942
> Hill, Gary, 1951
> Hiller, Susan, 1940
> Kelley, Mike, 1954
> Lucier, Mary, 1944
> Nauman, Bruce, 1941
> Ousler, Tony, 1957
> Paik, Nam Jun, 1932
> Viola, Bill, 1951

BODY ART (UNITED STATES, 1960s–PRESENT)

In this art form, the subject matter is frequently the artist's own body, which is changed somehow over time, with the changes usually recorded. (An example is the artist who recorded herself in a daily nude photograph as she lost weight over a period of months.)

> Acconci, Vito, 1940
> Kaprow, Allan, 1927
> Maciunas, George 1931–1978
> Mendieta, Ana, 1948–1985
> Oppenheim, Dennis, 1938

NEO-EXPRESSIONISM (1975–PRESENT)

Neo-Expressionism was basically a German movement distinguished primarily by large, rather crudely executed paintings that incorporate such things as straw or broken pottery.

Germany

Baselitz, Georg, 1938
Fetting, Rainer, 1949
Immendorf, Jorg, 1945
Kiefer, Anselm, 1945
Koberling, Bernd, 1938
Lupertz, Markus, 1941
Penck, A. R., 1939

Italy

Cucci, Enzo, 1949
Paladino, Mimmo, 1948

United States

Kushner, Robert, 1949
Schnabel, Julian, 1951

CONTEMPORARY ART (1965–PRESENT)

Contemporary art is created by living artists or those who have died within the relatively recent past. It does not have any one dominant style or feature, but includes many artistic movements, such as continued Photorealism, Appropriationism, Graffiti art, Neo-Classicism, Neo-Expressionism, Neo-Conceptualism, Post-Modernism, Earth Art and New Feminism. Artists are combining new media with old ideas, and of course using traditional media with new ideas. This list features contemporary artists. Birth (and death) dates are provided when available.

Africa

Aydu, Osi, 1955, Nigeria
Cookthorn, Robert, 1960
Samba, Cheri, 1956
Tokoudagba, Cyprien, 1954

Australia

Tjapaltjarri, Tim Leurah,
1939–1984
Warangkula Tjupurrola, Johnny,
1925

Belgium

Alechinsky, Pierre, 1927
Delvoye, Wim, 1965
Tordoir, Narcisse, 1954

Colombia

Botero, Fernando, 1932

Denmark

Kirkeby, Per, 1938

England

Auerbach, Frank, 1931
Barnbrook, Jonathan, 1966
Blake, Peter, 1932
Burgin, Victor, 1941
Chapman, Dinos, 1962
Chapman, Jake, 1966
Emin, Tracey, 1963
Freud, Lucian, 1922
Gilbert & George
   Gilbert Proesch, 1943
   George Pasmore, 1942
Hirst, Damien, 1965
Hockney, David, 1937
Hume, Gary, 1962
John, Gwen, 1876–1939
Kossoff, Leon, 1926
McLean, Bruce, 1944
LeBrun, Christopher, 1951
Ofili, Chris, 1968
Rego, Paula, 1935
Spencer, Stanley, 1891–1959
Starn, Mike, 1961
Starn, Doug, 1961 (Mike's twin)
Whiteread, Rachel, 196
Wilson, Jane, 1967
Wilson, Louise, 1967 (Jane's
   twin)

Finland

Ahtila, Eija Liisa, 1959

France

Aberola, Jean-Michel, 1953
Balthus (Balthasar Klossowski
   de Rola), 1908–2001

France (continued)

Blais, Jean-Charles, 1956
Cadmus, Paul, 1904–1999
Combas, Robert, 1957
Garouste, Gérard, 1946
Gilot, Françoise, 1921
Huyghe, Pierre, 1962
Klein, Yves, 1928–1962
Rustin, Jean, 1928

Germany

Ackerman, Franz, 1963
Althoff, Kari, 1966
Baselitz, Georg, 1938
Beuys, Joseph, 1921–1986
Haacke, Hans, 1936
Hofer, Candida, 1944
Immendorf, Jorg, 1945
Kiefer, Anselm, 1945
Polke, Sigmar, 1941
Richter, Gerhard, 1932

Israel

Absalon, 1964–1993

Italy

Burri, Alberto, 1915–1995
Chia, Sandro, 1946
Clemente, Francesco, 1952
Cucchi, Enzo, 1950
Mariani, Carlo Maria, 1931
Paladino, Mimmo, 1948

Japan

Funakoshi, Katsura, 1951
Mori, Mariko, 1967
Morimura, Yasumasa, 1951

Mexico

Gerzso, Gunther, 1915–2000
Gil de Montes, Roberto, 1950

Netherlands

Daniels, René, 1950

New Zealand

Kakuhiwa, Robyn, 1940

Norway

Nerdrum, Odd, 1944

Russia

Komar, Vitaly, 1943
Melamid, Aleksandr, 1946

Scotland

Campbell, Steven, 1951

Spain

Barcelo, Miguel, 1957
Sevilla, Feran Garcia, 1949
Lopez-Garcia, Antonio, 1936

Switzerland

Fischli, Peter, 1952
Weiss, Daniel, 1946

United States

Artschwager, Richard, 1923
Baechler, Donald, 1956
Baldessari, John, 1931
Bartlett, Jennifer, 1941
Basquiat, Jean-Michel, 1960–1988
Bell, Larry, 1936
Benglis, Linda, 1941
Bickerton, Ashley, 1959
Bidlo, Mike, 1953
Blechner, Ross, 1949
Brooks, Ellen, 1946
Casebere, James, 1953
Close, Chuck, 1940
Colescott, Robert, 1925
Currin, John, 1962
DeForest, Roy, 1930
Divola, John, 1949
Downes, Rackstraw, 1939
Fischl, Eric, 1948
Fish, Janet, 1938
Flavin, Dan, 1933–1996
Frey, Viola, 1933
Gantz, Joe, 1954
Gillespie, Gregory, 1936
Gilliam, Sam, 1933
Goldstein, Jack, 1945
Golub, Leon, 1922
Gonzalez-Torres, Felix, 1957–1996
Gornik, April, 1953
Groover, Jan, 1943
Halley, Peter, 1953
Haring, Keith, 1958–1990
Hartigan, Grace, 1922
Holzer, Jenny, 1950

United States (continued)

Jenney, Neil, 1945
Johns, Jasper, 1930
Kahn, Wolf, 1927
Kasten, Barbara, 1936
Katz, Alex, 1927
Kienholz, Ed, 1927–1994
Kienholz, Nancy, 1943
Kitaj, Ronald Brooks (R. B.),
    1932
Koons, Jeff, 1955
Kosuth, Joseph, 1945
Kruger, Barbara, 1945
Lasker, Jonathan, 1948
Levine, Sherrie, 1947
Longo, Robert, 1953
Mangold, Robert, 1957
Marden, Brice, 1938
Mitchell, Joan, 1926–1992
Moroles, Jesus Bautista, 1950
Morris, Robert, 1931
Murphy, Catherine, 1946
Nauman, Bruce, 1941
Nicosia, Nic, 1951
Nilsson, Gladys, 1940
Nutt, Jim, 1938
Otterness, Tom, 1952
Paschke, Ed, 1939
Pearlstein, Philip, 1924

Pettibone, Raymond, 1957
Pfaff, Judy, 1946
Ray, Charles, 1953
Ringgold, Faith, 1930
Rollins, Tim, 1955 & K.O.S.
    (Kids of Survival)
Rothenberg, Susan, 1945
Ruscha, Ed, 1937
Salle, David, 1952
Samaras, Lucas, 1936
Scharf, Kenny, 1958
Schnabel, Julian, 1951
Scholder, Fritz, 1937
Sherman, Cindy, 1954
Skoglund, Sandy, 1946
Smith, David, 1906–1965
Smith, Kiki, 1954
Smith, Tony, 1912–1980
Spero, Nancy, 1926
Stella, Frank, 1936
Taaffe, Philip, 1955
Tansey, Mark, 1949
Turrell, James, 1934
Twombly, Cy, 1928
Vallance, Jeffrey, 1955
Wegman, William, 1943
Witkin, Joel-Peter, 1939
Wofford, Philip, 1935
Wong, Su-en, 1973

*"Rembrandt painted about 700 pictures—of these,
3,000 are in existence."*

—WILHELM BODE, 1845–1929, German art historian,
specializing in Rembrandt

WELL-KNOWN WOMEN ARTISTS

Women artists have always existed, but were not known by name until relatively recent times. The Feminist group that emerged in the 1970s was a movement that sought to win recognition for female artists. The women on this list have received considerable notice both for their artwork and for their contributions to the field of art. Some of them may have been included in other lists according to art movements in which they have taken part. As elsewhere, birth (and death) dates are provided where available.

AUSTRALIA

King, Inge, 1918
Martin, Mandy, 1952
Norrie, Susan, 1953
Petyarre, Ada Bird, c. 1930

BAHAMAS

Antoni, Janine, 1964

BELGIUM

Peeters, Clara, 1594–c. 1657

BRAZIL

Clark, Lygia, 1920–1988

CANADA

Astman, Barbara, 1950
Carr, Emily, 1871–1945
Cohen, Lynne, 1944
Corne, Sharron Zenith, 1936
Dyck, Aganetha, 1937
Falk, Gathie (Agathe), 1928
Goodwin, Betty, 1923
Luke, Alexandra, 1901–1967

CANADA (continued)

McLaughlin, Isabella, 1903
Newdigate, Ann, 1934
Odjig, Daphne, 1928
Pflug, Christiane, 1936–1972
Pratte, Mary, 1950
Rayner, Stephanie
Reid, Leslie, 1947
Rockburne, Dorothea, 1934
Scheving, Ruth
Sterbak, Jana, 1955
Stockholder, Jessica, 1959
Whiten, Colette, 1945
Wieland, Joyce, 1931–1998

CROATIA

Kauoric-Kurtovic, Nives, 1938

ENGLAND

Beauclerk, Diana, 1734–1808
Bell, Vanessa, 1879–1961
Butler, Elizabeth Thompson,
    1846–1933
Cameron, Julia Margaret,
    1815–1879

ENGLAND *(continued)*

Carrington, Leonora, 1917
Emin, Tracey, 1963
Frink, Elizabeth, 1930–1993
Hepworth, Barbara, 1903–1975
John, Gwendolen, 1876–1939
Lee, Sadie, 1967
Lucas, Sarah, 1962
Osborn, Emily, 1834–c. 1909
Potter, Beatrix, 1866–1943
Rego, Paula, 1935
Riley, Bridget, 1931
Saville, Jenny, 1970
Siddall, Elizabeth, 1829–1862
Whiteread, Rachel, 1963
Wilding, Alison, 1948
Wilson, Jane, 1967
Wilson, Louise, 1967 (Jane's twin)
Wise, Gillian, 1936

FRANCE

Abbema, Louise, 1858–1927
Bashkirtseff, Marie, 1859–1884
Beaux, Cecilia, 1863–1942
Benoist, Marie-Guillemine, 1768–1826
Bonheur, Rosa, 1822–1899
Claudel, Camille, 1864–1943
da Silva, Veira, 1908–1992
Gerard, Marguerite, 1761–1837
Haudebourt-Lescot, Antoinette Cecile Hortense, 1784–1845
Jaudon, Valerie, 1945

FRANCE *(continued)*

Labille-Guiard, Adelaide, 1749–1803
Laurencin, Marie, 1885–1956
Loir, Marie Anne, c. 1715–1769
Lublin, Lea, 1929–1999
Marr, Dora, 1908–1997
Méssager, Annette, 1943
Morisot, Berthe, 1841–1895
Navarre, Marie-Genevieve, 1737–1795
Poirier, Anne, 1942
Richier, Germaine, 1904–1959
Saint-Phalle, Niki de, 1930–2002
Valadon, Suzanne, 1865–1938
Vallayer-Coster, Ann, 1744–1818
Vigée-Lubrun, Marie Louise Elizabeth, 1755–1842

GERMANY

Albers, Anni, 1889–1994
Becher, Hilla, 1934
Hoch, Hannah, 1889–1978
Horn, Rebecca, 1944
Kollwitz, Käthe, 1867–1945
Merian, Maria Sibylla, 1647–1717
Modersohn-Becker, Paula, 1876–1907
Munter, Gabriele, 1877–1962
Stolzl, Gunta, 1897–1983
Trockel, Rosemarie, 1952
Van Schurman, Anna Maria, 1607–1678

IRELAND

Cross, Dorothy, 1956

Prendergast, Kathy, 1958

ITALY

Anguissola, Sofonisba,
1550–1650

Brooks, Romaine, 1894–1970

Carriera, Rosalba, 1675–1757

Fontana, Lavinia, 1552–1614

Gentileschi, Artemisia,
1593–c. 1652

Merz, Marisa, 1925

Modotti, Tina, 1896–1942

Sirani, Elisabetta, 1638–1665

JAPAN

Araki, Nobuyoshi, 1940

Kubota, Shigeko

Mori, Mariko, 1967

Naito, Rei, 1966

Sasaki, Tomiyo, 1943

MEXICO

Escobedo, Helen, 1934

Izquierdo, Maria, 1902–1955

Kahlo, Frida, 1907–1954

Rodriguez, Patricia, 1944

NETHERLANDS

Dumas, Marlene, 1953

Leyster, Judith, 1609–1660

Ruysch, Rachel, 1666–1750

NEW ZEALAND

Albrecht, Gretchen, 1943

Kahukiwa, Robyn, 1940

PALESTINE

Hatoum, Mona, 1952

POLAND

Abakanowicz, Magdalena, 1930

Kurylok, Ewa, 1946

RUSSIA

Delaunay, Sonia Terk,
1885–1979

Exter, Alexandra, 1882–1949

Figurina, Elena, 1955

Golitsyna, Clara, 1925

Goncharova, Natalia, 1881–1962

Kopystiankaya, Svetlana, 1950

Nakhova, Irina, 1955

Nazarenko, Tatiana, 1944

Nesterova, Natalia, 1944

Popova, Lyubov, 1889–1924

Stepanova, Varvara, 1894–1958

Werefkin, Marianne, 1860–1938

SCOTLAND

Blackadder, Elizabeth, 1931

Redpath, Anne, 1895–1965

Watt, Alison, 1966

SOUTH AFRICA

Dumas, Marlene, 1953

SOUTH AMERICA

Pacheco, Maria Luisa,
    1919–1982, Bolivia
Penalba, Alicia, 1913–1982,
    Argentina
Porter, Liliana, 1941, Argentina
Tsuchiya, Tilsa, 1932, Peru

SPAIN

Solano, Susana, 1946
Varo, Remedios, 1908–1963

SWITZERLAND

Bailly, Alice, 1872–1938
Cahn, Miriam, 1949
Henri, Florence, c. 1893–1982
Kauffman, Angelica, 1741–1807
Oppenheim, Meret, 1913–1985
Taeuber-Arp, Sophie, 1889–1943

UNITED STATES

Abbott, Berenice, 1898–1991
Albers, Anni, 1889–1994
Anderson, Laurie, 1947
Antin, Eleanor, 1935
Apple, Jacki, 1941
Applebroog, Ida, 1929
Arbus, Diane, 1923–1971
Attie, Dotty, 1938
Aycock, Alice, 1946
Baca, Judith Francisca, 1946
Bacon, Peggy, 1895–1987
Barry, Judith, 1949
Bartlett, Jennifer, 1941

UNITED STATES *(continued)*

Beaux, Cecilia, 1855–1942
Beecroft, Vanessa, 1969
Benglis, Linda, 1941
Benning, Sadie, 1973
Bishop, Isabel, 1902–1988
Bloom, Barbara, 1951
Bontecou, Lee, 1931
Bouguereau, Elizabeth Gardner,
    1837–1922
Bourgeois, Louise, 1911
Bourke-White, Margaret,
    1904–1971
Brown, Joan, 1938–1990
Brownscombe, Jennie Augusta,
    1850–1936
Butterfield, Deborah, 1949
Butterworth, Elizabeth, 1949
Cassatt, Mary, 1844–1926
Catlett, Elizabeth, 1915
Chase, Louisa, 1951
Chase-Riboud, Barbara, 1930
Chicago, Judy, 1939
Chryssa, 1933
Cordero, Helen, 1915–1994
Cunningham, Imogen,
    1883–1975
Dahl-Wolfe, Louise, 1895–1989
Daw, Leila, 1950
de Kooning, Elaine, 1920–1989
Denes, Agnes, 1938
Duckworth, Ruth, 1919
Dwyer, Nancy, 1954
Edelson, Mary Beth, 1934
Eisenman, Nicole, 1965

UNITED STATES *(continued)*

Escobar, Marisol, 1930

Falkenstein, Claire, 1908–1997

Fasnacht, Heide, 1951

Ferrara, Jackie, 1929

Finley, Karen, c. 1960

Flack, Audrey, 1931

Forrester, Patricia Tobacco, 1940

Frank, Mary, 1933

Frankenthaler, Helen, 1928

Frey, Viola, 1933

Fried, Nancy, 1945

Fuller, Meta Vaux Warrick,
1877–1968

Garza, Carmen Lomas, 1948

Gillespie, Dorothy, 1920

Gilpin, Laura, 1891–1979

Goldin, Nan, 1953

Goodacre, Glenna, 1939

Gornik, April, 1953

Graves, Nancy, 1940–1995

Greene, Renée, 1959

Grossman, Nancy, 1940

Hale, Ellen Day, 1855–1940

Hall, Ann, 1792–1863

Hamilton, Ann, 1956

Hammond, Harmony, 1944

Hardin, Helen, 1943–1984

Harrison, Helen Mayer, 1929

Hartigan, Grace, 1922

Hesse, Eva, 1936–1970

Hoffman, Malvina, 1887–1966

Holt, Nancy, 1943

Holzer, Jenny, 1950

Hosmer, Harriet, 1830–1908

Hu, Mary Lee, 1943

Huntington, Anna Hyatt,
1876–1973

Hurd, Henriette Wyeth,
1907–1997

Jacobi, Lotte, 1896–1990

Jaquette, Yvonne, 1934

Jessup, Georgia Mills, 1926

Jones, Lois Mailou, 1905–1998

Kasebier, Gertrude, 1852–1934

Kelly, Mary, 1941

Kent, Corita, 1918–1986

Kozloff, Joyce, 1942

Krasner, Lee, 1908–1984

Krauss, Rosalind, 1940

Kruger, Barbara, 1945

Lange, Dorothea, 1895–1965

Larner, Liz, 1960

Lavenson, Alma, 1897–1989

Leibovitz, Annie, 1949

Lemieux, Annette, 1957

Levine, Sherrie, 1947

Levitt, Helen, 1913

Lewis, Edmonia, 1843–c. 1911

Lewis, Lucy, 1897–1992

Lewis, Samella, 1924

Lin, Maya, 1959

Linhares, Judith, 1940

Longman, Evelyn Beatrice,
1874–1954

Low-MacMonnies, Mary F.,
1858–1946

Lucier, Mary, 1944

Lundeberg, Helen, 1908–1999

UNITED STATES *(continued)*

Lutz, Winifred, 1942

Maciver, Loren, 1909–1998

Mangold, Sylvia Plimack, 1938

Mark, Mary Ellen, 1940

Martin, Agnes, 1912

Martinez, Maria Montoya,
1887–1980

Matthiasdottir, Louisa,
1917–2000

McClelland, Suzanne, 1973

Mears, Helen Farnsworth,
1872–1916

Mendieta, Ana, 1948–1985

Miss, Mary, 1944

Mitchell, Joan, 1926–1992

Morgan, Julia, 1872–1957

Moses, Anna Mary (Grandma),
1860–1961

Murphy, Catherine, 1946

Murray, Elizabeth, 1940

Natzler, Gertrud Amon,
1908–1971

Neel, Alice, 1900–1984

Nevelson, Louise, 1899–1988

Nilsson, Gladys, 1940

Nochlin, Linda, 1931

O'Keeffe, Georgia, 1887–1986

Peale, Anna Claypoole,
1791–1878

Peale, Sarah Miriam, 1800–1885

Pepper, Beverly, 1924

Perry, Lilla Cabot, 1848–1933

Peyton, Elizabeth, 1965

Pfaff, Judy, 1946

Pindell, Howardena, 1943

Pinney, Eunice, 1770–1849

Piper, Adrian, 1948

Prophet, Nancy Elizabeth,
1890–1960

Reichek, Elaine, 1943

Ringgold, Faith, 1930

Rockburne, Dorothy, 1921

Rothenberg, Susan, 1945

Saar, Alison, 1956

Saar, Betye, 1926

Sage, Kay, 1898–1963

St. Léger Eberle, Abastenia,
1878–1942

Sauer, Jane, 1937

Savage, Augusta, 1892–1962

Schapiro, Miriam, 1923

Sherman, Cindy, 1954

Silverthorn, Jeanne, 1950

Simmons, Laurie, 1949

Simpson, Lorna, 1960

Skoglund, Sandy, 1946

Sleigh, Sylvia, 1935

Smith, Alexis, 1949

Smith, Jaune Quick-to-See, 1940

Smith, Kiki, 1954

Snyder, Joan, 1940

Solomon, Holly

Spencer, Lilly Martin,
1822–1902

Spero, Nancy, 1926

Steir, Pat, 1940

Stephens, Alice Barber,
1858–1932

UNITED STATES *(continued)*

Stevens, May, 1924
Swartz, Beth Ames, 1936
Tafoya, Margaret, 1904–2001
Tanning, Dorothea, 1913
Thomas, Alma, 1891–1978
Truitt, Anne, 1921
Tucker, Marcia, 1940
Van Ness, Beatrice Whitney,
   1888–1981
von Rydingsvard, Ursula, 1942
von Wiegand, Charmion,
   1900–1983
Vonnoh, Bessie Potter,
   1872–1955
Walker, Kara, 1969
Walkingstick, Kay, 1935
Warashina, Patti, 1940
Wayne, June, 1918

Weems, Carrie Mae, 1953
Weems, Katherine Lane,
   1899–1990
Whitney, Gertrude Vanderbilt,
   1878–1942
Wildenhain, Marguerite,
   1896–1985
Wilke, Hannah, 1940–1993
Williams, Sue, 1954
Willson, Mary Ann,
   1810–c. 1840
Wilson, Jane, 1924
Winsor, Jackie, 1941
Wood, Beatrice, 1893–1998
Wright, Patience Lovell,
   1725–1786
Zorach, Marguerite Thompson,
   1887–1968

CONTEMPORARY PAINTINGS

By the end of the 20th century, the lines between art forms had become significantly blurred, with paintings no longer always two-dimensional and no longer always made with paint. Some are embellished with found materials, such as broken china or lines of fine copper wire. Sometimes the subject matter may make the viewer quite uncomfortable, or puzzled. Or there may even be no subject matter! Many of the works listed here are not yet in collections or museums, but have been shown in galleries and reproduced in several books on contemporary art.

AFRICA

Samba, Cheri, b. 1956, *Zaire, Liberation Spectaculaire de Nelson Mandela,* 1990, Annina Nosei Gallery, New York City

AUSTRALIA

Tjapaltjarri, Clifford, 1932–2002, *Possum Man's Dreaming,* 1992, Corbally Stourton Contemporary Art, London

CHINA

Yu Youhan, b. 1943, *Mao and Blonde Girl Analysed,* 1992, Marlborough Fine Art, London

COLOMBIA

Botero, Fernando, b. 1932, *Alof de Wignacourt* (after Caravaggio), 1974, Nohra Haime Gallery, New York City

Cardenas, Juan, b. 1939, *Variation on a Still Life,* 1990, Claude Bernard Gallery, New York

ENGLAND

Freud, Lucian, b. 1922, *Naked Portrait,* 1972–1973, Tate Gallery, London

Hockney, David, b. 1937, *The Twenty Third V.N. Painting,* 1992, collection, the artist

Rego, Paula, b. 1935, *The First Mass in Brazil,* 1993, Marlborough Fine Art, London

GERMANY

Richter, Gerhard, b. 1932, *Abstraktes Bild*, 1993, Marian Goodman Gallery, New York City

ITALY

Clemente, Francesco, b. 1952, *The Fourteen Stations, No. III, 1981–1982*, private collection

Mariani, Carlo Maria, b. 1931, *Composition 4—The Expulsion from Eden*, 1989, Studio d'Arte Cannaviello, Milan

NEW ZEALAND

Kahukiwa, Robyn, b. 1940, *Ko Hineteiwaiwa, Ko Hinekorako Ko Rona Whakamau tai*, 1993, Museum of New Zealand

UNITED STATES

Bartlett, Jennifer, b. 1941, *Spiral: An Ordinary Evening in New Haven*, 1989, private collection, New York

Basquiat, Jean-Michele, 1960–1988, *Untitled* (words and figures), 1984, Osaka City Museum, Japan

Close, Chuck, b. 1940, *Self-Portrait*, 1997, Pace-Wildenstein Gallery, New York

DeForest, Roy, b. 1930, *Big Foot, Dogs, and College Grad*, 1985, John Natsoulas Gallery, Davis, California

Estes, Richard Close, b. 1932, *Holland Hotel*, 1984, Louis K. Meisel Gallery, New York City

Fischl, Eric, b. 1948, *Squirt (For Ian Giloth)*, 1982, Thomas Ammann Fine Art, Zurich, Switzerland

Haring, Keith, 1958–1990, *Monkey Puzzle*, 1988, Tony Shafrazi Gallery, New York City

Marden, Brice, b. 1938, *Cold Mountain 6, (Bridge)*, 1989–1991, collection of the artist

Nilsson, Gladys, b. 1940, *The Swimming Hole*, 1986, Phyllis Kind Gallery, Chicago/New York

Peyton, Elizabeth, b. 1965, *Craig*, 1997, Gavin Brown's enterprise, New York

Rothenberg, Susan, b. 1945, *Butterfly*, 1986, Saatchi Collection, London

Scharf, Kenny, b. 1958, *Junkie,* 1992, Tony Shafrazi Gallery, New York City

Schnabel, Julian, b. 1951, *The Walk Home,* 1985, collection of the Eli Broad Family Foundation

GREEK AND ROMAN GODS, GODDESSES, AND HEROES

In Roman and Greek civilizations, the multitudes of gods played a very significant role in everyday life. Temples were built to honor and appease these gods, whose all-too-human characteristics included an affinity for vengeance. Although no Greek paintings have survived, the lives of gods and goddesses were frequently portrayed on Greek vases, enough of which have been discovered to give us an idea of how the Greeks lived, played, and worshipped. During the Renaissance, which was considered a revival of Classicism, mythology was an enormously popular subject. For painters, it provided rich subject matter—not to mention good reason to show more skin than previously approved of by the Church. Being acquainted with the personages of Greek and Roman mythology provides a helpful foundation for understanding and appreciating many works of art. This list is a brief primer that includes most of the well-known gods, goddesses, and heroes of the Greek and Roman cultures. Greek names are provided, with the Roman counterpart in parentheses.

THE BEGINNING

Gaea	Mother Earth
Uranus (Coelus)	the sky; heaven, Mother Earth's first husband

THE TITANS . . . AND TITANESSES
(CHILDREN OF MOTHER EARTH AND THE SKY)

Atlas	Hyperion	Pallas
Coeus	Iapetus	Phoebe
Crius	Leto	Prometheus
Cronus (Saturn)	Maia	Rhea (Cybele)
Dione	Mnemosyne	Tethys
Epimetheus	Oceanus	Theia
Eurynome	Ophion	Themis

THE OLYMPIANS

Aphrodite (Venus)	goddess of love and beauty
Apollo (Apollo)	god of the sun, truth (reason), archery, music, medicine, and prophecy
Ares (Mars)	god of war
Artemis (Diana)	goddess of the hunt, twin sister of Apollo, guardian of women
Athena (Minerva)	goddess of wisdom and war; patroness of artisans
Demeter (Ceres)	goddess of the underworld/agriculture
Hades (Pluto)	ruler of the underworld
Hera (Juno)	goddess of marriages, wife of Zeus
Hermes (Mercury)	messenger of the gods
Hestia (Vesta)	goddess of the family and home
Poseidon (Neptune)	ruler of the sea; carried a magic trident
Zeus (Jupiter or Jove)	ruler of the gods, god of the sky; symbol: thunderbolt and lightning

SPECIAL GODS

Acacesius	benefactor of mankind, deliverer from evil
Achelous	largest of the three thousand river gods
Adonis	a beautiful young man loved by Aphrodite, killed by a boar
Amazons	a strong, warlike tribe of women
Amphitrite	wife of Poseidon, goddess of the sea
Andromeda	bride of Perseus
Arachne	young girl changed by Athena into a spider
Argus	Hera's thousand-eyed watchman
Asklepios (Aesculapius)	god of healing, son of Apollo
Atlas	superhuman strength; carried the world on his shoulders, a Titan's son
Cassiopeia	the mother of Andromeda, Queen of Ethiopia
Circe	a sorcerer
Cronus (Saturn)	god of time, second god of the universe; dethroned by his son, Zeus

SPECIAL GODS *(continued)*

Cyclopes	one-eyed blacksmiths who made the thunderbolts
Danae	mother of Perseus
Dionysus (Bacchus)	god of wine
Eos (Aurora)	goddess of dawn, sister of the sun
Epimetheus	cousin of Zeus; slow-witted brother of Prometheus
Eros (Cupid)	god of love
Flora	Roman goddess of flowers
Fortuna	goddess of fate (fortune)
Ganymede	cupbearer of the gods, a prince carried to Olympus by Zeus's Eagle
Helios	god of the sun
Hephaistos (Vulcan)	god of fire
Hygeia	goddess of health
Linus	Heracles's music teacher
Medea	a sorceress
Menoetius	arrogant, brutal, evil man
Narcissus	fell in love with his own reflection
Nike (Victoria)	goddess of victory
Orion	friend of Artemis, a hunter
Pan (Faunus)	god of the shepherds, nature; half-human/half-goat
Paris	a prince of Troy; his judgment was the cause of the Trojan War
Persephone (Proserpina)	goddess of the underworld, daughter of Demeter
Priapus	god of fertility
Prometheus	creator of man
Psyche	goddess of the soul
Triton	son of Poseidon

ZEUS'S WIVES AND LOVES

Alcmene	mother of Heracles, and daughter of Semele
Danae	mother of Perseus
Demeter (Ceres)	mother of Persephone
Eruynome	mother of the three graces: Aglaia, Euphrosyne, Thalia
Europa	sister of Cadmus, the mother of famous sons such as King Minos
Harmonia	first Queen of Thebes, wife of Cadmus
Hera (Juno)	mother of Ares, Hebe, Eileithyia, and Hephaestus (not Zeus's daughter)
Io	mother of Epaphus, changed into a cow
Leda	mother of Helen of Troy, the most beautiful woman in the world, and Pollux
Leto (Latona)	mother of Artemis and Apollo
Maia	mother of Hermes
Metis	Zeus swallowed her before she could give birth; Zeus's first wife
Mnemosyne	associated with memory; mother of the nine Muses
Semele	mother of Dionysus
Themis	mother of the "Hours"—Thallo, Auxo, and Carpo—and the "Fates"—Clotho, Lachesis, and Atropos

HEROES (HALF HUMAN/HALF DIVINE)

Actaeon	Actaeon was changed into a stag upon coming across Artemis bathing
Atalanta	female hero who hunted with other heroes for the Calydonian boar
Bellerophon	ordered to kill the fire-breathing monster (the Cimera), mounted on Pegasus
Cadmus	founder of the city of Thebes, brother of Europa
Daphne	a nymph; to escape Apollo, she was turned into a laurel tree

HEROES (HALF HUMAN/HALF DIVINE) *(continued)*

Deucalion and Pyrrha	sole survivors of the flood that Zeus brought to destroy a wicked world
Heracles (Hercules)	son of Zeus; completed twelve tasks to atone for a crime his father committed
Io	female ancestor (with Zeus) of Heracles
Jason	leader of the heroes of the ship "Argo" in search of the Golden Fleece
Oedipus	a king who unknowingly killed his father and married his mother
Peleus	father of Achilles
Perseus	killed Medusa, one of the Gorgons
Terminus	god of boundaries
Theseus	kin of Heracles, King of Athens, sailed with Jason on the "Argo," slew the Minotaur

HEROES OF THE TROJAN WAR

Achilles	greatest of the Greek warriors
Aeneas	forefather of the Romans
Agamemnon	commander of the Greeks, brother-in-law of Helen
Ajax	second to Achilles in valor and beauty
Hector	enemy of Achilles
Laocoon	the priest who opposed the Trojan horse, saying he "feared Greeks even when they bear gifts"
Meleager	killed the Caledonian boar
Menelaus	brother of king Agamemnon
Odysseus	prince of Ithaca, invented the Trojan horse
Patroclus	loyal friend of Achilles, killed in his stead
Priam	king of Troy

THREE FURIES (PUNISHED THOSE WHO ESCAPED JUSTICE)

Alecto

Megara

Tisiphone

THREE FATES (SPUN THE THREADS OF HUMAN DESTINY)

Atropos (Morta)

Clotho (Nona)

Lachesis (Decuma)

THREE GRACES (GODDESSES OF BEAUTY, DANCE, SOCIAL ARTS)

Aglaia (Splendor)

Euphrosyne (Mirth)

Thalia (Good Cheer)

NINE MUSES (GODDESSES OF THE ARTS)

Calliope	muse of epic poetry, chief of the muses, mother of Orpheus
Clio	muse of history
Erato	muse of love, poetry, lyrics
Euterpe	muse of music
Melpomene	muse of tragedy
Polyhymnia	muse of sacred poetry, mime
Terpsichore	muse of dance
Thalia	muse of comedy
Urania	muse of astronomy

THREE GORGONS (HIDEOUS SISTERS WITH SNAKE-HAIR; MORTALS WHO SAW THEM TURNED TO STONE)

Euryale

Medusa

Stheno

Gray Sisters (sisters of the Gorgons, with one eye shared by the three)

MORTALS

Eurydice	wife of Orpheus
Orpheus	brought the joy of music to earth
Pandora	when she opened the box, she released all the plagues of the world

MYTHICAL CREATURES

Centaur	half horse/half man
Cerberus	three-headed underworld watchdog
Chimera	three-headed fire-breathing monster
Harpies	birds with women's heads
Hydra	nine-headed monster
Minotaur	half bull/half man
Nymphs	female spirits of nature
Satyr	half goat/half man
Sirens	singers who lured sailors to die
Sphinx	half lion/half human
Typhon	fire-breathing monster

SPECIAL LOCATIONS IN MYTHOLOGY

Cythera	the island where Aphrodite was washed ashore
Elysian Fields	land of dead heroes
Mount Olympus	home of the Gods
River Styx	underworld river of the dead

50 MYTHOLOGICAL PAINTINGS

Here are fifty of the countless paintings that feature a mythological character or event.

1. *Angelica,* 1819, Jean-Auguste-Dominique Ingres, Museu de Arte, Sao Paulo, Brazil

2. *Apollo and Daphne,* 1664, Nicolas Poussin, Louvre, Paris

3. *Apollo Pursuing Daphne,* c. 1755–1760, Giambattista Tiepolo, National Gallery, Washington DC

4. *Artemis and a Swan,* c. 480–450 B.C., Pan Painter, Hermitage, St. Petersburg

5. *Ascanius Shooting the Stag,* 1682, Claude Lorraine, Ashmolean Museum, Oxford, England

6. *Atalanta and Meleager,* c. 1628, Jacob Jordaens, Prado, Madrid

7. *Bacchanal,* 1630, Peter Paul Rubens, Nationalmuseum, Stockholm

8. *Bacchus and Ariadne,* 1523, Titian, National Gallery, London

9. *Cupid Complaining to Venus,* c. 1530, Lucas Cranach, National Gallery, London

10. *Diana after her Bath,* 1742, François Boucher, Louvre, Paris

11. *Diana and Actaeon,* 1556–1559, Titian, National Gallery of Scotland, Edinburgh

12. *Drunken Silenus,* c. 1620, Anthony van Dyck, Gemaldegalerie, Dresden

13. *Ganymede,* c. 1534, Antonio Corregio, Kunsthistoriches Museum, Vienna

14. *Ganymede,* 1635, Rembrandt, Gemaldegalerie, Dresden

15. *Garden of Love,* 1632–1634, Peter Paul Rubens, Prado, Madrid

16. *Judgment of Paris,* 1530, Lucas Cranach the Elder, Staatliche Kunsthalle, Karlsruhe, Germany

17. *La Primavera,* c. 1475–1478, Sandro Botticelli, Uffizi, Florence

18. *Laocoön,* c. 1608, El Greco, National Gallery of Art, Washington, DC

19. *Mars and Venus United by Love,* c. 1570, Paolo Veronese, Metropolitan Museum of Art, New York City

20. *Mercury and Argus,* 1635–1638, Peter Paul Rubens, Gemaldegalerie, Dresden

21. *Nymph of the Source,* after 1537, Lucas Cranach the Elder, National Gallery, Washington, DC

22. *Pallas and Centaur,* c. 1482, Sandro Botticelli, Uffizi, Florence

23. *Rinaldo Abandoning Armida,* 1745, Giambattista Tiepolo, Art Institute of Chicago

24. *Sacred and Profane Love,* c. 1514, Titian, Villa Borghese, Rome

25. *Saskia as Flora,* 1635, Rembrandt, National Gallery, London

26. *Saturn Devouring his Children,* 1819–1823, Francisco de Goya, Prado, Madrid

27. *Sleeping Venus,* 1944, Paul Delvaux, Tate, London

28. *Tempest,* 1506–1508, Giorgione, Accademia, Venice

29. *The Bathers,* c. 1765–1770, Jean-Honoré Fragonard, Louvre, Paris

30. *The Birth of Venus,* 1636–1638, Peter Paul Rubens, Musées Royaux des Beaux-Arts, Brussels

31. *The Birth of Venus,* c. 1480–1485, Sandro Botticelli, Uffizi, Florence

32. *The Departure from Cythera,* 1717, Jean-Antoine Watteau, Louvre, Paris

33. *The Dream of Antiope,* c. 1530, Antonio Corregio, Louvre, Paris

34. *The Fall of Icarus,* 1567–1578, Pieter Bruegel the Elder, Musées Royaux des Beaux-Arts, Brussels

35. *The Fall of Icarus,* c. 1608, Carlo Saracini, Museo Nationale di Capodimonte, Naples

36. *The Intervention of the Sabine Women,* 1797, Jacques Louis David, Louvre, Paris

37. *The Judgment of Paris,* 1632–1635, Peter Paul Rubens, National Gallery, London

38. *The Rape of Proserpina,* 1628–1629, Rembrandt, Staatliche Museen Dahlem, Berlin

39. *The Rape of the Sabine Women,* 1626–1637, Nicolas Poussin, Metropolitan Museum of Art, New York City

40. *The Three Graces,* 1638–1640, Peter Paul Rubens, Prado, Madrid

41. *The Toilet of Venus,* 1806, Diego Velasquez, National Gallery, London

42. *Venus and Adonis,* c. 1550–1575, Paolo Veronese, Prado, Madrid

43. *Venus and Cupid,* 1509, Lucas Cranach the Elder, Hermitage, St. Petersburg

44. *Venus and Mars,* 1485–1490, Sandro Botticelli, National Gallery, London

45. *Venus and Mars,* 1498, Piero di Cosimo, National Gallery, London

46. *Venus Bandaging the Eyes of Cupid,* c. 1565, Titian, Villa Borghese, Rome

47. *Venus Consoling Love,* 1751, François Boucher, National Gallery, Washington, DC

48. *Venus with Mercury and Cupid,* mid 1520s, Coreggio, National Gallery, London

49. *Venus, Cupid, Folly, and Time,* c. 1540, Agnolo Bronzino, National Gallery, London

50. *Youthful Bacchus,* c. 1589, Caravaggio, Uffizi, Florence

"Two of the greatest old masters are time and mastic varnish."

—MICHELANGELO, 1475–1564, Renaissance painter and sculptor

CHAPTER 3

Art from Many Cultures

"Of all lies, art is the least untrue."
—GUSTAVE FLAUBERT, 1821–1880, French novelist

T his chapter is meant to help people of diverse backgrounds understand what they are seeing when viewing artwork from a different time or culture. Most artwork that has survived through the ages—approximately 80 percent—was created for religious purposes and was well understood by the people within the culture in which it was created, but is a mystery to many people viewing it today.

Although some cultures, such as African American, Native American, and Asian, are integrated into the cultures of the United States and Canada, their roots come from ancient traditions. Many of today's artists continue to base their work on symbols used by their ancestors. An understanding of symbolism used by artists of many cultures and familiarity with their histories will increase appreciation of the work.

EGYPTIAN HISTORICAL PERIODS

The beginning of Western art dates back to the Egyptian culture. While the cultures on the Mediterranean were developing concurrently, most of what we know of the spread of Western art began in Egypt, moved to Greece, then Rome, throughout the European mainland, and then to the New World.

Dynastic Period	Ruler(s)	Capital City	Time Period
Predynastic Period			6100–2920 B.C.
Badarian			6100–3800 B.C.
Naqada I, Amratian			3800–3600 B.C.
Naqada II, Early Gerzean			3600–3400 B.C.
Naqada III, Late Gerzean			3400–3100 B.C.
Dynasty 0, Late Predynastic			3100–2920 B.C.
Early Dynastic Period			2920–2649 B.C.
Dynasties 1 and 2	King Narmer (Menes)	Thinis	2920–2649 B.C.
Old Kingdom			2649–2134 B.C.
Dynasty 3	Kings Zoser, Snefu	Memphis	2649–2575 B.C.
Dynasty 4	Cheops, Chefren and Mycerinus	Memphis	2575–2465 B.C.
Dynasty 5	Userkaf, Sahura, Niuserra, Unas	Memphis	2465–2323 B.C.
Dynasty 6	Kings Teti, Pepi I, et al.	Memphis	2323–2150 B.C.
Dynasties 7 and 8	many kings, short reigns	Memphis	2150–2134 B.C.
First Intermediate Period			2134–2040 B.C.
Dynasties 9 and 10		Heracleopolis	2134–2040 B.C.
Dynasty 11	Menuhotep	Thebes	2134–2040 B.C.
Middle Kingdom			2040–1640 B.C.
Dynasty 11	post-unification of north and south	Thebes	2040–1991 B.C.
Dynasty 12	Amenemhat I		1991–1783 B.C.
Dynasty 13	Sebekhotep, Neferhotep,	Thebes	1783–1640 B.C.
Dynasty 14	Xoite		ends 1640 B.C.
Second Intermediate Period			1640–1532 B.C.
Dynasties 15 and 16	Hyksos kings		1640–1532 B.C.
Dynasty 17	Ahmose I	Thebes	1640–1550 B.C.
New Kingdom (Empire)			1550–1070 B.C.
Dynasty 18	Amenophis I, Tuthmosis I, II, and III, Hatshepsut, Akhenaten, Tutankhamen, Horemheb	Diospolis, Luxor and Karnak	1550–1307 B.C.
Dynasty 19	Harmhab, Seti I, and Rameses I & II Tomb at Abu Simbel	Diospolis	1307–1196 B.C.

Dynastic Period	Ruler(s)	Capital City	Time Period
Dynasty 20	Rameses III, IV & V	Diospolis	1196–1070 B.C.
Third Intermediate Period (Post Empire)			1070–332 B.C.
Dynasty 21		Tanis	1070–945 B.C.
Dynasty 22	Sheshonk, Petubastis, Osorkon, Takecloth		945–745 B.C.
Dynasty 23		Tanis	745–712 B.C.
Dynasty 24	Psamtik	Sais	724–712 B.C.
Dynasty 25	Ethiopian kings		712–664 B.C.
Dynasty 26	Saite kings: Necho, Apries	Sais	664–525 B.C.
Dynasties 27 to 31	Persian kings		525–332 B.C.
Ptolemaic Period			332–30 B.C.
Alexander the Great		Alexandria	332–323 B.C.
Macedonian Dynasty			332–304 B.C.
Ptolemies I–XV	Cleopatra (last of the Ptolomies)		304–30 B.C.
Roman Domination			30 B.C.–A.D. 395

GREEK HISTORICAL PERIODS

The art created in these early Mediterranean civilizations on Greek islands and the mainland included statuary, pottery vessels, architecture, and sophisticated gold work. A famous example of art is listed in most of the periods.

Name of Period	Typical Artwork	Date of Artwork	Date of Period
Aegean, Early Cycladic	*Idol from Amorgos*	2500–1100 B.C.	1800–2000 B.C.
Greek-speaking tribes on the mainland			2000 B.C.
Mycenae	*The Vaphio Cups*	c. 1500 B.C.	2300–1100 B.C.
Minoan	*Palace of Minos*, Crete	c. 1500 B.C.	2000–1100 B.C.
Greek Vase			
Geometric Period	*Dipylon Amphora*	8th century B.C.	850–700 B.C.
Orientalizing Phase	*Owl Perfume Jar*	c. 650 B.C.	700–600 B.C.

Name of Period	Typical Artwork	Date of Artwork	Date of Period
Black Figured (Archaic)	*Heracles Strangling the Nemean Lion*	c. 525 B.C.	650–480 B.C.
Red Figured	*Lapith and Centaur*	c. 490–480 B.C.	c. 530 B.C.
Classical			480–323 B.C.
Red-Figure	*Eos and Memnon*	c. 490–480 B.C.	
White Ground	*Mistress and Maid*	440–430 B.C.	
Greek Sculpture			
Archaic	*Kouros*	c. 600 B.C.	700–480 B.C.
Classical	*Kritios Boy*	c. 480 B.C.	480–323 B.C.
Hellenistic	*Dying Gau*	c. 230–220 B.C.	323–30 B.C.
Greek Architecture			
Geometric Period	timber and mud-brick buildings		c. 750 B.C.
Archaic Period (Doric)	Temple of Apollo, Corinth		c. 540 B.C.
Classical Period (Doric, Ionic)		c. 480 B.C.	
Hellenistic Period (Ionic, Corinthian)	*Altar of Zeus,* Pergamon	c. 175 B.C.	323–30 B.C.

CHINESE DYNASTIES

Knowing what terms such as "Ming Dynasty" or "Warring States" mean as they relate to Chinese art history, and the historical period to which they refer in relation to Western history, will add depth to a Westerner's art viewing experience. Such knowledge will also foster an understanding of a culture with ancient roots, often expressed through its art.

Period	Dates
Neolithic	c. 7000–1600 B.C.
Yanshao Culture	5000–2000 B.C.
Longshan Culture	3000/2500–1500 B.C.
Hsia (Xia)	2205–1766 B.C.
Shang Dynasty	c. 1600–1027 B.C.
Zhou (Chou)	1122–770 B.C.
Western Zhou	1027–771 B.C.
Eastern Zhou	770–256 B.C.
Period of Spring and Autumn	770–475 B.C.
Warring States Period	475–221 B.C.
Qin (Ch'in)	221–207 B.C.
Han Dynasty	
Western (former) Han	206 B.C.–A.D. 9
Xin	A.D. 9–25
Eastern (later) Han	25–220
Six Dynasties Period	220–580
Three Kingdoms Period	220–265
Tsin (Jin)	265–420
Western Jin	265–316
Eastern Jin	317–420
Northern Dynasty	
Northern Wei	386–534
Eastern Wei	534–550
Western Wei	535–556
Northern Qui	550–557
Northern Zhou	557–581
Southern Dynasty	
Song	420–479
Qi	479–502
Liang	502–557
Chen	557–589

Period	Dates
Sui Dynasty	589–618
Tang (T'ang) Dynasty	618–906
Five Dynasties and Ten Kingdoms	906–960
Later Liang	907–923
Later Tang	923–936
Later Jin	936–947
Later Han	947–950
Later Zhou	951–960
Liao Dynasty	916–1125
Sung (Song)	960–1280
Northern Sung	960–1127
Southern Sung	1127–1279
Jin Dynasty	1115–1234
Yuan (Mongol) Dynasty	1271–1368
Ming Dynasty	1368–1644
Hungwu	1368–1398
Jianwen	1398–1402
Yongle	1403–1424
Hongxi	1425
Xuande	1426–1435
Zhengtong	1436–1449
Jingtai	1450–1456
Tianshun	1457–1464
Chenghua	1465–1487
Hongzhi	1488–1505
Zhengde	1506–1521
Jiajing	1522–1566
Longqing	1567–1572
Wanli	1572–1620
Tiachang	1620
Tianqi	1620–1627
Chongzhen	1628–1644

Period	Dates
Qing (Ch'ing)—(Manchu) Dynasty	1644–1911
Shunzhi	1644–1661
Kangxi	1662–1722
Yongzheng	1723–1735
Qianlong	1735–1795
Jiaqing	1796–1820
Daoguang	1821–1850
Xianfeng	1851–1861
Tongzhi	1862–1874
Guangxu	1875–1908
Xuantong	1908–1911
Republic of China	1912–1949
People's Republic of China	1949–present

SYMBOLS USED IN CHINESE ART

Chinese symbolism is used particularly in fine crafts (ceramics, textiles, metalwork), art, and architecture. The specific meanings of the symbols are clear to the Chinese, who understand why certain images are used repeatedly. The following lists of Chinese symbols used in art and their meanings may add to your understanding of Asian culture.

EIGHT BUDDHIST EMBLEMS OF GOOD LUCK

In India, where Buddhism began, the symbolism of these eight Buddhist emblems may vary slightly from Chinese beliefs.

Symbol	Meaning
Canopy	Royalty; sovereign power; protection
Conch shell	The voice of Buddha preaching the law
Lotus flower	Buddha is sometimes shown as a flame in the heart of a lotus

Symbol	Meaning
Mystic knot	Continuity of life; infinity and eternity
Pair of fish	Joys of union; marriage; fertility
Umbrella	Protection; the guardian of the South has the umbrella of earthquakes; darkness and chaos
Vase	Triumph over birth and death
Wheel of law	The cosmos; peaceful change; destiny; sovereignty

MISCELLANEOUS CHINESE SYMBOLS

In a cultural tradition as ancient as that of the Chinese, a variety of symbols might be found in a scroll painting, jade carving, or bronze ceremonial vessel. Only a few of the numerous symbols and what they represent are on this list.

Symbol	Meaning
Ax	Justice; judgment; authority
Bat (fu)	Good luck
Birds	Free; wandering spirit
Book	Learning
Butterfly	Joy
Carp	Determination; good luck
Chrysanthemum	Autumn; joy
Coin	Prosperity
Constellations	Spiritual wisdom of rulers
Cranes and pine trees together	Old age
Dragon (five-clawed)	Used only by the emperor
Dragon	Strength and beauty
Dragons, paired	Represent all opposites such as sun/moon, heaven/earth
Fish	Plenty; abundance
Gate gods	Gates symbolize an entry into new life
Ingot of gold	Riches
Kitchen god and his wife	Watch over daily activities

Symbol	Meaning
Lotus	Purity; creativity
Millet and flames	Presence of divinity; anger; danger
Moon	Femininity; the hare in the moon represents immortality
Mountain	The center of the world
Pair of mandarin ducks	Happy marriage
Peach	Longevity; happy marriage wishes; immortality
Peacock	Beauty and dignity
Peony	Spring; joy
Phoenix	Combination of pheasant and peacock
Pine tree	Long life
Plum blossom	Winter and beauty
Pomegranate	Fertility; numerous descendants
Sun	Power; the heavens
Teapot	Fertility
Three-legged toad	Spits gold coins, lives on the moon
Tiger	Wards away evil spirits
Tortoise	Luck and wisdom
Dragon of spring	Beginning of life
Phoenix of summer	Peak of life
Tortoise of winter	Hibernation, luck
White tiger of autumn	Harvest and death

COLORS

Red	South, joy, the luckiest of colors, life; happiness
White	West, the white tiger, mourning
Black	North, winter, water
Blue	Coolness of the heavens above and the waters below
Green	East, spring, wood and water
Orange	Love and happiness
Yellow	Earth, the center, the hare in the moon

THREE ABUNDANCES

The Three Abundances are happiness, longevity, and fertility, symbolized as follows.

Symbol	Meaning
Hands of Buddha	Happiness
Peaches	Longevity
Pomegranates	Fertility

FIVE HAPPINESSES

In Chinese tradition, the Five Happinesses are:

A natural death
Health
Longevity
Love of virtue
Officialdom

THREE PERFECTIONS

Chinese painters, poets, and philosophers often met to share their work. At the very heart of their craft were these Three Perfections.

Calligraphy	A long tradition of calligraphy (picture writing) exists in China.
Poetry	Chinese poetry often extolled the beauty of nature or a work of art.
Painting	Most Chinese paintings were based on nature. They might include animals, mountains, trees, or some of the many symbols listed here.

"The artist must train not only his eye but also his soul."
—WASSILY KANDINSKY, 1866–1944, Russian Expressionist painter

NINE PARTS OF A DRAGON

Asian dragons were believed to have these nine parts. In addition, a dragon with five claws was the symbol for royalty, and would only have been seen on objects or clothing belonging to the emperor.

Head of a camel
Horns of a deer
Eyes of a rabbit
Ears of a cow
Neck of a snake
Belly of a frog
Scales of a carp
Claws of a hawk
Palm of a tiger

JAPANESE DYNASTIES

Japanese dynasties were generally named after the rulers of each period. When it comes to Japanese art, Westerners are mostly familiar with works from the Edo, or Tokugawa, period—the 17th to 19th centuries. *Ukiyo-e* prints (translated as "pictures of the floating world," meaning subjects of everyday life) greatly influenced European painters, particularly the Impressionists.

Dynasty	Period
Jomon	5000 B.C.
Yayoi	c. 200 B.C.
Prehistoric period	ended A.D. 552
Asuka period	552–645
Nara period	645–784
Heian period	784–1185
Early Heian	784–897
Middle & Late Heian	897–1185
Kamakura period	1185–1333
Muromachi period	1333–1573

Dynasty	Period
Momoyama period	1573–1614
Edo, or Tokugawa, period	1614–1868
Meiji Restoration	1868–1912
Modern times	1912–present

WELL-KNOWN ASIAN ARTISTS

It is difficult to narrow down the thousands of Asian artists to one list; however, these are the ones who have been at the forefront in contemporary as well as ancient Asian art. Where information is available, the country of origin, dates of birth and death, and the profession of the artist are listed. (A single date is the artist's date of birth, unless otherwise noted.) Chinese and Japanese names are normally listed with the family (surname) first; therefore, even when not separated by a comma, these names are in last-name-first order. Where a comma is used, it's because the artist has an Anglicized first name (as in Bing, Bernice). This list was compiled with the assistance of Juliana Yuan, Professor of Asian Art at the University of Missouri, St. Louis.

CHINESE/NORTH AMERICAN

Bing, Bernice, 1936–1998, painter
Chen Chi, 1912, painter
Chen, Hilo, 1942, painter
Chuang Che, 1934, printer
Gu, Wenda, 1955, painter
Han, Raymond, 1931, painter
Hui, Ka-Kwong, 1923, ceramist
Kan, Diana, 1926, painter
Lin, Maya Ling, 1959, architect/sculptor
Lum, Ken, 1956, Canadian photographer
Moy, Seong, 1921, ceramist
Pei, I. M., 1917, architect
Wang Ming, 1921, painter
Wong, Wucius, 1936, painter

CHINESE

Ch'ien Hsuan, 1235–c. 1301, painter
Chang Da-chien, 1899–1993, painter
Chang Seng-Yu, active 479–557, painter
Chao Ch'ang, active 11th century, painter
Chao Ling-Jang, active 1070–1100, painter
Chao Tzu-Yun, active 12th century, painter
Chou Fang, active 780–805, painter
Chu-jan, active 960–985, painter
Fan K'uan, active 990–1030, painter
Fang LiJun, 1963, painter
Gao Xi, c. 1020–1090, painter
Guan Zilan, 1903–1986, painter
Han Kan, 715–781, painter
Hsia Kuei (Ka-Kei), active 12th century, painter
Hsu His, active, Five Dynasties, painter
Hua Yen, 1682–1756, painter
Huang Yon Ping, 1934, conceptual art
Kuo Hsi (Kwakki), 1020–1090, painter
Li Kung-lin, 1049–1105, painter
Li Lung-Mien, active c. 1070, painter
Li Shan, 1926, painter
Li Ti, active late 12th century
Liang K'ai, 1140–1210, painter
Lin Liang, 1410–c. 1490, painter
Lin Tinggui, active 12th century, painter
Liu Kuo-song, 1932, painter
Liu Wei, 1965, painter
Ma Yuan, 1189–1225, painter
Ni Zan, 14th century, painter
Qian Xuan, 1235–1305, painter
Shen Chou, 1427–1509, painter
Song Yong Ping, 1961, conceptual art
Ting Walasse, 1929, printmaker
Tung Ch'I-Ch'ang, 1555–1636, painter
Wang Jinsong, 1963, painter

Wang Meng, 1300–1385, painter
Wang Wei, 701–761, painter
Wang Yuan, 1642–1715, painter
Wang Ziwei, 1963, painter
Wen Zhengming, active 1470–1559, painter
Wong Su-en, 1973, painter
Wu Tao-Tzu, active c. 750, painter
Xu Beihong, 1895–1953, painter
Xu Bing, 1955, installation/calligraphy
Xu Tan, 1957, video installation
Yen Li-pen, active 626–668, painter
Yen Wen-Kuei, 967–1044, painter
Yu Youhan, 1943, photographer
Zeng Fanzhi, 1964, painter

JAPANESE/NORTH AMERICAN

Abe, Satoru, 1926, painter/sculptor
Akamu, Nina, sculptor
Arakawa, Shusaku, 1936, calligraphy/graphics, conceptualist
Arita, Akira, 1947, painter
Doi, Isami, 1903–1965, genre painter
Hibi, Hisako, 1907–1991, abstract expressionist
Inokuma, Genichiro, 1902–1993, painter
Iwamoto, Ralph, 1927, abstract paintings
Kanemitsu, Matsumi, 1922–1992, painter
Kasahara, Emiko, 1963, conceptualist
Kawabata, Minoru, 1911, painter
Kawashima, Takeshi, 1930, painter/sculptor
Kimura, Sueko M., 1912, painter
Kubota, Shigeko, 1937, installation, video
Kuniyoshi, Yasuo, 1893–1953, painter
Kusama, Yayoi, 1929, environmental artist
Mori, Mariko, 1967, conceptualist
Niizuma, Minoru, 1930–1998, painter
Noguchi, Isamu, 1904–1988, sculptor

Ochikubo, Tetsuo, 1923–1975, printmaker

Odate, Toshio, 1930, woodworker

Ohashi, Yutaka, 1923–1989, sculptor

Okada, Kenzo, 1902–1982, graphic artist

Okamura, Arthur, 1932, ceramist

Okubo, Mine, 1912–2001, painter

Sato, Masaaki, 1941, painter

Sato, Tadashi, 1923, painter

Suzuki, James Hiroshi, 1933, modernist painter

Takaezu, Toshiko, 1922, ceramics/sculpture

Takemoto, Henry Tadaaki, 1930, sculptor/ceramist

Tsutakawa, George, 1910–1997, sculpture/graphics

Uchima, Ansei, 1921, color woodcuts

Yamamoto, Noriko, 1929, performance art

Yamasaki, Minoru, 1912, architect

Yanagi, Yukinori, 1959, installation art

JAPANESE

Akiyama, Ryoji, 1942, photographer

Akiyama, Shotaro, 1920, photographer

Ando, Tadao, 1941, architect

Endo, Toshikatsu, 1952, sculptor

Fujii, Hiromi, 1935, architect

Fukuhara, Shinzo, 1883–1948, photographer

Funakoshi, Katsura, 1951, sculptor

Hanawa, Gingo, 1957, photographer

Hara, Hiroshi, 1936, architect

Harunobu (Suzuki Harunobu), 1725–1770, printmaker

Hasegawa, Itsuko, 1941, architect

Hibino, Katsuhiko, 1958, design

Hirabayashi, Kaoru, 1955, painter

Hiroshige (Utagawa [Ando] Hiroshige), 1797–1858, *Ukiyo-e* printmaker

Hokusai, Katsushika, 1760–1849, *Ukiyo-e* printmaker

Isozaki, Arata, 1931, architect

Ito, Makoto, 1950, glass artist

Ito, Toyo, 1941, architect

Kano, Eitoku, 1543–1590, painter

Kano, Mitsunobu, c. 1561–1608, painter

Kikutake, Kiyonori, 1950, architect

Kishi, Waro, 1950, architect

Kiyomizu, Kyube, 1922, sculptor

Kiyonobu (Torii Kiyonobu), 1664–1729, painter

Koetsu, Honnami, 1556–1637, painter

Kubota, Matusaka, 1945, video

Kuramata, Shiro, 1934–1991, architect

Kurokawa, Kisho, 1934, architect

Maemoto, Shoko, 1957, painter

Maki, Fumihiko, 1928, architect

Maruyama, Okyo, 1733–1795, painter

Mayekawa, Kunio, 1905–1986, architect

Miyajima, Tatsuo, 1951, photographer/sculptor

Mori, Sosen, 1747–1821, painter

Morimura, Yasumasa, 1951, photo artist

Murakami, Saburo, 1925–1996, sculptor

Nakagawa, Naoto, 1944, painter

Nakamura, Masato, 1963, installation art

Nakano, Emiko, 1925–1990, fiber artist

Narawahara, Takashi, 1930, sculptor

Noda, Tetsuya, 1940, printmaker

Nojima, Yasuzo, 1889–1964, photographer/painter

Ogata, Kenzan, 1663–1743, painter

Ogata, Korin, 1658–1716, painter

Otani, Sachio, 1924, architect

Saito, Takako, 1929, conceptual art

Sakakura, Junzo, 1904–1969, architect

Sharaku, Toshusai, d. 1801, printmaker

Shimabuku, Michihiro, 1969, conceptual art

Shingu, Susumu, 1937, sculptor

Shinohara, Kazuo, 1925, architect

Shiraga, Kazuo, 1924, happenings

Sotatsu, Tawaraya, 1623–1685, painter
Sudo, Reiko, 1953, textile designer
Sugimoto, Hiroshi, 1948, photographer
Takai, Teiji, 1911–1986, painter
Takamatsu, Shin, 1948, architect
Takeyama, Minoru, 1934, architect
Takuma, Eiga, active 14th century, painter
Tange, Kenzo, 1913, architect
Taniguchi, Yoshio, 1937, architect
Tschumi, Bernard, 1944, architect
Utamaro (Kitagawa Utamaro), 1753–1808, *Ukiyo-e* printmaker
Yokoo, Tadanori, 1936, graphic designer
Yoshihara, Jiro, 1905–1972, painter

KOREAN AMERICAN

Kim Po, 1917, painter
Kim Whanki, 1913–1974, painter/sculptor
Pai, John, 1937, sculptor
Paik, Nam Jun, 1932, video, conceptual art

KOREAN

Bong, Tae-Kim, 1937, painter, printmaker
Cho Duck-Hyun, 1957, graphic arts
Cho Soh, 1595–1668, painter
Ha, Chong-Hyun, 1935, painter
Kang Se-huang, 1713–1791, painter
Kim Chong-hui, 1786–1856, painter
Kim, Jong-Hak, 1954, painter
Kim Myong-guk, 1600–1663, painter
Lee, Nikki S., 1970, photographer
Sim, Sa-jong, 1707–1709, painter

MUSEUMS EMPHASIZING ASIAN ART

CHINA

Beijing	Imperial Palace Museum, Museum of Fine Arts
Hong Kong	The Chinese University of Hong Kong Art Museum; University Museum and Art Gallery
Shanghai	Shanghai Museum
Zhengzhou	Henan Museum

ENGLAND

Bath	The Museum of East Asian Art
Durham	Oriental Museum, University of Durham

FRANCE

Paris	Guimet National Museum of Asian Art

ITALY

Rome	Museo Nazionale d'Arte Orientale

JAPAN

Fukuoka	Fukuoka Prefectural Museum of Art; Fukuoka Art Museum
Kyoto	National Museum
Nara	Yamato Bunkakan Museum
Shiga	Miho Museum
Tokyo	Hara Museum of Modern Art; National Museum of Tokyo

LAOS

Vientiane	Musée National Lao

RUSSIA

Moscow State Museum of Oriental Art

SINGAPORE

Singapore National Heritage Board

SOUTH KOREA

Seoul National Museum of Korea; Seoul Metropolitan Museum of Art; Seoul Arts Center

Yongi-si Ho-Am Art Museum

TAIWAN

Taipei National Taiwan Art Gallery; Taipei Fine Arts Museum; National Palace Museum

UNITED STATES

California

Los Angeles Japanese American National Museum; Korean American Museum

Palo Alto Pacific Asia Museum

San Diego Fine Arts Gallery

San Francisco Asian Art Museum; M. H. de Young Museum; Chinese Cultural Center

Connecticut

New Haven Yale Art Gallery

District of Columbia

Washington Arthur M. Sackler Gallery; Freer Gallery; Smithsonian Institution

Hawaii

Honolulu — John Young Museum of Art, University of Hawaii at Manoa

Illinois

Chicago — Art Institute of Chicago; Chinese Museum; Oriental Institute Museum

Indiana

Indianapolis — Indianapolis Museum of Art

Maryland

Towson — Asian Arts and Culture

Massachusetts

Boston — Museum of Fine Arts
Cambridge — Fogg Art Museum
Milton — Museum of the American China Trade
South Hadley — Mount Holyoke College Art Museum
Springfield — Museum of Fine Arts
Worcester — Worcester Art Museum

Minnesota

Minneapolis — Minneapolis Institute of Arts
St. Paul — Minnesota Museum of Art

Missouri

Kansas City — Nelson-Atkins Museum of Art

New Jersey

Newark — Newark Museum
Princeton — Princeton University Art Museum

New York

    Brooklyn   Brooklyn Museum

    New York City   Asian American Arts Centre; Asia Society Galleries; China Institute; Japan Society Gallery; Metropolitan Museum of Art; Isamu Noguchi Garden

North Carolina

    Charlotte   Mint Museum of Art

Ohio

    Cleveland   Cleveland Museum of Art

    Coshocton   Johnson Museum

    Dayton   Dayton Art Institute

    Granville   Museum of Burmese Arts

    Toledo   Toledo Museum of Art

Oregon

    Eugene   Museum of Art, University of Oregon

    Portland   Portland Art Museum

Pennsylvania

    Scranton   Everhart Museum

Rhode Island

    Providence   Rhode Island School of Design Museum; Rockefeller Library

South Carolina

    Florence   Florence Museum

Texas

    Corpus Christi   Museum of Oriental Cultures

    Dallas   The Trammell and Margaret Crow Collection of Asian Art

Virginia

    Norfolk   Hermitage Foundation Museum

Washington

    Seattle   Seattle Asian Art Museum; Wing Luke Asian Museum

50 MAJOR AFRICAN AMERICAN ARTISTS

There are literally thousands of African American artists displaying fine works of art in museums around the world. Here are fifty whose work is acknowledged as being of top quality.

1. Alston, Charles, 1907–1977, painter. *The Family*, 1955, Whitney Museum of American Art, New York City

2. Andrews, Benny, 1930, painter. *Black*, 1971, collection of the artist

3. Bannister, Edward Mitchell, 1828–1901, painter. *Landscape*, 1882, Museum of Art, Rhode Island School of Design, Providence; *Sabin Point, Narragansett Bay*, 1885, Brown University, Providence, Rhode Island

4. Barthé, Richmond, 1901–1989, sculptor. *The Boxer*, 1942, Metropolitan Museum of Art, New York City

5. Bearden, Romare, 1911–1988, painter. *The Intimacy of Water*, 1973, St. Louis Art Museum, Missouri; *The Migration of the Negro (panel 50: Race Riots Were Very Numerous All Over the North)*, 1940–1941, Museum of Modern Art, New York City

6. Biggers, John, 1924–2001, painter and muralist. *Shotguns, Third Ward*, 1987 (Mural in the Christia V. Adair Park, Harris County, Texas); *Starry Crown*, 1987, Dallas Museum of Art, Texas

7. Blayton-Taylor, Betty, 1937, painter/mixed media. *Improvisation #5*, 1977, collection of the artist

8. Brown, Everald, 1917, painter. *Instrument for Four People*, 1986, National Gallery of Jamaica, Kingston

9. Brown, Grafton Tyler, 1841–1918, painter. *Grand Canyon of the Yellowstone from Hayden Point,* 1891, The Oakland Museum, California

10. Catlett, Elizabeth, 1915, sculptor. *Malcolm X Speaks for Us,* 1969, Museum of Modern Art, New York City; *Sharecropper,* 1968, National Museum of American Art, Washington, DC

11. Chase-Riboud, Barbara, 1936, sculptor. *Monument to Malcolm X (#11),* 1969, Newark Museum, New Jersey

12. Conwill, Houston, 1947, sculptor. *Installation,* 1995, Bernstein Associates, Mt. Vernon, New York

13. Cortor, Eldzier, 1916, painter/printmaker. *Southern Gate,* 1942–1943, National Museum of American Art, Washington, DC

14. Crite, Allan Rohan, 1910, painter. *Harriett and Leon,* 1941, The Boston Atheneum, Massachusetts

15. Douglas, Aaron, 1899–1979, painter. *The Negro in the African Setting: Panel #1,* 1934, collection of The New York Public Library, New York City; *The Creation,* 1935, The Howard University Gallery of Art, Washington, DC

16. Duncanson, Robert Stuart, 1823–1872, painter. *The Blue Hole, Flood Waters, Little Miami River,* 1851, Cincinnati Art Museum, Ohio; *The Land of the Lotus-Eaters,* c. 1861, His Majesty's Royal Collection, Stockholm

17. Edmondson, William, 1870–1951, carver. *Turtle,* 1940, collection of Mr. and Mrs. Robert L. Gwinn; *Eve,* early 20th century, Tennessee Botanical Gardens & Fine Arts Center, Nashville

18. Fuller, Meta Vaux Warrick, 1877–1968, sculptor. *Richard B. Harrison as "De Lawd,"* c. 1935, Howard University Gallery of Art, Washington, DC

19. Hayden, Palmer, 1890–1973, painter. *John Henry on the Right, Steam Drill on the Left,* 1947, collection of Museum of African Art, Los Angeles; *The Janitor Who Paints,* 1937, National Museum of American Art, Washington, DC

20. Johnson, Malvin Gray, 1896–1934, painter. *Self-Portrait,* 1934, National Museum of American Art, Washington, DC

21. Johnson, Sargent Claude, 1887–1967, sculptor. *Forever Free,* 1935, San Francisco Museum of Modern Art

22. Johnson, William Henry, 1901–1970, painter. *Street Musicians*, c. 1940, Oakland Museum of Art, California

23. Johnston, Joshua, c. 1765–1830, painter. *Portrait of a Cleric*, c. 1805, Bowdoin College Museum of Art, Brunswick, Maine

24. Jones, Ben, 1942, painter, scultor, printmaker, and mixed media. *Stars II* (15 elements), 1983, collection of the Newark Museum, New Jersey

25. Jones, Lois Mailou, 1905–1998, painter. *Symbols d'Afrique II*, 1983, collection of the artist; *Parade des Paysans*, 1965, collection of Max Robinson, Washington, DC

26. Lawrence, Jacob, 1917–2000, painter. *Builders #1*, 1972, St. Louis Art Museum, Missouri; *The Migration of the Negro*, Panel 1, 1940–1941, Phillips Collection, Washington, DC

27. Lee-Smith, Hughie, 1915–1999, painter. *Two Girls*, 1966, New Jersey State Museum, Trenton

28. Lewis, Edmonia, 1843–c. 1909, sculptor. *Hagar*, 1869, National Museum of American Art, Washington, DC

29. Lewis, Norman, 1909–1979, painter. *Yellow Hat*, 1936, collection of Ouida B. Lewis, New York

30. Lewis, Samella, 1924, painter. *Boy With a Flute*, oil, 1968, collection of the artist

31. Love, Ed, 1936, sculptor. *Mask for Mingus*, welded steel, 1974, collection of the artist

32. Motley, Archibald, Jr., 1891–1980, painter. *Chicken Shack*, 1936, Harmon Foundation Collection, the National Archives, Washington, DC; *Mending Socks*, 1924, Ackland Art Museum, University of North Carolina at Chapel Hill

33. Pigatt, Anderson, 1928, sculptor. *Caught in the Middle Earth*, wood and paint, 1970, New York Public Library, New York City

34. Pindell, Howardena, 1943, painter. *Autobiography: Water/Ancestors, Middle Passages/Family Ghosts*, 1988, The Wadsworth Atheneum, Hartford, Connecticut

35. Pippin, Horace, 1888–1946, painter. *The Holy Mountain*, 1944, Hirshhorn Museum and Sculpture Garden, Washington, DC; *John Brown Going to His Hanging*, 1942, The Pennsylvania Academy of the Fine Arts, Philadelphia

36. Porter, James A., 1905–1971, painter. *Woman Holding a Jug,* 1930, Fisk University, Nashville, Tennessee

37. Powers, Harriet, 1837–1911, quilter. *Bible Quilt,* c. 1895–1898, Museum of Fine Arts, Boston, Massachusetts

38. Prophet, Nancy Elizabeth, 1890–1960, sculptor. *Congolais,* 1931, Whitney Museum of American Art, New York City

39. Saar, Allison, 1956, sculptor. *Terra Firma,* 1991, Santa Barbara Museum of Art, California

40. Saar, Betye, 1926, sculptor. *The Liberation of Aunt Jemimah,* 1972, University Art Museum, University of California, Berkeley

41. Saunders, Raymond, 1934, painter. *Jack Johnson,* 1971, The Pennsylvania Academy of the Fine Arts, Philadelphia

42. Savage, Augusta, 1892–1962, sculptor. *Gamin,* 1929, Howard University Gallery of Art, Washington, DC

43. Scott, William Edouard, 1884–1964, painter. *When the Tide is Out,* c. 1931, Harmon Foundation Collection, the National Archives, Washington, DC

44. Searles, Charles, 1937, painter. *Dancer Series,* 1976, collection of Dr. and Mrs. Maurice Clifford, Philadelphia

45. Stout, Renée, 1958, sculptor. *Fetish #1,* 1988, Dallas Museum of Art, Texas

46. Tanner, Henry Ossawa, 1859–1937, painter. *Banjo Lesson,* 1893, Hampton University Museum Collection, Hampton, Virginia; *The Thankful Poor,* 1894, collection of Dr. William and Dr. Camille Cosby

47. Thomas, Alma W., 1896–1978, painter. *Light Blue Nursery,* 1968, National Museum of American Art, Washington, DC; *Elysian Fields,* 1973, National Museum of American Art, Washington, DC; *Three Red Hats,* 1964, collection of Mrs. J. E. Spingarn

"Art doesn't transform. It just plain forms."
—ROY LICHTENSTEIN, 1923–1997, American Pop Art painter

48. Wilson, Ellis, 1899–1977, painter. *Field Workers*, date unknown, National Museum of American Art, Washington, DC; *Haitian Funeral Procession*, c. 1950s, Amistad Research Center, Tulane University, New Orleans

49. Wilson, Fred, 1954, sculptor. *Guarded Men*, 1991, Whitney Museum of American Art, New York City

50. Woodruff, Hale, 1900–1980, painter. *Golden State Life Insurance Murals*, 1948–1949, Los Angeles, California; *Poor Man's Cotton*, 1934, Newark Museum, New Jersey

150 ADDITIONAL INFLUENTIAL AFRICAN AMERICAN ARTISTS

This list features another 150 notable African American artists. Many work in more than one medium, such as painting and photography, or sculpture and conceptual art. The list includes major influential artists from the past and well-known contemporary artists. Several were part of a specific group, and also appear in that list (such as those in The Harlem Renaissance). Birth and death dates are included where available. Where only one date is given, it is the artist's birthdate, unless otherwise noted.

PAINTING, DRAWING, AND PRINTMAKING

1. Allen, Tina, 1955
2. Banks, Ellen, 1941
3. Barnes, Ernie, 1938
4. Basquiat, Jean-Michel, 1960–1987
5. Beasley, Phoebe, 1943
6. Benoit, Rigaud, 1911–1987
7. Billops, Camille, 1933
8. Birch, Willie, 1942
9. Bolton, Shirley, 1945
10. Bradley, Peter, 1940
11. Braxton, William Ernest, 1978
12. Coleman, Floyd, 1939
13. Colescott, Robert H., 1925
14. Crichlow, Ernest, 1914
15. Cruz, Emilio, 1938
16. Davis, Alonzo, 1943
17. Davis, Bing (Willis), 1937
18. DeKnight, Avel, 1933
19. Delaney, Joseph, 1904–1991
20. Denmark, James, 1936

21. DePillars, Murry, 1938
22. Driskell, David, 1931
23. Farrow, William McKnight, 1885–1967
24. Favorite, Malaika, 1949
25. Fletcher, Gilbert, 1948
26. Freeman, Robert, 1946
27. Gilliam, Sam, 1933
28. Godwin, Michelle, 1961
29. Goodnight, Paul T., 1946
30. Gordon, Russell, 1936
31. Grigsby, J. Eugene, Jr., 1918
32. Harden, Marvin, 1935
33. Harper, William A., 1873–1910
34. Harris, Michael D., 1948
35. Heath, Thomas, 1949
36. Hendricks, Barkley, 1948
37. Herring, James V., 1887–1969
38. Hicks, Leon, 1933
39. Hoard, Adrienne, 1949
40. Holder, Robin, 1952
41. Hollingsworth, Alvin C., 1928
42. Honeywood, Varnett, 1950
43. Hudson, Julien, active 1811–1844
44. Hughes, Manuel, 1945
45. Jackson, Suzanne, 1944
46. Johnson, Daniel LaRue, 1938
47. Johnson, Lester, 1937
48. Lacy, Jean, 1932
49. Lam, Wilfredo, 1902–1982
50. Lee, Ron, 1951
51. LeVa, Barry, 1941
52. Lewis, Joseph S., III, 1953
53. Ligon, Glenn, 1960
54. Logan, Juan, 1946
55. Marshall, Kerry James, 1955
56. Mayhew, Richard, 1924
57. Miller, Tom, 1945
58. Mills, Lev, 1940
59. Mitchell, Dean, 1957
60. Moorhead, Scipio, active 1770
61. Morrison, Keith, 1940
62. Nefertiti (born Cynthia Freeman), 1949
63. Norman, Joseph E., 1957
64. O'Neal, Mary Lovelace, 1942
65. Olugebefola, Ademola, 1941
66. Oubre, Hayward, 1916
67. Parks, James Dallas, 1907
68. Phillips, James (Charles), 1945
69. Platt, Michael B., 1948
70. Pogue, Stephanie, 1944
71. Porter, Charles Ethan, 1847–c. 1923
72. Priestly, Debra
73. Proctor, Joseph, 1816
74. Riddle, John, 1933
75. Ringgold, Faith, 1930

76. Roberts, (Lucille) Malkia, 1927
77. Robinson, Christopher Wade, 1965
78. Rozzelle, John
79. Ryder, Mahler, 1937–1992
80. Sebree, Charles, 1914–1985
81. Smith, Alfred J., Jr., 1948
82. Tyler, Grafton, 1841–1918
83. Valentim, Rubem, 1922–1991
84. Walker, Annie E., 1855–1929
85. Waring, Laura Wheeling, 1887–1948
86. Wells, James Lesesne, 1902–1993
87. West, Pheoris, 1950
88. White, Charles, 1918–1979
89. Williams, Frank J., 1959
90. Williams, Philemona, 1951
91. Wilson, John Woodrow, 1922

MIXED MEDIA

92. Bailey, Radcliff, 1968
93. Carter, Carol Ann, 1947
94. Carter, Nanette, 1954
95. Howard, Mildred, 1945
96. Johnson, Stephanie A., 1952
97. Jones, Benjamin, 1942
98. Jones-Henderson, Napoleon, 1943
99. Maynard, Valerie, 1937
100. Piper, Adrian, 1948
101. Warmack, Gregory (Mr. Imagination), 1948

PHOTOGRAPHY

102. Amari, Amalia, 1949
103. Burns, Millie, 1950
104. Cox, Renée, 1958
105. DeCarava, Roy, 1919
106. Parks, Gordon, 1912
107. Rowe, Sandra, 1939
108. Simpson, Lorna, 1960
109. Sleet, Moneta, Jr. 1926–1996
110. Van Der Zee, James, 1886–1983
111. Walker, Christian, 1954
112. Walker, Kara, 1969
113. Weems, Carrie Mae, 1953
114. Williams, Pat Ward, 1948

SCULPTURE, INSTALLATION, AND PERFORMANCE ART

115. Adkins, Terry K., 1953
116. Artis, William E., 1914–1977,
117. Brown, James Andrew, 1953
118. Buchanan, Beverly, 1940
119. Burke, Selma, 1900–1995
120. Byard, Carole, 1941
121. Davis, Bing (Willis), 1937
122. Drew, Leonardo, 1961
123. Edwards, Mel, 1937
124. Eversley, Frederick, 1941
125. Green, Renée, 1959
126. Howard, Mildred, 1945
127. Humphrey, Margo, 1942
128. Hunt, Richard, 1935
129. Jackson-Jarvis, Martha, 1952
130. Johnson, Sargent Claude, 1888–1967
131. Lewis, Edmonia, 1843–c. 1909
132. Lloyd, Tom, 1929
133. Outterbridge, John (Wilfred), 1933
134. Perkins, Marion, 1908–1961
135. Purifoy, Noah, 1917
136. Puryear, Martin, 1941
137. Ravarra, Patricia, 1947
138. Rhoden, John, 1918–2001
139. Scott, Joyce, 1945

140. Simmons, Gary, 1964
141. Simms, Carroll H., 1924
142. Staton, Therman, 1953
143. Sullivan, Twotrees (Kaylynn), 1945
144. Thrash, Dox, 1892–1965
145. Warburg, Eugene, 1826–1859
146. Ward, Barbara, 1940
147. Ward-Brown, Denise, 1953
148. Washington, James W., Jr., 1909–2000
149. Williams, Michael Kelly, 1950
150. Wilson, Ed, 1925–1996

SPIRAL GROUP

This group, founded in 1963 by African American artists Romare Bearden and Norman Lewis, comprised artists who wanted to retain the unique characteristics of African American art, yet still have their work considered part of the American mainstream.

Alston, Charles, 1907–1977	Majors, William, 1930–1982
Amos, Emma, 1938	Mayhew, Richard, 1934
Bearden, Romare, 1911–1988	Miller, Earle
Douglas, Calvin	Morgan, Norma, 1928
Ferguson, Perry	Pritchard, William
Gammon, Reginald, 1921	Reid, Robert, 1924
Hines, Felrath, 1913–1993	Simpson, Merton, 1928
Hollingsworth, Alvin, 1928–2000	Thompson, Robert, 1937–1966
Hutson, Bill, 1936	Williams, William T., 1942
Lewis, Norman, 1909–1979	Woodruff, Hale, 1900–1980
Loving, Alvin, 1935	Yeargans, James

HARLEM RENAISSANCE, 1920s–1940

The Harlem Renaissance was a movement of all the arts that had its center in Harlem, New York. The African American experience was portrayed through the visual arts, literature, music, dance, and drama. Although many artists were considered part of the movement, these were the visual artists considered to be the forefront.

Barthé, Richmond, 1901–1989	Johnson, William H., 1901–1970
Delaney, Beauford, 1901–1979	Jones, Lois Mailou, 1905–1998
Douglas, Aaron, 1898–1979	Loving, Al, 1935
Hayden, Palmer, 1893–1973	Porter, James A. 1905–1971
Johnson, Malvin Gray, 1896–1934	Prophet, Elizabeth, 1890–1960
	Savage, Augusta, 1892–1962
Johnson, Sargent Claude, 1888–1967	Van Der Zee, James, 1886–1983
	Woodruff, Hale, 1900–1980

AFRICAN AMERICAN EXPRESSIONIST PAINTERS

The work of these contemporary painters is personally meaningful and may or may not relate to being African American. Birthdates are listed.

Andrews, Benny, 1930
Bailey, Malcolm, 1937
Chandler, Dona, 1941
DePillars, Murry, 1939
Edwards, Melvin, 1939
Hammons, David, 1943
Mason, Phillip, 1942

Overstreet, Joe, 1934
Rickson, Gary, 1942
Riddle, John, 1933
Ringgold, Faith, 1930
Searles, Charles, 1937
Smith, Vincent, 1929

MUSEUMS EMPHASIZING AFRICAN AMERICAN ART

Although these museums also emphasize African and African American culture, they sometimes have changing exhibitions of contemporary African American art.

UNITED STATES

Alabama

| Tuscaloosa | Will T. Murphy African American Museum |

California

| Los Angeles | Museum of African American Art |
| San Francisco | African American Historical and Cultural Society |

District of Columbia

| Washington | National Museum of African Art, Smithsonian |

Florida

| Miami | Black Heritage Museum |
| Tampa | Florida Museum of African American Art |

Illinois

| Chicago | DuSable Museum of African American History |

Michigan

    Detroit   Museum of African American History

Nebraska

    Omaha   Great Plains Black Museum

New York

    New York City   Museum for African Art; The Studio Museum in Harlem

Pennsylvania

    Philadelphia   Pennsylvania Afro-American Historical and Cultural Museum; The African American Museum in Philadelphia

Texas

    Dallas   African American Museum

NATIVE AMERICAN ROCK ART

Within the protected sites listed below, numerous prehistoric rock-art sites may be visited. Seeing petroglyphs (incised or painted images on rocks) is fascinating and brings the past to life. One particularly interesting site, *Newspaper Rock* near Monticello, Utah, was at a crossroads where people communicated with friends through picture-messages scratched into the desert "varnish" (a blackish surface) of a large, sheltered white rock. To locate specific locations and directions for viewing rock art, consult state maps. Several excellent field guides are available for specific Western regions.

ARIZONA

Chinley	Canyon de Chelly National Monument
Page	Glen Canyon National Recreational Area
Petrified Forest	Petrified Forest National Park
Tonalea	Navajo National Monument

COLORADO

Cortez	Mesa Verde National Park
Fruita	Colorado National Monument

MINNESOTA

Ely	Echo Trail, Cliff paintings

NEVADA

Baker	Lehman Caves National Monument
Moapa	Red Rock Canyon, Valley of Fire State Park

NEW MEXICO

Albuquerque	Petroglyph National Monument
Bloomfield	Chaco Canyon National Monument
Gila Hot Springs	Gila Cliff Dwellings National Monument
Los Alamos	Bandelier National Monument
Ramah Navajo Indian Reservation	El Morro National Monument
Three Rivers	Three Rivers Petroglyph Site

UTAH

Blanding	Hovenweep National Monument
Lake Powell	Natural Bridges National Monument; Grand Gulch Primitive Area
Moab	Arches National Park, Canyonlands National Park
Monticello	Newspaper Rock State Historical Monument, Indian Creek State Park
Springdale	Zion National Park
Torrey	Capitol Reef National Park
Utah/Colorado	Dinosaur National Monument

VERMONT

    Bellows Falls   Pennacook Tribe Petroglyphs

WASHINGTON

    Roosevelt   Roosevelt Petroglyphs

NATIVE AMERICAN CRAFTS

Like the people of many cultures, Native Americans who were doing what was necessary for everyday living would not have thought they were creating works of art that would one day appear in museums or be collected. Nevertheless, their clothing, baskets, pottery, and carvings, which continue to be made using some traditions of the past, are now appreciated the world over for their inherent beauty and fine craftsmanship. Embellishments of everyday items and those made for special occasions reflect the pride of the artisan (as well as the patriotism, as shown by the many American flags found on items of clothing). Among the many handcrafted items commonly produced by Native Americans were miniatures—miniature tipis, canoes, bows and arrows, dishes, and dolls, perhaps made as children's toys, or simply as a pastime. Many items were created in the 19th century for the tourist trade, when train travel opened up a large market for Native American wares.

This general list includes items that were part of the craftwork of Native American tribes across the North American continent. Variations in appearance depended upon the climate and available materials.

Beading. Native Americans traded pelts and craft items for imported glass beads (usually from Venice). These beads replaced hand-fashioned beads of clay, bone, or shell, and dyed porcupine quill that had formerly been used as decoration on moccasins, belts, shirts, vests, cradleboards, armbands, and other clothing.

Belts. These were made of woven yarn, beaded leather, or leather with silver decorations. A child's belt might be of leather studded with metal, and with beads, pouches, and suspended amulets.

Breechcloths (or breechclouts). The early Native American version of trousers, they were made of a length of flannel or hide about 1 × 6 feet and worn by men between the legs with each end tucked into a belt, hanging down in the front and back. Leggings, shirt, and a robe were worn if needed for warmth.

Coiled baskets. Traditionally used for gathering beans, and holding grain or trinkets, these baskets were woven or coiled. Their artistry was so admired that they became a commodity for the tourist market.

Cradle. The Native American cradle was a flat carrying board decorated with any combination of wood, textiles, beads, shells, wickerwork (sometimes dyed), and buckskin fringes.

Dresses. Traditional dresses varied depending on the climate and available materials. They were sometimes made of soft leather, beaded and fringed, or of woven fabric embellished with cowry shells, ribbon work, or fringed with "bells" made of tin.

Drums. Drums still play an important part of the rituals in Native American life. They are usually made of hollow logs with one or both ends covered with skin.

Fetishes. Fetishes, often used by Native Americans for religious purposes, are combinations of natural objects such as shells, feathers, beads, and bones, tied together with thongs.

Figural sculptures. Stone, wood, and pottery sculptures of humans and animals have been created throughout Native American cultures. Some were buried; others kept as prized possessions. Carvings of shamans (religious leaders known as medicine men) have been found in graves; their purpose is unknown.

Headdresses. Native American headdresses vary from simple cloth headbands or leather caps to warbonnets. Usually only one or two eagle feathers were worn into battle. Native Americans continue to be the only people legally qualified to use eagle feathers, as eagles are a protected species. The feathers were often cut in special patterns to signify feats of bravery.

Knife sheath. A sheath may be made of animal skin, and decorated with quills, beads, and leather fringe.

Leggings. Buckskin leg coverings traditionally had designs to match the moccasins that were worn with them. Women's leggings were knee high, and men's reached from hip to ankle.

Masks. Native Americans use masks for a variety of purposes such as festivals, to frighten the enemy, to give power, and sometimes for their comic effect. When a shaman wears a mask, he assumes special powers. Masks frequently represent animals and are made of different materials such as carved wood, painted leather, cloth, or corn husks.

Medicine bundle. This leather bag contains natural materials and images, and can be worn on clothing or attached to a shield, tipi, or horse.

Moccasins. Soft shoes worn by Native Americans are made of cured animal skins and frequently decorated with beads, porcupine quills, or fringe.

Pipe. Throughout the North American continent the pipe plays a special part in ceremonies. The material and style vary, depending on the peoples who use it.

Quiver case. This decorated slender tube of leather or birchbark was worn over the shoulder to hold arrows.

Vests. Leather vests usually are worn by Native American males. They are often elaborately decorated (sometimes with an American flag). In the past they featured quillwork, but now usually have beadwork and fringe.

War shirt. The war shirt was considered to have special powers. Rarely worn in battle, but usually reserved for a victory celebration, it was made of leather and featured beads and fringe.

Weaving. Woven bags and blankets were used by most of the Native American peoples.

NATIVE AMERICAN PEOPLES AND CRAFTS BY REGION

Although utilitarian crafts such as those in the preceding list were created by most Native American people, they are often distinctive by region, depending on the lifestyle, climate, wildlife, and materials available. These items were often traded between groups, and ownership of some crafts, such as a Navajo blanket, was a source of pride. These groupings are broadly organized by region, rather than by precise locale of each tribe.

CANADIAN PEOPLES

Native peoples of the Northern Plains and Northeast developed unique crafts. Because of their location, common elements of their crafts were moose hair for weaving and bear claws for jewelry. You can find more information on Canadian Tribes (The Subartic) under Northwest Coastal People, further on in this list.

Native American tribes of Canada include the following: Ahtna, Attikarmek, Beaver, Beothuk, Carrier, Chilcotin, Chipewyan, Cree, Dogrib, Han, Hare, Holikachuk, Ingalik, Kasha, Kutchin, Kolchan, Koyukon, Montagnais, Naskapi, Ojibwa, Saulteux, Sekani, Salvey, Tagish, Tahitan, Tanaina, Tanana, Tlingit, Tsetsault, Tutchine, and Yellowknife

> **Birchbark boxes.** In areas of the Northeast and upper Midwest, boxes and other items of use were decorated by biting interesting designs on birchbark. The same bark was also used to make canoes.

> **Effigy pipes.** The figural carving on an effigy pipe usually gazed at the smoker. It was buried with its owner.

CALIFORNIAN TRIBES

The Californian Indians were coastal, with territories extending from Mexico to Oregon. They include the following tribes: Cahuilla, Chumash, Costonoan, Cupeno, Esselen, Gabrieleino, Hupa, Karok, Luiseno, Maidu, Miwok, Modoc, Pomo, Salinan, Shasta, Tulare, Yuki, Yokuts, and Yurok.

> **Baskets.** The Californian tribes were known for their especially fine baskets. Their feather baskets were often given to commemorate rites of passage and were made from brightly colored feathers from meadowlarks, woodpeckers, mallards, and quail.

PLAINS TRIBES

This region runs roughly from as far south as coastal Texas, as far west and north as Northern Idaho, east to Missouri and Illinois, and north to North Dakota and Canada. Plains tribes include Apache, Arapaho, Atakapan, Blackfeet, Caddo, Cheyenne, Comanche, Crow, Hasinai, Iowa, Kansa, Kiowa, Kitchai, Kootenai, Missouri, Nez Perce, Oglala, Omaha, Osage, Oto, Pawnee, Piegan, Ponca, Quapaw, Santee, Shoshoni, Teton, Ute, Witchita, and Yankton.

Exploit robes. Individuals painted scenes of themselves involved in battle or other personal events in their lives.

Ledger drawings. When animal skins were not available, lined ledger paper used for bookkeeping was given to Native Americans for exploit drawings.

Muslin painting. Muslin that was given to the Native Americans by the United States government was sometimes decorated with exploits, and used as tipi linings when animal skins were not available.

Parfleche (decorative bag). The parfleche bag was used to hold dried food and was quite large. It generally has a long strap, frequently decorated with hanging fringes and designs. The modern version may be used as a type of briefcase.

Tipi covers. These shelters were usually decorated with symbols or personal "medicine" of the owner.

Warbonnet. The warbonnet contained from 30 to 50 eagle feathers, and was worn only by people who had accumulated honors; each feather was given by one person, and therefore represented a man; an extraordinary honor was to be able to attach buffalo horns to a bonnet. These headdresses were usually reserved for ceremonial occasions.

War shield. The war shield was made of the breast of a bull buffalo that was smoked to cure it. It was painted with special symbols, and often decorated with feathers and fringes.

Winter count. Each year a tribe decided on the single most significant event of its year, and one symbol to represent it was painted on the *winter count* tanned buffalo hide.

NORTHERN PLATEAU

This area, sometimes called the Great Basin, extends almost from Colorado to Canada and from the Great Lakes to California. Some of the groups that lived within this area are also listed elsewhere. Tribes include Arikara, Assiniboine, Blackfeet, Columbia, Flathead, Gros Ventre, Klamath, Mandan, Modoc, Nez Perce, Northern Cheyenne, Plains Ojibwa, Paiute, Shoshoni, Sioux (Lakota, Nakota, Dakota), Sisseton, Spokane, Ute, Walla Walla, and Yakima.

Coup stick. Coup sticks and lances were carried into battle; the coup stick was used only to touch an enemy in battle, and was decorative, sometimes with a carved head, feathers, or other decorations.

Finger weaving. Strands of yarn were woven together in geometric patterns using the fingers as heddles (to hold strands open).

Roach spreader (headdress). This decorative headdress of fur, leather, and horsehair stood straight up from the center to the back of the head.

Rock engravings. Many incised drawings of people, animals, and nature symbols may be found in these regions.

NORTHEAST WOODLANDS AND GREAT LAKES

These groups of Native Americans lived east of Missouri, all the way to the East Coast and north into Canada. Because of the climate and wooded area in which they lived, their crafts varied considerably from those of other tribes, such as Southwestern tribes, where wood was scarce and clay was plentiful.

Northeast Woodlands and Great Lakes tribes include: Abenaki, Algonquin, Conestoga, Cree, Huron, Illinois, Iroquois, Kickapoo, Lenni Lenape (Delaware), Malecite, Massachuset, Miami, Micmac, Minominee, Mismi, Mohawk, Nanticoke, Narraganset, Ojibwa (Chippewa), Oneida, Ottawa, Passamaquoddy, Penobscot, Potawatomi, Powhatan, Sauk-Fox, Seneca, Shawnee, Tuscarora, and Winnebago.

Bandoleer bag. A bag worn over the shoulder was decorated with floral or geometric designs executed in beads or porcupine quills.

Beadwork. This area is especially known for fine beadwork based on natural forms such as flowers.

Birchbark boxes. A natural resource in these areas, birchbark was sewn into containers.

False face masks. In these cultures, masks with features such as deep wrinkles, twisted features, or long shaggy hair are thought to have special powers.

Moosehair embroidery. Elaborately embroidered table or seat covers were done with dyed moosehair.

Porcupine quillwork. Before the advent of European glass beads, porcupine quills were flattened, sometimes dyed, and sewn onto clothing, boxes, textiles, and chair covers in decorative patterns.

Ribbon designs. Silk ribbons, often elaborately cut, are applied to cloth and leather clothing such as moccasins and leggings, robes, and skirts. The Iroquois combine this technique with beadwork.

Woven wampum belt. White and purple clam shells, shaped and with holes drilled in them (wampum) were used in place of money, and made into belts. A treaty or agreement was considered officially sealed when a string or belt of wampum beads accompanied it.

NORTHWEST COASTAL PEOPLE

Some of the crafts of the following groups, ranging from Oregon and Washington to Alaska, were of especially fine workmanship. Animal motifs representing a particular group's "totem" (lucky symbol) continue to be used to decorate houses, clothing, jewelry, wooden carvings, and baskets.

Northwest Coastal tribes include: Arctic, Aleut, Bellacoola, Chinook, Chilkat, Cowichan, Haida, Iglulik, Inuit, Klamath, Kwaikutl, Lillooet, Makah, Nauivak, Netsilik, Nootka, Quinault, Salish, Sallimiut, Thompson, Tlingit, Tillamook, and Tsimshian.

Basket making. Finely woven baskets decorated with totems were a specialty of Northwestern Coastal tribes. They also wove a type of hat that looked like an upside-down basket.

Bola. Two engraved stones or carved ivory weights tied together at each end of a thong were thrown to kill birds.

Button-trimmed robes. Robes worn by Northwest Coast tribes often bore appliqué totems (animals) on blankets, which were then outlined with buttons.

Carved and painted housefronts. Designs incised and brightly painted on meeting houses are based on the totem (animal) of the particular group.

Carving. Because wood was plentiful, storage vessels, masks, boxes, totem poles, and meeting houses were built of wood and carved. Blanket chests were slightly curved by steaming and bending the wood before carving designs. Carved wooden bowls were sometimes constructed in the same manner. Elaborately carved wooden rattles with totems might resemble a fish, bear, raven, sun, or moon.

Chilkat blankets. These tightly woven blankets, decorated in animal motifs, were worn as cloaks.

Clan hat. A carved wooden hat with animal totem on top was worn by leaders in Northwestern tribes for ceremonial occasions. These were painted or sometimes embellished with shells.

Coppers. Large, hammered, roughly rectangular copper plates were sometimes presented to a visiting dignitary at a "potlatch" (ceremonial party).

Dance apron. This ceremonial dress was usually completely covered with beadwork.

Figural carvings. Carved bone, ivory, wood, and soapstone figures and animals continue to be made in traditional forms and are prized by collectors. Intricate carvings could be made in black argillite, a very hard stone.

Frontlets. Small animal masks were worn at the front of the head, sometimes attached to a headdress.

Masks. Masks of the Northwest Coastal tribes were carved to represent the totem of a particular people, decorated with paint, sometimes feathers, and braided cedar bark added.

Seal scratchers. These Northern "decoys" were made of real seal claws attached to carved ivory, to scratch ice and entice seals to surface.

Shaman figures. Wooden and ivory carved figures were used for grave goods, ceremonial figures, and effigies.

Totem poles. Wooden poles with carved animal figures, topped by a tribe's representative animal, are often found in villages. Several favored totems are the raven, bear, beaver, whale, and fish.

Walrus ivory carvings. Ivory from tusks of walruses was carved in animal forms and used as handles for harpoons.

"Art is long and time is fleeting."

—HENRY WADSWORTH LONGFELLOW, 1807–1882, American poet

SOUTHEAST WOODLANDS

Woodlands Native Americans shared some of the same crafts as of Northern peoples, because many had migrated from the North. Of course their clothing needs were quite different because of the climate change.

Southeast Woodlands tribes include: Alabama, Apalachee, Atakapa, Biloxi, Caddo, Catawba, Cherokee, Chickasaw, Chitimacha, Choctaw, Creek, Hasinai, Miccosukee, Mobile, Natchez, Pensacola, Seminole, Timucua, Tunica, Tuskegee, Tutelo, and Yuchi.

Corncob dolls. Corncob dolls were dressed like adults, with beaded faces, fringed buckskin clothing, and even moccasins.

Seminole patchwork. The Seminoles applied beautiful, fine geometric patchwork trim to dark clothing.

SOUTHWEST

Some Native American peoples of Southwestern Desert tribes continue to live in pueblos, or reservations. The crafts of these groups originally became popular when train travel created a new market for their wares, and their popularity continues today.

Tribes of the Southwest include: Acoma, Apache, Chiricahua, Cochita, Cocopa, Havasupai, Hopi, Isleta, Jemez, Jicarillo, Mescalero, Mohave, Nambe, Navajo, Papago, Picuris, Pima, San Ildefonso, San Juan, Sandia, Santa Ana, Santa Clara, Santo Domingo, Taos, Tesque, Tewa, Tesuque, Zia, and Zuni.

Coiled pottery. Pottery was frequently placed in gravesites in ancient times, often with a hole punched in the bottom for offerings. Each pueblo has a different tradition in pottery decoration and technique. Pueblo people continue to create vessels and sculpture in their ancient (and new) traditions.

Kachina. In pueblo society, a Kachina is a costumed human dancer representing a spirit with special powers. Small Kachina images are replicas of the humans, featuring masks and appropriate dress.

Kokopelli. This humpbacked flute player design found on Southwest pottery represents rain, harvests, and human fertility.

Rock art. Native Americans incised petroglyphs, or painted pictographs, on rocks throughout America; they are plentiful in Utah, New Mexico, Arizona, and Colorado.

Sand painting. The sand painting process is a religious ceremony, usually conducted by a Medicine Man who paints by dribbling colored sands through the fingers to create significant patterns.

Silver and turquoise jewelry. Plentiful turquoise has made it a favorite of Indian jewelers, who use it alone for beads, or combine it with silver and sometimes coral.

Storyteller dolls. The figures may be human or animal, but always have their mouths open telling a story to small figures of the same species; not a traditional Native American craft until the 1960s, when Helen Cordero honored her father, who was a clown in the Cochiti Pueblo.

Woven blankets. Weavers use traditional patterns, techniques, and colors in their craft. Some contemporary Navajo pictorial blankets tell stories, which may feature birds, animals, flowers, mountains, trees, or sometimes trains, cars, and recreational vehicles. "Wearing blankets" (Chief's blankets) featured stripes, geometric designs, and diamonds, and were very popular among other Indian tribes as well as tourists.

WELL-KNOWN 20ᵀᴴ-CENTURY
NATIVE AMERICAN ARTISTS

This list includes well-known Native Americans whose work may be representative of a particular family or group of artists. Some work in the traditional manner, while others interpret their traditions using contemporary methods, ideas, and techniques. Dates of the artist's birth and death and tribal affiliations are included where available. A name in parentheses may be a family name. Some tribes have different names in the United States and in Canada, and these distinctions are given. Examples are Blackfeet (U.S.)/Blackfoot (Canada); Eskimo (U.S.)/Inuit (Canada); Chippewa (U.S.)/Ojibwa (Canada).

Abeyta, Narcisco, 1918–1998, Navajo
Abeyta, Tony, 1965, Navajo
Aguilar, José Vincent, 1924, San Ildefonso/Picuris
Amerman, Marcus, 1959, Choctaw
Amiotte, Arthur Douglas, 1942, Oglala Lakota Sioux
Anderson, Troy, 1948, Cherokee
Angeconeb, Allen, 1955, Ojibwa
Annesley, Robert, 1943, Cherokee
Ashevak, Kenojuak, 1927, Inuit
Ashoona, Mayoreak, 1946, Inuit
Ashoona, Pitseolak, 1904–1983, Inuit
Atencio, Gilbert, 1930–1995, San Ildefonso
Awa, Tsorej, 1898–1955, San Ildefonso

Baker, Joe, 1946, Delaware
Bales, Jean, 1946, Iowa
Battles, Asa, 1923, Choctaw
Beardy, Jackson, 1944–1984, Cree/Saulteaux/Ojibwa
Beaver, Fred, 1911–1980, Creek
Beck, Clifford, 1946, Navajo
Beeler, Joe, 1931, Cherokee
Begay, Harrison, 1917, Navajo
Begay, Keats, c. 1920, Navajo
Begay, Shonto W., 1954, Navajo
Big Lefthanded, active c. 1905–1912, Navajo
Bird, JoAnne, 1945, Sisseton Sioux
Biss, Earl, Jr., 1947, Crow/Chippewa
Black Owl, Archie, 1911–1992, Cheyenne
Blue Eagle, Acee, 1909–1959, Creek/Pawnee
Boni, Delmar, 1948, San Carlos Apache
Bosin, Blackbear, 1921–1980, Kiowa, Comanche
Boyer, Bob, 1948, Metis
Bradley, David, 1954, Chippewa, Sioux/Ojibwe
Broer, Roger L., 1945, Oglala/Lakota Sioux
Cannon, T. C., 1946–1978, Caddo/Kiowa/Choctaw
Cardinal-Schubert, Joane, 1942, Peigan
Chee, Robert, 1938–1972, Navajo

Cia, Manuel Lopez, 1937, Navajo

Clarke, Gerald L., 1967, Cahulla

Coffin, Barry, 1947, Potawatomi/Muskogee

Coffin, Douglas, 1946, Potawatomi/Creek

Collins, Adele, 1908, Chickasaw

Cordero, Helen, 1915–1994, Cochiti Pueblo

Crumbo, Woodrow W., 1912–1989, Potawatomi/Creek

Cutschall, Colleen, 1951, Oglala and Rosebud Sioux

Da, Tony, 1940, San Ildefonso

Danay, Richard Glazer, 1942, Mohawk

David, Neil R., Sr., 1944, Hopi

Davis, Jesse E., 1921–1976, Cheyenne

Debassige, Blake R., 1965, Ojibwa

Denetsosie, Hoke, 1919, Navajo

DesJarlait, Patrick, 1921–1973, Chippewa

DesJarlait, Robert, 1946, Red Lake Chippewa

Dewey, Wilson, 1915–1969, San Carlos Apache

Dick, Cecil, 1915–1992, Cherokee

Dishta, Duane, 1946, Zuni

Durham, Jimmie, 1940, Cherokee

Emerson, Anthony Chee, 1963, Navajo

Fadden, John, 1938, Mohawk

Fonseca, Harry, 1946, Maidu

Gawboy, Carl, 1943, Chippewa

Geionety, R. W., 1950, Kiowa

Glazer-Danay, Richard, 1943, Mohawk

Goodbear, Paul, 1913–c. 1940, Cheyenne

Gorman, Carl Nelson, 1907–1998, Navajo

Gorman, Rudolph Carl (R. C.), 1932, Navajo

Goshorn, Shan, 1957, Cherokee

Gray, Gina, 1954, Osage

Grummer, Brenda Kennedy, Potawatomi

Hachive Heap of Birds, Edgar, 1954, Cheyenne/Arapaho

Halsey, Minisa Crumbo, 1942, Creek/Potawatomi

Haney, Enoch Kelly, 1940, Seminole/Creek

Haozous, Robert, 1943, Apache

Hardin, Helen, 1943–1984, Santa Clara
Harjo, Benjamin, Jr., 1945, Seminole, Shawnee
Havard, James, 1937, Choctaw/Chippewa
Henderson, Kathy, 1954, Cherokee
Herrera, Joe Hilario, 1923, Cochiti
Herrera, Velino, 1902–1973, Zia
Hessing, Valjean McCarty, 1934, Choctaw
Hill, Joan, 1929, Creek/Cherokee
Hill, Rick, 1950, Tuscarora
Hokeah, Jack, 1902–1969, Kiowa
Honewytewa, Louis Calvin, 1930, Hopi
House, Conrad, 1956, Navajo
Houser, Allan, 1915–1994, Chiricahua Apache
Howe, Oscar, 1915–1983, Yankton Sioux

Ingram, Jerry, 1941, Choctaw/Cherokee
Jacobs, Arnold, 1942, Iroquois/Onondaga
Jemison, G. Peter, 1945, Cattaraugus Seneca
Johns, David, 1948, Navajo
Jojola, Tony, 1958, Isleta Pueblo
Jones, Ruthe Blalock, 1939, Delaware/Shawnee/Peoria
Kabotie, Fred, 1900–1986, Hopi
Kabotie, Michael, 1942, Hopi
Keahbone, George, 1916, Kiowa
Kenojuak (Ashevak), 1927, Inuit
Kimball, Yeffe, 1914–1978, Osage
Kuka, King, 1946, Blackfeet
LaPena, Frank, 1937, Nomtipom/Wintu
Larsen, Mike, 1944, Chickasaw
Lewis, Lucy, 1897–1992, Acoma
Littlebird, Harold, Santo Domingo/Laguna
Little Turtle, Carm, 1952, Apache-Tarahumarqa
Lomahaftewa, Linda, 1947, Hopi/Choctaw
Lomakema, Milland, Sr., 1941, Hopi
Lonewolf, Rosemary, 1953, Santa Clara
Longfish, George, 1942, Seneca/Tuscarora
Lucy (Qinnuayuak), 1915–1982, Inuit

Manygoats, Betty, 1945, Navajo
Marshall, Teresa MacPhee, 1962, Micmac
Martinez, Crescencio, c. 1879–1918, San Ildefonso
Martinez, Julian, 1897–1943, San Ildefonso
Martinez, Maria Montoya, 1887–1980, San Ildefonso
Martinez, Santana R., Tewa/San Ildefonso
McCombs, Solomon, 1913–1980, Creek
Medina, Rafael, 1929, Zia
Mikkigak, Qaunak, 1932, Inuit
Mirabel, Eva, 1920–1967, Santa Fe
Momaday, Al, 1913–1981, Kiowa
Montileux, Dan, 1968, Oglala Sioux
Montoya, Tommy, San Juan
Mootzka, Waldo, 1903–1940, Hopi
Mopope, Stephen, 1898–1974, Kiowa
Morez, Mary, 1946, Navajo
Morrison, George, 1919, Grand Portage Chippewa
Morrisseau, Norval, 1931, Ojibwa
Murdock, Cecil, 1913–1954, Kickapoo
Nailor, Gerald, 1917–1952, Navajo
Namingha, Dan, 1950, Hopi
Nampeyo, 1860–1942, Hopi/Tewa
Naranjo, Louis, 1932, Chochiti
Naranjo, Michelle Tsosie, 1959, Santa Clara/Navajo/Laguna/Mission
Naranjo-Morse, Nora, 1953, Santa Clara
Nequatewa, Verma, Hopi
Nevaquaya, Doc Tate, 1932–1999, Comanche
Odjig, Daphne, 1919, Ojibwa
Orduno, Robert, 1933, Gabrielino
Ortiz, Virgil, Cochiti Pueblo
Padilla, Fernando, Jr., 1958, Navajo/San Felipe
Paladin, David Chethlahe, 1926–1984, Navajo
Palmer, Dixon, 1920, Kiowa/Choctaw
Pena, Tonita, 1893–1949, San Ildefonso
Pitaloosie (Saila), 1942, Inuit
Pitsiulak, Oopik, 1946, Inuit

Poitras, Jane Ash, 1951, Plains Cree
Polelonema, Otis, 1902–1981, Hopi
Ponca, Wendy, Osage
Pootoogook, Napachie, 1938, Inuit
Quintana, Ben, 1923–1944, Cochiti
Quoyavema, Al, 1938, Hopi
Ray, Carl, 1943–1978, Cree
Red Bear, Martin, 1947, Oglala Sioux
Red Star, Kevin, 1943, Crow
Reid, Bill, 1920–1998, Haida
Romero, Diego, 1964, Cochiti Pueblo
Romero, Mateo, 1966, Cochiti Pueblo

Sahmie, Ida, 1960, Navajo
Sakyesva, Harry, 1921, Hopi
Sampson, William, Jr., 1933–1987, Creek
Saul, C. Terry, 1921–1976, Choctaw/Chickasaw
Scholder, Fritz, 1937, Luiseno
Seabourn, Bert, 1931, Cherokee
Seabourn, Connie, 1951, Cherokee
Shelton, Peter, Jr., 1920s, Hopi
Singletary, Preston, 1963, Tlingit
Smith, Jaune Quick-To-See, 1940, Salish/Cree/Shoshone
Smith, Kevin Warren, 1958, Cherokee
Smith, Richard Zane, Wyandot
Stevens, C. Maxx, 1951, Seminole
Stewart, Susan, 1953, Crow/Blackfeet
Stone, Willard, 1916–1985, Cherokee
Strait, Dorothy, 1935, Cherokee
Suazo, Jonathan Warm Day, Taos
Summers, Diosa, Santa Clara
Tafoya, Margaret, 1904–2001, Santa Clara
Tafoya, Teofilo, 1915–1998, Santa Clara
Tahoma, Quincy, 1921–1956, Navajo
Tailfeathers, Gerald, 1925–1975, Blood (Blackfoot)
Talaswaima, Terrance, 1939, Hopi
Taulbee, Dan, 1924–1987, Comanche
Tiger, Jerome, 1941–1967, Creek-Seminole

Toledo, José Rey, 1915–1994, Jemez
Toppah, Herman, 1923, Kiowa
Tsinajinnie, Andrew, 1916–2000, Navajo
Tsosie, Nelson, 1961, Navajo
Tunnillie, Ovilu, 1949, Inuit
Tuttle, Frank, 1957, Maidu/Yurok/Wailaki
Two-Arrows, Tom, 1920, Onondaga
Velarde, Pablita, 1918, Santa Clara
Vigil, Arthur, 1955, Santo Domingo
Vigil, Romando, 1902–1978, San Ildefonso
Vigil, Tomas, c. 1889–1960, Tesuque
Wallace, Denise, 1957, Sugpiaq
Walkingstick, Kay, 1935, Cherokee/Winnebago
West, Richard W. (Dick), 1912–1996, Cheyenne
Whitehorse, Emmi, 1956, Navajo
Whitethorne, Baje, Sr., 1950, Navajo
Wood, Margaret, 1950, Navajo/Seminole
Yazz, Beatien (Jimmy Toddy, Sr.), 1928, Navajo
Yazzie, James Wayne, 1943–1969, Navajo
Youngblood, Nathan, 1955, Santa Clara
Youngman, Alfred, 1948, Chippewa/Plains Cree

"What garlic is to salad, insanity is to art."
—AUGUSTUS SAINT-GAUDENS, 1848–1907, American sculptor

NATIVE AMERICAN ART: SITES AND MUSEUMS

Museums listed here include anthropological collections, ruins, burial grounds, and history museums. All are dedicated to keeping Native American culture alive and flourishing. Special Native American artifacts, mementos, and records are sometimes found in the tribal meeting place on a reservation. Visitors are usually welcome unless a special, restricted ceremony is taking place. For most of these museums or sites, the nearest town, rather than the exact locale, is given.

CANADA

Alberta

Calgary	Glenbow Museum

British Columbia

Alert Bay	U'Mista Cultural Center
Quathiaski Cove	Kwagiulth Museum and Cultural Center
Vancouver	University of British Columbia Museum of Anthropology
Victoria	Royal British Columbia Museum

Ontario

Brantford	Museum of the Woodland Indian
Kenora	Lake of the Woods Ojibwa Cultural Center

Quebec

Hull	Canadian Museum of Civilization

UNITED STATES

Alabama

Bridgeport	Russell Cave National Monument
Florence	Indian Mound and Museum
Moundville	Mound State Monument

Alaska

Anchorage	Anchorage Historical and Fine Arts Museum
Glove	Besh-Ba-Gowah
Juneau	Alaska State Museum; four-story totem
Ketchikan	Tongass Historical Society Museum; Totem Heritage Center
Sitka	Sheldon Jackson Museum; Sitka National Monument

Arizona

Camp Verde	Montezuma Castle National Monument
Clarkdale	Tuzigoot National Monument
Coolidge	Casa Grande Ruins
Dragoon	Amerind Foundation, Inc.
Flagstaff	Museum of Northern Arizona; Wupatki National Monument; Walnut Canyon
Fort Apache	Apache Culture Center
Grand Canyon National Park	South Rim and North Rim Visitors' Centers
Parker	Colorado River Tribes Indian Museum
Phoenix	Heard Museum; Pueblo Grande Museum
Puerco Ruin	Petrified Forest State Park
Roosevelt	Tonto National Monument
Sacaton	Gila River Indian Museum
Second Mesa	Hopi Museum and Cultural Center
Tuba City	Oraibi Pueblo; Walpi Pueblo
Tucson	Arizona State Museum; Tucson Mountain Park; Signal Mountain
Whiteriver	Kinishba Pueblo
Window Rock	Navajo Tribal Museum

Arkansas

Arkadelphia	Henderson State University Museum
Fayetteville	University of Arkansas Museum
Murphreesboro	Caddo Burial Mounds
Wilson	Hampson Memorial Museum of Archaeology

California

Alvarado	Coyote Hills Regional Park
Bakersfield	Kern County Museum
Banning	Malki Museum
Barstow	Calico Mountains Archaeological Project
Berkeley	Lowie Museum of Anthropology

California (continued)

China Lake	Big and Little Petroglyph Canyons
Eureka	Clarke Memorial Museum
Hoopa	Hupa Tribal Museum
Kelseyville	State Lake State Park
Lancaster	Antelope Valley Indian Research Museum
Los Angeles	Los Angeles County Museum of History and Science; Southwest Museum; Autry Museum of Western Heritage
North Fork	Sierra Mono Museum
Oakland	Oakland Museum, History Division
Pine Grove	Indian Grinding Rock State Historical Monument
Redlands	San Bernardino County Museum
Riverside	Riverside Municipal Museum
Sacramento	California State Indian Museum; Sacramento Indian Center
San Diego	San Diego Museum of Man
San Francisco	Adam E. Treganza Anthropology Museum
Santa Ana	Bowers Memorial Museum
Santa Barbara	Santa Barbara Museum of Natural History
Santa Catalina Island	Catalina Island Museum
Sheep Canyon	Renegade Canyon; Coso Range; Petroglyph Canyon
Stockton	Pioneer Museum and Haggin Galleries
Twentynine Palms	Joshua Tree National Monument
Visalia	Tulare County Museum

Colorado

Bayfield	Gem Village Museum
Colorado Springs	Colorado Springs Fine Art Center; Pioneers Museum
Cortez	Mesa Verde National Park
Denver	Colorado State Museum; Denver Art Museum; Denver Museum of Natural History
Dolores	Anasazi Heritage Center

Ignacio	Southern Ute Arts and Crafts
La Junta	Koshare Indian Kiva Museum
Montrose	Ute Indian Museum
Pleasant View	Lowry Pueblo Ruins

Connecticut

Greenwich	Bruce Museum
New Haven	Peabody Museum of Natural History
Norwich	Slater Memorial Museum
Uncasville	Tantaquidgeon Indian Museum

Delaware

South Bowers Island	Field Archaeological Museum

District of Columbia

Washington	Museum of Natural History; Smithsonian Institution; U.S. Department of the Interior Museum

Florida

Crystal River	Crystal River State Archaeological Site
Fort Lauderdale	Seminole Arts and Crafts Center
Fort Walton Beach	Temple Mound Museum and Park
Gainesville	Florida State Museum
Marathon	Southeast Museum of the North American Indian
Miami	Miccosukee Cultural Center and Museum
Tallahassee	Museum of Florida History
West Hollywood	Seminole Museum

Georgia

Blakely	Kolomoki Mounds State Park
Calhoun	New Echota Historic Site
Cartersville	Etowah Mounds Archaeological Area
Indian Springs	Creek Museum
Macon	Ocmulgee National Monument

Idaho

Fort Hall	Clothes Horse Trading Post
Spalding	Nez Perce National Historic Park

Illinois

Chicago	Field Museum of Natural History
East St. Louis	Cahokia Mounds State Park
Evanston	Mitchell Museum of the American Indian; Kendall College
Galena	Stockade
Lewistown	Dickson Mounds Museum of the Illinois Indian
Springfield	Illinois State Museum
Urbana	University of Illinois Museum of Natural History

Indiana

Anderson	Mounds State Park
Bloomington	Indiana University Museum
Evansville	Angel Mounds State Memorial
Indianapolis	Children's Museum; Eiteljorg Museum of American Indians and Western Art; Museum of Indian Heritage
Peru	Puterbaugh Museum

Iowa

Davenport	Davenport Museum
McGregor	Effigy Mounds National Monument

Kansas

Belleville	Pawnee Indian Village Museum
Ellsworth	Inscription Rock, Lake Kanpolis State Park
Highland	Kansas Sac and Fox Museum
Kansas City	Huron Park Indian Cemetery
Larned	Fort Larned National Historic Site
Salina	Indian Burial Pit

| Scott City | El Quartelejo Indian Kiva Museum |
| Topeka | Kansas State Historical Society |

Kentucky

Cairo	Ancient Buried City
Lexington	Adena Park, Museum of Anthropology, University of Kentucky
Louisville	J. B. Speed Art Museum

Louisiana

| Marksville | Marksville Prehistoric Indian Park State Monument |
| Shreveport | Louisiana State Exhibit Museum |

Maine

| Bar Harbor | Robert Abbe Museum of Stone Age Antiquities |
| Castine | Wilson Museum |

Maryland

| Baltimore | Baltimore Museum of Art |

Massachusetts

Andover	Robert S. Peabody Foundation for Archaeology
Attleboro	Bronson Museum
Cambridge	Peabody Museum of Archaeology and Ethnology; Fruitlands Museum, Harvard University
Deerfield	Memorial Hall
Grafton	Longhouse Museum
Plymouth	Plimoth Plantation, Inc.
Salem	Peabody Museum
Springfield	Springfield Science Museum

Michigan

| Alpena | Jesse Besser Museum |
| Ann Arbor | University of Michigan Exhibit Museum |

Michigan (continued)

Battle Creek	Kingman Museum of Natural History
Bloomfield Hills	Cranbrook Institute of Science
Cross Village	Great Lakes Indian Museum
Detroit	Fort Wayne Military Museum; Wayne State University Museum of Anthropology
Grand Rapids	Grand Rapids Public Museum, Norton Mounds
Harbor Springs	Chief Blackbird Home Museum

Minnesota

Brainerd	Crow Wing County Historical Society
Duluth	St. Louis County Historical Society
Mille Lacs	Mille Lacs State Indian Museum
Pipestone	Pipestone National Monument
St. Paul	The Science Museum of Minnesota

Mississippi

Laurel	Lauren Rogers Library and Museum
Natchez	Emerald Mound
Philadelphia	Choctaw Museum of the Southern Indian
Tupelo	Natchez Trace Visitor Center

Missouri

Columbia	Museum of Anthropology
Danville	Graham Cave State Park
DeSoto	Washington State Park
Jefferson City	Missouri State Museum
Kansas City	Kansas City Museum of History and Science; Nelson-Atkins Museum of Art
Marshall	Lyman Archaeological Research Center and Hamilton Field School (Utz Site)
Point Lookout	Ralph Foster Museum
St. Joseph	St. Joseph Museum
St. Louis	Museum of Science and Natural History

Montana

Broadus	Mac's Museum of Natural History
Browning	Museum of the Plains Indians
Glasgow	Pioneer Museum
Hardin	Custer–Sitting Bull Battlefield Museum
Havre	H. Earl Clack Memorial Museum
Lame Deer	Cheyenne Arts and Crafts Shop
Poplar	Poplar Indian Arts and Crafts Museum
Pryor	Chief Plenty Coups Museum

Nebraska

Chadron	Fur Trade Museum
Fort Robinson	Fort Robinson Museum
Lincoln	Nebraska State Historical Society; University of Nebraska State Museum
Neligh	Pioneers Antelope County Historical Museum

Nevada

Lake Mead	Lost City Museum of Archaeology

New Hampshire

Hanover	Dartmouth College Museum

New Jersey

Hopewell	Hopewell Museum
Newark	Newark State Museum
Paterson	Paterson Museum
Trenton	New Jersey State Museum

New Mexico

Albuquerque	Indian Pueblo Cultural Center; Abon State Monument; Maxwell Museum of Anthropology; Sandia Man Cave

New Mexico (continued)

Aztec	Aztec Ruins National Monument
Bernalillo	Coronado State Monument
Bloomfield	Chaco Canyon National Monument; Salmon Ruins Museum
Casa Blanca	Acoma Pueblo
Church Rock	Red Rock Museum
Cliff	Kwilleylekia Ruins
Dulce	Jicarilla Arts and Crafts Shop/Museum
Española	Puye Cliff Ruins; Santa Clara Reservation
Gallup	Zuni Pueblo
Las Cruces	New Mexico State University
Los Alamos	Bandelier National Monument
Mescalero	Mescalero Apache Cultural Center
Pecos	Pecos National Monument
Portales	Anthropology Museum, Eastern New Mexico University
San Juan Pueblo	O'ke Oweenge Crafts Cooperative
Sandia Pueblo	Bien Mur Indian Market Center
Santa Ana	Zia Pueblo
Santa Fe	Museum of American Indian Arts; Wheelwright Museum of the American Indian; Museum of Navajo Ceremonial Art; Palace of the Governors; San Ildefonso Pueblo Museum
Taos	Millicent Rogers Museum; Picuris Pueblo; Taos Pueblo
Zuni	Zuni Craftsmen Cooperative Association

New York

Albany	New York State Museum and Science Service
Auburn	Cayuga Museum of History and Art
Buffalo	Buffalo and Erie County Historical Society; Buffalo Museum of Science
Canandaigua	Canandaigua Historical Society
Castile	Castile Historical Society Museum

Cooperstown	Cooperstown Indian Museum
Elmira	Chemung County Historical Museum
Fonda	Mohawk-Caughnawaga Museum
Fort Plain	Fort Plain Museum
Hogansburg	Akwesasne Museum
Howes Cave	Iroquois Indian Museum
Lake George	Fort William Henry Restoration and Museum
New York City	American Museum of Natural History; American Indian Community House Gallery; Brooklyn Museum; Museum of the American Indian (The Heye Foundation)
Niagara Falls	The Turtle: Native American Center of the Living Arts
Onchiota	Six Nations Indian Museum
Oneonta	Yager Museum and Library
Orient	Oysterponds Historical Society
Owasco	Owasco Indian Village
Rochester	Rochester Museum and Science Center

North Carolina

Boone	Museum of the American Indian
Cherokee	Museum of the Cherokee Indian; Oconaluftee Indian Village
Mount Gilead	Town Creek Indian Mound

North Dakota

New Town	Three Affiliated Tribes Museum

Ohio

Bainbridge	Seip Mound
Chillicothe	Mound City Group National Monument, Story Mound
Cincinnati	Cincinnati Museum of Natural History
Cleveland	Cleveland Museum of Art; Cleveland Museum of Natural History; Western Reserve Historical Society

Ohio (continued)

Columbus	Ohio Historical Center and Village
Coshocton	Johnson–Humrickhouse Memorial Museum
Lebanon	Fort Ancient State Memorial
Lima	Allen County Museum
Miamisburg	Miamisburg Mound State Memorial
Peebles	Serpent Mound State Memorial
Piqua	Indian Museum
Youngstown	Butler Institute of American Art

Oklahoma

Anadarko	Anadarko Museum; Oklahoma Indian Arts and Crafts Cooperative, Southern Plains Indian Museum
Bartlesville	Woolaroc Museum
Caddo	Caddo Indian Museum
Lawton	Museum of the Great Plains
Miami	Ottawa County Historical Society
Muskogee	Five Civilized Tribes Museum; Bacone College; Ataloa Lodge Museum
Norman	J. Willis Stovall Museum
Oklahoma City	Red Earth Indian Center, Kirkpatrick Center, Oklahoma Historical Society
Okmulgee	Creek Indian Nation Council House
Park Hill	Tsa-La-Gi Indian Village
Pawhuska	Osage Tribal Museum
Pawnee	Pawnee Bill Museum
Ponca City	Ponca City Indian Museum
Poteau	Kerr Museum
Sallisaw	Sequoyah's Home
Tahlequah	Cherokee Heritage Center
Tulsa	Oklahoma Indian Arts and Crafts Cooperative; Tulsa Osage Tribal Museum; Thomas Gilcrease Institute, Philbrook Art Center
Wewoka	Seminole Nation Museum

Oregon

Bend	High Desert Museum
Corvallis	Horner Museum
Eugene	Museum of Natural History, University of Oregon
Klamath Falls	Klamath County Museum; Collier Memorial State Park
North Bend	Coos–Curry Museum
Portland	Portland Art Museum
Salem	Hallie Ford Museum, Willamette University

Pennsylvania

Brookville	E. M. Parker Indian Museum
Butler	Carnegie Museum of Natural History
Harmony	American Indian Museum
Hershey	Hershey Museum
Philadelphia	University Museum
Pittsburgh	American Indian Museum; Carnegie Museum of Natural History
Scranton	Everhard Museum
York	Indian Steps Museum

Rhode Island

Bristol	Haffenreffer Museum, Brown University
Exeter	Tomaquag Indian Museum
Providence	Museum of Natural History, Roger Williams Park

South Dakota

Eagle Butte	H. V. Johnston Cultural Center
Martin	Indian Arts Museum
Mobridge	Land of the Sioux Museum
Pierre	Robinson Museum
Pine Ridge	Mari Sandoz Museum; Red Cloud Indian Museum
Rapid City	Badlands National Monument; Sioux Indian Museum
Sioux Falls	Pettigrew Museum

South Dakota (continued)

St. Francis	Buechel Memorial Sioux Indian Museum
Vermillion	Museum of the University of South Dakota

Tennessee

Knoxville	Frank H. McClung Museum, University of Tennessee
Lookout Mountain	Lookout Mountain Museum
Memphis	Chucalissa Indian Town and Museum
Savannah	Shiloh Mounds; Shiloh National Military Park

Texas

Alpine	Museum of the Big Bend
Austin	Museum of the Department of Anthropology; Texas Memorial Museum, University of Texas
Canyon	Panhandle-Plains Historical Museum
Dallas	Dallas Museum of Fine Arts
El Paso	Tigua Indian Reservation Cultural Center; Ysleta Mission; The Wilderness Park Museum; El Paso Centennial Museum
Fort Worth	Fort Worth Museum of Science and History
Harwood	Indian Museum
Livingston	Alabama-Coushatta Indian Museum
Lubbock	Museum of Texas Tech University
San Angelo	Fort Concho Preservation and Museum
Sanford	Alibates Flint Quarries National Monument

Utah

Blanding	Hovenweep National Monument; Hatch Trading Post
Cedar City	Dr. and Mrs. William R. Palmer Memorial Museum
Escalante	Anasazi Indian Village State Historical Site
Moab	Canyonlands National Park
Provo	Anthropology Museum, Brigham Young University
Salt Lake City	Utah Museum of Natural History, University of Utah
Vernal	Natural History State Museum

Virginia

Hampton	Hampton Institute Museum
Richmond	Valentine Museum

Washington

Ariel	Chief Lelooska's Lodge
Coulee Dam	Colville Cultural Museum
Marysville	Tulalip Indian Reservation
Neah Bay	Makah Cultural Center and Museum
Olympia	State Capitol Museum
Pullman	Museum of Anthropology
Seattle	Seattle Art Museum; Washington State Museum; Burke Museum, University of Washington; Daybreak Star Arts Center Anthropology Museum, Washington State University
Spokane	Museum of Native American Cultures; Pacific Northwest Indian Center, Eastern Washington State Historical Society
Suquamish	Suquamish Museum
Tacoma	Washington State Historical Museum; Tacoma Totem Pole
Toppenish	Yakima Nation Museum
Vantage	Wanapum Dam Tour Center
Wenatchee	North Central Indian Museum
Yakima	Yakima Valley Museum

West Virginia

Morgantown	Archaeology Museum, West Virginia University
Moundsville	Grave Creek Mound State Park

Wisconsin

Aztalan	Aztalan State Park
Beloit	Logan Museum of Anthropology, Beloit College
Green Bay	Neville Public Museum
Hayward	Ojibwa National Museum

Wisconsin (continued)

Kenosha	Kenosha Public Museum
Madison	State Historical Society of Wisconsin
Oneida	Oneida Nation Museum
Oshkosh	Museum of Anthropology, Wisconsin State University
Sheboygan	Sheboygan Mound Park
Wausau	Venne Art Center
West Bend	Lizard Mound State Park
Wisconsin Dells	Winnebago Indian Museum

Wyoming

Casper	Fort Casper Museum and Historic Site
Cheyenne	Wyoming State Museum
Cody	Buffalo Bill Museum and Plains Indian Museum
Colter	Colter Bay Indian Arts Museum
Ethete	Arapahoe Cultural Museum
Fort Bridger	Fort Bridger Museum
Fort Laramie	Fort Laramie National Historic Site

"There is no life without arts and no arts without life."
—BOUNXOU CHANTHRAPHONE, weaver,
National Heritage Fellow, 2000

CRAFTS CREATED THROUGHOUT MEXICO

The variety of craft forms in Mexico is due to the diversity of its ethnic mix and geographical features. Fifty-six groups of Indians remain in Mexico, making up approximately 15 percent of the population, each with its own unique culture. Many of the crafts are made throughout Mexico, while others remain regional. Most can be seen in state-run crafts stores or regional fairs, but a visit to some of the centers is an exciting experience. Traditional techniques listed here are passed from generation to generation, and many folk art forms date back to pre-Columbian (before Columbus) times.

JEWELRY AND METALSMITHING

Coin necklaces. Coins often are combined with beads in necklaces and earrings.

Earrings. Earrings worn by men and women are made of beads, coins, gold, lacquer inlaid with abalone shell or painted horn pendants.

Ex-votos (milagros). Tiny forms represent something for which someone has prayed. Often these represent parts of the body—eyes, legs, hands—or animals, hearts, or houses; these were originally silver, but are now normally made of nickel or tin.

Gold and silver work. Some areas specialize in forged, cast, and fabricated silver and gold work.

Hammered copper. Specialists make pots, plates, all variety of practical yet decorative items.

Jade. Jade (a green stone) was valued more than gold; used for pendants, rings, and death masks.

Necklaces. Seeds and beads of glass and stone are often combined to make necklaces. Some strands are composed of only thin glass beads (papelillo).

Painted clay necklaces. A popular form was skeleton heads alternating with tigers or leopards.

Painted tin figures. These figures, with subjects such as people, animals, birds, fish, and butterflies, are approximately 4 inches high and feature repoussé details.

Papier-mâché. This popular technique was used to make masks, large lacquered animals, and amusing figural sculpture.

Silver ornaments. Buckles, buttons, and spurs are decorative features and part of the costume of mariachi bands or cowboys.

Steel spurs. These spurs, also favored by cowboys, were sometimes inlaid with silver.

Tin ornaments. Candlesticks, lanterns, mirror frames, niches for images, plates, and trays are made of tin.

Wrought iron. This specialty is used for balconies, doors, fittings for furniture, and crosses.

TEXTILE ARTS

Backstrap loom weaving. Narrow bands woven on a backstrap loom are used as sashes, bag handles, or are sewn together to make entire garments.

Embroidery. Embroidery designs feature animals, flowers, geometric designs, symbols, and religious figures. An embroidered costume or tablecloth might combine cross-stitch (an X made with thread) and satin stitch (a stitch that smoothly covers an area).

Huipil. This loosely woven or embroidered tunic is worn by both men and women.

Servilleta. An embroidered cloth used as a table covering for celebrations is a specialty.

Shoulder bags. General purpose bags that were woven, painted, or beaded.

Waist sashes. These sashes, worn by men and women, were usually made on a backstrap loom. The loom was held taut by being attached to the weaver's body.

MISCELLANEOUS CRAFTS

Amate paper. Amate paper is formed from bark. The brownish surface is used for paper cuttings and brilliant paintings of flowers and animals that are framed and hung.

Basketry and straw hats. Hats made of agave fibers, bamboo, cane, palm, wheatstraw, and willow are used throughout Mexico.

Beading. Beaded objects are created by pressing glass beads in an intricate pattern onto a wax-covered surface such as a mask, gourd bowl, or square of wood.

Ceramics. Mexico is renowned for ceramic dinnerware and small nativity sets.

Day of the Dead objects. Specialties for Day of the Dead (a Mexican religious celebration on the 1st and 2nd of November) include cardboard skeletons, metal-paper death figures, sugar skulls, sugar-paste figures, loaves of "bread of the dead," and tissue-paper cut-outs.

Foil masks. The repoussé technique is used to create depth in masks of human and animal faces.

Gourd designs. The outer shell of a gourd is either brightly painted with designs such as animals or flowers, or is carved and left in its natural colors (brown and light brown).

Lacquerware. Wood or gourds are carved or incised, gilded, coated with lacquer, and painted in brightly colored designs, a technique that goes back to pre-Columbian times.

Masks. Several different methods are used to make masks. They are carved from wood and smoothly lacquered, or made from rough papier-mâché pulp.

Paper cutting. Folded white tissue-paper cuttings are used for decorations for certain times of the year.

Straw painting. Dyed straws are individually glued down to make a design.

Tortoiseshell wares. Boxes, bracelets, clasps, earrings, watchstraps, letter openers, and ornamental combs are all made from tortoiseshell.

Tree of life. These intricate, traditional, brightly painted clay "trees" include figures and flowers.

Yarn pictures. "Drawings" done by pressing yarn into beeswax-coated cardboard or wood.

"The sculptor, and the painter also, should be trained in all these liberal arts: grammar, geometry, philosophy, medicine, astronomy, perspective, history, anatomy, theory of design, arithmetic."
—LORENZO GHIBERTI, c. 1440–1450, Italian sculptor

WELL-KNOWN HISPANIC ARTISTS

As the art world has become smaller through communication and travel, galleries and museums are broadening their scope and featuring work by contemporary and traditional Hispanic artists. This list features artists whose work is lauded in their own countries, and who are now receiving international recognition.

ARGENTINA

Candioti, Beatriz, 1950
DeCastro, Sergio, 1922
Segui, Antonio, 1934

BRAZIL

Amaral, Tarsila, 1886–1973
Britto, Romero, 1964
Clark, Lygia, 1921–1988
Portinari, Candido, 1903–1962

CHILE

Bravo, Claudio, 1936
Matta (Roberto Sebastian Matta-Echaurren), 1911–2002

COLOMBIA

Botero, Fernando, 1932

CUBA

Cardenas, Agustin, 1927
Mendieta, Ana, 1948–1985

MEXICO

Carrington, Leonora, 1917, b. England
Costa, Olga, 1913–1993
Gerzso, Gunther, 1915–2000
Hernandez, Ester
Izquierdo, Maria, 1902–1955
Kahlo, Frida, 1907 –1954
Lazo, Agustin, 1898–1971
Merida, Carlos, 1891–1984
Orozco, José Clemente, 1883–1949
Ramos-Martinez, Alfredo, 1875–1946
Rivera, Diego, 1886–1957
Romero, Carlos Orozco, 1896–1984
Romo, Jose Luis, 1953
Ruiz, Gilberto, 1950
Siqueiros, David Alfaro, 1896–1974
Tamayo, Rufino, 1899–1991
Toledo, Francisco, 1940
Urueta, Cordelia, 1908
Zarraga, Angel, 1886–1946
Zuniga, Francisco, 1911–1998

NICARAGUA

Morales, Armando, 1927
Moralez, Rodolfo, 1925

PERU

Szyslo, Fernando, 1925

PUERTO RICO

Oller, Francisco Manuel,
1833–1917
Pérez, Enoc, 1962

SPAIN

Chillida, Eduardo, 1924
Dali, Salvador, 1904–1989
El Greco, 1541–1614
Goya, Francisco, 1746–1828
Gris, Juan, 1887–1927
Miró, Joan, 1893–1983
Munoz, Juan, 1954
Murillo, Bartolomé, 1618–1682
Picasso, Pablo, 1881–1973
Ribera, Jusepe, 1588–1652
Tapies, Antoni, 1923
Velasquez, Diego, 1599–1660
Zurbarán, Francisco de,
1598–1664

UNITED STATES

Abizu, Olga, 1924, b. Puerto
Rico
Abularach, Rodolfo, 1923,
b. Guatemala
Aguirre, Emilio

Alfonzo, Carlos, 1950–1991,
b. Cuba
Algaze, Mario, 1947
Almaraz, Carlos, 1941, b. Mexico
Amaral, Jim, 1933, b. Colombia
Amaral, Tarsila do, 1973
Amezcua, Consuelo (Chelo)
Gonzalez, 1903–1975
Anguiano, Raul, 1915, b. Mexico
Alpuy, Julio, 1919, b. Uruguay
Aragon, Jose Rafael, active
1826–1850
Archuleta, Felipe, 1910–1991
Azeceta, Luis Cruz, 1942,
b. Cuba
Baca, Judith Francisca, 1946
Blanco, Elroy, 1933
Bravo, Claudio, 1936, b. Chile
Bravo, Marta Maria Perez, 1959,
b. Cuba
Briseno, Rolando, 1952
Buzio, Lidya, 1948, b. Uruguay
Canas, Maria Martinez, 1960
Casas, Melesio (Mel), 1929
Castillo, Consuelo Mendez, 1952
Cervantez, Pedro, 1914–1987
Chavez, Eduardo, 1917–1995
Chavez, Joseph A., 1938
Chavez, Margaret Herrera, 1912
Chavez, Ray, 1938
De Montes, Roberto Gil, 1950,
b. Mexico
Espada, Ibsen, 1952
Fernandez, Rudy, 1948
Frigerio, Ismael, 1955, b. Chile
Garcia, Antonio, 1901

UNITED STATES *(continued)*

Garcia, Rupert, 1944
Garza, Carmen Lomas, 1948
Gomez, Glynn, 1945
Gonzales, Julio, 1876–1942,
    b. Spain
Gonzales, Patricia, 1958,
    b. Colombia
Gonzalez, Ruben, 1923
Gonzalez-Torres, Felix,
    1957–1996, b. Cuba
Graham, Robert, 1938,
    b. Mexico
Gronk (Glugio Gronk
    Nicandro), 1954
Healy, Wayne Alaniz, 1949
Herrera, Carmen, 1915, b. Cuba
Herron, Willie, 1951
Jimenez, Luis, Jr., 1940
Juarez, Roberto, 1952
Lam, Wilfredo, 1902–1982,
    b. Cuba
Lasansky, Mauricio, 1914,
    b. Argentina
Lebron, Michael, 1954
Linares, Victor, 1929
Lopez, Felix, 1942
Lopez, Graciela Carrillo, 1949
Lopez, José Dolores, 1868–1937
Lopez, Michael, 1938
Lopez, Yolanda M., 1942
Lujan, Gilbert Sanchez, 1940
Marin, Augusto, 1921
Marisol (Marisol Escobar), 1930,
    raised in Venezuela

Martinez, Alfredo Ramos,
    1875–1946
Martinez, César Augusto, 1944
Martino, José Antonio Torres
Martorell, Antonio, 1939,
    b. Puerto Rico
Marzan, Gregorio, 1906–1997,
    b. Puerto Rico
Matta (Roberto Sebastian
    Antonio Matta Echaurren),
    1911
Medellin, Octavio, 1907–1999
Mendoza, Tony, 1941
Montoya, José, 1932
Morales, Raphael Colón, 1942
Moroles, Jesus Bautista, 1950,
    b. Mexico
Neri, Manuel, 1930
Otero, Nestor, 1948
Palomino, Ernesto, 1933
Pelaez, Amelia, 1897–1968
Pena, Amado, 1943
Perez, Irene, 1950
Perez, Pedro, 1951, b. Cuba
Ponce de León, Michael, 1922
Quesada, Eugenio, 1927
Raimondi, John, 1948
Ramirez, Joel Tito, 1923
Ramirez, Martin, 1885–1960,
    b. Mexico
Rivera, Angelica
Roche, Arnaldo, 1955, b. Puerto
    Rico
Rodriguez, Patricia, 1944

Rodriguez, Peter, 1926
Romero, Frank, 1941
Ruiz, Gilberto, 1950
Salinas, Porfirio, 1910–1973
Sanchez, Alex, 1946
Sierra, Paul, 1944, b. Cuba
Soto, Jorge, 1947
Stand, Luis, 1950, b. Colombia
Tacia, Jorge, 1958, b. Chile
Tanguma, Leo, 1941

Tapia, Luis, 1950
Torres-Garcia, Joaquin,
    1874–1949, b. Uruguay
Trevino, Rudy, 1945
Tufino, Nitza, 1949
Valdadez, John, 1951
Vallejo, Orlando, 1955
Velazquez, Juan Ramon,
    1820–1902
Villa, Esteban, 1930

URUGUAY

Alpuy, Julio, 1919

VENEZUELA

Borges, Jacobo, 1931
Cruz-Diez, 1923
Otero, Alejandro, 1921–1990
Soto, Jesus Rafael, 1923

MUSEUMS EMPHASIZING HISPANIC ART

PUERTO RICO

Old San Juan   Museo del Grabado; Latinoamericano Institute
                   of Puerto Rican Culture

SPAIN

Barcelona   Fundacio Joan Miró, Museu d'Art Contemporani
                   de Barcelona
Bilbao   Guggenheim Bilbao
Figueres   Fundacio Gala-Salvador Dali
Madrid   Museo del Prado; Museo Nacional Reina Sofia

UNITED STATES

California

Long Beach	Museum of Latin American Art
Los Angeles	Latino Museum of History, Art, and Culture
San Francisco	The Mexican Museum, Fort Mason Center

Florida

Miami	Latin American Art Museum

Illinois

Chicago	Mexican Fine Arts Center Museum

New York

New York City	El Museo del Barrio, Hispanic Society of America

JEWISH HOLIDAYS

To help in understanding the use of many of the objects created in the Jewish culture, definitions of special holiday seasons follow. The Hebrew seasons have specific names, but the actual dates change from year to year.

Sabbath. Observed every week beginning at sundown on Friday and ending at sundown on Saturday

Tu Bishevat. An agricultural festival (January–February)

Purim. Commemorates the saving of the Persian Jewish community from death (February–March)

Seder. A special observation of the first night of Passover, which includes specially prepared foods

Passover. Celebrating the Exodus of Israelites from Egypt (March–April)

Lag B'Omer. The thirty-third day between Passover and Shavuot, a special day commemorating two heroes (April–May)

Shavuot. Commemoration of the receiving of the Torah on Mount Sinai (seven weeks after Passover) (May–June)

Tisha B'Av. Ninth of Av; a fast day commemorating the destruction of the temples at Jerusalem (July–August)

Rosh Hashanah. Jewish New Year (September–October)

Yom Kippur. Day of Atonement; a day of fasting and prayer (September–October)

Sukkot. A seven-day feast that commemorates the divine protection the Jews received during their wanderings in the wilderness (September–October)

Shemini Atzeret. A festival that follows the seventh day of Sukkot (September–October)

Simchat Torah. A holiday to observe the annual completion of the reading of the Torah (September–October)

Hanukkah. An eight-day observance of the victory of Judah Maccabee over the Seleucids; one candle is lit on the menorah for each of the days (November–December)

JUDAIC MOTIFS

These symbols frequently appear in Judaic artwork, mosaic floors, coins, and illuminated manuscripts.

Motif	Meaning
Etrog (Citron)	Used during the harvest celebration of Sukkot
Eyes	Frequently found on marriage contracts to protect the newlyweds against the evil eye
Female busts	The four seasons, each represented by a different sculpture
Fish	Fertility symbol
Five arches	The number five has special powers against the evil eye.

Motif	Meaning
Grape clusters and vine leaf	Signify wine, which is used ceremonially
Hand	The hand could be "a guardian against the evil eye."
Leviathan	A legendary sea monster, often depicted on handcrafted objects
Lion	Represents the lion of the tribe of Judah
Lulav	A palm frond, myrtle, and willow held together, used for the harvest celebration of Sukkot
Magen David	The six-sided star that originated in the 6th century is based on a hexagram.
Mappah	A binder that is wrapped around the Torah to keep it from unrolling
Menorah	A candleholder that holds seven candles; the menorah used for Hanukkah (called a Hanukkian) holds nine candles.
Messianic meal	This meal is represented by a jar of manna (bread), fruit of the Tree of Life, flesh of Leviathan, and the blossoming rod of Aaron.
Rod of Aaron	A blossoming tree branch
Shofar	A horn (usually from a ram) is blown on Rosh Hashanah and other occasions.
Spice boxes	These boxes of wood or metal often resemble towers, with carved openwork to allow the fragrance to escape; used in a ceremony symbolizing the end of the Sabbath
Sukkah	A roofless booth often decorated with branches, decorative paper cutting, and fruits and vegetables; used during the festival of Sukkot
Tablets of the Law	Two tablets of stone bearing the Ten Commandments
Torah	The five books of Moses
Torah Ark	The Ark is the repository for the scrolls of the law.
Tree of life	This tree features various animals.

Motif	Meaning
Twisted columns	Reminders of the columns that were in front of the Temple of Solomon. Two columns represent the columns of Solomon's temple.
Zodiac signs	Such signs are often used on marriage contracts and other formal documents.

TRADITIONAL ART AND FOLK ART

Jewish folk art has been created for ceremonial use and for use in daily rituals. It reflects ancient, ongoing historical traditions. Many beautiful examples of the jeweler's or craftsman's skills have been carefully preserved. The decorative techniques and elements used frequently reflect the period and culture in which the artisans were living.

Artwork	Purpose
Amulets	For the bris (circumcision ceremony), paper cutouts, pillow covers
Amulets	Engraved pendants to be worn by women in childbirth, or a painting with verses to protect both mothers and children
Challah cover	Cover for the special bread made for the Sabbath
Dreidel	A spinning top with words on four sides that translate loosely as "nothing," "get all," "half," "put-in," used in a children's game. The symbols stand for words that mean "A great miracle happened here."
Embroidered bags	For prayer shawls

Artwork	Purpose
Illuminated book	Prayer books for the High Holy Days that were often richly illustrated
Itinerarium	An embroidery or painting that shows the main pilgrimage sites of the Holy Land
Ketubbah	A formal marriage contract, often richly decorated
Kiddush cup	A goblet, often richly decorated, filled with wine, used for Kiddush on the Sabbath and holidays
Mappah	An embroidered cover to protect the scrolls of the Torah from the table when it is unrolled and read
Megillat Esther	The story of Esther is one of the five books of the Tanakh known as the Ketuvim (writings); it is often a beautifully illuminated scroll on one roller, and is read from beginning to end in one session on Purim.
Memento mori	A paper cutout with verses that remind one of the shortness of life and the imminence of death
Mezuzah	A small case to contain bibilical passages, affixed to any doorpost in the house; made of reeds, glass, silver, ivory, stone, or even embroidered containers (in North Africa)
Micrography	Miniature writing used to "draw" a picture or decorate around figures
Mizrach (East)	Paper cutout, embroidery, drawing, or painting on a Jerusalem facing wall; it must say *mizrach* (the place where the sun rises) on it.
Omer calendar	A calendar containing a Bible verse for each day of the seven weeks of Omer (the period between Passover and Shavuot); often richly illustrated; sometimes in book form
Parokhet	The curtain that hangs behind the door of the Ark, often embroidered
Phylacteries (tefillin)	Small leather boxes containing Biblical verses, worn during morning prayers

Artwork	Purpose
Prayer books for women	These contain blessings and prayers for special occasions.
Quilts	Appliquéd wedding quilts or crib quilts rich with symbols
Rimmonim	Carved finials to ornament the staves on which the Torah scroll is rolled
Seder plate	Special ceremonial dish used for the Passover Seder; it holds the important ritual foods used for the Seder.
Shiviti (a Biblical saying)	A decorative amulet, embroidered, painted on paper or etched on copper, and usually placed on a Jerusalem-facing wall (generally an East wall)
Shpanyer arbeit	Spanish metal thread embroidery
Synagogue mosaic	The decorative mosaic pavement of synagogues, often included symbols
Tallit	The prayer shawl, with fringes attached to the four corners, worn during morning prayers; beautifully embroidered bags were sometimes made to contain the shawl.
Tik	An ornamental container for the Torah used in Oriental communities
Towel cover	An embroidered cover that was placed over soiled towels
Tzitzit	The fringes on four corners of the prayer shawl, which serve as a reminder to observe the commandments of the Torah.
Wimpel (torah binder)	Richly embroidered strips of cloth used to wrap a newborn son after the circumcision ceremony and given to the temple by mothers to be used to wrap the Torah
Wool embroidery on perforated paper	Various amulets or decorations were made by this technique.

"As the old saying goes, good work, good pay."
—GIOTTO, c. 1266–1337, Pre-Renaissance fresco painter

MUSEUMS EMPHASIZING JUDAIC ART AND CULTURE

As with the arts and crafts of many other peoples, Judaic art is inseparable from Judaic culture. Like the handiwork of several other cultures, many items from Judaic tradition now on display in museums and galleries were originally created to serve an everyday purpose, often one related to prayer.

AUSTRIA

Vienna   Jewish Museum Vienna

CZECH REPUBLIC

Prague   Jewish Museum

ENGLAND

London   Jewish Museum, Woburn House

ISRAEL

Jerusalem   The Israel Museum

NETHERLANDS

Amsterdam   Joods Historisch Museum

UNITED STATES

California

Berkeley   Judah L. Magnes Museum
Los Angeles   Skirball Museum
San Francisco   Jewish Museum

Colorado

Denver   Mizel Family Cultural Arts Center

District of Columbia

Washington   B'nai B'rith National Jewish Museum; Holocaust
                              Museum

Illinois

Chicago   Spertus Museum of Judaica

Maryland

Baltimore   Jewish Historical Society of Maryland

Michigan

Detroit   Janice Charach Epstein Museum Gallery

Mississippi

Jackson   Museum of the Southern Jewish Experience

New York

New York City   The Jewish Museum; Yeshiva University Museum

Ohio

Beechwood   The Temple Museum of Religious Art

Oklahoma

Tulsa   Gerson and Rebecca Fenster Museum of
                              Religious Art

Pennsylvania

Philadelphia   Philadelphia Museum of Jewish Art

JUDEO-CHRISTIAN SYMBOLISM IN ART

The Old Testament (on which both Judaism and Christianity are based) and the New Testament (which begins with the birth of Christ) of the Bible have provided endless subject matter for artists for centuries. Symbolism in Gothic, Renaissance, and Baroque art was understood by viewers of that time, and helped them understand the meaning of a painting. This list identifies some of the more frequently seen subjects and themes, and may contribute to your understanding of ancient and modern religious art.

OLD TESTAMENT PROPHETS

Daniel	A prophet who had visions and dreams
Ezekiel	A prophet, had a book in the Old Testament
Isaiah	A prophet, one of the great writing prophets
Jeremiah	A prophet, had a book in the Old Testament
Jonah	Was delivered from the belly of a whale
Minor Prophets	Hosea, Joel, Amos, Obadiah, Jonah, Micah, Nahum, Habakkuk, Zephaniah, Haggai, Zechariah, Malachi

SPECIAL PEOPLE IN THE OLD TESTAMENT

Abraham	Willing to sacrifice his son, Isaac, who was saved at the last minute
Adam and Eve	The first man and woman created
Angels	Heavenly creatures seen in many paintings
Bathsheba	Beautiful neighbor of King David, often depicted bathing
David and Goliath	Young David slew the giant Goliath with a rock from his slingshot
Isaac	Son of Abraham and Sarah
Job	Suffered numerous tribulations to try his patience
Moses	Led the Jews from slavery in Egypt through the desert

Noah	Built an ark and collected two of each animal to save from the flood
Salome	Daughter of Herod who had John the Baptist beheaded
Samson and Delilah	Delilah took away Samson's strength by cutting his hair as he slept
Saul	A king in the time of the young David
Solomon	King Solomon, son of Bathsheba and David, built the temple

PEOPLE FROM THE APOCRYPHA

The Apocrypha are stories written 220 B.C. to A.D. 100 that were excluded from the Jewish and Protestant canons of the Old Testament

Judith and Holerfernes	Judith cut off Holerfernes's head, which is shown in paintings as being carried in a basket by Judith's maid.
Suzanna and the Elders	The wife of a citizen of Babylon, Suzanna was seen bathing by two elders of the community who denounced her. She was saved by a young man, Daniel.
Tobias and the Angel	Tobias sought a cure for his father, Tobit, who was going blind.

NEW TESTAMENT

Anne	Mary's mother
Jesus	Considered by Christians to be the Messiah, the Savior
John the Baptist	Often seen pointing to Christ; he was usually painted as clothed in camel's hair
Joseph	Jesus' father, a carpenter, sometimes shown with a carpenter's tools
Lazarus	Raised from the dead by Christ
Mary	The Virgin Mary, Jesus' mother, often seen in blue and gold

THE ORIGINAL TWELVE APOSTLES*

Andrew
Bartholomew
James, son of Alphaeus
James, son of Zebedee
John
Judas Iscariot
Matthew (or Levi)
Peter
Philip
Simon the Canaanite
Thaddaeus (or Jude)
Thomas

*Paul, the "Apostle to the Gentiles," was not among the original twelve; Judas was replaced by Matthias.

HOW TO RECOGNIZE THE SAINTS

Illiterate people of the Middle Ages were often able to recognize saints by their "attributes," such as colors, accompanying animals, or a symbol of their martyrdom (death for their faith). Altarpieces frequently depicted the patrons (who paid for the altarpiece) accompanied by their patron saints. This is a partial list.

St. Anne	Carries book, wears green and red clothes
St. Anthony	Seen with crutch and bell and a hog; wears a monk's robe
St. Barbara	Carries a tower with three windows, a peacock feather
St. Benedict	White beard, dove, Benedictine abbot's robe
St. Catherine of Alexandria	Symbolized by a wheel; she carries crown, sword
St. Christopher	Palm tree staff, child (Christ) on shoulders
St. Francis of Assisi	Dark brown robe, skull, lily, wolf and lamb
St. George	Young knight in armor on a horse, slaying a dragon
St. Jerome	Red hat, crimson robe, a lion nearby, also a crucifix, skull and owl

St. John the Baptist	Lamb in his arms, camel's hair garment, leather belt
St. Joseph	Husband of the Virgin Mary; carpenter's plane, saw, hatchet
St. Jude	Lance or halberd; patron saint of lost causes
St. Lucy	Her eyes on a dish in her hand, a lamp, a wound in her neck
St. Luke	Winged ox; the patron saint of painters, often shown painting the Virgin Mary
St. Margaret	Cross, crown, palm, standing on a dragon
St. Mark the Evangelist	Winged lion, pen, and book of his Gospel
St. Martha	Ladle, keys at her waist
St. Mary Magdalene	Long hair that covers her, alabaster box of ointment
St. Matthew	Cherub (angel), bag of money, axe, book or pen
St. Nicholas	Red robe of a bishop, ship or anchor; patron saint of little children
St. Paul the Apostle	Sword, book or scroll
St. Peter the Apostle	Keys (to the Kingdom), fish, cock, yellow mantle
St. Philip the Apostle	Cross on a staff or reed, dragon
St. Sebastian	Bound to a tree or stake, body transfixed with arrows
St. Stephen	Stones (by which he was martyred)
St. Thomas, Apostle	Builder's rule or square
St. Veronica	Holds up a cloth showing the face of Christ with a crown of thorns

If you wish to read further about the symbolism of different cultures, the following two books are excellent references.

Cooper, J. C., *An Illustrated Encyclopedia of Traditional Symbols,* Thames and Hudson Ltd., London, 1978

Ferguson, G., *Signs & Symbols in Christian Art,* Oxford University Press, London, 1954

SPECIAL THEMES

Old Testament

    Noah's Ark
    The Flood
    Jonah and the Whale

New Testament

The Annunciation	An angel announces to Mary that she will bear a child
The Nativity	The birth of Christ in a stable
The Presentation	Christ being presented in the temple
The Last Supper	The night that Christ announces He will soon die and institutes the Eucharist
In the Garden	Christ's agony in the Garden of Gethsemene
The Crucifixion	Christ on the Cross
The Lamentation	Mourning at the Cross
The Descent from the Cross	Taking Christ off the Cross
The Resurrection	Christ after He has risen
The Assumption	Mary's entry into heaven
The Ascension	Christ's entry into heaven

ISLAMIC ART

The Islamic religion was founded in A.D. 622 following the teachings of the prophet and teacher Muhammad (c. 570–632). It spread from India to Spain, and as a result, shows influences already existing in those cultures. Early Islamic convention in art discouraged the depiction of live human or animal forms, though nothing is written in the Koran that forbids this, and they are occasionally seen. In later work such figures are combined with the preferred designs created of beautiful geometric forms, Arabic lettering, arabesques (scrolls), trees, swirling vines, and flowers. These decorative motifs were used in books, architecture, china, metalwork, and daily functional and religious objects. In approximately the 12th century, illuminated manuscripts, combined with these other decorative designs, depicted daily life.

These are a few of the beliefs of Islam, greatly simplified, to further the understanding of Islamic art by non-Muslims.

FIVE PILLARS (DUTIES) OF THE FAITH OF ISLAM

Profession of faith

Prayer, performed five times a day

Fasting, particularly during the Ramadan season

Almsgiving

Pilgrimage to Mecca (the Hajj). This is the birthplace of the prophet Muhammad; every Muslim should make the pilgrimage once in a lifetime.

HOLIDAY OBSERVANCES

Birth of the Prophet Muhammad.

New Year. The start of the Muslim calendar

Ramadan. Ninth month of the Muslim calendar; fasting begins shortly before dawn and ends after sundown each day

Night of Power. Twenty-seventh night of Ramadan

Friday. The holy day of the Muslim week

THREE CHIEF HOLY CITIES OF ISLAM

Mecca. A city in Saudi Arabia, to which a devout Muslim aspires to make a pilgrimage

Medina. Called the city of the Prophet (where Muhammad is buried); the first Islamic State

Jerusalem. Location of the *Dome of the Rock* mosque

GLOSSARY

Allah. Name of God in Islam

Hadith. Interpretations of words spoken by the Prophet Muhammad

Imam. The Muslim scholar who is foremost in the mosque

Kaaba. The cube-shaped mosque in the courtyard of the city of Mecca

Madrassa. Arabic for *school;* often used to mean the school where Islamic doctrine is taught

Mihrab. A prayer niche that shows the direction of the qibla, the "compass of the Muslim world"

Mimbar. The pulpit found in a mosque

Minaret. A slender tower attached to a mosque where the faithful are called to prayer five times daily

Mosque. The center of Islamic life where Muslims gather to learn and worship

Muezzin. The person who calls the faithful to prayer

Prayer beads. The "rosary" used by the faithful when reciting the ninety-nine full names of Allah (God)

Qibla. Direction of Mecca

Qur'an (Koran). The scripture of Islam

SOME ART FORMS

Architecture. Mosques and mausoleums made extensive use of building techniques such as cast-stucco panels, tile work, mosaics, elaborately carved wood panels, and ornamental brickwork.

Calligraphy. Considered by many Muslims as the most important Islamic art form, the Arabic lettering is used as decoration on buildings, metal and ceramic vessels, and manuscripts.

Manuscript illumination. Medical texts, poetry, fables, paintings of the life of the court, and scenes of workmen erecting a building are all examples of the painter's art. These exist from the early days of Islam until about 1600, roughly paralleling the development of this art form in Western art. Islamic miniatures are especially fine.

Metal working. Bronze, copper, and brass were sometimes combined with enamel work (champléve, a form of glass that was related to cloisonné, an Asian art form). Popular forms were the aquamanile (water pitcher) in the shape of a lion, ewers, and basins.

Pottery. Pottery decoration varies widely depending on the country and the time period in which it was done. Arabic script was used in all countries, however, and is seen on many different forms. Iznik ceramic decoration is found on wall tiles, bowls, and vessels.

Rug weaving. Carpets, which continue to be widely distributed, are of the finest quality.

Textile weaving. Woven patterned silk rarely exists today, but a few examples demonstrate the exceptional skill in weaving.

Wall paintings. Early wall paintings (frescoes) reflect Greek and Roman influence.

Wood carving. Frequently found in mosques, wooden carved panels made extensive use of geometric patterns combined with floral forms.

ISLAMIC COLORS

Islamic colors (red, white, black, and green): Seen in clothing, flags, traditional dress; four colors of Pan-Arabism.

White. The color of angels, the color of paradise, one of two colors worn by mullahs (leaders).

Black. The color of mourning, also worn by mullahs, and seen on *chadors* (enveloping robe) of women.

Green. Considered of particular importance in Islam, and consequently in its art. It represents creation, joy, success, happiness, hope, and eternity.

Red. Represents the bloodshed of heroes; also seen as the present time, just as green, its opposite, represents the past (blue) and the future (yellow).

CHAPTER 4

Naïve, Folk, and Outsider Art

"Folk art is learned at the knee and passed from generation to generation, or through established cultural community traditions."

—The National Endowment for the Arts

FOLK ART TERMS

Folk art comes out of an identifiable tradition, such as traditional Navajo rugs or pottery from the San Ildefonso Pueblo in New Mexico, and is created by non-academically trained artists. The American Visionary Museum defines "folk art" as coming out of a particular cultural tradition, in contrast with "visionary art," which comes from individual inspiration. However, it is commonplace to use the term *folk art* to describe any work that fits either category. This list includes words that may have several meanings in reference to art but have specific interpretations when applied to folk art.

Art brut. A French term that means "raw" or "strong" art, referring to the fresh, emotional appeal of some folk art. First used by Jean Dubuffet, founder of the Collection del'Arte Brut in Switzerland.

Assemblage. An assemblage is created from found objects, such as wood, metal, plastic, or glass, joined together by various means to create sculpture. Folk art assemblages are sometimes referred to as *junk sculpture*.

Contemporary folk art. This is artwork that is being produced now, by artists around the world following a cultural tradition.

Environmental art (sometimes called *yard art*). Some folk artists beautify their surroundings, creating artwork from materials such as cement, natural rocks, old tires, bottles, or other found materials. A prime example is Simon Rodia's *Watts Towers* in Los Angeles, a huge fantasy-construction that was created from broken china embedded in cement, and supported by metal rods. Tressa Prisbrey's *Bottle Village* is another example of the genre.

Faux folk art. This art is created by academically trained artists to look like work by self-taught artists.

Memory paintings. Paintings inspired by an artist's childhood surroundings or memories of special events, such as Grandma Moses' paintings of a reunion in the country. Such works are often rich in detail, filled with the people who are fondly remembered.

Naïve. The French term for the work of an artist whose work is unsophisticated and rather childlike.

Outsider art. This generally refers to the works of self-taught artists, some of whom may have spent their lives in prison or mental institutions or are developmentally, physically, or mentally disabled. Other outsider artists are simply people who have not had traditional artistic education who express themselves through sculpture, paintings, or constructions.

Primitive. A term used to describe the works of non-academically trained artists; was also applied to the work of Flemish painters of the 15th century (Flemish Primitives).

Self-taught. An artist who has not had formal training, but has learned a technique simply by "doing."

Visionary art. This art comes from within the artist, and is not based on a cultural tradition; paintings with subject matter based on fantasy, dreams, "voices," or "visions." Visionary works frequently have religious or sexual overtones.

UNIVERSAL FOLK ART AND CRAFTS

Most folk art developed in rural societies, with traditions passed down through generations. Training was acquired through watching and learning from family members or through apprenticeship. The folk artist continuing in a cultural tradition seldom signed the work. The work done by the artists in rural communities was as much a part of their lives as cooking, keeping house, and watching children, with the exception that the artwork often also served as a source of income.

The development of fine crafts and folk art came from simple human needs such as gathering, cooking, and storing food or carrying belongings. Common crafts that arose out of such a need include basketry, ceramics, and needlework. Other basic needs that inspired what we may now consider artwork were covering and sheltering the body, communication, worship, and celebrations. Regional differences in available materials (wood, shells, stone, animal skins, grasses, clay) and climate usually determined what art forms became traditional in specific cultures. As time passed, unique methods and patterns of decorating developed and differences among groups became more marked.

BASKETRY

Utilitarian objects woven from split-oak, river-cane, honeysuckle, twig and vine, bark, pine needles, sweetgrass, palmetto, and corn shucks exist all over the world and include such disparate objects as baskets, brooms, hats, floor mats, and chair seats.

Broom making. In the South, broom making is an art form related to basketry that originally was brought to the United States by slaves from Africa. Brooms were made of palmetto, broomcorn, buckeye, and sedge. Although it is no longer necessary to make brooms by hand, many people appreciate and collect them.

Splint baskets. Craftspeople in many parts of the American South continue to make splint baskets from long thin pieces of wood woven together.

Sweetgrass baskets. In South Carolina, an enduring tradition of coiling sweetgrass to make baskets is carried out by descendants of slaves. This same tradition is seen in the north of Brazil, where it was also learned from African ancestors.

"It is not the individual piece that is important but the general quality of all the pieces in a particular kiln. The best hitter in baseball fails more often than not. His average, and not any particular performance, marks him as great. So it is with the hardworking artisan. A high average makes him an artist."

—HENRY GLASSIE, folk-art professor, writer, and researcher
(in speaking of potter Dan Garner)

CERAMICS

Because ceramics endure, much of what is known of ancient cultures is learned from clay shards. Vessels were universally made from local clay for storage of liquids, grains, and fruit. Clay was also formed into human and animal shapes, with most cultures developing a recognizable tradition either in the decoration, form, or colors of their clay figures. Common types of ceramic folk art include:

Face pots. In the American South, fired clay jugs frequently have a face on one side and are sometimes called ugly or grotesque jugs. In Peru, such "face pots" might have been actual portraits.

Pottery. Techniques for making pottery, forms, and glazes developed according to a culture's social and religious needs. For example, small ceramic female forms were created as "grave goods" 27,000 years ago in Austria.

FIBERS

As people have needed to clothe and keep themselves warm, fiber techniques such as weaving and felting came into being. In most traditions this work was done by women. The application of decorative designs was added as people had time to add embellishment. Techniques for creating or decorating fabrics include the following.

Batik. In this decorative technique, which originated in Indonesia, designs are applied to cloth with molten wax; then the cloth is dyed. The waxed areas retain the original cloth color, giving a crackled effect.

Beading. Small beads made of hollow glass are sewn onto a background in decorative patterns. This technique is used worldwide by most cultures. A form of beading with porcupine quills originated with Native Americans.

Felting. This is a universal process wherever animals with long hair, such as goats, alpaca, or sheep, are found. Wool and other fibers are combined to make felt cloth through the addition of moisture, chemicals, and pressure. Felt continues to be made in cultures from Austria and Australia to Peru.

Hooked rug. Yarn or rags are sewn to a support such as burlap by pulling the fiber through to the underside with a hook. These rugs usually feature animals, flowers, or geometric designs, and were especially popular in America in the late 19th and early 20th centuries.

Macramé. Macramé (decorative knot-making with cord) is thought to have originated with sailors who passed the long hours at sea perfecting their ability to make knots. More contemporary applications of this technique include creating jewelry, purses, plant hangers, and wall hangings.

Weaving. Weaving has been done in most cultures since ancient times. Various types of looms have been used to make homespun cloth, coverlets (bedspreads), and rugs.

METALWORK

Metalworking is a universal craft that has been used for practical and decorative purposes. Humans discovered that metal could be isolated and transformed by melting, heating, or hammering. Common methods of metalworking include:

Cast iron. A mold is used to make a hollow (sometimes in a fine sand). Molten iron is poured into the pattern created in the mold and allowed to harden.

Casting. Casts made from molds have existed in ancient societies, with each society's designs reflecting its particular culture. This technique encompasses ancient Chinese bronze vessels, African goldweights, colossal statuary, and fine jewelry.

Forged iron (wrought iron). This method of working metal involves alternately heating in a forge, then hammering on iron rods. It is used by blacksmiths to make decorative metalwork for such things as gates, farm implements, weathervanes, candleholders, utensils, horseshoes, and farm machinery.

Goldsmithing and silversmithing. Goldsmiths and silversmiths use various metalworking techniques to create jewelry, fine vessels, and ornamental objects. Craftsmen such as Paul Revere created bowls, porringers, tableware services, and napkin rings out of silver.

Repoussé. This technique of "pushing" thin metal to stretch it was used in some ancient societies to make masks, decorative cups, and jewelry.

Tinsmithing. Sometimes called tole work, this is a type of metalwork in which candleholders, pitchers, trays, and light fixtures were produced out of tin and usually handpainted with traditional designs.

Weathervanes. Three-dimensional vanes, made either of flat sheet metal or carved and painted wood, featured subjects such as trains, angels, fish, Indian hunters, roosters, or farm animals. They were placed on barn roofs by farmers to determine the direction of the wind.

MUSICAL INSTRUMENTS

Throughout the world, the need to make music has resulted in all manner of musical instruments. Today's craftsmen continue this age-old tradition of handmade dulcimers, banjos, fifes made of cane, mandolins and fiddles, accordions, and limberjacks (a dancing wooden doll used to beat a rhythm). The primary material is wood, but leather, metal, gut, and reed are also used in their production.

NEEDLEWORK

While this is traditionally "women's work," in some cultures only men are allowed to do weaving, while women instead cultivate the fields. Needlework encompasses many specialties, including the following.

Embroidered sampler. Originating in Europe, this was a means of teaching young girls how to do various decorative embroidery stitches. In Colonial America it usually included an alphabet and numbers, and the seamstress's name as well as decorative designs such as a house, school, trees, or flowers. Samplers were relatively small, and probably most were displayed in a frame.

Embroidery. A craft mostly practiced by women, involving the use of silken threads to apply decorative designs on linens and clothing.

Molas. These colorful reverse appliqué panels are created by the Cuna Indians of the San Blas Islands (offshore from Panama). The panels, which originally were created as blouse fronts, consist of several layers of cloth. Decorative designs are cut in the top and successive layers underneath to allow various colors to show through.

Smocking. In this needlework technique, cloth is finely gathered, and then rows of decorative embroidery are applied to emphasize the gathers.

Quilting. Sewing layers of cloth together, with pieced designs on the top to create patterns, is an ancient technique that originally developed in the East, but has become a signature of American folk art. Types of quilts include:

- **Album quilt.** Sometimes called a Baltimore quilt, this was usually made by several people, and involved appliqué and fancy stitching. This type of quilt was sometimes given by friends to commemorate a wedding or coming-of-age party, or as a farewell gift to someone who was moving to a different part of the country. It sometimes featured ribbons, photographs, or personal items that were meaningful to the recipient.

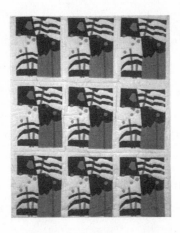

- **Appliquéd quilt.** In this quilting technique, cutouts such as hearts and flowers are sewn onto a quilt.

- **Crazy quilt.** This type of quilt, most popular in the late 19th century, often featured fine silks, satins, and velvets put together in no logical manner, and decorated with fancy embroidery. It often included special fabrics such as a piece from a wedding dress or some other meaningful garment. It was rarely intended to be used on a bed, but rather as a fancy throw for a sofa or piano. Trade with China was flourishing in America at that time, and small scraps of silks were readily available for use in these quilts.

- **Embroidered quilt.** This often features simple cross-stitch embroidered designs done in one color on a plain background.

- **Pieced quilt.** This quilting style originally featured old clothing cut up and pieced together in geometric patterns, but evolved into a fancier art form whereby new fabrics were used to create traditional patterns such as *The Windmill* or the *Texas Star.*

- **Shaker quilt.** Favored by collectors for their strong geometric designs and bold colors.

PAINTING

Once the basic needs had been met, craftspeople often applied decoration to make things more beautiful and appealing. Not surprisingly, flowers, plants, animals, and geometric designs are the primary themes common to the artwork of most cultures. Frequently, painting techniques were developed to beautify people's surroundings.

Overmantle painting. Painting done directly on the wall above a mantle.

Painted fireboard. A fancy small screen to protect ladies' faces from the fire, sometimes used to cover the fireplace opening when not in use.

Painted furniture. In Colonial times, furniture was often simple. The tradition of painting designs on chests and armoires was brought to America from Europe.

Painted tinware. Tole (tin) painting was used to enhance trays, coffee pots, and other household objects.

Rosemahling (Norway). Painted interior walls and furniture were decorated with flowers or other designs from nature.

Stenciling. This revival of an old craft is once again popular. Decorative patterns are painted on a wall or floorcloth through an opening cut in a water-resistant stencil.

PAPER

Paper is a basic material for creating art, and it has been found that almost any vegetal material can be formed into paper such as Asian rice paper, Egyptian papyrus, or bark paper (such as amate and tapa paper). High quality paper has a high rag (cotton) content. Paper making was originally perfected by the Chinese c. A.D. 100.

Traditional ways of cutting paper have evolved in most societies, ranging from Chinese red paper decorations to Mexican tissue paper for the Day of the Dead to the silhouettes that were so popular with Victorians.

Amate paper cutouts. These symmetrical figure cutouts are created by the Mayan Otomi Indians of Central America.

Chien-chih (Chinese). Individual cuttings made with scissors or knife.

Fraktur. A decorative certificate of German origin on which weddings, births, or engagements were recorded. Decorations might include people, flowers, birds, mermaids, or borders.

Katazome (Japanese). Stencils cut for use in dyeing fabrics.

K'e-chih (Chinese). Many layers cut at a time using a knife.

Knippen, schneiden (Dutch). Cutwork to decorate commemorative documents.

Mon-kiri (Japanese). Emblems and crests cut from paper.

Papel picado (Mexican). Intricate tissue paper cutouts for holiday decorations.

Paper flowers (Mexican). Artificial flowers made with paper are particularly prized for holidays.

Papercutting (American). Commonly featured nature scenes cut from black paper; mounted on foil or glass; silhouettes.

Papercutting (English). Specialized in paper mosaics, collage, especially fine botanical illustrations, silhouettes, and pin pricking.

Papier-mâché (France). Paper that has been applied to an underlying armature or that has been soaked until it is pulp, used by many cultures to make forms ranging from masks to furniture.

Papercutting (Jewish). Used to commemorate special events; often included written text.

Scherenschnitte (German, Swiss, Pennsylvania Dutch). These cut-paper designs typically featured trees, animals, and nature scenes (usually black and white).

Spirit drawings (universal). Ink or crayon drawings such as these represent a "divine vision or spiritual communication" to the person who creates them.

Tapa cloth (Mexican). Brown tapa cloth is covered with brightly painted flowers and animals.

Wycinanki (Polish). These designs are on brightly colored layers of paper, mostly using flowers, stars, birds, and other nature themes.

SCRIMSHAW

In this folk art form designs are incised, usually by sailors, with a sharp instrument on whale teeth, ivory, bones, or baleen. Favorite designs were sailing ships, mermaids, flowers, or geometric patterns, and were sometimes combined with wood or other materials. Common scrimshaw works included:

Corset busks. Used for making women's waists smaller.

Ivory pipe stoppers. Used for packing tobacco into pipes.

Scrimshaw pie crimpers. Serrated wheel with female figure, a hand, a horse, or decorated handle.

Whalebone yarn swifts. Used to wind yarn.

TOYS AND DOLLS

Dolls have been made in all cultures from materials as varied as cloth, corn cobs, cornhusks, cardboard, or paper. Here are a few examples.

Apple doll. A doll with a head carved out of an apple, dried, then attached to a cloth body.

Corn-husk dolls. These small dolls, which are created from rolled or stuffed corn husks, with the face painted on, are still popular with collectors.

Puppets. This timeless craft is still popular and includes hand puppets, marionettes, and stick puppets used in performances.

Rag dolls. Simple dolls made from rags or leftover cloth (such as *Raggedy Ann*) are still homemade or manufactured.

Shadow puppets. Indonesians made these large pierced and highly decorative flat puppets out of leather. Supported by sticks, these were manipulated behind a back-lit screen.

WOODCARVING

Woodcarvers did decorative carving for ships and homes, as well as trade signs, trade store figures, and figureheads. Typical woodcarving works include:

Barber poles. Barbers displayed a red-and-white spiral striped pole outside their shops.

Carved animals. These were typically made as toys or carved for carousels, and often featured tigers, horses, lions, and giraffes.

Carved canes. A tradition of the American South, these functional canes are frequently made of found wood, carved with animals, people, or snakes, and sometimes painted.

Decoys. These are carved wooden birds of all types, painted realistically, and used to attract real birds for hunters.

Figureheads. These were placed at the bows of ships, and usually featured beautiful women or top-hatted men.

Model ships. Intricate ships, complete with sails and rigging, were probably made by sailors.

Tavern signs. These signs usually featured the name of the tavern along with a painted figure such as a general.

Trade figures. Many of these carved wooden effigies were used as tobacconists' figures to attract customers. Popular figures in Colonial America were sailors (Jack Tar), Native Americans or Scottish Highlanders, the eagle, Uncle Sam, George Washington, and Miss Liberty.

Trade signs. Wood or metal oversized signs of such things as a tooth, eyeglasses, boot, fish, bread, or watches, designed to "advertise" services or wares.

Whirligigs. Mechanical wind-powered vanes that, when moved, cause attached painted and carved figures to move and "perform"—for example, ride a bicycle or use a saw.

Whittled crafts. Toys, dolls, whistles, small figures, and animals carved with a knife.

OTHER FOLK ART AND CRAFTS

Calligraphy. Fancy lettering was done on important documents such as diplomas and birth or wedding certificates. Some skilled calligraphers could make animals such as eagles or horses from calligraphy strokes. In China, the mark of a scholar was to be able to do beautiful calligraphy.

Candlemaking. Candles made from animal fat were a necessity in a society without electricity. Popularity continues for aesthetic reasons.

Decoupage. Designs are cut from decorative paper and glued onto a background of glass, wood, or heavy cardboard. Many coats of varnish are applied and sanded between coats, to give the work a smooth glossy finish.

Engraved coconuts. Like scrimshaw, this work was done by sailors and featured similar themes—such as ships, mermaids, flowers.

Floorcloth. A canvas on which a design was painted or stenciled, then varnished to be dirt-resistant. This was the forerunner of linoleum.

Gourds, carved or painted. This craft form has always been common among country people, who dried and hollowed the gourds to use as water dippers, bird houses, and decorative objects.

Pen and ink sampler. Boys and girls made samplers in ink on parchment, using alphabets and numbers, along with decorative borders.

Pysanky (Poland). The decorating of eggs with unique designs and patterns using a batik method.

Quilling. Fancy designs are made of narrow pieces of paper rolled around a needle to make small circles. These circles are grouped together, then glued onto a stiff background to create a picture.

Saddle making. In the days when the horse was the most common means of transport, saddle making was an important skill. Saddles were made of leather molded over handmade wooden forms, tooled, and stitched.

Screenwire masks. Painted, formed masks were used for Mardi Gras by Cajuns in the countryside around New Orleans.

Shaker wooden boxes. These simple round wooden boxes were used for storage, and have become collectors' items.

Squirrel cage. Commonly used among American colonists, this was an elaborately carved cage with an exercise wheel for a pet squirrel.

Stone carving. In the United States, stone carvers at first made gravestones, but eventually expanded to decorative carving for homes and monumental sculpture.

Straw work. Straw weaving was a craft brought from Sweden and England. This tradition continues in modern-day Mexico, China, the United States, and wherever straw is grown. Straw is also flattened to form a decorative surface for items such as boxes.

Wheat weaving. A European tradition brought to the United States by English and Swedish immigrants, wheat weaving includes such items as *House Blessings* (an intricate small woven hanging), ornaments, dolls, and other decorations.

COLLECTING FOLK ART

If you already own some folk art, try to find out more about what you already have before you begin collecting in earnest. Or you may just be ready to start collecting. To learn more—and make your collecting experience more rewarding—visit galleries and museums, read about collections and collectors, or talk with other people about their collections. You can also learn a great deal about folk art on the Internet simply by typing in the names of some of the folk artists and museums found in this chapter.

If you have already begun collecting, consider what you now have, and what your taste appears to lean to. Perhaps you are eclectic and want to collect art from every culture and craft. (Alexander Girard was one such collector, and his 100,000 objects from more than one hundred countries comprise the bulk of the Museum of International Folk Art in Santa Fe, New Mexico.) Or you may prefer to limit your collection to work from one country or region. These tips come from various collectors, gallery owners, and museum professionals, and will help you in building your own collection.

- If choosing from several similar items, you might mentally sort them as "good, better, best" (a trick used by some experienced collectors). Buy the best you can afford.
- Select a dealer who belongs to a professional association or is recommended for honesty by other collectors. Such a dealer may be willing to buy back work that is unsatisfactory.
- Consider purchasing through a gallery. This offers the advantage of a dealer who may have selected the best artwork available in the region or who may represent specific artists. As you build a collection, a dealer may keep an eye out for the type of thing that is of interest to you.
- If you purchase an object, such as a sculpture, for which a drawing also exists, buy both, as it will increase the value.

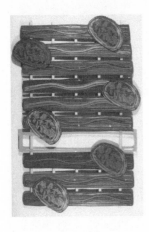

- Photograph how the artwork looked when you acquired it. Folk art materials seldom are "archival," and you will want to take action if there are significant changes.
- Although a signed and dated piece may be worth more than one that is unsigned, the signature is unlikely to add much to the value if the quality is poor.
- If you are buying a painting on canvas, check to see if the canvas is taut and be aware of tears, missing areas of pigment, or rips. It may be necessary to have a professional conservator do restoration work.
- Educate yourself by reading and asking questions about how forgers are able to "age" metal with chemicals and wood with paint. Repainting can diminish the value of a carved wooden piece. If you see paint inside splits or cracks (natural signs of aging in wood), it may well have been repainted.
- Keep records with as much information as you have or can find out about the artist, the materials used, the original cost, where it was purchased, who might have owned it before you (provenance). Notice if the work is signed. Keep anything that relates to the work, even a receipt with a signature.

PRESERVING THE WORK

Once you have acquired a work of folk art, you must take the steps necessary to preserve your folk art collectibles. Here are a few pointers.

- If you suspect that bugs may have infested and begun to damage a work, consider having it professionally exterminated to prevent further changes and damage.
- When framing an artwork, always use acid-free board as a backing, archival mats, and UF-3 plexiglass or UV glass used to filter ultraviolet radiation. To preserve without framing, store works on paper flat in an archival folder, covered with acid-free paper.
- Do not remove pastels framed under glass from their existing frames as this may cause a loss of pigment.
- Keep artwork out of direct sunlight, as some colors will fade.
- If an object's wear appears to be from neglect rather than natural aging, consider having it restored by a qualified professional conservator to maintain its value.
- If a work on paper is torn, have it professionally restored. Avoid tapes and glues that might harm the work. Rice paper applied with wheat glue is often used for restoration.
- Display or store the work in a climate-controlled area to avoid mildew and cracks.
- Store artworks on enameled metal shelves, wrapped in acid-free paper. Plywood or particle board emit chemicals that could damage metal or natural materials.

DISPLAYING THE COLLECTION

How you present a work of art can have an impact on its aesthetic appeal. Here are some tips to help you display your folk art to maximum advantage.

- If a piece was originally meant to be seen from below (such as a ship figurehead or shop sign) hang it above eye level.
- If a work needs protection from dust, have a plastic or glass display case made to size. A large, sculptural piece such as a stone sculpture, of course, would not need to be covered.

∾ Objects such as masks can be more easily seen if hung or displayed on a stand.

∾ Rotate the collection so a piece that has been in sunlight might "rest" in a dark corner from time to time.

CHARACTERISTICS OF PAINTINGS BY SELF-TAUGHT ARTISTS

Works of self-taught (or non-academic) artists tend to have certain qualities that set them apart from other works of art in their field. Although these characteristics don't apply to all such works, similar qualities are seen in many. The following lists provide typical characteristics for the works of self-taught artists in various types of folk art.

∾ Portraits might appear to be outlined, with flat rather than contoured faces.

∾ Heads might appear to not quite "match" the bodies. It is speculated that in Colonial America, some itinerant painters painted "bodies" during the winter, and traveled in the milder seasons to paint portrait heads to match the bodies.

∾ Figures may not be in proportion (heads and hands often larger than normal). Self-taught painters have greater difficulty with proportions simply because of lack of formal training.

∾ Hair typically doesn't appear to grow out of the head, but rather appears to rest on top of it.

∾ Children often resemble miniature old men and women.

∾ Figures are sometimes not in proportion to the background.

∾ The pictures often lack depth and have a skewed perspective. For example, a rug may not appear to lie flat or a tabletop may look tilted.

∾ Frequently, attention is given to minute detail such as objects found on a table or a woman's jewelry. In a landscape, plants will have every leaf; or animals, every spot. Grandma Moses' memory paintings of her childhood or Edward Hicks's farm scenes are examples of the work of two self-taught painters.

∾ Bright, flat areas of color give a childlike charm to the work. In fact some painters charged less if they didn't do "shading." (In painting it is called *modeling*). An artist trained in the French Academy (therefore an *academic* artist) would have learned how to subdue colors through mixing.

~ Outsider and folk artists use very little shading, and often use simple media such as felt pens or oil pastels.

~ The artwork often shows either simplicity of design or the exact opposite—intricately detailed or patterned compositions.

~ Found materials such as old fabric swatches, pieces of wood, glass, or metal are occasionally incorporated into a painting or sculpture.

~ In so-called outsider art, the artist had a single-minded dedication to a social, religious, or cultural message, shown either by the images (angels, devils, sexually explicit figures) or by a written message incorporated into the artwork. Many artists paint in a deliberately "primitive" style.

FAMOUS NAÏVE ARTISTS

Self-taught artists sometimes become famous for their individualistic style and because they didn't have to "unlearn" what they might have been taught in an academy for formal art education. The following lists feature some of the more famous self-taught folk (or naïve) artists, grouped by country or region where they lived and worked. Where only a single date is given, it is the year of the artist's birth, unless otherwise noted as the year(s) in which the artist was active; if the year of his or her death is given, a "d." will precede the date.

FRANCE

These two artists have become "mainstream" painters, but they were self-taught, and their work had a distinguishing naïve quality.

Gauguin, Paul, 1848–1903. A banker by training, Gauguin broke all the rules with the use of flat, unrealistic color. He, along with others of his generation, was attracted by the "primitive." His escape to the simple life in Tahiti gave new impetus to his colorful work. Gauguin was a colleague of van Gogh, and he exhibited with the Impressionists.

Rousseau, Henri, 1844–1910. Rousseau was a customs agent by profession before he became a painter. He painted wild animals and forests from the "jungles" of the Paris Botanical and Zoological Gardens.

UNITED STATES

When America was still a relatively young country, many of these people were the "fine artists" of their day, even though they might have been self-taught or "primitive." Many are considered major painters in the history of American Art.

A. J. (the only name by which his work is identified), active c. 1820. A. J. created retablos (altar paintings) in the New Mexico region for missionaries to use in their churches as teaching tools for Christianity.

Aragon, José, active 1820–1835. Carved Santos (figures of saints), sometimes inscribed with poems.

Durrie, George Henry, 1820–1863. Known for his oil-painted landscapes (particularly snowcaps) and portraits, his work inspired Currier and Ives lithographs and was even copied outright by Grandma Moses.

Field, Erastus Salisbury, 1805–1900. Painter of complex allegorical scenes and portraits.

Hicks, Edward, 1780–1849. A sign painter who became famous for historical scenes featuring people, animals, and frequently "inspirational" messages written around the borders.

Phillips, Ami, 1788–1865. Colonial itinerant portrait artist. He is one of the few limners known by name. (*Limner* is a word taken from "illuminer," the European medieval craftsmen who painted illuminated manuscripts.)

Robb, Samuel, active 1875–1900. Robb was considered one of the most important carvers of cigar store figures—such as Native American men and women.

Savage, Edward, 1761–1817. Painted portraits of families, often strangely distorted.

Shimmel, Wilhelm, active c. 1850–1895. An itinerant carver of eagles and other animals (over 500 roosters), his work is highly prized for its fine detail. Although he died in poverty, his carvings are among the highest priced folk carvings.

20ᵀᴴ-CENTURY OUTSIDER AND FOLK ARTISTS

As used today, an "outsider" artist is an individual who may be completely self-taught, or who has a unique inner vision that simply must be expressed through artwork. It means literally that the artist has not received traditional academic training, or that the subject matter is outside the norm for the culture in which the artist lives. Some outsider artists may have spent part of their lives in institutions or may have allowed their religious and cultural beliefs to dominate their lives and their art. The work of some individuals shows a sexual or religious obsession that comes out in the only way they know to express it.

Some folk artists are simply country people who enjoy working with their hands to make something they consider beautiful or instructional. Much folk art of this type is made with recycled and found materials such as wood, bottle caps, sheet metal, aluminum foil, matchsticks, painted boards, or broken pottery. Other descriptive terms for such artists are folk, self-taught, primitive, naïve, and visionary.

One other type of folk artist is the person who may have continued work learned through family tradition either in the United States or another country in which the artist grew up. This could include such artists as the Hispanic Santero carver, Native American basket weaver, or Cambodian silk weaver.

CROATIA

In Croatia, contemporary naïve (self-taught) painters have received considerable recognition for their skillful renditions of the countryside and village life.

Fejes, Emerik, 1904–1969. An "urban modern primitive," Fejes painted pictures of his travels.

Gazi, Dragan, active 1970s. Paintings of village life on glass

Generalic, Ivan, 1914. Known for his "art of the people"—highly detailed paintings of village life, celebrations, portraits

Kovacic, Mijo, active 1980s. Biblical stories reminiscent of the Flemish painter Breughel

Lackovic, Ivan, 1932. Colorful oil paintings that include minute detail in scenes of village life

Vecenaj, Ivan, active 1970s. Childlike biblical interpretations painted with oil on glass

ENGLAND

Gill, Madge, 1882–1961. A London housewife and "spiritualist" (she was inspired from the "spirit world"), she made richly patterned, detailed ink drawings that featured staring female faces.

FRANCE

Bauchant, André, 1873–1958. A gardener by profession, Bauchant specialized in historical paintings and scenes of peasant life.

Bombois, Camille, 1883–1970. A former wrestler and circus strongman, Bombois painted peasants and their surroundings.

Lagru, Dominique, 1873–1960. Lagru was a herdsman, obviously spending a great deal of time outdoors. His prehistoric landscapes featuring dinosaurs (often seen in books) are rich in texture and pattern.

NETHERLANDS

van Genk, Willem, 1927. Extremely detailed pen-and-ink drawing/collages

SWITZERLAND

Wolfli, Adolf, 1864–1930. An "outsider" who, during his 35 years in an asylum, produced collages of imaginary travels, accompanied by extensive written text

"Primitive art . . . is something made by people with a direct and immediate response to life."
—HENRY MOORE, 1898–1986, English sculptor and graphic artist

UNITED STATES

Adkins, Garland, 1928–1997. Adkins's specialty was horse images that he carved and painted.

Adkins, Minnie, 1934. Kentucky artists, Minnie and Garland carved and painted animals and Bible scenes. Quilts with her animal designs are made by her and her neighbors.

Aiken, Gayleen, 1934. A Vermont artist, Aiken became known for her word-and-picture paintings of cats and her life.

Amezcua, Consuelo "Chelo," 1903–1975. Colored ballpoint pens, paper, or cardboard were selected by Mexican-born Texas artist Chelo for her intricate "Texas filigree art" drawings.

Anderson, John, 1953. Anderson, a Virginian, sculpts in both wood and metal. His background as a certified welder is evident in his large sculptures created from rusted auto parts.

Archuleta, Felipe, 1910–1991. Called "the best of the New Mexican carvers," Archuleta's large carved animal sculpture in the Santero tradition are avidly collected.

Archuleta, Leroy, 1949. Continuing his father Felipe's tradition, Leroy also carves and paints in cottonwood.

Arning, Eddie, 1898–1993. Arning, who was schizophrenic, was institutionalized most of his life. His fantasy drawings were his personal vision of newspaper stories and the popular culture.

Ashby, Steve, 1904–1980. This Western artist called his sculptures from wood, cloth, and found objects "fixing ups."

Badami, Andrea, 1913. Badami, born in Nebraska, traveled extensively. His "storytelling" oil paintings and portraiture of children are greatly prized.

Bell, Ralph, 1913–1995. Bell, an Ohio artist who lived in an institution most of his life, did childlike paintings on wood of people and animals.

Besharo, Peter (Attie), d. 1962. A Syrian-born Pennsylvania resident, Besharo's fantasy paintings on wood are seen in galleries and books.

Black, Minnie, 1899–1996. Black, a Kentucky artist, grew her own gourds, which she transformed into fantasy animals.

Blackmon, William "Prophet," 1913. Stories of the Bible and his personal visions inspire Blackmon's paintings. His Revival Center in Wisconsin was the center of his life.

Blayney, William A., 1918–1985. Blayney's colorful paintings based on heaven and hell include Biblical quotations.

Blizzard, Georgia, 1919. Blizzard makes low-fired clay figural pots and plaques based on Native American techniques learned from her Apache father. She is a Virginia resident.

Bolden, Hawkins, 1914. Hawkins, who is blind, uses found materials for his scarecrows and mask-like constructions. He lives in Memphis, Tennessee.

Boudreaux, A. J. "Sainte-James Boudrot," 1948. This New Orleans resident, a former attorney, specializes in "funerary art," paintings in bright colors that feature funeral notices on the back.

Bowlin, Loy A. "Rhinestone Cowboy," 1909–1995. Everything about Mississippi artist Bowlin glittered—his clothing and car, his walls, and furniture. The glitter, sequins, and rhinestones on his drawings and paintings were just another part of his life.

Bridgers, Herman, 1912–1990. Bridgers made people "cutouts" of wood, statues for his "Shady Grove House of Prayer" in North Carolina.

Brito, Frank, Sr., 1922. This Southwestern carver of "santos" and animals is considered more innovative than some of the "santeros" (saint carvers).

Brown, Russell (Smoky), 1919. Collages of found materials, paintings of oil on canvas, and painted "monsters" are the specialty of this Ohio artist.

Butler, David, 1898–1997. Butler's whimsical shaped, pierced, and painted tin sculptures decorated his Louisiana home and yard.

Butler, Edward, 1941. Butler did carvings about black history. His early work was made of bundles of matchsticks.

Carpenter, Miles B., 1889–1985. Carpenter's home in Virginia featured root monsters (painted carvings).

Clawson, Rex, 1933. Clawson is a New Yorker born in Texas. His richly embellished paintings are represented by a number of galleries.

Coins, Raymond, 1904–1998. This Southern folk carver of angels, stone baby dolls, and animals has work represented in museums and galleries.

Coker, Jerry, 1938. Coker, a Florida resident, makes tin masks and brightly painted "Impressionistic" sculptures.

Cordero, Helen, 1916–1994. Cordero, a Native American, originated story-teller dolls (seated human or animal ceramic figures surrounded by babies) in memory of her grandfather, a Cochiti Pueblo clown. Her concept has been widely copied throughout the Southwest.

Craig, Burlon, 1914. Craig, a North Carolina native, has been making traditional pots since he was 14. His ceramic face pots are found in many collections.

Criss, Abraham Lincoln, 1914–2000. Criss, who was born in Virginia but lived in New Jersey, became known for his carved wooden animals and people. He made drawings as well as carvings.

Darger, Henry J., 1892–1973. Darger, a Chicagoan, who was institutionalized, created 20,000 drawings that were not discovered until after his death. His disturbed, intricate cartoon-like drawings of children playing have been widely exhibited.

Darmafall, Powell (Paul) "Glassman," 1925. He is known for his broken bottle/mixed media collages.

Davis, Patrick, c. 1943. Davis, a Guyanian by birth, now lives in Texas where he uses found materials to produce his humorous sculpted figures such as men with hats and ties.

Dawson, William, 1901–1990. This Chicago artist is known for his "totem-like" painted carvings, which sometimes included chicken bones.

DePrie, Gerald "Creative," 1935–1999. DePrie's boldly outlined action pencil drawings usually involve people and architecture. He lived in West Virginia.

Dey, Uncle Jack, 1912–1978. Virginian Jack Dey's paintings, inspired by his dreams, often featured crows.

Dial, Thornton, Jr., 1953. This patriarch of a large family of folk artists in Georgia is a painter and sculptor who often uses themes about human relationships.

Doyle, Sam (Uncle Sam), 1906–1985. Doyle's colorful paintings, mostly portraits on roofing tin, are based on the Gullah culture off the Southeast coast of the United States.

Dulaney, Burgess, 1914. Dulaney's unfired painted figural mud sculptures are created in his native Northern Mississippi.

Edmondson, William, 1870–1951. Edmondson is one of the most famous folk carvers, known for his limestone carvings of angels and Biblical figures. He lived near Nashville, Tennessee.

Evans, Minnie, 1892–1987. Evans was born in North Carolina. Her richly colored, dream-inspired patterned paintings of figures and flowers are represented in several books about folk art.

Farmer, Josephus, 1894–1989. Southern-born, he created bas-relief carved and painted panels about Biblical and political subjects. He was a minister, founding a church in Missouri.

Ferdinand, Roy, 1959. His drawings in ink and tempera are based on the brutality he has seen and experienced as a native of New Orleans.

Finster, Howard, 1916–2001. One of the better-known folk artists, he founded an "environment," the Paradise Garden and Folk Art Church, and his sacred art paintings are exhibited and sold through dozens of galleries.

Godie, Lee, 1908–1994. Godie is a homeless Chicago "bag lady/street artist." Her watercolor and ink paintings, her self-portraits, and "Prince Charming" (an idealized male figure) are in many collections.

Gordon, Ted, 1924. A Californian, his specialty is obsessive pen-and-ink "doodle" drawings of faces and some animals.

Hampton, James, 1909–1964. Hampton's 180-piece aluminum assemblage *Throne of the Third Heaven of the Nationals Millennium General Assembly* was created in his garage.

Harvey, Bessie, 1929–1994. Tennesseean Harvey's found wood assemblages and drawings were based on spiritual visions.

Harvey, John, 1951. His paintings with Biblical texts often include dogs, which he feels represent evil.

Hawkes, Gerald, 1943–1998. Baltimore resident Hawkes's stained matchstick sculpture has been exhibited in Baltimore's Visionary Art Museum.

Hawkins, William, 1895–1990. His bold, expressionistic cityscape and house paintings are painted with semi-gloss enamel on plywood and masonite. Hawkins was from Ohio.

Herrera, Nicholas, 1964. This Southwestern painter, also known as the El Rio Santero, carves saints and retablos (paintings on board).

Hirshfield, Morris, 1872–1946. Hirshfield worked in the New York garment industry after emigrating from Lithuania, and was a carver early in his career. His paintings of women and animals sometimes featured painted fabric draperies.

Holley, Lonnie, 1950. Alabamian Holley's found object installations are in numerous galleries.

Howard, Jesse, 1885–1983. "Free Thought, Free Speech, And Jesse Howard Is My Name" is a typical expression of Howard's thousands of painted signs expressing his thoughts. A Missourian, his work is in numerous folk art collections.

Hunter, Clementine, 1885–1987. A Southerner, Hunter painted her experiences and the lives of black people in the countryside.

Hussey, Billy Ray, 1955. Wheel-thrown face and character jugs are typical forms of expression for this North Carolina potter.

Isik, Levent, 1961. Canadian-born Isik lives in Ohio, where he creates intricate patterned paintings of cityscapes and Biblical themes, as well as mixed media constructions.

Jennings, James Harold, 1931–1999. Jennings lived in North Carolina, creating brightly colored wooden "constructs," angels, bird houses, and Ferris wheels.

Jimenez, Alonzo, 1949. This New Mexican artist learned to make animal woodcarvings from Felipe Archuleta, the great "santero." He began carving at a very young age, and is best-known for African animals, cats, and coyotes.

Johnson, Anderson, 1915–1998. Johnson was a preacher in Virginia. He did many paintings of women ("because that's what I do best"), animals, landscapes, and people from the Bible.

Jones, Frank, 1900–1969. Jones, a Texan, was imprisoned for life and became known for the "devil houses" he drew, based on his personal experiences and view of life.

Jones, Joan Julene, 1950. Jones is a "Louisiana Living Treasure" whose metal sculptures painted with acrylics express her joy of living and great pleasure in working with children.

Jones, M. C. "5¢," 1917. In his watercolor and oil portraits of rural life, he is inspired by dreams, his religious beliefs, and his memory of plantation life in Louisiana.

Jones, S. L. (Shields Landon), 1901–1997. Jones, from West Virginia, did not become an artist until he retired from his work for the railroad. His carvings of horses, men, and women and his drawings frequently include his favorite subject, horses.

Kane, John, 1860–1934. One of the best-known self-taught artists, he was born in Scotland but worked in Pittsburgh, specializing in industrial scenes. His self-portrait, once seen, is never to be forgotten. His work is in many museums.

Kennedy, Leon, 1945. His large paintings feature religious life and everyday activities.

Kinney, Charlie, 1906–1991. Kentucky-born Kinney's "haints" (ghosts) and storytelling watercolors featured Bible stories, local history, and legends.

Kinney, Hazel, 1929. Hazel, also of Kentucky, makes detailed and realistic "Bible pictures" and small unfired clay figures that she paints.

Kinney, Noah, 1912–1991. Noah was Charley Kinney's brother, specializing in carved wooden figures and hand-carved puppets.

Krans, Olof, 1838–1916. A Swedish immigrant, Krans settled in Bishop Hill, Illinois, where he painted portraits and historical scenes of that community.

Lebduska, Lawrence, 1894–1966. Baltimore-born Lebduska's richly embellished paintings that include horses are found in a number of important museums and collections.

Lewis, Junior, 1948–1999. Lewis's specialty was carved devil heads and animal figures commonly found in Kentucky, where he lived. His Biblical scenes, such as his *Last Supper*, are considered masterpieces.

Lewis, Tim, 1952. Lewis continues this Kentucky family's carving tradition by making carved canes based on Bible stories, animals, and devils. His stone carvings are also a specialty.

Lopez, George, 1900–1993. This New Mexican carver's religious figures are unpainted.

Lucas, Charles, 1951. This Alabama artist does paintings of black history, but is better known for his scrap metal larger-than-life figures.

Mackintosh, Dwight, 1906–1999. Mackintosh, institutionalized for 56 of his 93 years, used a felt-tipped pen for his line drawings of human figures, animals, and yellow buses.

Maldonado, Alex A., 1901–1989. Beginning as a painter at age 60, Maldonado, who was born in Mexico, painted fantasies of the future, space travel, and astronomy.

Materson, Raymond, 1954. He uses one of the more unusual materials for his religious "paintings"—unraveled socks!

Meaders, Lanier, 1917–1998. Lanier was one of the Meaders family of artists who lived in Georgia. His jugs, pitchers, and face jugs placed him at the forefront of Southern potters of the 20th century.

Memkus, Frank, 1865–1965. The patriotic whirligig in the Chicago Art Institute's collection is the only piece of folk art ever known to have been created by Memkus, a European immigrant who lived in Milwaukee, Wisconsin.

Miller, Reuben "R.A.," 1912. Miller, a resident of Georgia, specializes in making whirligigs and cutout tin forms of animals, devils, angels, and humans.

Morgan, Sister Gertrude, 1900–1980. Sister Morgan's visionary paintings of angels, children, and herself, dressed in white, were several forms of religious expression for this Alabama native. She was a gospel singer and preacher in several different southern cities.

Moses, Anna Mary Robertson (Grandma Moses), 1860–1961. Moses is probably the best-known folk artist of the United States. Her colorful paintings were inspired by country life in upstate New York. Like many other self-taught artists, she did not begin painting until late in life.

Murry, J. B., 1908–1988. Murry, who lived in Georgia, was inspired by a vision in 1970 to make colorful paintings and "spirit drawings."

O'Kelly, Mattie Lou, 1908–1997. This Georgia painter specialized in landscapes and nostalgic memory paintings of her life in the country.

Ortega, José, 1858–1941. Also known as "The Master of the Dotted Line" (because he frequently decorated his figures with fine black dots), Ortega was considered the last of the New Mexican santeros (saint carvers).

Person, Leroy, 1907–1985. Person, a North Carolina resident, carved, incised, painted, and crayon-colored furniture, plants, and animals.

Philpot, David, 1940. A Chicago artist, Philpot was inspired to make carved and painted staffs in the African American tradition by seeing the movie *The Bible*.

Pickett, Joseph, 1848–1918. Pickett decorated the concessions that he ran at carnivals before becoming a painter. Few of his landscapes have survived, but are appreciated for their limited palette of yellow, green, red, and brown.

Pierce, Elijah, 1892–1984. This well-known Columbus, Ohio, folk artist was a barber for 50 years. His carved and painted wood artworks using religious and patriotic themes have been called "sermons in wood."

Pippin, Horace, 1888–1946. Pippin, an African American, had painted prior to World War I, but after a return from the war with a paralyzed arm, he began his technique of burning lines in wood prior to painting, which helped him regain use of his arm. He painted scenes of everyday life, but also recorded some history of African Americans (such as a scene that featured John Brown).

Ramirez, Martin, 1885–1960. Ramirez's symbolic drawings of his inner thoughts were created during the 30 years he was confined to a California mental hospital for schizophrenia.

Rizzoli, A. G. "Achilles," 1896–1981. An Italian-Swiss immigrant, Rizzoli saw himself as the "earthly architect and transcriber for God." His visionary architectural drawings and fantasy community were accompanied by writings and other illustrations.

Robertson, Royal, 1930. A Louisiana resident, he was divorced after 19 years of marriage. His roadside signs, Biblical messages, and visionary paintings feature a futuristic world and his bitterness about women.

Rodia, Simon, 1874–1954. Rodia worked in the construction industry and was a tile setter. He spent 33 years constructing towers and walls of metal, concrete, stone, tile, and broken ceramics on his small lot in Los Angeles. His *Watts Towers* (so-called because they are in the Watts section) in Los Angeles have become world-renowned. The *Towers* have recently been restored and are open to the public.

Rogers, Sulton, 1922–2003. Rogers was born in Mississippi but lived in New York. He was famous for religious carvings of men and women with long tongues, snakes, and male and female devils. His work is in many museums.

Rowe, Nellie Mae, 1900–1982. Rowe was inspired by visions and dreams to create the paintings and sculptures that have made her work so widely appreciated.

Ruley, Ellis, 1882–1959. Ruley's paintings of popular images of animals, the scenery near his Norwich, Connecticut, home, and scantily dressed women were not appreciated until after his death.

Sanchez, Mario, 1908. Sanchez's brightly painted carved wood reliefs of old Key West are based on the history of descendants of Cuban cigar makers who came to Florida.

Savitsky, John, 1910–1991. Savitsky began painting when the coal mines in which he had worked were shut down. Although he had painted with oil and acrylic paints, he later worked mostly in pencil and colored pencil to make drawings of the life of the coal miner in Pennsylvania.

Scott, Lorenzo, 1934. Scott is a Georgia resident. His religious images are the result of "conversations with God" and are framed in his own "Baroque" handmade frames.

Serl, Jon, 1894–1993. Serl's paintings of men, women, and animals are from his personal experiences as a child vaudeville performer and dancer.

Simpson, Vollis, 1919. Simpson's huge wind-driven whirligig subjects are such things as an airplane, buggy, or bicyclist. Many visitors come to his Lucama, North Carolina, home.

Singleton, Herbert, 1945. Singleton's bas-relief carved commentaries on life in New Orleans, the wickedness of women, religious themes, and his perception of the African American life are so well crafted that he is considered by many to be one of the best folk carvers.

Sudduth, Jimmy Lee, 1910. Sudduth's surreal mud/craft paint pictures are usually on plywood or board. His wife (now dead) was sometimes his subject. He lives in Alabama.

Swearingen, Rev. Johnnie, 1908–1993. Swearingen's paintings are inspired by the Bible and his life as a Texas rural preacher.

Thomas, James "Son," 1926–1993. A Mississippi musician, Thomas created clay skulls and portrait busts, sometimes using real teeth.

Tolliver, Mose, 1915. Tolliver's brightly colored, sometimes erotic figure-paintings are on wood and are much sought-after.

Tolson, Edgar, 1904–1984. Tolson is considered one of Kentucky's finest wood sculptors. He specialized in Biblical themes with figures and animals.

Traylor, Bill, 1854–1947. Traylor is a master storyteller through his drawings. His work, which strongly resembles West African images, is in many major museums.

Turrell, Terry, 1946. Turrell's work is a combination of wood sculpture and painting. He lives and works in Seattle.

Van Wie, Carrie, 1880–1947. Most of Van Wie's detailed architectural drawings of San Francisco, where she lived, were done early in the 20th century.

Walker, Inez Nathaniel, c. 1907–1990. Walker's pencil-and-marker drawings of elaborately coiffed women were done during her imprisonment (for murder) in a South Carolina correctional institution.

Warmack, Gregory, 1948. "Mr. Imagination" lives in Chicago, where he finds the materials he incorporates into his bottle-cap sculpture and large collages.

Watson, Willard "Texas Kid," 1921–1995. A North Carolina toymaker, Watson made accurate reproductions of farm implements and mechanical jointed wooden toys. His stagecoaches, mule-drawn wagons, and mechanical mule and farmer were designed from memory.

West, Myrtice, 1923. West, from Alabama, makes highly detailed paintings based on her visions of occurrences in Revelations, Daniel, and Ezekiel (books of the Bible), as well as memory paintings.

Willeto, Charlie, 1906–1964. Willeto's work included carved figures of spirits and people.

Williams, Chuck, 1957. Williams specializes in paintings of rock music video personalities.

Willis, Wesley, 1963. Willis, a native of Chicago, uses colored pen to draw trains and architecture. He sometimes sells his drawings in the subway.

Yoakum, Joseph, 1886–1972. Yoakum, who was born on a Navajo reservation, moved to Chicago, where he made almost 2,000 dreamscape drawings (landscapes from places, events, travels) in the last ten years of his life.

Zeldis, Malcah, 1931. Following her own rules, this New Yorker does paintings of her life, her religion, her environment, and her heroes.

FAMOUS FOLK ART ENVIRONMENTS

Folk art environments are relatively small areas that surround the home of a self-taught artist. They usually begin when an artist is inspired to change natural objects by painting them, or evolve when an artist's production has to move outside to make more room indoors. Art environments are usually created with found materials such as bottles, broken china (used as tiles set in concrete), leftover paint, aluminum foil, furniture, and metal and wood scraps. Many of these "grassroots" structures appear to grow in a somewhat chaotic manner. Some folk art environments or structures have been relocated to museums. (For example, James Hampton's *Throne of the Third Heaven of the Nationals Millennium General Assembly* is now in the National Museum of American Art.) A few environments have been "adopted" by companies or civic groups in order to preserve them. The following are some well-known folk art environments, grouped by country.

FRANCE

Region	Artist	Date	Title of Work	Description
Hauterives	Cheval, Ferdinand	1836–1924	*Palais Idéal*	concrete-over-steel environment
Rothéneuf	Fouré, Adolphe-Julien	1839–1910	*Les Roches sculptés*	figures sculpted on rock

UNITED STATES

Region	Artist	Date	Title of Work	Description
California				
Los Angeles	Rodia, Simon	1874–1965	*The Watts Towers of Simon Rodia,* 1921–1955	Tile-over-metal sculpture, recently renovated
Niland County	Knight, Leonard	1931	*Salvation Mountain*	Paint poured on a hill; religious messages placed near the bottom of the hill
Simi Valley	Prisbrey, Tressa "Grandma"	1896–1988	Bottle Village 1955–1972	Bottle Village is now not open to the public but may be seen from the outside
Woodland Hills	Ehn, John	1896–1981	Old Trapper's Lodge, c. 1941–1956	Historical and fictional characters constructed of wire and cement, moved to Pierce College
District of Columbia				
Washington	Hampton, James	1909–1964	*Throne of the Third Heaven . . . Millennium General Assembly,* 1954	180-piece aluminum assemblage, now displayed at National Museum of American Art
Georgia				
Buena Vista	Martin, Eddie Owens	1908–1986	*Pasaquan,* 1957–1986	A self-styled spiritual center that includes shrines, gates, and walls

Region	Artist	Date	Title of Work	Description
Georgia (continued)				
Pennvillee	Finster, Howard	1916–2001	*Paradise Garden and Folk Art Church,* 1970s–present	*Paradise Garden* may still be visited
Kansas				
Humboldt	Woods, Dave	1885–1975	Untitled	Found-object environment filled with artwork created from items ranging from hula-hoops to venetian blinds. Many of his pieces have also been purchased by the Kansas Glass-Roots Association.
Wilson	Root, Ed	1867–1959	Untitled	A cast-concrete environment with found objects and glass embedded. Many pieces have been purchased by the Kansas Glass-Roots Association in Lucas, Kansas.
New York				
Woodstock	Schmidt, Clarence	1897–1978	*Woodstock Environment (House of Mirrors),* c. 1938–1968	This one-room cabin grew to 35 rooms filled with foil-covered assemblages and mirrors. Destroyed by fire in 1968.
North Carolina				
Lucama	Simpson, Vollis	1919	*Whirligig Environment,* 1980–1990	This display contains whirligigs, windmills, small airplanes, and a merry-go-round
Oregon				
Redmond	Peterson, Rasmus	1883–1952	*Peterson's Rock Garden*	A collection of rocks such as agate, jasper, and so on, were combined with mortar to create a miniature environment of buildings and bridges.

Region	Artist	Date	Title of Work	Description
Texas				
Houston	McKissack, Jeff	1902–1980	*The Orange Show,* 1955–1980	Built from found materials such as wheels and tiles over a 25-year period
Houston	Milkovisch, John	1912–1988	*Beer Can House,* c. 1960–1988	Milkovisch's home and garden have been transformed through the addition of rocks, marbles, and beer cans.
Virginia				
Waverly	Carpenter, Miles	1889–1985	*The Miles B. Carpenter Folk Art Museum,* c. 1960–1985	This is the artist's former home and serves as a setting for his own work and that of others.
Wisconsin				
Phillips	Smith, Fred	1885–1976	*Wisconsin Concrete Park,* 1950–1976	Contains 200 sculptures of historical and mythological characters created in concrete; maintained as a park

"Everything made by man's hands has a form, which must be either beautiful or ugly."

—WILLIAM MORRIS, 1834–1896, English craftsman and designer

MAJOR ARTS AND CRAFTS FESTIVALS

Small towns and large cities alike have become home to annual or semi-annual arts and crafts festivals. Many artists produce work throughout a certain portion of the year to be sold at these fairs. This list includes festivals that have become nationally known.

JANUARY

> Outsider Art Fair, Museum of American Folk Art, New York City
> Sotheby holds a sale of 20th-century folk art early in the year.

FEBRUARY

> Mid-States Craft Exhibit, Evansville, Indiana
> San Francisco Tribal, Folk, and Textile Art Show

MARCH

> Arts and Crafts Festival, Fairhope, Alabama
> Heard Museum Indian Fair, Phoenix, Arizona

APRIL

> Arkansas Folk Festival & Crafts Show, Mountain View, Arkansas
> Jazz and Heritage Festival, features a folk art section, New Orleans

MAY

> Kentucky Guild of Artists and Craftsmen's Fair, Berea, Kentucky
> Tribal Antiques Show, New York City

JUNE

> Contemporary Crafts Market, Santa Monica, California
> Frederick Craft Fair, Frederick, Maryland
> Mountain Heritage Arts and Crafts Festival, Harpers Ferry, West Virginia
> Northeast Crafts Fair, Rhinebeck, New York
> Omnicraft Festival, Owensboro, Kentucky (sponsored by Owensboro Museum)

JULY

Craftsman's Fair of the Southern Highlands, Asheville, North Carolina
Festival of American Folklife, The Mall, District of Columbia
Folk Art Fair, Santa Fe, New Mexico
Gatlinburg Craftsmen's Fair, Gatlinburg, Tennessee
Mountain State Art and Craft Fair, Ripley, West Virginia
Pacific Northwest Arts and Crafts Festival, Seattle, Washington
Spanish Market, Santa Fe, New Mexico

AUGUST

Appalachian Arts and Crafts Festival, Beckley, West Virginia
Craftsmen's Fair of the League of New Hampshire, Sunapee State Park,
  New Hampshire
Folk Fest, Atlanta, Georgia
Georgia Mountain Fair, Hiawassee, Georgia
Lowell Quilt Festival, Lowell, Massachusetts
Ozark Empire Fair, Springfield, Missouri
Santa Fe Indian Market, Santa Fe, New Mexico
South Carolina Arts and Crafts Festival, Easley, South Carolina
United Marine Craftsmen's Fair, Cumberland, Maine
Virginia Highlands Arts and Crafts Festival, Abingdon, Virginia
York State Craft Fair, Ithaca, New York

SEPTEMBER

Kentucky State Fair, Louisville
Morgan County Sorghum Festival, West Liberty, Kentucky
Ohio State Fair, Columbus

OCTOBER

Festival of Fine Craft, Millville, New Jersey
Kentuck Festival (sponsored by Kentuck Museum), Northport, Alabama
National Festival of Craftsmen, Silver Dollar City, Missouri
Ozark Arts and Crafts Show, War Eagle Mills, Arkansas
The Craftsman's Fall Festival, Gatlinburg, Tennessee

NOVEMBER

Los Angeles Tribal and Folk Art Show
Southeastern Arts and Crafts Fair, Macon, Georgia

MUSEUMS WITH SPECIAL FOLK ART COLLECTIONS

Many of these museums feature work created locally or, as in many of the Shaker settlements, simply demonstrate a way of life. The collections focus on festivals or the heritage of a country or culture as shown in the objects people created for daily use. They may also feature contemporary folk art.

Buenos Aires, Argentina	Museo de Motivos Argentinos José Hernandez
Vienna, Austria	Osterreichisches Museum für Volkskvade
Havana, Cuba	Museo de Arte Popular
Bath, England	American Museum in Britain (Claverton Manor)
Warwickshire, England	British Folk Art Collection, Compton Verney
Nice, France	Musée International d'Art Näif
Paris, France	Musée National des Arts et Traditions Populaires
Essen, Germany	Museum Folkwang
Athens, Greece	Benaki Museum; Museum of Greek Folk Art
Rome, Italy	Museo Nazionale delle Arti e Tradizioni Popolari
Tokyo, Japan	Folk Crafts Museum
Seoul, Korea	National Folklore Museum of Korea
Guadalajara, Mexico	Museo Regional de Guadalajara
Mexico City, Mexico	Museo de Arte Popular
Rotorua, New Zealand	Rotorua Museum of Art and History
Skien, Norway	Telemark County Museum
Lausanne, Switzerland	Collection d l'Art Brut

UNITED STATES

Alabama

Birmingham	Birmingham Museum of Art
Fayette	Fayette Art Museum
Mobile	Mobile Museum of Art
Montgomery	Museum of Fine Arts

Arizona

Flagstaff	Museum of Northern Arizona
Phoenix	Heard Museum
Tempe	Art Museum
Tucson	Arizona State Museum

Arkansas

Little Rock	Arkansas Arts Center
Mountain View	The Ozark Folk Center

California

Berkeley	University Art Museum
Los Angeles	Autry Museum of Western Heritage; Craft and Folk Art Museum; Los Angeles County Museum of Art; Southwest Museum
Oakland	Oakland Museum
San Diego	Mingei International Museum of World Folk Art; San Diego Museum of Art
San Francisco	Fine Arts Museum of San Francisco; San Francisco Craft and Folk Art Museum

Colorado

Colorado Springs	Colorado Springs Fine Art Center; Taylor Museum
Denver	Denver Art Museum

Connecticut

Bridgeport	Barnum Museum
Bridgeport	Connecticut Historical Society
Litchfield	Litchfield Historical Society
Mystic Seaport	Marine Historical Association, Inc.
New London	Lyman Allyn Art Museum
Riverton	Hitchcock Museum

Delaware

Winterthur	The Henry Francis du Pont Winterthur Museum

District of Columbia

Washington	Archives of American Art, Smithsonian Institution
	Daughters of the American Revolution Museum
	Index of American Design, National Gallery of Art
	National Museum of American Art, Smithsonian Institution
	National Museum of American History
	Phillips Collection

Florida

Coral Gables	Lowe Art Museum
Key West	East Martello Museum
Orlando	Menello Museum of American Folk Art
Sarasota	John and Mable Ringling Museum of Art

Georgia

Atlanta	High Museum of Art, Folk Art, and Photography Galleries; Atlanta Historical Society
Columbus	Columbus Museum
Macon	Museum of Arts and Sciences
Savannah	King-Tisdell Cottage Foundation

Illinois

Bishop Hill	Bishop Hill Heritage Museum
Charleston	Tarble Arts Center
Chicago	Art Institute of Chicago; Center for Intuitive and Outsider Art; Chicago Historical Society; Lithuanian Museum; Museum of Contemporary Art; Terra Museum of American Art

Indiana

Fort Wayne	Allen County–Fort Wayne Historical Society Museum
Peru	Circus City Festival Museum

Iowa

Amana	Amana Villages
Decorah	Vesterheim Norwegian American Museum

Kansas

Lawrence	Spencer Museum of Art
Lucas	Museum of Grassroots Art

Kentucky

Berea	Appalachian Museum
Bowling Green	Kentucky Museum
Frankfort	Kentucky Historical Society
Harrodsburg	Shaker Village of Pleasant Hill
Louisville	The Filson Club
Morehead	Kentucky Folk Art Center
Owensboro	Owensboro Mueum of Fine Art
Paducah	Museum of the American Quilter's Society
South Union	Shakertown at South Union

Louisiana

Alexandria	Alexandria Museum of Art
Baton Rouge	Riverside Museum/Louisiana Arts and Science Center
Lafayette	University Art Museum
New Orleans	New Orleans Museum of Art
Shreveport	Meadows Museum of Art

Maine

Augusta	Maine State Museum
Bath	Maine Maritime Museum
Blue Hill	Parson Fisher House
Poland Spring	United Society of Shakers, Sabbathday Lake
Rockland	William A. Farnsworth Library and Art Museum
Saco	York Institute
Southwest Harbor	Wendell Gilley Museum
Waterville	Bixler Art and Music Center; Colby College Museum of Art

Maryland

Baltimore	American Visionary Art Museum; Baltimore Museum of Art
Havre de Grace	Havre de Grace Decoy Museum
Rockville	Latvian Museum
St. Michaels	Chesapeake Bay Maritime Museum
Salisbury	Ward Museum of Wildfowl Art

Massachusetts

Cambridge	Fruitlands Museum, Harvard
Dedham	Museum of Bad Art, "Art Too Bad to Be Ignored"
Deerfield	Historic Deerfield
Essex County	Cogswell Grant
Hancock	Hancock Shaker Village Museum

Lowell	New England Quilt Museum
Nantucket	Whaling Museum of the Nantucket Historical Association
New Bedford	New Bedford Whaling Museum
Salem	Peabody Essex Museum
Sandwich	Heritage Plantation of Sandwich
Sharon	Kendall Whaling Museum
Sturbridge	Museum of Fine Arts, Old Sturbridge Village
Worcester	Worcester Art Museum; Worcester Historical Museum

Michigan

Dearborn	Henry Ford Museum and Greenfield Village
Detroit	Detroit Historical Museum; Detroit Institute of the Arts

Minnesota

Minneapolis	The Minnesota Institute of Arts
St. Paul	Minnesota Historical Society

Mississippi

Clarksdale	Delta Blues Museum
Greenwood	Cottonlandia Museum
Jackson	Mississippi State Historical Museum; Smith Robertson Museum
Oxford	University of Mississippi

Missouri

Kansas City	Nelson-Atkins Museum of Art
St. Louis	St. Louis Art Museum

Nebraska

Lincoln	Sheldon Memorial Art Gallery

New Hampshire

Canterbury	Shaker Village
Manchester	The Currier Gallery of Art
Portsmouth	Strawbery Banke

New Jersey

Freehold	Monmouth County Historical Association
New Brunswick	American/Hungarian Heritage Center Museum
Newark	Newark Museum
Trenton	New Jersey State Museum

New Mexico

Albuquerque	Albuquerque Museum of Art, History and Science; Maxwell Museum of Anthropology
Santa Fe	Museum of International Folk Art; Wheelwright Museum of the American Indian
Taos	Millicent Rogers Museum

New York

Albany	Shaker Heritage Society
Brooklyn	Brooklyn Museum
Cooperstown	New York State Historical Association; Fenimore House
Mumford	Genesee Country Museum
New York City	Museum of American Folk Art; Cooper Union Museum
Old Chatham	Shaker Museum
Utica	Munson-Williams-Proctor Institute

North Carolina

Asheville	Asheville Art Museum; Southern Highland Craft Guild at the Folk Art Center
Chapel Hill	Ackland Art Museum

Charlotte	Mint Museum of Craft and Design
Raleigh	North Carolina Museum of Art; Visual Arts Center, North Carolina State University
Robbins	Southern Folk Pottery Collectors Society/Shop and Museum
Rocky Mount	The Lynch Collection
Wilmington	St. John's Museum of Art
Winston-Salem	Old Salem and Museum of Early Southern Decorative Arts

Ohio

Akron	Akron Art Museum
Cleveland	Western Reserve Historical Society
Columbus	Columbus Museum of Art, Ohio Historical Center
Oberlin	Allen Memorial Art Museum
Oxford	Miami University Art Museum
Zoar	Zoar Village State Memorial

Oklahoma

| Oklahoma City | National Cowboy Hall of Fame and Western Heritage Center |

Pennsylvania

Bethlehem	Lehigh University Art Galleries
Doylestown	Bucks County Historical Society
Hershey	Hershey Museum of American Life
Lancaster	Pennsylvania Farm Museum of Landis Valley
Lenhartsville	Pennsylvania Dutch Folk Culture Society
Philadelphia	Philadelphia Maritime Museum
West Chester	Chester County Historical Society

Rhode Island

| Providence | Rhode Island Historical Society |

South Carolina

Columbia	The University of South Carolina McKissick Museum
Edgefield	Pottersville Museum

South Dakota

Mitchell	Museum of Pioneer Life

Tennessee

Knoxville	Knoxville Museum of Art
Nashville	Tennessee State Museum; Carl Van Vechten Gallery of Fine Arts; Cheekwood Fine Arts Center
Norris	Museum of Appalachia

Texas

Beaumont	Art Museum of Southeast Texas
Canyon	Panhandle-Plains Historical Museum
Dallas	Dallas Museum of Art; Museum of African-American Life and Culture
Houston	Bayou Bend Collection; Museum of Fine Arts; Menil Collection

Utah

Salt Lake City	Chase Home Museum of Utah Folk Art

Vermont

Bennington	Bennington Museum
Brownington	Old Stone House Museum
Middlebury	The Sheldon Museum; Vermont Folklife Center
Montpelier	Vermont Museum
Shelburne	Shelburne Museum

Virginia

Clintwood	Cumberland Museum
Ferrum	Blue Ridge Institute and Farm Museum
Glen Allen	Meadow Farm Museum
Newport News	The Mariners Museum
Norfolk	Chrysler Museum
Richmond	Folk Art Society of America; Owensboro Museum of Fine Art; Valentine Museum; Meadow Farm Museum
Roanoke	Art Museum of Western Virginia; Roanoke Museum of Fine Arts
Waverly	Miles B. Carpenter Folk Art Museum
Williamsburg	Abby Aldrich Rockefeller American Folk Art Center

West Virginia

Huntington	Huntington Museum of Art
Wheeling	Oglebay Institute Mansion Museum

Wisconsin

Baraboo	Circus World Museum
Madison	State Historical Society of Wisconsin
Milwaukee	Milwaukee Art Museum; University of Wisconsin Art Museum; Villa Terrace Decorative Arts Museum
Mount Horeb	Wisconsin Folk Art Museum
Sheboygan	John Michael Kohler Arts Center

"Limitations of technique often comprise the charm and energy of primitive painting. Expansion, on the other hand, draws the art into decadence."

—GEORGES BRAQUE, 1882–1963, French Cubist painter

NATIONAL HERITAGE FELLOWS OF AMERICA

Since 1982, America's "Living National Treasures" (artists selected for their skills in the performing or visual arts) have been recognized as National Heritage Fellows at an annual ceremony on the George Washington University campus in Washington, DC. The following list includes fellows from the visual arts only. Artists are identified by their year of induction and the description of the artisans and their work as it is listed in the official National Heritage Fellowships 2000 Program.

1982	George Lopez, santos woodcarver, Cordova, New Mexico
1982	Elijah Pierce, carver/painter, Columbus, Ohio
1982	Georgeann Robinson, Osage ribbonworker, Bartlesville, Oklahoma
1982	Duff Severe, saddlemaker and rawhide worker, Pendleton, Oregon
1982	Philip Simmons, blacksmith, ornamental ironworker, Charleston, South Carolina
1983	Mike Manteo, Sicilian marionettist, Staten Island, New York
1983	Lanier Meaders, potter, Cleveland, Georgia
1983	Alex Stewart, cooper (wooden barrel maker) and woodworker, Sneedville, Tennessee
1983	Ada Thomas, Chitimacha basket maker, Charenton, Louisiana
1983	Lucinda Toomer, African American quilter, Dawson, Georgia
1983	Lem Ward, decoy carver, painter, Crisfield, Maryland
1984	Bertha Cook, knotted-bedspread maker, Boone, North Carolina
1984	Burlon Craig, potter, Vale, North Carolina

1984	Mary Jane Manigault, African American seagrass basket maker, Mount Pleasant, South Carolina
1984	Genevieve Nahra Mougin, Lebanese American lace maker, Bettendorf, Iowa
1984	Margaret Tafoya, Santa Clara Pueblo potter, Espanola, New Mexico
1984	Paul Tiulana, Eskimo mask maker/dancer/singer, Anchorage, Alaska
1985	Eppie Archuleta, Hispanic weaver, Alamosa, Colorado
1985	Meadi'i Kalama, Hawaiian quilter, Honolulu, Hawaii
1985	Leif Melgaard, Norwegian American woodcarver, Minneapolis, Minnesota
1985	Alice New Holy Blue Legs, Lakota-Sioux quill artist, Ogala, South Dakota
1986	Ernest Bennett, Anglo American whittler, Indianapolis, Indiana
1986	Helen Cordero, potter, Cochiti Pueblo, New Mexico
1986	Sonia Domsch, Czech American bobbin lace maker, Atwood, Kansas
1986	Jennie Thlunaut, Tlingit Chilkat blanket weaver, Haines, Alaska
1987	Juan Alindato, carnival maskmaker, Ponce, Puerto Rico
1987	Genoveva Castellanoz, Mexican American *corona* (crown-headdress) maker, Nyssa, Oregon
1987	Allison "Totie" Montana, Mardi Gras costume maker, New Orleans, Louisiana
1987	Emilio and Senaida Romero, Hispanic American craftworkers in tin embroidery, Santa Fe, New Mexico
1987	Newton Washburn, split-ash basket maker, Littleton, New Hampshire
1988	Kepka Belton, Czech American egg painter, Ellsworth, Kansas
1988	Amber Densmore, New England quilter/needleworker, Chelsea, Vermont
1988	Sister Rosalia Haberl, German American bobbin lace maker, Hankinson, North Dakota
1988	Yang Fang Nhu, Hmong weaver, embroiderer, Detroit, Michigan
1989	Vanessa Paukeigope Morgan, Kiowa regalia maker, Anadarko, Oklahoma

1989	Ethel Kvalheim, Norwegian rosemaler (flower painter), Stoughton, Wisconsin
1989	Mabel Murphy, Anglo American quilter, Fulton, Missouri
1989	Harry V. Shourds, wildfowl-decoy carver, Seaville, New Jersey
1989	Chesley Goseyun Wilson, Apache fiddle maker, Tucson, Arizona
1990	Em Bun, Cambodian silk weaver, Harrisburg, Pennsylvania
1990	Maude Kegg, Ojibwe loom beadwork, designer, storyteller, writer, Onamie, Minnesota
1990	Marie McDonald, Hawaiian lei maker, Kamuela, Hawaii
1990	Emilio Rosado, woodcarver, Utuado, Puerto Rico
1991	George Blake, Hupa-Yurok Native American regalia and featherwork craftsman, Hoopa, California
1991	Rose Frank, Nez Perce corn-husk weaver, Lapwai, Idaho
1991	Donald L. King, Western saddlemaker, Sheridan, Wyoming
1991	Esther Littlefield, Tlingit beadworker, regalia maker, basket maker, Sitka, Alaska
1991	Gussie Wells, African American quilter, Oakland, California
1991	Arbie Williams, African American quilter, Oakland, California
1992	Jerry Brown, southern stoneware tradition potter, Hamilton, Alabama
1992	Belle Deacon, Athabascan basket maker, Grayling, Alaska
1992	Nora Ezell, African American quilter, Eutaw, Alabama
1992	Gerald R. Hawpetoss, Menominee/Potowatomi regalia maker, Milwaukee, Wisconsin
1993	Nicholas and Elena Charles, Yupik woodcarver/maskmakers and skin sewers, Bethel, Alaska
1993	Elmer Miller, bit and spur maker/silversmith, Nampa, Idaho

1993	Mone and Vanxay Saenphimmachak, Lao weaver/needleworkers and loommakers, St. Louis, Missouri
1994	Mary Mitchell Gabriel, Passamaquoddy Native American basket maker, Princeton, Maine
1994	Frances Varos Graves, Hispanic American colcha (tapestry) embroiderer, Ranchos de Taos, New Mexico
1994	Lily Vorperian, Armenian Marash-style embroiderer, Glendale, California
1995	Mary Holiday Black, Navajo basket weaver, Mexican Hat, Utah
1995	Bea Ellis Hensley, Appalachian blacksmith, Spruce Pine, North Carolina
1995	Nathan Jackson, Tlingit Alaska Native woodcarver and metalsmith, Ketchikan, Alaska
1995	Nellie Star Boy Menard, Lakota Sioux quilter, Rosebud, South Dakota
1996	Joaquin "Jack" Lujan, Guamian blacksmith, Barrigada, Territory of Guam
1996	Eva McAdams, Shoshone regalia maker, Fort Washakie, Wyoming
1996	Vernon Owens, Anglo American potter, Seagrove, North Carolina
1996	Betty Pisio Christenson, Ukrainian American pysanky (egg decoration), Suring, Wisconsin
1996	Dolly Spencer, Inupiat dollmaker, Homer, Alaska
1997	Gladys LeBlanc Clark, Acadian (Cajun) spinner and weaver, Duson, Louisiana
1997	Georgia Harris, Catawba potter, Atlanta, Georgia
1997	Ramon José López, santero (carver of wooden saints) and metalsmith, Santa Fe, New Mexico
1997	Hystercine Rankin, African American quilter, Lorman, Mississippi
1997	Francis Whitaker, blacksmith/ornamental ironworker, Carbondale, Colorado
1998	Bruce Caesar, Sac and Fox/Pawnee German silversmith, Anadarko, Oklahoma
1998	Sophia George, Yakama-Colville beadworker, Gresham, Oregon
1998	Nadjeschda Overgaard, Danish American Hardanger needleworker, Kimballton, Iowa

1999	Lila Greengrass Blackdeer, Hocak Black Ash basketmaker/needleworker, Black River Falls, Wisconsin
1999	Ulysses "Uly" Goode, Western Mono (a California Native American tribe) basket maker, North Fork, California
1999	Eudokia Sorochaniuk, Ukrainian weaver/textile artist, Pennsauken, New Jersey
2000	Bounxou Chanthraphone, Laotion weaver, Brookland Park, Minnesota
2000	José González, hammock weaver, San Sebastián, Puerto Rico
2000	Nettie Jackson, Klickitat (Yakama) basket maker, White Swan, Washington
2000	Konstantinos Pilarinos, Greek Orthodox Byzantine icon woodcarver, Astoria, New York
2000	Dorothy Thompson, weaver, Davis, West Virginia
2001	Celestino Avilés, santero, Orocovis, Puerto Rico
2001	Mozell Benson, African American quilter, Opelika, Alabama
2001	Evalena Henry, Apache basket weaver, Peridot, Arizona
2001	Dorothy Trumpold, rug weaver, East Amana, Iowa
2002	Loren Bommelyn, Tolowa tradition bearer, Crescent City, California
2002	Francis Cree, Ojibwe basket maker/storyteller, Dunseith, North Dakota
2002	Rose Cree, Ojibwe basket maker/storyteller, Dunseith, North Dakota
2002	Clara Neptune Keezer, Passamaquoddy basket maker, Perry, Maine
2002	Losang Samten, Tibetan sand mandala painter, Philadelphia, Pennsylvania

"The most common theme of visionary artists worldwide is the backyard recreation of the Garden of Eden and other utopian visions—quite literally building heaven on earth."

—AMERICAN VISIONARY MUSEUM, Baltimore, Maryland,
Web site definition, 2001

CHAPTER 5

Applied Design and Fine Crafts

"Form ever follows function."
—LOUIS H. SULLIVAN, 1856–1924, American architect

I n this chapter you will discover some of the designers, craftspersons, and museums dedicated to "applied design," which is simply fine design applied to ceramics, furniture, jewelry, even cars. Perhaps it will affect your thinking the next time you buy something with which you intend to spend your life (or at least a few years of your life).

We are all consumers, and even if we are buying something for practical use, it should be what we would consider the most beautiful of its kind. The functional quality of practical items does not mean that they cannot be aesthetically pleasing. If we are purchasing something that serves no purpose *other* than to be beautiful (such as fine art or fine crafts), we should think it is so wonderful that we simply must have it. We might even be willing to do without something else in order to be able to own that particular object.

This chapter gives an overview of only a few areas of design, particularly those that generate a great deal of interest today: glass, ceramics, and textiles. At the end of the chapter you will find a list of master craftspersons in other related fields.

100 DESIGN ICONS OF THE 20ᵀᴴ CENTURY

These "icons of design" are so familiar in the Western world that most people instantly recognize them by sight or by name. They appear repeatedly in design books and are often included in shows of industrial design or decorative arts exhibitions. They fall in no particular category except that they are memorable, serve a purpose, and have that indefinable "something" that has made them icons. Sometimes their designers are known by name, and at other times the design is associated with its manufacturer.

Design	Date	Location	Designer
ARCHITECTURE			
1. *Arch*	1965	St. Louis, Missouri	Eero Saarinen
2. *Big Ben*	c. 1854	London	E. B. Denison
3. *Chrysler Building*	1932	New York City	William van Alen
4. *Eiffel Tower*	1899	Paris	Gustave Eiffel
5. *Fallingwater*	1936	Bear Run, Pennsylvania	Frank Lloyd Wright
6. *Guggenheim Museum*	1997	Balboa, Spain	Frank Gehry
7. *Statue of Liberty*	1886	New York City	Frederic A. Bartholdi
8. *Sydney Opera House*	1956–1973	Sydney, Australia	Jorn Utzon
CLOTHING AND PERSONAL-USE ITEMS			
9. *Blue Jeans*	1853		Levi Strauss
10. *Chanel Suit*	1920s and 1930s		Coco Chanel
11. *Dr. Martens Shoes*	1960–1990		Dr. Maertens and Dr. Funck
12. *Love Ring*	c. 1966		Robert Indiana
13. Madonna's *Corset dress*	1990		Jean-Paul Gautier
14. *Miniskirt*	1960s		Mary Quant
15. *Ray-Ban Sunglasses*	founded 1937		
16. *Swatch Watch*	1983		Ernest Thonke, Jacques Muller, and Elmer Mock
17. *Swiss Army Knife*	1891		Carl and Victoria Eisener

Design	Date	Designer
ENTERTAINMENT/TECHNOLOGY		
18. *Boom Box*	1980	Panasonic
19. *Sony Walkman Radio*	1978	Sony Design Center
FURNITURE		
20. *Barcelona Chair*	1929	Mies van der Rohe
21. *Beanbag Chair* (Sacco)	1968–1969	Piero Gatti, Cesare Paolini, and Franco Teodoro
22. *Bentwood Chair*	c. 1859– early 1900s	Michael Thonet
23. *Biomorphic Table*	1947	Isamu Noguchi
24. *Butterfly Chair*	1938	Antonio Bonet, Juan Kurchan and Jorge Ferrari-Hardoy
25. *Carlton Sideboard*	1981	Ettore Sottsass
26. *Diamond Chair* (wire)	1952	Harry Bertoia
27. *Little Beaver Chair* (corrugated cardboard)	1987	Frank Gehry
28. *Lounge Chair* and *Foot Stool*	1956	Charles Eames
29. *Mae West Sofa* (shaped like red lips)	1936	Salvador Dali
30. *Marshmallow Sofa*	1956	George Nelson
31. *"Potato Chip" Chair* (steamed plywood)	1945	Ray and Charles Eames

Design	Date	Designer
32. *Powerplay Armchair* (molded plywood strips)	1992	Frank Gehry
33. *Red-and-Blue Chair*	1918	Gerrit Rietveld
34. *Sitzmaschine Chair*	c. 1908	Josef Hoffmann
35. *Stacking Stool*	1932–1933	Alvar Aalto
36. *Stained-glass Windows*	1892–1950	Frank Lloyd Wright
37. *Tall-back Spindle Rocking Chair*	c. 1908	Gustave Stickley
38. *Tulip Group* (chair and table)	1956	Eero Saarinen
39. *Wassily Chair* (leather and tubular steel)	1925	Marcel Breuer
40. *Womb Chair*	1947–1948	Eero Saarinen
41. *Zig-Zag Chair*	1934	Gerrit Rietvelt

GRAPHIC AND COMMERCIAL DESIGN

Design	Date	Designer
42. *Campbell Soup Can Label*	1898	Herberton Williams
43. *Chanel No. 5 perfume bottle*	1921	Coco Chanel
44. *Coca-Cola "Hobbleskirt" bottle*	1915–1923	Raymond Loewy
45. *Michelin Man* (Mr. Bib—Bibendum)	early 20th century	Marius Rossillon
46. *Fed Ex Mailing Packages*	1995	Lindon Gray (leader)
47. *Lacoste* Logo	1933	René Lacoste
48. *Lucky Strike Cigarette Packet*	1941	Raymond Loewy

HOME FURNISHINGS

Design	Date	Designer
49. *Arco Floor Lamp*	1962	Achille Castiglioni and Pier Giacoma Castiglioni
50. *Bacchantes Vase* (figural)	c. 1932	René Lalique

Design	Date	Designer
51. *Electrolux Vacuum Cleaner*	1939	Raymond Loewy
52. *Handkerchief Vase*	1946	Paolo Venini
53. *Akari Hanging Lamp*	1951	Isamu Noguchi
54. *Lava Lamp*	1963	Edward Craven Walker
55. *Russell Wright Pottery*	1937	Russell Wright
56. *Savoy Vase*	1936	Alvar Aalto
57. *Tiffany Lamp*	c. 1900	Louis Comfort Tiffany
58. *Tupperware*	1950s	Earl Tupper
59. *Arts and Crafts furniture, stained glass, wallpaper, and fabric*	1875	William Morris and Co.

MISCELLANEOUS

60. Dimpled *Jim Beam Bottle*		
61. *Fender Stratocaster Guitar*	1954	Leo Fender
62. *McDonald's Golden Arches*	1962	Jim Schindler
63. *Penguin Cocktail Shaker*	1936	E. A. Schueke

OFFICE

64. *Anglepoise Lamp*	1933	George Carwardine
65. *Apple eMate 300*	1996	Jonathon Ive and others
66. *Apple Macintosh Classic Computer*	1984	Steve Jobs
67. *Bic Pen*	1938	Laszlo Biro
68. *Candlestick Telephone*	c. 1910	Western Electric
69. *Desk Telephone*	1937	Henry Dreyfuss

Design	Date	Designer
70. *IBM Selectric Typewriter*	1961	Eliot Noyes
71. *Nokia 9000 Communicator* (phone, fax, e-mail)	1997	Nokia partners
72. *Olivetti Valentine Typewriter*	1970	Ettore Sottsass
73. *Rolodex* (address filing system)	1952	Arnold Neudstadter

PHOTOGRAPHIC EQUIPMENT

Design	Date	Designer
74. *Canon CB10*	1982–1983	Luigi Colani
75. *Hasselblad 500 camera*	1972	Victor Hasselblad
76. *Kodak Bantam Special*	1936	Walter Dorwin Teague
77. *Kodak Brownie Camera*	1900	Frank Brownell
78. *Leica Camera*	1930	Oskar Barnack
79. *Rolleiflex 2.8F Camera*	1953	

SMALL APPLIANCES

Design	Date	Designer
80. *Sunbeam Mixmaster*	c. 1955	Ivar Jepson
81. *Coach Whistle Teakettle*	1985	Michael Graves

TOYS

Design	Date	Designer
82. *Barbie Doll*	1959	Ruth Handler
83. *Kewpie Doll*	c. 1913	Joseph Kallus
84. *Legos*	1930	Ole Kirk Christiansen
85. *Mad Circle Skateboard*	1995	
86. *Monopoly*	1934	Charles B. Darrow
87. *Slinky*	1943	Richard James

TRANSPORTATION

Design	Date	Designer
88. *Airstream Trailer*	1936	Airstream Trailer Company
89. *Concorde Airplane*	1969	CNRS

Design	Date	Designer
90. *Harley-Davidson Motorbike*	1903	William Harley and Arthur Davidson
91. *Jeep*	1941	Willy's and Ford both manufactured the Jeep
92. *Land Rover*	1955	David Bache
93. *Model T Ford*	1908	Henry Ford
94. *Mustang*	1964	Ford Motor Company
95. *Titanic*	1907–1912	Thomas Andrews
96. *Streamline Locomotive*	1935	Henry Dreyfuss
97. *Thunderbird*	1955	Ford Motor Company
98. *U.S. Space Shuttle*	1981	NASA
99. *Vespa Grand Sport Motor Scooter*	1963	Corradino d'Ascanio
100. *Volkswagen Beetle*	1933–1966	Ferdinand Porche

SOME GREAT DESIGNERS

The following list features some of the world's most famous architects, decorative arts designers, fashion designers, and more. If your favorite seems to be absent from this list, check out the other lists in this chapter, such as "Ceramics," "Glass," "Textiles," or "Master Craftspersons of the 20th Century."

ARCHITECTURAL, DECORATIVE ARTS, INDUSTRIAL, GRAPHIC DESIGNERS

Austria

Hoffman, Josef, 1870–1956	Architect, furniture design, art objects
Thonet, Michael, 1796–1871	Originator of bentwood furniture

Czech Republic

Mucha, Alphonse, 1860–1939	Graphic designer

*"I like to think that design is 98 percent common sense. . . .
That [last] two percent makes the difference between
something which is perfectly acceptable and something
which is so special that everyone wants to possess it."*
—TERRENCE CONRAN, b. 1931, British designer and critic

Denmark

Jacobsen, Arne, 1902–1971	Architect, furniture designer; *Ant Chair*, 1951
Jensen, Georg, 1866–1935	Designer, silver hollow and flatwear, jewelry
Panton, Verner, 1926–1998	Architect, *Cantilevered Plastic Chair* for Herman Miller, 1967

England

Conran, Terence, 1931	Founder of Habitat stores
Gray, Eileen, 1878–1976	Designer of geometric furniture
Morris, William, 1834–1896	Designer of Craftsman era; wallpaper, textiles, and home furnishings

Finland

Aalto, Alvar, 1898–1976	Architecture, glassware and furniture designer

France

Boulanger, Pierre, 1886–1950	Engineer, car designer
Guimard, Hector, 1867–1942	Architect and designer of furniture and the Art Nouveau *Paris Metro* (subway) entrances
Starck, Philippe, 1949	Interior design; creator of the *Juicy Salif* (lemon squeezer), c. 1990

Germany

Behrens, Peter, 1868–1940	Industrial designer
Brandt, Marianne, 1893–1983	Bauhaus teacher, metalwork designer
Braun, Artur, 1921–1971	Appliance manufacturer and designer

Hungary

Breuer, Marcel, 1902–1981	Architect, chair designer

Italy

Bellini, Mario, 1935	Industrial designer; *Olivetti Praxis Typewriter*
Bertone, Giuseppe, 1914–1997	Car designer; *Alfa Romeo,* 1954, *Lamborghini,* 1966
Castiglioni, Achille, 1918–2002	Industrial designer; *Tractor Seat* stool, 1957
De Lucchi, Michele, 1952	Memphis designer; *First Chair,* 1983
Pesce, Gaetano, 1939	Architect, sofa and chair designer; *Umbrella chair,* 1995
Rossetti, Dante Gabriel, 1828–1882	Pre-Raphaelite designer of Craftsman Era furnishings
Sottsass, Ettore, 1917	Founder of Memphis group; *Casablanca sideboard,* 1981

Netherlands

Rietveld, Gerrit, 1888–1964	Architect, chair designer; *Zig-Zag,* 1934 and *Red and Blue* chairs, 1918

Russia

Erté, (Romain de Tirtoff), 1892–1990	Theater and graphic designer, sculptor

Scotland

Mackintosh, Charles Rennie,
1868–1928

Architect, interior designer,
jewelry designer

Sweden

Bulow-Hube, Vivianna Torun, 1927

Designer of jewelry, glassware, and
porcelain for Georg Jensen

Switzerland

Botta, Mario, 1943

Architect, chair designer

United States

Bayer, Herbert, 1900–1985 — Bauhaus graphic designer

Bel Geddes, Norman, 1893–1958 — Theater and industrial designer

Bertoia, Harry, 1915–1978 — Metalwork designs, chairs

Breuer, Marcel, 1902–1981,
b. Hungary — Architect and chair designer

Chadwick, Don, 1936 — Furniture designer for Herman Miller

Dreyfuss, Henry, 1903–1972 — Industrial designer; telephone
designer, writer

Eames, Ray, 1912–1988, and Charles,
1907–1978 — Furniture designers and film makers

Esherick, Wharton, 1887–1970 — Woodcarver

Gehry, Frank O., 1929 — Architect, furniture designer

Glaser, Milton, 1929 — Illustrator and graphic designer

Graves, Michael, 1934 — Architect; small household
appliances

Loewy, Raymond, 1893–1986 — Commercial designer; *Lucky Strike*
package

Mattia, Alphonse, 1947 — Furniture designer

Nelson, George, 1907–1986 — Architect, furniture designer

Noguchi, Isamu, 1904–1988 — Sculptor, lamp designer

Saarinen, Eero, 1910–1961 — Architect; *Tulip Group* chair
and table

Stickley, Gustave, 1857–1942	Arts and Crafts furniture designer
Stumpf, Bill, 1935	Furniture designer for Herman Miller
Teague, Walter Dorwin, 1883–1960	Industrial designer; streamlining
van der Rohe, Ludwig Mies, 1886–1969	Architect and Bauhaus Director; *Barcelona Chair*, 1929
Whistler, James McNeill, 1834–1903	Painter, interior designer
Wright, Frank Lloyd, 1904–1976	Architecture, furniture, stained glass, lamps

DESIGNERS OF FABRIC, CLOTHING, SHOES

England

Ashley, Laura, 1926–1985	Fabrics, clothing, and home furnishings
Galliano, John, 1961	Head designer at Givenchy

France

Balmain, Pierre, 1914–1981	Couturier, unisex clothing
Cardin, Pierre, 1922	Clothing, home furnishings
Chanel, Gabrielle (Coco), 1883–1971	Luxurious women's clothing, fragrances
Dior, Christian, 1905–1957	Women's high fashion, introduced the *New Look* (dramatically long skirts)
Dufy, Raoul, 1877–1953	Textile designer, painter
Fath, Jacques, 1912–1954	High fashion women's clothing; designed costumes for the ballet *The Red Shoes*
Givenchy, Hubert, 1927	Women's and men's wear
Saint Laurent, Yves, 1936	Ran the house of Dior, then his own men's and women's fashion lines

Italy

Armani, Giorgio, 1934	Women's and men's fashions
Ferragamo, Salvatore, 1898–1960	Shoes and leather goods
Valentino, 1932	Women's and men's wear
Versace, Gianni, 1946–1997	Men's and women's fashions, fabric

Japan

Miyake, Issey, 1935	Fashion and textile

Spain

Balenciaga, Cristobal, 1895–1972	Women's wear
Blahnik, Manolo, 1940	Shoe designer
Fortuny y Madrazo, Mariano, 1871–1949	Pleated silk, etched velvet

United States

De la Renta, Oscar, 1932	Men's and women's clothing, accessories, fragrances
Dorn, Marion Victoria, 1899–1964	Textile and tufted carpet
Ellis, Perry, 1940–1986	Men's and women's sportswear collections
Karan, Donna, 1948	DKNY women's fashions
Klein, Calvin, 1942	Women's clothes: jeans, underwear, and fragrances
Lagerfeld, Karl, 1939	Women's ready-to-wear
Lauren, Ralph, 1939	Women's and men's wear, *Polo*, home furnishings, tableware, and luggage
Wang, Vera, 1949	Wedding fashions

100 FABULOUS ART OBJECTS

Every object in this list is the product of a highly skilled artist. Many of them were created to serve a utilitarian purpose, while others were intended simply as objects of beauty to be admired and enjoyed. That some of these artworks have endured for millennia speaks to their value as true works of art. The list provides either the location where the artwork still stands or the museum where it is permanently housed.

ARCHAEOLOGICAL ARTIFACTS

1. *Mummy Cartonnage of Amen-Nestawy Nahkt,* c. 1000 B.C., artist unknown, St. Louis Art Museum, Missouri

2. *Sarcophagus of Djedkhonsouioufankh* (Egyptian mummy cover), c. 560–525 B.C., artist unknown, Louvre, Paris

3. *Stone Calendar,* pre-Columbian, artist unknown, Museum of Archaeology, Mexico City

4. *The Cyrus Cylinder,* 539 B.C., artist unknown, British Museum, London

5. *Throne of Tutankhamen,* Egyptian, c. 1350 B.C., artist unknown, Egyptian Museum, Cairo

ARCHITECTURAL DETAILS

6. *Gates of Paradise* (Cathedral Baptistery Doors), 1450, Lorenzo Ghiberti, Florence, Italy

7. *North Transept Rose Window,* Notre Dame de Chartres, c. 1230, Chartres, France

8. *Royal Gates,* 1784, Gregory Chizhevski, Church of the Nativity of the Mother of God, Kiev, Russia

BOOKS

9. *Dead Sea Scrolls,* c. 100 B.C.–A.D. 68, Israel Museum, Jerusalem

10. *Gutenberg Bible,* 1456, Johannes Gutenberg, British Museum, London

11. *Imperial Gospel Book,* 9th century, Hans von Reutlingen, Museum of Art History, Vienna

BOWLS (SILVER OR PORCELAIN)

12. *Liberty Bowl,* 1768, Paul Revere, Museum of Fine Arts, Boston

13. *Lotus Bowl,* c. 1107–1127, The National Palace Museum, Taipei, Taiwan

14. *Sèvres Bowl,* 1792, Jacques, Dieux, J. Paul Getty Museum, Malibu, California

15. *Studley Bowl,* c. 1400, Victoria and Albert Museum, London

CERAMICS

16. *Black Vase,* 1929, Maria Martinez and Julian Martinez, The Indian Art Center of California, Studio City

17. *Blue Delft Collection,* c. 1700–present, Rijksmuseum, Amsterdam

18. *Geometric Amphora,* 800 B.C., National Museum, Athens, Greece

19. *Heracles and the Nemean Lion* (Greek vase), c. 520 B.C., "Antimenes painter," British Museum, London

20. *House Model* (Han dynasty), 206 B.C.–A.D. 221, artist unknown, Nelson-Atkins Museum of Art, Kansas City, Missouri

21. *Lekythos with Artemis and a Swan* (Greek vase), c. 409 B.C., "Pan painter," Hermitage, St. Petersburg, Russia

22. *Portland Vase* (Roman), c. 1st century A.D., British Museum, London

23. *Red-Figured Calyx-krater: Sleep and Death Lifting the Body of Sarpedon,* c. 515 B.C., Euphronios (painter), Euxitheos (potter), Metropolitan Museum of Art, New York City

GOLD AND JEWELS

24. *Celestial Globe,* c. 1279, Muwajd el Ordhi, The Municipal Mathematics Room, Dresden, Germany

25. *Chalice of Abbot Suger,* c. 1140, National Gallery, Washington, DC

26. *Easter Egg,* 1912, Peter Carl Fabergé, Museum of Fine Arts, Richmond, Virginia

27. *Emerald Topkapi Dagger* (Ottoman), 1746–1747, Topkapi Palace, Istanbul, Turkey

28. *Gold Beaker,* 1200–1000 B.C., Archaeological Museum, Tehran, Iran

29. *Gold Cradle,* 17th century, Topkapi Palace, Istanbul, Turkey

30. *Gold Crown with Two Pendants,* 5th to 6th century, National Museum of Korea, Seoul

31. *Gold Man from Gaul,* late 4th to early 5th century, Dumbarton Oaks, Washington, DC

32. *Gold Mask of King Tutankhamen,* 1362–1253 B.C., Egyptian Museum, Cairo

33. *Gold Rhyton,* 5th century B.C., Archaeological Museum, Tehran, Iran

34. *Golden Egg Decorated with Enamel and Diamonds,* 1902, Mikhail Perkhin (for Fabergé), Armory Chamber, Moscow, Russia

35. *Guelph Treasure,* c. 1579, Berlin (a portion is also in Cleveland, Ohio)

36. *Lyre with Gold Bull's Head,* c. 2500 B.C., Iraq Museum, Baghdad

37. *Mask of Agamemnon,* 1580–1550 B.C., National Museum of Athens, Greece

38. *Mildenhall Treasure,* 4th century, British Museum, London

39. *Pala d'Oro* (altar), 976–1209, Cathedral of St. Mark, Venice, Italy

40. *Rospiogli Cup,* 16th century, Benvenuto Cellini, Metropolitan Museum of Art, New York City

41. *Saltcellar of Francis I,* 1339–1543, Benvenuto Cellini, Kunsthistorisches Museum, Vienna

42. *Scythian Stag, Scythian Panther,* c. 7th–6th century B.C., Hermitage, St. Petersburg, Russia

43. *St. George and the Dragon,* c. 1590, Hans Reimer and Munich Masters, Residence Palace, Munich, Germany

44. *Turquoise Throne of Murat III,* Topkapi Palace, Istanbul, Turkey

45. *Vaphio Cups* (gold repoussé "sporting" cups), c. 1500 B.C., National Museum of Athens, Greece

ILLUMINATED MANUSCRIPTS

46. *Book of Kells,* 8th century A.D., Trinity College, Dublin, Ireland

47. *Koran Collection,* 1436–1520, Topkapi Palace, Istanbul, Turkey

48. *Lady Wen-Chi's Return,* 12th century, Sung dynasty (Chinese) illuminated manuscript, Museum of Fine Arts, Boston

49. *Les Très Riches Heures du Jean, Duc de Berry I* (richly illuminated hourly prayer book), 1413–1416, Limbourg Brothers, Musée Condé, Chantilly, France

50. *Lindisfarne Gospels,* c. A.D. 698, British Museum, London

51. *Lorsch Bookcover,* 9th century, Victoria and Albert Museum, London

52. *Miniatures Collection* (illuminated manuscripts of Court life), 13th–18th centuries, Topkapi Palace, Istanbul, Turkey

53. *Très Belles Heures du Duc de Berry* (literally "The beautiful hour book of the Duke of Berry," illuminated, with five of its pages attributed to Jan van Eyck), 15th century, Turin, Italy

IVORY

54. *Barbarini Ivory,* c. 527, Louvre, Paris

55. *Ivory Panel with Archangel,* c. 5th century A.D., British Museum, London

56. *Minoan Snake Goddess,* 1500 B.C., Museum of Fine Arts, Boston

JEWELRY

57. *Blackamoor* (the face of a black slave) *with South American Emeralds,* c. 1724, Gemaldegalerie, Dresden, Germany

58. *Bracelet* (Persian), 10th–11th centuries, Los Angeles County Museum of Art

59. *Cross of Princely Crowns,* 13th and 15th centuries, Treasury of Wawel Cathedral, Cracow, Poland

60. *Crown of St. Edward,* 1667, Robert Vyner, Crown Jewels of England, London

61. *Crown of the Holy Roman Empire,* c. A.D. 962, Kunsthistorisches Museum, Vienna

62. *Grand Condé Rose Diamonds,* 1621–1686, Condé Museum, Chateau of Chantilly, France

63. *Lothar Cross,* end of 10th century, Treasury of the Royal Palace, Aachen, Germany

64. *Order of the Golden Fleece,* c. 15th century, Residence Palace, Munich, Germany

65. *Sutton Hoo Treasure* (Anglo-Saxon ship-burial treasure), A.D., 625–633 British Museum, London

66. *The Royal Heart,* c. 1952, Salvador Dali, Owen Cheatham Foundation, New York City

67. *Trojan Gold Diadem,* Bronze Age, Pushkin Museum, Moscow, Russia

MISCELLANEOUS

68. *Feather Crown of King Montezuma,* c. 1500, Ethnological Museum, Vienna

69. *Great Bed of Ware* (sleeps eight people). (In 1689 it is supposed to have slept "26 butchers and their wives" at the White Hart Inn in Ware, England.), late 16th century, Victoria and Albert Museum, London

70. *Lycurgus Cup,* 4th century, British Museum, London

71. *St. Ursula and the 11,000 Virgins* (reliquary for the bones of a saint), Hans Memling, c. 1430, St. Jans Hospital, Bruges, Belgium

72. *The Wellington Shield, Victory,* 1822, Thomas Stothard, Wellington Museum, Apsley House, London

MOSAICS AND CERAMICS

73. *Battle Between Darius and Alexander,* 4th century B.C., Muzeo Nazionale, Naples, Italy

74. *Court of the Emperor Justinian and Court of the Empress Theodora,* (mosaics), A.D. 6th century, Church of San Vitale, Ravenna, Italy

75. *Lion Gate,* Ishtar (ceramic), 6th century B.C., State Museums, Berlin, Germany

76. *Mosaic of the Good Shepherd,* 5th century A.D., Mausoleum of Galla Placida, Ravenna, Italy

MUSICAL INSTRUMENTS

77. *Bulls Head on a Harp,* 2500 B.C., Egyptian Museum, Cairo

78. *Stradivarius Violin,* Antonio Stradivarius, 1644–1737, Metropolitan Museum of Art, New York City

PAINTINGS

79. *Shield of David,* 1420–1457, Andrea del Castagno, National Gallery of Art, Washington, DC

80. *Wilton Diptych,* c. 1377–1413, National Gallery, London

PRINTS

81. *Fifty-three Stages of the Tokaido Shono,* c. 1834, Utagawa Hiroshige, Museum of Fine Arts, Boston

SCULPTURE

82. *Animal Head* from the Oseberg Ship-Burial, c. A.D. 825, University of Antiquities, Oslo

83. *Antependium* (frontal altar) of Henry II, early 11th century, Cluny Museum, Paris

84. *Arms of Peru,* Chimu culture, c. 1200–1300, Miguel Mujica Gallo Museum, Lima

85. *Bronze Panel* (Benin culture, Africa), c. A.D. 1500, British Museum, London

86. *Buddha Enthroned,* 10th century, Kimbell Art Museum, Fort Worth, Texas

87. *Bust of Tiberius,* 1st century A.D., Pitti Palace, Florence, Italy

88. *Code of Hammurabi* (carved stone), c. 1930–1888 B.C., Louvre, Paris

89. *Discobolus* ("*Discus Thrower*"), 450 B.C., Myron, Museu della Terme, Rome

90. *Flute Player* (Benin culture), 15th–16th centuries, cast bronze, British Museum, London

91. *Geese of Meydum* (frieze), c. 2600 B.C., Cairo Museum, Egypt

92. *Horse Biting Its Leg* (Sung Dynasty), A.D. 960–1260, Collection, King Gustaf VI Adolf of Sweden, Stockholm

93. *Palace Ladies Hunting from a Pavilion,* 1760–1770, Cleveland Museum of Art, Ohio

94. *Palette of King Narmer* (basalt bas-relief), c. 3000 B.C., Egyptian Museum, Cairo

95. *Ram Caught in a Thicket* (Ur), c. 2600 B.C., British Museum, London

96. *Two-headed Serpent* (Aztec), 15th century, British Museum, London

97. *Venus De Milo,* 2nd century B.C., Louvre, Paris

TAPESTRIES

98. *Bayeux Tapestry,* end of 11th century, Queen Mathilde and her attendants, Bayeux, France

99. *Lady with the Unicorn Tapestries,* 1509–1515, Cluny Museum, Paris

100. *Syon Cope* (embroidery), 1300–1320, Victoria and Albert Museum, London

"Have nothing in your houses that you do not know to be useful, or believe to be beautiful."
—WILLIAM MORRIS, 1834–1896, British designer

MUSEUMS OF DECORATIVE ARTS AND CONTEMPORARY CRAFTS

These museums house some of the world's most important examples of design, including jewelry, toys, home furnishings, needlework, and fine crafts. Some specialize in only contemporary work, but other collections include armor and decorative items that range from thousands of years old to 20th-century contemporary craft.

Sydney, Australia	Sydney Powerhouse Museum
Vienna, Austria	Kunsthistorisches Museum
Copenhagen, Denmark	The Danish Museum

Bath, England	Holburne Museum of Art
London, England	Victoria and Albert Museum; British Museum
Paris, France	Musée des Arts Décoratifs; Centre Georges Pompidou
Reims, France	Musée des Beaux Arts
Weil am Rhein, Germany	Vitra Design Museum

UNITED STATES

San Francisco, California	San Francisco Craft & Folk Art Museum
Brookfield, Connecticut	Brookfield Craft Center
Winterthur, Delaware	The Henry Francis Du Pont Winterthur Museum, Inc.
District of Columbia	Daughters of the American Revolution Museum; Renwick Gallery; Smithsonian Institution
Wichita, Kansas	Decorative Arts Collection
Louisville, Kentucky	Kentucky Art & Craft Foundation, Inc.
Boston, Massachusetts	Museum of Fine Arts
Ridgeland, Mississippi	Mississippi Crafts Center
New York City	Cooper-Hewitt National Design Museum, Smithsonian Institution; New York Design Center; Metropolitan Museum of Art; Museum of Modern Art; The Cloisters
Asheville, North Carolina	Biltmore House
Charlotte, North Carolina	Mint Museum of Craft & Design
Winston-Salem, North Carolina	Museum of Early Southern Decorative Arts
Lancaster, Ohio	Decorative Arts Center of Ohio
Bethlehem, Pennsylvania	Kemerer Museum of Decorative Arts
Chattanooga, Tennessee	Houston Museum of Decorative Arts
Memphis, Tennessee	National Ornamental Metal Museum
Houston, Texas	Museum of American Architecture and Decorative Arts; Houston Center for Contemporary Craft (HCCC)

MAJOR ARTS AND CRAFTS GALLERIES

If your travels take you to any of the destinations featured in this list, a visit to these arts and crafts galleries should prove a satisfying way to spend your time. To plan your gallery tour ahead of time, simply log on to the gallery's Web site, check out the list of exhibits and floor plan, and you'll know exactly where to go in the museum or gallery to see what interests you most.

Tucson, Arizona	Obsidian Gallery
San Francisco, California	Virginia Breier Gallery
Louisville, Kentucky	Kentucky Art and Craft Foundation, Inc.
Newton, Massachusetts	Jubilation
Stockbridge, Massachusetts	Holsten Galleries
Worcester, Massachusetts	Worcester Center for Crafts
St. Louis, Missouri	Craft Alliance
Albuquerque, New Mexico	Weyrich Gallery/The Rare Vision Art Gallery
Santa Fe, New Mexico	Contemporary Glass Gallery
Cannon Beach, Oregon	White Bird Gallery
Portland, Oregon	Contemporary Crafts Gallery
Pittsburgh, Pennsylvania	Society for Contemporary Craft
Waynesboro, Virginia	Artisans Center of Virginia

MAJOR CRAFTS FAIRS

If you live near one of the cities listed here, you can let the galleries come to you. While crafts fairs occur in even the smallest towns or schools, the ones in this list would be considered major fairs that either attract dealers from all over the world or are highly specialized, such as the Indian Market in Santa Fe. Dealers vie for acceptance in these fairs, and you can be assured of high quality from a reputable dealer. The month in which the fairs traditionally take place is included so you can get more information about them in art magazines or on the Internet.

London, England	Ceramics Fair, June
	Haughton International Ceramics Fair, June

UNITED STATES

Scottsdale, Arizona	Annual Indian Artists of America Show, February
San Francisco, California	Contemporary Crafts Market, March
Santa Monica, California	Contemporary Crafts Market, May
District of Columbia	Smithsonian Craft Show, April; Washington Craft Show, December
Miami, Florida	SOFA (Sculpture, Objects & Functional Art) show, March
Atlanta, Georgia	ACC (American Crafts Council) show, March
Chicago, Illinois	SOFA (Sculpture, Objects & Functional Art) show, October
Baltimore, Maryland	ACC (American Crafts Council) show, February
Gaithersburg, Maryland	Sugarloaf Contemporary Crafts, November
Millville, New Jersey	Festival of Fine Craft, October; Glass Weekend, July
Santa Fe, New Mexico	SITE Santa Fe, August; Indian Market, August; Spanish Market, July
New York City, New York	The New York Ceramics Fair, January
Westchester, New York	Craft Show, October
Cincinnati, Ohio	Cincinnati Contemporary Crafts Market, March
Gatlinburg, Tennessee	Gatlinburg Craftsmen's Fair, July
Chantilly, Virginia	Sugarloaf Crafts Festival, May

"Less is more."

—LUDWIG MIES VAN DER ROHE, 1886–1969, American architect, born Germany

MAGAZINES OF INTEREST TO COLLECTORS

American Ceramics, 9 E. 45th St., New York, NY, 10017–2403
American Craft, 72 Spring St., New York, NY, 10012–4019
Art & Antiques, 3 E. 54th St., New York, NY, 10022
Ceramics Monthly, 735 Ceramic Pl., Westerville, OH, 43086
Collector Magazine, Krause Publications, 700 E. State St., Iola, WI 54981
Neus Glas (in German), 153 South Dean Street, Englewood, NJ 07631

MUSEUMS EMPHASIZING GLASS COLLECTIONS

Whether you're interested in Tiffany stained glass works or contemporary mouth-blown glass, these museums may give you the opportunity to observe the glass-making process while seeing outstanding examples of the glassblower's art covering more than two thousand years.

Vienna, Austria	Decorative Art Museum
Liège, Belgium	Museum of Glass
Prague, Czech Republic	Decorative Arts Museum; National Technological Museum
Ebeltoft, Denmark	Moderne International Glaskunst Museum
Fensmark, Denmark	Holmegaard-Kastrup Glass Museum
London, England	Victoria and Albert Museum
Merseyside, England	Pilkington Glass Museum
Biot, France	Ecomusée du Verre de Biot
Meisenthal, France	Musée du Verre et du Cristal
Paris, France	Musée des Arts Décoratifs
Sars Poteries, France	Musée du Verre
Sèvres, France	Musée National de Ceramique
Bavaria, Germany	Glasmuseum Fravenau
Inamenhausen, Germany	Glasmuseum
Wertheim, Germany	Glasmuseum
Venice, Italy	Peggy Guggenheim Collection
Sapporo, Japan	Hokkaido Museum of Modern Art

Tokyo, Japan	Sasaki Glass Museum
Leerdam, Netherlands	National Glass Museum
Jevnaker, Norway	Hadeland Glaswerk
Lausanne, Switzerland	Musée des Arts-Decoratifs

UNITED STATES

Menlo Park, California	Saxe Collection (private collection, sometimes on view)
Redlands, California	Historical Glass Museum Foundation
Atlanta, Georgia	High Museum of Art
Dunkirk, Indiana	The Glass Museum
Greentown, Indiana	Greentown Glass Museum, Inc.
Sebago, Maine	The Jones Museum of Glass and Ceramics
Sandwich, Massachusetts	Sandwich Glass Museum
Millville, New Jersey	Museum of American Glass at Wheaton Village
Corning, New York	Corning Museum of Glass
New York City	Cooper-Hewitt Museum, Museum of Contemporary Crafts
Cambridge, Ohio	Cambridge Glass Museum; Degenhart Paperweight & Glass Museum, Inc.
Columbus, Ohio	Ross C. Purdy Museum of Ceramics
Newark, Ohio	National Heisey Glass Museum
Toledo, Ohio	Toledo Museum of Art
Seattle, Washington	Seattle Art Museum
Stanwood, Washington	Pilchuk Collection
Tacoma, Washington	Museum of Glass
Milton, West Virginia	Blenko Glass
Williamstown, West Virginia	Fenton Glass Museum

CRYSTALLERIES YOU CAN VISIT

If you appreciate the form and function of fine crystal, these are places where you can watch the creation of fine crystal pieces. Most crystalleries have a museum and sales room attached. This list contains mostly large, established firms that have been continually in business for many years.

AUSTRIA

Vienna	J & L Lobmeyr

BELGIUM

Liège	Cristalleries du Val-Saint-Lambert

CZECH REPUBLIC

Chlum	Bohemia Crystal
Karlsbad	Moser Glassworks
Neuwelt	Harrachov Glassworks
Podebrady	Bohemia Glassworks, near Prague
S'krdlovice	Beranek
Zelezny Brod	Zelezny Brod Glass

ENGLAND

Amblecote, Stourbridge	Royal Doulton Crystal
Stourbridge	Royal Brierley Crystal
Sunderland	James A. Jobling & Co. Ltd.
Wealdstone	Whitefriars Glass Ltd.; Webb Corbett Ltd.
Wordsley, Stourbridge	Stuart & Sons Ltd.

FINLAND

Nuutajarvi	Iittala Nuutajarvi; Nuutajarvi-Notsjo Glass (Arabia Glass)
Riihimaki	Riihimaen Lasi Oy

FRANCE

Baccarat Luneville	Baccarat
Lorraine	Cristalleries de Saint-Louis-les-Bitche
Nancy	Daum & Cie Cristalleries de Nancy
Sèvres	Cristallerie de Sèvres et Clichy Réunis
Wingen-sur-Moder	Lalique & Cie

GERMANY

Amberg	Rosenthal
Duren	Peill and Putzler
Waldgassen	Villeroy & Boch

IRELAND

Waterford	Waterford Glass Ltd.

ITALY

Murano	Barovier & Toso; Cenedese & Figlio; Compagnia di Venezie e Murano; La Fucina degli Angeli; Venini & Co.; Vetraria Vistosi; Salviati & Co.

NETHERLANDS

Leerdam	Royal Dutch Glasfabriek Leerdam

NORWAY

Jevnaker	Hadelands Glasverk

SCOTLAND

Perth	Caithness Glass

SWEDEN

Eriksmala, Smaland	Afors Glasbruk (Kosta Boda)
Orrefors	Orrefors Glasbruk

UNITED STATES

Corning, New York	Steuben (Corning Glass Works)
Ceredo West Virginia	Pilgrim Glass Company
Milton, West Virginia	Blenko Glass
Moundsville, West Virginia	Fostoria

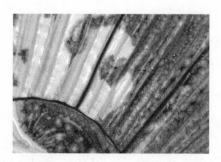

GLASSMAKING TERMS

Whether you're looking for just the right glass or crystal piece to accentuate the character of your dining room, or just browsing and admiring a work of glass, a knowledge of the following terms will enhance your appreciation of high-quality work.

Acid-etched. Glass etched by mean of applying acid to create the particular pattern or design.

Blown glass. Glass formed by gathering a molten blob of glass onto the end of a long hollow metal tube, holding it against a rounded or flat surface, then enlarging it by blowing through the tube.

Cast (or molded) glass. Glass poured into a pre-formed mold that determines its shape.

Cold work. Transforming the surface of glass by means of grinding, polishing, etching, laminating, or sandblasting.

Cut glass. Glass that features designs created by the use of a grinding wheel. The edges and planes created by such cutting create many light-reflecting surfaces.

Depression glass. Inexpensive iridescent glass produced in the 1930s.

Electroplated. A thin layer of metal heated and applied to the glass surface.

Engraved. Glass featuring engraved designs applied by use of a wheel, sandblasting, or etching.

Flame worked. Glass rods heated with a small torch and transformed by the use of various tools.

Fused. Two pieces of glass heated sufficiently to bond together.

Glass mosaic. Glass containing large pieces or streaks of varied colored glass.

Glory hole. A small furnace for reheating glass in order to continue working on it.

Millefiore. Also known as "thousand flower" designs, the complex multi-colored circles of glass are combined to make an allover flower-like design. Millefiore designs are seen in paperweights or glass jewelry.

Polishing. Abrading glass using a polishing wheel and progressively finer grit (like sandpaper) until the surface is smooth.

Pontil. The steel tube used in blown-glass production. It also refers to the flat or hollow area where the piece was separated from the tube.

Pressed glass. Glass forced into a mold with a plunger, creating the effect of cut glass, but with smooth, rounded edges.

Sandblasted. Glass with a matte finish, created by using air pressure to bombard sand or aluminum oxide particles onto the glass surface.

Slumped glass. Sheet glass heated to a temperature that causes it to droop to conform to a mold.

Stained glass. Patterns or pictures created by piecing together pieces of colored sheet glass.

Studio glass. Might be considered a "fine art," as it serves no practical purpose other than to be admired for its beauty.

"Always design a thing by considering it in its next larger context—a chair in a room, a room in a house, a house in an environment, an environment in a city plan."

—EERO SAARINEN, 1910–1961, American architect, born Finland; Professor, Cranbrook Academy of Art

COLLECTING GLASS

If you are serious about collecting glass, become informed by reading some of the many books available on the subject, attending glass exhibitions, talking with dealers and other collectors, and visiting museums. Here are some pointers to get you started.

If you are buying glass from a dealer as an investment:

- ✤ It is important to have a "name" designer.
- ✤ Make sure the glass is signed. On clear glass, acid-etched names may be signed backwards so the name may be read from the inside.
- ✤ Go by the reputation of the dealer.
- ✤ Know the reputation of the glass blower.
- ✤ Get a certificate of authenticity or guarantee.

When buying at auction:

- ✤ Take the time to inspect a piece carefully before bidding.
- ✤ Look for chips, being aware that chips diminish the value.
- ✤ Inspect for evidence that it has been ground down. The telltale signs are dips in an edge.
- ✤ Find the signature.

When buying on the Internet:

- ✤ Know what you are looking for.
- ✤ Read the description carefully.

✤ Note the size, as pictures can be deceiving and you may be disappointed if something is not as large as you thought it would be.

✤ Find out whether or not the piece is signed.

✤ Ask whether areas are ground down.

✤ Find the ranking of the dealer (often ranked by purchasers).

When buying at flea markets or garage sales:

✤ Carefully inspect a piece for chips or evidence that it has been ground down.

✤ Look for markings and stickers. Original stickers add to the value for collectors. If you are purchasing with an eye toward appreciation in value, leave stickers in place.

How to recognize genuine mouth-blown glass:

✤ It has a pontil (flat area) on bottom where the glass was attached to the rod; sometimes the pontil is ground away, leaving a smooth hollow.

✤ Sizes of the same "model" may vary.

✤ Small flaws may be evident.

✤ No two pieces are exactly alike.

Tricks of the trade:

✤ Dealers often examine glass under black light, which exposes repairs.

✤ Genuine green Depression glass will glow under a black light, evidence of the uranium that was found in glass at that time. This same technique does not work on Depression glass of other colors.

Tips from collectors:

✤ Blenko glass produced in 1959 and 1960 is usually not signed. Instead, it has an acid-etched stamp on the bottom. It may also have plastic or foil stickers. In the late 1960s to 1980s, Blenko glass was mouth blown. This glass has rich colors: orange, turquoise blue, amethyst, green. Richard Blenko now signs some work when selling in stores, obviously adding to its ultimate value.

❖ Steuben crystal is marked with an acid stamp featuring a leaf on the bottom or along the side.

❖ Daum glass is usually signed on the side.

❖ Waterford glass is signed on the side and usually has a foil sticker featuring a sea horse.

❖ Decanters sometimes have a numbered stopper (found on the side or bottom). Make sure the stopper and the decanter have the same number.

PROMINENT GLASS ARTISTS

Although fragile, an amazing amount of glass has been preserved through the years. It is a truly international medium, with glass artists studying in countries other than their own to learn techniques to improve their art. Until the relatively recent past, glass artists were not known by name; however, many contemporary artists now receive the same recognition as artists in other media. These are a few of the best known. The dates of an artist's birth and death are given where available. A single date is the artist's date of birth unless otherwise noted.

AUSTRALIA

Hirst, Brian, 1956

Moje, Klaus, 1936

BELGIUM

Leloup, Louis, 1929

CZECH REPUBLIC

Brychtova, Jaroslava, 1924
Ciglar, Vaclav, 1929
Fisar, Jan, 1933
Harcuba, Jiri, 1928
Kaplicky, Josef, 1899–1962
Karel, Marian, 1944
Klinger, Miroslav, 1922

Kopecky, Vladimir, 1931
Kotik, Jan, 1916
Libensky, Stanislav, 1921–2002
Machac, Vaclav, 1954
Mares, Ivan, 1956
Novak, Bretislav, 1952
Pala, Stepan, 1944

CZECH REPUBLIC *(continued)*

Palova, Zora, 1944

Pavlik, Michael, 1941

Roubicek, René, 1922

Roubickova, Miluse, 1922

Rozsypal, Ivo, 1942

Sabokova, Gizela, 1952

Sramkova, Ivana, 1960

Vachtova, Dana, 1937

Vizner, Frantisek, 1936

Zamecnikova, Dana, 1945

Zertova, Jirina, 1932

Zoritchak, Yan, 1944

Zoritchak, Caterine, 1947

ENGLAND

Alston, Margaret, 1956

Amsel, Galia Elsa, 1967

Clegg, Tessa, 1946

Coper, Hans, 1920–1981

Hobson, Diana, 1943

Kirk, Christina, 1961

Lane, Danny, 1955

Pennell, Roland, 1939

Proctor, Stephen, 1970

Reekie, David, 1947

Reid, Colin, 1953

Taylor, David, 1949

Wood, Emma, 1969

FINLAND

Aalto, Alvar, 1898–1976

Orvola, Heikki, 1943

Salo, Markku, 1954

Sarpaneva, Timo, 1926

Toikka, Oiva, 1931

Wirkkala, Tapio, 1915–1985

FRANCE

Bégou, Alain, 1945

Bégou, Marisa, 1948

Daum, Jean-Louis-Auguste

Dejonghe, Bernard, 1942

Delsol, Edmée, 1939

Gallé, Emile, 1846–1904

Grimaldi, Marie Aimée, 1958

Lalique, Marc, 1900–1977

Lalique, René Jules, 1860–1945

Marinot, Maurice, 1882–1960

Navarre, Henri, 1885–1971

Ruhlman, Emile-Jacques,
1879–1933

GERMANY

Eisch, Erwin, 1927
Holler, Franz Xaver, 1950
Model, Hanns

Moje-Wohlgemuth, Isgard, 1941
Wolff, Ann, 1937
Zimmermann, Jorg, 1940

HUNGARY

Bohus, Zoltan, 1941

IRELAND

Rainey, Clifford, 1948

ISRAEL

Sikorsky, Todd, 1951

ITALY

Ballarin, Giuliano, 1942
Barovier, Ercole, 1889–1974
Barovier, Ercole, 1930
Barovier, Giuseppe, 1913
Bianchin, Cristiano, 1956
Ferro, Renzo, 1954
Fuga, Anzolo, 1914
Giuman, Giuliano, 1944
Licata, Riccardo, 1929
Martinuzzi, Giampaolo, 1933

Nordio, Massimo, 1947
Rosin, Maria Grazia, 1958
Santarossa, Renato, 1934
Santillana, Alessandro Diaz de, 1959
Santillana, Laura Diaz de, 1955
Scarpa, Carlo, 1906–1978
Venini, Paolo, 1895–1959
Zennaro, Orlando, 1932

JAPAN

Fujita, Kyohei, 1921
Iezumi, Toshio, 1954
Masuda, Hideko
Mukaide, Keiko, 1954

Ohiro, Yoichi, 1946
Shibuya, Ryoji, 1956
Yamano, Hiroshi, 1956

NETHERLANDS

Ginneke, Vincent Van, 1956

Groot, Mieke, 1949

Smit, Bibi, 1965

Van Meurs, Sien, 1953

NEW ZEALAND

McClure, Elizabeth, 1957

ROMANIA

Negreanu, Matei, 1941

SWEDEN

Cyrén, Gunner, 1931

Gate, Simon, 1843–1945

Hald, Edward, 1885

Hydman-Vallien, Ulrica, 1938

Lindblad, Gun, 1954

Vallien, Bertil, 1938

SWITZERLAND

Guggisberg, Monica, 1955 (with partner Philip Baldwin)

Nierderer, Roberto

UNITED STATES

Abildgaard, Mark, 1957

Anderson, Doug, 1952

Anderson, Winslow, 1917

Arnold, David

Baldwin, Philip, 1947

Barbini, Alfredo, 1912, b. Italy

Barton, Paula, 1946

Beecham, Gary, 1955

Billeci, Andre

Blomdahl, Sonja, 1952

Carder, Frederick, 1864–1963

Carlson, William, 1950

Cash, Sydney, 1941

Castle, Wendell, 1932

Chihuly, Dale, 1941

Clayman, Daniel, 1957

Cohen, Carol, 1939

Cohn, Michael, 1949

Cribbs, Kéké, 1951

Dailey, Dan, 1947

Darricarrere, Roger, 1912–1983

De Obaldia, Isabel, 1957

Durand, Victor, 1870–1931,
    b. France

Eckhardt, Edris, 1929

Fritz, Robert, 1920–1986

Glancy, Michael, 1950
Goldhagen, David
Halem, Henry, 1938
Huchthausen, David R., 1951
Hutter, Sidney R., 1954
Jervis, Margie, 1956
Jolley, Richard, 1952
Kallenberger, Kreg, 1950
Kehlmann, Robert, 1943
Kilby, Ruth Maria
Kirkpatrick, Joey, 1952, and
   Mace, Flora C., 1949
Krasnican, Susie, 1954
Kuhn, Jon, 1949
Kulasiewicz, Frank, 1930
Labino, Dominick, 1910–1987
LaFarge, John, 1835–1910
Leperlier, Antoine, 1953
LeQuier, William, 1953
Levi, David W., 1951
Lipofsky, Marvin, 1938
Littleton, Harvey K. 1922
MacNeil, Linda, 1954
Magdanz, Andrew, 1951
Marioni, Dante, 1964
Marquis, Richard, 1945
McCutchen, Earl, 1918–1985
Meitner, Richard, 1949

Morris, William, 1957
Musler, Jay, 1949
Myers, Joel Philip, 1934
Paley, Albert, 1944
Patti, Tom, 1943
Peiser, Mark, 1938
Porter, Priscilla Manning
Price, Kenneth, 1935
Ruffner, Ginny, 1952
Schmidt, Jack, 1968
Seide, Paul, 1949
Shaffer, Mary, 1947
Stankard, Paul J., 1943
Tagliapietra, Lino, 1934
Thompson, Catherine (Cappy),
   1952
Tiffany, Louis Comfort,
   1848–1933
Tobey, Mark, 1890–1976
Tré, Howard Ben, 1949
Trinkley, Karla, 1956
Van Cline, Mary, 1954
Watkins, James, 1955
Wax, James, 1956
Weinberg, Steven I., 1954
Willson, Robert, 1912
Zynsky, Mary Ann (Toots), 1951

"Technique is cheap."
—HARVEY LITTLETON, 1921, glassmaker

MUSEUMS EMPHASIZING CERAMICS COLLECTIONS

Many of these are small museums, either attached to a ceramics factory or perhaps a private collection in a home that has been opened to the public. They are all worth a visit.

Antwerp, Belgium	Smidt van Gelder Museum
Ottawa, Canada	Canada National Museum
Toronto, Canada	Royal Ontario Museum; George R. Gardiner Museum of Ceramic Art
Cambridge, England	Fitzwilliam Museum
Liverpool, England	Museum of Ceramics at East Liverpool
London, England	Wallace Collection, Contemporary Ceramics
Norwich, England	Sainsbury Centre for Visual Arts
Stoke-on-Trent, England	Gladstone Pottery Museum; Minton Museum; Royal Doulton Ltd.; The Potteries Museum and Art Gallery; Wedgewood Museum
Worcestershire, England	Worcester Factory and Museum
Paris, France	Musée des Arts Décoratifs
Dusseldorf, Germany	Hetjens Museum; Deutsches Keramikmuseum
Frechen, Germany	Karamion; Keramische Kunst
Meissen, Germany	Meissen Factory and Museum
Kossuth, Hungary	Herend Porcelain Museum
Faenza, Italy	Museo Internazionale della Ceramica
Delft, Netherlands	Het Porcelyne Vles Museum and Factory
Moscow, Russia	State Museum of Ceramics

UNITED STATES

Phoenix, Arizona	Heard Museum of Anthropology and Primitive Art
San Francisco, California	DeYoung Museum
District of Columbia	Arthur M. Sackler Gallery; Renwick Gallery of the National Museum of American Art, Smithsonian Institution

Chicago, Illinois	Chicago Art Institute
Baltimore, Maryland	Walters Museum of Art; National Museum of Ceramic Art and Glass
Alfred, New York	International Museum of Ceramic Art, Alfred University
Seagrove, North Carolina	North Carolina Pottery Center
East Liverpool, Ohio	Museum of Ceramics at East Liverpool
Roseville, Ohio	Ohio Ceramic Center
Westerville, Ohio	The Ross C. Purdy Museum of Ceramics (at the American Ceramic Society)
Oklahoma City, Oklahoma	The World Organization of China Painters
Memphis, Tennessee	Dixon Gallery and Gardens

CERAMICS TERMS

Bisque. Sometimes called biscuit ware, this is a first firing of clay without glazes.

Cast. Clay slip poured into plaster molds; allows mass reproduction of one form.

Ceramic. Clay products that have been fired for permanence.

China. Translucent ware fired at 2230 degrees F.; porcelain.

Clay. A moist earth of decomposed rock; used in products such as pottery, bricks, tiles, and sculpture.

Coiling. A method of creating pots by building up bottom and sides with even, ropelike coils.

Decal. Designs that are transferred to ware before firing; often used in china decorating.

Earthenware. Low-fire pottery, usually red or tan, that has been fired to below 2000 degrees F.

Engobe. A glaze made of clay diluted with water and used for painting on greenware.

Firing. Placing ceramic ware into a special oven and heating at high temperatures until it is mature.

Glaze. Ground minerals in a solution that enables them to adhere to the clay body; when fired, they give a glassy effect.

Greenware. A ceramic form that has been dried but not fired. It is sometimes decorated at this stage.

Kiln. Electric, gas, or wood-fired oven for firing ceramics.

Porcelain. Fine white clay used primarily for china. Fires at a high temperature and is quite hard.

Pottery. Term used to distinguish earthenware from porcelain or stoneware. Earthenware, which is low-fire, is more prone to chipping than stoneware or porcelain, which are fired at higher temperatures.

Raku. A low fire often done outdoors that produces dark areas and iridescence.

Reduction firing. Firing with insufficient oxygen; causes interesting color changes in glazes.

Sgraffito. Scratching designs through colored slip (clay thinned with water) that has been painted onto a clay form of a different color. An example would be a white clay pot that has been coated with red slip, then a design scratched into the red, exposing the white undercolor.

Slab. Clay evenly rolled and formed by draping or joining.

Slip. Clay diluted with water to the consistency of cream; used for joining or as an engobe (glaze).

Stoneware. Gray, reddish, or tan clay that has been fired at a very high temperature.

Terra cotta. Reddish clay that contains grog (ground clay), commonly used for ceramic sculpture.

Throwing. Beginning with a lump of clay and creating vessels on a potter's wheel.

Underglaze. Colors that can be painted on greenware that will show through a clear glaze.

Wheel. A wheel for making (throwing) pots; may be driven by hand, foot, or electric power.

CERAMICS ARTISTS

This list includes some of the better-known ceramists worldwide.

AUSTRIA

Rie, Lucie, 1902–1995

CANADA

Levine, Marilyn, 1935

DENMARK

Salto, Axel, 1889–1961

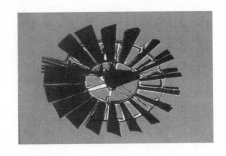

ENGLAND

Cardew, Michael, 1901–1983
Cliff, Clarice, 1899–1972
Cooper, Susie, 1902–1995
Coper, Hans, 1920–1981
Leach, Bernard, 1887–1979
Murray, William Staite,
　1881–1962

Odundo, Magdalene, 1950
Pleydell-Bouverie, Katharine,
　1895–1985
Tchalenko, Janice, 1942
Vyse, Charles, 1882–1971

*"Pottery is at once the simplest and the most difficult
of all the arts."*

—SIR HERBERT READ, 1893–1968, British poet and critic

FRANCE

Dalpayrat, Pierre Adrien, 1844–1910
Larocque, Jean-Pierre
Sainte Phalle, Nikki de, 1930

HUNGARY

Zeisel, Eva, 1906

JAPAN

Hamada, Shoji, 1892–1978

SPAIN

Picasso, Pablo, 1881–1973

UNITED STATES

Adams, Hank Murta, 1956
Arneson, Robert, 1930–1992
Ase, Arne, 1940
Autio, Rudy, 1926
Baggs, Arthur, 1886–1947
Bean, Bennett, 1941
Butterly, Kathy, 1963
Chicago, Judy, 1939
de Staebler, Stephen, 1933
DeVore, Richard, 1933
Dillingham, Rick, 1952–1994

Duckworth, Ruth, 1919
Earl, Jack, 1934
Frank, Mary, 1933
Frey, Viola, 1933
Fritz, Robert C., 1920–1986
Gilhooley, David, 1943
Gill, Andrea, 1948
Higby, Wayne, 1943
Holcomb, Jan, 1945
Hudson, Robert, 1938
Hughto, Margie, 1944

Jeck, Douglas, 1963

Karnes, Karen, 1925

Koons, Jeff, 1955

Lewis, Lucy, d. 1992

Lucero, Michael, 1953

Lukens, Glen, 1887–1967

MacKenzie-Childs, Victoria and Richard L.

Martinez, Maria Montoya, 1887–1980

McLaughlin, Mary Louise, 1847–1939 .

Moonelis, Judy, 1953

Nagle, Ron, 1939

Nam, Yun-Dong,

Natzler, Gertrud, 1935–1971

Natzler, Otto, 1908

Ohr, George, 1857–1918

Price, Ken, 1935

Rhodes, Daniel, 1911–1989

Rippon, Tom, 1954

Robineau, Adelaide Alsop, 1865–1929

Rothman, Jerry, 1933

Saxe, Adrian, 1943

Shaw, Richard, 1941

Schrekengost, Viktor, 1906

Soldner, Paul, 1921

Staffel, Rudolf (Rudy), 1911–2002

Stratton, Mary Chase Perry, 1867–1961

Turner, Robert C., 1913

Van Briggle, Artis, 1869–1904

Voulkos, Peter, 1924–2002

Warashina, Patti, 1940

Weller, Samuel A., 1851–1925

Wildenhain, Marguerite, 1898–1985

Wood, Beatrice, 1893–1998

Wright, Russell, 1904–1976

Youngblood, Nathan, 1954

TEXTILES AND FIBER ARTS

Everyone has textiles. Everyone wears them. Some people consciously collect them as works of art and yet others collect them because of sentimental value— as in the case of wedding gowns, christening dresses, doll clothes, handmade rugs, or family quilts. Textiles are made to be used, and eventually, because most are of natural fibers such as silk, wool, or cotton, they begin to disintegrate. Artificial materials such as rayon, nylon, or acetate last longer, but also can fade or become brittle. Contemporary fiber arts are a recognized art form, with more and more artists creating art from soft natural materials. Some of these are "wearable art," others sculpture, others simply artworks on cloth. Artists weave, bead, wrap, dye, stamp, screen, use photo-images, needlepoint, and quilt, turning fibers into amazing forms.

"Develop an infallible technique, then place yourself at the mercy of inspiration."

—RALPH RAPSON, b. 1914, architect, designer and teacher

MUSEUMS WITH EXCEPTIONAL TEXTILE COLLECTIONS

The museums in this list, throughout their history, and through the dedication of curators and restoration staff, have become known for their extraordinary textile collections.

Vienna, Austria	Kunsthistorisches Museum
Toronto, Canada	Museum for Textiles
Bath, England	The Museum of Costume
Helmshore, England	Helmshore Textile Museums
London, England	Victoria and Albert Museum
Aix-en-Provence, France	Musée des Tapisseries, Chateau d'Angers
Angers, France	Musée Jean Lurçat et de la Tapisserie Contemporaine
Paris, France	Musée de Cluny; Musée des Gobelins; Le Musée de La Mode et du Textile; Musée des Arts Décoratifs; Louvre; Mobilier National; Petit Palais
Pau, France	Musée des Beaux-Arts
Reims, France	Musée des Beaux-Arts
Berlin, Germany	German Historical Museum, Textiles & Clothing
Oslo, Norway	Norsk Folkemuseum
Cracow, Poland	Wawel Museum; Wawel Cathedral
Lisbon, Portugal	National Museum of Art; Palacio National da Ajuda
Madrid, Spain	El Escorial
Santiago de Compostela, Spain	Cathedral
Saragossa, Spain	Cathedral el Pilar Y la Seo; Tapestry Museum
Bern, Switzerland	Historical Museum

UNITED STATES

Los Angeles, California	Los Angeles County Museum of Art
San Francisco, California	California Palace of the Legion of Honor
District of Columbia	Smithsonian; Daughters of the American Revolution; The Textile Museum
Paducah, Kentucky	Museum of the American Quilter's Society
Lowell, Massachusetts	New England Quilt Museum
Dearborn, Michigan	Greenfield Village
Santa Fe, New Mexico	Girard Collection, Museum of International Folk Art
New York City	Cloisters; Metropolitan Museum of Art; Museum of the City of New York, Costume Collection; Cooper Hewitt
Cleveland, Ohio	Cleveland Museum of Art
Newport, Rhode Island	Rhode Island School of Design
Houston, Texas	Museum of Fine Arts

TEXTILE TERMS

The following are brief descriptions of some fiber items from various cultures that are often seen in museums, or treasured and displayed.

African Kente cloth. Brightly colored narrow strips of cloth woven (only by men) into lengths that are joined together as robes to be worn by leaders.

Batik. Designs applied to cloth with molten wax before the cloth is dyed; thus waxed areas retain the color beneath the wax, yet with a crackled effect; originated in Indonesia.

339

Carpets. Handmade rugs are created by knotting each strand of yarn onto a "warp" individually. The vast majority of handmade rugs continue to be created in the "rug belt," which ranges from China through the Middle East and Central Asia to Spain. It was originally thought that the technique originated in Islamic countries in approximately the 12th century, and then spread to Western Europe. However, this theory has been challenged by the finding of an ancient knotted rug, found in Siberia, dating from 500 B.C.

Clothing/costume. Special articles of clothing have always been used for festive occasions, and while they might not have been considered "costumes" at the time, they now fit into that category.

Embroidered mirror work. Small pieces of mirror are incorporated into heavily embroidered cloth designs. Primarily done in India.

Embroidery. Garments and cloth for special occasions the world over have been embellished (usually by women) with tiny decorative stitches. Embroidery is becoming a lost art, and people are beginning to treasure such pieces as they may have or collect.

Felting. Felted garments and rugs are made from carded (combed) wool that is pressed and steamed.

Hooked rug. Yarn or rags sewn to a support such as burlap; these rugs usually feature animals, flowers, or geometric designs.

Kantha. Common to Bangladesh, the kantha is constructed of used saris assembled in layers and embroidered.

Mola. Made by the Cuna Indians, San Blas Islands near Panama, these small reverse appliquéd cloth panels are made of layers that are cut out and embroidered. Originally used as blouse fronts.

Mourning pictures. Sentimental scenes often including Grecian urns or a weeping willow tree were embroidered on silk. These mementos were created during Victorian times to commemorate the passing of someone dear.

Navajo rugs. These rugs continue to be treasured. Dyes, designs, and type of yarn are updated, and these are truly an art form.

Needlepoint. This labor-intensive form of needlework has traditionally been used to create chair coverings, tapestries, small pillows, or cushions.

Quilts. Quilts began as utilitarian bedcovers made from used fabrics. They evolved to fancy designs, and are appreciated today as works of art.

Sampler. Usually a small piece of embroidered cloth created by young girls as they learned fancy embroidery stitches.

Sari. A traditional garment made of a 6-ft. length of cloth that ranges from plain white to brilliant colors; can be of simple cloth or the finest embroidered silk.

Sumak. Tapestry woven in Iran.

Weaving. Tapestries, rugs, serapes, and table covers, for example, generally woven on a loom. Primitive looms existed as long ago as 5000 B.C., as seen in cave pictures. Woven clothing is considered wearable art.

Wrapping. Single strands of fiber (yarn, sisal, horsehair, hemp) are wrapped around a core made of cord, rope, or multiple strands of fiber. The stiff strands may be combined to create large standing fiber wool sculptures or to create small vessels or fine jewelry.

PRESERVING TEXTILES

To preserve a textile, you may choose to store the object, or display it by hanging or framing it. Here are some tips to add to the longevity of your textile collectibles.

To display the textile:

- For a flat object such as a quilt, tapestry, or rug, hand-sew a cotton band across the top through which a rod can be placed for hanging.
- A Velcro support system is an alternative that allows support to be placed evenly.
- Hang only textiles that are sturdy and in good condition.
- If you're going to hang it, consider lining the textile to protect the back, just as you would line draperies, especially if it will hang on a paneled wall. The lining should be lighter than the textile.
- You can display a costume on a thickly padded hanger. Drape a thin ribbon

over the hanger on each end, supporting the inside of the waist with the ribbon rather than by the shoulders of the garment.

- Even if displaying a costume on a dummy, support the skirt at the waist in order to minimize strain at the shoulders. A "dummy" can be made of stuffed cloth or acid-free tissue paper.

For framing:

- Smaller flat items, such as a sampler, pieces of lace, or embroidery, should be framed under glass, but not touching it. To protect the fabric, sew it onto a piece of unbleached muslin first, then stretch the muslin over canvas stretchers, foam board, or archival mountboard.
- Protect the back of the textile by covering the back of the frame with acid-free cardboard and paper.
- Use UV-filtered glass and keep out of direct sunlight.

General suggestions:

- Keep an inventory and photograph of rugs, tapestries, or other textile collectibles.
- Keep textiles as clean as possible.
- You can vacuum dust from a textile, protecting the surface with a filtration fabric (a monofilament screen similar to a silk screen).
- Check from time to time for possible damage from silverfish, beetles, and moths.
- Try to avoid storing where there are extreme fluctuations of temperature and humidity. Ideal conditions would be 50 percent humidity and 60 to 65 degrees F.
- Treat fresh stains immediately.

To store textiles:

- Avoid storing textiles in basements or attics.
- Store clean items washed, unstarched, and unironed.
- Costumes should be stored flat, folded at the waist, with sleeves folded across the front. Pad with cotton cloth or acid-free tissue inside the fold to avoid breakage of the fibers.

- Cotton-wrapped textiles can be stored in an unsealed plastic wrapping.
- Delicate textiles ideally could be stored individually or as the top layer of less delicate items in a drawer.
- Remove the textiles from time to time and air them out, refolding on different lines.
- Tapestries and rugs should be rolled onto tubes rather than folded. Roll rugs, quilts, and flat textiles by placing acid-free tissue on top and rolling with the decorative side facing outward.

Ideal materials for storing textiles:

- Old sheets
- Unbleached muslin
- Archival tissue paper
- Acid-free boxes
- Enameled metal shelves

Avoid the following:

- Direct contact with wood or plastic
- Cardboard (anything made with wood has acids that affect cloth)
- Blue tissue paper
- Bleached cloth
- Avoid commercial dry cleaning if possible
- Air-tight plastic bags
- Extreme temperature fluctuations
- Stacking large bundles of textiles (the weight can break fibers)
- Direct sunlight
- Adhesives that will permanently damage cloth over time
- Pesticides, which can damage some fabrics

"The hands make the head clever."
—MICHAEL CARDEW, 1901–1983, English potter and teacher

COLLECTING TEXTILES

As with other forms of collecting, before you begin investing you should become educated about the art you want to collect. Go to museums, read, and talk with other people who have textile collectibles you admire. Here are some tips to get you started.

- Know your dealer.
- Always ask for a receipt, identifying an item such as a rug and the price paid.
- Hold it up to the light to find holes and areas of wear.
- Look also for areas that may have been "fiddled" by having dye, tea or coffee, or even marking pen added to disguise wear.
- Consider what you intend to use your collectibles for and where you will display them.

MASTER FIBER ARTISTS

This is just a short list of the many fiber artists whose names have become known in the last few generations. Their work is frequently seen in museums and books.

CANADA

Newdigate, Ann, 1934

CZECH REPUBLIC

Mrazek, Bohdan, 1931

FRANCE

Gromaire, Marcel, 1892–1971
Léger, Fernand, 1881–1955
Lurçat, Jean, 1892–1966
Poiret, Paul, 1879–1944

GERMANY

Knodel, Gerhardt, 1940
Stolzl, Gunta, 1897–1983

HUNGARY

Ban, Istvan, 1922

JAPAN

Arai, Junichi, 1932
Kobayashi, Naomi, 1945
Kubota, Itchiku, 1917
Murata, Hirozo, 1920
Otani, Keiji, 1967
Takahashi, Hideko, 1950

NORWAY

Hansen, Frida, 1855–1930
Munthe, Gerhard, 1849–1929

POLAND

Sadowska, Krystyna, 1912–2000
Sledziewska, Anna, 1900

UNITED STATES

Abakanowicz, Magdalena, 1930
Albers, Anni, 1899–1994
Amaral, Olga de, 1932
Blount, Akira, 1945
Cook, Lia, 1942
Dickerson, Ann
Hicks, Sheila, 1934
Itter, Diane, 1946–1989
James, Michael, 1949

UNITED STATES *(continued)*

Larsen, Jack Lenor, 1927
Liebes, Dorothy, 1899–1972
O'Banion, Nance, 1949
Rapoport, Debra E., 1945
Reichek, Elaine, 1943
Ringgold, Faith, 1930
Rossbach, Ed, 1914–2002
Sauer, Jane, 1937
Schira, Cynthia, 1934
Sekimachi, Kay, 1926
Tawney, Lenore, 1925
Turner, Robert, 1913
Zeisler, Claire, 1903–1991

MASTER CRAFTSPERSONS OF THE 20TH CENTURY

This list cannot possibly include all the artisans who make a living in the crafts field. These artists' names come to the forefront because of the consistency and quality of their work over time. Some of these artists work with the materials of their craft in the traditional way, while others are more progressive and "break the barriers."

BASKETRY

United States

McQueen, John, 1943
Niehues, Sharon, 1952, and
    Leon, 1951

Sauer, Jane, 1937
Seitzman, Lincoln, 1923

JEWELRY AND METALWORK

Denmark

Jensen, Georg, 1866–1935
Koppel, Heinz, 1919–1980
Nielsen, Harald, 1892–1977

England

Knox, Archibald, 1864–1933

France

Cartier, Louis, 1875–1942
Lalique, René, 1860–1945
Puiforcat, Jean, 1897–1945

Germany

Brandt, Marianne, 1893–1983
Friedlander, Marguerite,
1896–1985

Italy

Vitali, Ubaldo

Norway

Vigeland, Tone, 1938

Spain

Cuyas, Ramon Puig, 1953

Sweden

Torun Bulow-Hube, Vivianna,
1927

United States

Aguado, Deborah, 1939
Baldwin, Phillip, 1953
Brush, Daniel
Eickerman, Alma, 1908–1995
Herbst, Gerhard, 1959
Hu, Mary Lee, 1943
Paley, Albert, 1944
Pardon, Earl, 1926–1991
Pearson, Ronald Hayes,
1924–1996
Prip, John, 1922
Scherr, Mary Ann, 1931
Seppa, Heikke, 1927
Smith, Richard (Rick), 1960
Threadgill, Linda, 1947
Tiffany, Louis Comfort,
1848–1933

"It's my art. . . . Why should I care if people don't like it?"
—JOHN STEWART, 20th century New York collector

PAPERMAKING

United States

Babcock, John, 1941
Seventy, Sylvia, 1947

WOODWORKING

United States

Bencomo, Derek, 1962
Castle, Wendell, 1932
Exton, Peter, 1951
Groth, David, 1950
Isham, Tex
Jones, Arthur
Lindquist, Mark, 1949
Lindquist, Melvin, 1911

Maloof, Sam, 1916
Moulthrop, Edward, 1916
Nakashima, George, 1905–1990
Prip, John, 1922
Sils, Al
Stocksdale, Bob, 1913
Vesery, Jacques

"Collections generally need to be put together slowly and include similar works."
—RUTH SACKNER, 20th-century Miami collector

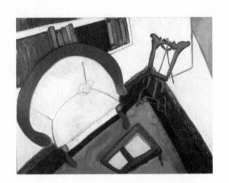

CHAPTER 6

Museums to Visit Around the World

"We should comport ourselves with the masterpieces of art as with exalted personages—stand quietly before them and wait till they speak to us."
—ARTHUR SCHOPENHAUER, 1788–1860,
German philosopher and writer

HOW TO VISIT A MUSEUM

Even the most dedicated museum-goer or tourist can become visually saturated after two hours or so in a large museum. Here are some suggestions to help you get the most out of your museum visit and recognize what the museum considers its masterpieces, and why.

IN A LARGE MUSEUM

❖ At the front desk, pick up a map and any literature about the museum's permanent collection or special exhibitions. Notice the artwork that is reproduced on the front, as that may be the "best" work in the museum. If a catalogue of the collection is at the desk, look briefly through it to familiarize yourself with the different works.

❖ If you know in advance that you will be going, get a museum catalogue from a library and go through it.

❖ Most museums have one period or one artist's works of which they are especially proud. This may have been the result of a curator's choice, or the good fortune of having a privately amassed collection donated.

❖ In a museum that contains a large private collection, try to see common threads in the artwork that might have appealed to the collector who chose these particular items.

❖ Make a quick visit to the museum shop to look at the postcards of the museum's collection. See what they have considered worth reproducing.

❖ Begin your visit in the galleries in which you are most interested. If this is a museum you revisit from time to time, begin each visit in a different gallery, as you will absorb more at the beginning of the tour than later on.

❖ Keep in mind that frequently much of a museum's collection is in storage. Curators rotate and rehang work on a regular basis, and it is always worthwhile to visit a gallery you haven't seen for a while.

❖ If you have a short time, many museums have acoustiguides—headphones with a recording that speaks about specific masterpieces in the collection.

❖ A conducted tour will explain the highlights of the collection, but you may wish to return another day for a revisit to your personal favorites.

❖ To increase your appreciation, pause briefly as you enter a gallery and look all the way around the room. See if one work in the room immediately gets your attention. Look again as you leave.

❖ Notice how a gallery is arranged. Curators take great care to juxtapose works that complement each other.

❖ Sit down from time to time where there are benches, to take time to look around the room, or to really look at one piece.

❖ Take a refreshment break after two hours.

❖ Play a game with yourself as to which one work in a gallery or exhibition you would add to your "personal collection" if availability and price were no issue. Famous writer Brendan Gill said that he had a "mental collection" of only three works, which he "de-accessed" (just as a museum might) or upgraded from time to time.

❖ Artist Betty Polites says that when she and her husband visit a gallery or museum together, each one selects "the best" artwork in each gallery and they then compare their selections.

❖ To examine a painting closely without making the guards nervous, put your hands behind your back while you look at details.

❖ If a work of art is of special interest to you, these details will be on the wall label next to the painting:

- The title of the artwork

- The artist's name, birth, and death dates

- The date the artwork was created

- The medium, such as watercolor or oil on canvas

- A number, such as 14:67, which usually means that this was the 14th work acquired in 1967

- Whether it was a museum purchase or given by a donor

- Historical information

VIEWING A BLOCKBUSTER EXHIBITION

Many large museums host a "blockbuster" exhibition from time to time. Tickets may be purchased in advance that will enable the ticket holder to join a line to enter the exhibit at a designated time. Many of the works at such exhibits are on loan from private collectors and museums you may never get to visit. Such exhibitions often include much more information and related art than one museum collection might contain, and it is truly worth your time to visit them. Generally, audio tours are included with the admission price and will make viewing more meaningful. Here are some tips on how to maximize the experience of visiting such an exhibition.

❖ People enter a gallery in surges, going to the special paintings that a curator has chosen to discuss on the audio tour. These large crowds usually prevent a close look. Instead, listen to the lecture, while looking at other items in the gallery; then when the crowd moves on, stay behind to look at the work more closely.

❖ After your tour, take time to visit the museum shop and purchase a catalogue of the collection, or at least a memento, such as note cards or a refrigerator magnet.

❖ If the blockbuster exhibit is in your own town, revisit it more than once. At the same time, always take the opportunity to revisit a different gallery featuring the permanent collection.

LOOKING AT SCULPTURES

Looking at sculpture takes a somewhat different mind-set than looking at paintings. Sometimes it is necessary to read the label first for the title of a sculpture, which may help your understanding. In addition, it's helpful to look at a sculpture from all angles. In a one-color material, notice how the artist created differences through the use of texture and shadow. As you view a sculpture, it's helpful to remember the following.

- ❖ How does the sculpture affect you? Perhaps you are repulsed, or long to own this sculpture, or are amused. If you feel something when you see a sculpture, perhaps the artist has succeeded in projecting his or her own creative intent.

- ❖ Tempting as it is to touch, don't!

- ❖ Contemporary sculpture is sometimes made of a material that you know would be repulsive to the touch. The sculpture may also be intangible and untouchable, as would be the case with one created from projected images, or an environment with changing lights, movement, smell, or sound, or a combination of all of these.

- ❖ Notice if there are areas that are especially refined or polished—perhaps the artist was calling your attention to that portion.

LOOKING AT CONTEMPORARY ART

Contemporary art by definition means that the artist is still living or has recently died. It is frequently an art of ideas and concepts, with the material being secondary. Most contemporary art museums are building permanent collections while offering frequently changing exhibits that carry out their mission. When viewing contemporary art, keep the following points in mind.

- ❖ Instead of making judgments about whether something is beautiful or ugly, try to understand the artist's message. It may be something about the environment, or sexuality or the materialism of today's populace.

- ❖ Take time to read any literature about the artist or the collection made available at the museum so you can more fully understand the purpose and the origin of the work.

LOOKING AT THE MUSEUM ITSELF

Often, the buildings that house some of the world's greatest artistic masterpieces are themselves works of art, painstakingly designed to enhance the art-viewing experience. Next time you visit a museum, take time to examine the architecture of the building.

- ❖ Look at the building exterior, and if possible, walk around the outside, where sculptures are frequently sited.
- ❖ Observe how the architect used or did not use outside light in the interior. What devices were used to protect the artwork from sunlight?
- ❖ If you were designing this museum, what would you change to make it more patron-friendly?

VISITING MUSEUMS IN A CITY YOU MAY VISIT ONLY ONCE

Of course, if you are visiting a city you think you probably won't be visiting again (or at least not for a very long time), how you spend your limited amount of time is particularly important, and deciding which museums to visit can be a tough task. Here are some tips to get you started.

- ❖ Find out which is considered the major museum in that city.
- ❖ Find out about minor museums or homes of artists.
- ❖ See if you can visit several small museums in one neighborhood.
- ❖ Combine a visit to a small museum with an opportunity to take public transportation and walk in a local neighborhood.

❖ When time is of the essence and you want to see them all, take taxis.

❖ In a small museum such as an historic house or the collection of one artist, take advantage of a docent's knowledge of the collection.

VISITING A MUSEUM WITH CHILDREN

Children can quickly lose interest while visiting an art museum, where "hands-on" involvement is forbidden. Here are a few guidelines for keeping the museum experience a positive one for children (and the adults accompanying them).

❖ Set some basic rules: look but don't touch; speak quietly; don't run; watch where you're going; don't sit on any furniture except benches.

❖ Make a viewfinder by cutting a 1 × 1½-inch rectangle in an index card, and encourage the child to look through the viewfinder to isolate a portion of an artwork (like taking a photo of it).

❖ Let the child bring a small notebook and pencil to draw something he or she sees in a painting. You can also "assign" something to draw, such as eyes or hats from several different paintings.

❖ A child's audiotour (offered for some exhibitions) calls a child's attention to something in a painting that may be of special interest. The paintings to which these apply are usually identified by a wall-label of a different color than the adult audio tour (and the adults may find these tidbits interesting too).

❖ Some museums offer a small "children's educational pack" in the museum shop, which typically has reproductions of some of the exhibited work and suggestions for gallery activities for children.

❖ If this is a frequently visited museum and you have a collection of post-cards from the museum, carry along a set so the child can match the postcard to the picture in a gallery. Children love this "matching game."

❖ Use a modified form of scavenger hunt in each gallery. Ask the child to hunt for a work with geometric shapes, a painting with a dog or horse, a red/yellow/blue combination, movement in a painting or sculpture, an artwork that shows a tree/sky/water (whatever you can see at a glance when you enter the gallery). Or (if a gallery has both paintings and sculpture) ask the child to find a painting that goes with a sculpture.

❖ For an older child, suggest finding one painting to hang in his or her own room, and ask why that one was chosen.

❖ When you get home, ask the child to draw something based on what he or she saw that day.

❖ Ask questions about what the child saw; don't make statements. Let the child express personally what feelings the art evoked.

"Art is a way of expression that has to be understood by everyone, everywhere."
—RUFINO TAMAYO, 1899–1991, Mexican muralist

ARTISTS' HOMES AND MUSEUMS AROUND THE WORLD

It is always interesting to envision the life and work of an artist by visiting the place where he or she worked. Seeing the artist's original palette, a paint-spattered floor, or the artwork collected can add a new dimension to your appreciation. Here is a list of individual artists' museums or studios that you can visit to get a sense of the environment from which the artist drew inspiration, and to see some of the artists' work. Occasionally, these settings contain the artist's personal art collection, or work that was kept especially for the family.

BELGIUM

Breughel, Pieter. Breughel Museum, Brussels
Ensor, James. Ensor-Museum, Oostend
Memling, Hans. The Memling Museum, The Medieval Hospice, Bruges
Permeke, Constant. Museum Constant Permeke, Jabbeke
Rubens, Peter Paul. Rubenshuis, Antwerp

CZECH REPUBLIC

Mucha, Alphonse. Mucha Museum, Prague

ENGLAND

Hepworth, Barbara. Barbara Hepworth Museum and Sculpture Garden, Cornwall
Moore, Henry. Henry Moore Foundation, Hertfordshire

FRANCE

Bourdelle, Emile-Antoine. Musée Bourdelle, Paris

Cézanne, Paul. Atelier de Cézanne, Aix-en-Provence

Chagall, Marc. Musée Marc Chagall, Nice

Cocteau, Jean. La Chapelle Saint-Pierre, Villefranche-sur-Mer; Musée
    Jean Cocteau, Merton

Corbusier. Fondation Le Corbusier, Paris

Delacroix, Eugène. Musée Eugène-Delacroix, Paris (Includes a large
    collection of Toulouse-Lautrec's work and that of other modern artists.)

Léger. Le Musée National Fernand Léger, Biot

Maillol, Aristide. Musée Maillol, Paris

Matisse, Henri. La Chapelle du Rosaire, Vence; Musée Matisse, Nice

Monet, Claude. Musée Claude-Monet, Musée des Impressionistes
    Américains, Giverny, near Paris; Musée Marmottan (Claude Monet's
    Paris Home), Paris

Moreau, Gustave. Musée Gustave-Moreau, Paris

Picasso, Pablo. Le Musée National Picasso, Vallauris; Musée Picasso,
    Paris; Musée Picasso, Chateau Grimaldi, Antibes

Renoir, Pierre Auguste. Le Musée Renoir; Le Domaine des Collettes,
    Cagnes-sur-Mer

Rodin, Auguste. Rodin Museum, Paris

Toulouse-Lautrec, Henri de. Musée Toulouse-Lautrec, Palais de la
    Berbie, Albi

van Gogh, Vincent. Vincent van Gogh Foundation, Arles

GERMANY

Dürer, Albrecht. Albrecht Dürer House, Nuremberg

Kollwitz, Käthe. Käthe Kollwitz Museum Berlin, Berlin

Lehmbruck, Wilhelm. Wilhelm Lehmbruck Museum, Duisburg

Modersohn-Becker, Paula. Paula Modersohn-Becker Haus, Roselius-
    Haus, Bremen

ITALY

Chirico. Casa de Chirico, Rome

Marini, Marino. Marino Marini Museum, Florence

NETHERLANDS

Escher, M. C. Escher's Art Museum, Leeuwarden
Hals, Frans. Frans Hals Museum, Haarlem
Rembrandt. Rembrandthuis, Amsterdam
van Gogh, Vincent. Vincent van Gogh Museum, Amsterdam

NORWAY

Munch, Edvard. Munch Museum, Oslo
Vigeland, Gustave. Vigeland Sculpture Park and Vigeland Museum, Oslo

SPAIN

Miró, Joan. Joan Miró Foundation, Barcelona
Picasso, Pablo. Museo Picasso, Barcelona; Museo Picasso, Malaga
Sorolla, Joaquin. Museo Joaquin Sorolla y Bastida, Madrid

SWEDEN

Milles, Carl. Millesgarden, Stockholm

SWITZERLAND

Klee, Paul. Paul Klee Centre, Bern
Tinguely, Jean. Museum Jean Tinguely, Basel

UNITED STATES

Benton, Thomas Hart. Thomas Hart Benton Home and Studio, Kansas City, Missouri
Dali, Salvador. Salvador Dali Museum, St. Petersburg, Florida
Gorman, R. C., Navajo Gallery, Taos, New Mexico
Gross, Chaim. Chaim Gross Studio Museum, New York City
Hopper, Edward. Hopper House, Nyack, New York
Noguchi, Isamu. Isamu Noguchi Garden Museum, Long Island City, New York
O'Keeffe, Georgia. Georgia O'Keeffe Foundation, Santa Fe, New Mexico
Remington, Frederic. Remington Art Memorial, Ogdensburg, New York

UNITED STATES *(continued)*

Rockwell, Norman. Norman Rockwell Museum at Stockbridge, Stockbridge, Massachusetts

Rodin, Auguste. Rodin Museum, Philadelphia

Rothko, Mark. Rothko Chapel, Houston, Texas

Russell, Charles. Charles Russell Museum, Great Falls, Montana

Saint-Gaudens, Augustus. Saint-Gaudens Historic Site, Cornish, New Hampshire

Twombly, Cy. Cy Twombly Gallery, Houston, Texas

Warhol, Andy. Andy Warhol Museum, Pittsburgh, Pennsylvania

Whistler, James McNeill. Whistler House Museum of Art, Lowell, Massachusetts

Wyeth, Andrew. Brandywine River Museum, Chadds Ford, Pennsylvania (Also features work by other members of the Wyeth family)

Wright, Frank Lloyd. Frank Lloyd Wright Foundation, Oak Park, Illinois

MUSEUMS OF LATE MODERN AND CONTEMPORARY ART

Although some of these museums have permanent collections, many museums of contemporary art do not, as they can remain truly contemporary only by featuring changing exhibitions of the "latest" artists. A few will only show work of living artists.

AUSTRALIA

Adelaide	Art Gallery of South Australia
Canberra	National Gallery of Australia
Melbourne	Museum of Modern Art at Heide; Australian Center for Contemporary Art
Sydney	Museum of Contemporary Art

AUSTRIA

Salzburg	Museum of Modern Art
Vienna	KunstHaus Wien; Museum of the 20th Century; Osterreichische Galerie; Leopold Museum; Museum of Modern Art

BELGIUM

Antwerp	The Museum van Hedendaagse Kunst Antwerpen
Brussels	Musée d'Art Moderne; Musées Royaux des Beaux-Arts de Belgique
Ghent	The Stedelijk Museum voor Actuele Kunst

BRAZIL

Rio de Janeiro	Museu de Arte Moderna

CANADA

Montreal	Montreal Museum of Fine Arts
Ottawa	National Gallery of Canada
Toronto	Center for Contemporary Art; The Power Plant; Ydessa Hendeles Art Foundation

DENMARK

Humlebaek	Louisiana Museum of Modern Art (near Copenhagen)
Ishoj	Arken Museum of Modern Art

ENGLAND

Aylesbury	Peter Stuyvesant Foundation Limited
Bebington	Lady Lever Art Gallery
Cambridge	Fitzwilliam Museum
Liverpool	Tate Gallery Liverpool
London	Barbican Art Gallery; Cotton's Atrium; Courtauld Institute Galleries; Hayward Gallery; South Bank Centre; National Gallery; Saatchi Collection; Tate Britain (Millbank); Tate Modern (Bankside)
Nottingham	City Art Gallery, Nottingham Castle
Oxford	Museum of Modern Art

ENGLAND *(continued)*

Salford	Salford Art Gallery and Museum
Southampton	Southampton City Art Gallery
St. Ives	Tate Gallery St. Ives

FINLAND

Helsinki	Kiasma Museum of Contemporary Art; Finnish National Gallery

FRANCE

Cergy-Pontoise	Musée de Pontoise
Grenoble	Centre National d'Art Contemporain de Grenoble
Lyon	Musée d'Art Contemporaine
Marseille	Musée Cantini
Nantes	Musée des Beaux-Arts
Nice	Musée d'Art Moderne et d'Art Contemporaine
Paris	Musée d'Orsay; Musée d'Art Moderne de la Ville de Paris; Musée National d'Art Moderne (Centre Georges Pompidou)
Saint Paul de Vence	Maeght Foundation
Saint-Etienne	Musée de Saint-Etienne

"There is no abstract art. You must always start with something."

—PABLO RUIZ Y PICASSO, 1881–1973,
Spanish Cubist painter

GERMANY

Berlin	Akademie der Kunste; Bildende Kunst; Berlinische Galerie; Deutsche Guggenheim Berlin
Bremen	Kunsthalle Bremen
Cologne	Museum Ludwig Koln
Frankfurt	Museum für Moderne KunstHagen; Karl Ernst Osthaus-Museum
Hamburg	Hamburger Kunsthalle
Karlsruhe	Museum für Moderne Kunst
Krefeld	Kaiser Wilhelm Museum
Munich	Goetz Collection
Munster	Westfallsches Landesmuseum
Stuttgart	Staatsgalerie Stuttgart
Wuppertal	Von der Heydt-Museum

INDIA

West Bengal	Rabindra Shavan Archive

IRELAND

Dublin	Irish Museum of Modern Art; Hugh Lane Municipal Gallery of Modern Art

ISRAEL

Jerusalem	Israel Museum

ITALY

Rome	Contemporary Art Center (to open in 2005); Galleria Nazionale d'Arte Moderna e Contemporanea
Turin	Fondo Rivetti per l'Arte
Udine	Galleria Civica d'Arte Moderna
Varese	Panza's Villa/Guggenheim
Venice	Galleria Internazionale d'Arte Moderna di Ca'Pesaro; Peggy Guggenheim Collection

JAPAN

Hiroshima	Hiroshima City Museum of Contemporary Art
Kagawa	Museum Marugame Hirai
Kyoto	The National Museum of Modern Art
Nagaoka	The Niigata Prefectual Museum of Modern Art
Naoshima	Naoshima Museum
Sakura	Museum of Contemporary Art
Tokyo	Bridgestone Museum of Art; Contemporary Sculpture Centre; Tokyo National Museum of Contemporary Art; Gumma Prefectural Museum of Modern Art, Takasaki; Hara Museum of Modern Art

LUXEMBOURG

Luxembourg City	Museé d'Art Modern Grand Duc Jean

MEXICO

Mexico City	Centro Cultural Arte Contemporaneo; Museo de Arte Moderno

NETHERLANDS

Amsterdam	Stedelijk Museum of Modern Art
Groningen	Groninger Museum
Rotterdam	Kunsthal Rotterdam; Museum Boymans-van Beuningen
Tilburg	De Pont Foundation

NEW ZEALAND

Auckland	Waikato Museum of Art and History

NORWAY

Oslo	Nasjonalgalleriet; Astrup Fearnley Museum of Modern Art

POLAND

Lodz	Muzeum Sztuki w Lodzi

RUSSIA

St. Petersburg	State Russian Museum

SCOTLAND

Edinburgh	Scottish National Gallery of Modern Art
Glasgow	Gallery of Modern Art

SLOVENIA

Ljubljana	Moderna Galerija

SOUTH AFRICA

Johannesburg	Standard Bank Collection; Witwatersrand

SOUTH KOREA

Seoul	National Museum of Contemporary Art

SPAIN

Abarca de Campos	Museu d'Art Contemporani
Barcelona	Museum of Modern Art; Centre de Cultura Contemporania
Bilbao	Guggenheim Museum Bilbao
Castellon	Castellon Contemporary Art Center
Madrid	Fundacion Caja de Pensiones; IFEMA Collection; Museo Nacional Centro de Arte Reina Sofia
Valencia	Instituto Valenciano de Arte Moderno

SWEDEN

Stockholm	Modern Art Museum; Moderna Museet, Nordenhake

SWITZERLAND

Basel	Fondation Beyeler
Berne	Adolf Wolfli Foundation
Geneva	Musée d'Art Moderne et Contemporain (MAMCO); Petit Palais
Lausanne	Hermitage Foundation
Lugano	Museo d'Arte Moderna
Zurich	Kunsthaus

THAILAND

Bangkok	Bhirasi Museum of Modern Art

UNITED STATES

Arizona

Scottsdale	Scottsdale Museum of Contemporary Art
Tucson	Museum of Art

California

Escondido	California Center for the Arts
La Jolla	Museum of Contemporary Art of San Diego
Los Angeles	J. Paul Getty Museum; Los Angeles County Museum of Art; The Museum of Contemporary Art MOCA at the Geffen Contemporary
Palm Springs	Palm Springs Desert Museum
Pasadena	Pasadena Museum of Modern Art
San Diego	Museum of Contemporary Art
San Francisco	San Francisco Museum of Modern Art
Santa Ana	Orange County Center for Contemporary Art
Santa Monica	Santa Monica Museum of Art

Connecticut

Bridgeport	Housatonic Museum of Art
Brooklyn	New England Center for Contemporary Art
Hartford	Wadsworth Atheneum
New Haven	Yale University Art Gallery
Ridgefield	Aldrich Museum of Contemporary Art

District of Columbia

Washington	Corcoran Gallery of Art; Hirshhorn Museum and Sculpture Garden; National Gallery of Fine Arts; Phillips Collection

Florida

Fort Lauderdale	Museum of Art
Jacksonville	The Jacksonville Museum of Contemporary Art
Miami	Miami Art Museum
Miami Beach	Bass Museum of Art
Naples	Naples Museum of Art
North Miami	Museum of Contemporary Art/North Miami
Palm Beach	The Palm Beach Institute of Contemporary Art
West Palm Beach	Norton Gallery of Art

Georgia

Athens	Georgia Museum of Art

Hawaii

Honolulu	The Contemporary Museum; The Contemporary Museum at First Hawaiian Center; University of Hawaii Art Gallery at Manoa

Illinois

Chicago	Museum of Contemporary Art; Art Institute of Chicago
Elmhurst	Elmhurst Art Museum

Indiana

Bloomington	Indiana University Art Museum
Muncie	Art Gallery, Ball State University

Iowa

Iowa City	Museum of Art, University of Iowa

Louisiana

New Orleans	Contemporary Arts Center

Maine

Ogunquit	Ogunquit Museum of American Art

Maryland

Baltimore	The Museum for Contemporary Arts

Massachusetts

Boston	The Institute of Contemporary Art (ICA)
Northampton	Smith College Museum of Art
Springfield	Museum of Fine Arts

Michigan

Detroit	Detroit Institute of Arts

Minnesota

Minneapolis	University Gallery, Walker Art Center

Missouri

Kansas City	Kemper Museum of Contemporary Art and Design
St. Louis	Forum for Contemporary Art; Pulitzer Foundation for the Arts

Nebraska

Lincoln	Sheldon Memorial Art Gallery and Sculpture Garden

Nevada

Las Vegas	Guggenheim Las Vegas; Guggenheim-Hermitage Museum

New Jersey

Trenton	New Jersey State Museum

New Mexico

Santa Fe	Georgia O'Keeffe Foundation, Museum of Contemporary Art (MOCA)

New York

Buffalo	Albright-Knox Art Gallery
Long Island City	Contemporary Art Center
New York City	Dia Center for the Arts; Adolf and Esther Gottlieb Foundation; Metropolitan Museum of Art; Museum of Modern Art (MOMA); Neue Galerie New York; New School for Social Research; P.S. 1 Contemporary Art Center; Solomon R. Guggenheim Museum; Guggenheim Museum/Soho; The New Museum of Contemporary Art; Whitney Museum of American Art

New York *(continued)*

Poughkeepsie	Vassar College Art Gallery
Utica	Munson-Williams-Proctor Institute Museum of Art

North Carolina

Greensboro	Weatherspoon Art Gallery
Raleigh	Contemporary Art Museum
Winston-Salem	Southeastern Center for Contemporary Art (SECCA)

Ohio

Akron	Akron Art Museum
Cincinnati	The Contemporary Art Center
Cleveland	Cleveland Museum of Art
Dayton	Dayton Art Institute

Oregon

Eugene	Museum of Art

Pennsylvania

Philadelphia	Institute of Contemporary Art, Philadelphia Museum of Art; Philadelphia Art Alliance

Tennessee

Knoxville	The Knoxville Museum of Art

Texas

Austin	Archer M. Huntington Art Gallery
Dallas	Dallas Museum of Fine Arts
Fort Worth	Modern Art Museum of Fort Worth
Houston	Contemporary Arts Museum
San Antonio	San Antonio Museum of Art

Vermont

   Waitsfield   Bundy Art Gallery

Virginia

   Norfolk   Chrysler Museum at Norfolk
   Virginia Beach   Contemporary Arts Center of Virginia

Washington

   Seattle   Henry Art Gallery

West Virginia

   Huntington   Huntington Museum of Art

Wisconsin

   Milwaukee   Milwaukee Art Center

Wyoming

   Rock Springs   Fine Arts Center

VENEZUELA

   Caracas   Museo de Arte Contemporaneo de Caracas
                                   Sofia Imber

Hitler's representative in Paris one day visited Picasso, where on the wall he saw a sketch for Guernica, which symbolizes the Luftwaffe's destruction of its defenseless victim, the Basque town of Guernica. "Did you do that?" he asked Picasso, who replied, "No, you did."

MUSEUMS WITH SPECIAL COLLECTIONS
OF ANCIENT AND CLASSICAL ART

These museums have treasures from the nation in which they are located, as well as a collection of art and artifacts from ancient civilizations in Asia, Europe, the Middle East, Egypt, Greece, and Italy.

ENGLAND

Cambridge	Fitzwilliam Museum, Trumpington Street

ITALY

Florence	Galleria Accademia; Bargello National Museum
Naples	National Museum
Rome	Capitoline Museums; Galleria Nazionale d'Arte Antica; Vatican Museums; Villa Giulia National Museum

GREECE

Athens	Acropolis Museum; National Museum of Athens
Delphi	Delphi Museum

UNITED STATES

Los Angeles, California	J. Paul Getty Art Museum
San Francisco, California	M. H. De Young Memorial Museum and California Palace of the Legion of Honor
Brunswick, Maine	Bowdoin College Museum of Art
Boston, Massachusetts	Boston Museum of Fine Arts; Fogg Art Museum
Detroit, Michigan	Detroit Institute of Arts
New York City	Brooklyn Museum; The Cloisters; The Metropolitan Museum of Art
Cleveland, Ohio	Cleveland Museum of Art

MUSEUMS SPECIALIZING IN WESTERN ART
OF NORTH AMERICA

Some of these museums, in addition to displaying a representative collection of American and European art, specialize in collecting artworks specifically of the Western region of the North American Continent. These works depict the life of Native Americans, cowboys, pioneers, and the powerful landscape, as explorers first saw them. Listings are organized alphabetically by state or province.

CANADA

Calgary, Alberta	Glenbow Museum
Hull, Quebec	Canadian Museum of Civilization

UNITED STATES

Flagstaff, Arizona	Museum of Northern Arizona
Phoenix, Arizona	Heard Museum, Phoenix Art Museum
Los Angeles, California	Autry Museum of Western Heritage; Southwest Museum
Colorado Springs, Colorado	Colorado Springs Fine Arts Center
Denver, Colorado	Denver Art Museum; Museum of Western Art
District of Columbia	National Museum of the American Indian
Sarasota, Florida	John and Mable Ringling Museum
Moscow, Florida	Appaloosa Museum and Heritage Center
Shreveport, Louisiana	R. W. Norton Art Gallery
Kansas City, Missouri	Nelson-Atkins Museum of Art
St. Louis, Missouri	The St. Louis Art Museum
Bozeman, Montana	Montana State University
Great Falls, Montana	Charles Russell Museum
North Platte, Nebraska	Buffalo Bill Ranch State Historical Park
Omaha, Nebraska	Joslyn Art Museum
Roswell, New Mexico	Roswell Museum and Art Center
Santa Fe, New Mexico	Museum of New Mexico; Museum of Indian Arts & Culture/Laboratory of Anthropology; Museum of Fine Arts, Palace of the Governors; Georgia O'Keeffe Museum

Taos, New Mexico	Blumenschein Home & Museum; Harwood Foundation; Fetchin Institute; Millicent Rogers Museum; Van Vechten-Lineberry Taos Art Museum
Corning, New York	Rockwell Museum
New York City	National Museum of the American Indian
Anadarko, Oklahoma	Southern Plains Indian Museum
Bartlesville, Oklahoma	Woolaroc Museum
Oklahoma City, Oklahoma	National Cowboy Hall of Fame & Western Heritage Museum
Tahlequah, Oklahoma	Cherokee Heritage Center
Tulsa, Oklahoma	Philbrook Museum of Art; Thomas Gilcrease Institute of American History and Art
Austin, Texas	The Huntington Art Gallery
Canyon, Texas	Panhandle-Plains Historical Museum
Dallas, Texas	Dallas Museum of Art
Fort Worth, Texas	Amon Carter Museum; Sid Richardson Collection of Western Art
Orange, Texas	Stark Museum of Art
Seattle, Washington	Seattle Art Museum
Cody, Wyoming	Buffalo Bill Historical Center: Whitney Gallery of Western Art, Plains Indian Museum, Buffalo Bill Museum
Jackson Hole, Wyoming	National Museum of Wildlife Art

"A room hung with pictures is a room hung with thoughts."
—Sir Joshua Reynolds, 1723–1792,
English portraitist and critic

HISTORIC AMERICAN HOMES OPEN AS MUSEUMS

The following list includes historic sites that were at one time home to America's rich and famous, from business tycoons to political leaders to Southern landed gentry. They are all fascinating places to visit—some for their architecture, others for their unmistakable aura of aristocracy. Where available, the building's date and architectural style are included.

Alabama

Arlington Antebellum Home and Gardens, 1820, Birmingham, Greek Revival

Bellingrath Gardens and Home, c. 1920, Mobile (800 acres of gardens)

Gainswood, 1860, Demopolis (Greek Revival mansion)

Alaska

House of Wickersham, 1898, Juneau (Victorian Queen Anne)

Rika's Roadhouse, 1909–1910, Big Delta State Park, near Fairbanks

Totem Bight, reconstructed 1940, Ketchikan (Reconstruction of Native village, includes clan house and totem poles, Tlingit and Haida peoples)

Arizona

Riordan Ranch, 1904, Flagstaff (Craftsman style)

Rosson House, 1895, Phoenix (Victorian Queen Anne-Eastlake)

Taliesin West, 1938, Paradise Valley, near Phoenix (Frank Lloyd Wright's western home and school, run much as he did during his lifetime)

Arkansas

McCollum-Chidester House, 1847, Camden (Civil War era house)

Rosalie House, 1883, Eureka Springs (Brick Victorian home)

Villa Marre, 1881, Little Rock (Italianate)

California

Avila Adobe, 1818, Los Angeles (oldest house in Los Angeles)

Governor's Mansion, 1877, Sacramento (High Victorian Second Empire)

California (continued)

Haas-Lilienthal House, 1886, San Francisco (Victorian Queen Anne)

Hearst Castle, 1920s, San Simeon ("Eclectic-Hispano-Mooresque")

Hollyhock House, 1919–1921, Los Angeles (Eclectic style)

Leland Stanford Mansion, 1856, Sacramento (Italianate/French Second Empire)

Colorado

Grant-Humphreys Mansion, 1902, Denver (Renaissance Revival, Beaux Arts)

Miramount Castle Museum, 1895, Manitou Springs (Gothic and Tudor Revival)

Molly Brown House Museum, 1899, Denver (Victorian Queen Anne)

Connecticut

Hill-Stead Museum, 1901, Farmington (Colonial revival)

Mark Twain House, 1874, Hartford (Victorian Mansion)

Nathan Hale Homestead, 1776, South Coventry (period furnishings)

Old Morris House, c. 1750, New Haven (period furnishings)

Stanley-Whitman House, c. 1720, Farmington (early 18th century)

Delaware

Amstel House Museum, 1730, New Castle (Colonial style)

Nemours Mansion and Gardens, 1910, Wilmington (modified Louis XVI chateau)

Old Dutch House, late 17th century, New Castle (Delaware's oldest dwelling)

Winterthur Museum, Wilmington (estate of Henry Francis duPont)

District of Columbia

Christian Heurich Mansion, 1892 (Neo-Renaissance Victorian)

Decatur House Museum, 1818 (Federal town house)

Dumbarton Oaks (Federal Style home)

Hillwood Museum and Gardens, 1925 (Neo-Classical Style, formal gardens)

Mount Vernon, c. 1735, Mount Vernon (Colonial)

Tudor Place, 1805 (Federal style, original furnishings)

Woodlawn, 1802, 3 miles from Mount Vernon (late Georgian architecture)

Florida

Edison/Ford Winter Estates, 1885, Fort Myers (winter estates of Thomas Alva Edison and Henry Ford)

Gamble Plantation State Historic Site, 1865, Bradenton (only surviving antebellum home in south Florida)

John and Mable Ringling home, 1927, Sarasota (home and art collection)

Vizcaya Museum and Gardens, 1914–1916, Coconut Grove, near Miami (70-room Italian Renaissance villa)

Georgia

Andrew Low House, c. 1848, Savannah (home of Juliette Gordon Low, founder of the Girl Scouts of America) (Victorian/West Indian influence)

Church-Wadel-Brumby House, c. 1820, Athens (Federal-style house)

Harris House, c. 1795, Augusta (period furnishings)

Little White House Historic Site, 1932, Warm Springs (Franklin D. Roosevelt's summer home)

Taylor-Grady House, 1839, Athens (Greek-revival mansion)

Telfair Mansion and Art Museum, 1818, Savannah (Regency style)

Hawaii

Chamberlain House Museum, 1831, Honolulu (modified Greek Revival)

Hanaiakamalama (Queen Emma Summer Palace), 1848, Oahu (Greek Revival)

'Iolani Palace, 1879–1882, Honolulu, 104 rooms (American Florentine)

Maui Historical Society Museum, 1834, Maui (missionary home; home of the Rev. Dwight Baldwin and family)

Idaho

Basque Museum and Cultural Center, 1864, Boise (old boarding house for Basque immigrants)

Bishops' House, 1889, Boise (Victorian Queen Anne)

Idaho (continued)

McConnell Mansion, 1886, Moscow (eclectic Victorian)

Standrod House, 1900, Pocatello (Late Victorian, Queen Anne)

Illinois

Belvedere Mansion and Gardens, 1857, Galena (Italianate "steamboat Gothic")

Dana-Thomas State Historic Site, 1902, Springfield (Frank Lloyd Wright design, complete with furnishings)

Flanagan House, 1837, Peoria (Federal Pre-Civil War)

Lincoln Home, c. 1860, Springfield (Federal style)

Magnolia Manor, 1869, Cairo (Italianate/Victorian)

Robie House, 1909, Chicago (Frank Lloyd Wright's Prairie style)

Indiana

Barker Mansion, 1900, Michigan City

Governor Hendricks' Home, 1817, Corydon (original furnishings)

Morris-Butler House Museum, 1864, Indianapolis (Victorian)

President Benjamin Harrison Memorial Home, 1874, Indianapolis

William Henry Harrison Mansion, 1803, Vincennes (period furnishings)

Iowa

Brucemore, 1886, Cedar Rapids (Queen Anne style)

George Wyth House, 1907, Cedar Falls (furnished in Art Deco style)

Phelps House, c. 1850, Burlington (Italianate/Victorian)

Salisbury House, Des Moines (replica of king's house in Salisbury, England)

Scholte House, 1897, Pella (oldest Dutch-style dwelling in Pella; Dutch, French, and Italian furniture)

Kansas

Brown Mansion, 1897, Coffeyville (Victorian)

Carroll Mansion, 1867, Leavenworth (Victorian)

Shawnee Indian Mission State Historical Site, c. 1800, Shawnee Mission

Kentucky

Farmington, 1810, Louisville (Federal style)

Federal Hill, 1795, Bardstown (Georgian)

Hunt-Morgan House, c. 1812, Lexington (Federal period mansion)

Old Governors' Mansion, 1798, Frankfort (Georgian style)

Owensboro Museum of Fine Art, pre-Civil War, Owensboro (restored mansion now used as an art museum)

Riverview, 1857, Bowling Green (Italianate style)

Louisiana

Home Place, 1801, Charles Parish (French architecture)

Magnolia Mound, c. 1790, Baton Rouge (French architecture)

Pontalba Apartments, 19th century, New Orleans (Greek Revival style)

Shadows-on-the-Teche, 1834, New Iberia (French-style plantation mansion)

Maine

Lady Pepperell House, 1760, Kittery (Georgian)

Morse House, 1858, Portland (Victorian Mansion)

Wadsworth-Longfellow House, 1785, Portland

Wedding Cake House, c. 1820, Kennebunk (Adamesque-Federal)

Maryland

Chase-Lloyd House, 1769, Annapolis (period furnishings)

Hammond-Harwood House, 1774, Annapolis (late Georgian)

Homewood House, 1803, Baltimore (Federal period)

William Paca House, 1763, Annapolis (William Buckland carvings)

Massachusetts

Boardman House, 1686, Saugus (design attributed to Bulfinch; 19th-century paintings and furniture)

Elihu Coleman House, 1722, Nantucket Island

Hadwen House, c. 1770, Nantucket Island (Greek Revival)

Harrison Gray Otis House, 1795, Boston (Adamesque house)

House of the Seven Gables, 1668, Salem (four historic houses nearby)

Massachusetts (continued)

John Ward House, 1684, Salem (Jacobean house)

John Whipple House, 1640, Ipswich (one of the best-preserved 17th-century American homes)

Nichols House Museum, early 19th century, Boston (Federal)

Paul Revere House, c. 1676, Boston (Colonial)

Pierce-Nichols House, 1782, Salem (carpenter-builder, Samuel McIntire)

Pingree House, 1804, Salem (furnished in period pieces)

Michigan

Cranbrook House, 1908, Bloomfield Hills (Craftsman style decorative arts)

Friant House, 1892, Grand Rapids (Queen Anne/Medieval Revival)

Honolulu House Museum, 1860, Marshall (Italianate/plantation style)

Kempf House, 1853, Ann Arbor (Greek Revival architecture)

Kimball House Museum, 1886, Battle Creek (Victorian home)

Meyer May House, 1908, Grand Rapids (Frank Lloyd Wright–designed home)

Minnesota

Alexander Ramsey House, 1872, St. Paul (French Renaissance)

Charles A. Lindbergh House, 1906–1920, Little Falls

Hubbard House, 1871, Mankato (Victorian home)

Mayowood, 1911, Rochester (home of Dr. Charles Mayo) (eclectic)

Olaf Swensson Farm Museum, Granite Falls (brick farmhouse and farm)

Mississippi

Beauvoir, c. 1850, Biloxi (southern French architecture)

Governor's Mansion, 1842, Jackson (Greek Revival style)

Longwood, 1855–1861, Natchez (octagonal house, Victorian eclectic)

Magnolia Hall, 1858, Natchez (Greek Revival mansion)

Rosalie, 1820–1823, Natchez (Greek Revival antebellum style)

The Briers, 1812–1815, Natchez (Southern planter style)

Missouri

Balduc House Museum, 1770, Sainte Geneviève (French style log home)

Campbell House Museum, c. 1850, St. Louis (Victorian town house)

Chatillon-De Menil House, 1848, St. Louis (Greek Revival antebellum mansion)

Rockcliffe Mansion, c. 1900, Hannibal (Beaux-arts mansion)

Tower Grove House, c. 1850, Missouri Botannical Garden, St. Louis (Victorian furnishings)

Montana

Daly Mansion, c. 1886, Hamilton (42 room eclectic Colonial mansion)

Grant-Kohrs Ranch National Historic Site, 19th century, Deer Lodge (Greek Revival)

Moss Mansion Museum, 1901, Billings (Eclectic Renaissance Revival)

Original Governor's Mansion, 1888, Helena (22-room brick home)

William Andrews Clark House, 1884, Butte (High Victorian Queen Anne)

Nebraska

General Crook House, 1878, Omaha (period furnishings)

Louis E. May Historical Museum, 1874, Fremont (Victorian home)

Nevada

Bowers Mansion, 1864, Carson City (Italianate)

House of the Silver Door Knobs, 1868, Virginia City (Second Empire)

MacKay Mansion, 1860, Virginia City (modified Italianate)

New Hampshire

Governor John Langdon Mansion, 1784, Portsmouth (Colonial Revival)

John Paul Jones House, 1758, Portsmouth (Colonial residence)

Macphaedris-Warner House, 1718–1732, Portsmouth (Queen Anne style)

Richard Jackson House, 1664, Portsmouth (Medieval style)

Wentworth-Gardner House, 1760, Portsmouth (Georgian style)

Wheeler House, 1814–1815, Orford (Federal Style)

New Jersey

Ackerman House, 1704, Hackensack (Dutch Colonial)
Boxwood Hall State Historic Site, 1783, Elizabeth
Covenhoven House, 18th century, Freehold
Schuyler-Hamilton House, 1760, Morristown (period furnishings)
Steuben House State Historic Site, 1713, Hackensack (Colonial)
The Hermitage, 1760, Hohokus (stone Victorian house)

New Mexico

Ernest L. Blumenschein Home, 1797, Taos (Spanish colonial)
Governor's Palace, 1610–1614, Santa Fe
La Hacienda de Don Antonio Severino Martinez, 1804, near Taos
El Zaguan, pre 1850, Santa Fe (adobe Spanish Colonial)

New York

Boscobel, 1807, Route 9D between Garrison and Cold Spring
(Adamesque architecture)
Falaise, c. 1923, Sands Point, Long Island (mansion with eclectic
European influence)
Hempstead House, c. 1900, Sands Point, Long Island, early 20th century
(Wedgwood collection)
Lyndhurst, 1838, Tarrytown (Victorian mansion)
Morris-Jumel Mansion, 1765, New York City (Colonial)
Schuyler Mansion, 1761, Albany (Georgian)
Van Cortlandt Mansion, 1748, New York City (17th- and 18th-century
furnishings)
Wilcox Mansion, c. 1890s, Buffalo (Greek Revival)

North Carolina

Biltmore, 1890–1895, Asheville (250-room mansion for the Vanderbilts)
Duke Homestead State Historic Site, 1852, Durham
Newbold-White House, 1680s, Edenton (oldest house in the state)

North Dakota

Chateau de Mores State Historic Site, Medora (mansion of Marquis de
Mores)

Governors' Mansion State Historic Site, 1884, Bismarck

Ohio

John Hauck House, 19th century, Cincinnati (Italianate)

Perkins Mansion, 1837, Akron (Greek Revival style)

Stan Hywet Hall and Gardens, 1912, Akron (Tudor-revival style,
65 rooms)

Taft Museum, 1820, Cincinnati (Federal period mansion)

Oklahoma

Frank Phillips Mansion, 1908, Bartlesville

Hefner family mansion, 1917, Oklahoma City

Murray-Lindsay Mansion, 1880, Erin Springs (Classic Revival)

Overholser Mansion, 1902–1904, Oklahoma City

Oregon

Captain George Flavel House Museum, 1884, Astoria (Queen
Anne/Italianate)

Captain John C. Ainsworth House, 1850, Oregon City

Deepwood Estate, 1894, Salem (Queen Anne)

Pittock Mansion, 1914, Portland (French Renaissance chateau)

Pennsylvania

Fallingwater, 1936, Connellsville (Frank Lloyd Wright design)

Fox Hunter Mansion, 1786, Harrisburg (Federal-style stone mansion)

Landingford Plantation, 1683, Chester (Caleb Pusey Home) (early
Colonial)

Mount Pleasant, 1761, Fairmont Park, Philadelphia (18th-century High
Georgian house)

The Cloister, 1741–1743, Ephrata (Medieval-style dormitories for
communal living)

Woodford, 1756, Philadelphia (Colonial)

Rhode Island

The Breakers, 1895, Newport (Italian Renaissance Vanderbilt "cottage")
John Brown House, 1786, Providence (Georgian)
Colony House, 1739–1743, Newport (pre-Revolutionary Capitol building)
Governor Stephens Hopkins House, 1707–1742, Providence (Colonial)
Marble House, 1892, Newport (French style)

South Carolina

Heyward-Washington House, 1772, Charleston (Georgian town house)
John Mark Verdier House Museum, c. 1790, Beaufort (Federal period)
Joseph Manigault House, 1803, Charleston (Adamesque-Federal style)
Miles Brewton House, 1733, Charleston (Georgian, Pre-Revolutionary)

South Dakota

Mellette House, 1883, Watertown (Victorian home)
Pettigrew Home and Museum, 1889, Sioux Falls (Queen Anne)

Tennessee

Governor William Blount Mansion, 1792, Knoxville (two-story frame house)
James K. Polk's Ancestral Home, 1816, Columbia
Mallory-Neely House, c. 1852, Memphis (Italianate)
Woodruff-Fontaine House, 1870, Memphis (Second Empire/Victorian)

Texas

Ashton Villa, 1859, Galveston (Italianate)
DeGolyer House, 1939, Dallas (Spanish Eclectic)
Mission San Francisco de la Espada, 1731, San Antonio
Mission San Juan Capistrano, 1731, San Antonio
Moody Mansion, 1893, Galveston (Richardsonian Romanesque)
Spanish Governor's Palace, 1749, San Antonio (Spanish Colonial)
Steves Homestead, 1876, San Antonio (Italianate/Second Empire)

Utah

Alfred McCune Home, 1901, Salt Lake City (Tudor revival with East Asian influence)

Beehive House, 1853–1855, Salt Lake City (Brigham Young's home) (Greek Revival)

Kearns Mansion, 1902, Salt Lake City (eclectic Renaissance)

Vermont

Dana House, 1807, Woodstock (period furnishings)

Dutton House, 1782 (Colonial Salt box)

Historic Hildene, 1904, Manchester (Robert Todd Lincoln's Home) (Georgian manor house with original furnishings)

John Strong Mansion, 1795, Vergennes (Federal Style House)

Virginia

Adam Thoroughgood House, 1636–1640, Norfolk

Bacon's Castle, c. 1655, Surry County (Colonial)

Governor's Palace, 1706–1720, Williamsburg (Colonial Georgian style)

Gunston Hall, 1755, Alexandria (Chinese to Gothic influence, Palladian dining room)

Monticello, 1767–1826, Charlottesville (Roman classicism)

Oatlands, 1803, Leesburg (Classical revival)

Stratford, 1725, 40 miles southeast of Fredericksburg (plantation house on Potomac River)

Wythe House, 1752–1754, Williamsburg (Colonial Georgian)

Washington

Chateau Ste. Michelle, 1930, Sunnyside

Henderson House Museum, 1905, Olympia (Carpenter Gothic style)

Hoquiam's Castle, 1897, Hoquiam (Victorian/Queen Anne)

Maryhill Museum of Art, c. 1920, Goldendale (mansion featuring exhibitions of Rodin sculpture, chess collection, Native American baskets)

West Virginia

General Adam Stephen House, 1789, Martinsburg (period furnishings)
Governor's Mansion, 1925, Charleston (Georgian style)
Stealey-Goff Vance House, 1807, Clarksburg

Wisconsin

Captain Frederick Pabst Mansion, 1893, Milwaukee
Charles A. Grignon Mansion, 1837, Appleton (Greek Revival)
Cotton House, Green Bay (Greek Revival)
Kilbourntown House, Milwaukee (period furnishings)
Lincoln-Tallman House, 1855–1857, Janesville (antebellum mansion, Italianate design)
Octagon House, 1856, Fond du Lac (period furnishings)
Octagon House, 1854, Watertown (eight-sided house)

Wyoming

Historic Governors' Mansion, Cheyenne (Colonial Revival, Georgian)
Ivinson Mansion, 1892, Laramie (Victorian/Queen Anne-Eastlake)
Trail End Historic Site, 1908–1913, Sheridan (Colonial Revival, Flemish/Neo-Classical)

AMERICAN MUSEUM TOWNS

Although visiting a museum usually means touring through the contents of a building, often a whole town can serve as a museum. Visiting a museum town is a little like traveling back in time. Some of the towns in this list may be on the original site and authentically restored (such as Williamsburg); others contain some homes and buildings that have been moved and brought together in one place. In some of the following listings, historically accurate reproductions of period or regional homes may have been constructed on the site.

California

Bridgeport	Bodie State Historic Park
Columbia	Columbia State Historic Park
Solvang	Solvang Village (Scandinavian)

Connecticut

Mystic	Mystic Seaport

Florida

St. Augustine	Historic St. Augustine

Georgia

Lumpkin	Westville Village

Hawaii

Laie, Oahu	Polynesian Cultural Center

Illinois

Galesburg	Lincoln's New Salem State Historic Site; Bishop Hill
Naperville	Naper Settlement, Aurora Avenue
Nauvoo	Nauvoo Historic District

Indiana

New Harmony   Founded by Harmonie Society members

Iowa

Amana Colonies   Amish Colonies

Kentucky

Harrodsburg   Shakertown at Pleasant Hill

Maine

Augusta   Old Town
New Gloucester   Sabbathday Lake Shaker Village
Poland Spring   Shaker Village

Massachusetts

Deerfield   Deerfield Village
Nantucket Island   Nantucket Town
Pittsfield   Hancock Shaker Village
Plymouth   Plimoth Plantation
Salem   Historic Salem
Sturbridge   Old Sturbridge Village
West Springfield   Storrowton Village

Michigan

Salem   Henry Ford Museum and Greenfield Village

Minnesota

Brainerd   Lumbertown, U.S.A.

Missouri

Chesterfield   Faust Park Historic Village

Nebraska

Minden	Harold Warp Pioneer Village
Grand Island	Stuhr Museum of the Prairie Pioneer

New Hampshire

Canterbury	Canterbury Shaker Village
Portsmouth	Strawbery Banke Museum

New Jersey

Hammonton	Batsto Historic Site
Smithville	Historic Towne
Waterloo	Waterloo Village

New Mexico

Santa Fe	Historic downtown area
Taos	Taos Pueblo

New York

Albany	Shaker Heritage Society
Cooperstown	Farmer's Museum and Village Crossroads
Mumford	Genesee County Museum
New York City	Richmondtown Restoration

North Carolina

Winston-Salem	Old Salem

Ohio

Burton	Geuga County Pioneer Village
Cincinnati	Sharon Woods Village
New Philadelphia	Schoenbrunn Village State Memorial
Zoar	Zoar Village State Memorial

Pennsylvania

Ambridge	Old Economy Village
Elverson	Hopewell Furnace National Historic Site
Ephrata	Ephrata Cloister
Fallsington	Historic Fallsington
Lancaster	Farm Museum of Landis Valley

South Dakota

Madison	Prairie Village

Texas

Woodville	Heritage Garden Village

Vermont

Shelburne	Shelburne Museum

Virginia

Jamestown	Jamestown Festival Park
Williamsburg	Colonial Williamsburg
Yorktown	Yorktown

Washington

Cashmere	Old Mission Pioneer Village

West Virginia

Harpers Ferry

Wisconsin

Cassville	Stonefield

GREAT SMALL MUSEUMS

The following are some great museums to visit in cities around the world when you only have an hour or two to spare in a busy day of sightseeing . . . although you could end up spending considerably longer.

AUSTRIA

Vienna	Belvedere. Upper Belvedere, Austrian 19th and 20th Centuries, Klimt's *Judith and Holerfernes*, Schiele paintings; Lower Belvedere, Medieval and Baroque art. These two small museums are both located on a royal estate, with one housing modern art and the other older, more traditional art.

BELGIUM

Antwerp	Museum Smidt Van Gelder (one person's collection of fine china, furniture)
Bruges	Municipal Fine Arts Museum (early Flemish Masters: van Eyck, Memling, Van Der Weyden, Bosch, Gerard David)
	Rubenshuis Museum (Rubens's home with some original furnishings)

ENGLAND

London	Appsley House (town house of the Duke of Wellington, perfectly restored; includes collection of Rubens, large collection of Canaletto paintings of Venice)
	Courtauld Institute Galleries (choice collection of Impressionist painters)
	Tower of London (the Crown Jewels and a collection of armor)
	Wallace Collection, Hertford House (Boucher, Watteau, Fragonard, Sèvres, Rembrandt, Titian, Rubens, Reynolds, Canaletto)
Woburn	Woburn Abbey (250-room castle, 21 original Canaletto paintings)

FRANCE

Bayeux	Musée de la Reine Mathilde (*Bayeux Tapestry*)
Paris	Cluny (Medieval art in a Gothic residence; applied arts, tapestries, altars, Limoges enamels)
	Jacquesmart-André (collection of Renaissance art)
	Marmottan (Monet's private home; "Monet's Monets"—the ones he reserved for his family)
	Musée de l'Orangerie (Monet's *Waterlilies,* Soutine's *The Little Pastry Cook,* Utrillo's *Flag Over the Town Hall*)
	Sainte Chapelle (interior surrounded by stained glass gives visitors the feeling of being in a small jewel box)

GREECE

Athens	Benaki Museum (Byzantine art; icons, jewelry, sculpture, applied art)

IRELAND

Dublin	Trinity College Library (*Book of Kells*)

ITALY

Florence	Galleria dell'Accademia (famous statuary, primarily Michelangelo's *David*)
Rome	Borghese Palace (Bernini sculptures, fine collection of oils)

NETHERLANDS

Arnhem	Kroller Mueller Museum (van Gogh, other Dutch artists)
Haarlem	Frans Hals Museum (This almshouse where Hals spent the last years of his life contains many of his finest paintings.)
The Hague	Mauritshuis Museum (private home of Prince Johan Maurits van Nassau; the best of 17th-century Dutch and Flemish paintings)

SPAIN

Madrid   Thyssen-Bornemisza (collection of European paintings and decorative arts)

UNITED STATES

Arizona

Phoenix   Heard Museum (annual Native American art exhibition, Native American jewelry, pots, paintings, baskets, weavings, Kachina dolls)

California

Los Angeles   J. Paul Getty's home in Santa Monica

Pasadena   The Gamble House (craftsman style home—a treasure)

                       Norton Simon Museum of Art (European art, sculpture)

San Simeon   Hearst Castle (William Randolph Hearst's home and guest houses; worth the visit to see the eccentric millionaire's collection)

Delaware

Winterthur   The Henry Francis du Pont Winterthur Museum (Stuart's *George Washington*, West's *Peace Treaty Between England and the American Colonies*, American furniture, silver)

District of Columbia

Washington   Freer (worth the visit if only to see Whistler's *Peacock Room* from a London house; wonderful selection of Asian art)

                       Phillips Collection (one man's selection—Impressionist and modern, artwork by Georgia O'Keeffe, Renoir's *The Boating Party*)

Florida

St. Petersburg	Salvador Dali Museum (large collection of Dali's art)
Winter Park	Charles Hosmer Morse Museum of Art (world's most comprehensive collection of Louis Comfort Tiffany stained glass)

Hawaii

Honolulu	Honolulu Academy of the Arts (Asian, Oceanian, and African art)

Illinois

Chicago	Terra Museum (choice, small collection of American art, including work by Arthur Dove, Georgia O'Keeffe)

Kansas

Wichita	Wichita Art Museum (18th- to 20th-century American painting, sculpture, drawing, and prints)

Maryland

Baltimore	Walters Art Gallery (a personal collection of treasures, attached to a residence)

Massachusetts

Boston	Isabella Stewart Gardner (private home, turned into a museum; features a Titian Room (Titian's *Rape of Europa*), Dutch Room, and Italian Renaissance paintings and sculpture; Botticelli's *Madonna and Child of Eucharist*)
Williamstown	Sterling and Francine Clark Institute of Fine Art (14th- to 19th-century European old master collection, English silver, French Impressionist collection)

New Jersey

Morristown	Morris Museum (fine and applied arts, permanent and temporary exhibitions)

New Mexico

Santa Fe   International Museum of Folk Art (huge assemblage of folk art; must be revisited many times to appreciate the genius of the collector and the collection)

Taos   Millicent Rogers Museum (hacienda housing a superb collection of Southwestern art; includes pueblo pottery, silver jewelry, paintings, and weavings)

New York

Buffalo   Albright-Knox Art Gallery (American and European art of the last 50 years; collection of paintings, drawings, sculpture, prints)

New York City   The Frick Collection (Financier Henry Clay Frick's New York town house containing a notable collection of paintings by Rembrandt, Vermeer, Boucher; an oasis in the city)

Cloisters (Nelson Rockefeller's collection of medieval artifacts, housed in a medieval building)

Cooper Hewitt, National Design Museum, Smithsonian Institution (housed in Andrew Carnegie's former home; a chance to see good design and visit a wonderful Upper East Side mansion)

Neue Galerie (Austrian and German paintings and furniture in a Beaux Arts mansion)

Whitney Museum of American Art (Calder's original *Circus* and an exhibition of American art ranging from traditional to contemporary)

"Art's whatever you choose to frame."
—FLEUR ADCOCK, 1934, New Zealand writer and poet

Ohio

Toledo	Toledo Museum of Art (great Spanish collection; outstanding glass collection)
Youngstown	Butler Institute of American Art (complete survey of American painting, drawing, and prints)

Oklahoma

Tulsa	Philbrook Museum of Art (18th- and 19th-century European and American painting)
	Gilcrease Museum (collection of Western American sculpture and painting; Native American artifacts and art)

Oregon

Goldendale	Maryhill Museum of Art (Rodin collection, Russian icons, Native American baskets and other artifacts, outdoor full-sized reproduction of *Stonehenge*)

Pennsylvania

Merion Station	Barnes Foundation (a well-kept secret featuring a wonderful collection of Post-Impressionist, modern, primitive, African, Asian, and American art)

Tennessee

Memphis	Dixon Gallery and Gardens (German porcelain, French Impressionists, pewter)

Texas

Fort Worth	Kimbell Art Museum (European, Asian, Mesoamerican and African Art; prehistoric to 20th-century art)
Houston	Menil Collection (antiquities, Byzantine, tribal, and 20th-century collection)

Vermont

    Shelburne   Shelburne Museum (Early American and Colonial collection)

Virginia

    Williamsburg   Abby Aldrich Rockefeller Museum of Folk Art (One of the first and foremost of folk art collections, it features a variety of media.)

Washington

    Seattle   Seattle Art Museum (great collection of Northwestern Native American art; art glass)

Wyoming

    Cody   Whitney Gallery of Western Art at the Buffalo Bill Historical Center (excellent collection of Russell, Remington, Bierstadt and Catlin)

"I believe that if it were left to artists to choose their own labels, most would choose none."

—BEN SHAHN, 1898–1969, American Social Realist painter

50 MUSEUMS TO SEE IN YOUR LIFETIME

Each of the following museums is a must-see for anyone interested in art. Add them to your list of things to do during your lifetime, and get started by going to the one nearest you. Then make it your goal to visit others as your travels permit—or perhaps, you can even plan your travels around these museums. You won't be disappointed.

Vienna, Austria

   1. Kunsthistorisches Museum

Beijing, China

   2. Imperial Palace Museum

Prague, Czech Republic

   3. Narodni Galerie (National Gallery)

Cairo, Egypt

   4. The Egyptian Museum

London, England

   5. British Museum
   6. Courtauld Institute Galleries
   7. National Gallery of Art
   8. Tate Gallery, Millbank
   9. Victoria and Albert Museum

Paris, France

  10. Louvre
  11. Marmottan, Monet's Home
  12. Musée d'Orsay
  13. Musée National d'Art Moderne (Beaubourg)
  14. Picasso Museum
  15. Rodin Museum

Berlin, Germany

  16. Dahlem Museum, National Gallery

Dresden, Germany

  17. Art Gallery of the Old Masters

Athens, Greece

  18. National Museum of Athens

Budapest, Hungary

  19. Budapest Museum of Fine Arts

Florence, Italy

  20. Galleria dell'Accademia
  21. Galleria degli Ufizzi
  22. Pitti Palace

Rome, Italy

  23. Galleria Borghese
  24. Vatican Museums

Tokyo, Japan

  25. National Museum of Tokyo

Mexico City, Mexico

  26. National Museum of Anthropology

Amsterdam, Netherlands

  27. Rijksmuseum

Auckland, New Zealand

  28. War Memorial Museum

Oslo, Norway

    29. Munch Museum

Moscow, Russia

    30. Pushkin

St. Petersburg, Russia

    31. Hermitage

Edinburgh, Scotland

    32. National Gallery of Scotland

Madrid, Spain

    33. Museo del Prado

Istanbul, Turkey

    34. Topkapi Palace

UNITED STATES

Juneau, Alaska

    35. Alaska State Museum

Los Angeles, California

    36. J. Paul Getty Museum
    37. Los Angeles County Museum of Art

San Francisco, California

    38. Museum of Modern Art
    39. M. H. De Young Memorial Museum and California Palace of the Legion of Honor

Washington, D.C.

    40. Freer Gallery
    41. National Gallery of Art
    42. National Museum of American Art
    43. Phillips Collection

Chicago, Illinois

    44. Art Institute of Chicago

Boston, Massachusetts

    45. Boston Museum of Fine Arts

New York City

    46. Frick Museum
    47. Metropolitan Museum
    48. MOMA (Museum of Modern Art)
    49. The Cloisters

Philadelphia, Pennsylvania

    50. Philadelphia Museum of Art

MAJOR MUSEUMS OF THE WORLD

Many of these museums were begun when either a wealthy collector or a member of royalty amassed beautiful artworks that were then made available for the public to see. The museums typically grew through additional personal collections, museum purchases, and individually donated artworks. Most in this list are national museums, often government supported and well established. Some are just so outstanding that you must make time to see them if you're anywhere in the area. Along with a brief description of the museum's major collections, some listings also include masterpieces that are part of the museum's permanent exhibits.

AFGHANISTAN

Kabul	National Museum of Afghanistan (5,000 years of Afghanistan's history, Islamic collection, Buddhist paintings, archaeological treasures)

ARGENTINA

Buenos Aires	National Museum of Fine Arts (Argentine art, European paintings, prints, drawings, furniture, musical instruments, van Gogh's *Le Moulin de la Galette*)
Rosario	Juan B. Castagnino Municipal Museum of Fine Arts (Argentine artists, European painters)

AUSTRALIA

Adelaide	Art Gallery of South Australia (Australian 18th- and 19th-century paintings and English art from the 15th century, Sickert's *Mornington,* Tom Robert's *The Breakaway*)
Brisbane	Queensland Art Gallery (Aborginal art from central and western Australia, Tjukurrpa's *Desert Dreamings,* Tjapaltjarri's *Mouse Dreaming*)
Canberra	National Gallery of Australia (Australian, Asian, and international art, Aboriginal art, *The Aboriginal Memorial,* Jackson Pollock's *Blue Poles,* 1952)
	National Portrait Gallery (faces of Australia: artists, politicians, Torres Strait Islanders, Aboriginals)

Melbourne	National Gallery of Victoria (Aboriginal, colonial Australian, Asian, and European work, Tom Robert's *Shearing the Rams*)
Perth	Art Gallery of Western Australia (particular emphasis on Aboriginal art, also Australian and international works)
Sydney	Art Gallery of New South Wales (traditional and modern European art, Australian painters, Aboriginal artworks)
	The Australian Museum (20th-century art, Aboriginal tribal art, Asian art, sculpture garden)

AUSTRIA

Vienna	Albertina Graphische Sammlung (prints, drawings, watercolors, Dürer's *Praying Hands,* Rembrandt's etchings, Rubens's drawings)
	Gallery of Paintings of the Academy of Fine Arts (14th- to 18th-century Italian, 18th- to 19th-century French artworks)
	Kunsthistorisches Museum (Hapsburg collections, Brueghel's *Tower of Babel* and *Peasant Wedding,* Velazquez's *Infanta Margarita,* Vermeer's *The Artist in His Studio, The Gemma Augustea* (Roman Cameo), Holbein's *Jane Seymore,* Cranach's *Young Woman*)
	New Gallery of the Museum of the History of Art (19th- and 20th-century paintings)

BELGIUM

Antwerp	The Royal Museum of Fine Arts (Flemish and Dutch artists van Eyck, Van der Weyden, van Dyck, Rubens, Ensor, Permeke, and Delvaux)
Brussels	Musées Royaux des Beaux-Arts de Belgique (Belgian and Dutch masters van Dyck, Rubens, Jordaens, Van der Weyden, Master of Flemalle (Robert Campin), Brueghel)
	Musées Royaux des Beaux-Arts de Belgique (Modern Art Museum) (19th- century Belgian and international art from 1860–present, Ensor, Delvaux, Magritte, Jacques-Louis David)

BRAZIL

Rio de Janeiro	Museu de Arte Moderne (contemporary and modern art, Brancusi's *Mlle Pogany,* Picasso, Cubist *Head,* Brazilian artists Vieira, Aterro, and Da Silva)
Sao Paulo	Museu de Arte de Sao Paulo Assis Chateaubriand (traditional and modern European collection, changing exhibitions)

CANADA

British Columbia

Vancouver	The Vancouver Art Gallery (Canadian artists; Emily Carr's paintings of Canadian village life and Indian totem poles)
Victoria	Art Gallery of Greater Victoria (Japanese and Chinese artworks, European painting and sculpture, 15th- to 20th-century art, Rodin's *Mercury Descending from a Cloud*)

Manitoba

Winnipeg	Winnipeg Art Gallery (Eskimo carvings, Dufy's *The Jetty at Trouville,* North German panel: *Flagellation of Christ*)

Ontario

Ottawa	National Gallery of Canada (European collection, Benjamin West's *The Death of General Wolfe,* paintings by Memling, Martini, Rembrandt, El Greco, Corot)
Toronto	Art Gallery of Ontario (Rubens's *The Elevation of the Cross,* Gainsborough's *The Harvest Wagon,* Moore's *Working Model for Three-Piece Sculpture No. 3— Vertebrae,* New York School collection)
	Royal Ontario Museum (Outstanding Asian collections, Canadian paintings and furniture)

Quebec

Montréal	Musée des Beaux Arts de Montreal (13th- to 20th-century paintings; Memling, Rembrandt, Tiepolo)
Quebec	Le Musée du Quebec (The museum contains paintings, sculpture, decorative arts, drawings, and prints by primarily Quebec artists, ranging from the 17th century to the present.)

CHINA

Beijing	Imperial Palace Museum (traditional pavilions complete with decorative carving, furniture and art objects, sculpture)
	Museum of Fine Arts (large collection of traditional arts of China)
Hong Kong	Hong Kong Museum of Art (Chinese antiquities, fine arts, decorative arts)
Shanghai	Shanghai Museum (bronze vessels, paintings, ceramics, furniture, jade, seals, and coins)
Sichuan	The Sanxingdui Museum (relics of the ancient Shu people, dating from 4,000 years ago; include bronze vessels, jade ritual utensils, pottery, ivory, a bronze mask)

"When love and skill work together, expect a masterpiece."
—John Ruskin, 1819–1900, British writer and critic

CZECH REPUBLIC

Prague	Narodni Galerie (Schiele's *Seated Woman with Bent Knee,* works from the Bohemian Master, Brueghel's *Haymakers,* Kokoschka's *The Charles Bridge, Prague*)

DENMARK

Copenhagen	National Museum of Fine Art (Danish and international collection of painting and sculpture dating from 1600; a new contemporary space, The X room, recently opened)
	Ny Carlsberg Glyptothek (Egyptian and Greek collections, early paintings by Gauguin and paintings by other Impressionists)
	Rosenborg Castle Collections (crown jewels, ivory *Coronation Chair,* life-sized silver lions, Venetian glass, silver, furniture)
Skagen	Skagens Museum (Kroyer's *Summer Evening on the Southern Beach*)

EGYPT

Cairo	Egyptian Museum (Egyptian antiquities from 1800 B.C., King Tut tomb treasures and *Golden Mask,* gold, sculpture, numerous mummies)

ENGLAND

Birmingham	Barber Institute of Fine Arts (English and European collection, Bellini's *St. Jerome in the Wilderness,* Murillo's *The Marriage Feast at Cana*)
	Birmingham Museum and Art Gallery (Italian collection, tapestries, furniture, Mideast archaeological collection)

Bristol	Bristol Art Gallery (Asian collection, Chinese glass, broad European collection of paintings and prints)
Cambridge	Fitzwilliam Museum (Egyptian, Greek ,and Roman antiquities, European paintings, Medieval manuscripts and music collection)
Leeds	Leeds City Art Gallery (20th-century British artists: painters Paula Rego and Bridget Riley; sculptors Henry Moore and Barbara Hepworth; English watercolors and Pre-Raphaelite paintings; Grimshaw's *Nightfall Down the Thames*)
Liverpool	Tate Gallery Liverpool (National collection of modern and contemporary British 20th-century artists; Gilbert & George's *Death, Hope, Life, Fear*)
	Walker Art Gallery (15th- to 20th-century English art, English and international paintings, Italian primitives, Simone Martini's *Christ Discovered in the Temple*)
London	British Museum (*Elgin Marbles (Parthenon) Lindisfarne Gospels, Rosetta Stone, Magna Carta,* Egyptian sphinxes, and other ancient treasures from around the world)
	Courtauld Institute Galleries (Manet's *Bar at the Folies Bergère,* Seurat's *Young Woman with a Powderpuff,* Cézanne's *The Card Players,* Gauguin's *Nevermore,* van Gogh's *Self-Portrait with a Bandaged Ear,* Modigliani's *Nude*)
	National Gallery (Italian masters, Rembrandt, Velasquez, Cézanne, van Eyck, Botticelli's *The Mystic Nativity,* Holbein's *The Ambassadors,* Campin's *The Virgin and Child before a Fire-screen,* van Gogh's *Sunflowers,* Rubens's *The Judgment of Paris*)
	Victoria and Albert Museum (fine and applied arts, arms and armor, musical instruments, woodwork, sculpture, *Syon Cope* (embroidered vestment), *Studley Bowl* (silver))
	National Portrait Gallery (portraits of important figures in English history)

ENGLAND *(continued)*

	Tate Gallery, Millbank (British artists from 15th century, large collection of J.M.W. Turner, Picasso, Rothko, Stubbs, Constable, Blake, Gainsborough, Epstein, Moore)
	Tate Modern, Bankside (international modern art from 1900 to present)
Manchester	Manchester City Art Gallery (Dutch 17th century, sculpture, glass, furniture, pre-Raphaelite paintings, Turner)
Oxford	Ashmolean Museum of Art and Archaeology (Minoan, Mycenaean, and Cycladic, Egyptian collections, *Bodleian Bowl*, armor)
St. Ives	Tate Gallery (Artists from St. Ives, 20th-century work from the Tate Gallery
Windsor	Windsor Castle (Royal collection of paintings by Holbein, Rubens, van Dyck, arms and armor, French and English furniture and porcelain, *Queen Mary's Doll House*, and Agasse's *The Nubian Giraffe*)

FINLAND

Helsinki	Finnish National Gallery (European and Finnish collection of old masters to present-day painters)

FRANCE

Calais	New Museum (400,000 pieces of machine and handmade lace, 19th-century sculpture, Rodin's *Burgher's of Calais*, paintings by Balthus)
Chantilly	Condé Museum, Chateau de Chantilly (Régence woodwork, Chantilly porcelain, Flemish and Italian Primitives, Memling, Clouet, *Les Très Riches Heures du Duc de Berry*)
Colmar	Musée d'Unterlinden (Grunewald's *The Crucifixion*)
Paris	Louvre (Egyptian collection, Leonardo's *Mona Lisa*, Whistler's *Portrait of the Artist's Mother*, van Dyck's *Charles I of England*, Holbein's *Portrait of Emmaus*,

Rembrandt's *Bathsheba Bathing, Nike of Samothrace, Venus de Milo, Code of Hammurabi,* frieze from the *Parthenon, The Seated Scribe*)

Musée D'Orsay (collection of French Impressionists including five of Monet's *Rouen Cathedral,* 19th-century sculpture, photography, and applied arts, van Gogh collection)

Centre Georges Pompidou (Beaubourg) (20th-century Modern artists: Modigliani, Utrillo, Vuillard, Derain, Delaunay, Braque, Dufy, Léger, Matisse, Picasso's *Harlequin,* Claes Oldenburg's *Soft Drum Set*)

Musée des Arts Africaine et Océaniens (recently reopened collection of African art and Oceanic art)

Rouen	Musée des Beaux-Arts (Daubigny's *The Lock at Optevoz*)
Saint Paul de Vence	Maeght Foundation (20th-century French art, Braque, Chagall, Kandinsky, Miró, and Giacometti)
Strasbourg	Museum of Fine Art (Tintoretto, el Greco, Goya, Rubens, Watteau)

GERMANY

Berlin

Pergamon Museum (Greek and Roman antiquities, *Pergamon Altar, Ishtar Gate* (from Babylon), *Façade of Mshatta*)

Altes Museum (Alte Nationalgalerie/Bode Museum) (early Christian, Byzantine, and Egyptian art, Ravenna mosaics, Cranach's *Doomsday*)

Charlottenburg Palace Museums (bust of *Nefertiti, Guelph Treasure,* Egyptian, Greek, and Roman antiquities, Early Christian and Byzantine, sculpture collection, European paintings, Cranach, Elsheimer, Ravenna *Mosaics,* Donatello sculpture)

Dahlem Museum (regularly scheduled ethnological exhibitions, collection of European, Islamic, and Far Eastern art, Dürer, Cranach, Hals, Holbein, van Eyck, Van der Weyden, Vermeer, Rembrandt)

GERMANY *(continued)*

	National Gallery (collection of Modern art, Renoir, Manet, Munch's *Panorama of Life*, Kokoschka's *Adolf Loos*, Klee's *The Ship's Departure*, Beckmann's *Death-Birth*)
Bonn	Kunstmuseum Bonn (German art after 1945: August Macke's *Turkisches Café*, George Baselitz's *Die Hand Gottes*, Sigmar Polke's *o.t.*)
Bremen	Kunsthalle Bremen (15th- to 20th-century European paintings; emphasis on 19th-century French and German)
Brunswick	Herzog Anton Ulrich Museum (ducal collection of antiquities, European paintings, clocks, ceramics, carvings)
Cologne	Wallraf-Richartz Museum (German, Dutch, Flemish primitives, Hals's *Hille Bobbe*, German Expressionists, Lochner's *The Virgin and Child in a Rose Arbor*)
Dresden	Art Gallery of the Old Masters (Royal Treasury, 16th- to 18th-century Italian, and 17th-century Flemish and Dutch works, Rembrandt's *Self Portrait with Saskia*, Vermeer, Holbein, van Eyck, Velasquez, Giorgione, Raphael's *Sistine Madonna*)
	Staatliche Kunstsammlungen Dresden (Correggio's *The Nativity*)
Dusseldorf	Art Museum of Dusseldorf (Baroque and 19th-century painting, Medieval and Baroque sculpture, Art Nouveau collection, German Expressionists, Dutch 17th-century paintings, De Hooch's *Interior*)
Hamburg	Hamburg Art Gallery (Kirchner's *Self-portrait with Model*, Overbeck's *The Adoration of the Magi*)
Munich	Alte Pinakothek (Old Master collection, Van Der Weyden's *The Adoration of the Magi*, Dürer's *Self-Portrait in Fur Coat*, Altdorfer's *Battle of Alexander at Issus*)
	Haus der Kunst (the gallery was intended to be a "House of German Art," and includes work by Surrealist, Cubist, and Fauve artists)

Stuttgart	Staatsgalerie Stuttgart (collection of paintings and sculpture includes Franz Marc's *Little Yellow Horses*)

GREECE

Athens	Acropolis Museum (collection of early Greek sculpture mostly from the Acropolis: *The Calf-Bearer, The Critius Boy by Critius, the Master of Myron, c. 480 B.C. Parthenon* fragments, *Caryatids, The Rampin Rider*)
	National Museum of Athens (bronzes, ivory, stone, from Neolithic times to the Roman Imperial period, gold *Death mask, Vaphio Cups, Funeral Stele*, bronze *Poseidon, Artemis* from Delos)
Delphi	Delphi Museum (Archaic sculpture from the Temple of Apollo, *Delphi Charioteer*, 5th century B.C.)

HUNGARY

Budapest	Fine Arts Museum (National historical collection, European masterworks from the Esterhazy Collection, Leonardo da Vinci's *Equestrian Statue*, Rembrandt, Breughel's *The Sermon of St. John the Baptist*, Goya, Raphael's *Portrait of a Youth*, Giorgione)

INDIA

Baroda	Baroda Museum and Picture Gallery (ancient and modern Indian and other Asian art and a small European collection)
Bombay	Prince of Wales Museum Fort (sculpture, ivories, Indian and European paintings)
Calcutta	Asutosh Museum of Indian Art (Eastern India and Bengal collections, stone sculpture, textiles, scrolls, coins, seals, ivory)
Madras	Government Museum (Indian stone and bronze tools and sculpture, wood carvings, metalwork, pottery, armor, gold coins and paintings)
New Delhi	National Gallery of Modern Art (contemporary Indian art)

IRAN

Tehran   Archaeological Museum (Persian gold, sculpture and artifacts from Persepolis, carpets, silver, porcelain)

IRAQ

Baghdad   Iraq Museum (Mesopotamian antiquities)

IRELAND

Dublin   National Gallery of Ireland (collection of icons, Cranach's *Judith with the Head of Holerfernes*, Sargent's *President Woodrow Wilson*, Rembrandt's *Rest on the Flight to Egypt*)

National Museum of Ireland (Stone Age antiquities, shrines, handicrafts)

ISRAEL

Jerusalem   Israel Museum (*Dead Sea Scrolls,* Torah Scrolls and ornaments, Menorahs, contemporary Israeli artists, reconstructed synagogues from Vittorio Veneto (Italy) and Horb (Germany))

ITALY

Bologna   Pinacoteca Nazionale (This collection is primarily of Italian work from the 13th century to the present. Raphael's *St. Cecilia in Estasi,* Perugino's *The Virgin and Child with Saints,* Guido Reni's *Flagellation of Christ,* and an altarpiece attributed to Giotto are some of the museum's masterpieces.)

Florence   Bargello National Museum (sculpture by Renaissance masters: Donatello's *David,* Cellini, Bernini, Brunelleschi, Della Robbia ceramics and treasures of the applied arts such as ivory, enamel, glass, jewelry, tapestries and textiles)

Galleria Accademia (large sculpture collection, Michelangelo's *David,* Italian primitives, other works by Michelangelo)

Pitti Palace (Florentine Renaissance Palace containing Medici family collections, finest collection of Raphael's work, masterpieces by Titian, Tintoretto, Rubens, van Dyck, Fra Filippo Lippi, Veronese, Brueghel, Velasquez. The Silver Museum and the Boboli gardens behind the museum are worth seeing.)

Ufizzi Gallery (Medici collection. Uccello's *Battle of San Romano,* van Der Goes *Portinari Altarpiece,* Raphael's *The Madonna of the Goldfish,* and Botticelli's *Primavera and Birth of Venus,* and The *Medici Venus,* Duccio's *The Rucellai Madonna*)

Genoa
Palazzo Bianco Gallery (Zurbaran, Gerard David, Rubens, Genoese painters from 15th to 17th centuries)

Milan
Pinacoteca Ambrosiana (Raphael's Cartoon (full-sized drawing) for the *School of Athens,* Breughel's *Daniel in the Lion's Den*)

Brera Picture Gallery (Mantegna's *The Dead Christ,* Caravaggio's *Supper at Emmaus,* Guardi, Bramante, Raphael's *The Betrothal of the Virgin*)

Museum of Ancient Art, Castello Sforzesco (artwork by Michelangelo, Bellini)

Poldi Pezzoli Museum (Pollaiuolo, Botticelli, Bellini, Mantegna, Tiepolo, Murano glass collection, Limoges enamel, Persian *Court Rug*)

Naples
Capodimonte National Museum and Gallery (Titian's *Danae and the Shower of Gold,* Brueghel's *Parable of the Blind Leading the Blind*)

National Museum (sculptures, cameos, *Farnese Cup, Farnese Bull* (restored by Michelangelo), treasures from Herculaneum and Pompeii)

Rome
Borghese Gallery (Canova's *Paolina Borghese as Venus,* Bernini's *Apollo and Daphne,* Caravaggio's *St. Jerome,* Raphael's *The Deposition,* Cranach's *Venus and Cupid with a Honeycomb*)

Capitoline Museums (Michelangelo's *Staircase and Piazza,* ancient Greek, Etruscan, and Italian vases, *She-Wolf, The Dying Gaul,* Titian's *Baptism of Christ*)

ITALY *(continued)*

National Museum of Rome (housed in the *Baths of Diocletian,* ancient Roman art, frescoes from *Villa of Livia,* large collection of Roman sarcophagi, Myron's *The Discus Thrower*)

Vatican Museums (Michelangelo's Sistine Chapel ceiling and *Last Judgment,* Raphael's *School of Athens,* ancient sculpture *Apollo Belvedere, Laocoön,* Giotto's *Stefanaschi Polyptych*)

Villa Giulia National Museum (Etruscan art, sculptures from Veii, *Sarcophagus of the Bride and Bridegroom*)

Siena   Palazzo Pubblico (Renaissance City Hall, Lorenzetti's *Allegory of Good Government*)

Turin   Civic Museum of Ancient Art, Palazzo Madama (Roman and Barbarian jewelry, *The Turin Hours* (*Très Belles Heures du Duc de Berry*), Messina's *Portrait of an Unknown Man,* Della Robbia's *Annunciation* (ceramic))

Venice   Galleria dell'Accademia (Venetian painting from 14th to 18th centuries, Giorgione's *The Tempest,* Veronese's *The Feast in the House of Levi,* Titian's *Presentation of the Virgin at the Temple,* Bellini's *The Miracle of the True Cross near the San Lorenzo Bridge*)

JAPAN

Kyoto   Miho Museum (an I. M. Pei designed museum, itself a work of art, houses fine quality art objects)

Nara   Yamato Bunkakan Museum (Japanese national treasures, Japanese and Chinese painting, sculpture, ceramics)

Tokyo   Bridgestone Museum of Art (Western art, Cézanne, Renoir, De Chirico, Rouault, Rousseau, Sisley, Manet)

National Museum of Tokyo (Japanese art from pre-551 B.C. to present, Japanese national treasures, *Cinerary Urn, Figure of Armoured Man, Bronze Mirror*)

National Museum of Western Art (Rodin's *The Kiss, The Thinker* and *The Gates of Hell,* Gauguin's *Two Little Breton Girls by the Sea,* Monet's *Waterloo Bridge*)

KENYA

Nairobi   Kenya National Museum (ancient and contemporary African art, artifacts, masks)

KOREA

Seoul   National Central Museum of Korea (metallurgic art, ceramics, paintings, Buddhist paintings, also central Asian art)

LEBANON

Beirut   Archaeological Museum of the American University of Beirut (archaeological finds from Middle Eastern cultures, Stone Age through Bronze and Iron Ages)

Musée des Beaux Arts (artifacts of the Middle East)

MEXICO

Mexico City   Modern Art Museum (Mexican paintings and sculpture, paintings by Tamayo, O'Gorman, Camarena)

National Museum of Anthropology (Mexican art from prehistory to the present: *Aztec Calendar, Jade Mask,* Mayan, Olmec, Teotihuacan, *Chac-Mool* (reclining stone effigy))

NETHERLANDS

Amsterdam   Rijksmuseum (collection of Dutch paintings from the 15th to the 18th centuries: Vermeer, Hals, Ruisdael, prints, Rembrandt's *The Night Watch,* Hals's *The Merry Toper,* Vermeer's *The Letter* and the *Little Street*)

Stedelijk Museum (painting, sculpture, and the applied arts from 1850 to the present, collection of 20th-century art including Pop Art, De Stijl, and Cobra art)

Vincent van Gogh Museum (400 paintings, 200 drawings by van Gogh)

NETHERLANDS *(continued)*

Rotterdam   Boijmans-Van Beuningen Museum (Netherlandish paintings: Bosch's *The Prodigal Son,* Brueghel's *The Small Tower of Babel,* Steen's *Easy Come, Easy Go,* van Gogh's *Armand Roulin,* Kandinsky, De Stael, Hubert and Jan van Eyck's *The Three Marys at the Sepulchre,* Hals's *Portrait of a Man.* Also included are large Modern and decorative arts collections)

The Hague   Mauritshuis Royal Picture Gallery (the home and collection of a Prince of Orange; includes the finest Dutch and Flemish artists of his day; especially strong in work by Vermeer and Rembrandt. Other paintings include those by Steen, van Dyck, Van der Weyden, Rubens, Hals, and Memling.)

Otterlo Kroller-Mueller Rijksmuseum (outdoor sculpture garden including artwork by Henry Moore and Barbara Hepworth, van Gogh's *Potato Eaters,* Seurat's *Le Chahut,* Dutch painter Piet Mondrian's *Composition in Line and Color*)

NEW ZEALAND

Auckland   Auckland City Art Gallery (European and New Zealand paintings)

Auckland War Memorial Museum (*Maori Meeting House, Storage House, War Canoe,* wood and stone carvings)

Wellington   National Art Gallery (Australian and British artists, Hepworth's *Oval Form*)

National Museum (Maori collection, European and New Zealand paintings)

NIGERIA

Jos   Jos Museum (Nok culture, contemporary Nigerian art, architecture and archaeology)

NORWAY

Oslo — National Gallery (Norwegian paintings, Manet, Renoir, Russian icons, El Greco)

Munch Museum (1,200 paintings by Munch including *The Voice* and *Melancholy,* and a vast collection of prints, drawings, sculptures)

POLAND

Krakow — Wawelu Castle State Art Collections (Flemish tapestries, *Coronation Sword,* gold chalice, arms and armor, European paintings)

Warsaw — National Museum at Warsaw (Polish art, European, Egyptian and Greek art, Canaletto's *26 Views of Warsaw*)

The Royal Castle in Warsaw (Royal apartments, painting and decorative arts collection)

PORTUGAL

Lisbon — Gulbenkian Museum (eclectic collection of Western and Eastern antiquities, paintings, ceramics, bronzes)

Museu Nacional de Arte Antigua (collection of Portuguese and European paintings from 12th to 19th centuries, including Bosch's *The Tribulations of St. Anthony,* Hans Memling's *Virgin with Child,* Albrecht Dürer's *Hieronymus*)

"Artists, by definition innocent, don't steal. But they do borrow without giving back."

—NED ROREM, 1923, American composer and author

PUERTO RICO

Ponce — Museo de Arte de Ponce (European, Peruvian, and South American collection)

ROMANIA

Bucharest — Art Museum of the Socialist Republic of Romania (10th- to 18th-century Romanian, European, and Asian painting, sculpture and decorative arts, collection of Romanian sculptor Constantin Brancusi's work including *Sleeping Muse*)

Craiova — Muzeul de Arta (Brancusi's famous work, *The Kiss*)

RUSSIA

Moscow — Kremlin Museums (The museums consist of a number of churches and other buildings. The Armoury Chamber (the treasure-house and the oldest museum in Russia) contains a collection of masterpieces including paintings and decorative and applied arts such as Fabergé eggs, carriages, silver and gold work, arms and armor, and personal effects of the Tsar.)

Pushkin Museum of Fine Arts (Western European paintings from 15th to 20th century; antiquities, foreign art and archaeology from 4000 B.C. to the present)

Tretiakov Gallery (national collection of Russian art including icons, sculpture, and miniatures; particularly strong collection of "Revolutionary Art")

St. Petersburg — Hermitage Museum (6th to 4th century B.C. Scythian Gold Objects and *Pazyryk Tumuli* (tombs) objects, magnificent collection of old European masters, French Impressionists, Matisse's *Harmony in Red,* De Hooch's *Woman and a Maid with a Pail in a Courtyard,* 27 works by Rembrandt including *The Sacrifice of Abraham and Danae*)

Russian State Museum (collection of Russian art in all forms including painting, sculpture, folk art. After the 1917 Revolution, the museum substantially increased its holdings.)

SCOTLAND

Edinburgh

National Gallery of Scotland (many works by Raphael, El Greco, Dégas, Claude Lorraine, Tiepolo, Constable, Ramsay)

Royal Museum of Scotland (international collections, decorative arts, china, and glass)

SOUTH AFRICA

Cape Town

South African National Gallery (Dutch and English paintings, German Expressionism, modern European schools of art)

Johannesburg

Johannesburg Art Gallery (South African art, 19th-century French painting and sculpture, Boudin's *Regatta at Argenteuil,* Signac's *Leaving La Rochelle Harbor,* British works of the late 19th century)

SPAIN

Barcelona

Museo Pablo Picasso (includes some of Picasso's finest artworks, many of which were donated by his friend and patron Jaime Sabartes, such as *Portrait of Sabartes.* Picasso's *Las Meninas* series, based on work by another Spaniard, Velasquez, are also in the collection.)

Madrid

Fundacion Coleccion Thyssen-Bornemisza (Ghirlandaio's *Portrait of Giovanna Tornabuoni*)

Prado Museum (Spanish masters El Greco, Goya, Zurbarán, Murillo, Velasquez's *Las Meninas* from the Spanish Royal collection and many Flemish paintings from the period when the Spaniards occupied Flanders: Ruben's *The Garden of Love,* Brueghel's *The Triumph of Death,* Bosch's *Garden of Earthly Delights,* Dürer's *Self-portrait with Gloves,* Baldung's *The Three Ages of Man and Death*)

SWEDEN

Gothenburg	Gothenburg Art Gallery (Northern European paintings, modern Swedish and other Scandinavian artists)
Stockholm	Modern Art Museum (Brancusi's *The Newborn Child*, Calder's *The Four Elements*, Picasso's *The Guitar Player*, Kienholz's *The State Hospital*, Rauschenberg's *Monogram*, Matisse's *Moroccan Landscape*)
	National Museum (Royal collections, Swedish paintings, Dürer's *Young Girl*, Delacroix's *The Lion Hunting*, La Tour's *St. Jerome in Penitence*, Raphael's *Adoration of the Shepherds*)

SWITZERLAND

Basle	Basle Fine Arts Museum (Holbein, Grunewald, Cranach, Rousseau, Paul Klee's *Senecio*, Paul Gauguin's *Ta Matete*, Franz Marc's *The Animal's Destiny*, and Joan Miró's *Figures* and *Dog Before the Sun*)
	Ernst Beyeler Museum (Impressionists, work by Amedeo Modigliani)
Bern	Bern Museum of Fine Arts (works by Swiss artist Paul Klee, Swiss works of art from 15th- to 20th-centuries, early Italian paintings, Cubist art)
Geneva	Musée d'Art et d'Histoire (Hodler's *Lake Thun*, Witz's *The Miraculous Draught of Fishes*)
Zurich	Kunsthaus Zurich (Old Masters, Swiss artists, 20th-century art including Rousseau's *Portrait of Pierre Loti*, Toulouse-Lautrec's *Bar*, Munch's *Lubeck Harbor*, Bonnard's *Signac and Friends in a Sailing Boat* and one hundred works, including *The Chariot Bronze*, by Swiss sculptor and painter Alberto Giacometti)

"If it had not been for American collectors, the Impressionists would have starved."
—PAUL DURANT-RUEL, 1831–1922, French art dealer

TAIWAN

    Taipei   National Palace Museum (Comprehensive collections of bronzes, porcelains, hanging scrolls covering 3,600 years)

THAILAND

    Bangkok   National Museum (Thailand's religious, cultural, and archaeological treasures)

TUNISIA

    Tunis   National Museum of Bardo (Phoenician, Roman, early Christian and Moslem antiquities, Arab museum, Roman mosaics)

TURKEY

    Ankara   Ankara Archaeological Museum (archaeological finds from 8,000–600 years B.C., Hittite remains excavated in Turkey and Ephesus)

    Istanbul   Topkapi Palace Museum (Sultan Suleyman's treasure in his palace: *Emerald Dagger, Gold Cradle, Turquoise Throne,* Asian porcelain, mosaics, miniatures collection, illuminated manuscripts)

    Selçuk   Ephesus Museum (Ephesus antiquities: *Head of Eros,* Roman *Sun Dial,* Mycenaean vases, sculptures)

UNITED STATES

Alabama

Birmingham	Birmingham Museum of Art (Comprehensive collection of European, American, and Asian Art, 12th century to present, Wedgwood collection, Remington bronzes)
Mobile	Mobile Museum of Art (Southern furniture, contemporary American crafts, American and European art)
Montgomery	Montgomery Museum of Fine Arts (Southern regional art, 19th- to and 20th-century American art)

Alaska

Anchorage	Anchorage Museum of History and Art (comprehensive Alaskan Art and artifacts collection, contemporary photograph archive)
Fairbanks	University of Alaska Museum (Native American art, regional paintings, sculpture, prints and fine art photography including work by Ansel Adams)
Juneau	Alaska State Museum (Eskimo, Aleut, Northwest Coast, Athabaskan art, Alaskan fine art)

Arizona

Phoenix	Phoenix Art Museum (Asian collection, 20th-century art, European and American paintings)

Arkansas

Little Rock	Arkansas Arts Center (contemporary crafts, American and European drawings, 19th- and 20th-century paintings)

California

Berkeley	• University of California at Berkeley (Soviet, Japanese, and American avant-garde film and video, 20th-century American and European paintings, sculpture, drawings, and prints)

Los Angeles	J. Paul Getty Museum (classical antiquities, photographs, illuminated manuscripts, paintings, drawings, sculpture, French furniture, Tintoretto's *Toilet of Venus,* Pierre Bonnard's *Nude*)
	Los Angeles County Museum of Art (De Hooch's *Woman Giving Money to Her Servant Girl,* Holbein's *Young Woman With a White Coif,* Rembrandt's *Portrait of Maarten Looten,* Cézanne's *Still Life With Cherries and Apricots,* Giorgione's *Head of a Woman*)
	The Museum of Contemporary Art (20th-century art in all media, including sculpture and painting)
Oakland	Oakland Art Museum (California artists, Diebenkorn, Viola Frey ceramics, Dorothea Lange and Eadweard Muybridge photography)
Pasadena	Norton Simon Museum of Art (European art from the Renaissance to the 20th century; many works by Botticelli, Dégas, Goya, Manet, Matisse, Rembrandt, Rousseau's *Exotic Landscape,* van Gogh, Zurbarán)
	Pasadena Art Museum (20th-century art collection including Klee's *Refuge,* Kandinsky's *Severe in Sweet,* Feininger's *Blue Skyscraper*)
San Diego	Fine Arts Gallery (Rembrandt's *Young Man With a Cock's Feather in His Hat,* Titian's *Portrait of the Doge Francesco Donato,* Rubens's *Holy Family with St. Francis*)
	San Diego Museum of Art (German Expressionists, European and American paintings, Mark Rothko, Paul Gauguin)
	Timken Art Gallery (American paintings, European old masters and Russian icons, Bosch's *Christ Taken Captive,* Canaletto's *Bacino di San Marco, Tribute Money*)
San Francisco	Asian Art Museum (bronze *Rhinoceros Vessel,* Khmer sculpture, painted scrolls, pottery *T'ang Camel,* 12,000 objects covering 6,000 years of art history)
	M. H. de Young Memorial Museum (closed until 2006) and California Palace of the Legion of Honor (ancient Asian Bronzes, American art, textiles, print collection,

419

California (continued)

Cranach's *Madonna and Child,* Cellini's bust of *Cosimo de Medici,* El Greco's *St. John the Baptist,* Rubens's *The Tribute Money,* Harnett's *After the Hunt,* Lorenzo Lotto's *Portrait of a Man,* Fragonard's *Self-Portrait,* large collection of Rodin bronzes: *The Thinker, Burghers of Calais, The Age of Bronze*)

San Francisco Museum of Modern Art (20th-century modernist and contemporary art, Diego Rivera's *Flower Vendor,* Braque's *The Table*)

San Marino — Henry E. Huntington Art Gallery (Gainsborough's *Blue Boy,* Thomas Lawrence's *Pinkie,* Joshua Reynolds' *Sarah Siddons as The Tragic Muse,* William Morris Decorative Arts collection)

Santa Barbara — Santa Barbara Museum of Art (Sumerian *Head of Gudea,* comprehensive collection of American, Asian, and 19th-century French art)

Colorado

Colorado Springs — Colorado Springs Fine Arts Center (American and Native American art, large collection of santos (carved saints), Southwestern, and Hispanic Colonial art, Walt Kuhn's *Trio,* Arthur Dove's *Fog Horns*)

Denver — Denver Art Museum (collection of Western art, contemporary art, and photography, Giuseppi Arcimboldo's *Summer,* Dégas's *Examen de Danse,* collection of santos)

Connecticut

Hartford — Wadsworth Atheneum (Bierstadt's *In the Yosemite Valley,* Copley's *Portrait of Mrs. Seymore Fort,* Goya's *Gossiping Women,* Rubens's *Tiger Hunt,* Zurbarán's *St. Serapion,* African American collection, 20th-century masters)

New Britain	The New Britain Museum of American Art (American art from 1740 to present, Benton's *The Arts of Life in America,* Harnett's *Still Life With Violin,* Eakins's *Old Lady Sewing,* Eastman Johnson's *Hollyhocks*)
New Haven	Yale Center for British Art(16th- to 20th-century British paintings, sculpture, prints, drawings)
	Yale University Art Gallery (13th- to 20th-century European art, prints, drawings, photographs, 20th-century American painting, van Gogh's *The Night Cafe,* Eakins's *John Biglen in a Single Scull,* Brancusi's *Yellow Bird,* Moore's *Draped Seated Woman,* Ralph Earl's *Roger Sherman,* Trumbull's *Surrender of Burgoyne,* Joseph Stella's *Battle of Light, Coney Island* and *Brooklyn Bridge*)

Delaware

Wilmington	Delaware Art Museum (American art: Hopper, Gorky, Homer, John Sloan, Howard Pyle)

District of Columbia

Washington	Corcoran Gallery of Art (Samuel F. B. Morse's *The Old House of Representatives,* Bierstadt's *The Last of the Buffalo,* Bellow's *Forty-two Kids,* Frankenthaler, Sargent, Warhol, Copley)
	Freer Gallery (Persian miniature paintings, *A Buddhist Procession,* Whistler's *The Peacock Room* and *Nocturne—Blue and Gold*)
	Hirshhorn Museum and Sculpture Garden (20th-century contemporary paintings and sculpture, outdoor sculpture garden; Rodin, Matisse, De Kooning)
	National Gallery of Art (Raphael's *Alba Madonna,* Titian's *Venus with a Mirror,* Vermeer's *A Woman Weighing Gold,* Toulouse-Lautrec's *Quadrille at the Moulin Rouge,* Titian's *Doge Andrea Gritti,* Rembrandt's *The Mill* and *Lady with an Ostrich Fan,* van Eyck's *The Annunciation*)

District of Columbia *(continued)*

National Museum of African Art, Smithsonian (African gold collection, masks, ivory sculpture, wood carvings, Central African pottery)

National Museum of American Art, Smithsonian Institution (American art from 18th century to present, George Catlin, Albert Bierstadt, John LaFarge, Edmonia Lewis, Hiram Powers, Albert Pinkham Ryder)

National Museum of Women in the Arts (more than 1,200 works from over 400 women, artists from 28 countries, Rosa Bonheur, Judy Chicago, Helen Frankenthaler, Frida Kahlo, Berthe Morisot, Louise Nevelson)

National Portrait Gallery, Smithsonian Institution (Portraits of persons important in the history of the United States, George Catlin collection of Indian portraits and village life)

The Phillips Collection (Bonnard's *The Open Window,* Marin's *Maine Islands,* Picasso's *The Blue Room,* Corot's *View from the Farnese Gardens,* Klee's *Arab Song,* Arthur Dove's *Cows in Pasture,* Renoir's *The Boating Party Luncheon*)

Renwick Gallery (changing exhibitions of American contemporary crafts and decorative arts)

Arthur M. Sackler Gallery (Asian, Islamic bronzes and silver, Chinese jades and bronzes, Persian manuscripts)

United States Capitol Art Collection (744 works of American art: portraits, marble and bronze busts, frescoes, murals, lunettes (half-moon shaped paintings) dealing with American history)

Florida

Miami Beach

The Wolfsonian (founded 1996; 70,000 objects including books, furniture, games, and works on paper, machine-influenced designs since 1885, Art Deco movie-theater window grille, radios, etc.)

Naples	Naples Museum of Art (Modern American art from 1900 to the present, ancient Chinese art and artifacts)
Sarasota	John and Mabel Ringling Museum of Art (Rubens's *Meeting of Abraham and Melchizedek*, Velazquez's *Philip IV,* Cranach's *Cardinal Albrecht as St. Jerome,* collection of circus wagons and other memorabilia)
St. Petersburg	Museum of Fine Arts (O'Keeffe's *Poppy,* Jacobean and Georgian period rooms, *Steuben* crystal, sculpture courts)
	Salvador Dali Museum (collection of Dali's paintings, sculpture, prints, drawings, and art objects)
Tampa	Tampa Museum of Art (contemporary American painting and photography, classical antiquities)
West Palm Beach	Norton Museum of Art (Dégas's *Little Dancer,* Brancusi's *Mme. Pogany,* Braque's *Still Life on Red Tablecloth,* El Greco's *Purification of the Temple*)

Georgia

Athens	Georgia Museum of Art (Max Weber's *Drapeau,* Stuart Davis's *Snow on the Mountain*)
Atlanta	High Museum of Art (comprehensive collection, Faith Ringgold's *Picnic,* other American artists, Harnett, Childe Hassam, Jacob Lawrence, John Marin, John Singer Sargent)

Hawaii

Honolulu	The Contemporary Museum (sculpture garden, permanent collection from 1940s to present)
	Honolulu Academy of the Arts (Kress and Michener collections, Asian, European and American art, Oceanic and African art)

Idaho

Boise	Boise Art Museum (American Realism and contemporary Northwest art)

Illinois

Chicago

Art Institute of Chicago (Toulouse-Lautrec's *At the Moulin Rouge,* Renoir's *Rower's Lunch,* Seurat's *Sunday Afternoon on the Island of La Grande Jatte,* Cassatt's *La Toilette,* Monet's *Gare St. Lazare,* Hans Memling's Diptych of *Madonna and Child and Donor*)

Field Museum of Natural History (Archaeological treasures, and an important reconstructed Egyptian *Temple, Tomb,* and exhibition)

Museum of Contemporary Art (Post World War II art, Pop Art, Surrealism, Minimalism)

Oriental Institute (colossal *Portrait of Tutankhamen, Assyrian Winged Bull,* Persian *Bull's Head* and *Man-Bull* capital)

Terra Museum of American Art (The Daniel J. Terra Collection of American art from the 18th to 20th centuries: Bingham, Audubon, Cassatt, Copley, Hassam, Prendergast, Whistler)

Indiana

Bloomington

Indiana University Art Museum (Greek and Roman art, Laurent's *Birth of Venus,* Maillol's *Nude,* and Barlach's *Singing Man*)

Indianapolis

Indianapolis Museum of Art (Asian, Pre-Columbian, African, American, European, J.M.W. Turner collection)

Iowa

Cedar Rapids

Cedar Rapids Museum of Art (regional artists Grant Wood, printmaker Mauricio Lazansky, and Malvina Hoffman, collections of 19th- and 20th-century sculpture)

Des Moines

Des Moines Art Center (Yasuo Kuniyoshi's *I,* Calder *Mobile,* Prendergast, Bellows, Burchfield, Hassam, Hopper, Shahn, Max Weber, Jasper Johns, Brancusi, Cindy Sherman)

Kansas

Lawrence	Spencer Museum of Art (comprehensive collection of ancient artifacts, quilts, Japanese prints, and Edo paintings)
Wichita	Wichita Art Museum (pre-20th-century American painting, John Steuart Curry's *Kansas Cornfield,* Marin, Hopper, Walt Kuhn, Gaston Lachaise)

Kentucky

Lexington	University of Kentucky Art Museum (African and pre-Columbian, American, and European art)
Louisville	The Speed Art Museum (ancient to contemporary African and Native American art, European and American collection of paintings, graphics, decorative arts)

Louisiana

New Orleans	New Orleans Museum of Art (Naum Gabo's *Construction in Space,* Veronese's *Sacred Conversation,* photographs, art of the Americas, Fabergé Gallery, 13th- to 19th-century European painting)

Maine

Brunswick	Bowdoin College Museum of Fine Arts (Stuart's *Jefferson and Madison,* sculpture by French and Saint-Gaudens, ancient artifacts, Colonial painters Copley, Earl, Feke, Smibert, Trumbull, and Stuart)
Ogunquit	Ogunquit Museum of American Art (Charles Burchfield, Charles Demuth, Jack Levine, John Marin, Reginald Marsh, Marsden Hartley)
Portland	Portland Museum of Art (18th- through 20th-century fine and decorative arts)
Rockland	Farnsworth Art Museum (painting, sculpture, and photography by contemporary Maine artists)

Maryland

Baltimore
American Visionary Art Museum (folk art, self-taught artists, and outsider art)

Baltimore Museum of Art (The Cone Collection of French Post-Impressionist art; van Gogh's *The Shoes,* Gauguin's *Woman With a Mango,* Lipchitz's *Gertrude Stein,* Matisse's *The Blue Nude,* Cézanne's *Mont Ste. Victoire Seen from Bibemus Quarry,* Asian, Pre-Columbian, American, European decorative arts)

Baltimore City Life Museums (Charles Willson Peale's *Exhuming the Mastodon,* Rembrandt Peale's *Roman Daughter,* Sarah Miriam Peale's *Self Portrait,* large collection of decorative arts and period rooms)

Walters Art Gallery (Ingres's *The Odalisque with the Slave,* Manet's *Le Café-Concert,* Daumier's *Second-Class Railway Carriage,* sculpture collection Medieval objects)

Massachusetts

Andover
Addison Gallery of American Art (Eakins's *Professor Rowland,* Homer's *Eight Bells,* Ryder's *Toilers of the Sea,* Luks's *The Spielers*)

Boston
Museum of Fine Arts (paintings and sculpture from India, Old Kingdom Egyptian sculpture, American, European, and Asian decorative arts)

Cambridge
The Arthur M. Sackler Museum Ancient Asian, Islamic, and Indian art collection)

Fogg Art Museum (print and drawing collection, Ingres' *Odalisque with a Slave,* Dégas' *Cotton Merchants,* Sheeler's *Upper Deck,* Copley's *Portrait of Mrs. Thomas Boylston,* T'ang Dynasty *Adoring Bodhisattva*)

Northampton
Smith College Museum of Art (Sheeler's *Rolling Power,* American and European Paintings)

Springfield
Museum of Fine Arts (19th-century American prints, Erastus Field's *Historic Monument of the American*

	Republic, Gericault's *The Madman-Kidnapper,* American artists, 20th-century prints, sculpture, Tiffany glass)
Williamstown	Sterling and Francine Clark Art Institute (Old Master paintings, Dégas's *Self-Portrait,* bronze *Ballet Dancer,* Piero Della Francesca's *Madonna and Child With Four Angels,* Homer's *The Bridle Path*)
Worcester	Worcester Art Museum (comprehensive collection of Egyptian and classical antiquities to Impressionist paintings, Pop Art, Clouet's *Diane de Poitiers,* Gainsborough's *The Artist's Daughters,* Sheeler's *City Interior*)

Michigan

Detroit	Detroit Institute of Arts (Brueghel's *The Wedding Dance,* da Vinci's *The Adoration With Two Angels,* Whistler's *Nocturne in Black and Gold: The Falling Rocket,* Sheeler's *Home Sweet Home,* graphic arts and photography)

Minnesota

Minneapolis	Minneapolis Institute of Arts (painting, sculpture, decorative arts, period rooms, Beckman's *Blindman's Bluff,* Munch's *Jealousy,* Gauguin's *Tahitian Mountains,* Seurat's *Port-en-Bessin,* Larry Rivers's *The Studio,* *Pieta* by the Master of the St. Lucy Legend, Dégas's *Portrait of Mlle. Hortense Valpincon*
	Walker Art Center (Stuart Davis's *Colonial Cubism,* Franz Marc's *Blue Horses,* Jacques Lipchitz's *Prometheus and the Vulture,* contemporary painting, sculpture garden)

Mississippi

Jackson	Mississippi Museum of Art (19th- and 20th-century American, Southern, and Mississippi art, Old Master to contemporary paintings, Asian and Native American art)

Missouri

Kansas City — Nelson-Atkins Museum of Art (Thomas Hart Benton paintings, strong Asian collection, Goya's *Don Ignacio Omulryan y Rourera*, Caravaggio's *St. John the Baptist*, Rodin's *The Thinker*, Raphaelle Peale's *After the Bath*, Memling's *Madonna and Child Enthroned*, sculpture garden featuring work by Henry Moore and Claes Oldenburg)

St. Louis — St. Louis Art Museum (German Expressionists, including large Max Beckman collection, John Greenwood's *Sea Captains Carousing at Suriname*, George Caleb Bingham's *Raftsmen Playing Cards*, van Gogh's *Stairway at Auvers*, de Hooch's *A Game of Skittles*, Hals's *Portrait of a Woman*, Anselm Kiefer's *The Broken Vessel*)

Washington University Gallery of Art (Guston's *Fable*, varied collection of European drawings and paintings)

Montana

Helena — Montana Historical Society (Western art, Montana history, Charles M. Russell, Phimister Proctor)

Nebraska

Omaha — Joslyn Art Museum (19th- and 20th-century collections of Western art by George Catlin, Seth Eastman, Carl Bodmer, Thomas Hart Benton's *Hailstorm*, Grant Wood's *Stone City*, Jackson Pollock's *Galaxy*)

Nevada

Las Vegas — Las Vegas Art Museum (contemporary art, also houses traveling Smithsonian exhibitions)

Reno — Nevada Museum of Art (19th- and 20th-century American art, paintings of the Great Basin region)

New Hampshire

Hanover Hood Museum of Art (American and European paintings, Asian, African, Oceanic and Pre-Columbian artifacts)

New Jersey

Newark Newark Museum (20th-century American paintings and sculpture, Joseph Stella's *Brooklyn Bridge,* Tibetan artifacts)

Princeton The Art Museum (Classical, Chinese, Pre-Columbian, American collection, sculpture court, Medieval art)

New Mexico

Santa Fe Georgia O'Keeffe Foundation (comprehensive collection of work by O'Keeffe)

Museum of Fine Arts, Palace of the Governors (20th-century American, Native-American, and Hispanic art)

Taos University of New Mexico, Harwood Foundation Museum (20th-century art of Taos and surrounding areas)

New York

Brooklyn Brooklyn Museum (comprehensive collection of artifacts from ancient times, period rooms, costumes and textiles, Hopi Kachina dolls, Oceania *Ancestor Figures,* African masks and sculpture, Ralph Blakelock's *Moonlight,* Hiram Powers's *The Greek Slave,* Bingham's *Shooting for the Beef*)

Buffalo Albright-Knox Art Gallery (20th-century American and European art, Gauguin's *The Yellow Christ,* Gorky's *The Liver is the Cock's Comb,* Moore's carved *Reclining Nude,* Lehmbruck's *Kneeling Woman,* David Smith's *Tank Totem IV*)

New York (continued)

Corning	Corning Museum of Glass (outstanding collection of glass from 1500 B.C. to present, demonstrations of glass blowing)
Glen Falls	The Hyde Collection Art Museum (Eakins's *In the Studio*, Rubens's *Head of a Negro*, Rembrandt's *Christ*, Peto's *Still Life*, Leonardo, Dégas, Homer, Picasso, Renoir, Rubens, van Gogh, Whistler)
Ithaca	The Herbert F. Johnson Museum of Art (print collection (Baskin, Hassam, Marin, Pennell and Whistler), 115 Tiffany glass pieces)
New York City	American Craft Museum (contemporary American crafts from mid-20th century, changing exhibitions)
	American Museum of Natural History (ethnic art and artifacts, Northwest Native American art
	The Cloisters (Medieval treasures, including portions of an actual cloister, stone and wood carvings, stained glass, *Unicorn Tapestries*)
	Cooper Hewitt Museum of Design (historic and contemporary collection of American Design, changing exhibitions)
	Frick Collection (Constable's *Salisbury Cathedral*, van Eyck's *Virgin and Child with Saints and a Donor*, Fragonard's *The Progress of Love*, La Tour's *The Education of the Virgin*, Rembrandt's *The Polish Rider* and *Self-Portrait*, work by Boucher, Vermeer (6 paintings), El Greco, Gainsborough, van Dyck)
	Metropolitan Museum of Art (5,000 years of art, Egyptian *Temple of Dendur*, Demuth's *I Saw the Figure 5 in Gold*, Sargent's *Madame X*, El Greco's *View of Toledo*, Memling's *Tommaso and Maria Portinari*, Rembrandt's *Aristotle Contemplating the Bust of Homer*, Vermeer's *Young Woman with a Water Jug*, Leutze's *Washington Crossing the Delaware*, Impressionist collection)

Museum of Modern Art (MOMA) (outstanding modern collection, Picasso's *Three Musicians* and *Les Demoiselles d'Avignon,* Rodin's *Monument to Balzac,* de Chirico's *Nostalgia of the Infinite,* Braque's *Woman With a Mandolin,* Monet's *Waterlilies,* van Gogh's *Starry Night*)

National Academy of Design (permanent collection of 19th- and 20th-century American art, changing exhibitions of drawing, painting, architecture, and sculpture)

National Museum of the American Indian, Smithsonian Institution (collection of art and cultural material from Native Americans of the entire North and South American continents)

New School for Social Research (J. C. Orozco's *Table of Universal Brotherhood* mural)

New York Historical Society Museum (18th- to 20th-century American paintings, drawings, prints, Audubon's *Birds of America,* Thomas Cole's *The Course of Empire,* Bierstadt, Charles Willson Peale, Louis Comfort Tiffany)

Pierpont Morgan Library (Medieval and Renaissance manuscripts, drawings, prints)

Solomon R. Guggenheim Museum (Léger's *The Great Parade,* Cézanne's *The Clock Maker,* 120 paintings by Kandinsky, artwork by Toulouse-Lautrec, Giacometti, Paul Gauguin, Paul Klee, Georges Braque)

Whitney Museum of American Art (20th-century American paintings, sculpture, Alexander Calder's *Circus,* Ben Shahn's *The Passion of Sacco and Vanzetti,* Max Weber's *Adoration of the Moon,* Edward Hopper's *Early Sunday Morning,* DeMuth's *My Egypt,* Joseph Stella's *Brooklyn Bridge*)

Rochester Rochester Memorial Art Gallery (American collection, Copley, Homer, Eakins, Ryder, Stuart Davis, Elie Nadelman, Isamu Noguchi)

New York (continued)

Syracuse	Everson Museum of Art (American paintings, ceramics, prints, photography and sculpture, African and Asian art)
Utica	Munson-Williams-Proctor Institute (American paintings; Charles Burchfield, Arthur Dove, Arshile Gorky, Morris Graves)

North Carolina

Charlotte	Mint Museum of Art (Applied arts: pottery, porcelain, costumes, pre-Columbian artifacts, Renaissance to contemporary art)
Raleigh	North Carolina Museum of Art (14th- to 19th-century European and American paintings, classical sculpture, Boucher's *The Abduction of Europa*, Rembrandt's *Esther's Feast*, Bellotto's *Views of Dresden*)

North Dakota

Grand Forks	North Dakota Museum of Art (contemporary art by regional, national, and international artists)

Ohio

Cincinnati	Cincinnati Art Museum (500 years of art; Botticelli's *Judith With the Head of Holofernes*, Joos van Cleve's *Francis I*, Cézanne's *Bread and Eggs*, Grant Wood's *Daughters of the Revolution*, Sir Henry Raeburn's *The Elphinstone Children*, Frank Duveneck's *Whistling Boy*)
	Taft Museum (Duncan Phyfe furniture (25 pieces), Robert S. Duncanson paintings, Corot, Gainsborough, Hals, Ingres, Rembrandt, Sargent, Whistler, Turner)
Cleveland	Cleveland Museum of Art (arts of the ancient Mediterranean, Egypt, Greece, and Rome, J.M.W. Turner's *Burning of the Houses of Parliament*, George Bellows's *Stag at Sharkey's*, Manet's *Portrait of Berthe*

	Morisot, Berthe Morisot's *Young Lady in White,* Japanese treasures)
Columbus	Columbus Museum of Art (Impressionism and American Modernism, paintings by George Bellows, John Marin, Charles Demuth, Maurice Prendergast, Jules Pascin, Monet, O'Keeffe, Pissarro, Renoir)
Oberlin	Allen Memorial Art Museum (17th-century Dutch paintings, 14th- to 20th-century European and American painting and sculpture, Japanese print collection)
Toledo	Toledo Museum of Art (Thomas Cole's *The Architect's Dream,* Hopper's *Two on the Aisle,* Rubens's *Crowning of St. Catherine,* Jacques Louis David's *Oath of the Horatii,* large collection of glass; Wyeth, Frank Stella, Hopper, Feininger)
Youngstown	Butler Institute of American Art (American paintings, drawings, and prints from 1719 to present, Hopper's *Pennsylvania Coal Town,* Homer's *Snap the Whip*)

Oklahoma

Oklahoma City	Oklahoma City Art Museum (regional, American, and European art, George Bellows, Eugene Boudin, Alexander Calder, Sam Francis, Andy Warhol, Robert Indiana)
Tulsa	Gilcrease Museum (American sculpture and painting, Native American artifacts and art, Remington, Charles M. Russell, Albert Bierstadt, Thomas Eakins)
	Philbrook Museum of Art (18th- and 19th-century European and American painting, Italian Renaissance sculpture and painting, paintings by Dürer, Goya, Tiepolo)

Oregon

Portland	Portland Art Museum (Northwestern Coast collection: masks, baskets, contemporary art, Bronzino's *Madonna and Child With the Infant St. John the Baptist*)

Pennsylvania

Chadds Ford	Brandywine River Museum (work by members of the Wyeth family, American 19th- and 20th-century landscape paintings)
Merion Station	Barnes Foundation (collection of Impressionists, Old Masters, African, Asian, and primitive art, Cézanne's *Les Grandes Baigneuses,* Matisse's *Three Sisters* triptych, Renoir's *Bathers of 1918,* Seurat's *Les Poseuses*)
Philadelphia	Historical Society of Pennsylvania (Philadelphia furniture, 500 pieces of silver, early Colonial painters: Hesselius, Peale family, Sully, West, Copley)
	Pennsylvania Academy of the Fine Arts (18th- to 20th-century American painting, sculpture, drawings, and prints, Charles Willson Peale's *The Artist in His Museum,* Benjamin West's *Penn's Treaty With the Indians,* Eakins's *Portrait of Walt Whitman*)
	Philadelphia Museum of Art (Brancusi's *Bird in Space,* Duchamp's *Nude Descending a Staircase,* Peale's *Staircase Group,* Asian collection: Persian, Indian, Chinese, and Japanese artifacts, Picasso's *Three Musicians,* Rousseau's *Carnival Evening,* van Gogh's *Sunflowers,* Cezanne's *Bathers,* 40 paintings by Thomas Eakins)
	University of Pennsylvania Museum (extensive archaeological treasures: Mideastern, East African, American, and Oceanic)
Pittsburgh	Carnegie Institute Art Museum (Asian art, photography, paintings, sculpture, prints, drawings, Rouault's *Old King,* Kokoschka's *Thomas Masary*) Frick Art Museum (Italian Renaissance, Flemish, and French paintings; bronzes, tapestries)

Rhode Island

Newport	Newport Art Museum (permanent collection of New England and Newport artists, contemporary and historical)

Providence	Rhode Island School of Design Museum of Art (antiquity to 20th-century collection, classical Greek sculpture, Dégas's *Six Friends of the Artist* and *Before the Race*)

South Carolina

Columbia	Columbia Museum of Art (13th- to 20th-century European and American paintings, sculpture, graphic arts, Botticelli's *Nativity,* Canaletto's *View of Venice,* Joachim Patinir's *The Flight into Egypt,* Tiffany glass)
Greenville	Bob Jones University Museum of Sacred Art (13th- to 19th-century French, Flemish, Italian, Dutch, Spanish art: Botticelli, Rubens, Tintoretto, Titian, van Dyck)

South Dakota

Sioux Falls	Civic Fine Arts Center (regional, American, and international artists, paintings, sculpture, other media)

Tennessee

Memphis	Brooks Museum of Art (European painting from 13th to 20th centuries, English and American Decorative arts, collection of Greek vases)

Texas

Austin	Blanton Museum (European paintings from the 14th to the 18th centuries, Latin American art, 15th- to 20th-century prints and drawings)
Dallas	Dallas Museum of Fine Arts (contemporary, pre-Columbian, American, and European paintings, Morris Graves's *Bird,* Matisse's *Collage,* Pollock's *Cathedral,* Rufino Tamayo's *El Hombre,* van Gogh's *Sheaves of Wheat*)
El Paso	El Paso Museum of Art (Kress collection of 14th- to 17th-century European art, 19th- and 20th-century American paintings, Hispanic art)

Texas (continued)

Fort Worth   Amon Carter Museum (19th- and 20th-century American art, Remington's *The Old Stage Coach of the Plains*)

Kimbell Art Museum (Asian, African, Mesoamerican, prehistoric to 20th-century art, Matisse, Rubens, Velazquez, Caravaggio, Cézanne, Fra Angelico; building by Louis Kahn)

Modern Art Museum of Fort Worth (20th-century artists, Avery, Diebenkorn, Donald Judd, Kandinsky, Motherwell, Pollock, Picasso, Rauschenberg, Clyfford Still)

Houston   Menil Collection (tribal antiquities, Byzantine, and 20th-century art collection)

Museum of Fine Arts (more than 27,000 works of art from prehistoric artifacts to contemporary art, Cézanne's *Madame Cézanne in Blue*)

San Antonio   San Antonio Museum of Art (Jacob Lawrence's *Bar 'n Grill*)

Utah

Provo   Brigham Young University Museum of Fine Arts (Hudson River School, American Realism, American Impressionism)

Vermont

Burlington   Shelburne Museum, (18th- and 19th-century American art, Church, Cole, Bierstadt, Quidor, Homer, folk art collection)

St. Johnsbury   St. Johnsbury Athenaeum (19th-century American landscapes, Hudson River School)

Virginia

Richmond   Virginia Museum of Fine Arts (ancient, Medieval, and contemporary art, Five *Fabergé Imperial Easter Eggs*, Copley's *Mrs. Isaac Royall*, Francesco Guardi's *Piazza San Marco*, Henry Moore's *Reclining Figure*, sculpture court)

Washington

Seattle — Charles and Emma Frye Art Museum (German and 19th-century American paintings, Alaskan and Russian American collections)

Seattle Art Museum (20,000 works of art covering 5,000 years, Native American art, Asian art, Mark Tobey's *Forms Follow Man*, Morris Graves's *Sea Fish* and *Constellation*)

Tacoma — Tacoma Art Museum (19th- and 20th-century art, Dale Chihuly, Jacob Lawrence, Robert Motherwell, Renoir, Raphael Soyer, Mark Tobey)

West Virginia

Charleston — Sunrise Art Museum (regional art, contemporary sculpture, 19th- to 20th-century American paintings, Chuck Close, Stuart Davis, Viola Frey, Nancy Graves, Larry Rivers, Ben Shahn)

Huntington — Huntington Museum of Art (French, English, and American paintings, Frank Benson, George Inness, Willard Metcalf, Alfred Stieglitz)

Wisconsin

Milwaukee — Milwaukee Art Center (20th-century American and European painting and sculpture, ancient art, decorative arts, film, video)

Wyoming

Cody — Buffalo Bill Historical Center (Gallery of Western Art)

Plains Indian Museum (Catlin, Remington, Moran)

Jackson Hole — National Museum of Wildlife Art (sculpture and paintings of North American wildlife; artists exhibited: Audubon, Catlin, A. Phimister Procter, Charles M. Russell)

VENEZUELA

Caracas　　　　　　　Fine Arts Museum (Venezuelan art, 20th-century Latin American sculpture, pre-Columbian and Egyptian art)

WALES

Cardiff　　　　　　　National Museum of Wales (Richard Wilson's *View in Windsor Great Park,* archaeology, art, geology, botany, Welsh and British painting)

YUGOSLAVIA

Belgrade　　　　　　Belgrade National Museum (archaeological collection from prehistory, Serbian art, European collection)

"For every artist with something to say but the inability to say it well, there are two who could say something well if they had something to say."

—PAUL C. MILLS, graphic designer and musician

CHAPTER 7

Prints and Drawings

"To draw, you must close your eyes and sing."
—PABLO PICASSO, 1881–1973, Spanish Cubist painter/sculptor

PRINTS: AN INTRODUCTION

With the exception of the monotype (one-of-a-kind print), original prints are created through one of four techniques of printing: intaglio, relief, planographic, and stencil. Intaglio and relief prints have had the depth of the printing surface altered chemically or by cutting. Lithography (a planographic technique) relies on the natural antipathy of oil and water to alter the printing surface. Serigraphy (silk screen) is a stenciling technique. In contrast to a drawing, which is a one-of-a-kind original, artists have been making *multiple originals* of their work for hundreds of years. The first mass-reproduced work of art may well have been a charcoal-covered hand that stamped black prints onto the wall of a cave 30,000 years ago.

At least 1,200 years ago the Chinese used woodcuts to illustrate Buddhist texts, and in Medieval times in Europe, woodcuts were used in textile designs. In the 16th and 17th centuries, with the advent of the printing press, Albrecht Dürer's famous woodcuts and Rembrandt van Rijn's etchings were widely distributed. In the 1800s, anonymous engravers interpreted paintings by famous artists for distribution as prints. Some original prints were made for use in books and may number in the thousands.

PRINTMAKING TERMS

Although choosing a print to hang in your home or office is essentially a decision you make based on aesthetics—how it looks, whether it appeals to your taste, and whether it matches your decorating style—wouldn't you also like to be just a little more "in the know" about what you're looking at and choosing? This list features some key terms about basic printing processes. Getting acquainted with these terms will help you choose your next print with a bit more savvy.

Aquatint. A method of creating a fine, pebbled background by etching a metal plate for printing. An etching made by this process is usually combined with other techniques to give rich differences in tone and texture.

Burr. The metal fuzz left after the plate's surface has lines deliberately scratched with a metal tool. This technique is called drypoint, and is sometimes combined with other printing methods. The burr may be scraped off or left on the plate and inked to create rich, velvety blacks.

Cancellation proof. Following the printing of an edition, the printing plate is traditionally defaced by putting a hole in it or a mark across it. A cancellation proof (print) is pulled to demonstrate that the plate was canceled.

Collagraph. A collage-like assemblage built up on a surface such as Masonite®, wood, or matboard, then varnished and inked. It may be printed multiple times onto a piece of paper. The collagraph plates might have materials such as Mylar©, organza, cardboard of various weights, plaster, or anything else that will give an interesting texture.

Deckle. In handmade paper, the deckle is an open frame used to shape the paper. When the deckle is removed, it leaves a slightly fringed edge.

Dot pattern. The minute dots that may be seen with a magnifying glass in any photographically reproduced artwork.

Drypoint. The technique of scratching directly into a metal or plastic plate with a sharp metal- or diamond-pointed tool to create burrs, often after a design is completely etched. Rembrandt was particularly noted for the drypoint additions to his etchings that gave a soft quality to lines.

Embossing. Creating impressions on paper, normally without color, by running damp paper through a press on a prepared uninked plate such as a woodcut or collagraph. (Sometimes called blind-printing.)

Engraving. To create an engraving, lines are incised into a metal plate with a lozenge-shaped tool called a burin. Ink is then forced into these lines.

Etching. A process of making designs or pictures on a metal plate by immersing it in acid. An etching will have thin marks, dots, and/or lines, and the edges of the printing plate will leave marks from the pressure of the press.

Giclée (zhee-clay) print. (Sometimes called an Iris print.) A computer technique in which an artwork in any medium is digitized (scanned), then printed using an inkjet printing system with ink, acrylic, or oil paint. It is considered a reproduction because it is a photographic technique. Tests have shown the ink will last from 15 to 40 years under normal circumstances, compared to the indefinite life-span of a print produced with traditional printing methods.

Ground. In most forms of acid-etching, a copper or zinc plate is coated with a waxy substance that is called the ground. (See *Hard ground* and *Soft ground*.)

Hard ground. A waxy acid-resistant substance painted or rubbed, then melted onto a warmed etching plate, through which a design is scratched with a sharp tool.

Intaglio printing. *Intaglio* (pronounced in-*tal*-yo) is an Italian term used to describe hollowing out a surface by etching (acid-corroding) or engraving (incising). In an intaglio print, the ink is rubbed onto a plate, but most of the ink is wiped from the surface of the plate, leaving ink remaining in the lines or marks below the surface. The design is transferred to damp paper by running it through a printing press.

Iris print. (See also *Giclée print*.) A computerized digital print made with paint or ink.

Lithography. A printing technique in which the artist draws with a lithocrayon or a grease-based liquid called tusche directly on a lithographic stone, or metal plate. After chemical treatment, the drawing surface has water wiped over it, then is inked. The greasy design holds the ink while the wet background repels it. A true lithograph is printed on high-quality paper and may have a deckle edge.

Mezzotint. An etching in which the entire metal plate is textured with a tool called a rocker or roulette, which has many tiny points. Some areas are then scraped or burnished so they hold little or no ink. When used for printing, this plate produces rich, velvety blacks contrasting with light areas.

Monotype and monoprint. In these techniques, which are the exception to "printmaking as multiples," a one-of-a-kind print is made by inking or painting directly on a plate (glass, plastic, or metal), then transferring the image to paper while the ink is still wet. "Ghost prints" are sometimes made when pigment still left on the plate is reprinted. A monoprint differs from a monotype in that it involves a traditional printing plate such as a relief print, etching or lithograph, but is changed slightly each time it is printed.

Offset-lithography. A photographic mechanical reproduction process that results in identical prints, and (usually) large editions. Offset-lithographs are sometimes signed by the artist, but because they are considered reproductions rather than original prints, are of far less value than an original. A dot pattern (such as you would see in a magazine print) is evident under close examination.

Original print. A piece of art created by an artist directly onto a printing surface such as a plate, stone, or screen, using a technique such as engraving, etching, or woodcut. Inks are applied to the surface of the plate, then transferred to paper through pressure. Silk screens (serigraphy) and lithos (lithography is drawing or painting on stone or metal) would also be considered original prints.

Planographic technique. In a planographic technique such as lithography, the image is neither etched nor carved from the plate, but is drawn on the same flat surface as the plate. Serigraphs (silk screens) or monoprints would be considered planographic prints.

Plate. The plate is created specifically by an artist for a print. It can be a wooden plank or linoleum block, cardboard collagraph, or etched metal.

Poster. One popular meaning is a reproduction of an artist's original work, such as posters that are sold in museums. Prior to advertising on television and radio, posters were used for disseminating information, propaganda, advertising, and for selling new ideas. A poster was usually inexpensively reproduced in quantity to be *posted* to advertise a product or event. The image was created by an artist (graphic designer), and would include words (often a headline and smaller words explaining the event). Occasionally a poster was printed in a limited edition, and signed in pencil by the artist. Old posters have become popular with collectors and are valued not only for the history they represent, but sometimes for their wonderful graphic design.

Proof. A print made when the plate has been changed, by further etching or carving, for example.

Reduction block printing. In this technique, a single wood or linoleum plate is inked and used to print several times, but a portion is removed and colors are changed in each printing (printed from lightest to darkest).

Registration. Correctly aligning a printing plate when successive colors are printed one atop another (such as the reduction print mentioned above).

Relief print. (Also called block print.) Made by using a plate such as linoleum (lino-cut) or wood (woodcut) in which areas have been cut away, creating a design on the raised areas. When the surface of the plate is inked and the image is transferred onto paper, the cut-away areas remain uncolored.

Remarque. A personal drawing accompanying an artist's signature.

Restrikes. Prints made from a plate after an original edition has been sold. Although the plate should be defaced after the original edition is produced, additional copies—restrikes—are sometimes made, often on a different type of paper to distinguish them from the first edition.

Serigraph (silk screen). This technique, which is a glorified form of stenciling, is also used to make screen-printed T-shirts. To create a silk-screen image, all areas except the one to be printed are blocked out on silk or nylon tautly stretched on a frame. Paint is forced through the open areas with a squeegee. To create a multi-colored image, several screens are prepared. Contemporary artists may prepare screens with a special technique created from a photographic image.

Soft ground. A waxy acid-resistant substance that is rubbed onto a warmed metal plate. It is sensitive to pressure, and materials (such as net, leaves, grasses) may be pressed into the surface to leave an image. If a paper is placed on the soft ground and drawn on with pencil, when the paper is lifted off, it removes areas of the soft-ground that will be etched, giving a much softer line than one that is scratched with a metal tool.

State. A completed print may have gone through many trial printings by the artist before being considered a finished print. Each printing in this trial process is called a state.

Stencil. A design cut into a water-resistant material such as plastic. Paint is applied to a surface such as a wall, cloth, or paper through the openings in the stencil.

Sugar-lift. A process whereby a design is painted on a metal plate using a sugar-water solution. When the solution is dry, a waxy ground is painted on top, allowed to dry, and the sugar-water is dissolved with water. The plate is then immersed in acid to etch the open areas left in the acid-resistant ground.

Wood engraving. A relief printing engraved into end blocks of wood, which are denser than regular woodcut plates.

LOOKING AT PRINTS

Although new technology has brought about new printmaking techniques, such as giclée, many artists continue to use time-honored printing methods and continue to sign in pencil. To distinguish between different printmaking techniques, take time to visit museums and galleries, and try to attend exhibits featuring a particular artist.

NOTATIONS

Prior to the late 19th century, artists did not traditionally sign their prints; therefore, many fine vintage prints are unsigned. Since that time, a specific tradition of signing has developed that is unique to printmaking. The first place to find out more about a print that intrigues you is by reviewing the notations below the picture. These can tell you quite a bit, and typically include:

- ✧ The artist's signature in pencil. (Inks fade, graphite does not.)
- ✧ A number or notation indicating the size of the run (number of copies printed). For example, if you see a number such as 6/50, it would mean that this was the sixth print of an edition of fifty. This notation is normally found in the center or left-hand side. One expert feels that it could mean that it was the sixth best print, not necessarily the sixth one printed. Theoretically all prints in an edition are identical and numbers are meaningless.

Notations may also include:

- ✧ The particular state at which you are looking. For example, a notation such as *3rd st* means that the print is a third trial proof taken before the print was completed for the edition.
- ✧ The edition number. If you see a notation stating *2nd ed.*, for example, it means that the print is from a second printing of a plate, using either new colors or paper, or both.
- ✧ *Open edition:* This means there are no limits to the number of printings the publishers may print from the same plate. With no limit on the edition, the print would have little value to a collector and would be considered a "decorative work."
- ✧ *AP (artist's proof):* This means the work is a proof of a work in progress, or one of a few finished proofs (traditionally ten percent) reserved for the use of the artist. An artist's proof may be considered of more value to a collector because there are fewer of these proofs than those in the regular edition.
- ✧ *Bon à tirer:* This French phrase means "good to pull," and would be the artist's guide for the printing of the entire edition.
- ✧ *E.A. (épreuve d'artist):* French term for artist's proof.
- ✧ *H/C hors de commerce:* Such copies were not intended for resale. They may have the same value as an artist's proofs.
- ✧ *Lith:* This stands for lithographer and is usually followed by the name of a master printer.

✧ *Litho (lithograph):* Some authentic lithographs, such as John James Audubon's or Currier and Ives' works, will have the authorized printer's name on the front.

✧ *PP (printer's proof):* There are usually only two of these reserved by the printer.

✧ *Publisher's proof:* This notation is usually written out rather than abbreviated. A publisher's proof is similar to an artist's proof, and is sometimes used as a promotional item.

✧ *TP (trial proof):* This means the print was made for the use of the artist during preparation of the plate.

COLLECTING PRINTS

For many art lovers, prints are the most accessible works to own, in part because they are generally less costly than an original oil painting. Original prints by living artists or relatively unknown printmakers are surprisingly inexpensive and of greater value than a reproduction. If a print is an *original,* that means the artist personally created the plate from stone, wood block or other material, made the decision as to color and type of paper, and approved the finished print. Contemporary artists sometimes work with a master printmaker, for example in a lithography studio, but the artist is on hand, making decisions about ink color, quality of prints, and so on. The personalized signature means that the artist has approved the print. Artists have been known to retouch or hand-color in one area prior to signing.

COLLECTING ORIGINAL PRINTS

Print collectors are advised that the three most important aspects affecting the value of a specific print are "condition, condition, condition." In order for an original print to be of any real value as a work of art, it must meet certain criteria, including the following:

✧ It should be printed on archival paper and mounted archivally.

✧ The paper should be in excellent condition, not faded or discolored.

✧ It should really be a limited edition, which means the print run is normally no more than 100 to 150. If the artist personally does the printing, the edition might be no larger than 30 prints. A run of 5,000 or even 1,000 is not very limited, and a print in a run of that size was probably reproduced through a photomechanical process.

✧ When you are uncertain of whether a print is a reproduction or an original, if you examine an offset-lithography print with a magnifying glass, you will see small dot patterns, just as you would in examining a magazine photo, indicating that it is a reproduction.

✧ On an intaglio print, because the paper was dampened for printing, the edges should be indented (the plate mark), and margins should be slightly higher from being forced through the press.

✧ The margins should be wide and completely free of ink. Many old prints have had the margins completely trimmed and are mounted on backing paper.

Here are some questions you should ask and some details you should be on the lookout for as you consider a print that catches your eye.

✧ Be wary of "chalky" looking paper. It may have been bleached, which could affect the life of the paper.

✧ Ask what technique(s) were used in producing the print. A knowledgeable gallery owner will be able to describe the technique or combination of techniques used.

✧ Find out the provenance—a list of previous owners from the time the artist printed it until the present.

✧ Find out when it was printed (whether during the artist's lifetime or from the artist's plate by someone else). A contemporary print from the artist's original plate would still be considered an original, but obviously could not compare in value to one printed in the edition and signed by the artist.

✧ Ask if the artist might have interpreted this print in another medium at a different date.

✧ Ask if a version of the print might also be in any museums.

✧ Look for the artist's signature in pencil directly below the image. If the print is signed within the picture, it may have been reproduced by a photographic technique. Many photo-offset lithography prints have a signature on the plate and again below the plate in pencil.

"Drawing is the true test of art."

—J.A.D. INGRES, 1780–1867, French academically trained painter

COLLECTING A "LIMITED EDITION" OFFSET-LITHOGRAPHY PRINT

Although it is called a "print," a photographic process print is not considered an original print because it does not involve a plate. The standard edition is 1,000 prints; the record-setting edition so far was by Bev Doolittle in 1989, which had a run of 69,996 offset-lithographic fine art "prints." A reproduction, which is not considered a work of art, will never hold the value of an original print.

Advantages to purchasing an offset lithography print are that it may cost less than an original print, and the entire run will be identical, even to include identical deckle edges in every print.

To choose a print that is aesthetically pleasing as well as a good value, consider the following:

- ✧ Ask what medium was used for the original artwork. (For example, was the original a watercolor, oil, or acrylic?)
- ✧ Because all prints are identical in the photo-lithography process, the number in the print-run is not important. Instead, consider buying a "special number" such as 100 or 1,000.
- ✧ Closely examine the print for clean, wide margins and good overall condition. Check both the front and back of the print, as "dings" may be more easily seen from the back.

Any print you purchase should be in "mint" condition, meaning that even if it is not new, the print has been properly framed and maintained, and thus appears new.

CARING FOR PRINTS AND DRAWINGS

If you buy prints or drawings because you love to look at them, you probably won't be content to keep them packed away in a portfolio, to be looked at occasionally (unless you have a large collection). Instead, you'll probably want to display them. Whether you store your prints or frame and display them, you'll want to keep the following pointers in mind to ensure the prints' longevity.

- ✧ Use only archival (non-acidic) materials (such as matboard, tape, backing material).
- ✧ Avoid direct sunlight.
- ✧ Use UV protective glass, and do not allow the prints or drawings to directly touch glass.
- ✧ Consider rotating your "exhibition" several times a year as museums do.
- ✧ To repair damage caused by smoke, mildew, tape marks, or dampness, let a professional restorer do the job.
- ✧ Wash your hands or wear gloves before handling the prints, and handle them only by the edges.
- ✧ If you're storing the prints, have them archivally matted and store them in a special box, separated with acid-free paper.

"It's like golf. The fewer strokes I can take,
the better the picture."
—JOHN MARIN, 1870–1953, American Abstractionist

ARTISTS IN PRINT

Unlike the creation of a sculpture or a painting, creating a print is rarely a solitary enterprise. They are often created by artists in collaboration with master printers at an atelier or lithography studio. Combining the artist's design with the printer's expertise to create a work of art in print allows a wider distribution than the artist would normally have in his or her usual medium.

This list features printmakers, but also includes many familiar artists who may be better known for their work in other media.

AUSTRIA

Kokoschka, Oskar, 1886–1980

BELGIUM

Ensor, James Sydney, 1860–1949
Vlaminck, Maurice de,
1876–1958

ENGLAND

Beardsley, Aubrey Vincent,
1872–1898
Hamilton, Richard, 1922
Hockney, David, 1937
John, Augustus Edwin,
1878–1968
Moore, Henry, 1898–1986
Paolozzi, Eduardo, 1924
Sutherland, Graham, 1903–1980

FRANCE

Bonnard, Pierre, 1867–1947
Braque, Georges, 1882–1963
Cézanne, Paul, 1839–1906
Chagall, Marc, 1889–1985
Cocteau, Jean, 1889–1963
Corot, Jean Baptiste Camille,
1796–1875
Daumier, Honoré, 1808–1879
David, Jacques Louis,
1748–1824
Dégas, Edgar, 1834–1917
Delacroix, Ferdinand Victor
Eugène, 1798–1863
Delaunay, Robert-Victor Felix,
1885–1941

FRANCE (continued)

Derain, André, 1880–1954
Dubuffet, Jean, 1901–1985
Dufy, Raoul, 1877–1953
Gauguin, Paul, 1848–1903
Gericault, Jean 1791–1824
Ingres, Jean Auguste, 1780–1867
Léger, Fernand, 1881–1955
Maillol, Aristide, 1861–1944
Manet, Edouard, 1832–1883
Masson, André, 1896–1987
Matisse, Henri, 1869–1954
Monet, Claude, 1840–1926
Redon, Odilon, 1840–1916
Renoir, Pierre Auguste,
1841–1919
Rodin, Auguste, 1840–1917
Rouault, Georges, 1871–1958
Rousseau, Henri, 1844–1910
Seurat, Georges Pierre,
1859–1891
Soulages, Pierre, 1919
Toulouse-Lautrec, Henri de,
1864–1901
Vasarely, Victor, 1908–1997
Villon, Jacques (Gaston
Duchamp), 1875–1963
Vuillard, Jean-Edouard,
1867–1940

GERMANY

Albers, Josef, 1888–1976
Barlach, Ernst, 1870–1938
Beckmann, Max, 1884–1950
Corinth, Lovis, 1858–1925

GERMANY *(continued)*

Dix, Otto, 1891–1969
Ernst, Max, 1891–1976
Hartung, Hans, 1904–1989
Heckel, Erich, 1883–1970
Hofer, Karl, 1878–1955
Kirchner, Ernst Ludwig,
1880–1938
Kollwitz, Käthe, 1867–1945
Lehmbruck, Wilhelm,
1881–1919
Marc, Franz, 1880–1916
Nolde, Emil (Emil Hansen),
1864–1956
Pechstein, Max, 1881–1955
Schmidt-Rottluf, Karl,
1884–1976
Schwitters, Kurt, 1887–1948

ITALY

Boccioni, Umberto, 1862–1916
Chirico, Giorgio Di, 1888–1978
Giacometti, Alberto, 1901–1966
Marini, Marino, 1901–1980
Modigliani, Amedeo, 1884–1920
Morandi, Giorgio, 1890–1964
Severini, Gino, 1883–1966

JAPAN

Hamaguchi, Yozo, 1909–2000
Ikeda, Masuo, 1934–1997
Munakata, Shiko, 1903–1975

MEXICO

Orozco, José Clemente,
1883–1949
Rivera, Diego, 1886–1957
Siqueiros, David, 1898–1974

NETHERLANDS

Escher, Maurits Cornelius
(M. C.), 1898–1972
Gogh, Vincent van, 1853–1890

NORWAY

Munch, Edvard, 1863–1944

RUSSIA

Kandinsky, Wassily, 1866–1944
Lissitzky, El (Lazar Markovitch),
1890–1941
Malevich, Kasimir, 1878–1935

SPAIN

Dali, Salvador, 1904–1988
Goya y Lucientes, Francisco José
de, 1746–1828
Gris, Juan, 1887–1927
Miró, Joan, 1893–1983
Picasso, Pablo, 1881–1973

SWITZERLAND

Klee, Paul, 1879–1940

UNITED STATES

Anuszkiewicz, Richard, 1930
Baskin, Leonard, 1922–2000
Bellows, George Wesley,
    1882–1925
Blume, Peter, 1906–1992
Burchfield, Charles, 1893–1967
Cassatt, Mary, 1845–1926
Close, Chuck, 1940
Davis, Stuart, 1894–1964
de Kooning, Willem, 1904–1997
Demuth, Charles Henry,
    1883–1935
Dine, Jim, 1935
Eakins, Thomas, 1844–1916
Feininger, Lyonel, 1871–1956
Francis, Sam, 1923–1994
Frankenthaler, Helen, 1928
Glackens, William James,
    1870–1938
Gottleib, Adolph, 1903–1974
Graves, Morris, 1910–2001
Grosz, George, 1893–1959
Homer, Winslow, 1836–1910
Hopper, Edward, 1882–1967
Indiana, Robert, 1928
Johns, Jasper, 1930
Katz, Alex, 1927
Kent, Rockwell, 1882–1971
Kitaj, R. B., 1932

Lasansky, Mauricio, 1924
Lichtenstein, Roy, 1923–1997
Marin, John, 1870–1953
Matta (Sebastian Antonio
    Echaurren Matta), 1911–2002
Moholy-Nagy, Lazlo, 1895–1946
Motherwell, Robert, 1915–1991
Nevelson, Louise, 1899–1988
Newman, Barnett, 1905–1970
Pollock, Jackson, 1912–1956
Prendergast, Maurice Brazil,
    1859–1924
Rauschenberg, Robert, 1925
Rivers, Larry, 1923–2002
Rockwell, Norman, 1894–1978
Rosenquist, Jim, 1933
Sargent, John Singer, 1856–1925
Shahn, Ben, 1898–1960
Sheeler, Charles, 1883–1965
Sloan, John, 1871–1951
Steinberg, Saul, 1914–1999
Tchelitchew, Pavel, 1898–1937
Warhol, Andy, 1930–1987
Weber, Max, 1881–1961
Whistler, James Abbott McNeill,
    1834–1903
Wood, Grant, 1892–1942
Wyeth, Andrew, 1917

"Drawing well does not mean drawing correctly."
—ALEXEI VON JAWLENSKY, 1864–1941, Russian painter

DRAWING TERMS

Almost every aspect of art involves drawing in one form or another, ranging from a preliminary sketch for a sculpture, or a final drawing for a painting, to an architect's rendering of a building. Differences between drawing and painting are that drawing is normally on paper rather than canvas and usually has a predominantly linear quality. Drawing is often done in a combination of media, some wet, some dry. This list defines some materials, techniques, and terms used to discuss drawing.

Bistre. A brown pigment popular from the 14th through 19th centuries, but seldom used today because it tends to fade.

Caricature. A drawing in which certain features are deliberately exaggerated.

Cartoon. A drawing done on brown paper and used for interpretation in fresco. Also, humorous drawing of a subject with exaggerated features.

Chalk. Sometimes called whiting; often used in combination with other materials to give broad areas of texture or add highlights.

Charcoal. Drawing material in stick form made of burnt vine or willow.

Chiaroscuro. Effects of dark and light used by an artist to call attention to specific areas of a drawing or painting.

Collage. A composition created by gluing a variety of materials onto a support or background. Collage is frequently combined with drawing.

Colored pencil. Thick, soft leads of light-resistant pigments.

Conté crayon. Hard grease-free chalk in pencil or stick form, commonly used in white, black, gray, and sanguine (blood red). Conté was often used by the old masters such as Leonardo da Vinci or Rembrandt.

Contour drawing. An outline drawing usually without shading. It also refers to a drawing done of the human figure that gives it a three-dimensional quality. Contour drawings are sometimes combined with an ink or watercolor wash applied to the paper.

Crayon. Pigment combined with paraffin wax, usually available in stick form.

Cross hatching. Using parallel lines on top of parallel lines but at different angles to create ranges of color intensity, or value differences. *Hatching* refers to short parallel lines closely or widely spaced to create dark or light areas.

Estompe (stump or tortillon). Tightly rolled paper, leather or felt, pointed at one or both ends, used for blending and softening edges in a drawing.

Gouache. Watercolor pigment that contains chalk to make it opaque.

Gradation. The soft blending of pigment to create lights and darks.

Graphite. Grayish black, crystallized form of carbon; combined with clay to make "lead" pencils.

Highlight. The lightest spot in a drawing—the reflection in an eye, for example.

Illuminated manuscript. A drawing or painting on a manuscript from pre-printing press days, often painted on parchment or vellum with ground pigment mixed with egg yolk, highlighted with gold.

Illustration. A drawing intended for publication in a book or magazine.

India ink. Dense black permanent ink made from carbon.

Iron gall ink. Ferrous oxide mixed with gall (an oak tree fungus) and carbon.

Laid paper. Watermarked handmade paper that shows closely spaced parallel lines in both directions created by the wire screen used in making the paper.

Life-drawing. A drawing in which the artist draws what he or she actually sees, whether it is from a live model, a still life, or a real object.

Lithographic crayon. Black grease crayon normally used in lithographic printing, but also used in drawing.

Modeling. Showing soft roundness of forms through different ranges of intensity.

Modello. A compositional presentation drawing that shows what a larger, completed drawing would look like.

Old Masters. A term generally used to describe European Renaissance artists through the 18th century.

Original drawing. Produced by the artist's hand; not mechanically reproduced.

Parchment. Paper originally made from goat or sheepskin. Paper parchment is a textured, oil- and grease-resistant bond paper commonly used in calligraphy.

Pastel. Ground pigment held together in stick form with a binder, such as gum arabic. Oil pastel is held together with an oil binder. Although pastel has come to mean "a light color" to some, pastels of all kinds actually come in a full range of values, including black.

Preliminary drawing. An early-stage drawing done as a study for a later artistic interpretation.

Prismacolor®. Intense colors in a wax-based colored pencil or stick form.

Recto. A catalog description meaning "signed work" (not necessarily signed by the artist).

Reed pen. Bamboo section that has a carved point; used for drawing with ink.

Scraping. Scraping through the drawing medium with a sharp instrument to show the color of the underlying paper.

Silver point. A drawing made with a pointed silver wire or rod on specially treated white or tinted paper, leaving a soft grayish line that becomes darker as it tarnishes with age. This was a favorite of Renaissance masters.

Sketch. A rough quick drawing intended to get an idea down on paper for later use in another medium.

Still life (nature morte). An artwork featuring a grouping of inanimate objects, such as flowers in a vase.

Study. A sketch done quickly for use in later compositions.

Sumi ink. Ink from vegetable oil and soot (used in Asian painting).

Value. Range in intensity from the lightest to darkest possible tones within a particular hue.

Vellum. Originally made of calfskin; modern paper vellum, used for diplomas or certificates, is usually cream or natural colored and has a smooth finish.

Wash. Light ink or watercolor combined with other materials in a drawing.

Watercolor. A pigment for which water is used as a vehicle. The art or technique of painting with such pigments.

Wove paper. Handmade paper made on a tightly meshed screen. Unlike laid paper, it does not have cross lines.

LOOKING AT DRAWINGS

Most museums display drawings in small, dimly lit galleries to keep them from being damaged by bright light. Permanent collections are usually rotated several times a year, occasionally featuring a particular artist. Some museums, such as the Albertina in Vienna, hang only *reproductions* of some of their most famous works, keeping the originals in their library for study by scholars.

When you look at a drawing in a museum, check the label for the title, the name of the artist, when it was drawn, the medium used, and the ground (paper) used. When you examine a drawing, here are some questions you might consider.

✦ Is it a finished drawing? Or did the artist appear to leave the drawing deliberately unfinished? Does the composition appear to be complete?

✦ Is it an original concept?

✦ Would you know it was by this particular artist even if you did not read the label?

✦ How did the artist call your attention to the main subject?

✦ How did the artist create contrast? Was it through a wash, cross-hatching, use of a different medium?

✦ Did the artist combine a variety of media for emphasis of certain areas or to create highlights and dark areas?

✦ How did the artist fill the space? Is empty space important for drama in this composition?

✦ Is a grid visible (used for enlarging a drawing)?

✦ Examine how the directions of the strokes are used to create folds in clothing, plowed fields, or delicate roundness in an arm.

✦ Does the artist have mastery over the medium used? Are some lines bold and sure? Is there variation in the lines? Or can you picture that if more had been done, it would have been too much?

✦ Do you feel the artist's sensitivity and flexibility?

COLLECTING DRAWINGS

If you're interested in owning drawings rather than just viewing them in museums, take a little time to learn how to choose a quality drawing. Print and drawing fairs are wonderful places to begin your education as you can see work by a variety of artists and have discussions with many different dealers. Another way to learn about drawings is to ask questions of other collectors and gallery owners.

✦ Of course, the most important matter to consider is whether the drawing appeals to you. However, your decision to purchase a particular drawing should be based on more than that. Here are some tips to help you choose drawings of artistic value. When you're just getting started, narrow your selection to one subject or school of art to make beginning a little easier.

✦ A connection between a figure study and a painting, sculpture, or etching naturally adds value to a drawing.

✦ Does the paper give some clue as to the age of the drawing?

✦ Creased paper may have been deliberately used, as done by Tiepolo. (He deliberately drew on creased paper to cause the brush to skip, giving an effect of wear and tear.)

✦ What is the condition of the background?

✦ What media were used?

✦ What is the provenance of the drawing? (Where did it come from?)

"Draw from memory. It is the best thing in the world for you. Draw a foot from memory, but be careful to get a particular foot to remember, not just any old foot."

—BOARDMAN ROBINSON, 1876–1952,
American painter, illustrator

ARTISTS NOTED FOR THEIR DRAWINGS

Although original drawings date back some 30,000 years to the cave painters, drawings in collections are rarely more than 500 years old, simply because of the nature of paper. The exceptions are illuminated manuscripts, which were painted on vellum or parchment (animal skin). The artists included in this list have created a significant body of drawings that are avidly collected, although you may associate many of these artists with artwork in a different medium, such as sculpture, painting, or photography.

AUSTRIA

Klimt, Gustav, 1862–1918
Kokoschka, Oskar, 1886–1980
Schiele, Egon, 1890–1918

BELGIUM

Ensor, James, 1860–1949

ENGLAND

Barry, James, 1741–1806
Beardsley, Aubrey, 1872–1898
Blake, Peter, 1932
Blake, William, 1753–1828
Constable, John, 1776–1837
du Maurier, George, 1834–1896

ENGLAND *(continued)*

Freud, Lucian, 1922
Gainsborough, Thomas,
    1727–1788
Hayter, Stanley William,
    1901–1988
Hogarth, William, 1697–1764
Keene, Charles, 1823–1891
Lely, Sir Peter, 1618–1680
Moore, Henry, 1898–1986
Sutherland, Graham, 1903–1980
Tenniel, Sir John, 1820–1914
Turner, Joseph Mallord William,
    1775–1851

FRANCE

Balthus (Count Balthasar
  Klossowski de Rola),
  1908–2001
Bonnard, Pierre, 1867–1947
Boucher, François, 1703–1770
Braque, Georges, 1882–1963
Bresdin, Rodolphe, 1825–1885
Cézanne, Paul, 1839–1906
Chagall, Marc, 1889–1985
Chardin, Jean-Baptiste-Siméon,
  1699–1779
Clouet, Jean, 1485–1541
Corot, Camille-Jean Baptiste,
  1796–1875
Courbet, Gustave, 1819–1877
Daumier, Honoré, 1808–1879
David, Jacques-Louis,
  1748–1825
Dégas, Edgar, 1834–1917
Delacroix, Eugène, 1798–1863
Derain, André, 1880–1954
Dubuffet, Jean, 1901–1985
Dufy, Raoul, 1887–1953
Fantin-Latour, Henri,
  1836–1904
Forain, Jean Louis, 1852–1931
Fragonard, Honoré, 1732–1806
Gauguin, Paul, 1848–1903
Géricault, Théodore, 1791–1824
Ingres, Jean-Auguste-
  Dominique, 1780–1867
La Fresnaye, Noel, 1885–1925
Léger, Fernand, 1881–1955
Lorrain, Claude, 1600–1682

FRANCE *(continued)*

Maillol, Aristide, 1861–1944
Manet, Edouard, 1832–1883
Marquet, Albert, 1875–1947
Matisse, Henri, 1869–1954
Millet, Jean François,
  1814–1875
Moreau, Gustave, 1826–1898
Redon, Odilon, 1840–1916
Renoir, Pierre Auguste,
  1842–1919
Rodin, Auguste, 1840–1917
Rouault, Georges, 1871–1958
Seurat, Georges, 1859–1891
Toulouse-Lautrec, Henri de,
  1864–1901
Villon, Jacques (Gaston
  Duchamp), 1875–1963
Watteau, Antoine, 1684–1721

GERMANY

Barlach, Ernst, 1870–1938
Beckmann, Max, 1884–1950
Corinth, Lovis, 1858–1925
Dix, Otto, 1891–1969
Dürer, Albrecht, 1471–1528
Feininger, Lyonel, 1871–1956
Friedrich, Caspar David,
  1774–1840
Grien, Hans Baldung,
  c. 1484–1545
Groz, George, 1893–1959
Heckel, Erich, 1883–1970
Holbein, Hans (the Younger),
  c. 1497–1543

GERMANY *(continued)*

Kirchner, Ernst Ludwig,
  1880–1938
Kollwitz, Käthe, 1867–1945
Lehmbruck, Wilhelm,
  1881–1919
Modersohn-Becker, Paula,
  1876–1907
Nolde, Emil, 1867–1956
Schongauer, Martin, c. 1453–1491

ITALY

Boccioni, Umberto, 1882–1916
Canaletto (Giovanni Antonio
  Canale), 1697–1768
Carracci, Annibale, 1560–1609
Castiglione, Giovanni Benedetto,
  c. 1610–1665
Chirico, Giorgio di, 1888–1978
Correggio (Antonio Allegri),
  1489–1534
Cortona, Pietro da (Pietro
  Berrettini), 1596–1669
Guardi, Francesco, 1712–1793
Leonardo da Vinci, 1452–1519
Marini, Marino, 1901–1980
Michelangelo Buonarroti,
  1775–1564
Modigliani, Amedeo, 1884–1920
Piazzetta, Giovanni Battista,
  1683–1754
Piranesi, Giovanni Battista,
  1720–1778
Pisanello (Antonio Pisano),
  c. 1395–c. 1455
Raphael (Raffaello Sanzio),
  1483–1520

ITALY *(continued)*

Severini, Gino, 1883–1966
Tiepolo, Giovanni Battista,
  1696–1770
Veronese, (Paolo Caliari),
  c. 1528–1588

MEXICO

Castellanos, Julio, 1905–1947
O'Gorman, Juan, 1905–1982
Orozco, José Clemente,
  1883–1949
Posada, José Guadalupe,
  1851–1913
Rivera, Diego Maria, 1886–1957
Siqueiros, David Alfaro,
  1896–1974

NETHERLANDS

Avercamp, Hendrik, 1585–1634
Bosch, Hieronymus,
  c. 1450–1516
Cuyp, Albert, 1620–1691
Doesburg, Theo van, 1883–1931
Escher, M. C. 1898–1972
Gheyn, Jacob de, II, 1565–1629
Gogh, Vincent van, 1853–1890
Goyen, Jan van, 1596–1656
Heemskerck, Maerten van,
  1498–1574
Ostade, Adriaen van, 1610–1685
Rembrandt van Rijn, 1606–1669
Ruisdael, Jacob van,
  c. 1628–1682
Weyden, Roger van der,
  1397–1464

NORWAY

Munch, Edvard, 1863–1944

RUSSIA

Kandinsky, Wassily, 1866–1944

SPAIN

Dali, Salvador, 1904–1988
Goya, Francisco de, 1746–1828
Gris, Juan, 1887–1927
Miró, Joan, 1893–1935
Murillo, Bartolomé Esteban, 1617–1682
Picasso, Pablo, 1881–1973

SWITZERLAND

Giacometti, Alberto, 1901–1966
Klee, Paul, 1879–1940

UNITED STATES

Avery, Milton, 1893–1965
Baskin, Leonard, 1922–2000
Bellows, George Wesley, 1882–1925
Blume, Peter, 1906–1992
Burchfield, Charles, 1893–1967
Calder, Alexander, 1898–1976

Cassatt, Mary, 1845–1926
Davis, Stuart, 1894–1964
Demuth, Charles, 1883–1935
Feininger, Lyonel, 1871–1956
Glackens, William James, 1870–1938
Gorky, Arshile, 1904–1948
Graves, Morris, 1910–2001
Grosz, George, 1893–1959
Homer, Winslow, 1836–1910
Hopper, Edward, 1882–1967
Levine, Jack, 1915
Marin, John, 1870–1953
Martin, Agnes, 1912
Newman, Barnett, 1905–1970
Pollock, Jackson, 1912–1956
Prendergast, Maurice, 1859–1924
Sargent, John Singer, 1856–1925
Shahn, Ben, 1898–1969
Sheeler, Charles, 1883–1965
Sloan, John, 1871–1951
Steinberg, Saul, 1914–1999
Tchelitchew, Pavel, 1898–1957
Tobey, Mark, 1890–1976
Whistler, James Abbott McNeill, 1834–1903
Wyeth, Andrew, 1917

"I prefer drawing to talking. Drawing is faster, and allows less room for lies."
—Le Corbusier, 1887–1966, Swiss architect

MUSEUMS ESPECIALLY NOTED FOR FINE PRINT
AND DRAWING COLLECTIONS

Naturally, all art museums have prints and drawings that are put on display from time to time, along with the museum's collections of paintings, sculpture, and decorative arts (their furniture, silver, armor, jewelry, tapestries, glass, and ceramics). What distinguishes the museums in this list is that they have very large collections of prints and drawings.

INTERNATIONAL MUSEUMS

Albertina, Vienna, Austria

National Gallery of Canada, Ottawa, Canada

The British Museum, London, England

Ashmolean Museum, Cambridge, England

The Louvre, Paris, France

Uffizi, Florence, Italy

Rijksmuseum, Amsterdam, Netherlands

UNITED STATES

Notable Collections

Each of the following museums has 100,000 or more prints and drawings on display.

Achenbach Foundation for Graphic Arts, San Francisco

Art Institute of Chicago

Metropolitan Museum of Art, New York City

National Gallery of Art, Washington, DC

New York Public Library

Museum of Fine Arts, Boston

Philadelphia Museum of Art

The museums listed here have 50,000 or more works on paper.

Baltimore Museum of Art, Maryland

Boston Public Library

Fogg Art Museum, Cambridge (Harvard), Massachusetts

Grunwald Center for Graphic Art, University of California, Los Angeles

Los Angeles County Museum of Art

Minneapolis Museum of Art, Minnesota

Other Special Collections

Indianapolis Museum of Prints, Drawings, and Photographs, Indiana

Pierpont Morgan Library, New York City

Note: This information was furnished courtesy of Karen Breuer, Prints and Drawings curator of the San Francisco Fine Arts Museums.

"To me, pencil drawing is a very emotional, very quick, very abrupt medium. I will work on a tone of a hill and then perhaps I will come to a branch or a leaf or whatever, and then all of a sudden I'm drawn into the thing penetratingly. I will perhaps put in a terrific black and press down on the pencil so strongly that the lead will break, in order to emphasize my emotional impact with an object. And to me, that's what a pencil will do."

—ANDREW WYETH, 1917, American realist painter

CHAPTER 8

Paintings and Painters

"Every time I paint, I throw myself into the water in order to learn how to swim."

—EDOUARD MANET, 1832–1883, French Impressionist painter

PAINTING TERMS

These simple definitions are mostly about the materials and techniques used in painting. They will add to your understanding when you read or hear about art, and will help you more confidently join in a discussion about paintings and painters.

Acrylic. Acrylic painting first appeared on the scene in the 1950s as a modern-day answer to the more time-consuming traditional technique of painting with oil. This water-soluble polymer-based paint dries quickly, adheres to most surfaces, and may be used as either a "watercolor" or "oil."

Aerial perspective. A sense of depth created through using subdued colors to indicate distance.

Alla prima (all at once). This Italian term refers to paint applied to canvas in one coat rather than the more common layer-by-layer method. In oil paint this means that it is not allowed to dry between coats. The surfaces of van Gogh's paintings remain in perfect condition because he applied his paint *alla prima*.

Analogous colors. Colors closely related on a color wheel, such as red, red-orange, and yellow.

Bleeding. The tendency of some colors to show through a second layer of paint.

Blending. The transition of color from one tone to another; the different tones of a sky, for example.

Buon (true) fresco. The application of pigment into a freshly plastered still-damp surface.

Canvas. Heavy fabric that is "stretched" on a wooden frame as a surface for painting.

Casein. A milk-based opaque paint that may be diluted with water.

Chiaroscuro. The use of light and dark areas to create a dramatic focal point or mood. Artists such as Caravaggio and Rembrandt were masters of the technique, calling the attention of the viewer to a certain area of a composition through mysterious lighting, much as a spotlight is used in a theatrical production.

Color wheel. The color wheel is an artificial means of organizing the colors of the spectrum (a rainbow contains these colors). Imagine a triangle made with the *primary* colors of red, blue, and yellow at each apex. A second triangle (to make a six-pointed star) is superimposed on the first, with its points representing orange, green, and violet, the *secondary* colors that are achieved by mixing red with yellow, yellow with blue, and blue with red. A circle drawn to enclose the intersecting points results in the color wheel. *Tertiary* colors are those achieved by mixing a primary and secondary color (for example, red and orange make red-orange).

Complementary colors. Colors opposite each other on the color wheel: red/green, blue/orange, yellow/violet. One only has to look at paintings and clothing to see that artists and designers frequently base color schemes upon opposite, complementary colors.

Cool colors. Colors that recede such as blue, green, violet.

Drybrush. Making the brush almost free of pigment before painting with it.

Earth colors. Pigments that occur naturally in earth or ore, such as raw sienna, burnt sienna, burnt umber, and yellow ochre.

Egg tempera. Pigment mixed with egg yolk and water is used in painting frescoes, canvases, or panels.

Encaustic. A colored pigment mixed with melted wax and resin, then applied to a surface while warm. This was used by the Romans in ancient Egypt, and has been used by contemporary artists, notably Jasper Johns, in the 20th century.

Figure/ground relationship. The contrast between a subject and its background.

Fresco secco. The application of pigment into a dried plastered surface.

Gesso. A thick mixture of glue, whiting (powdered calcium carbonate), and water used to prime a panel or canvas with an undercoat for painting. Many artists purchase pre-primed (first-coated) canvases.

Glaze. A transparent film of paint color applied over a dried underpainting, allowing the underneath to show through. Artists of the Renaissance, who applied thin coats of glaze, achieved glowing effects in their paintings with this technique.

Gouache. A watercolor medium made more brilliant by the addition of finely ground white pigment.

Grisaille (literally *gray*). A painting in shades of gray, sometimes on the outside of an altarpiece.

Ground. A primed surface that gives tonal qualities to paintings. For example, white, umber (brown), or ochre (golden tone) underpainting may be used prior to the application of color in an oil paint. A pastel artist, for example, frequently works on a "ground" of colored paper.

High key. Color applied in its purest intensity. Also, a composition that contains mostly light colors.

Highlight. A brightened area of an artwork that represents the reflection of light, as in the eye of a model.

Hue. Color at its purest intensity. A *tint* of a hue is created when white is added (red and white makes pink); a *shade* is achieved by adding black to the hue (red and black makes dark red).

Illumination. In the days before the printing press, books were hand-copied (mostly in monasteries) and the pages richly decorated with paintings of flowers, animals, and designs. Brilliant colors and gold leaf brought to life the lives of courtiers and peasants in the Middle Ages. *The Book of Kells* in Dublin is one of the most famous of these *illuminated manuscripts.*

Impasto. The thick, textured buildup of a picture's surface through repeated applications of oil or acrylic paint.

Intensity. The concentration of color. Color used in its purest hue without mixing can be said to have its purest intensity.

Linear perspective. The use of lines and diminishing size to create a feeling of depth; based on a geometric system of measurement.

Low key. Subdued, grayed color, or a very dark composition.

Magna. A trade name for a line of acrylic colors.

Masonite®. A trade name for a fiberboard made from pressed wood fiber used as a surface for painting.

Medium. A painting method such as oil, watercolor, or gouache; or a *liquid* such as linseed oil with which oil paints are mixed.

Mineral colors. Mineral pigments are made from inorganic chemicals or raw materials. Examples are ultramarine violet, mineral white (gypsum), Antwerp blue, mineral green (malachite).

Modeling paste. A paste of a lightweight thick texture used with acrylics to build up the surface of a painting.

Monochromatic. A color scheme that involves different values (degrees of light and dark) of a single hue.

Neutral colors. Complementary colors mixed to produce a dull, subdued color (variations of gray). Also, the noncolors of black and white.

Oil paint. Jan van Eyck is credited with discovering—almost 500 years ago—that ground minerals (pigment) mixed with linseed oil allowed the artist greater freedom in painting. Larger paintings were possible because canvas isn't so heavy as panels or plaster. New effects allowed by this medium, such as transparency and opacity in the same painting, gave a glowing richness to paintings. Unlike some water-based paints, oil colors remain unchanged when they have dried, and do not fade over time.

Opaque. Pigment that does not allow underneath colors to show through.

Oriental papers. Rice paper, mulberry paper, and others used as a surface for painting. They range from heavy to quite delicate.

Palette. The wooden, metal, plastic, or paper surface on which paint is placed and mixed. Also, a description of the color preferences of a particular artist.

Panel. A painting surface of prepared wood, Masonite®, or canvas-covered board.

Pigment. Earth, minerals, or chemicals finely ground and evenly suspended in a wet or dry medium.

Pointillism. The application of small dots of pure color on canvas, allowing the eye to do the mixing (such as seeing violet, when in reality, red and blue dots are side-by-side). Post-Impressionist Georges Seurat devised this method of painting that he considered scientific, and titled it *Divisionism.*

Polychrome. A work done in many colors.

Powdered pigments. Ground pure color powder to be mixed with a medium such as egg yolk, oil, or water.

Primary colors. The colors that cannot be produced by mixing: red, blue, yellow.

Saturated color. Hues undiluted with white, consequently deep and intense.

Scumbling. Adding a thin layer of color over a dry underlayer, allowing the underlayer to show through.

Secondary colors. The colors achieved when two primaries are mixed, for example, orange, violet, green.

Sfumato. A smoky, hazy effect in a painting. Leonardo da Vinci was a master of the technique of sfumato, as shown in the softness of *Mona Lisa's* eyes and mouth and the hazy background.

Shade. Any color mixed with black.

Stretchers. Wooden strips of varying lengths fitted together to make a support frame for canvas.

Tempera. Pigment mixed with water or egg yolk to make a creamy, opaque paint.

Tenebrism. Describes a dark painting with most detail obscured by shadow, yet attention called to the important area of the painting with a shaft of light. Masters known for this work were Caravaggio, 1573–1610, and Georges de La Tour, 1593–1652.

Tint. Any hue mixed with white.

Transparent colors. Colors that allow a strong underneath color to show through.

Triptych. A painting done in three sections hinged together.

Trompe l'oeil (fool the eye). A painting so real that you want to touch the objects.

Warm colors. Colors that advance visually such as red, red-orange, orange, yellow.

Wash. A thin application of paint or ink; pigment diluted with water and applied to a painting surface to give a translucent effect.

Watercolor. Pigment mixed with a binder such as gum arabic and applied with water to give a transparent effect.

Wet-in-wet. The action of paint spreading when adding new pigment to an area of wet paper.

*"There is nothing more difficult for a truly creative painter
than to paint a rose, because before he can do so, he must
first forget all the roses that were ever painted."*
—HENRI MATISSE, 1869–1954, French Post-Impressionist painter

TERMS USED IN DECORATIVE PAINTING TECHNIQUES

Some old decorative painting techniques are enjoying a revival. The ones in this list are mostly used on walls, furniture, and frames. If trying to reproduce natural stone such as marble, malachite, porphyry, or lapis lazuli, it is helpful to find a library book on faux-painting or geology that shows the patterns that occur naturally in these stones. Some of the terms found in this list also apply to traditional painting techniques.

Antique. To paint a thin glaze of burnt sienna or burnt umber over a base coat and wipe most of it off with a soft rag to create an antiqued look.

Color wash. To apply a thin second color on top of a first, allowing the undercoat to show.

Comb. To make designs with professional rubber or steel combs or ones made of cardboard or a squeegee by cutting the edges.

Decoupage. To cut out designs, glue them on a surface, and varnish them to protect the cutouts.

Drag. To apply a second color of paint on top of a first, allowing the brush-strokes to show.

Faux (false) bamboo. To paint round legs on furniture to look as if they were bamboo.

Faux stone. To paint blocks on a wall to resemble stone.

Flog. To apply glaze and hit it with a flat brush while it is still wet to create texture.

Gild. To apply thin gold or silver leaf over a reddish undercoat and size (sticky varnish). Gilding is frequently used on wooden frames, furniture, or carvings.

Glaze. To apply one transparent color over another, changing the color of each as the colors build up.

Grain. To make designs with rubber rollers or rubber squeegees that have lines carved in them.

Lapis lazuli. To create the jewel-like effect of lapis lazuli (a blue gemstone sometimes found in nature alongside or mixed with turquoise), a Prussian blue glaze (deep royal blue) may be used.

Lime. To apply white latex mixed with plaster of Paris, allowing it to remain in the grain of the wood, then wiping it off before applying a pale varnish.

Malachite. This greenish natural stone effect is made by using a green underglaze. Different values of green are added, with whorls and lines defined with a brush or feather.

Marbleize. To paint designs on a wall to resemble marble by using a combination of brushes, a sponge, and a feather.

Moiré. To use a fine comb to make designs resembling moiré silk.

Pickle. To wipe a whitish paint onto a surface and wipe off (same as *lime*).

Porphyry. To create the effect of this dark purplish-red granite-like rock, a plain dark red glaze is applied and smoothed with a sponge. Two or three related colors in different values (light to dark) and gold, used sparingly, are then spattered over the base coat.

Rag. To roll a rag in freshly applied paint, removing part of the paint in an abstract pattern.

Spatter. To flick paint from a brush that has been dipped in contrasting paint in an abstract pattern of spots.

Sponge. To create a two-tone effect by painting over the base coat with a sponge dipped in a contrasting color.

Stencil. To apply paints to a surface by dabbing paint through designs cut in oiled sheets or plastic stencils.

Stipple. To make individual small dots with a stiff brush in a slightly darker color(s) than the base coat.

Trompe l'oeil. To paint a subject on a wall or furniture so realistically that it "fools the eye."

Verdigris. To apply turquoise and green paints to make something resemble oxidized copper.

Wood grain. To use brushes to make the "grain" of the wood, then use a "mottler" to create irregularities that would be found in natural wood.

GREAT THEMES IN PAINTING

Certain universal themes, such as romance, religious beliefs, or death, have been used in the artwork of many cultures, though not in all time periods. Some themes have been taboo in certain places or time periods and acceptable in others. Other inspirations for art may be based on literature or folktales common to one culture, and not understood by those outside the culture. However, in such cases, if the art is good, it certainly isn't always necessary to understand it.

UNIVERSAL PAINTING THEMES

Adoration of religious figures
Allegorical
Animals
Artists' families
Carnivals
Children
Circus
Cities
The elements: earth, air, fire, water
Families
Farming
Festivals
Figural (human or animal)
Flowers
Gardens
Genre (ordinary daily activities)
Grief
Groups of people involved in wars, game-playing, conversation, and so on
Historical events
Hunting
Landscapes
Love
Musicians
Mythology
Narrative (storytelling in a painting)
Nighttime
Other artists at work
Outdoors
Portraiture
Processions
Religious subjects
Room interiors
Seascapes
Self-portraits
Sports
Still life
Theater
Transportation
Trees
War
Water

ASIAN THEMES

Animals
Birds
Buddha
Fans
Flowers

Mountains
Nature
Trees
Water

INDIAN THEMES

Adventure scenes
Animals
Hunting scenes
Illustrations of love poetry
Legends
Life of Buddha

Lives of the gods
Manuscript illumination
Portraits of court officials
Romantic scenes
Scenes at court
Story illustration

NATIVE AMERICAN THEMES

Animal totems
Dances
Exploits on horseback

Nature
Symbols for nature

CHRISTIAN RELIGIOUS THEMES

Adam and Eve in the Garden of
  Eden
Adoration of the Golden Calf
Adoration of the Magi
Adoration of the Shepherds
Annunciation
Bathsheba
Beheading of St. Paul
Biblical stories
Birth of the Virgin
Carrying of the Cross
Christ Before Pilate
Christ in Majesty

Circumcision
Coronation of the Virgin
Crucifixion
David and Goliath
Death of the Virgin
Descent from the Cross
Dormition of the Virgin
Doubting Thomas
Entombment
Entry into Jerusalem
Flight into Egypt
Flood
Garden of Eden

Garden of Gethsemene
Holy Family
Immaculate Conception
John the Baptist in the
    Wilderness
Last Judgment
Life of St. Stephen
Lives of the Saints
Madonna in the Clouds
Martyrdom of Saint Paul
Martyrdom of Saints
Moses Striking the Rock
Nativity
Pietá

Portraits of Popes and Cardinals
Presentation in the Temple
Presentation of the Virgin in the
    Temple
Raising of Lazarus
Rest on the Flight into Egypt
Sacrifice of Abraham
Supper at Emmaus
The Last Supper
The Trial of Moses
Tree of Jesse
Virgin Among Virgins
Virgin and Child
Visitation

TIMELINE: DISCOVERIES IN PIGMENT

Pigments are ground animal, vegetable, or mineral sources combined with a binder, such as gum arabic for watercolor pigments and oil for oil painting pigments. This list includes important dates in the history of using pigments for painting.

30,000 B.C.	Colors used in cave paintings: black and yellow manganese, red and yellow ochre, violet, mixed with water, egg white, or blood.
5,000 B.C.	Egyptian palette found in ancient scrolls and tomb paintings: black, blue, brown, green, red, white, yellow.
850–700 B.C.	Greek Palette: black overall geometric designs on vases.
700–600 B.C.	Greek Palette: black figures on red clay vases.
650–480 B.C.	Greek Palette: black figures with incised details on red clay vases.
530 B.C.	Greek Palette: red figures on vases with background painted black.
480–323 B.C.	Greek Palette: colors such as violet and yellow painted on white background vases.

100–44 B.C.	Realistic colors used by Romans on fresco in public and private decorations.
200 B.C.–A.D. 200	Egyptian encaustic panel portraits (colored pigment mixed with melted wax and painted on wood—sometimes placed on a mummy's sarcophagus).
C. A.D. 700–1400	Rich colors and gold leaf used by monks in European monasteries, particularly Germany, Flanders, and Ireland, to illuminate manuscripts on vellum or parchment.
c. 900	Encaustic seldom used after this date, until the 1950s when the technique was revived by such artists as Jasper Johns.
1000–1520	Fresco painting on walls flourished in Italy.
1380–1600	Manuscript illumination on paper common in Europe and Middle Eastern countries.
1300–1600	Egg tempera painting on wood panels. Prior to the common use of oil paint, this was the preferred method of painting portraits and altarpieces. It was particularly popular in Italy and Northern Europe.
1498–1520	Oil on wood panel. Jan van Eyck (1390–1441) is given credit by Georgio Vasari (a 16th-century art chronicler) for discovering oil paint, but numerous artists such as the Italian painter Giovanni Bellini had used oil earlier. Common usage did not come for many years until after his death.
1500	Watercolor (pigment mixed with water-soluble substances such as gum arabic) became more commonly used on paper or parchment. Pigment previously had been mixed with egg yolk and applied with small brushstrokes. Asian cultures used watercolor on textiles and hand-made paper.
1533–present	Oil and tempera pigment combined on canvas.
1829	Introduction of cadmium colors (red, yellow) into oil painting. Discovered in Germany by de Haen and Friedrich Strohmeyer.

1835	Watercolors had glycerine added and were pressed into cake form, sold in pans.
1840s	Aniline dyes from coal tars used in painting: emerald greens, magenta.
1856	First coal-tar dye: Perkin's Violet.
c. 1900	Silk-screen enamel used for textile printing.
1930s	Silk screen as an artistic medium.
1940s	Acrylic paint (magna) introduced.
1950s	Encaustic revival led by American pop artist Jasper Johns.

"A painter paints a picture with the same feeling as that with which a criminal commits a crime."

—EDGAR DÉGAS, 1834–1917, French Impressionist painter

PAINTING BEFORE THE "OLD MASTERS"

As far back as we can find evidence of civilization, we find paintings. Sometimes the paintings are as simple as a line drawing preserved on the wall of a cave, or a painted fragment of a wall. Egypt's dry climate has preserved sophisticated, exotic paintings on tomb walls. A great deal of what we know about the lives of ordinary people in ancient civilizations comes to us through these visual records.

The list that follows is an attempt to recognize some of the great paintings of the world—the ones done before the "Old Masters." More complete lists of artists may be found in the art history section of this book.

PREHISTORY

artist(s) unknown, *Lascaux Cave,* c. 15,000–13,000 B.C., Lascaux, France

MIDDLE AGES, A.D. 400–1000

The period sometimes known as the "Dark Ages" was actually a time of assimilation and growth. The principles of new religions, Christianity and Islam in particular, replaced superstition and paganism. During this time period, art consisted primarily of manuscript illumination and altarpieces.

Gospel Book of Otto III, c. 1000, artist unknown, Bavarian State Library,
   Munich
Lindisfarne Gospels, c. 700, artist unknown, British Library, London
Madonna, 6th–7th century, artist unknown, Sta. Francesca Romana, Rome
St. Matthew the Evangelist, 800, artist unknown, British Museum, London
The Book of Kells, c. 760–820, artist unknown, Trinity College, Dublin
The Gospel Book of Charlemagne, c. 800–810, artist unknown,
   Kunsthistorisches Museum, Vienna
The Thirteen Emperors, T'ang period, China, 7th century A.D., Yen Li-Pen
   died 673, Museum of Fine Arts, Boston

ROMANESQUE, 1000-1150

This term applies primarily to Roman-style church architecture. Romanesque paintings and sculptures are highly stylized, featuring a rigid torso and large staring eyes. It is as if artists of the Middle Ages were disregarding the human figure, hiding it under stiff garments and completely ignoring the realism of earlier Greek and Roman art.

Initial R with St. George and the Dragon, 12th century, artist unknown,
   Citeux, France
St. John the Evangelist (Gospel Book of Abbot Wedricus), c. 1147, artist
   unknown, Societé Archéologique, Avesnes, France
St. Luke Washing the Feet of Peter, Gospel Book of Otto III, c. 1000, artist
   unknown, Bavarian State Library, Munich
Virgin and Child Enthroned, c. 1130, artist unknown, Metropolitan
   Museum of Art, New York City

GOTHIC, c. 1100-1400

Gothic architecture was the style prevalently used in the churches of Western Europe from the 12th to the 15th centuries. The most common characteristics of Gothic churches were the many stained glass windows and pointed arches. When referring to art, the term *Gothic* applies to sculpture and illuminated manuscripts of the same time period.

Belleville Breviary, c. 1323–1326, artist unknown, Bibliothèque Nationale, Paris

Wilton Diptych, c. 1377–1413, artist unknown, National Gallery, London

Très Riches Heures du Jean, Duc de Berry, 1413–1416, artist unknown, Limbourg Brothers, Musée Condé, Chantilly, France

ASIAN AND MIDDLE EASTERN

The Ascension of Mohammed, 1539, artist unknown, British Library, London

River and Mountains on a Clear Autumn Day, 1555–1636, Tung Ch'i-ch'ang, Nelson-Atkins Museum of Art, Kansas City, Missouri

OLD MASTERS

Although the term "Old Masters" has traditionally been applied to European painters who worked from the Renaissance to the 18th century, this list is expanded to include other artists whose artwork is found in many museums.

ITALY, PRE-RENAISSANCE, c. 1250–1470

Painters were becoming known by name in this time period. They were decorating chapels and public buildings, and not always painting religious subjects, but cityscapes, battle scenes, and other events as well. The use of perspective was rudimentary at this time. Giotto's work in the late 13th century broke ground when he painted people with expressive faces and in natural positions.

Cimabue (Cenni di Peppi), 1251–1302
> *The Madonna of the Angels,* c. 1275, Louvre, Paris

Giotto (di Bondone), c. 1276–1337
> Giotto was one of the first artists whose name is known. In a series of frescoes he did for a chapel, Giotto portrayed the people in the religious scenes as real flesh-and-bone human beings, portraying emotions and participating in real events. This was a departure from the two-dimensional images of people portrayed in paintings earlier.
>> *Arena Chapel,* 1305–1306, Padua, Italy: *The Massacre of the Innocents,* 1305, *The Flagellation of Christ,* 1305, *The Betrayal by Judas,* 1305

Lorenzetti, Ambrogio, active 1320–1348
> *Good Government in the City,* 1338–1340, Palazzo Pubblico, Siena

Martini, Simone, 1315–1344
> *Christ Carrying the Cross,* c. 1340, Louvre, Paris

Uccello, Paolo, 1397–1475
> *Battle of San Romano,* 1327, Uffizi Gallery, Florence

NORTHERN RENAISSANCE, 1350–1600

Two influences that dominated the Northern Renaissance artwork were the Black Death of 1348, in which nearly half of Europe's population died, and religion, evidence of the influence of the Church in Europe during this time. Paintings clearly showed the religious fervor felt by the people, the majority of whom were illiterate. The symbolism that is murky to today's population would have been clearly understood by people whose lives were inseparable from the Church, and who understood every nuance of Biblical reference in paintings. Artists of this time period traveled more, and their work reflected a more "International Style."

Bosch, Hieronymus, c. 1450–1516, Netherlands
> *Garden of Earthly Delights,* 1500, The Prado, Madrid

Campin, Robert (Master of Flemalle), 1375–1444, Flanders
> *The Merode Altarpiece,* c. 1425–1428, Metropolitan Museum of Art, New York City

Cranach, Lucas, 1472–1553, Germany
> *Adam and Eve,* 1528, Uffizi Gallery, Florence

Dürer, Albrecht, 1471–1528, Germany
> Dürer was an outstanding draftsman, especially known for his copper and wood engravings. His portraits, particularly one of himself that was painted to resemble Jesus Christ, demonstrated his creativity.
> *Four Horsemen of the Apocalypse,* c. 1497–1498, British Museum, London
> *Knight, Death, and the Devil,* 1513, Museum of Fine Arts, Boston
> *Melencolia I,* 1514, Metropolitan Museum of Art, New York City
> *Self Portrait in a Fur Coat,* 1471, Alte Pinakothek, Munich

Eyck, Jan van, 1390–1441, Flanders (present-day Northern France and Western Belgium)

Jan van Eyck is considered the first artist to mix pigment with oil rather than egg yolk, and is credited with "inventing" oil painting. He primarily created large altarpieces and religious paintings. Although considered a Flemish Primitive, his work was filled with symbolism and is quite sophisticated.

Giovanni Arnolfini and His Bride, 1434, National Gallery, London

Madonna of Chancellor Rolin, c. 1433–1434, Louvre, Paris

Man in a Red Turban (Self-portrait?), 1433, National Gallery, London

Mystic Lamb Altarpiece (with brother Hubert), 1432, Church of
St. Bavo, Ghent, Belgium

Goes, Hugo Van der, c. 1440–1482, Flanders

Portinari Altarpiece, 1476, Uffizi Gallery, Florence

Grunewald, Mathis, (Mathis Gothart Neithart), c. 1470–1528, Germany

Grunewald's *Isenheim Altarpiece* shows German Realism at its strongest.

Crucifixion, c. 1525, Staatliche Kunsthalle, Karlsruhe, Germany

Isenheim Altarpiece, 1515, Musée d'Unterlinden, Colmar, France

Stuppach Madonna, c. 1518–1520, Church, Stuppach, Germany

Holbein, Hans, the Younger, c. 1497–1543, Germany

Holbein was a court painter. His portraiture of important people, royalty, and religious subjects is found in major museum collections. He dabbled in visual illusions, as seen in *The Ambassadors,* where he painted a distorted skull that can only be discerned at certain angles.

Anne of Cleves, 1539, Louvre, Paris

Erasmus, 1523–1526, Louvre, Paris

Madonna of Burgomaster Meyer, 1526, Schlossmuseum, Darmstadt,
Germany

The Ambassadors, 1533, National Gallery, London

Memling, Hans, c. 1430–1494, Flanders

Shrine of St. Ursula, c. 1430, St. Jan's Hospice, Bruges, Belgium

Weyden, Rogier van der, c. 1399–1464, Flanders

Descent from the Cross, 1435, The Prado, Madrid

ITALIAN RENAISSANCE, 1450–1520

The Italian Renaissance was a period in which the Classicism of the ancient Greeks and Romans was being reborn in literature, mathematics, and, of course, in art. Perspective was introduced into painting, and the human form lost the rigidity that had been seen in most earlier work. Renaissance artists were not only painters, but also designed buildings, fortifications, costumes for pageantry, and even Vatican uniforms (designed by Michelangelo and still in that style today).

Bellini, Giovanni, c. 1430–1516
Bellini was one of a family of Venetian painters and a teacher of Titian. He is best known for his ability to combine portraiture with landscape.
Agony in the Garden, 1460, National Gallery, London
Doge Leonardo Loredan, c. 1501, National Gallery, London
Woman With a Mirror, 1515, Kunsthistorisches Museum, Vienna

Botticelli, Sandro, 1444–1510
Botticelli painted primarily portraits and religious and mythological subjects. The Medici family and the Church were his patrons.
Birth of Venus, c. 1480, Uffizi Gallery, Florence
Madonna of the Magnificat, c. 1483, Uffizi Gallery, Florence
Mystic Nativity, 1500, National Gallery, London
Primavera, 1477–1478, Uffizi Gallery, Florence

Francesca, Piero Della, 1420–1492
Discovery and Proving of the True Cross, c. 1460, S. Francesco, Arezzo

Ghirlandaio, Domenico, 1449–1494
An Old Man and His Grandson, c. 1480, Louvre, Paris

Giorgione (Barbarelli), c. 1478–1510
Giorgione was one of the first artists to specialize in pictures for private collectors—"cabinet painting." Few of his works have survived, but his romantic landscapes featuring the nude figure were a great influence on his followers.
The Tempest, n.d., Accademia, Venice
Pastoral Concert, c. 1510, Louvre, Paris

"Painting is concerned with the ten things you can see; these are: darkness and brightness, substance and color, form and place, remoteness and nearness, movement and rest."

—LEONARDO DA VINCI, 1452–1519, Renaissance master

Leonardo da Vinci, 1452–1519

Da Vinci is the standard by which the Renaissance Man is measured. He was an inventor, painter, sculptor, and designer for a royal court (which included designing costumes and scenery for pageants, or fortifications, weapons for war). His notebooks included drawings on anatomy, meteorology, mechanics, botany, and geology. Although only a few of his paintings are known, those that exist are famous masterpieces.

Last Supper, c. 1495–1498, Santa Maria delle Grazie, Milan

Madonna and Saint Anne, c. 1501, Louvre, Paris

Madonna of the Rocks, c. 1483, Louvre, Paris

Mona Lisa, 1503–1506, Louvre, Paris

Mantegna, Andrea, 1431–1506

St. Sebastian, c. 1455–1460, Kunsthistorisches Museum, Vienna

Masaccio, Tomaso, c. 1401–1428

Holy Trinity with the Virgin and St. John, 1425, Santa Maria Novella, Florence

Tribute Money, c. 1427, Brancacci Chapel, Santa Maria del Carmine, Florence

Michelangelo Buonarroti, 1475–1564

Michelangelo lived to a ripe old age, producing both sculpture and paintings. Among his best known are the *Pietà* and the Sistine Chapel ceiling and *Last Judgment.*

David (sculpture), 1504, Accademia, Florence

Holy Family, 1506, Uffizi Gallery, Florence

Pietà (sculpture), 1498–1499, St. Peter's, Rome

Sistine Chapel fresco, 1508–1512, Vatican, Rome

Perugino, Pietro, c. 1450–1523

Delivery of the Keys, 1482, Vatican, Rome

Raphael (Raffaello Sanzio), 1483–1520

Raphael painted either small religious portraits or grandiose murals such, as *The School of Athens* in the Vatican. He was described by Vasari as "so gentle and so charitable that even animals loved him."

Madonna of the Chair, 1515–1516, Pitti Palace, Florence

School of Athens, 1510–1511, Stanza della Segnatura, Vatican, Rome

Sistine Madonna, c. 1512–1514, Gemaldegalerie, Dresden

St. George and the Dragon, 1505–1506, National Gallery, Washington, DC

The Alba Madonna, c. 1509, National Gallery, Washington, DC

MANNERISM, 1525–1600

Mannerism was a derogatory term implying that artists of the time period painted in the "manner" of the great Renaissance masters and their Classical perfection, but without the substance. This period actually saw great developments in the use of color and composition to create emotional reaction from viewers.

Arcimboldo, Giuseppe, 1527–1593, Italy

Summer, 1573, Louvre, Paris

Winter, 1563, Kunsthistorisches Museum, Vienna

Clouet, Jean, c. 1522–1572, France

Portrait of Francis I, 1524, Louvre, Paris

Greco, El (Domenikos Theotokopoulos), 1541–1614, Spain, b. Greece

El Greco was a Mannerist painter whose subjects appear to be elongated and distorted. It was long believed that he had an astigmatism that caused these exaggerations, but current theory says he painted this way because he chose to.

Grand Inquisitor Don Fernando Nino de Guevara, c. 1600, Metropolitan Museum, New York City

Resurrection, c. 1597–1604, Prado, Madrid

The Burial of Count Orgaz, 1586, Toledo, Spain

View of Toledo, 1600–1710, Metropolitan Museum of Art, New York City

Poussin, Nicolas, 1594–1665, France

Poussin was considered a Classical painter. His early paintings followed the Mannerist tradition, and he proposed that painting should be for the mind, not the eye.

Holy Family on the Steps, 1648, National Gallery of Art, Washington, DC

The Baptism of Christ, 1641–1642, National Gallery of Art, Washington, DC

Titian (Tiziano Vecellio), c. 1485–1576, Italy

Titian was the greatest painter of the Venetian School, and was considered a profound influence on painters who followed him.

Sacred and Profane Love, c. 1516, Villa Borghese, Rome

Bacchus and Ariadne, c. 1560, National Gallery, London

The Rape of Europa, c. 1550–1562, Gardner Museum, Boston

NEWER "OLD MASTERS"

The masters of the periods following the Renaissance were less dependent than previously on the patronage of the church or royalty. While religious paintings still dominated, the growth of commerce enabled middle-class merchants to purchase paintings for their homes. Numerous "little masters" emerged in such regions as the Netherlands and Italy.

BAROQUE ARTISTS, 1590–1750

The Baroque era was a flourishing period for painters. The art is much more emotional and rich in color than that of the Renaissance. Paintings might be very quiet, such as church interiors, or filled with people in swirling, energetic, vigorous compositions. Religious symbolism still existed (especially in the Netherlands), but was gradually disappearing. Those painters who worked in Royal courts throughout Europe sometimes acted as ambassadors, painting portraits of royal family members (particularly those of marriageable age), and assisting in cementing alliances between countries.

Ast, Balthasar van der, 1593–1657, Netherlands
Flowers, 1622, St. Louis Art Museum

Brueghel, Pieter, c. 1520–1569, Flanders
"Peasant" Brueghel was known for his delightful scenes and moralizing stories of peasant life in Belgium. His paintings included beautiful landscapes, and were often based on proverbs or religion.
Dulle Griet (Mad Meg), 1562, Musée Meyer Van den Bergh
   Museum, Antwerp, Belgium
Hunters in the Snow, 1565, Kunsthistorisches Museum, Vienna
Landscape with the Fall of Icarus, 1555, Musées Royaux des Beaux
   Arts, Brussels, Belgium
Netherlandish Proverbs (The Blue Cloak), 1559, Kaiser Friedrich
   Museum, Berlin
Peasant Wedding, c. 1567–1568, Kunsthistorisches Museum, Vienna

Caravaggio, Michelangelo Merisi da, 1573–1610, Italy
The term *chiaroscuro* is nearly always used when describing the paintings of Caravaggio, whose use of dark and light introduced drama to his (mostly) religious paintings.
Bacchus, 1589, Uffizi Gallery, Florence
Calling of Saint Matthew, c. 1599–1600, S. Luigi dei Francesi, Rome
Crucifixion of St. Peter and Conversion of St. Paul, 1600–1601, Sta.
   Maria del Popolo, Rome
Entombment, 1602–1604, Vatican, Rome
The Death of the Virgin, 1605–1606, Louvre, Paris

Claesz, Pieter, 1590–1661, Netherlands
Claesz and a colleague, Willem Claesz Heda, specialized in "interrupted breakfast" or "vanitas" paintings. They featured a table set with the finest crystal, half-eaten food, perhaps a glass broken or wine spilled. These

symbolized to the people of that day that life was fleeting and could stop at any moment.

> *Still Life*, 1643, St. Louis Art Museum

Dyck, Anthony van, 1599–1641, Netherlands

Van Dyck worked in Peter Paul Rubens's studio, but eventually moved to England where he became a court painter. Although he did historical and religious paintings, he is best known for the 350 portraits he completed while in England.

> *Charles I in Hunting Dress*, 1635, Louvre, Paris
>
> *Madonna of the Rosary*, 1624–1627, Oratorio della Compagnia del Rosario di S. Domenico, Palermo, Italy
>
> *Portrait of Charles I in Hunting Dress*, 1635, National Gallery, London

Gentileschi, Artemisia, c. 1565–1647, Italy

> *Judith with the Head of Holofernes*, c. 1625, Detroit Institute of Art

Hals, Frans, 1582–1666, Netherlands

Hals was a painter of individual and group portraits, many of which reveal the personality of the sitter perfectly. His *Malle Baba*, 1650, a portrait of a madwoman is one of the most memorable.

> *Banquet of the Officers of the Saint George Guard Company*, 1616, Frans Hals Museum, Haarlem
>
> *The Women Regents of the Old Men's Almshouse*, c. 1664, Frans Hals Museum, Haarlem
>
> *Regents of the St. Elizabeth Hospital*, 1641, Frans Hals Museum, Haarlem
>
> *The Laughing Cavalier*, 1624, Wallace Collection, London
>
> *The Jolly Toper*, 1627, Rijksmuseum, Amsterdam

Heda, Willem Claesz, 1594–c. 1680, Netherlands

The moralizing, symbol-filled paintings of Dutch masters had special meaning to the newly emerged middle-class merchants who purchased them.

> *Still Life*, 1634, Boymans-van Beuningen Museum, Rotterdam
>
> *Still Life*, c. 1648, Fine Arts Museum of San Francisco

"There are painters who transfer the sun into a yellow spot, but there are others who, thanks to their art and intelligence, transform a yellow spot into the sun."
—PABLO PICASSO, 1881–1973, Spanish Cubist painter

Heyden, Jan van der, 1637–1712, Netherlands
View of the Martelaarsgracht in Amsterdam, c. 1670, Rijksmuseum, Amsterdam

Hobbema, Meindert, 1638–1709, Netherlands
A View on the High Road, 1665, National Gallery, London

Hooch, Pieter de, 1629–1684, Netherlands
De Hooch is often compared to his contemporary, Vermeer. He also painted simple domestic interiors and homes, but without the distinctive prosperity seen in Vermeer's interiors, which Vermeer often painted in his own home.
A Country Cottage, c. 1665, Rijksmuseum, Amsterdam

La Tour, Georges de, 1593–1652, France
La Tour's paintings featured figures lit from the side by a candle, with the background filled with shadow. These unique dramatic studies are immediately recognizable as his work.
Newborn, 1630, Musée des Beaux-Arts, Rennes, France

Leyster, Judith, 1609–1660, Netherlands
Leyster was a student of Frans Hals, and her work reflects the same joyous outlook.
Boy with Flute, 1630, Nationalmuseum, Stockholm

Rembrandt van Rijn, 1606–1669, Netherlands
Rembrandt's *Nightwatch* broke the Netherlandish tradition of portraying everyone in a group portrait equally. The drama of using chiaroscuro (light and dark) obscured some faces while highlighting others. He is considered one of the great masters, primarily for his portraiture, prints, and

drawings. He was one of the few Dutch Baroque artists to interpret religious subjects.

Anatomy Lesson of Dr. Tulp, 1632, Mauritshuis, The Hague

The Conspiracy of Claudius Civilis, 1661–1662, Nationalmuseum, Stockholm

The Night Watch, 1642, Rijksmuseum, Amsterdam

The Polish Rider, c. 1655, Frick Collection, New York City

The Syndics of the Drapers' Guild, 1662, Rijksmuseum, Amsterdam

The Three Crosses, 1660–1661, Metropolitan Museum of Art, New York City

Rubens, Peter Paul, 1577–1640, Belgium

Rubens, a major Baroque painter, was certainly an exception to the concept of a starving artist. He was a successful painter of portraits and large allegorical and religious paintings in his native Antwerp. Rubens sometimes acted as a diplomat between royal courts by painting portraits of prospective brides and grooms.

Garden of Love, c. 1638, Prado Museum, Madrid

Helene Fourment with Two of Her Children, c. 1637, Louvre, Paris

Henry the IV Receiving the Portrait of Maria de Medici, 1621–1625, Louvre, Paris

The Descent from the Cross, c. 1612, Cathedral, Antwerp, Belgium

Wedding Portrait, 1609, Alte Pinakothek, Munich

Ruisdael, Jacob van, 1628–1682, Netherlands

Ruisdael's landscapes of the Dutch countryside showed forests, windmills, trees, streams, and the ever-changing sky. He is credited with over 700 paintings.

View of Haarlem, c. 1670, Mauritshuis, The Hague

Mill at Wijk by Duurstede, c. 1670, Rijksmuseum, Amsterdam

Steen, Jan, 1626–1679, Netherlands

Steen, a tavern owner with a large family, often did humorous paintings of large groups of people making merry in which he left a hidden moralizing message (sometimes written on a dropped letter or a letter someone was reading).

The World Upside Down, c. 1663, Kunsthistorisches Museum, Vienna

Vermeer, Jan, 1632–1675, Netherlands

Vermeer has a life's work of 35 to 40 paintings, but what paintings! He is primarily noted for interior scenes that include one or two figures, side-lit from a window.

> *Allegory of the Art of Painting, The Artist's Studio,* c. 1670–1675, Kunsthistorisches Museum, Vienna
>
> *Kitchen Maid,* c. 1658, Rijksmuseum, Amsterdam
>
> *Street in Delft,* c. 1660, Rijksmuseum, Amsterdam
>
> *View of Delft,* c. 1662, Mauritshuis, The Hague

Velázquez, Diego, 1599–1660, Spain

Velázquez was a portrait painter in the Spanish court, doing numerous portraits of the royal family and court retainers. His series of the *Infanta* (princess) are dynamic. His great masterpiece was *Las Meninas.*

> *Juan de Pareja,* 1650, Metropolitan Museum of Art, New York City
>
> *King Philip IV of Spain,* 1644, Metropolitan Museum of Art, New York City
>
> *Las Meninas,* 1656, Prado Museum, Madrid
>
> *Portrait of Queen Mariana,* 1632–1633, Louvre, Paris
>
> *Surrender of Breda,* 1634–1635, Prado, Madrid
>
> *Triumph of Bacchus,* c. 1628, Prado Museum, Madrid

AMERICAN COLONIAL ART, c. 1550–1775

As in most colonies, the early years of American colonialism were devoted to simple existence: planting, building, making whatever was needed to allow pioneers to live in the frontier. It wasn't until basic needs were met that people found time for luxuries such as art. Most early American art was either created by artists trained in Europe or by so-called "Primitive" painters who were self-taught.

artist unknown

> *Mrs. Freake and Baby Mary,* 1674, Worcester Art Museum, Worcester, Massachusetts

artist unknown

> *Pocahontas,* c. 1616, National Portrait Gallery, Washington, DC

Feke, Robert, c. 1707–1752
> *Family of Isaac Royall,* 1741, Harvard Law School, Boston
> *Self Portrait,* (date unknown), Museum of Fine Arts, Boston

Greenwood, John, 1727–1792
> *Sea Captains Carousing in Surinam,* c. 1752, St. Louis Art Museum

Hesselius, Gustavus, 1682–1755, United States, b. Sweden
> *Tishcohan,* 1735, Historical Society of Pennsylvania, Philadelphia

Le Moyne, Jacques, 1533–1588
> *Saturiba, the Indian Chief, and René Laudonniere at Ribaut's
>   Column,* 1564, New York Public Library, New York City

Pratt, Matthew, 1734–1805
> *The American School,* 1765, Metropolitan Museum of Art,
>   New York City

Revere, Paul, 1735–1818
> *The Bloody Massacre,* 1770, Library of Congress, Washington, DC

Smibert, John, 1688–1751
> *The Bermuda Group,* 1729, Yale University Art Gallery, New Haven,
>   Connecticut

White, John, active 1570s–1593
> *Indians Fishing,* 1585, British Museum, London

ROCOCO, 1700–1800

Rococo art is identified with the decorative arts popular in the time of Louis XV of France. It was considered a reaction against the heaviness of Baroque colors, and is known for its light and airy intimacy.

Boucher, François, 1703–1770, France
> *Venus Consoling Love,* 1751, National Gallery of Art,
>   Washington, DC
> *Reclining Girl,* 1751, Alte Pinakothek, Munich

Fragonard, Jean-Honoré, 1732–1806, France
> *A Young Girl Reading*, c. 1776, National Gallery of Art, Washington, DC

Watteau, Jean-Antoine, 1684–1721, France
> Watteau was a court painter, specializing in paintings of young people idling away time in the country. His figures were often clothed in theatrical costumes. He became known as a painter of the *Fête Galante*.
>
> *A Pilgrimage to Cythera*, 1717, Louvre, Paris
>
> *Signboard of Gersaint*, c. 1721, Staatliche Museen, Berlin

NEO-CLASSICISM, 1770–1820

The creation of art is a system of action and reaction. Neo-Classicism was a reaction against the excesses of Rococo art, and a return to the naturalism of Greek and Roman art. In the Neo-Classical period, painters once again returned to historical and mythological subject matter.

Copley, John Singleton, 1738–1815, United States
> Copley was a major portrait painter in Colonial America, but left the United States with his family when the Revolution began. He spent the rest of his life in England where he painted historical subjects and actual events such as his masterpiece, *Brook Watson and the Shark*.
>
> *Brook Watson and the Shark*, 1782, Detroit Institute of the Arts
>
> *Mrs. Ezekiel Goldthwait*, 1771, Museum of Fine Arts, Boston
>
> *Paul Revere*, 1768–1770, Museum of Fine Arts, Boston

David, Jacques Louis, 1748–1825, France
> David was part of the Napoleonic and Revolutionary periods in France. His work became more realistic as his career progressed.
>
> *Coronation of Napoleon and Josephine*, 1805–1807, Louvre, Paris
>
> *Death of Marat*, 1793, Musées Royaux des Beaux-Arts de Belgique, Brussels
>
> *Mme. Récamier*, 1800, Louvre, Paris
>
> *Oath of the Horatii*, 1784–1785, Louvre, Paris
>
> *Socrates*, 1787, Metropolitan Museum of Art, New York City

Ingres, Jean Auguste Dominique, 1780–1867, France

Ingres was an academically trained painter and member of the French Academy. His favorite subject was said to be the nude, although he was unrivaled in accurately depicting fashionable clothing and accessories in his portraits of society women.

Comtesse d'Haussonville, 1845, Frick Collection, New York City

Mme Moitessier, 1851, National Gallery of Art, Washington, DC

Napoleon on His Throne, 1806, Musee de l'Armée, Paris

Odalisque, 1814, Louvre, Paris

Oedipus and the Sphinx, 1808, Louvre, Paris

Peale, Charles Willson, 1741–1827, United States

Peale was the founder of a dynasty of painters. He also founded one of the first American museums to exhibit such natural wonders as the locally discovered Mastodon (of which he painted a picture). His portraiture, historical scenes, and paintings of the Revolution helped to record the early days of the new country.

Exhuming the Mastodon, 1806–1808, Peale Museum, Baltimore City Life Museums

George Washington at the Battle of Princeton, 1780–1781, Yale University Art Gallery, New Haven, Connecticut

The Staircase Group, (1795), Philadelphia Museum of Art

Washington After Trenton, 1767, Metropolitan Museum of Art, New York City

Reynolds, Sir Joshua, 1723–1792, England

> *Lady Sarah Bunbury Sacrificing to the Graces*, 1765, The Art
> Institute of Chicago
>
> *Mrs. Siddons as the Tragic Muse*, c. 1789, Huntington Library and
> Art Gallery, San Marino, California

Stuart, Gilbert, 1755–1828, United States

Stuart's painting of George Washington is found on the dollar bill. As one of America's best early painters, he strongly influenced succeeding generations.

> *George Washington* (the "Athenaeum" Portrait), 1796, Museum of
> Fine Arts, Boston
>
> *George Washington* (the "Lansdowne" Portrait), 1796, Pennsylvania
> Academy of the Fine Arts, Philadelphia
>
> *The Skater*, 1782, National Gallery of Art, Washington, DC

Trumbull, John, 1756–1843, United States

> *Death of General Mercer at the Battle of Princeton*, 1777, Yale
> University Art Gallery, New Haven, Connecticut
>
> *The Declaration of Independence*, 1786–1794, Yale University Art
> Gallery, New Haven, Connecticut
>
> *The Surrender of Cornwallis at Yorktown*, 1817–1820, United States
> Capitol, Washington, DC

Vigeé-Lebrun, Elizabeth, 1755–1842, France

LeBrun was a painter in Marie Antoinette's court, specializing in portraits of women and children.

> *Marie Antoinette and Her Children*, 1788, Musée National
> du Chateau de Versailles, Paris
>
> *Portrait of a Lady*, 1789, National Gallery of Art, Washington, DC

West, Benjamin, 1738–1820, United States

While West was considered one of the pre-eminent artists of the United States, he spent most of his life in London, and was a founder of the London Academy of Arts. He was generous in offering assistance and encouragement to American painters who came to study or visit abroad.

> *Penn's Treaty with the Indians*, 1772, Pennsylvania Academy of the
> Fine Arts, Philadelphia
>
> *The Death of General Wolfe*, 1771, National Gallery of Canada, Ottawa

ROMANTICISM, c. 1800–1850

Artists of the Romantic period rejected the calm, controlled principles of Neo-Classicism, favoring instead personal vision and interpretation. Art was closely related to literature and music of the period, often telling a story in paint.

Allston, Washington, 1779–1843, United States
> *The Rising of a Thunderstorm at Sea,* 1804, Museum of Fine Arts, Boston

Bingham, George Caleb, 1811–1879, United States
Bingham was probably best known for his portraiture and wry interpretations of life in the Midwest, be it a political rally or raftsmen on the Missouri and Mississippi Rivers.
> *Fur Traders Descending the Missouri,* 1845, Metropolitan Museum of Art, New York City
> *The County Election,* 1851–1852, St. Louis Art Museum
> *The Jolly Flatboatmen in Port,* 1857, St. Louis Art Museum

Constable, John, 1776–1837, England
> *Stoke-by-Nayland,* 1836, Art Institute of Chicago

Delacroix, Eugène, 1798–1863, France
Delacroix's energetic, swirling canvases made him a leader of the French school of Romantic painting. He based his subjects on literature, medieval and contemporary history, and the Crusades.
> *Greece on the Ruins of Missolonghi,* 1826, Musée des Beaux-Arts, Bordeaux
> *Jacob and the Angel,* 1853–1861, Luxembourg Palace, Paris
> *Liberty Leading the People,* 1830, Louvre, Paris
> *The Massacre at Chios,* c. 1824, Louvre, Paris
> *Tiger Hunt,* 1854, Louvre, Paris

Gainsborough, Thomas, 1727–1788, England
Gainsborough is best known for his portraiture, although landscape was his true love. He was considered a great rival of Sir Joshua Reynolds, excelling in paintings of persons at court.
> *George Washington, Patriae Pater,* c. 1824, Pennsylvania Academy of the Fine Arts, Philadelphia

Jonathan Buttall: The Blue Boy, 1770, The Huntington Library, San
Marino, California
Mrs. Siddons, c. 1783–1785, National Gallery, London
The Court of Death, 1821, Detroit Institute of the Arts
The Morning Walk, c. 1785, National Gallery, London

Géricault, Théodore, 1791–1834, France
Mounted Officer of the Imperial Guard, 1812, Louvre, Paris
The Raft of the Medusa, 1818–1819, Louvre, Paris

Goya, Francisco, 1746–1828, Spain
Goya began as a designer of tapestries for the royal factory. He later
painted portraits of the royal court and, on behalf of the king, protested
foreign rule by showing the bloody uprisings in his *Second of May* and
Third of May paintings.
Executions of the Third of May, c. 1808, Prado, Madrid
Family of Charles IV, 1799, Prado, Madrid
Naked Maja, 1800, Prado, Madrid
The Disasters of War, 1810–1814, Prado, Madrid

Hicks, Edward, 1780–1849, United States
Hicks was a sign painter, part-time preacher, and painter of narrative art.
He often included beautifully painted messages around the edges of his
paintings of animals, people, and farms.
The Peaceable Kingdom, c. 1830–1840, Brooklyn Museum, Brooklyn,
New York
Peaceable Kingdom, 1845, Albright-Knox Art Gallery, Buffalo,
New York
The Peaceable Kingdom, date unknown, Abby Aldrich Rockefeller
Folk Art Center, Williamsburg, Virginia
The Cornell Farm, 1848, National Gallery of Art, Washington, DC

Leutz, Emanuel Gottlieb, 1816–1868, United States
Although the work of Emanuel Leutz comes in and goes out of favor, he
did one of the most famous paintings of the American Revolution, *Washington Crossing the Delaware.* A member of the Dusseldorf school of
painters, he did many of his American historical paintings while living in
Germany.

> *Nathaniel Hawthorne,* 1862, National Portrait Gallery, Washington, DC
>
> *On the Banks of a Stream,* c. 1860, Corcoran Gallery, Washington, DC
>
> *Washington Crossing the Delaware,* 1851, Metropolitan Museum of Art, New York City
>
> *Westward the Course of Empire Takes its Way,* 1861–1862, mural, Capitol Building, Washington, DC

Millet, Jean François, 1814–1875, France

> *The Sower,* c. 1850, Museum of Fine Arts, Boston
>
> *The Angelus,* 1859, Musée d'Orsay, Paris

Peale, Rembrandt, 1778–1860, United States

Rembrandt Peale and his brothers Rubens, Ramsey, Titian, and Raphaelle all continued the family tradition of painting begun by their father, Charles Willson Peale.

> *Rubens Peale with a Geranium,* 1801, National Gallery of Art, Washington, DC

Quidor, John, 1801–1881, United States

Quidor supported himself as a painter of signs, fire engines, and coaches while painting his genre scenes that illustrated popular legends.

> *The Legend of Ichabod Crane,* c. 1828, Yale University Art Gallery, New Haven, Connecticut
>
> *The Money Diggers,* 1832, Brooklyn Museum, Brooklyn, New York
>
> *The Return of Rip Van Winkle,* c. 1849, National Gallery of Art, Washington, DC

Sargent, John Singer, 1856–1925, United States

Sargent was one of the foremost society portrait painters of the United States, as well as a prolific watercolorist. His *Madame X* caused a sensation in the Paris Salon (exhibition) because of her sensuous (some said erotic) beauty.

> *Gassed,* 1918, Imperial War Museum, London
>
> *Madame X,* 1884, Metropolitan Museum of Art, New York City
>
> *Mrs. George Swinton,* 1896, Art Institute of Chicago
>
> *Portrait of Lady Agnew,* c. 1892–1893, National Galleries of Scotland, Edinburgh

Turner, Joseph Mallord William, 1775–1851, England

Turner's swirling, windblown luminous paintings of sea and sky, most of which were painted inside a studio, reflect his penchant for strapping himself to a mast in a storm to experience the atmosphere firsthand.

Rain, Steam, and Speed, 1844, National Gallery, London

The Slave Ship, 1839, Museum of Fine Arts, Boston

Venice: The Piazzetta from the Water, c. 1835, Tate Gallery, London

Yacht Approaching the Coast, 1840–1845, Tate Gallery, London

"Every child is an artist. The problem is how to remain an artist once he grows up."

—PABLO PICASSO, 1881–1973, Spanish Cubist painter

REALISM, c. 1850–1880

This group of painters rebelled against the historical, religious, and poetic themes favored by the academically trained members of the French salon. Instead they preferred to paint what is seen in daily life (genre painting), an approach that greatly influenced the Impressionists who were to come after them.

Bonheur, Rosa, 1822–1899, France

One of the first feminist painters, her primary subject was animals: lions, tigers, horses, wolves.

The Horse Fair, 1853–1855, Metropolitan Museum of Art, New York City

Boudin, Eugene, 1824–1898, France

Boudin's small paintings of society members at play could certainly be considered early *plein air* paintings (and in fact he introduced Monet to this technique).

The Beach at Trouville, 1863, Ittleson Collection, New York

Corot, Jean Baptiste Camille, 1796–1875, France

Corot was considered a great influence on the Impressionists because of his landscape painting.

Forest of Fontainebleau, c. 1830, National Gallery of Art, Washington, DC

Courbet, Gustave, 1819–1877, France

Courbet was considered a "revolutionary socialist" because of his choice of subject matter. He was a leader of the realist painters.

The Artist's Studio, 1855, Louvre, Paris

The Burial at Ornans, 1850, Musée d'Orsay, Paris

Daumier, Honoré, 1808–1879, France

The Third Class Carriage, c. 1863, Metropolitan Museum of Art, New York City

Eakins, Thomas, 1844–1916, United States

Thomas Eakins was a Realist painter and professor for ten years at the Pennsylvania Academy of the Fine Arts. His landscapes and sporting events appeared to be the most acceptable of his subjects.

Fairman Rogers Four-in-Hand, 1879, Philadelphia Museum of Art

Max Schmitt in a Single Scull, c. 1871, Metropolitan Museum of Art, New York City

The Agnew Clinic, 1889, Jefferson Medical College, Philadelphia

The Gross Clinic, 1875, Jefferson Medical College, Philadelphia

Hokusai, Katsushika, 1760–1849, Japan

The Great Wave Off Kanagawa, 1823–1829, Metropolitan Museum of Art, New York City

Homer, Winslow, 1836–1910, United States

Homer loved the sea, hunting, fishing, and people. His paintings reflected the life of the times; what he saw, where he lived. His oils and watercolors are treasured icons of Americana.

Breezing Up (A Fair Wind), 1876, National Gallery of Art, Washington, DC

Country School, 1871, St. Louis Art Museum

Taking on Wet Provisions, Key West, 1903, Metropolitan Museum of Art, New York City

The Croquet Game, 1866, Art Institute of Chicago

The Morning Bell, c. 1866, Yale University Art Gallery, New Haven, Connecticut

Tanner, Henry Ossawa, 1859–1937, United States

Tanner was the first well-known African American painter. He studied with Thomas Eakins, but spent most of his career in Europe.

The Banjo Lesson, c. 1893, Hampton Institute, Hampton, Virginia

Daniel in the Lion's Den, 1895, Los Angeles County Museum of Art

Whistler, James Abbott McNeill, 1834–1903, United States

Whistler's paintings usually included the title of a musical composition (arrangement, nocturne, symphony). His restrained palette and skill at portraiture and atmospheric scenes assured his place in the history of art.

Arrangement in Grey and Black, No. 1: The Artist's Mother, 1871, Louvre, Paris

Nocturne in Black and Gold: Falling Rocket, c. 1874, Detroit Institute of Arts

Portrait of Thomas Carlyle: Arrangement in Grey and Black, No. 2, 1872, Glasgow Art Gallery and Museum

The White Girl: Symphony in White No. 1, 1862, National Gallery, Washington, DC

NATIVE AMERICANS AND THE AMERICAN WEST IN ART, c. 1800–1900

The surveying teams that opened the West sometimes included an artist whose sole job was to record wildlife, people, and scenery encountered in these explorations. Among their works are many paintings and drawings of Native Americans and the Western Frontier.

Audubon, John James, 1785–1851, United States

Audubon, a hunter, was also one of the great chroniclers of American birds and wildlife. Although he did not consider what he was doing as "art," his watercolors became enormously popular, and he became known as a great ornithologist.

Brown Thrasher, 1829, New York Historical Society, New York City

Great Blue Heron, 1821, New York Historical Society, New York City

The Birds of America, 1826, New York Historical Society, New York City

Bierstadt, Albert, 1830–1902, United States

Bierstadt, a painter who accompanied surveying expeditions of the American West, was one of the first to do grand paintings of the West's natural wonders.

Storm in the Rocky Mountains, 1866, Brooklyn Museum, New York

The Rocky Mountains, Lander's Peak, 1863, Metropolitan Museum of Art, New York City

Thunderstorm in the Rockies, 1859, Museum of Fine Arts, Boston

Catlin, George, 1796–1872, United States

George Catlin left a tremendous legacy through his 310 oil paintings and 200 scenes of Native American life, painted from 1832 to 1846. He wrote and illustrated an account of his experiences with the 48 tribes among whom he lived.

Buffalo Bull's Back Fat, Head Chief, Blood Tribe, 1832, American Museum, Washington, DC

La Salle's Party Feasted in the Illinois Village, 1847–48, National Gallery of Art, Washington, DC

Tal-lee, a Warrior of Distinction, 1834, American Museum, Washington, DC

Eastman, Seth, 1808–1875, United States

Travelling Tents of the Sioux Indians Called a Tepe, 1847–1849, St. Louis Art Museum

King, Charles Bird, 1785–1862, United States

Young Omahaw, War Eagle, Little Missouri, and Pawnees, 1821, Smithsonian Institution, Washington, DC

Remington, Frederic, 1861–1909, United States

Remington was a master painter and sculptor of the Western Experience. His interpretations of soldiers, Native Americans, horses, and the desert have proven enormously popular over the years.

Cavalry Charge on the Southern Plains, 1907, Metropolitan Museum of Art, New York City

His First Lesson, 1903, Amon Carter Museum, Fort Worth

The Bronco Buster (sculpture), 1895, St. Louis Art Museum

The Fight for the Waterhole, c. 1895–1900, Museum of Fine Arts, Houston

Ryder, Albert Pinkham, 1847–1917, United States

Moonlit Landscape, 1819, Museum of Fine Arts, Boston

Death on a Pale Horse, c. 1896, Cleveland Museum of Art

Wimar, Charles F., 1828–1862, United States

Chief Billy Bowlegs, 1861, St. Louis Art Museum

The Buffalo Dance, 1860, St. Louis Art Museum

HUDSON RIVER SCHOOL, c. 1825–1875

The Hudson River School was a group of painters who tried to show the grandeur of the mountainous region around the Hudson River. Some of the group felt that nature was closely related to God, and their work was intended to give an emotional or spiritual effect.

Cole, Thomas, 1801–1848, United States

Cole was considered a founder of the Hudson River School. Members of the group were also called Romantic Landscapists.

View from Mount Holyoke, Massachusetts, after a Thunderstorm—The Oxbow, 1836, Metropolitan Museum of Art, New York City

The Voyage of Life, 1840, Williams-Proctor Institute, Utica, New York

The Course of Empire, 1836, New York Historical Society, New York City

Cropsey, Jasper Francis, 1823–1900, United States

Autumn on the Hudson River, 1860, National Gallery of Art, Washington, DC

Durand, Asher B., 1796–1886, United States

Kindred Spirits, 1849, New York Public Library, New York City

Kensett, John F., 1816–1872, United States

White Mountain Scenery, 1859, New York Historical Society, New York City

TROMPE L'OEIL PAINTINGS, c. 1875–1900

This painting technique was quite popular with the Victorians, but until relatively recently, was not considered in the "masterpiece" category. The subject matter of these paintings is reminiscent of the Dutch still lifes so popular in the Baroque period, or the Hyperrealism popular a hundred years later.

Harnett, William Michael, 1848–1892, United States

Harnett was a photo-realist before photography really was developed. His work was so realistic that he was arrested by U.S. Treasury agents when they thought he had used a counterfeit five-dollar bill in one of his paintings.

Just Dessert, 1891, Art Institute of Chicago

After the Hunt, 1885, California Palace of the Legion of Honor, San Francisco

Still Life—Violin and Music, 1888, Metropolitan Museum of Art, New York City

The Artist's Card Rack, 1879, Museum of Modern Art, New York City

My Gems, 1888, National Gallery of Art, Washington, DC

Peto, John F., 1854–1907, United States

John F. Peto was a trompe l'oeil painter of the first rank. Unfortunately, he had to compete with William Harnett's popularity, and Peto's work was often signed with Harnett's name (by unscrupulous sellers), because the pictures would bring more money that way. Peto's subjects were not quite so lofty as Harnett's.

Reminiscences of 1865, after 1890, Minneapolis Institute of the Arts

Poor Man's Store, 1885, Museum of Fine Arts, Boston

Still Life With Lanterns, 1889, Brooklyn Museum, New York

"A painting is never finished—it simply stops in interesting places."

—PAUL GARDNER, contemporary writer

THE NABIS, FRANCE, c. 1890S

A short-lived Parisian group, the Nabis (Hebrew for *prophet*) included the musician DeBussy, several other artists, and the sculptor Maillol. They had in common a joy in the emotional use of color and distortion of line, based on their admiration for Gauguin. Many in this group were considered Fauves (literally translated as *Wild Beasts*), whose colors were brilliant and usually wildly unrealistic.

Bonnard, Pierre, 1867–1947

A Post-Impressionist, Bonnard was known as an "Intimiste" because of his interest in painting domestic interior scenes in Fauvist (unrealistic) colors.
La Revue Blanche, 1894, Yale University Art Gallery, New Haven, Connecticut
Nude in the Bath, 1937, Louvre, Paris
The Breakfast Room, 1930–1931, The Museum of Modern Art, New York City

Vuillard, Edward, 1868–1940

Vuillard specialized in domestic scenes. His bright colors, also favored by Gauguin and some of the Fauves, used flat planes and contours.
Woman in a Striped Dress, 1895, National Gallery of Art, Washington, DC

IMPRESSIONISM, 1870–1905

The Impressionist movement began in France about 1870, but eventually artists in most Western countries were working in this method; hence there are Spanish, Italian, American, English, and Swedish Impressionists, among others. The French artists called themselves members of the Salon des Réfusés (the Refused Ones), which meant that their work had been rejected in juried competitions for exhibition in the Salon (The French Academy's Exhibition).

Typically, subjects of Impressionist painters were outdoor scenes, such as landscapes, people in a cafe, the racetrack—rather commonplace subjects, in the eyes of the art establishment. Painting outdoors just wasn't considered something serious artists indulged in! The paintings were generally (though not always) executed *en plein air* (outdoors), and were noted for the treatment of light. Few of the Impressionists used black in their compositions.

The term *Impressionism* was a derogatory term taken from a Monet painting, *Impression, Sunrise.* Impressionism endured a long time, continuing simultaneously with the emergence of other movements. Monet, one of the original Impressionists, lived to be 86 years old, and his work remained Impressionistic, although it spanned many art movements.

Cassatt, Mary, 1845–1926, United States

Cassatt frequently painted portraits of women and children, using pastels or oils. The only American who exhibited with the Impressionists, some of her work resembled the Japanese woodcuts so popular at the time.

Emmie and Her Child, 1889, Wichita Art Museum, Wichita, Kansas

La Loge, c. 1882, National Gallery of Art, Washington, DC

Lady at the Tea Table, 1885, Metropolitan Museum of Art,
New York City

Mother and Child, 1900, Brooklyn Museum, New York

The Bath, 1891, Art Institute of Chicago

Dégas, Edgar, 1834–1917, France

Dégas mostly worked in pastels. His subjects often were ballet dancers and horses (which he also interpreted in sculpture). He used dramatic lighting and short, parallel, diagonal strokes. His sculptures used the same "sketchy" approach.

Ballet Dancers in the Wings, 1900, St. Louis Art Museum

Little Fourteen-year-old Dancer (sculpture), 1881, St. Louis Art
Museum

Portrait of Mlle. Hortense Valpincon, c. 1871, Minneapolis Institute
of Arts

Singer with Glove, 1878, Fogg Art Museum, Harvard University,
Cambridge, Massachusetts

The Glass of Absinthe, 1876, Musée d'Orsay, Paris

Manet, Edouard, 1832–1883, France

Manet used dramatic contrast, often depicting people in a "snapshot" effect. His work was basically realistic, and he sometimes used a neutral background and flat colors.

Bar at the Folies Bergère, 1882, Courtauld Institute, London

Le Déjeuner sur l'Herbe (Luncheon on the Grass), 1863, Musée d'Orsay, Paris

Le Moulin de la Galette, 1876, Louvre, Paris

The Fifer, 1866, Louvre, Paris

The Reading, 1868, Louvre, Paris

Monet, Claude, 1840–1926, France

Monet used pastels applied with small strokes of color. He painted people early in his career, but mostly did landscapes and water lilies based on his famous water garden at Giverney.

Impression Sunrise—Le Havre, 1872, Musée Marmottan, Paris

Madame Gaudibert, 1868, Louvre, Paris

Rouen Cathedral, Sunset, 1892–1894, Museum of Fine Arts, Boston

The River, 1868, Art Institute of Chicago

Water Lilies, c. 1920, Carnegie Institute, Pittsburgh, Pennsylvania

Morisot, Berthe, 1841–1895, France

Morisot painted portraits and interiors, but ultimately painted out-of-doors with the Impressionists and exhibited with them.

The Artist's Sister at a Window, 1869, National Gallery of Art, Washington, DC

The Artist's Sister, Mme. Pontillon, Seated on the Grass, 1873, Cleveland Museum of Art

The Butterfly Chase, 1874, Musée d'Orsay, Paris

Pissarro, Camille, 1830–1903, France

Pissarro was the eldest of the Impressionists, known for his city and country landscapes. He also spent a time experimenting with Pointillism, a technique in which small dots of color were placed closely together and "mixed by the eye."

A View from the Artist's Window, Eragny, 1888, Ashmolean Museum, Cambridge, England

Red Roofs, 1877, Musée d'Orsay, Paris

The Boulevard Montmartre at Night, 1897, National Gallery, London

The Orchard, 1877, Louvre, Paris

The Potato Harvest, 1886, New York Public Library, New York City

Renoir, Pierre-Auguste, 1841–1919, France

Renoir was a portrait artist, frequently painting members of his family, flowers, Mediterranean landscapes, and holiday scenes. Among his peers, he was the one most concerned that the Impressionists earn the respect of the French people for their new approach to painting.

At the Grenouillère, 1879, Louvre, Paris

Gabrielle with a Rose, c. 1911, Louvre, Paris

Luncheon of the Boating Party, 1881, Phillips Collection, Washington, DC

The Ball at the Moulin de la Galette, Montmartre, 1876, Musée d'Orsay, Paris

Venus Victorious, 1914, Tate Gallery, London

POST-IMPRESSIONISM, 1880–1905

Post-Impressionism is generally lumped together with Impressionism in books or exhibitions, but the Post-Impressionists did not exhibit with the original group. They took the movement further toward Abstraction through such advances as Pointillism (Seurat, Pissarro, Sisley), vigorous brushstrokes (van Gogh), paint applied in a patchwork of colors (Cézanne), and unrealistic colors (Gauguin, Matisse).

Cézanne, Paul, 1839–1906, France

Cézanne used "patches" of color, concentrating on relationships of forms and patterns. His work was considered a major influence in Cubism.

Mont Sainte-Victoire, 1885–1887, Metropolitan Museum of Art, New York City

Mont Ste. Victoire, 1885–1887, Courtauld Institute Galleries, London

Self-Portrait, 1877, Bayerische Staatsgemalde-Sammlungen, Munich

The Woman with a Coffee Pot, 1890–1894, Louvre, Paris

Gauguin, Paul, 1848–1903, France

The work of Gauguin was distinguished by bright, often unrealistic colors and patterns, and flat areas of color. Much of his work was done in Brittany and Tahiti.

Fatata te Miti (By the Sea), 1892, National Gallery of Art, Washington, DC

Girl with Mango, 1892, Baltimore Museum of Art

La Orana Maria, 1891, Metropolitan Museum of Art, New York City

The Day of the God, 1894, Art Institute of Chicago

Vision After the Sermon, 1888, National Gallery of Scotland, Edinburgh

Gogh, Vincent van, 1853–1890, Netherlands

Vincent van Gogh used vivid colors applied in a thick impasto; swirling brush marks distinguished his paintings. Although his paintings now command the highest prices of all painters, he sold only one painting in his lifetime.

Bedroom at Arles, 1888, Art Institute of Chicago

Irises, 1889, Metropolitan Museum of Art, New York City

Self-Portrait, 1899, Private collection, New York

The Night Cafe, 1888, Yale University Art Gallery, New Haven, Connecticut

The Potato Eaters, 1885, Vincent Van Gogh Foundation, Amsterdam, Netherlands

The Starry Night, 1888–1889, Museum of Modern Art, New York City

Matisse, Henri, 1869–1954, France

Matisse's art took several forms, including his sure use of line; bright, unrealistic colors reflecting his association with the Fauves; the large cutouts on hand-painted paper that he did in his old age; and his sculpture.

Bathers by a River, 1916–1917, Art Institute of Chicago

Decorative Figure Against an Ornamental Background, 1925, Musée National d'Arte Moderne, Paris

Lady in Blue, 1937, Collection of Mrs. John Wintersteen, Philadelphia

Luxe, Calme et Volupte, 1904–1905, Musée d'Orsay, Paris

The Back, I–IV (sculpture), 1900–c.1929, Hirshhorn Sculpture Garden, Washington, DC

The Dance, 1909–1910, The Hermitage, St. Petersburg, Russia

The Green Stripe (Mme Matisse), 1905, Royal Museum of Fine Arts, Copenhagen

Redon, Odilon, 1840–1916, France

Redon isolated his subjects against a plain background, then sometimes filled in around the edges of the picture plane with flowers. The pastel colors give a soft, dream-like Surrealistic effect.

Ophelia Among the Flowers, 1905–1908, National Gallery, London

Portrait of Mademoiselle Violette Heymann, 1909, Cleveland Museum of Art

Profile and Flowers, 1912, McNay Art Institute, San Antonio

Roger and Angelica, 1910, Museum of Modern Art, New York City

The Birth of Venus, 1912, Kimbell Art Foundation, Fort Worth

Rousseau, Henri, 1844–1910, France

Rousseau, the "Douanier" (customs official), painted "jungle scenes" based on what he had seen at the Paris Botanical Garden and Zoo. His work was frequently considered Surrealistic.

The Dream, 1910, Museum of Modern Art, New York City

The Waterfall, 1910, The Art Institute of Chicago

Tropical Storm with a Tiger, 1891, National Gallery, London

Seurat, Georges, 1859–1891, France

Seurat worked in what he called "Divisionism" (Pointillism). He died at a young age and therefore completed few large paintings.

Bathers at Asnières, 1883–1884, National Gallery, London

Sunday Afternoon on the Island of La Grande Jatte, 1884–1886, Art Institute of Chicago

Woman Powdering Herself, 1890, Courtauld Institute, London

Woman with Parasol, 1884, Emil G. Buehrle Collection, Zurich

Sisley, Alfred, 1839–1899, France

Sisley's work was at times almost indistinguishable from that of Monet, as they often painted the same scenes at the same time. He also painted in the Pointillist style. His specialty was landscapes, mostly in and around Paris.

Floods at Port-Marley, 1876, Musée d'Orsay, Paris

Toulouse-Lautrec, Henri de, 1864–1901, France

Toulouse-Lautrec's subject matter of the sporting life, cafes, and brothels of Paris reflected the dissolute life he lived. (He was an alcoholic, had syphilis, and died at age 36.) Much of his work was done in pastels in short, slanted, parallel strokes on a tan background. His lithography posters are masterpieces of design.

Moulin de la Galette, 1889, Art Institute of Chicago

The Moulin Rouge, 1892, Art Institute of Chicago

20TH-CENTURY MODERN MASTERS

Modernism, which includes such techniques as Expressionism, Fauvism, and Cubism, began early in the 20th century as a reaction against the historical styles and romantic subject matter so popular in the late 19th century. Art Nouveau, which was also popular at the end of the 19th and early 20th centuries, included architecture and interior design, and fine crafts (jewelry, blown glass, book design, and tapestries). Painters, illustrators, and printmakers of this era also employed the sinuous forms of Art Nouveau that were based on forms from nature such as lilies, cattails, and irises. The decorative arts in Art Nouveau were soon replaced by the stark simplicity and geometry seen in Art Deco design and architecture.

EXPRESSIONISM, 1905–1925

Expressionist painters purposely emphasize, distort, and use unrealistic, jarring color schemes, to show feelings. Had they lived longer, Vincent van Gogh and Paul Gauguin would surely have been considered Expressionists (because of their unique ways of expressing themselves), as was Norwegian Edvard Munch, who used distortion of line and color to express basic emotions such as fear, love, and sadness. Expressionist painters have existed in most art movements since the beginning of the 20th century.

Klimt, Gustave, 1862–1918, Austria

Klimt's work primarily consisted of decorative portraiture of society women, but it went far beyond that to include sly commentary on their lives.

Judith I, 1901, Osterreichische Galerie, Vienna

The Kiss, 1907–1908, Osterreichische Galerie, Vienna

Baby, 1917–1918, Private collection, New York

Kokoschka, Oscar, 1886–1980, Austria

Self-Portrait, 1913, Museum of Modern Art, New York City

Munch, Edvard, 1863–1944, Norway

Munch, whose mother and two sisters died young, showed the distress he felt through his paintings, which were lonely, mysterious, and philosophical. His *Scream* has become so well known that it is often parodied.

Between the Clock and the Bed, 1940–1942, Munch Museum, Oslo

Melancholy, c. 1891, National Gallery, London

The Scream, 1895, National Gallery, Oslo

Rouault, Georges, 1871–1958, Austria

The Old King, 1937, Museum of Art, Carnegie Institute, Pittsburgh, Pennsylvania

FAUVISM, c. 1905-1907

The Fauves (translated "wild beasts") favored landscapes, harbor scenes, even portraits, using bold, flat areas of color (often straight from the tube). Matisse was sometimes included in this group.

Derain, André, 1880–1954, France

Pool of London, 1906, Tate Gallery, London

Vlaminck, Maurice, 1876–1958, France

Houses at Chatou, c. 1905, The Art Institute of Chicago

Still Life with Lemons, 1907, Norton Simon Museum of Art, Los Angeles

CUBISM, 1907-1920s

Cubism might be described as trying to show all sides of a real object. Instead of painting what is *seen,* Cubists painted what is *known* of a real object by breaking it into sections and reassembling it. An example would be to show a face from the front and profile together, as Picasso was so fond of doing.

Braque, Georges, 1882–1963, France

Braque is considered a co-founder of Cubism. He and Picasso were close colleagues, and it is sometimes difficult to tell their early work apart

Area de Bach, 1913, National Gallery of Art, Washington, DC

Picasso, Pablo, 1881–1973, Spain

Picasso is credited (with Braque) with the invention of Cubism, which might be considered the birth of Modernism. A subject may always be found in this work, although it may be quite abstract.

Guernica, 1937, Prado Museum, Madrid

Les Demoiselles d'Avignon, 1907, Museum of Modern Art,
New York City

Three Musicians, 1921, Philadelphia Museum of Art

Woman's Head (sculpture), 1909, Museum of Modern Art,
New York City

THE TEN, 1898–1919, UNITED STATES

Sometimes called the "American Impressionists," most members of this group had studied in Europe and were profoundly influenced by European Impressionism, though their work had more solid forms and they were less concerned with the effects of light.

Benson, Frank, 1861–1951

Sunlight, 1909, Indianapolis Museum of Art

Hassam, Childe, 1859–1935

Hassam was considered a North American Impressionist, though his work was somewhat later than the original Impressionists. His joyous, fresh cityscapes capture the moment.

Allies Day, May 1917, 1917, National Gallery of Art, Washington, DC

The Union Jack, New York, April Morn, 1918, Hirshhorn Museum
and Sculpture Garden, Washington, DC

Tarbell, Edmund, 1862–1938

Across the Room, 1899, Metropolitan Museum of Art, New York City

"Art is either plagiarism or revolution."

—PAUL GAUGUIN, 1848–1903, French Post-Impressionist painter

THE EIGHT, c. 1900–1920, UNITED STATES

The Eight was a group originally called "The Philadelphia Realists" where most of them had worked as newspaper artists before the common use of the camera in journalism. When they moved to New York, they became "The New York Realists." The original group was Arthur B. Davies, Maurice Prendergast, Ernest Lawson, Robert Henri, George Luks, William J. Glackens, John Sloan, and Everett Shinn. George Bellows later joined the group.

Davies, Arthur B., 1862–1928
> *Intermezzo,* 1915, Graham Gallery, New York City

Glackens, William, 1870–1938
> *Hammerstein's Roof Garden,* 1901, Whitney Museum of American Art, New York City
> *The Green Car,* 1910, Metropolitan Museum of Art, New York City

Prendergast, Maurice, 1859–1924
> Prendergast, considered an American Impressionist, was a member of "The Eight," and exhibited in the 1913 Armory show. His scenes of ordinary places where people gathered for leisure activities featured brilliant clear colors.
> *Central Park,* 1908–1910, Metropolitan Museum of Art, New York City
> *On the Beach No. 3,* 1918, Cleveland Museum of Art
> *Seashore,* c. 1910, St. Louis Art Museum
> *The Promenade,* 1913, Whitney Museum of American Art, New York City

THE ASHCAN SCHOOL, 1900–1940, UNITED STATES

The nickname "Ashcan School" referred to the subject matter of these early 20th-century realists. Many of the group had been members of "The Eight." They painted life as they saw it on the crowded streets of New York.

Bellows, George, 1882–1925
> *Cliff Dwellers,* 1913, Los Angeles County Museum of Art
> *Stag at Sharkey's,* 1909, Cleveland Museum of Art

Henri, Robert, 1865–1929

Henri was considered the master of the Ashcan School. He was a teacher and major influence in American art of his time. His New York City scenes clearly depicted the atmosphere of a busy metropolis.

New York Street in Winter, 1902, The National Gallery of Art, Washington, DC

The Masquerade Dress, 1911, The Metropolitan Museum of Art, New York City

Luks, George, 1886–1933

Mrs. Gamely, 1930, Whitney Museum of American Art, New York City

Sloan, John, 1871–1951

Hairdresser's Window, 1907, Wadsworth Atheneum, Hartford, Connecticut

Sunday, Women Drying Their Hair, 1912, Addison Gallery of American Art, Phillips Academy, Andover, Massachusetts

MODERN PAINTERS, 1900–1950

These artists primarily worked in the first half of the 20th century. Their work showed a distinctive difference from the Realistic or Romantic artwork of the previous century, breaking ground by using distortion and exaggeration and (sometimes) a total elimination of a subject.

Albers, Josef, 1888–1976, United States

Albers was interested in showing color relationships. His subject matter was usually composed of squares-within-squares, thus enabling him to experiment with the effect of one color when placed next to another.

Study for Homage to the Square, 1963, Tate Gallery, London

Beckmann, Max, 1884–1950, Germany

Beckmann's paintings involved social criticism, probably as a result of the horrors he experienced as a medical orderly in World War I. An Expressionist, his paintings depicted cruelty, horror, and other aspects of the negative side of the human condition, yet were painted in bright colors to give an apparent lighthearted mood until one looks closely.

Acrobats, 1939, St. Louis Art Museum

Self-Portrait, 1937, The Art Institute of Chicago

Davis, Stuart, 1894–1964, United States

Davis was a pre-Pop artist. His combinations of visual images and words often resembled collages. His cityscapes, bold patterns of letters, and abstract forms have become standard in contemporary art.

Blips and Ifs, 1963–1964, Amon Carter Museum, Fort Worth

Colonial Cubism, 1954, Walker Art Center, Minneapolis

House and Street, 1931, Whitney Museum of American Art,
    New York City

The Paris Bit, 1959, Whitney Museum of American Art,
    New York City

Visa, 1951, Museum of Modern Art, New York City

Demuth, Charles, 1883–1935, United States

Demuth mostly painted Cubist watercolors of houses, grain elevators, and circus performers. He was sometimes grouped with the "Precisionists" whose style was so exacting. His *I Saw the Figure Five in Gold* is based on a poem written by a friend about a fire truck (No. 5) racing through the city at night.

Acrobats, 1919, Museum of Modern Art, New York City

Buildings, Lancaster, 1930, Whitney Museum of American Art,
    New York City

I Saw the Figure Five in Gold, 1928, Metropolitan Museum of Art,
    New York City

Dove, Arthur, 1880–1946, United States

Arthur Dove was a contemporary of Georgia O'Keeffe. Both artists were members of Gallery 291 in New York City, a gathering place for Modernist painters, sculptors, and photographers. Dove's subject matter was similar to O'Keeffe's: abstract organic natural forms painted in soft colors.

Fog Horns, 1929, Colorado Springs Fine Arts Center

Sand Barge, 1930, Phillips Collection, Washington, DC

The Red One, 1944, William H. Lane Foundation, Leominster,
    Massachusetts

Escher, Maurits Cornelis (M. C.), 1898–1972, Netherlands

M.C. Escher became enamored of the tessellation (interlocking forms such as one might see in a complex mosaic floor), and created many works of art using this technique. His witty drawings, graphic designs, and illusionistic treatment of frogs, geese, and knights were mostly done in black and white.

> *Concave and Convex*, 1955, National Gallery of Art, Washington, DC
> *Day and Night*, 1938, National Gallery of Art, Washington, DC
> *Drawing Hands*, 1948, Vorpal Galleries, San Francisco and Chicago
> *House of Stairs*, 1951, National Gallery of Art, Washington, DC

Hartley, Marsden, 1877–1943, United States

Hartley was profoundly affected by World War I, when he lost a dear friend. An Abstract Modernist, he often included symbolism of this period in his paintings.

> *Berlin Abstraction*, 1914–1915, Corcoran Gallery of Art,
>   Washington, DC
> *Berlin Ante-War*, 1915, Columbus Gallery of Fine Arts, Columbus,
>   Ohio
> *Painting, Number 5*, 1914–1915, Whitney Museum of American Art,
>   New York City
> *Portrait of a German Officer*, 1914, Metropolitan Museum of Art,
>   New York City
> *The Window*, 1928, Columbus Gallery of Fine Arts, Columbus, Ohio

Hopper, Edward, 1882–1967, United States

Hopper painted extraordinary images of the ordinary—a couple sunning themselves, people sitting in a night café, sunshine and shadow on an old house by the seashore.

> *Bow of Beam Trawler Osprey*, 1926, St. Louis Art Museum
> *Early Sunday Morning*, 1930, Whitney Museum of American Art,
>   New York City
> *Nighthawks*, 1942, Art Institute of Chicago

Kandinsky, Wassily, 1866–1944, Russia

Although he began as a landscape artist, Kandinsky was one of the first artists to completely eliminate a recognizable subject of any kind, painting pure abstractions in the early 1900s. Following the Russian Revolution, Kandinsky was involved in the Russian art world, but eventually moved to Germany where he taught at the Bauhaus, then settled in France.

Composition VI, 1913, Guggenheim Museum, New York City
Light Picture and Black Lines, 1913, Guggenheim Museum,
　　New York City

Marin, John, 1870–1953, United States

Marin was a member of the Alfred Stieglitz circle. Stieglitz founded the Secessionist movement in photography, and was a key figure in the introduction of Modernism to the United States. The group included Georgia O'Keeffe, Arthur Dove, Marsden Hartley, and a number of European Modernists. Marin painted both watercolor and oil cityscapes and harbors filled with energetic lines. He often left parts of the paper/canvas unpainted.

Brooklyn Bridge, 1910, Metropolitan Museum of Art, New York City
Lower Manhattan, 1922, Museum of Modern Art, New York City
Maine Islands, 1922, Phillips Collection, Washington, DC
Singer Building, 1921, Philadelphia Museum of Art

Marsh, Reginald, 1898–1954, United States

Marsh's subject matter was the teeming nightlife of New York City and Coney Island. Although a member of the "Ashcan School," his aim was to paint contemporary life in the manner of the Old Masters.

Twenty Cent Movie, 1936, Whitney Museum of American Art,
　　New York City
10 Shots 10 Cents, 1939, St. Louis Art Museum
Tattoo and Haircut, 1932, Art Institute of Chicago

Modigliani, Amedeo, 1884–1920, Italy

Modigliani's paintings and sculptures always used the human face or figure as a subject, usually exaggeratedly elongated, much as Fernando Botero paints all his portrait subjects as fat people.

Gypsy Woman with Baby, 1919, National Gallery of Art,
　　Washington, DC

Mondrian, Piet, 1872–1944, Netherlands

Mondrian's paintings are recognizable by their simplicity (mostly grids) and color (red, white, blue, and yellow with black lines). His designs have widely inspired furniture, interior design, and clothing.

Composition in Line and Color, 1913, Kroller Muller Rijksmuseum, Otterlo, The Netherlands

Composition with Red, Yellow and Blue, 1922, Rijksmuseum, Amsterdam

O'Keeffe, Georgia, 1887–1986, United States

O'Keeffe is one of the few female artists whose work is represented in most museum collections. A modernist, she eliminated unnecessary detail in her paintings, whether the subject was hills and sky, flowers, shells, or a cow's skull floating in a sea of clouds. Her paintings of New York and her beloved New Mexico demonstrate her unique viewpoint.

Black Iris III, 1926, Metropolitan Museum of Art, New York City

Cow's Skull—Red, White and Blue, 1931, Metropolitan Museum of Art, New York City

New York Night, 1928–1929, Nebraska Art Association, Sheldon Gallery, Lincoln, Nebraska

Red Hills and Bones, 1941, Philadelphia Museum of Art

Sky Above Clouds IV, 1965, Art Institute of Chicago

Paxton, William, 1869–1941, United States

Paxton was known for his paintings of upper-class life, and was known by some as "the court painter of Philadelphia."

The Front Parlor, 1913, St. Louis Art Museum

The Housemaid, 1910, Corcoran Gallery, Washington, DC

Rivera, Diego, 1886–1957, Mexico

Rivera's large murals and paintings of Mexican peasants and the spirit of revolution were brilliantly colored social commentary, and brought him to the forefront of Mexican artists. He was married to painter Frida Kahlo.

The Liberation of the Peon, 1931, Philadelphia Museum of Art

Creation, 1922, National Training School, Mexico City

Russell, Morgan, 1886–1953, United States

Russell was a Synchromist, a believer in using color to create form and composition. His swirling forms and softly modeled (shaded) paintings influenced many later artists.

Four Part Synchromy No. 7, 1914–1915, Whitney Museum of American Art, New York City

Shahn, Ben, 1898–1969, United States

Shahn was a painter/photographer whose paintings featured social commentary about current events. In 1933 he assisted Diego Rivera when he painted murals for Rockefeller Center (these were later destroyed). He was a member of the FSA (Farm Security Administration) photography group formed during the Depression of the 1930s.

The Passion of Sacco and Vanzetti, 1931–1932, Whitney Museum of American Art, New York City

Sheeler, Charles, 1883–1965, United States

Sheeler was known as one of the "Immaculates" or "Precisionists" because of his photo-like renderings of the industrial landscape. His use of subdued colors caused his paintings to be constrained and unemotional.

Barn Abstraction, 1918, Philadelphia Museum of Art

Classic Landscape, 1931, St. Louis Art Museum

River Rouge Plant, 1932, Whitney Museum of American Art, New York City

Upper Deck, 1929, Fogg Art Museum, Cambridge, Massachusetts

Stella, Joseph, 1877–1946, United States

Battle of Lights, Coney Island, 1914, Yale University Art Gallery, New Haven, Connecticut

Brooklyn Bridge, 1917, Yale University Art Gallery, New Haven, Connecticut

The Bridge, 1920–1922, Newark Museum, New Jersey

Tooker, George, 1920, United States

Tooker's paintings feature self-absorbed people who never appear to interact with one another, and are considered somewhat surrealistic. His repetition of isolated people, sometimes in cubicles, gives the viewer a feeling of disquiet.

The Subway, 1950, Whitney Museum of American Art, New York City

The Waiting Room, 1959, National Museum of American Art, Washington, DC

Weber, Max, 1881–1961, United States

    Chinese Restaurant, 1915, Whitney Museum of American Art,
        New York City

    Rush Hour, New York, 1915, National Gallery of Art, Washington, DC

HARLEM RENAISSANCE PAINTERS, 1915–1940, UNITED STATES

The Harlem Renaissance refers to a time when the arts—literature, music, performance, painting, and sculpture—placed an emphasis on the life and the work of the African American in the United States. Harlem, New York, was the epicentre of this movement.

Douglas, Aaron, 1899–1979

    Douglas painted murals that combined African motifs with the Art Deco style popular at that time. He was a teacher at Fisk University.

    Aspects of Negro Life: From Slavery Through Reconstruction, 1934,
        New York Public Library, New York City

Fuller, Meta Vaux Warrick, 1877–1968

    Ethiopia Awakening, 1914, The New York Public Library,
        New York City

Hayden, Palmer, 1890–1973

    The Janitor Who Paints, 1939–1940, National Museum of American
        Art, Washington, DC

Johnson, William H., 1901–1970

    Johnson lived and studied in Europe for approximately twelve years. On his return to the United States, he increasingly painted from his personal experiences as a black person.

    Young Man in a Vest, c. 1939–1940, National Museum of American
        Art, Washington, DC

Jones, Lois Mailou, 1905–1998

> *Les Fetiches,* 1938, National Gallery of American Art, Washington, DC

Woodruff, Hale, 1900–1980

Woodruff is primarily known for his large historical murals, which were influenced by his studies with Diego Rivera of Mexico. His genre paintings of life in the South were from personal experience.

> *The Mutiny Aboard the Amistad, 1839,* 1938–1939, from the *Amistad Mutiny* Mural, Talladega College, Talladega, Alabama

AMERICAN SCENE PAINTERS—REGIONALISTS, 1930-1950

The American Scene Painters were primarily Midwesterners who painted between the World Wars. They depicted people, events, and scenery—what they saw or what they remembered. Many American painters could be included in such a group, two of whom are elsewhere in this list, Edward Hopper and Charles Burchfield, a member of "The Eight."

Benton, Thomas Hart, 1899–1975

Benton was a Regionalist. His large murals and paintings of life in the Midwest are complex compositions of vivid color and wit. In his drawings and prints, he depicted people at work in places ranging from cottonfields to Hollywood.

> *Arts of the West,* 1932, New Britain Museum of American Art,
>   New Britain, Connecticut
> *Cotton Pickers (Georgia),* 1928–1929, Metropolitan Museum of Art,
>   New York City
> *Hollywood,* 1937, Nelson-Atkins Museum of Art, Kansas City, Missouri
> *Independence and the Opening of the West* (mural), 1959–1962,
>   Harry S. Truman Library, Independence, Missouri
> *The American Historical Epic,* 1924–1927, Nelson-Atkins Museum of
>   Art, Kansas City, Missouri

Burchfield, Charles, 1893–1967

Burchfield was considered an American Scene painter. His often stormy skies and small town scenes are familiar sights.

> *Sun and Rocks,* 1950, Albright-Knox Art Gallery, Buffalo, New York
> *The Sphinx and the Milky Way,* 1946, Munson-Williams-Proctor
>   Institute, Utica, New York

Moses, Anna Mary (Grandma), 1860–1961

"Grandma Moses" was an American *primitive*. Her memory paintings of life on the farm, richly peopled with friends and family, came from a vivid imagination, and are popular with collectors.

Battle of Bennington, 1953, Daughters of the American Revolution, Washington, DC

First Snow, 1957, Bennington Museum, Bennington, Vermont

Home of Hezekiah King, 1942, Phoenix Art Museum, Arizona

The Eisenhower Farm, 1956, Dwight D. Eisenhower Library, Abilene, Kansas

Soyer, Moses, 1899–1974

Artists on W.P.A., 1935, National Museum of American Art, Washington, DC

Wood, Grant, 1892–1942

A Regionalist, Grant Wood's paintings (particularly of the *Daughters of the Revolution*) reveal a sly wit. His landscapes demonstrate the ability to simplify and stylize a composition almost to abstraction.

American Gothic, 1930, Art Institute of Chicago

Daughters of the Revolution, 1932, Cincinnati Art Museum

Dinner for Threshers, 1934, Whitney Museum of American Art, New York City

Midnight Ride of Paul Revere, 1931, Metropolitan Museum of Art, New York City

The Birthplace of Herbert Hoover, 1931, New York Historical Society, New York City

"So I said to myself, I'll paint what I see, what the flower is to me but I'll paint it big and they will be surprised into taking time to look at it. I will make even busy New Yorkers take time to see what I see of flowers."

—Georgia O'Keeffe, 1887–1986, American Modernist painter

DADA, 1910–1925

Dada, a nonsense French word for "hobbyhorse," was almost anti-art in its rebellion against traditional forms of art and culture. Marcel Duchamp was in the forefront of this movement with his "ready-mades" that essentially said "If I say it is art, it is art!" In fact, Pop Art, with its emphasis on ordinary objects, was sometimes known as "Neo-Dada."

> **Duchamp, Marcel,** 1887–1968, France
>
> Duchamp set the American art world on its ear with his *Nude Descending a Staircase* shown at the 1913 Armory Show. The painting was between abstraction and figurative art, showing movement at the same time as it showed a very nontraditional nude. He continued to shock throughout his career, with his "ready-mades" (for example, a urinal that he signed and a bicycle wheel mounted on a stool). He was a founder of the Dada movement.
>
> > *Chocolate Grinder, No. 1,* 1913, Philadelphia Museum of Art
> > *Fountain,* 1917, Louise and Walter Arensberg Collection
> > *Nude Descending a Staircase,* No. 2, 1912, Philadelphia Museum of Art
> > *The Bride Stripped Bare by Her Bachelors, Even (The Large Glass),* 1915–1923, Philadelphia Museum of Art

SURREALISM, 1922–1940s

Surrealism translates literally as "above reality," and Surrealist artists combined seemingly unrelated subjects into one composition. These artworks were considered the visual representation of a dreamlike state—disarranged and jumbled, much as is the subconscious. Surrealism arose from the literary movement of stream-of-consciousness writing developed by André Breton.

> **Chagall, Marc,** 1887–1985, France, b. Russia
>
> Chagall often painted scenes of his native Russia. His upside-down villages, paintings of peasants, and illustrations of Jewish proverbs and Russian folktales were all done in his brightly colored, highly personal style.
>
> > *I and the Village,* 1911, Museum of Modern Art, New York City
> > *Self Portrait with Seven Fingers,* 1912, Stedelijk Museum, Amsterdam

The Asher Window, 1960, Hadassah University Medical Center, Jerusalem

The Cock, 1928, Thyssen Collection, Lugano, Switzerland

Chirico, Giorgio de, 1888–1978, Italy

Nostalgia of the Infinite, 1913, Museum of Modern Art, New York City

The Disquieting Muses, 1916, Gianni Mattioli Foundation, Milan

The Philosopher's Conquest, 1914, The Art Institute of Chicago

Dali, Salvador, 1904–1989, Spain

Dali is probably the best known of the Surrealists, with his melting watches, and his later treatment of religious themes. A fine painter, his Surrealistic work was full of visual puns.

Crucifixion of St. John of the Cross, 1951, Glasgow Art Gallery, Scotland

Illumined Pleasures, 1929, Museum of Modern Art, New York City

The Persistence of Memory, 1931, Museum of Modern Art, New York City

Ernst, Max, 1891–1975, Germany

Elephant of the Celebes, 1921, Museum of Modern Art, New York City

Kahlo, Frida, 1907–1954, Mexico

Kahlo was married to artist Diego Rivera. Many of her strongest self-portraits were made at a time when she was afflicted with very poor health. She has become a heroine for feminists because of the courage and spirit that kept her creating through adverse conditions.

Fulang-Chang and I, 1937, Museum of Modern Art, New York City

Self Portrait with Cropped Hair, 1940, Museum of Modern Art, New York City

Self Portrait with Monkey and Parrot, 1942, Collection of IBM Corp., Armonk, New York

Magritte, René, 1898–1967, France

Magritte had a fertile wit. His paintings invariably were a visual play-on-words, whether it was raining men carrying umbrellas or his *Ce n'est pas un Pipe* (a painting of a pipe that says "This is not a pipe.").

The False Mirror, 1928, Museum of Modern Art, New York City

The Human Condition, 1934, National Gallery of Art, Washington, DC

The Menaced Assassin, 1926, Museum of Modern Art, New York City

The Promenades of Euclid, 1955, Minneapolis Institute of Arts

Miró, Joan, 1893–1983, Spain

Miró's abstract paintings always have a subject. However, when looking at his work, it is important to read the titles to help identify what the subject is. His canvases consist of abstracted forms (people, animals, organic shapes, disembodied heads and hands) often joined by random lines.

Dog Barking at the Moon, 1926, Philadelphia Museum of Art

Dutch Interior, 1928, Collection of Peggy Guggenheim, Venice

The Beautiful Bird Revealing the Unknown to a Pair of Lovers, 1940–1941, Museum of Modern Art, New York City

The Harlequin's Carnival, 1924–1925, Albright-Knox Art Gallery, Buffalo, New York

POP ART, 1945–1965

Pop artists felt that the subject was unimportant, and frequently chose as their subject matter banal objects such as a soap box or comic books. Improved techniques such as silk screen enabled them to make multiple images of their work.

Diebenkorn, Richard, 1922–1993

Ocean Park No. 122, 1980, Museum of Fine Arts, Houston

Dine, Jim, 1935, United States

Blue Clam, 1981, Museum of Contemporary Art, Chicago

Indiana, Robert, 1928, United States

Indiana's strength is his combination of words and letters, often making sly commentary about society. His LOVE icon has been interpreted in everything from postage stamps to jewelry.

Louisiana, 1966, Krannert Art Gallery, University of Illinois, Champaign

LOVE, 1966, Indianapolis Museum of Art

The Calumet, 1961, Rose Art Museum, Brandeis University, Waltham, Massachusetts

The Demuth American Dream No. 5, 1963, Art Gallery of Ontario, Toronto

Triumph of Tira, 1961, Sheldon Memorial Art Gallery, Lincoln, Nebraska

Johns, Jasper, 1930, United States

Johns explores the ordinary by extraordinary means. He often uses encaustic (melted wax mixed with pigment) to build up wonderfully textured surfaces. Always look for the unexpected in his work!

Flag, 1954–1955, Museum of Modern Art, New York City

Numbers 0 Through 9, 1961, Hirshhorn Museum, Washington, DC

Painted Bronze (Ballantine Ale cans), 1960, Museum Ludwig, Cologne, Germany

Target with Four Faces, 1955, Museum of Modern Art, New York City

White Flag, 1955, Leo Castelli Gallery, New York City

Lichtenstein, Roy, 1923–1997, United States

Lichtenstein took commercial subjects such as cartoons and interpreted them with enlarged "Benday dots" like those used to make colored magazine photos. He was also fond of "quoting" (copying the work of other artists in his own recognizable style). His *Mural With Blue Brushstroke* includes "quoted" work from a number of well-known artists.

Blam, 1962, Yale University Art Gallery, New Haven, Connecticut

Dreaming Girl, 1963, Museum of Modern Art, New York City

Goldfish Bowl II (sculpture), 1978, St. Louis Art Museum

Mural with Blue Brushstroke, 1986, Equitable Life Assurance Society building, New York City

Popeye, 1961, Collection of David Lichtenstein, New York City

Rauschenberg, Robert, 1925, United States

Rauschenberg's work is part painting, part collage, part assemblage, and part photograph. He combines unlikely subjects in bizarre assemblages, such as his goat with a tire around its middle, standing in the center of a large mattress.

Bed, 1959, Collection of Mr. and Mrs. Leo Castelli, New York

Doric Circus, 1979, National Gallery of Art, Washington, DC

Monogram, 1955–1959, Moderna Museet, Stockholm

Odalisk, 1955–1956, Collection of Peter Ludwig, Wallraf-Richartz
Museum, Cologne, Germany

Retroactive I, 1964, Wadsworth Atheneum, Hartford, Connecticut

Tracer, 1964, Nelson-Atkins Gallery of Art, Kansas City, Missouri

Warhol, Andy, 1930–1988, United States

Andy Warhol began his career as a shoe illustrator. He is one of the best
known of the Pop artists, taking ordinary objects (Campbell soup can
labels, for example), or well-known public figures (Liz Taylor, Marilyn
Monroe), and photographing them, then doing repeat images in silk
screen.

Campbell's Soup Can, 1965, Museum of Modern Art, New York City

Dollar Bills, 1962, Collection of Mr. and Mrs. Robert C. Scull,
New York

Green Coca-Cola Bottles, 1962, Private collection, New York

Marilyn Diptych, 1962, Tate Gallery, London

Marilyn Monroe's Lips, 1962, Hirshhorn Museum of Art,
Washington, DC

ABSTRACT EXPRESSIONISM, c. 1940–1970

Some Abstract Expressionists used a subject, while others avoided one altogether. What unified them was their rebellion against traditional painting techniques and ideas.

Bacon, Francis, 1909–1992, England

Bacon's paintings have an unfinished quality that is disturbing to the
viewer. His application of paint is beautiful and unique, but his subject
matter, ranging from his paintings of a screaming Pope Innocent X (based
on Velasquez's originals) to twisted figures in isolation or in groups, is
unsettling.

Head Surrounded by Sides of Beef, 1954, Art Institute of Chicago

Three Studies for Figures at the Base of a Crucifixion, 1944, Tate
Gallery, London

Bearden, Romare, 1914–1988, United States

Bearden, an African American, became known for his prints and collages
depicting everyday life of American Blacks. He was among the first artists
to include photographs in his compositions, often combining them with
his painting and prints.

House in Cotton Field, 1968, Estate of Romare Bearden, ACA
Galleries, New York City

The Falling Star, 1980, Estate of Romare Bearden, ACA Galleries,
New York City

The Piano Lesson, 1983, Estate of Romare Bearden, ACA Galleries,
New York City

Gorky, Arshile, 1904–1948, United States

The Artist and His Mother, 1926–1929, Whitney Museum of
American Art, New York City

Kline, Franz, 1910–1962, United States

Mahoning, 1956, Whitney Museum of American Art, New York City

Kooning, Willem de, 1904–1997, United States, b. Netherlands

Willem de Kooning was an Abstract Expressionist whose paintings
nonetheless often had a subject such as a grinning woman bicyclist—a
somewhat hidden, yet still recognizable female form in his *Woman and
Bicycle.*

Queen of Hearts, 1943–1946, Hirshhorn Museum, Washington, DC

Woman and Bicycle, 1952–1953, Whitney Museum of American Art,
New York City

Woman I, 1950–1952, Museum of Modern Art, New York City

Woman II, 1952, Museum of Modern Art, New York City

Pollock, Jackson, 1912–1956, United States

In his haste to apply paint to canvas, Pollock began laying canvases flat on
the floor and applying it through the "controlled drip" method. His
apparently haphazard method of working was deliberate, and altogether
broke away from including a subject in a painting.

Autumn Rhythm (Number 20), 1950, Metropolitan Museum of Art,
New York City
Number 1 (Lavender Mist), 1950, National Gallery, Washington, DC
Number 27, 1950, Whitney Museum of American Art, New York City
One (Number 31), 1950, Museum of Modern Art, New York City
Portrait and a Dream, 1953, Dallas Museum of Art
The She-Wolf, 1943, Museum of Modern Art, New York City

Rivers, Larry, 1923–2002, United States
River's storytelling in his paintings is somewhat obscured by his Abstract
Expressionist method of loosely applying paint. Yet the subject (and so
much more) becomes evident when you examine the work for a while.

Berdie with the American Flag, 1955, Nelson-Atkins Museum of Art,
Kansas City, Missouri
First New York Film Festival Billboard, 1963, Hirshhorn Museum,
Washington, DC
Last Civil War Veteran, 1961, Collection of Martha Jackson,
New York City
The History of the Russian Revolution: From Marx to Mayakovski,
1965, Hirshhorn Museum, Washington, DC
The Studio, 1956, Minneapolis Institute of Arts

Rothko, Mark, 1903–1970, United States
During his career, Rothko was best known for the large, vertical paintings
that incorporated rectangles of color with softly painted edges. It was easy
to think of these parallel rectangles as landscapes. His last fourteen paintings for a chapel in Houston, now known as the Rothko Chapel, were
somber and limited to browns, maroon, gray, and black, reflecting the
depression from which he suffered most of his career.

Centre Triptych for the Rothko Chapel, 1966, Rothko Chapel,
Houston

"How you do your work is a portrait of yourself."
—author unknown

COLOR FIELD PAINTING, c. 1955–1964

Artists of this movement avoided subject matter altogether, either applying smooth, unbroken color or staining canvas by pouring pigment.

Frankenthaler, Helen, 1928, United States
Frankenthaler's Abstract Expressionist style is to stain large or small canvases in soft colors that have a calming effect.
Blue Territory, 1955, Whitney Museum of American Art,
New York City
Flood, 1967, Whitney Museum of American Art, New York City
For E.M., 1981, Collection of the artist
Jacob's Ladder, 1957, Museum of Modern Art, New York City
Mountains and Sea, 1952, National Gallery of Art, Washington, DC

Kelly, Ellsworth, 1923, United States
Kelly's hard-edge paintings often consist of geometrically shaped panels of clear color. The hard edge refers to the uniform color used in adjoining sections of various hues.
Colors for a Large Wall, 1951, Museum of Modern Art,
New York City
Mural, 1969, UNESCO, Paris
Spectrum II, 1967, St. Louis Art Museum
White Angle, 1966, The Solomon R. Guggenheim Museum,
New York City

Stella, Frank, 1936, United States
Stella's canvases cover a wide range: from predominantly black paintings to geometric-shaped canvases with hard-edge painted rainbow-colors, to wildly painted hanging constructions that are as much sculpture as they are painting.
Guadalupe Island, Caracara, 1979, Tate Gallery, London
Jarama II, 1982, National Gallery of Art, Washington, DC

"Every time I paint a portrait I lose a friend."
—JOHN SINGER SARGENT, 1856–1925, American society portraitist

HYPERREALISM, c. 1965–1977, UNITED STATES

The work of the Hyperrealists can almost pass for photography. The work can be purely realistic portraiture (figurative), or Surreal scenes (cityscapes or suburban neighborhoods) barren of people.

Eddy, Don, 1944
>*New Shoes for H,* 1973–1974, Cleveland Museum of Art

Estes, Richard Close, 1932
>*Holland Hotel,* 1984, Louis K. Meisel Gallery, New York City
>*Prescriptions Filled (Municipal Building),* 1983, Private collection
>*Times Square at 3:53 pm, Winter,* 1985, Private collection

Flack, Audrey, 1931
Flack's large paintings of subjects (such as a dressing table cluttered with objects) are faithfully based on her photographs. She achieves extreme realism using an airbrush (a mechanical spray for pigment).
>*Jolie Madame,* 1972, Australian National Gallery, Canberra
>*Leonardo's Lady,* 1975, Museum of Modern Art, New York City
>*Marilyn* (Monroe), 1977, University of Arizona Museum of Art, Tucson
>*Buddha,* 1975, St. Louis Art Museum

"OLD MASTERS" FOR FUTURE GENERATIONS

This list includes some artists whose work is considered significant and groundbreaking for its time. It will remain to be seen what "history" thinks of them. What is that magic quality that causes one artist to emerge (over time) from a group of artists doing similar work in the same period? Which ones in this group do you think will emerge from the pack?

Bartlett, Jennifer, 1941, United States
>*Spiral: An Ordinary Evening in New Haven,* 1989, Private collection, New York

Basquiat, Jean-Michele, 1960–1988, United States
>*Untitled* (words and figures), 1984, Osaka City Museum, Japan
>*Slave Auction,* 1982, Musée National d'Art Modern, Centre Georges Pompidou, Paris

Botero, Fernando, 1932, Colombia

Botero's work is comprised mostly of portraiture (individual and group) and still life. His work is instantly recognizable because all the figures in his work are fat. Even the objects in his still lifes are slightly rotund.

Alof de Wignacourt (after Caravaggio), 1974, Nohra Haime Gallery, New York City

Cardenas, Juan, 1939, Colombia

Variation on a Still Life, 1990, Claude Bernard Gallery, New York City

Clemente, Francesco, 1952, Italy

Clemente was an architect and great admirer of Frank Lloyd Wright before he became a painter. It is hard to imagine that his Expressionistic portraits and figural work might be done by someone with architectural training.

The Fourteen Stations, No. III, 1981–1982, Private collection

Close, Chuck, 1940, United States

Close works in many different media and techniques, but has restricted himself to one subject: the portrait head.

Fanny, Fingerpainting, 1985, National Gallery of Art, Washington, DC

Keith, 1970, St. Louis Art Museum

Linda, 1975–1976, Akron Art Museum, Ohio

Self-Portrait, 1968, Walker Art Center, Minneapolis

Self-Portrait, 1997, Pace-Wildenstein Gallery, New York City

Stanley (large version), 1980–1981, Solomon R. Guggenheim Museum, New York City

DeForest, Roy, 1930, United States

Big Foot, Dogs, and College Grad, 1985, John Natsoulas Gallery, Davis, California

Fischl, Eric, 1948, United States

Fischl's disturbing visions of what appears to be ordinary family life have underlying messages about sexuality that may make the viewer ask, "What did he really mean by that?"

A Visit To/A Visit From/The Island, 1983, Whitney Museum of American Art, New York City

Growing Up in the Company of Women II, 1987, St. Louis Art
> Museum

Squirt (For Ian Giloth), 1982, Thomas Ammann Fine Art, Zurich,
> Switzerland

Fish, Janet, 1938, United States

Fish paints the ordinary in extraordinary ways. She is a gardener and a
collector of interesting vases that she uses in her tabletop still-life arrange-
ments. The sheer size of her watercolors and oils and the reflections and
relationships of the objects in her compositions are the distinguishing
characteristics of her work.

Chinoiserie, 1984, Collection of Paine Webber Group Inc., New York
> City

Kara, 1983, Museum of Fine Arts, Houston

Painted Water Glasses, 1974, Whitney Museum of American Art,
> New York City

Raspberries and Goldfish, 1981, Metropolitan Museum of Art,
> New York City

Freud, Lucian, 1922, Austria

Naked Portrait, 1972–1973, Tate Gallery, London

Haring, Keith, 1958–1990, United States

In Haring's too-short life, his work reflected his origin as a graffiti artist.
He was best-known for abstract figures positioned in every direction in
(mostly) large compositions. His influence is widely seen in contemporary
work.

Monkey Puzzle, 1988, Tony Shafrazi Gallery, New York City

Mural, 1984, Collingwood Technical School, Melbourne, Australia

Mural, 1987, Exterior Stairwell, Necker Children's Hospital, Paris

Mural, 1989, Church of Sant'Antonio, Pisa, Italy

New York City Subway Panels, 1984, Fifth Avenue, New York City

The Ten Commandments, 1985, Contemporary Art Museum,
> Bordeaux, France

Hockney, David, 1937, England

Hockney, one of the most famous contemporary British painters, lives
and works in California. His paintings reflect what he sees there, includ-

ing swimming pools, friends, and scenery (such as his large painting of Mulholland Drive). He is also noted for large photo-collages that are assembled from dozens of photographs of the same subject taken at slightly different angles.

A Bigger Splash, 1967, Tate Gallery, London

The Twenty-Third V.N. Painting, 1992, Collection of the artist

Kahukiwa, Robyn, 1940, New Zealand

Ko Hineteiwaiwa, Ko Hinekorako Ko Rona Whakamau tai, 1993, Museum of New Zealand

Kahn, Wolf, 1927, United States, b. Germany

Kahn is a master of the landscape, and works mostly in pastels, using vivid colors that make his work distinctive and recognizable.

Across from the Gannetts, 1995, Marianne Friedland Gallery, New York City

Kiefer, Anselm, 1945, Germany

Kiefer 's enormous, dark, textured, Expressionist paintings are full of hidden references to the war-torn landscape of Germany's past.

Burning Rods, 1984–1987, St. Louis Art Museum

Grane, 1980–1993, Museum of Modern Art, New York City

March Heath, 1984, Van Abbemuseum, Eindhoven, Netherlands

The Broken Vessel, 1990, St. Louis Art Museum

Kitaj, R. (Ron) B., 1932, England, b. United States

Kitaj, though born in America, lives and works in England. His work is a combination of realism and abstraction.

The Murder of Rosa Luxemburg, 1960, Marlborough Fine Art Ltd., London

If Not, Not, 1975–1976, Scottish National Gallery of Modern Art, Edinburgh

Lawrence, Jacob, 1917–2000, United States

Lawrence's paintings were not large, but they were mighty. He chronicled the movement of Blacks from the American South, their work environments, family life, and sports.

Cabinet Makers, 1946, Hirshhorn Museum and Sculpture Garden, Washington, DC

Dreams #2, 1965, National Museum of American Art, Smithsonian,
 Washington, DC
John Brown, 1941, Detroit Institute of the Arts
Study for the Munich Olympic Games (poster), 1972, Seattle Art
 Museum
The Studio, 1977, Brooklyn Museum, New York

Marden, Brice, 1938, United States
Cold Mountain 6, (Bridge), 1989–1991, Collection of the artist

Mariani, Carlo Maria, 1931
Composition 4—The Expulsion from Eden, 1989, Studio d'Arte
 Cannaviello, Milan

Mathieu, Georges, 1921, France
Capetians Everywhere, 1954, Musée National d'Art Moderne, Centre
 Georges Pompidou, Paris

Neel, Alice, 1900–1984, United States
Alice Neel's trademark was her uncompromising portraits of family, artist
friends, curators, and critics that are remarkable for their psychological
insight. For example, her portrait of Warhol has him seated facing her,
looking frail and with vivid scars showing that were a result of an assassi-
nation attempt.
Andy Warhol, 1970, Whitney Museum of American Art,
 New York City
Last Sickness, 1954, Estate of the Artist
Red Grooms and Mimi Gross, No. 2, 1967, Robert Miller Gallery,
 New York City

Nilsson, Gladys, 1940, United States
The Swimming Hole, 1986, Phyllis Kind Gallery, Chicago/New York

Rego, Paula, 1935, England
The First Mass in Brazil, 1993, Marlborough Fine Art Ltd., London
The Dance, 1988, Tate Gallery, London

Richter, Gerhard, 1932, Germany
Abstraktes Bild, 1993, Marian Goodman Gallery, New York City
Atelier, 1985, Staatliche Museen, Nationalgalerie, Berlin

Ringgold, Faith, 1930, United States

Ringgold's inspiration for her quilts and paintings is her African American heritage. In addition to being a creative artist, she often writes stories directly on her quilts that give insight into her life.

Jo Baker's Birthday, 1994, St. Louis Art Museum

Tar Beach, 1988, Guggenheim Museum, New York City

The Church Picnic, 1987, High Museum, Atlanta

The French Collection, Part I #4 *Sunflowers Quilting Bee at Arles,* 1991, Collection of Oprah Winfrey

Rodrigue, George, 1944, United States

Although Rodrigue's *Blue Dog* is just one of his many artistic works, it has become his trademark, the subject for which he is most recognized.

Angel on My Shoulder, 1999, Collection of the artist

Blue Dog, 1984, Collection of the artist

Oak Tree in the Morning, 1999, Collection of the artist

Rollins, Tim, 1955, United States

K.O.S. Amerika IV, 1986–1987, Saatchi Collection, London

Rothenberg, Susan, 1945, United States

Butterfly, 1986, Saatchi Collection, London

Holding the Floor, 1985, Sperone Westwater Gallery, New York City

Mondrian Dancing, 1985, St. Louis Art Museum

Salle, David, 1952, United States

Salle, a Neo-Expressionist, creates collage-like paintings distinguished by their enormous size.

What Is the Reason for Your Visit to Germany? 1984, Mary Boone Gallery, New York City

Samba, Cheri, 1956, Democratic Republic of the Congo, Africa

Liberation Spectaculaire de Nelson Mandela, 1990, Annina Nosei Gallery, New York City

Scharf, Kenny, 1958, United States

Junkie, 1992, Tony Shafrazi Gallery, New York City

"When I sit down to make a sketch from nature, the first thing I try to do is to forget I have ever seen a picture."
—JOHN CONSTABLE, 1776–1837, English landscape painter

Schnabel, Julian, 1951, United States

Schnabel's work is distinguished by his incorporation of found elements (primarily broken china) into his paintings.

> *The Walk Home,* 1985, Collection of the Eli Broad Family
> Foundation

Shapiro, Miriam, 1923, United States

Shapiro's art reflects her Feminist perspective. She uses cloth and other "feminine" materials such as buttons, lace, and so on, in the complex patterns of her quilt-like collages.

> *Big Ox No. 2,* 1968, La Jolla Museum of Art, La Jolla, California
> *Black Bolero,* 1980, Art Gallery of New South Wales, Sydney,
> Australia
> *I'm Dancin' as Fast as I Can,* 1980s, Collection of the artist
> *Murmur of the Heart,* 1980, Collection of the artist
> *The Azerbajani Fan,* 1980, Collection of the artist

Skoglund, Sandy, 1946, United States

Skoglund is a sculptor/photographer who creates room-sized environments that she then photographs. These installations are humorous, yet carry a social message.

> *Radioactive Cats,* 1980, St. Louis Art Museum

Tansey, Mark, 1949, United States

> *Action Painting II,* 1984, Montreal Museum of Fine Arts

Thiebaud, Wayne, 1920, United States

Thiebaud's subject matter for his paintings varies from a cafeteria array of cakes in all their fake-frosted glory to figures and stark landscapes of San Francisco, where he lives.

> *Apartment Hill,* 1980, Nelson-Atkins Museum of Art, Kansas City,
> Missouri

Bikini, 1964, Nelson-Atkins Museum of Art, Kansas City, Missouri
Various Cakes, 1981, Private collection

Tjapaltjarri, Clifford, 1932–2002, Australia
Possum Man's Dreaming, 1992, Corbally Stourton Contemporary Art, London

Wyeth, Andrew, 1917, United States
Wyeth could technically be considered a Regionalist because most of his paintings are of friends, neighbors, home, and landscapes in or near Chadds Ford, Pennsylvania. His egg-tempera paintings feature realistic, soft colors and straightforward presentation. His father, N. C. Wyeth, was his first teacher, and several members of his family are artists.
Christina's World, 1948, Museum of Modern Art, New York City
Grape Wine (Willard Snowden), 1966, Metropolitan Museum of Art, New York City
Nick and Jamie, 1963, Museum of Fine Arts, Richmond, Virginia
Dodges Ridge, 1947, National Gallery of American Art, Washington, DC

Yu Youhan, 1943, China
Mao and Blonde Girl Analysed, 1992, Marlborough Fine Art Ltd., London

"When you first commence painting everything is a muddle. Even the commonest colors seem to have the devil in them."
—THOMAS EAKINS, 1844–1916, American realist painter, teacher

CHAPTER 9

Sculpture

"A good statue can be rolled down hill without damage."
—MICHELANGELO (BUONARROTI), 1475–1564,
Italian Renaissance sculptor

SCULPTURE TERMS

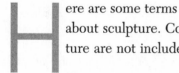ere are some terms you are likely to see or hear in books or discussions about sculpture. Commonplace terms describing contemporary sculpture are not included in the list.

Academic sculptors. Sculptors who interpret forms in the classical tradition—for example, depicting the human form in as life-like a manner as possible.

Armature. A base made of wire, iron, cardboard, or sticks for supporting the sculptural material such as clay, papier–mâché, or mixed media.

Assemblage. A sculpture created of related or unrelated materials, such as wood, metal, and glass.

Bas-relief. Also called low-relief. A sculpture in which the figures project slightly from the background.

Carrara. A quarry in Italy that is a source of fine marble, even as it was in Michelangelo's time.

Carving. Removing material from a surface, such as wood, stone, or plaster, to create a sculptural form.

Casting. Pouring liquid, such as molten metal, plaster, polyester resin, or clay, into a mold.

Form. A three-dimensional shape, such as the human form or an abstract form.

Found materials. Materials that were developed for some specific purpose but have been discarded and adapted by the sculptor for another use (such as auto-part sculpture).

Hardwood. The wood that comes from deciduous trees, such as maple, walnut, ash.

Maquette. A small preliminary model for a sculpture; a prototype.

Modeling. The forming of a (usually) realistic sculpture using clay or wax.

Modeling stand. A revolving chest- or eye-level stand for supporting clay while modeling.

Monumental. A very large sculpture, or a monument to someone.

Moulage. A rubberized material used on the face, hands, or a clay model to make a reusable mold for plaster.

Negative space. The space that defines a piece of sculpture; lets air into it. In Michelangelo's *David,* for example, the *negative* space surrounds the outside contours of the figure and defines the interior triangles that his legs and arms create.

Patina. The colored surface (sometimes greenish) that is given to a bronze sculpture through the use of chemicals or is acquired over time by weathering.

Polyester casting resin. Liquid material that hardens into a clear substance when its chemical components are mixed and cast into a mold.

Roughing out. Removing the extraneous material from a carving surface prior to refining, such as sawing a form from a block of wood prior to final shaping and polishing.

LOOKING AT SCULPTURE

If you think of sculpture as including only such works as Michelangelo's *David* or Rodin's *Thinker,* it's time to update your definition. New contemporary art museums and sculpture gardens are being built around the world to house "tough art"—stuff that may not be fun to look at, but expresses something that the artist has to say, and that people in turn react to.

Sculpture is an all-encompassing term into which many disparate media are now grouped. It includes traditional sculpture such as carved wood or marble, ceramic sculpture, or cast bronze, as well as sculptures that do not neatly fall into a particular category. Contemporary sculptors use such "media" as photography, TV, video, water, motors, sound, light and such tools as time-lapse and movement to create their art. In addition, for environmental artists, a sculpture can be produced by making changes to the landscape. You can view sculptures in many settings—in a museum or art gallery, of course, on city streets, in churches, or even at the beach. No matter where you are viewing sculptures, and whether you are seeking out the experience or are just an accidental spectator, the tips in the following list will add depth to your understanding and appreciation of what you see.

GENERAL SUGGESTIONS

✔ To increase your understanding of sculpture, visit museums, look at art books, and find public sculpture in your town or in cities you visit.

✔ Look at a sculpture from as many angles as you can—it will look completely different from each direction. Figural sculpture in particular may be as beautiful from the back as from the front.

✔ Consider whether a sculpture evokes a particular emotion such as joy, sadness, amusement, amazement, or revulsion.

✔ When possible, make a second or even third visit to view the sculpture. It's likely that you will see and interpret something different as you view the sculpture over a period of time.

✔ Read whatever informational material is provided—a plaque or a brochure—to find out what medium was used to create a sculpture, when it was created, and who the artist is.

✔ Don't just look at what you like. Take time to look at artwork that doesn't appeal to you. Try to understand what it might mean.

✔ Think about your reaction to a particular work or collection and try to know why you react to it the way you do—regardless of whether your reaction is positive or negative.

✔ Notice the *shape*. Does it incorporate any geometric forms? Is it organic (open to interpretation as to whether the subject is human, animal, or plant life)?

✔ Does it appear to *balance* (visually and literally)? Even if it is an environmental work, the use of space, light, texture, repetition, and balance are important.

✔ Look at the use of *space* within, through, and surrounding the sculpture. This *negative space* could be perceived as important as the sculpture itself.

✔ Is there a *focal point* or *emphasis*? Is part of the surface shinier or more complex than the rest? Or is every part of the sculpture as important as every other part?

✔ Did the sculptor *exaggerate* some aspect? For example, Michelangelo's *David* has massive hands, and the ancient statue of the Emperor Constantine has enormous, staring eyes (perhaps considered in that era as the mirror to his soul). *Distortion* might exist because of the original plan for the sculpture's placement (high on a building, looking down, for example).

✔ What is the *texture*? Is it smooth, rough, or a combination?

✔ Do you see the use of geometry? The human form is full of geometric triangles—such as legs spread wide, a hand placed on a hip, or a hand on the head.

SUGGESTIONS FOR VIEWING CONTEMPORARY SCULPTURE

✔ Contemporary sculpture doesn't seem to fit any mold. Ask yourself what a particular artist did that is different or unique.

✔ Does it appeal to more than one of your senses? Much contemporary sculpture incorporates sound, movement, light, texture (and frequently uses several sensations at once).

✔ Is it mechanical? Is part of it recorded? Photographed? Filmed? Does it use laser beams?

✔ Do you think of it as "factory-made" because of the materials or sheer size?

✔ If it is an environmental work and is large enough to enter, do so by all means so you can not just see it, but experience it as well.

✔ Do you think the work is intended to be humorous?

✔ Where is the focal point in this sculpture? Is there one area where the sculptor seemed to direct your attention through making it more complex?

FAMOUS SCULPTURES

Everyone has heard of the *Venus de Milo, The Pietà,* and *The Great Sphinx.* In this list you'll find a few dozen more sculptures that every art lover should be familiar with. These are among the hundreds of famous sculptures throughout the world, and are selected because they are representative of certain time periods in the history of the art. The works are grouped by country of origin. Dates and artists' names are given (if known), along with the museum or other location where the sculpture is housed. For some, no museum or gallery is named because the sculpture remains on its original site. In such cases, only the name of the town (or country) is provided. The Sphinx in Giza, Egypt, is one example.

AFRICA

Head of Queen Olokun, Ife, c. A.D. 11th–15th century, British Museum, London

Head of the King of Ife, 13th century, British Museum, London

Leopard, Benin, 16th–17th century, British Museum, London

Portrait of a Yoruba of Ancient Ife, c. 15th century, British Museum, London

Princess, Benin, c. A.D. 14th–16th century, Nigeria, British Museum, London

ANCIENT NEAR EAST

Assyrian Human-Headed Winged Lion, 883–859 B.C., Metropolitan Museum, New York City

Billy Goat and Tree, Ur, c. 2600 B.C., University Museum, Philadelphia

Darius and Xerxes Giving Audience, c. 490 B.C., Treasury, Persepolis, Iran
Gold Rhyton (cup), 5th–3rd century B.C., Archaeological Museum, Tehran
Gudea, King of Lagash, 2141–2122 B.C., British Museum, London
Head of Gudea, 2150 B.C., Neo-Sumerian, Museum of Fine Arts, Boston
Lion Gate, 1400 B.C., Boghazkoy, Turkey
Stele of Hammurabi, c. 1760 B.C., Louvre, Paris

AUSTRIA

Venus of Willendorf, c. 25,000–20,000 B.C., Museum of Natural History,
Vienna

BELGIUM

Baptismal Font, 1107–1118, René de Huy, St. Barthlemy Church, Liège,
Belgium

CHINA

Bactrian Camel with Packsaddle, c. A.D. 700–755, Nelson-Atkins Museum
of Art, Kansas City, Missouri
Buddha, A.D. 386–535, Louvre, Paris
Divine Winged Animal, A.D. 220–420, Hebei Research Institute of
Cultural Relics
Elephant, c. 1122–249 B.C., Freer Gallery of Art, Washington, DC
Four Ladies of the Court Playing Polo, A.D. 650–700, Nelson-Atkins
Museum of Art, Kansas City, Missouri
Musicians, A.D. 618–906, T'ang Dynasty, Rietberg Museum, Zurich
Stone Mythical Creatures (18 pairs), 1368–1644, Ming tombs, near
Beijing
Tomb of Emperor Qin Shi Huangdi, c. 221–207 B.C., *effigies* (men and
horses), Qin Dynasty, Xian
Tomb Figure of a Horse, A.D. 618–906, Art Institute of Chicago

COLOMBIA

Man on Horseback, 1984, Fernando Botero, Nassau County Museum of
Fine Art, Roslyn Harbor, New York

"Simplicity is not a goal, but one arrives at simplicity in spite of oneself, as one approaches the real meaning of things."

—CONSTANTIN BRANCUSI, 1876–1957, Romanian sculptor

EGYPT

Chefren, c. 2530 B.C., Egyptian Museum, Cairo

Colossal Statues of Ramesses II, 1275 B.C., Abu Simbel

Colossi of Memnon, 1411–1375 B.C., Luxor

Gold Coffin Cover of Tutankhamen, c. 1340 B.C., Egyptian Museum, Cairo

Hippopotamus, 20th–18th century B.C., Cairo Museum

Mycerinus and Queen, c. 2470 B.C., Museum of Fine Arts, Boston

Narmer's Palette, c. 3000 B.C., Egyptian Museum, Cairo

Nefertiti, c. 1375–1357 B.C., Dahlem Museum, Berlin

Prince Rahotep and His Wife, Nofret, c. 2580 B.C., Egyptian Museum, Cairo

Rosetta Stone, 196 B.C., British Museum, London

Seated Scribe, c. 2400 B.C., Louvre, Paris

The Great Sphinx, c. 2500 B.C., Giza

ENGLAND

Cornwall Slate Line, 1990, Richard Long, installation at Tate Gallery, London

Family Group, 1947, Henry Moore, The British Council, London

Head (Elegy), 1952, Barbara Hepworth, University of Nebraska Art Gallery, Lincoln

Internal and External Forms, 1953–1954, Henry Moore, Albright-Knox Art Gallery, Buffalo, New York

Pendour, 1947, Barbara Hepworth, Hirshhorn Museum and Sculpture Garden, Washington, DC

The Physical Impossibility of Death in the Mind of Someone Living, 1991, Damien Hirst, Saatchi Collection, London

FRANCE

Bison, c. 15,000–10,000 B.C., Les Eyzies
Venus of Laussel, 25,000–20,000 B.C., Dordogne

French Romanesque Sculpture

Four Figures, c. 1150, Chartres Cathedral

Northern Renaissance Sculpture

Portal of the Chartreuse de Champmol, 1391–1397, Claus Sluter, Dijon
Virgin and Child, 14th century, artist unknown, Victoria and Albert
  Museum, London
Well of Moses, 1395–1403, Claus Sluter, Dijon

French Neo-Classical Sculpture

George Washington, 1788–1792, Jean Antoine Houdon, State Capitol,
  Richmond, Virginia
Thomas Jefferson, 1785, Jean Antoine Houdon, New York Historical
  Society, New York City
La Marseillaise, 1833–1836, François Rude, Arc de Triomphe, Paris

French "Impressionist" Sculpture

Be in Love, You Will Be Happy, 1901, Paul Gauguin, Museum of Fine
  Arts, Boston
Burghers of Calais, 1884–1886, Auguste Rodin, Hirschhorn Museum and
  Sculpture Garden, Washington, DC
Little Dancer of Fourteen Years, 1840–1845, Edgar Dégas, St. Louis Art
  Museum
The Gates of Hell, 1840–1845, Auguste Rodin, Musée Rodin, Paris

French Modern Sculpture

Back I, 1909, *Back II,* 1913, *Back III,* 1916–1917, *Back IV,* 1930, Henri
  Matisse, Hirshhorn Museum and Sculpture Garden, Washington, DC
Bell and Navels, 1931, Jean Arp, Museum of Modern Art, New York City

Bottle Rack ("ready-made"—Duchamp purchased the bottle rack and
  signed it, thereby designating it as art—a Dada concept), 1914, Marcel
  Duchamp, Galeria Schwarz, Milan
Cock, c. 1932, Pablo Picasso, Tate Gallery, London
Danseuse, 1913, Jacques Lipchitz, Musée d'Arte Modern, Paris
Head #2, 1916, Naum Gabo, Tate Gallery, London
Jeanette III, 1910–1913, Henri Matisse, Museum of Modern Art,
  New York City
La Riante Contre, Théatres de Memoirs, 1975–1978, Jean Dubuffet,
  Collection of Arne and Milly Glimcher, New York City
La Serpentine, 1909, Henri Matisse, Hirshhorn Museum and Sculpture
  Garden, Washington, DC, and Museum of Modern Art, New York City
Long Term Parking, 1975–1982, Arman, Fondation Cartier, Jouy-en-Josas,
  France

GERMANY

Pietà, early 14th century, Provinzial Museum, Bonn
The Gero Crucifix, c. 975–1000, Cologne Cathedral
Uta and Ekkehard of Naumburg, c. 1250–1260, Naumburg Master,
  Naumburg Cathedral

German Contemporary Sculpture

The Turtle Sighing Tree, 1994, Rebecca Horn, Marian Goodman Gallery,
  New York City

GREECE OR MYCENAE

"Agamemnon" Gold Mask, c. 1500 B.C., National Museum, Athens
Alexander the Great, 2nd century B.C., Acropolis Museum, Athens
Calf Bearer, c. 570 B.C., Acropolis Museum, Athens
Caryatid Figures, 421–409 B.C., Acropolis Museum, Athens
Charioteer of Delphi, c. 470 B.C., Delphi
Cyclades Statuettes, c. 3000 B.C., National Museum, Athens
Cycladic Figure of a Seated Man Playing a Harp, 2400–2200 B.C.,
  National Museum, Athens

GREECE OR MYCENAE *(continued)*

Discus Thrower (Discobolus), c. 450 B.C., Myron, (Roman Copy) National
Museum, Rome

Dying Gaul, c. 230–220 B.C., Capitoline Museum, Rome

Dying Warrior, c. 490 B.C., Staatliche Museum, Munich

Elgin Marbles (Parthenon sculptures), Phidias, c. 438–432 B.C., British
Museum, London

Four Horses, c. 330 B.C., attributed to Praxiteles, Church of San Marco,
Venice

Hera of Samos, c. 565 B.C., Louvre, Paris

Kore from Chios, c. 520 B.C., Acropolis Museum, Athens

Kouros of Sounion, c. 600 B.C., National Archaeological Museum, Athens

Kritios Boy, c. 480 B.C., Acropolis, Athens

Lion Gate, c. 1250 B.C., Mycenae, Greece

Medusa, c. 600–580 B.C., Archaeological Museum, Corfu

Nike of Samothrace (Winged Victory), c. 200 B.C., Louvre, Paris

Pergamon Altar of Zeus, 180 B.C., (stone temple façade), Berlin

Poseidon, c. 460–450 B.C., National Museum, Athens

Snake Goddess, c. 1600 B.C., Museum, Heraklion, Crete

Spear Bearer, c. 450–440 B.C., Polykleitos, National Museum, Naples

Stele from Sounion, 460 B.C., National Museum of Athens

The Rampin Head, c. 560 B.C., Louvre, Paris

Three Goddesses, c. 438–432 B.C., British Museum, London

Vaphio Cups, c. 1500 B.C., National Museum, Athens

Venus de Milo, c. 150 B.C., Louvre, Paris

INDIA

The Descent of the River Ganges from Heaven,
10ᵗʰ century, Mamallapuram

INDONESIA

Prajnaparamita (Goddess of transcendental wisdom),
c. 1300, Museum Nasional, Jakarta

ITALY

Etruscan Sculpture

Apollo Belvedere, 1st century B.C., Apollonius of Athens, Vatican Museum, Rome

Apollo of Veii, c. 515–490 B.C., Villa Giulia, Rome

Boy Removing a Thorn, c. 200 B.C.–A.D. 27, Capitoline Museum, Rome

Bronze Boxer, 1st century B.C., National Museum, Rome

Sarcophagus from Ceveteri, c. 520 B.C., Villa Giulia, Rome

She-Wolf, c. 500–480 B.C., Capitoline Museum, Rome

Early Italian Sculpture

Ara Pacis Augustae (Altar of Augustan Peace), 13–9 B.C., Rome

Augustus of Prima Porta, c. 20 B.C., Vatican Museums, Rome

Constantine the Great (bust), A.D. 325–326, Palazzo dei Conservatori, Rome

Equestrian Statue of Marcus Aurelius, A.D. 161–180, Piazza del Campidoglio, Rome

Ivory Panel with Archangel, c. 5th century A.D., British Museum, London

Laocoon, 1st century B.C., Vatican Museums, Rome

Philippus the Arab, c. A.D. 244–249, Vatican Museums, Rome

Portrait of a Lady, c. A.D. 90, Capitoline Museum, Rome

Portrait of Aulus Metellus (the Etruscan Orator), c. 80 B.C., Archaeological Museum, Florence

Italian Romanesque Sculpture

Crucifixion (nave fresco), c. 1087, Sant' Angelo Church in Foris, near Capua

Italian Renaissance Sculpture

David, c. 1430–1432, Donatello, Bargello, Florence

David, 1501–1504, Michelangelo, Galleria dell'Accademia, Florence

David, 1476, Andrea del Verrocchio, Bargello, Florence

Equestrian Monument of Bartolomeo Colleoni, c. 1483–1488, Andrea del Verrocchio, Venice

Italian Renaissance Sculpture (continued)

Gates of Paradise, c. 1435, Lorenzo Ghiberti, Baptistery, Florence

Gattemelata (Equestrian Statue of Erasmo da Narni), c. 1445–1450, Donatello, Padua

Hercules and Antaeus, c. 1475, Antonio Pollaiuolo, Museo Nazionale, Florence

Madonna and Child, c. 1455–1460, Luca della Robbia, Florence

Moses, c. 1513–1515, Michelangelo, St. Peter in Chains Church, Rome

Pietà, Michelangelo, 1499–1500, St. Peter's, Vatican, Rome

Saltcellar of Francis I, 1539–1543, Benvenuto Cellini, Kunsthistorisches Museum, Vienna

Tomb of Lorenzo and Giuliano de Medici, 1524–1534, Michelangelo, Florence

Italian Baroque Sculpture

Apollo and Daphne, 1622–1624, Gianlorenzo Bernini, Galleria Borghese, Rome

David, 1623, Gianlorenzo Bernini, Galleria Borghese, Rome

Ecstasy of Saint Theresa, 1645–1652, Gianlorenzo Bernini, Sta. Maria della Vittoria, Rome

Rape of Proserpina, 1621–1622, Gianlorenzo Bernini, Galleria Borghese, Rome

Italian Neo-Classical Sculpture

Pauline Borghese as Venus, 1788–1792, Antonio Canova, Borghese
Gallery, Rome

The Three Graces, 1813, Antonio Canova, Hermitage, St. Petersburg,
Russia

Italian Modern Sculpture

Caught Hand, 1932, Alberto Giacometti, The Alberto Giacometti
Foundation, Kunsthaus, Zurich

Development of a Bottle in Space, 1912, Umberto Boccioni, Collection of
Harry L. Winston, New York City

Head, c. 1913, Amedeo Modigliani, The Tate Gallery, London

Horseman, 1947, Marino Marini, Tate Gallery, London

Little Horse and Rider, 1949, Marino Marini, Hirshhorn Museum and
Sculpture Garden, Washington, DC

Tall Figure, 1947, Alberto Giacometti, Hirshhorn Museum and Sculpture
Garden, Washington, DC

JAPAN

Amida Buddha, c. 1053, Jocho, Byodo-in, near Kyoto

Haniwa (figure), A.D. 6th century, Tokyo National Museum

Kuya Preaching, c. 1207, Kosho, Rokuhara Mitsu-ji, Kyoto

MEXICO

Chac Mool, the Rain Spirit, 948–1697, Museo Nacional de Antropologia,
Mexico City

Colima Dog, c. 500 B.C.–A.D. 1521, Museo Nacional de Antropologia,
Mexico City

Colossal Head (Olmec), c. 900–500 B.C., La Venta Park, Tabasco

Colossal Head (Olmec), c. 800 B.C., Museo de Antropologia, Jalapa

Colossi at Tula, 12th–13th centuries, Toltec, Tula, near Mexico City

Mask of Green Serpentine, c. 800–1200, Toltec, National Gallery of Art,
Washington, DC

Rock Crystal Carved Skull, c. 1324–1521, Aztec, British Museum, London

"The Human Body is the mirror of the soul, and it is from this fact that it derives its greatest beauty."
—AUGUSTE RODIN, 1840–1917, French sculptor

NORWAY

Animal Head from the Oseberg ship-burial, c. A.D. 825, University of Antiquities, Oslo

Frogner Park sculptures, c. 1900–1940, Gustave Viegland, Oslo

POLYNESIA

Stone images, 17th century or earlier, Easter Island

ROMANIA

Modern Sculpture

Bird, 1912, Constantin Brancusi, Philadelphia Museum of Art

Mlle. Pogany, 1913, Constantin Brancusi, Museum of Modern Art, New York City

Sleeping Muse, 1910, Constantin Brancusi, Musée National d'Art Moderne, Paris

Torso of a Young Man, 1925, Constantin Brancusi, Hirshhorn Museum and Sculpture Garden, Washington, DC

RUSSIA

Construction in an Egg, 1948, Antoine Pevsner, Albright-Knox Art Gallery, Buffalo, New York

Construction Suspended in Space, 1952, Naum Gabo, Baltimore Museum of Art

Head of a Woman, 1916–1917, Naum Gabo, Museum of Modern Art, New York City

Woman Combing Her Hair, 1915, Alexander Archipenko, Museum of Modern Art, New York City

SPAIN

Head of Fernande Olivier, 1909, Pablo Picasso, Hirschhorn Museum and
Sculpture Garden, Washington, DC

Portal of Gloria, 1188, Master Mateus, Santiago de Compostela

Venus de Milo with Drawers, 1936, Salvador Dali, Museum Boymans-van
Beuningen, Rotterdam

SWITZERLAND

Endless Loop I, 1947–1949, Max Bill, Hirshhorn Museum and Sculpture
Garden, Washington, DC

Homage to New York, 1960, Jean Tinguely, Museum of Modern Art,
New York City

Horse, 1914, Raymond Duchamp-Villon, Art Institute of Chicago

The Table, 1932, Alberto Giacometti, Musée National d'Art Moderne,
Paris

UNITED STATES

Colonial Sculpture

Grasshopper Weathervane, 1749, Shem Drowne, Faneuil Hall, Boston

Gravestone of John Foster, 1681, unknown artist, Dorchester,
Massachusetts

Indian Weathervane, 1716, Shem Drowne, Province House, Boston

Little Admiral, c. 1750, unknown sculptor (possibly Shem Drowne), Old
State House, Boston

Sculpture of the Revolutionary Period

Agriculture, Liberty, and Plenty, 1791, John and Simeon Skillin, Jr., Yale
University Art Gallery, New Haven, Connecticut

Andrew Jackson, 1834, John Frazee, Art Museum, Princeton University,
Princeton, New Jersey

Benjamin Franklin, 1778, Jean-Antoine Houdon, St. Louis Art Museum

Benjamin Franklin, 1785–1790, attributed to William Rush, Historical
Society of Wilmington, Delaware

Sculpture of the Revolutionary Period (continued)

Benjamin Franklin and *George Washington* (wax busts), c. 1725, Patience
Lovell Wright, Maryland Historical Society, Baltimore

Governor John Winthrop, 1798, Samuel McIntire, American Antiquarian
Society, Worcester, Massachusetts

Hope, c. 1790, attributed to John and Simeon Skillin, Jr. Henry Francis du
Pont Winterthur Museum, Winterthur, Delaware

Sacred Cod, 1784, John Welch, Boston State House

Thomas Jefferson, 1785, J. A. Houdon, New York Historical Society, New
York City

Sculpture of the Period of U.S. Expansion

Andrew Jackson, 1835, Hiram Powers, Metropolitan Museum of Art,
New York City

Daniel Webster, 1858, Hiram Powers, State House, Boston

George Washington, 1814, William Rush, Philadelphia Museum of Art

George Washington, 1832–1841, Horatio Greenough, Smithsonian
Institution, Washington, DC

John Trumbull, 1834, Robert Ball Hughes, Yale University Art Gallery,
New Haven, Connecticut

Schuylkill Freed, c. 1828, William Rush, Philadelphia Museum of Art

The Greek Slave, 1843, Hiram Powers, Yale University Art Gallery,
New Haven, Connecticut

Washington Monument, 1814–1842, Robert Mills, Baltimore

Water Nymph and Bittern, c. 1828, William Rush, Philadelphia Museum
of Art

Victorian Sculpture

Bacchante and Infant Faun, 1894, Frederick MacMonnies, Philadelphia
Museum of Art

Daphne, 1854, Harriet Hosmer, Washington University Gallery of Art,
St. Louis

George Washington, 1883, John Quincy Adams Ward, Federal Hall
National Memorial, New York City

Minute Man, 1889, Daniel Chester French, Concord, Massachusetts

Nydia, the Blind Girl of Pompeii, 1895, Randolph Rogers, Pennsylvania
Academy of the Fine Arts, Philadelphia

Roma, 1869, Anne Whitney, Wellesley College Museum, Wellesley,
Massachusetts

The White Captive, 1859, Erastus Dow Palmer, Metropolitan Museum of
Art, New York City

Zenobia, 1858, Harriet Hosmer, Metropolitan Museum of Art,
New York City

Modern Sculpture

Dancer and Gazelles, 1916, Paul Manship, Corcoran Gallery of Art,
Washington, DC

End of the Trail, 1915, James Earle Fraser, Brookgreen Gardens,
South Carolina

Hostess, 1918, Elie Nadelman, Hirshhorn Museum and Sculpture Garden,
Washington, DC

In Advance of a Broken Arm, 1915, Marcel Duchamp, Yale University Art
Gallery, New Haven, Connecticut

Lincoln, 1908, John Gutzon Borglum, Washington, DC

Lincoln, 1922, Daniel Chester French, Lincoln Memorial, Washington, DC

Man in the Open Air, 1915, Elie Nadelman, Museum of Modern Art,
New York City

Young Lincoln, 1927, Lorado Taft, Urbana, Illinois

Sculpture Between the Wars

Cloud, 1939, José de Creeft, Whitney Museum of American Art,
New York City

Floating Figure, 1935, Gaston Lachaise, Museum of Modern Art,
New York City

Gertrude Stein, 1920, Jo Davidson, Whitney Museum of American Art,
New York City

Handlebar Riders, 1935, Chaim Gross, Museum of Modern Art,
New York City

Indian Hunter with Dog, 1926, Paul Manship, Metropolitan Museum of
Art, New York City

Sculpture Between the Wars (continued)

Kneeling Figure, 1935, Robert Laurent, Whitney Museum of American Art, New York City

Lobster Trap and Fish Tails, 1939, Alexander Calder, Museum of Modern Art, New York City

Mid-20th-Century Sculpture

An American Tribute to the British People, 1960–1965, Louise Nevelson, Tate Gallery, London

One and Others, 1955, Louise Bourgeois, Whitney Museum of American Art, New York City

Sacrifice II, 1948, Jacques Lipchitz, Whitney Museum of American Art, New York City

Pop Art Sculpture

Ale Cans, 1960, Jasper Johns, Collection of Peter Ludwig, New York City

Cinema, 1963, George Segal, Albright-Knox Gallery, Buffalo, New York

Clothespin, 1976, Claes Oldenburg, Center Square Plaza, Philadelphia

Corridor, 1967, Lucas Samaras, Los Angeles County Museum of Art

Cubi XIX, 1964, David Smith, Tate Gallery, London

Figure, 1926–1930, Jacques Lipchitz, Museum of Modern Art, New York City

Fur-Lined Teacup, 1936, Meret Oppenheim, Museum of Modern Art, New York City

Pony, 1959, Ellsworth Kelly, Dayton's Gallery 12, Minneapolis

Soft Giant Drum Set, 1967, Claes Oldenburg, Collection of Kimiko and John G. Powers, New York City

Target with Four Faces, 1955, Jasper Johns, Museum of Modern Art, New York City

Three Way Plug, Scale A, Prototype in Blue, 1971, Claes Oldenburg, Des Moines Art Center, Iowa

Two Cheeseburgers with Everything, 1962, Claes Oldenburg, Museum of Modern Art, New York City

Expressionist Sculpture

Bird E-Square Bird, 1958–1966, Isamu Noguchi, Collection of
Mr. Carl E. Solway, Cincinnati

Camel VII, Camel VI, Camel VIII, 1968–1969, Nancy Graves,
National Gallery of Canada, Ottawa

Depression Bread Line, 1991, George Segal, Sidney Janis
Gallery, New York City

The Dinner Party, 1974–1979, Judy Chicago, Collection of the
artist

Hammering Men, 1984, Jonathan Borofsky, shown at Moderna
Museet, Stockholm

Labyrinth, 1974, Robert Morris, Institute of Contemporary Art,
Philadelphia

Medici Slot Machine, 1942, Joseph Cornell, Solomon R. Guggenheim
Museum, New York City

The Nest, 1994, Louise Bourgeois (b. France), Robert Miller Gallery,
New York City

Object to Be Destroyed, 1958, Man Ray, (metronome and photograph),
Collection of Morton G. Neumann, Chicago

Praise for Elohim Adonai, 1966, Mark De Suvero, St. Louis Art Museum

Reclining Figure: Angles, 1979, Henry Moore, Collection of Patsy and
Raymond Nasher

The Reign of Narcissism, 1988–1989, Barbara Bloom, Collection of the
Museum of Contemporary Art, Los Angeles

Rush Hour, 1983, George Segal, Sidney Janis Gallery, New York City

Sitting Bull, 1959, Peter Voulkos, Santa Barbara Museum of Art, Santa
Barbara, California

The State Hospital, 1966, Edward Kienholz, Moderna Museet, Stockholm

Times Square Sky, 1962, Chryssa, Walker Art Center, Minneapolis

Torso, 1930, Gaston Lachaise (b. France), Whitney Museum of American
Art, New York City

Untitled, 1969, Donald Judd, Hirshhorn Museum and Sculpture Garden,
Washington, DC

Venturi Window, 1992, Dale Chihuly, Installation (blown glass forms) at
the Seattle Art Museum

The Wait, 1964–1965, Edward Kienholz, Whitney Museum of American
Art, New York City

Environmental Art

> *The City, Complex One,* 1972–1974, Michael Heizer, Central Eastern
> Nevada
> *Double Negative,* 1969–1971, Michael Heizer, Virgin River Mesa, Nevada
> *Hart Plaza,* 1980, Isamu Noguchi, Detroit
> *Isla de Umunnum, The Mound,* 1986–1990, Heather McGill and John
> Roloff, Estuarine Research Reserve, California
> *Mill Creek Canyon Earthworks,* 1982, Herbert Bayer, Kent, Washington
> *Revival Field,* 1990–present, Mel Chin, St. Paul, Minnesota
> *Spiral Jetty,* 1970, Robert Smithson, Great Salt Lake, Utah

Sculpture with Light

> *Head with Blue Shadow,* 1965, Roy Lichtenstein, Collection of Patsy and
> Raymond Nasher
> *Ohayo,* 1986, Judy Pfaff, Holly Solomon Gallery and Max Protetch
> Gallery, New York City
> *Pergusa,* 1981, Frank Stella, Collection of Holly Hunt Thackberry,
> Winnetka, Illinois
> *Pink and Gold,* 1968, Dan Flavin, Museum of Contemporary Art, Chicago
> *The Survival Series, (Protect Me From What I Want),* 1986, Jennie
> Holzer, Caesar's Palace, Las Vegas

Post-Modern Sculpture

> *Cell (Eyes and Mirrors),* 1989–1993, Tate Gallery, London
> *Extravaganza Televisione,* 1984, Kenny Scharf, Tony Shafrazi Gallery,
> New York City
> *Le Defi,* 1992, Solomon R. Guggenheim Museum, New York City
> *Man With a Briefcase,* 1987, Jonathan Borofsky, General Mills,
> Minneapolis
> *Self Portrait with Sculpture,* 1980, John De Andrea, Collection of Foster
> Goldstrom, San Francisco
> *Women,* 1985, Magdalena Abakanowicz, Xavier Fourcade, Inc.,
> New York City

"What we have is given by God and to teach it to others is to return it to him."

—GIANLORENZO BERNINI, 1598–1680, Italian Baroque sculptor

MASTER SCULPTORS AND A FEW OF THEIR WORKS

There are literally thousands of sculptors whose work has been exhibited at galleries, museums, and other prominent places where it may be viewed and enjoyed by the masses. So, what is the criteria for making it onto this list? Basically, sculptors listed here are those whose work is or has been seen in museums in many different countries. Further, these sculptors' work is usually unique and can be instantly recognized as the work of that particular artist. Finally, artists on this list have also been influential beyond their immediate time and place.

ENGLAND

Caro, Sir Anthony, 1924
> *Early One Morning,* 1962, Tate Gallery, London
> *Midday,* 1960, Museum of Modern Art, New York City
> *Rape of The Sabines,* 1985–1986, Metropolitan Life Building, Seattle
> *TB Cyclamen,* 1990–1991, André Emmerich Gallery, New York City
> *The Caliph's Garden,* 1989–1992, André Emmerich Gallery,
>   New York City

Deacon, Richard, 1949
> *Art for Other People No. 10,* 1984, Private collection, New York City
> *Body of Thought,* 1987–1988, Marian Goodman Gallery,
>   New York City
> *Fish Out of Water,* 1987, Hirshhorn Museum and Sculpture Garden,
>   Washington, DC
> *The Interior Is Always More Difficult,* 1992, Marian Goodman
>   Gallery, New York City

ENGLAND *(continued)*

Epstein, Jacob, 1880–1959
Portrait Bust of Paul Robeson, 1928, York City Art Gallery, York, England
St. Michael and the Devil, 1958, Coventry Cathedral
The Visitation, 1926, Tate Gallery, London

Flanagan, Barry, 1941
Acrobat on Pyramid, 2000, Waddington Galleries, London
Six Foot Leaping Hare on Steel Pyramid, 1990, Grant Park, Chicago
The Drummer, 1989–1990, Beverly Gardens Park, Beverly Hills, California

Goldsworthy, Andy, 1956
Hand to Earth, 1970, The Henry Moore Centre for the Study of Sculpture, Leeds, England
Herd of Arches, 1994, Hat Hill Copse, near Glasgow, Scotland
A Line and a Wall, 2000, Storm King Art Center, New York State
Yellow Elm Leaves Laid Over River Rock, Low Water, Scaur Water, 1991, Dumfriesshire, England

Gormley, Antony, 1950
A Case for an Angel II, 1990, Contemporary Sculpture Centre, Tokyo

Hepworth, Barbara, 1903–1975
Assemblage of Sea Forms, 1972, Norton Simon Museum of Art, Los Angeles
Doves, 1927, Manchester City Art Gallery, England
Pelagos, 1946, Tate Gallery, London
Single Form (Memorial to Dag Hammarskjöld), 1962–1963, United Nations Building, New York City

Moore, Henry, 1898–1986
Draped Seated Woman, 1957–1958, Hebrew University, Jerusalem
Fallen Warrior, 1956–1957, Hirschhorn Museum and Sculpture Garden, Washington, DC
Reclining Figure, 1929, Leeds City Art Galleries, England

Reclining Mother and Child, 1960–1961, Walker Art Center, Minneapolis

Recumbent Figure, 1938, Tate Gallery, London

The King and Queen, 1952–1953, Hirschhorn Museum and Sculpture Garden, Washington, DC

Whiteread, Rachel 1963

Inverted Plinth, 2000–2001, design for display at Trafalgar Square, London

Untitled (Pair), 1999, New Art Centre Sculpture Park and Gallery, Wiltshire, England

Untitled (Slab II), 1991, Van Abbe Museum, Eindhoven, Netherlands

FRANCE

Bourdelle, Emile-Antoine, 1861–1929

Adam, 1889, Museum of Fine Arts, Houston

Le Fruit, 1902–1911, Musée Bourdelle, Paris

Monument to Rodin, 1909, Los Angeles County Museum of Art Sculpture Garden

The Tragic Mask (Beethoven), 1908, Hermitage, St. Petersburg, Russia

Dégas, Edgar, 1834–1917

Dressed Ballerina, 1920 (Although Dégas created the ballerina in wax prior to his death, like all his bronzes, it was cast posthumously.) Metropolitan Museum of Art, New York City

Prancing Horse, 1865–1881, Hirschhorn Museum and Sculpture Garden, Washington, DC

The Masseuse, c. 1896–1911, Hirschhorn Museum and Sculpture Garden, Washington, DC

Laurens, Henri, 1885–1954

La Baigneuse, 1947, Musée d'Arte Moderne, Paris

Maillol, Aristide, 1861–1944

Summer, 1910, National Gallery of Art, Washington, DC

The River, 1939–1943, Norton Simon Museum of Art, Los Angeles

Venus With the Necklace, 1928–1929, St. Louis Art Museum

FRANCE *(continued)*

Matisse, Henri, 1869–1954

Luxe, Calme et Volupte, 1904–1905, Musée d'Orsay, Paris

Seated Nude, 1925, Art Institute of Chicago

The Back, I–IV, 1909–c. 1929, Hirshhorn Museum and Sculpture Garden, Washington, DC

Rodin, Auguste 1840–1917

Balzac, 1840–1845, Hirschhorn Museum and Sculpture Garden, Washington, DC

Eve, 1881, Musée Rodin, Paris

She Who Was Once the Helmet Maker's Beautiful Wife, 1888, Musée Rodin, Paris

The Three Shades, 1880, Musée Rodin, Paris

The Walking Man, 1877, National Gallery of Art, Washington, DC

Saint Phalle, Niki de 1930–2002

Black Venus, 1969, Whitney Museum of American Art, New York City

Hon en Kathedral, 1955–1966, Moderna Museet, Stockholm

King Kong, 1963–1964, Moderna Museet, Stockholm

Stravinsky Fountain, 1982, Centre Georges Pompidou, Paris

Tarot Garden, begun 1979, near Garavicchio, Tuscany

GERMANY

Kiefer, Anselm, 1945

Breaking of the Vessels, 1990, St. Louis Art Museum

Lehmbruck, Wilhelm, 1881–1919

Bathing Woman, 1914, Montreal Museum of Fine Arts, Canada

Seated Youth, 1917, National Gallery of Art, Washington, DC

ITALY

Bernini, Gianlorenzo, 1598–1680
    Apollo and Daphne, 1622–1625, Borghese Gallery, Rome
    Costanza Buonarelli, c. 1645, Bargello, Florence
    Ecstasy of St. Theresa, 1645–1652, Sta. Maria della Vittoria, Rome
    Fountain of the Four Rivers, 1648–1651, Piazza Navona, Rome
    Rape of Proserpine, 1621–1622, Borghese Gallery, Rome

Boccione, Umberto, 1882–1916
    The City Rises, 1910–1911, Museum of Modern Art, New York City
    Unique Forms of Continuity in Space, 1913, Museum of Modern Art,
      New York City

Donatello, c. 1386–1466
    David, c. 1430–1432, Bargello, Florence
    Mary Magdalene, c. 1454–1455, San Lorenzo Baptistery, Florence
    St. George, c. 1415–1417, Bargello, Florence
    Zuccone, 1423–1425, Campanile, Florence Cathedral

Michelangelo (Buonarroti), 1475–1564
    David, 1501–1504, Galleria dell' Accademia, Florence
    Medici Tombs, 1519–1534, San Lorenzo, Florence
    Moses, c. 1513–1515, Church of St. Peter in Chains, Rome
    Pietà, 1498–1499, St. Peter's, Rome
    The Rebellious Slave, 1513–1516, Louvre, Paris

JAPAN

Funakoshi, Katsura, 1951
    Distant Rain, 1995, Collection of the artist
    The Distance from Here, 1991, Annely Juda Fine Art, London

"There is a right physical size for every idea."
—HENRY MOORE, 1898–1986, English sculptor and graphic artist

ROMANIA

Brancusi, Constantin, 1876–1957

Bird in Space, 1928, Museum of Modern Art, New York City

Mlle. Pogany, 1913, Philadelphia Museum of Art

Mlle. Pogany, 1920, Albright Art Gallery, Buffalo, New York

The Kiss, 1909, Tomb of T. Rachevskaia, Montparnasse Cemetery, Paris

Torso of a Young Man, 1924, Hirschhorn Museum and Sculpture Garden, Washington, DC

SPAIN

Picasso, Pablo, 1881–1973

Baboon and Young, 1951, Museum of Modern Art, New York City

Head of a Woman, 1909, Art Institute of Chicago

Horse, 1967, Art Institute of Chicago

The Goat, 1950, Musée Picasso, Paris

Woman With a Baby Carriage, 1950, Hirshhorn Museum and Sculpture Garden, Washington, DC

SWITZERLAND

Giacometti, Alberto, 1901–1966

Hands Holding the Void, 1934–1935, St. Louis Art Museum

Man Pointing, 1947, Museum of Modern Art, New York City

Tinguely, Jean, 1925–1991

Eureka, 1964, Zurich, Switzerland

Le Cyclop de Jean Tinguely, Milly-la-Foret

M.K. III, 1964, Museum of Fine Arts, Houston

UNITED STATES

Borglum, Gutzon, 1867–1941

Abraham Lincoln Bust, 1908, U.S. Capitol Building, Washington DC

The Aviator, 1919, Charlottesville, Virginia

John Ruskin, 1904, Metropolitan Museum of Art, New York City
(on loan from the Rhode Island School of Design)

Mount Rushmore, 1927–1939, Keystone, South Dakota

Bourgeois, Louise, 1911

Cell II, 1991, Carnegie Museum of Art, Pittsburgh

Femme Voltage, 1951, Solomon R. Guggenheim Museum,
New York City

Mortise, 1950, National Gallery of Art, Washington, DC

Nature Study (Dog), 1984, Whitney Museum of American Art,
New York City

Sleeping Figure, 1950, Museum of Fine Arts, Boston

Spiral Woman, 1951–1952, Miller Gallery, New York City

Butterfield, Deborah, 1949

Horse #6–82, 1982, Dallas Museum of Art

Horse #9 –82, 1982, Collection of Ethan and Sherry Wagner

Punahele (horse), 1993, Edward Thorp Gallery, New York City

Resting Horse, 1977, Whitney Museum of American Art,
New York City

Small Horse, 1977, Private collection

Calder, Alexander, 1898–1976

Circus, 1932, Whitney Museum of American Art, New York City

Flamingo, 1974, Federal Center Plaza, Chicago

Josephine Baker, 1928, Musée d'Arte Moderne, Paris

Lobster Trap and Fish Tails, 1939, Museum of Modern Art,
New York City

Red, Black and Blue, 1967, Dallas-Fort Worth Airport

The Crab (stabile), 1962, Museum of Fine Arts, Houston

Christo (Javacheff), 1935

Package on Wheelbarrow, 1963, Museum of Modern Art,
New York City

Strip-tease (empaquetage), 1963, Private collection

Surrounded Islands, Biscayne Bay (temporary), 1983, Biscayne Bay,
Florida

Wrapped Reichstag (temporary; with Jeanne-Claude de Guillebon
Christo), 1994, project for Berlin

UNITED STATES *(continued)*

Cornell, Joseph, 1903–1972

Isabelle (Dien Bien Phu), 1954, St. Louis Art Museum

Medici Slot Machine, 1942, Solomon R. Guggenheim Museum, New York City

Soap Bubble Set, 1950, Art Institute of Chicago

Space Object Box, 1959, Allan Stone Gallery, New York City

Duchamp, Marcel, 1887–1968, b. France

The Bride Stripped Bare by Her Bachelors, Even (The Large Glass), c. 1920–1923, Philadelphia Museum of Art

Fountain (urinal), 1917, Philadelphia Museum of Art (duplicate; original lost)

Nude Descending a Staircase #2, 1912, Philadelphia Museum of Art

Graves, Nancy, 1940–1995

Fayum, 1982, Knoedler Gallery, New York City

Fought Cight Cockfight, 1984, St. Louis Art Museum

Zaga, 1983, Nelson-Atkins Art Museum, Kansas City, Missouri

Grooms, Red, 1937

City of Chicago, 1967, Art Institute of Chicago

Discount Store, 1970, Collection of Norman Braman

Loft on 26th Street, 1965–1966, Hirshhorn Museum and Sculpture Garden, Washington, DC

Mr. and Mrs. Rembrandt, 1971, Cheekwood Art Museum, Nashville, Tennessee

Ruckus Manhattan: A Sculptural Novel, 1976, Collection of the artist, New York City

Hanson, Duane, 1925–1996

Motorcycle Accident, 1969, Gallery of Contemporary Art, Portland, Oregon

Museum Guard, 1976, Nelson-Atkins Museum of Art, Kansas City, Missouri

Queenie, 1995, Private collection

The Seated Artist, 1972, Collection of Byron and Eileen Cohen,
Mission Hills, Kansas

Tourists, 1970, National Gallery of Modern Art, Edinburgh

Woman with Dog, 1977, Whitney Museum of American Art,
New York City

Hill, Gary, 1951

Black Performance, 2001, performance art

Viewer, 1996, video, Collection of the artist

Wall Piece, 2000, video, Collection of the artist

Holzer, Jenny, 1950

Protect Me from What I Want, 1988, LED display, Picadilly Circus,
London

Johns, Jasper, 1930

Ale Cans, 1960, Collection of Peter Ludwig, New York City

Kienholz, Edward, 1927–1994

Sollie 17, 1979–1980 (with Nancy Kienholz), Private collection

The State Hospital, 1966, Museum of Modern Art, Stockholm

Koons, Jeff, 1955

Michael Jackson and Bubbles, 1988, San Francisco Museum of
Modern Art

Popples, 1998, porcelain, Jeff Koons Productions

Rabbit, 1986, Jeff Koons Productions

Split Rocker, 2000, Avignon, France

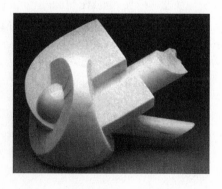

UNITED STATES *(continued)*

Lipchitz, Jacques, 1891–1973

Figure, 1926–1930, Norton Simon Museum of Art, Los Angeles

Man With Guitar, 1916, Museum of Modern Art, New York City

Prometheus Strangling the Vulture, 1944–1953, Walker Art Center, Minneapolis

Still Life With Musical Instruments, 1918, Estate of the Artist

Marisol (Escobar), 1930

The Bicycle Race, 1962–1963, The Harry N. Abrams Family Collection, New York City

Children Sitting on a Bench, 1994, Museo de Arte Contemporaneo, Caracas, Venezuela

The Family, 1962, Museum of Modern Art, New York City

The Generals, 1961–1962, Albright-Knox Art Gallery, Buffalo, New York

John Wayne, 1963, Colorado Springs Fine Arts Center

The Party, 1965–1966, Collection of Mrs. Robert Mayer, Winnetka, Illinois

Nauman, Bruce, 1941

Having Fun/Good Life/Symptoms, 1990, Carnegie Museum of Art, Pittsburgh, Pennsylvania

Nevelson, Louise, 1899–1988, b. Russia

An American Tribute to the British People, 1960–1965, Tate Gallery, London

Black Chord, 1964, Collection of Joel Ehrenkranz

New Continent, 1962, St. Louis Art Museum

Sun Garden, No. 1, 1964, Collection of Mr. and Mrs. Charles M. Diker

Transparent Sculpture VI, 1967–1968, Whitney Museum of American Art, New York City

Oldenburg, Claes, 1929

Giant Hamburger, 1962, Art Gallery of Ontario, Toronto

Giant Ice Bag, 1969–1970, Thomas Segal Gallery, Boston

Soft Pay Telephone, 1963, Collection of William Zierler, New York City

Soft Toilet, 1966, Collection of Mr. and Mrs. Victor W. Ganz,
New York City

Paik, Nam Jun, 1932

Electro-Symbio Phonics for Phoenix, 1992, commissioned by Phoenix,
Arizona (seen in various exhibitions)

King Ramses III, 1991 (seen in various exhibitions)

Leonardo da Vinci, 1991, Reynolda House, Museum of American Art,
Winston-Salem, North Carolina

Mars, 1990 (seen in various exhibitions)

Remington, Frederic, 1861–1909

The Bronco Buster, 1895, St. Louis Art Museum

The Cheyenne, 1901, Denver Art Museum

Coming Through the Rye, 1902, Art Museum, Princeton University,
Princeton, New Jersey

Trooper of the Plains, 1909, National Cowboy Hall of Fame and
Western Heritage Center, Oklahoma City

Saar, Alison, 1956

Strange Fruit, 1995, Baltimore Museum of Art

Travelling Man, 1999, Collection of the artist

Saar, Betye, 1926

Bessie Smith Box, 1974, Collection of Monique Knowlton

Imitation of Life, 1975, Collection of the artist

Indigo Mercy, 1975, Studio Museum in Harlem, New York City

Veil of Tears, 1976, Collection of Mr. and Mrs. Alvin P. Johnson

Segal, George, 1924–2000

Cinema, 1963, Albright-Knox Art Gallery, Buffalo, New York

The Bus Driver, 1962, Museum of Modern Art, New York City

The Dancers, 1971, National Gallery of Art, Washington, DC

The Gas Station, 1963–1964, National Gallery of Canada, Ottawa

Smith, David, 1906–1965

Agricola, 1951, Hirshhorn Museum and Sculpture Garden,
Washington, DC

Cockfight, 1945, St. Louis Art Museum

Cubi I, 1963, Detroit Institute of Fine Arts

UNITED STATES *(continued)*

Cubi XIX, 1964, Tate Gallery, London

Medals for Dishonor, 1937–1940, Hirshhorn Museum and Sculpture
Garden, Washington, DC

Voltri-Bolton, 1962, Museum of Fine Arts, Boston

Zig, 1960, Lincoln Center, New York City

Stella, Frank, 1936

Damascus Gate 1, 1969, Norton Simon Museum of Art, Pasadena,
California

Harran II, 1967, Guggenheim Museum, New York City

FAMOUS SCULPTORS, LISTED BY COUNTRY

Paring down the list of thousands of accomplished sculptors to the select few
who appear here was not an easy feat. However, the sculptors you'll see here
are those who have been the most notable in the art world, and the ones whose
names you are likely to encounter most frequently as you visit museums, galleries, or talk to people "in the know" about art. Artists are listed under the country in which they do most of their work. The years of an artist's birth and death
are given where available. A single date is the artist's year of birth, unless otherwise noted.

BELGIUM

Broodthaers, Marcel, 1924–1976

Bury, Pol, 1922

BRAZIL

Clark, Lygia, 1921–1988

CANADA

Bullock, Angela, 1966

McKenzie, Robert Tait, 1867–1938

Goodwin, Betty, 1923

Stockholder, Jessica, 1959

CHINA

Huang Yong Ping, 1945

DENMARK

Thorwaldsen, Bertel, 1768–1844

ENGLAND

Annesley, David, 1936
Armitage, Kenneth, 1916–2002
Blake, Peter, 1932
Butler, Reg, 1913–1981
Caro, Anthony, 1924
Chadwick, Lynn, 1914
Cox, Steve, 1946
Cragg, Tony, 1949
Deacon, Richard, 1949
Epstein, Jacob, 1880–1959
Flanagan, Barry, 1941
Frink, Elisabeth, 1930–1993
Goldsworthy, Andrew, 1956
Gormley, Antony, 1950
Hatoum, Mona, 1952
Hepworth, Barbara, 1903–1975
Hirst, Damien, 1965
Kapoor, Anish, 1954
King, Phillip, 1934
Long, Richard, 1945
Moore, Henry, 1898–1986
Paolozzi, Eduardo, 1924
Scott, Tim, 1937
Tucker, William, 1935
Whiteread, Rachel, 1963

FRANCE

Arp, Jean, 1887–1966
Baldaccini, César, 1921–1998
Boltanski, Christian, 1944
Bourdelle, Emile-Antoine,
  1861–1929
Brancusi, Constantin, 1876–1957
Dégas, Edgar, 1834–1917
Dubuffet, Jean, 1901–1985
Duchamp-Villon, R., 1876–1918
Ernst, Max, 1891–1976
Gaudier-Breska, Henri,
  1891–1915
Gauguin, Paul, 1848–1903
Guimard, Hector, 1867–1942
Lachaise, Gaston, 1882–1935
Laurens, Henri, 1885–1954
Magritte, René, 1898–1967
Maillol, Aristide, 1861–1944
Matisse, Henri, 1869–1954
Messager, Annette, 1943
Pevsner, Antoine, 1884–1962
Picabia, Francis, 1879–1953
Richier, Germaine, 1904–1953
Rodin, Auguste, 1840–1917
Rude, François, 1784–1855
Saint Phalle, Niki de, 1930–2002

GERMANY

Barlach, Ernst, 1870–1938
Beuys, Joseph, 1921–1986
Bonin, Cosima, 1962
Ernst, Max, 1891–1976

GERMANY *(continued)*

Fritsch, Katharina, 1956

Hildebrand, Adolph von,
1847–1921

Hofer, Candida, 1944

Horn, Rebecca, 1944

Kippenberger, Martin,
1953–1997

Lehmbruck, Wilhelm,
1881–1919

Trockel, Rosemarie, 1952

GREECE

Lysippus, 4th century B.C.

HUNGARY

Moholy-Nagy, Lázló, 1895–1946

ITALY

Bernini, Gianlorenzo, 1598–1680

Boccioni, Umberto, 1882–1916

Canova, Antonio, 1757–1882

Cattelan, Maurizio, 1960

Cellini, Benvenuto, 1500–1591

Donatello, (Donato di Niccolo),
c. 1386–1466

Marini, Marino, 1901–1980

Michelangelo (Buonarroti),
1475–1564

Modigliani, Amedeo, 1884–1920

Pollaiuolo, Antonio,
c. 1429–1498

Rosso, Medardo, 1858–1928

JAPAN

Funakoshi, Katsura, 1951

Shingu, Susumu, 1937

KOREA

Paik, Nam Jun, 1932

LITHUANIA

Lipchitz, Jacques, 1891–1973

MEXICO

Escobedo, Helen, 1934

Orozco, Gabriel, 1962

NORWAY

Vigeland, Gustave, 1869–1943

POLAND

Balka, Miroslaw, 1958

ROMANIA

Brancusi, Constantin, 1876–1957

RUSSIA

Kabakov, Ilya, 1933

Pevsner, Antoine, 1886–1962

Tatlin, Vladimir, 1885–1953

SPAIN

Chillida, Eduardo, 1924–2002

Gonzales, Julio, 1876–1942

Miró, Joan, 1893–1983

Picasso, Pablo, 1881–1973

SWITZERLAND

Armleder, John M., 1948
Arp, Jean, 1887–1966
Balkenhol, Stephan, 1957
Bill, Max, 1908–1995
Fischli, Peter, 1952
Fleury, Silvie, 1961
Giacometti, Alberto, 1901–1966
Oppenheim, Meret, 1913–1985
Rist, Pipilotti, 1962
Tinguely, Jean, 1925–1991
Weiss, David, 1946

UNITED STATES

Adams, Herbert, 1858–1945
Africano, Nicholas, 1948
Akamu, Nina, 1955
Akers, B. Paul, 1825–1861
André, Carl, 1935
Archipenko, Alexander,
    1887–1964
Arneson, Robert, 1930–1993
Artschwager, Richard, 1923
Augur, Hezekiah, 1791–1858
Aycock, Alice, 1946
Baizerman, Saul, 1889–1957
Ball, Thomas, 1819–1911
Barnard, George Grey,
    1863–1938
Barney, Matthew, 1967
Bartholomew, Edward Sheffield,
    1822–1858
Bartlett, Paul Wayland,
    1865–1925
Baskin, Leonard, 1922–2000

UNITED STATES *(continued)*

Beecroft, Vanessa, 1969
Bell, Larry, 1939
Benglis, Lynda, 1941
Bertoia, Harry, 1915–1978
Bickerton, Ashley, 1959
Bitter, Karl, 1867–1915
Bladen, Ronald, 1918–1988
Bloom, Barbara, 1951
Bochner, Mel, 1940
Borglum, Gutzon, 1867–1941
Borglum, Solon H., 1868–1922
Borofsky, Jonathan, 1942
Bourgeois, Louise, 1911
Brenner, Michael, 1885–1969
Brenner, Victor D., 1871–1924
Browere, John H. I., 1790–1834
Brown, Henry Kirke, 1814–1886
Burton, Scott, 1939–1989
Butterfield, Deborah, 1949
Calder, A. Stirling, 1870–1945
Calder, Alexander, 1898–1976
Calder, Alexander Milne,
    1846–1923
Callery, Mary, 1903–1977
Castle, Wendell, 1932
Ceracchi, Giuseppi, 1751–1802
Chamberlain, John, 1927
Chicago, Judy, 1939
Christo (Javacheff), 1935
Christo, Jeanne-Claude de
    Guillebon, 1935
Chryssa, Varda, 1933
Clevenger, Shobal Vail,
    1812–1843

UNITED STATES *(continued)*

Coffee, William John, 1744–
c. 1846

Cogdell, John, 1778–1847

Conner, Bruce, 1933

Cornell, Joseph, 1903–1972

Crawford, Thomas, c. 1813–1857

Creeft, José de, 1884–1982

Dallin, Cyrus, 1861–1944

Davidson, Jo, 1883–1952

de Andrea, John, 1941

De Maria, Walter, 1935

Dexter, Henry, 1806–1876

di Suvero, Mark, 1933

Dodge, Charles J., 1806–1886

Duchamp, Marcel, 1887–1968

Duff, John, 1943

Eberle, Abastenia St. Léger,
1878–1942

Faggi, Alfeo, 1885–1966

Ferber, Herbert, 1906–1991

Fiene, Paul, 1899–1949

Flavin, Dan, 1933–1996

Foley, Margaret, 1820–1877

Frank, Mary, 1933

Fraser, James Earl, 1876–1953

Frazee, John, 1790–1852

French, Daniel Chester,
1850–1931

Frey, Viola, 1933

Gabo, Naum, 1890–1977

Gallo, Frank, 1933

Gilhooly, David, 1943

Gober, Robert, 1954

Goodnough, Robert, 1917

Grafly, Charles, 1862–1929

Graham, Dan, 1942

Graham, Robert, 1938

Graves, Nancy, 1940–1995

Greene, Gertrude, 1911–1956

Greenough, Horatio, 1805–1852

Greenough, Richard, 1819–1904

Grooms, Red, 1937

Gross, Chaim, 1904–1991

Grosvenor, Robert, 1937

Hamilton, Ann, 1956

Hampton, James, 1909–1964

Hanson, Duane, 1925–1996

Hare, David, 1917–1992

Hart, Joel Tanner, 1810–1877

Harvey, Eli, 1860–1957

Haseltine, Herbert, 1877–1962

Heizer, Michael, 1944

Hesse, Eva, 1936–1970

Hoffman, Malvina, 1885–1966

Holland, Tom, 1936

Holzer, Jenny, 1950

Hosmer, Harriet, 1830–1908

Hudson, Robert, 1938

Hughes, Robert Ball, 1806–1868

Hunt, Bryan, 1947

Hunt, Richard, 1935

Huntington, Anna Hyatt,
1876–1973

Indiana, Robert, 1928

Irwin, Robert, 1928

Ives, Chauncey, 1810–1894

Jennewein, Carl Paul,
1890–1978

Jimenez, Luis, Jr., 1940
Johns, Jasper, 1930
Jones, Thomas Dow, 1811–1891
Judd, Donald, 1928–1994
Kelley, Mike, 1954
Kelly, Ellsworth, 1923
Kemeys, Edward, 1843–1907
Kienholz, Edward, 1927–1994
Kienholz, Nancy, 1943
Kiesler, Frederick, 1896–1965
Kiester, Steve, 1949
Konti, Isidore, 1862–1938
Koons, Jeff, 1955
Lachaise, Gaston, 1882–1935
Laessle, Albert, 1877–1954
Lassaw, Ibram, 1913
Laurent, Robert, 1890–1970
Lawler, Louise, 1947
Lee, Arthur, 1881–1961
LeVa, Barry, 1941
Lewis, Edmonia, 1845–c. 1900
LeWitt, Sol, 1928
Lichtenstein Roy, 1923–1997
Lipchitz, Jacques, 1891–1973
Lippold, Richard, 1915
Lipton, Seymour, 1903–1986
Lombard, James, 1865–1920
MacMonnies, Frederick,
    1863–1937
MacNeil, Hermon Atkins,
    1866–1947
Man Ray, 1890–1976
Manship, Paul, 1885–1966
Marisol (Escobar), 1930
Mason, John, 1927

McIntire, Samuel, 1757–1811
McKillop, Edgar Alexander,
    1878–1950
Mills, Clark, 1815–1883
Moore, Bruce, 1905–1980
Moore, Henry, 1898–1986
Morris, George L. K., 1905–1975
Morris, Robert, 1931
Moses, Thomas 1844–1917
Nadelman, Elie, 1882–1946
Nakian, Reuben, 1897–1986
Nauman, Bruce, 1941
Nevelson, Louise, 1899–1988
Niehaus, Charles, 1855–1935
Noguchi, Isamu, 1904–1988
Oldenburg, Claes, 1929
Olitski, Jules, 1922
Oppenheim, Dennis, 1938
Palmer, Erastus Dow, 1817–1904
Partridge, William Ordway,
    1861–1930
Peterman, Dan, 1960
Pfaff, Judy, 1946
Piccirilli Attilio, 1866–1945
Potter, Edward, 1857–1923
Powers, Hiram, 1805–1873
Pratt, Bela, 1867–1917
Price, Kenneth, 1935
Proctor, A. Phimister, 1860–1950
Puryear, Martin, 1941
Rauschenberg, Robert, 1925
Ray, Charles, 1953
Remington, Frederic, 1861–1909
Rhind, John Massey, 1860–1936
Rhoades, Jason, 1965

UNITED STATES *(continued)*

Rickey, George, 1907–2002
Rimmer, William, 1816–1879
Rinehart, William, 1825–1874
Rivera, Jose de, 1904–1985
Rivers, Larry, 1923–2002
Robb, Samuel Anderson,
    1851–1928
Robus, Hugo, 1885–1964
Rogers, John, 1829–1904
Rogers, Randolph, 1825–1892
Roszak, Theodore, 1907–1981
Rubins, Nancy, 1952
Ruckstull, Frederic Wellington,
    1853–1942
Rush, William, 1756–1833
Russell, Charles M., 1864–1926
Saar, Alison, 1956
Saar, Betye, 1926
Saint-Gaudens, Augustus,
    1848–1907
Samaras, Lucas, 1936
Sampson, Charles A. L.,
    1825–1881
Schamberg, Morton L.,
    1881–1918
Scott, Tim, 1937
Segal, George, 1924–2000
Serra, Richard 1939
Shapiro, Joel, 1941
Shaw, Richard, 1941
Simmons, Franklin, 1839–1913
Simonds, Charles, 1945
Skillin, John, 1746–1800
Skillin, Simeon, Jr., c. 1756–1806

Skillin, Simeon, Sr., 1716–1778
Smith, David, 1906–1965
Smith, Tony, 1912–1980
Smithson, Robert, 1938–1973
Sonnier, Keith, 1941
Stankiewicz, Richard, 1922–1983
Steinberg, Saul, 1914–1999
Stella, Frank, 1936
Stockholder, Jessica, 1959
Stone, Sylvia, 1928
Storrs, John, 1885–1956
Story, William Wetmore,
    1819–1895
Sugarman, George, 1912–1999
Surls, James, 1943
Taft, Lorado, 1860–1931
Therrien, Robert, 1947
Thorwaldsen, Bertel, 1768–1844
Trova, Ernest, 1927
Truitt, Anne, 1921
Tucker, William, 1935
Turrell, James, 1943
Tuttle, Richard, 1941
Volk, Leonard, 1828–1895
Von Rydingsvard, Ursula, 1942
Vonnoh, Bessie Potter,
    1872–1955
Voulkos, Peter, 1924–2002
Ward, John Quincy Adams,
    1830–1910
Warner, Olin Levi, 1844–1896
Weber, Max, 1881–1961
Weinman, Adolph A., 1870–1952
Westermann, H. C., 1922–1981

Wharton, Margaret, 1943
Whitney, Anne, 1821–1915
Whitney, Gertrude Vanderbilt, 1875–1942
Wickey, Harry, 1892–1968
Wiley, William T., 1937
Wilmarth, Christopher, 1943

Winsor, Jackie, 1941
Wolfe, James, 1944
Wright, Patience Lovell, 1725–1786
Young, Mahonri, 1877–1957
Yunkers, Adja, 1900–1943
Zorach, William, 1889–1966

VENEZUELA

Cruz-Diez, Carlos, 1923
Soto, Jesus-Rafael, 1923

SCULPTURE PARKS

The following parks are either partially or entirely devoted to sculpture, and include permanent and temporary installations. Many are affiliated with or adjacent to museums. A few large commercial sculpture parks are included, because they often feature the work of contemporary artists.

ARGENTINA

Museo de Bellas Artes de la Voca, Buenos Aires

AUSTRALIA

Herring Island Environmental Sculpture Park, Melbourne
Macquarie University Sculpture Park, Sydney
Museum of Modern Art at Heide, Melbourne

AUSTRIA

Museum Moderner Kunst Stiftung Ludwig Wien Sculpture Garden, Vienna

BELGIUM

Middelheim-Openluchtmuseum Voor Beeldhouwkunst, Antwerp

BRAZIL

Museo de Arte Moderna, Rio de Janeiro

CANADA

Boreal Sculpture Garden, St. Johns, Newfoundland
Canadian Centre for Architecture Sculpture Garden, Montreal, Quebec
Geert Maas Sculpture Gardens, Kelowna, British Columbia
Macdonald Stewart Art Centre Sculpture Park, Guelph, Ontario
Toronto Sculpture Garden, Toronto
Windsor Sculpture Garden, Windsor, Ontario

CHINA

The Sculpture Walk, Kowloon Park, Hong Kong

CZECH REPUBLIC

Klenova Castle, Klatovy
Novyles Civic Association, Prague

DENMARK

Forest Art, Arhus
Krakamarken Nature Art Park, Brusgard Production School, Randers
Louisiana Museum of Modern Art Sculpture Garden, Humlebaek
Torskind Gammel Grusgrav Sculpture Park, Near Egtved, 25 km from
    Vejle
Tranekaer International Center for Art and Nature (TICKON), Langeland

ENGLAND

Barbara Hepworth Museum and Sculpture Garden, Barnoon Hill,
    St. Ives, Cornwall
Gateshead Riverside Sculpture Park, Gateshead, Tyne & Wear
Grizedale Forest Project, Hawkshead, near Ambleside, Cumbria
Henry Moore Foundation, Dane Tree House, Much Hadham,
    Hertfordshire

Roche Court Sculpture Garden, East Winterslow, near Salisbury,
Wiltshire

Yorkshire Sculpture Park, Bretton Hall College, West Bretton, near
Wakefield, West Yorkshire

FINLAND

Turku Art Museum, Turku

FRANCE

Centre d'Art Contemporain de Vassiviere en Limousin, Beaumont du Lac
(near Limoges)

Chateau de Kerguehennect, Bignan, Morbihan

Chateau de Pourtales, Schiller University, Strasbourg

Essaim-Art, Beaulieu-sur-Mer

Fondation Cartier Pour L'Art Contemporain, Paris

Galerie Beaubourg Sculpture Garden, Chateau Notre-Dame-des-Fleurs,
Vence

Jardin de Sculptures Musée D'Art Contemporain, Dunkerque, Nord

Maeght Foundation, Saint-Paul-de-Vence

Musée de Sculpture de Plein Air de la Ville de Paris, Paris

Musée National d'Art Moderne, Centre d'Art et de Culture, George
Pompidou, Paris

Musée Rodin, Paris

Musée Zadkine, Paris

Tuileries Gardens, Paris

GERMANY

Skulpturenpark, Katzow

Skulpturenpark AM Seestern, Dusseldorf

Stadelsches Kunstinstitut Und Stadtische Galerie, Frankfurt am Main

Stiftung Europaischer Skulpturenpark, Willebadessen

Wilhelm Lehmbruck Museum, Duisberg

GREECE

Basil & Elise Goulandris Museum of Modern Art, Andros

HUNGARY

Szoborparkban, Muvelodesi Has Nagyatad, Baross Gabor

IRELAND

The Lough Mac Nean Sculpture Trail, near Sligo

ISRAEL

Billy Rose Sculpture Garden, Israel Museum, Jerusalem
Tefen/The Open Museum, Tefen Industrial Park, Jerusalem

ITALY

Fattoria Di Celle, Villa Celle, Pistoia, near Florence
Giardino Dei Tarochi, near Garavicchio, Tuscany (Nikki de Saint Phalle's
    Tarot Garden)
Open Air Park Museum of Stone Sculpture, Fanano, Modena
Raymond Nasher Sculpture Garden at The Peggy Guggenheim
    Collection, Venice

JAPAN

Contemporary Sculpture Center, Tokyo
The Hakone Open-Air Museum, Hakone
Hara Museum of Contemporary Art, Tokyo
The Isamu Noguchi Garden Museum, Kita-gun, Kagawa
Sapporo Art Park Sculpture Garden, Sapporo
The Utsukushi-Ga-Hara Open Air Museum, Tokyo

KOREA

Che Ju Sculpture Park, Kwangnyong, Che-Ju
Korean National Museum of Contemporary Art, Seoul
Olympic Park, Seoul

LATVIA

The Pedvale Open-Air Art Museum, Pedvale, Sabile

LITHUANIA

Central Europe Open-Air Sculpture Museum, Europos Parkas, Vilniaus raj

MEXICO

Museo de Arte Moderno, Bosque de Chapultepec

NETHERLANDS

Collection of Joop van Caldenborgh, Wassenaar (near The Hague)
Haags Gemeentemuseum, The Hague
Kroller-Muller Museum, National Park De Hoge Veluwe, Otterlo
St. Ives Open Air Museum Drechtbanks Sculpture Park, Zwijndrecht
Van Abbe Museum, Eindhoven

NORWAY

Vigeland Sculpture Park, Vigeland Museum, Oslo

POLAND

Center of Polish Sculpture, Topolowa

PORTUGAL

Serralves Museum of Contemporary Art, Oporto

SPAIN

Barcelona Open Air Sculpture Gallery, Barcelona
Chillida Foundation Sculpture Park, Hernani
IVAM Museo de Julio Gonzales, Valencia

SWEDEN

Millesgarden, Stockholm
Moderna Museet, Stockholm

"It is easy. You just chip away the stone that doesn't look like David."

—MICHELANGELO (BUONARROTI), 1475–1564,
Italian Renaissance sculptor, explaining how he made
his statue of David

SWITZERLAND

Fondation Beyerler, Basle
Fondation Pierre Gianadda, Martigny
Modern Art Advising Sculpture Garden, Zolfingen

UNITED STATES

Alabama

Charles Ireland Sculpture Garden, Birmingham Museum of Art
University of Alabama Sculpture Tour, Department of Art, Tuscaloosa

Arizona

Arlene Dunlop Smith Garden, Tucson
Tempe Arts Center and Sculpture Park
Scottsdale Center for the Arts

California

Art Center College of Design Sculpture Garden, Pasadena
B. Gerald Cantor Rodin Sculpture Garden, Stanford Museum, Palo Alto
B. Gerald Cantor Sculpture Gardens, Los Angeles County Museum of Art
California Scenario and South Coast Plaza, Costa Mesa
California State University, Long Beach
Clos Pegase Sculpture Garden, Calistoga
di Rosa Preserve, Napa
Djerassi Sculpture Garden, Woodside

Edwards Garden, Museum of Contemporary Art, University of California
 at San Diego, La Jolla
Franklin D. Murphy Sculpture Garden, University of California,
 Los Angeles
La Quinta Sculpture Park, La Quinta
Living Memorial Sculpture Garden, Weed
Norton Simon Museum Sculpture Garden, Pasadena
Oakland Museum Sculpture Garden
Skirball Museum, Hebrew Union College, West Los Angeles
Stuart Collection of Sculpture, University of California at San Diego,
 La Jolla
University of California at Davis Arboretum
Westin Mission Hills Resort, Rancho Mirage

Colorado

Benson Park Sculpture Garden, Loveland
Colorado Springs Fine Art Center Sculpture Courtyard and Sculpture
 Garden
Museum of Outdoor Arts, Greenwood Plaza, Englewood

Connecticut

Aldrich Museum of Contemporary Art, Ridgefield
Kouros Sculpture Center, Ridgefield
Stamford Museum & Nature Center

District of Columbia

Hirshhorn Museum and Sculpture Garden
National Gallery of Art Sculpture Garden, The Mall
The Kreeger Museum

Florida

Ann Norton Sculpture Gardens, Inc., West Palm Beach
Artpark, The Art Museum at Florida International University, Miami

Hawaii

The Contemporary Museum Sculpture Garden, Honolulu

Idaho

Kagan Sculpture Garden, Ketchum

Illinois

Mitchell Museum, Cedarhurst Sculpture Park, Mount Vernon
Nathan Manilow Sculpture Park, Governors State University,
    University Park
Northwestern University Sculpture Garden, Mary and Leigh Block
    Gallery, Evanston
Ravinia Festival, Highland Park
Skokie Northshore Sculpture Park, Skokie
University of Chicago, Ida Noyes Hall, Hyde Park

Iowa

Des Moines Art Center
Effigy Mounds National Monument, c. A.D. 1300, Mississippi River across
    from Prairie du Chien, Wisconsin
Iowa State University, University Museums Art on Campus Program,
    Ames

Kansas

Edwin A. Ulrich Museum of Art, Martin Bush Outdoor Sculpture
    Garden, Wichita State University
Johnson County Community College Sculpture Collection, Overland Park

Louisiana

The Virlane Foundation Collection, New Orleans

Maryland

Janet and Allen Wurtzburger and Ryda and Robert H. Levi Sculpture
Gardens, Baltimore Museum of Art
Sculpture at Quiet Waters Park, Annapolis

Massachusetts

Butler Sculpture Park, Sheffield
Chesterwood Museum (Daniel Chester French's Home), Stockbridge
De Cordova and Dana Museum and Sculpture Park, Lincoln
List Visual Arts Center, Massachusetts Institute of Technology, Cambridge

Michigan

Cranbrook Educational Community, Bloomfield Hills
Frederick Meijer Gardens, Grand Rapids

Minnesota

General Mills Art Collection Sculpture Program, Minneapolis
Minneapolis Sculpture Garden, Walker Art Center
St. Paul Cultural Garden

Missouri

The E. F. Pierson Sculpture Garden and the Kansas City Sculpture Park
and Henry Moore Sculpture Garden, Nelson-Atkins Museum of Art,
Kansas City
Laumeier Sculpture Park, St. Louis
Missouri Botanical Garden, St. Louis

Nebraska

Prairie Peace Park Sculpture Garden, Lincoln
Sheldon Sculpture Garden, Sheldon Art Center, University of Nebraska,
Lincoln

New Hampshire

Saint-Gaudens National Historic Site, Cornish

New Jersey

Burlington County College Sculpture Garden, Pemberton
Grounds for Sculpture, Hamilton
John B. Putnam, Jr., Memorial Collection, Princeton University,
Princeton, New Jersey
Newark Museum Sculpture Garden, Alice Ransom Dreyfuss Memorial
Garden
Quietude Garden Gallery, East Brunswick

New Mexico

Albuquerque Museum of Art
Lightning Field (Walter De Maria's 400 stainless steel poles), Dia Center
for the Arts, Corales
Nedra Matteucci's Fenn Galleries, Santa Fe (commercial)
Shidoni Foundry, Gallery and Sculpture Garden, Tesuque (commercial)

New York

Abby Aldrich Rockefeller Sculpture Garden (to reopen 2005),
The Museum of Modern Art, New York City
Albright-Knox Art Gallery, Buffalo
Battery Park City, New York City
Brooklyn Museum, Frida Schiff Warburg Sculpture Garden
Donald N. Kendall Sculpture Garden, PepsiCo World Headquarters,
Purchase
Empire State Plaza Art Collection, Governor Nelson A. Rockefeller
Empire State Plaza, Albany
Griffis Sculpture Park, East Otto
Hans Van de Bovenkamp Sculpture Garden, Tillson
Hofstra University Sculpture Park, Hempstead
Iris and B. Gerald Cantor Roof Garden, Metropolitan Museum of Art,
New York City

Isamu Noguchi Garden Museum, Long Island City
Kykuit Sculpture Gardens, Rockefeller Estate, North Tarrytown
Nassau County Museum of Art, Rosslyn Harbor
P.S. 1 Museum, Institute for Contemporary Art, Long Island City
Poughkeepsie Sculpture Park, Poughkeepsie
Robert Moses Plaza, Fordham University, New York City
Socrates Sculpture Park, Long Island City
Stone Quarry Hill Art Park, Cazenovia
Storm King Art Center, Mountainville
Studio Museum in Harlem, New York City

North Carolina

Rosen Outdoor Sculpture Garden, Appalachian State University, Boone
Southern Center for Contemporary Art, Winston-Salem

Ohio

Columbus Museum of Art Sculpture Park
Pyramid Hill Sculpture Park, Hamilton (near Cincinnati)

Oregon

Evan H. Roberts Memorial Sculpture Garden, Portland Art Museum

Pennsylvania

Abington Art Center Sculpture Garden, Jenkintown
Drexel University, Philadelphia
James Wolf Sculpture Trail, Johnstown
Lookout Sculpture Park, Damascus
Madeline K. Butcher Sculpture Garden and the Morris Arboretum,
    University of Pennsylvania, Philadelphia
Philip and Muriel Berman Sculpture Collection, Lehigh University,
    Bethlehem
Philip and Muriel Berman Museum of Art, Ursinus College, Collegeville
Philip and Muriel Berman Sculpture Park, Lehigh Valley Hospital,
    Allentown

South Carolina

Brookgreen Gardens, Murrells Inlet

Tennessee

Chattanooga State Technical Community College Sculpture Garden
University of Tennessee Sculpture Tour, Knoxville

Texas

Chianti Foundation, Marfa (near El Paso)
Connemara Conservancy Foundation, Dallas
Dallas Museum of Art Sculpture Garden
Elizabeth Meadows Sculpture Garden, Southern Methodist University,
    Dallas
Lillie and Hugh Roy Cullen Sculpture Garden, Museum of Fine Arts,
    Houston
San Antonio Museum of Art Sculpture Garden
Umlauf Sculpture Garden and Museum, Austin

Vermont

Marble Street Sculpture Park, West Rutland

Virginia

Virginia Museum of Fine Arts, Richmond

Washington

Chapman University, Orange
Gardens of Art at Big Rock Garden Park, Bellingham
Warren G. Magnuson Park, Western Regional Center, Seattle
Western Washington University Outdoor Sculpture Collection,
    Bellingham

Wisconsin

> Bradley Family Foundation Sculpture Park, Milwaukee
> Fred Smith's Wisconsin Concrete Park (Sponsored by the Kohler
>   Foundation), Phillips
> Woodlot Outdoor Sculpture Gallery, Sheboygan (commercial)

VENEZUELA

> Jardin de Esculturas del Museo de Bellas Artes de Caracas, Caracas

100 PUBLIC ART PIECES

Long before the meaning of art was articulated, public art in the form of sculpture has existed in civilizations all over the world. One obvious example is *The Sphinx* in Egypt. Other public sculptures include live-rock carvings (into outcroppings of rock) in India, *Stonehenge* in England, or *Crazy Horse*, an entire mountain carving still in progress in South Dakota. Sculptures, such as the Jefferson Memorial in Washington, DC, are built as lasting monuments to an individual. Although it was not intended that way, some public sculptures become temporary. One such example is Richard Serra's *Tilted Arc* in New York City, a public sculpture that was removed after eight years of controversy because it interfered with normal pedestrian traffic.

In this list you will find some of the more famous public art. Some of the smallest sculptures (such as the *Manniken Pis* in Brussels) receive as much acclaim or notoriety as the largest. Dates and artists' names are given (if known), along with the city where the sculpture or monument is located.

AFGHANISTAN

> 1. *Buddha* (world's tallest standing Buddha), c. A.D. 500, Bamiyan, near
>   Kabul. Destroyed in March, 2001

AUSTRIA

> 2. *Mozart Monument*, 1842, Ludwig Schwanthaler, Park Burggarten,
>   Salzburg

BELGIUM

3. *Atomium,* 1958, André Waterkeyn, Brussels
4. *Brabo* (the Hand Thrower), 1887, Jef Lambeaux, Grote Markt, Antwerp
5. *Manniken Pis,* 1619, Jerome Duquesnoy, Brussels

BRAZIL

6. *Christ the Redeemer (Corcovado),* 1931, Rio de Janeiro

CANADA

7. *Totem Poles,* ongoing, Duncan, British Columbia

CHINA

8. *Phoenix Ascending the Sky,* 1990, Yang Yingfeng, Olympic Center, Beijing
9. *Public Art Memorial Hall Group Sculpture,* 1978, 108 artists collaborated, Tiananmen Square, Beijing
10. *The Boat of Purity and Ease* (a 36-meter long boat created in marble), 1755, Summer Palace, Beijing

CZECH REPUBLIC

11. *Charles Bridge,* 1357, Peter Parler, Prague

DENMARK

12. *Gefion Fountain,* 1908, Anders Bundgaard, Copenhagen
13. *The Little Mermaid,* 1913, Edvard Eriksen, Copenhagen

"Whatever the artist makes is always some kind of self-portrait."

—MARISOL (ESCOBAR), 1930, American sculptor

EGYPT

14. *Sphinx,* c. 2500 B.C., Giza

ENGLAND

15. *Admiral Nelson,* 1830s, John Nash, Trafalgar Square, London
16. *Angel of the North,* 1995, Antony Gormley, Gateshead, Newcastle-on-Tyne
17. *Eros (Cupid),* 1892, Alfred Gilbert, Memorial to Lord Shaftesbury, Picadilly Circus, London
18. *Marble Arch,* 1880, John Nash, Hyde Park, London
19. *Prince Albert Monument,* 1872–1876, George Gilbert Scott, London

FRANCE

20. *Arc de Triomphe,* 1806–1836, Jean-François-Therese Chalgrin (commissioned by Napoleon), Paris
21. *Burghers of Calais,* 1884–1888, Auguste Rodin, Calais (installed in several different locales worldwide)
22. *Egyptian Obelisk,* 1831–1840, Place du Concorde, Paris
23. *Eiffel Tower,* 1899, Gustave Eiffel, Paris
24. *The Triumph of Apollo,* 1900, Georges Recipon, Grand Palais, Paris

GERMANY

25. *Brandenberg Gate,* 1788–1791, Karl Langhans, Berlin
26. *Inverted Collar and Tie,* 1994, Claes Oldenburg/Coosje van Bruggen, Dusseldorf

GREECE

27. *Arch of Hadrian,* c. 81 B.C., Athens
28. *Monument of Lysicrates,* c. 334 B.C., Athens

ITALY

29. *Arch of Constantine*, A.D. 312–315, Rome

30. *Constantine the Great* (head only), early 4th century A.D., Rome

31. *David*, 1501–1504, Michelangelo, Florence

32. *Elephant and Obelisk*, 1667, Bernini, Rome

33. *Equestrian Monument of Bartolomeo Colleoni*, 1483–1488, Andrea del Verrocchio, Venice

34. *Gattemelata (Equestrian Monument of Erasmo da Narni)*, 1445–1450, Donatello, Padua

35. *Lion Pillar*, St. Mark's Square, Venice

36. *Trajan's Column*, A.D. 113, Rome

37. *Trevi Fountain*, 1732–1751, Pietro da Cortona, Bernini, Nicola Salvi, Rome

38. *Victor Emmanuel II Monument*, 1884–1922, Giuseppe Sacconi, Rome

POLYNESIA

39. *Stone Face Images*, 17th century, Easter Island

RHODES

40. *Colossus of Rhodes*, 248–304 B.C., Chares the Lindios (one of the Seven Wonders of the World, destroyed by earthquake)

RUSSIA

41. *Peter the Great Equestrian Statue*, 1782, Etienne Falconet, St. Petersburg

SPAIN

42. *The Columbus Monument*, 1888, Rafael Atché, Barcelona

43. *Reina Mariana*, 2001, Manolo Valdés, Madrid

TURKEY

44. *Egyptian Obelisk*, c. 1500 B.C., Istanbul

UNITED STATES

Alaska

    45. *Totem Poles,* ongoing, Ketchikan

Arizona

    46. *Windows to the West,* 1977, Louise Nevelson, Scottsdale

California

    47. *Dragon Entrance Gate* to Chinatown, 1969, San Francisco

    48. *Great Wall of Los Angeles,* 1976, Judith F. Baca, Los Angeles

    49. *HOLLYWOOD* sign, 1923, Los Angeles

    50. *Long Beach,* 1982, Frank Stella, Wells Fargo Bank, Los Angeles

    51. *Night Sail,* 1985, Louise Nevelson, Crocker Center, Los Angeles

    52. *Peace on Earth,* 1966–1969, Jacques Lipchitz, Music Center, Los Angeles

    53. *Sequi,* 1984–1985, Nancy Graves, Crocker Center, Los Angeles

    54. *To the Issei,* 1980–1982, Isamu Noguchi, Japanese American Cultural and Community Center, Los Angeles

    55. *Watts Towers,* 1921–1955, Simon Rodia, Los Angeles

Connecticut

    56. *The Lipstick (Ascending) on Caterpillar Tracks,* 1969, Claes Oldenburg, Yale University, New Haven

District of Columbia

    57. *Franklin Delano Roosevelt Memorial,* 1996, Robert Graham

    58. *Jefferson Memorial,* c. 1939, John Russell Pope, sculpture by Rudolph Evans, 1941

    59. *Lincoln Memorial,* 1922, Piricilli Brothers

    60. *Vietnam War Memorial,* 1982, Maya Lin

    61. *Vietnam Women's Memorial,* 1993, Glenna Goodacre

    62. *Washington Monument,* 1848–1885, Robert Mills

Georgia

    63. *Confederate Memorial,* c. 1905–1925, Gutzon Borglum, Stone Mountain

Illinois

    64. *Batcolumn,* 1977, Claes Oldenburg, Chicago

    65. *Buckingham Fountain,* 1927, Marcel François Loyau, Chicago

    66. *Chicago,* 1981, Joan Miró, Chicago

    67. *Flamingo,* 1973, Alexander Calder, Chicago

    68. *Four Seasons* (ceramic mural), 1974, Marc Chagall, Chicago

    69. *Monument with Standing Beast,* 1969, Jean Dubuffet, Chicago

    70. *Untitled* (giant horse's head), 1967, Pablo Picasso, Chicago

Maryland

    71. *Under Sky/One Family,* 1979, Mark di Suvero, Baltimore

    72. *Washington Monument,* 1815–1825, Robert Mills, Baltimore

Massachusetts

    73. *Big Sail,* 1966, MIT, Alexander Calder

    74. *Dunes I,* 1971, MIT, Beverly Pepper

    75. *Minute Man,* 1889, Daniel Chester French, Concord

Michigan

    76. *La Grande Vitesse,* 1969, Alexander Calder, Grand Rapids

    77. *Horace E. Dodge and Son Memorial Fountain,* 1975, Isamu Noguchi, Detroit

Minnesota

    78. *Spoonbridge and Cherry,* 1988, Claes Oldenburg with Coosje van Bruggen, Minneapolis

Missouri

79. *Badminton Shuttlecocks,* 1994, Claes Oldenburg, Kansas City
80. *Gateway Arch,* 1966, Eero Saarinen, St. Louis
81. *Meeting of the Waters Fountain,* 1939, Carl Milles, St. Louis
82. *Spider,* 1996, Louise Bourgeois, Kansas City
83. *Twain* (7 large Cor-ten steel walls), 1982, Richard Serra, St. Louis

New Jersey

84. *Atmosphere and Environment X,* 1969–1970, Louise Nevelson, Princeton

New Mexico

85. *Lightning Field,* 1977, Walter De Maria, Quemado

New York

86. *Atlas,* 1936, Lee Lawrie, Rockefeller Center, New York City
87. *Red Cube,* 1968, Isamu Noguchi, New York City
88. *Shadows and Flags,* 1978, Louise Nevelson, Louise Nevelson Plaza, New York City
89. *Statue of Liberty,* 1886, Frederic Bartholdi, New York Harbor
90. *Tilted Arc,* 1981 (destroyed 1989), Richard Serra, New York City

North Dakota

91. *Sodbuster (Farmer Plowing with Oxen),* 1977, Fargo

Ohio

92. *Cincinnati Gateway,* 1988, Andrew Leicester, Cincinnati
93. *Great Serpent Burial Mound,* c. A.D. 900–1200, near Locust Grove

Pennsylvania

94. *LOVE,* 1978, Robert Indiana, Philadelphia
95. *William Penn,* 1893, Alexander Milne Calder, Philadelphia

UNITED STATES *(continued)*

South Dakota

> 96. *Crazy Horse Mountain,* 1948–ongoing, Korczak Ziolkowski and family, Keystone
> 97. *Mount Rushmore,* c. 1927–1941, Gutzon Borglum, Keystone

Texas

> 98. *Broken Obelisk,* 1963–1967, Barnett Newman, Houston

Virginia

> 99. *Marine Corps War Memorial,* 1954, Felix de Weldon, Arlington

Washington

> 100. *Space Needle,* 1961, Edward E. Carlson, Seattle

EARTHWORKS, PAST AND PRESENT

Earthworks such as the *Pyramids* in Egypt, the *Great Wall of China,* or the *Great Serpent Mound* at Chillicothe, Ohio, were created for burial, defense, or religious purposes. In the 1960s, when the "Land Art" movement began, artists began transforming the land itself for conceptual (and sometimes) practical purposes. Some contemporary earthworks were not intended as permanent installations, but as artistic statements about that particular environment in that particular time. Some have already disappeared and are known only by photographs taken of them. In some instances, land that was considered a wasteland from mining, construction, or landfills, has been transformed into large-scale artworks.

CHINA

> *Great Wall of China,* unified c. 210 B.C., unknown workers. This is the only earthwork that can be seen from the moon.

EGYPT

Pyramids, 2530–2470 B.C., unknown workers, Giza. It is known that these were tombs for Egyptian rulers.

ENGLAND

Elder Patch, 1983, Andy Goldsworthy, Cumbria. Goldsworthy moves things in nature such as stones, sticks, leaves, pebbles, to create his earthwork sculpture, then produces color photos of his creation.

Hadrian's Wall, begun A.D. 122, Northumberland. Portions of this 5-meter-high, 73-mile-long wall and its accompanying fortresses were built by occupying Roman soldiers.

Running Table, 1978, David Nash, Cumbria. Nash sculpts wood where he finds it, sometimes carving, sometimes burning, but always altering its appearance.

Stonehenge, 1650 B.C., unknown workers, Wiltshire. This circular grouping of gigantic monoliths was possibly used in a form of religious observance or astronomical study.

FRANCE

Marianne, 1989, Jacques Simon, Orly Airport. This temporary earthwork was a giant face "painted" on the land through plantings of petunias, geraniums, and cineraria.

GERMANY

Gartenschlauch (Garden Hose) 1983, Claes Oldenburg, Breisgau. This huge tubular steel construction is similar to other outdoor sculptures by Oldenburg which are simply gigantic interpretations of ordinary objects.

ISRAEL

To Life (L'Chaim), 1999, Andrew Rogers, near Moshav Paran cooperative. This stone sculpture "geoglyph" is 125 × 108 feet × several yards in height and consists of the two Hebrew letters that form the Hebrew word for "life."

ITALY

Terrace of One Hundred Fountains, 16th century, unknown workers, Villa d'Este, Tivoli.

MEXICO

Teotihuacan, A.D. 300–900, unknown workers. The Pyramid of the Sun dominates this ancient city.

NETHERLANDS

Five Columns for the Kroller Mueller, 1982, Ian Hamilton Finlay, Otterlo. This site-specific sculpture consists of five trees with the bases sculpted to resemble columns.

PERU

Lines in the Nazca Desert, c. 300 B.C. to A.D. 800, unknown workers. Mysterious lines called "geoglyphs" abound in certain parts of Peru. It is believed that they relate to fertility or astrological observations.

Walking a Line in Peru, 1972, Richard Long. In this sculpture, Long walks a straight line, sometimes slightly altering the landscape when he does. He regards walking as a form of art, and records his walks in maps, photographs, or by writing.

ROMANIA

Endless Column, 1935–1938, Constantin Brancusi, Tirgu Jiu. This sculptured column of repetitive forms is 96 feet high and appears that it really could continue endlessly. It consists of 17 copper-coated iron modules and is a World War I memorial.

Table of Silence, 1935–1938, Constantin Brancusi, Tirgu Jiu. Circular stone table surrounded by 12 stone "seats" on which one couldn't sit because each seat is made of two half-round balls of stone precariously balanced.

"Brancusi, like the Japanese, would take the quintessence of nature and distill it. Brancusi showed me the truth of materials."

—ISAMU NOGUCHI, 1904–1988, American sculptor

UNITED STATES

Arizona

Roden Crater, 1977–c. 2000, James Turrell. This natural-appearing crater near Flagstaff is a long-extinct volcano. Turrell is reshaping it to be perfectly concave and to align with spaces between the sun and certain stars.

California

Running Fence, 1972–1976, Christo (Javacheff), Sonoma and Marin Counties, California (dismantled). This "fence" was made of 24½ miles of 18-foot-high woven nylon held in place by poles and cables, running along the top of a ridge to the water,

The Umbrellas Japan-USA, 1984–1991, Christo and Jeanne-Claude. Thirty one hundred octagonal umbrellas almost 20 feet high by 30 feet in diameter were installed in a line 12 miles long in Japan and 18 miles long in the United States.

Colorado

Earth Mound, 1955, Herbert Bayer, Aspen. Bayer has proven that site rehabilitation of land damaged by humans (for example, by mining, landfills, erosion) can be a work of art. His earth sculpture contours the land, creating shadows and contrasts, while serving a useful purpose.

District of Columbia

Vietnam War Memorial, 1982, Maya Lin. This 250-foot-long black granite wall inscribed with the names of American military personnel who died in Vietnam is stirring in its simplicity.

Florida

Surrounded Islands, 1983, Christo (Javacheff), Biscayne Bay, Miami. Pink "skirts" made of six-and-a-half million square feet of pink polypropylene were temporarily placed around the bay islands.

Illinois

Buffalo Rock Effigy Tumuli, c. 1985, Michael Heizer, Ottawa, near Chicago. Heizer has reconfigured land destroyed by strip-mining by building five giant creatures of earth: a snake, a turtle, a water strider (a long-legged bug), a frog, and a catfish.

Cahokia Mounds, A.D. 700–1500, Cahokia. These earthen mounds, preserved in a 2,200-acre tract, were built by the Mississipian Native American culture.

Dwelling, Chicago, 1981, Charles Simonds, Museum of Contemporary Art, Chicago. Forty-four-foot-long clay and wood model of houses for "Little People" whom he believes have disappeared, leaving behind their architecture.

Michigan

Grand Rapids Project, 1973–1974, Robert Morris, Grand Rapids. Using earth, asphalt, and natural grasses, Morris's functional piece of artwork allows viewers to go down a steep hill to the ballfields below.

The Wave Field, 1995, Maya Lin, Ann Arbor. This field is a 90-foot plot of mounds covered with grass that appear to undulate because of the shadows that appear on each wave. It is like an ocean of grass.

Minnesota

Pigs Eye Landfill, 1990–present, Mel Chin, St. Paul. Chin has chosen to locate his artwork (a round garden of perennial and annual flowers surrounded by chain-link fence) in a landfill to demonstrate that what has been desolate can again become beautiful.

Missouri

> *Cromlech Glen,* 1985–1990, Beverly Pepper, Laumeier Sculpture Park,
> St. Louis. Cromlech Glen is composed of grass-covered earthen ridges
> that form a natural amphitheater. Steps allow access to the tops of the
> hills.

> *Face of the Earth #3,* 1988, Vito Acconci, Laumeier Sculpture Park,
> St. Louis. Acconci's giant face with simplified eyes, nose, and mouth
> looks up from the ground. The face is surrounded by four increasingly
> larger terraces of concrete, gravel, and grass that take the place of the
> original Astroturf-covered wooden platforms.

Nevada

> *Complex 1,* 1972–1974, Michael Heizer, Garden Valley. Concrete and
> compacted earth create an elongated pyramid-like form.

> *Double Negative,* 1969–1970, Michael Heizer, near Overton. These
> vertical slits in two facing buttes are impressive for the shadows they
> create.

> *Las Vegas Piece,* 1969, Walter de Maria, Las Vegas. Two 1-mile lines,
> 8 feet wide, were made in the desert with a 6-foot bulldozer blade.

> *Rift,* 1968, Michael Heizer, Jean Dry Lake. Geometric zigzags are cut into
> a dry lake bed.

New Jersey

> *A Simple Network of Underground Wells and Tunnels,* 1975, Alice Aycock,
> Far Hills. Aycock had six 7-foot deep wells dug, connected by tunnels.
> Viewers descended by ladder into a well, then were expected to crawl
> through a tunnel to the next well. The concept was to determine
> people's reactions to confined spaces.

> *Sky Mound Landfill,* 1988–present, Nancy Holt, Hackensack. Using earth
> mounds and steel poles, Holt created a work of art and astronomical
> observatory for a 57-acre landfill.

New Mexico

> *The Lightning Field,* 1974–1977, Walter de Maria, near Quemado. Twenty
> ½-foot high stainless steel poles were placed in a field—to attract
> lightning.

New York

Secant, 1977, Carl Andre, Roslyn. A line of 12 × 12 × 36 wooden beams were laid end to end to form a "log piece."

South Cove, Battery Park, 1988, Mary Miss, New York City. Mary Miss is a well-known environmental artist. In this sculpture, she incorporates rocks, natural plantings, blue lights, and pilings in the water to provide a meditative landscape.

Spray of Ithaca: Falls Freezing and Melting on Rope, 1969, Hans Haacke, Ithaca. Haacke works with water, air, temperature to create "sculpture." This sculpture may be viewed in photos.

Ohio

Earthwoman, 1976–1977, James Pierce, Pratt Farm, near Clinton. 5 × 30 × 15 ft. grass-covered mound of dirt appears to be a woman on her stomach.

Great Serpent Mound, A.D. 10th century, Chillicothe. Unknown Native American workers formed a serpent along the tops of hills.

Streams, 1976, Athena Tacha, Oberlin. Pumice, rocks, sandstone, and lake pebbles create a formation of "steps" in the side of a hill.

Rhode Island

Sod Maze, 1974, Richard Fleischner, Newport. Concentric circles form a mounded turf maze, 142 feet in diameter, 18 inches high.

Texas

Amarillo Ramp, 1973, Robert Smithson, Amarillo. This 3/4 circle, 150 feet in diameter, is partially submerged in a lake.

Cadillac Ranch, 1974, Chip Lord, Hudson Marquez, and Doug Michels, Amarillo. In this bizarre sculpture, ten painted Cadillacs are half-buried at an angle, nose-down, with rear ends projecting into the air.

Utah

> *Spiral Jetty*, 1970, Robert Smithson, Rozel Point, Great Salt Lake. This famous sculpture consisted of a 1,500-foot spiral made of rock and earth that entered the Great Salt Lake from the lakeshore and is now covered with water.
>
> *Sun Tunnels*, 1973–1976, Nancy Holt, Lucin. Four large concrete pipes were aligned to the rising and setting of the sun on the summer and winter solstices.

Washington

> *Mill Creek Canyon Earthworks*, 1979–1982, Herbert Bayer, Kent. This reconstruction of the earth allowed a stream to be dammed in a natural, beautiful way.
>
> *Untitled Reclamation Project*, 1979, Robert Morris, King County. A grass-covered concentric circle earthwork was formed to reclaim an unused gravel pit.

"Above all, sculpture is a conquest of space, a space that is delineated by forms."

—HENRI LAURENS, 1885–1954, French sculptor

CHAPTER 10

Architecture

"Architecture is inhabited sculpture."
—CONSTANTIN BRANCUSI, 1876–1957, Romanian sculptor

ARCHITECTURAL TERMS

Following are some commonly used architectural terms that you may encounter in decorating and architecture magazines. And if you enjoy touring historic homes and buildings, you've also probably heard the tour guides use a few of them. The more of these you know, the better you can understand (and even tell others about) architecture you admire.

Abbey. A religious center for monks or nuns; an abbey church and surrounding buildings.

Acropolis. The Greek acropolis, usually located at a city's high point, is an open plaza that was the center of culture and religion in ancient Greek cities. This gathering place might include several temples. For example, the *Acropolis* in Athens contains the *Parthenon*, the *Erechthion* (a temple to many gods), and the *Temple to Athena Nike.*

Adobe. Sun-dried brick made from mud and straw; used to construct homes.

Aisle. In a church, the space between the nave and supporting columns and the outside wall.

Altar. A location where offerings are made to a spirit; in Christian churches, a table-like structure.

Altarpiece. A decorative screen behind an altar, often with movable wings and featuring many scenes.

Ambulatory. A walking space behind the high altar in a Gothic cathedral; covered walkway.

Amphitheater. An oval or circular arena with tiers of seats; used for competitions or entertainment.

Apse. A round or polygonal vaulted space behind an altar at the eastern end of a cathedral.

Aqueduct. A conduit for water transported from a distant source.

Arcade. A series of columns combined with arches to support a roof.

Arch. A (usually) curved structural element that spans an opening and supports the weight above.

Art Deco. Architecture of the 1930s featuring flat roofs, geometric design, and simplified shapes.

Atrium. An open court in the center of a building; or an entry court.

Baldachin. An architectural canopy above a throne or high altar.

Balusters. Short, rounded, pillar-like columns that support a balcony railing (or balustrade).

Baptistery. A portion of a church that is used specifically for baptism; often octagonal or round.

Baroque. Type of architecture characterized by curved lines, movement, and excessive decoration.

Basilica. A long colonnaded hall used in Roman times for commerce; later used for church design.

Bauhaus. A German school that brought together all the arts and united them through architecture.

Bay. An opening in a building that is created by walls or columns; a projecting window unit.

Beam. A support for a roof or floor, usually going from wall to wall.

Blind arcade. A series of decorative columns attached to a wall.

Boiserie. Wooden paneling often found in French interiors of the 17th and 18th centuries.

Brickwork. Decorative arrangement of bricks; particularly popular in Victorian architecture.

Broken pediment. A pediment (triangular gable) may be found at the top of a building, above a portico, or on a tall piece of furniture. A broken pediment is a triangle that is interrupted at its upper apex by a rounded opening. One variation of the broken pediment is called a "swan's neck" for the graceful curve of the "break."

Bungalow. A single-story house that often included a porch; often featuring a variety of exterior materials, including stucco, brick, and shingles. Popular in the early 1900s.

Buttresses. Projecting supports that allow exterior walls to be built higher. See *flying buttress*.

Campanile. A bell tower, sometimes freestanding, or sometimes an integral part of a church.

Cantilever. A projecting structure such as a balcony, supported by a downward force behind a fulcrum, appearing to be unsupported.

Capital. The top of a column; can be in a variety of styles from various cultures.

Caryatid. A carved female figure that substitutes for a column to support a roof.

Catacomb. An underground cemetery with wall niches used for burial.

Cathedral. A church that contains the throne of a bishop (cathedra).

Chancel. The eastern part of a church reserved for the clergy.

Choir. The part of a church behind the altar for singers and the clergy.

Classical architecture. Based on ancient Greek and Roman architectural forms.

Clerestory. The window-filled upper portion of a wall. While this first became common in Romanesque churches, it is found in contemporary houses as well by the placement of a series of small windows on the upper part of the wall.

Cloister. An open courtyard surrounded by a covered colonnade.

Coffer. A box-like ceiling, often octagonal or rectangular.

Colonnade. A series of columns at regular intervals supporting a roof or arches.

Column. A usually round or fluted post to support beams or a roof.

Corbel. A projecting support usually of carved blocks of stone or wood.

Cornice. A horizontal roof overhang; raking cornice is a diagonal overhang found in a pediment.

Crenellation. Battlements—openings for archers alternating with solid walls—found in a castle.

Crossing. The central area of a church where a transept intersects a nave.

Cupola. A small dome atop a roof.

Curtain wall. Curving brick walls; non-load-bearing outer walls.

Dome. An evenly curved vaulted roof, usually round or elliptical.

Dormer. An attic window usually with a gable and roof.

Eaves. The lower portion of a roof that projects beyond the wall.

Elevation. A straight-on drawing of one side of a building without using perspective.

Engaged column. A column attached to the wall directly behind it.

Entablature (architrave, frieze, and cornice). The structure above columns in Classical architecture.

Entasis. The gentle convex swelling of a column that makes it appear straight rather than concave; used in columns of the Parthenon.

Façade. The front view (elevation) of a building.

Federal style. Neo-Classical style of building used in the United States from 1780 to c. 1820.

Fenestration. The use of windows in a building.

Finial. An ornament that caps something such as a newel post, buttress, roof apex, or canopy.

Flying buttress. A projecting support for a wall with an arched opening to give it strength, which allows exterior walls to be built higher.

Folly. An apparently useless building that enhances the view; for example, a fake "ruin."

Formal balance. Symmetrical arrangement of architectural elements on each side of a center axis.

Forum. A Roman place of assembly for markets, religion, commerce, and justice. The Forum in Rome, for example, was a central open plaza that contained government buildings, triumphal arches, colonnades, and temples.

Fresco. Decorative painting done on wet plaster made of lime or gypsum.

Frieze. Decorative ornamentation that is part of the entablature; a decorative strip on walls above columns.

Gable. The upper, pointed part of a wall underneath a pitched roof.

Gallery. An open second story above the aisle of a church and below the clerestory.

Gambrel roof. Barn-like roof imported to the United States from Holland.

Gargoyle. A water spout of lead or carved stone that resembled a beast or monster.

Gazebo. A small open-air summer house.

Geodesic dome. A geometric dome created with light metal bars, connectors, and glass.

Georgian style. Architecture associated with Kings George I, II, III, and IV (1714–1830).

Girder. A supporting beam, usually made of steel.

Gothic cathedral. A church featuring flying buttresses and pointed-arch windows (c. 1250–c. 1500).

Groin. An angle formed by two intersecting vaults.

Half-timbering. Exterior decorative timber allowed to show, contrasting with white walls.

Hall church. A church with nave and aisles of the same height.

Hippodrome. An enclosed racecourse or theater that featured animal acts.

Hypostyle hall. A large hall with the roof supported by a vast number of columns (Egyptian origin).

International style. Box-like buildings often with walls of glass.

Jambs. The vertical sides of an opening such as a church entrance; frequently carved.

Keystone. The stone that goes at the very top of an arch to complete its load-bearing quality.

Lantern. A round turret that extends above a dome, with side openings to let in light.

Lintel. The horizontal beam at the top of two vertical supports to support the wall above it.

Loggia. A gallery or arcade that is open to the air on at least one side.

Lunette. A semicircular space above a door or window (similar to a tympanum).

Machicolation. The opening behind battlements in a castle entrance that allows oil or pitch to be poured on invaders.

Mansard roof. A roof with two slopes, the first quite steep, the second less steep.

Mausoleum. An imposing tomb, usually for an important person (the *Taj Mahal*, for example).

Mihrab. A small niche in a mosque wall (see *qibla*) that shows the direction of Mecca.

Minaret. Slender tower(s) attached to a mosque from which prayers are sung.

Molding. A decoratively carved ornamental strip mostly used in classical architecture.

Mosaic. A decorative floor or wall mural made of pieces of stone or colored glass.

Narthex. A porch in the front of a church, or a vestibule just outside the nave of the church.

Nave. The long space in a Christian church reserved for worshippers. Aisles may be in the middle or along the sides.

Neo-Classicism. A revival of the principles of Greek and Roman architecture. Such architecture features columns, pediments, and lack of excessive decoration.

Niche. A rounded, concave opening in a wall for sculpture.

Obelisk. A monumental tapering squared column, pyramid-shaped at the top; originated in Egypt.

Oculus. Literally an eye (round window) to let in light, such as that in the ceiling of the *Pantheon*.

Onion dome. A bulbous, pointed dome frequently seen in Byzantine architecture in Eastern Europe and Russia.

Pagoda. A Chinese or Indian temple built of many stories, each smaller than the one below.

Palladian. An architectural movement based on the work of Andrea Palladio, who synthesized the balance of ancient Roman architecture with Renaissance innovations. Thomas Jefferson's *Monticello,* an example of Palladianism, features a portico with columns and symmetrical balance.

Parapet. A low wall at the edge of a balcony or terrace.

Pedestal. The lowest part of a support for a column, often square.

Pediment. The triangular decoration above a door or temple, often decoratively carved.

Pendentive. Triangular pieces of masonry at each corner of four walls that support a rounded dome.

Peristyle court. A many-columned court (colonnade) around an open courtyard.

Pier. A massive support, sometimes square, but often formed of several columns (compound pier).

Pilaster. A squared, flat attached (engaged) column with capital and base.

Pillar. A vertical structural support such as columns, piers, and pilasters.

Porte cochère. (French for *carriage entrance*). A roofed open-air area usually at the entrance of a building to allow passengers to be sheltered while entering or leaving a vehicle.

Post and lintel. A support system that consists of vertical uprights (columns or walls) and a horizontal beam (lintel or pediment). This ancient support system was used in Egyptian, Greek, and Roman temples. An entry door is an example of a post and lintel.

Post-Modernism. A 1970s style that is based on traditional classical or decorative architecture.

Proscenium. A Roman or Greek stage; the space between the curtain and an orchestra.

Pylon. Sloping walls (as in Egyptian temples); or flanking structures at an entrance or bridge.

Pyramid. A structure with a square base with four sides that slope upward to a point.

Qibla. The wall in a mosque that contains the mihrab niche and faces Mecca.

Rose window. A stained glass circular window with tracery, often found in Gothic churches.

Rotunda. A circular interior space, usually surmounted by a dome.

Rustication. The deliberate roughness left on stone; also indented edges where stones were joined.

Sacristy. A room near the altar where clothing and vessels for a church service are kept.

Sanctuary. The most sacred inner part of a church surrounding the altar.

Shaft. The vertical portion of a column or pilaster.

Spire. The pointed top portion of a tower or steeple.

Steeple. A spire and its supporting tower.

Stringcourse. A decorative horizontal band on a building, often in a contrasting color.

Terrazzo. Marble chips and cement combined and poured, then highly polished.

Tokonoma. A niche in a Japanese home or a tea-ceremony room to display artwork.

Tracery. Stone or wood carving used decoratively in stained glass windows, panels, and screens.

Transept. The arm of a church that forms a right angle "crossing" in a basilica-style church.

Turret. A small tower attached to the top of a castle.

Tympanum. A rounded space above (church) doors, usually filled with sculpture.

Vault. An arched ceiling usually of brick, stone, or concrete.

Veranda. An attached open porch supported by columns.

Volute. A scroll ornament used in Ionic and (often) Corinthian capitals, at the top of columns.

Wattle and daub. A wall composed of woven branches filled with mud or plaster.

Westwork. The west end of a church that contains the main doorway, towers, and narthex.

Ziggurat. A flat-topped pyramid formed of a series of platforms on which a temple was built.

MUSEUMS FEATURING ARCHITECTURE

Although few museums are dedicated solely to architecture, a number of museums have collections of architectural artifacts, such as stained glass, carved stone portals, scale models, and drawings. The Museum of Modern Art in New York and The Art Institute of Chicago are two such museums.

INTERNATIONAL

Centre Canadien d'Architecture, Montreal, Canada

Das Architekturmuseum in Basel, Basel, Switzerland

Latvian Architecture Museum, Riga, Latvia

Museum of Architecture, Vilnius, Lithuania

Museum of Finnish Architecture, Helsinki, Finland

Netherlands Architecture Institute, Rotterdam, Netherlands

Norsk Arkitekturmuseum, Oslo, Norway

Outdoor Museum of Architecture, Tel Aviv, Israel

Swedish Museum of Architecture, Stockholm, Sweden

UNITED STATES

Architecture Museum (in City Museum), St. Louis, Missouri

Art Institute of Chicago

Department of the Treasury, Washington, DC

Fallingwater, Mill Run, Pennsylvania

Heinz Architectural Center, Carnegie Museum of Art, Pittsburgh,
    Pennsylvania

MAK Center for Art & Architecture at the Schindler House,
    West Hollywood, California

Museum of Modern Art, New York City

National Building Museum, Washington, DC

Schifferstadt Architectural Museum, Frederick, Maryland

SED Gallery/School of Environmental Design, University of Georgia, Athens

The Chicago Athenaeum: Museum of Architecture and Design, Chicago

The Gardner Museum of Architecture and Design, Quincy, Illinois

The Skyscraper Museum, New York City

HISTORIC CITIES WORTH A VISIT

From the ancient ruins of Pompeii to the more recent Colonial homes of Annapolis, Maryland, cities around the world are recognizing the value of preserving history and the architectural heritage of their past. Thus, whether your interest is in first-century artifacts or more recent ones, there are plenty of cities and small towns where you can take a walk back in time. These are some that have special appeal.

AUSTRIA

Melk. A charming small town; beautiful Baroque monastery.

Salzburg. Here you can see castles, churches, and a charming city center.

Vienna. In this city, there are palaces and Baroque architecture everywhere you look.

BELGIUM

Antwerp. Guild houses, Medieval castle, home of Rubens are just some of the highlights.

Bruges. A city of canals and Medieval buildings. Even new buildings look old.

Brussels. Guild houses on the Grande Place are a must-see.

Ghent. The oldest house in Europe (1066) is in Ghent, along with a medieval castle and canals.

BRAZIL AND PERU

Brazilia, Brazil. A totally new capital city designed in the 1950s by Oscar Niemeier, to open the interior of Brazil to commerce. It is a well-preserved example of visionary planning.

BRAZIL AND PERU *(continued)*

Cuzco, Peru. This city high in the Andes looks as it must have for hundreds of years.

Embu, Brazil. A Colonial city of small, charming buildings.

Manaus, Brazil. A city on the Amazon with an opulent opera house and many Colonial buildings.

Ouro Preto, Brazil. A World Heritage city from Colonial times, home to beautiful Baroque churches.

Salvador-Bahia, Brazil. This city, settled in the 1500s, is built on two levels (cliff and seaside), preserving the heritage of both. One either walks the steep road or takes an elevator to the upper city.

CANADA

Duncan, B.C. This city is the home of totem poles and a Native American enclave.

Montreal. A cosmopolitan city with lovely old homes. Cobbled streets and stone facades abound in Old Montreal.

Quebec City. This city is situated high on a bluff and has very old homes.

Victoria. An island city that has preserved many historic homes and the old town.

CROATIA

Dubrovnik. A picturesque walled port city on the Adriatic Sea dating back to the 4th century B.C. About A.D. 900, Croatian rule was established.

Split. A port city; home to *Diocletian's Palace*, which dates back to c. A.D. 300.

"Light, God's eldest daughter, is a principal beauty in a building."

—THOMAS FULLER, 1822–1898, Canadian architect

CZECH REPUBLIC

Prague. A Medieval city untouched by the ravages of war; beautiful Baroque buildings.

FRANCE

Honfleur. Charming preserved port city on an estuary of the Seine across the bay from Le Havre. Its tall narrow buildings overlooking the port are an artist's or photographer's dream subject.

Mont-Saint-Michel. This small island in the Gulf of St. Malo dates back to about the 11th century. It is connected to the mainland by a road that is covered at high tide.

Paris. Paris truly deserves to be called the "City of Light," and proudly maintains its neighborhoods and architectural heritage.

GERMANY

Dinklesbuhl. A charming stop on the Romantic Road.

Heidelburg. This old town by the Neckar river features town gates and a grand castle.

Meissen. Visit the porcelain factory, palace, and museum.

Rothenburg ob der Tauber. A walled city on the Tauber river, founded in the late 10th century, Rothenburg features Medieval and Gothic architecture.

GREAT BRITAIN

Bath. Georgian architecture *(Crescent Circles)* and restored ancient *Roman Baths.*

Broadway. A charming Cotswold village, with a wide main street and beautiful old stone buildings.

Cambridge. Home to many colleges, this is a vibrant new/old city.

Canterbury. This ancient city is a wonderful place to tour on foot. Home to historic *Canterbury Cathedral.*

Edinburgh, Scotland. A city in gray stone, ideal for walking. Home to *Edinburgh Castle.*

London. Many neighborhoods preserved for hundreds of years.

GREAT BRITAIN (*continued*)

Lower Slaughter. A postcard town of golden cottages beside small streams, with roses growing to the rooftops.

Oxford. Home to *Bodleian Library* and many colleges.

Stowe-on-the-Wold. A very Shakespearean town featuring Cotswold architecture, golden stone, and a town square.

Stratford-upon-Avon. Shakespeare's hometown features many half-timbered houses.

York. Walk the Roman city walls, see half-timbered houses.

ITALY

Florence. Golden city with Medieval and Renaissance structures.

Herculaneum. An ancient city destroyed at the same time as Pompeii; excavation ongoing.

Pompeii. Excavation continues in this city buried in ash in A.D. 79.

Rome. Ancient structures incorporated into a modern city.

Siena. A Medieval city with a very well preserved city center and structures.

Venice. Canals and palaces remain much as they were in the Renaissance.

UNITED STATES

Annapolis, Maryland. A charming Colonial city with many historic houses.

Baltimore, Maryland. An historic Colonial town; old neighborhoods of row houses featuring Colonial architecture are proudly maintained.

Boston, Massachusetts. You can take a walk back in time to Colonial America in many parts of this city.

Charleston, South Carolina. A charming historic Colonial seaport that treasures its antebellum houses and plantations.

Chicago, Illinois. Chicago's architectural heritage of early skyscrapers and buildings by many famous architects in the downtown area is proudly maintained.

New Harmony (near Pittsburgh), Pennsylvania. Settled by the Bavarian Pietists (Harmonie sect) in 1804, this is an example of a Utopian community, in which everyone worked for the common good. A total of

8 Harmonist sites and 25 Harmonist buildings remain in New Harmony. The Harmonists' motto was "Work, work, work! Save, save, save!"

New Harmony, Indiana. Another town founded and settled by the Bavarian Pietists from 1814–1824, features community houses, long cabins, the Atheneum, and other Harmonist structures.

Newport, Rhode Island. "Cottages" (mansions) built by American aristocrats for summer residence.

Oak Park, Illinois. Home to numerous Frank Lloyd Wright homes.

Old Deerfield Village, Massachusetts. Home to many Colonial New England homes.

Old Economy Village (Ambridge), Pennsylvania. Settled by the Bavarian Pietists (Harmonie sect); 17 original buildings dating 1824–1830 and recreated gardens are open to the public.

Old Mystic Seaport, Connecticut. A harbor, old wharf, and buildings dating back to 1838 form the nucleus of the Museum of America and the Sea. Historic wooden ships, a lighthouse, and 60 buildings or historic structures are worth the visit.

Salem, Massachusetts. Colonial houses and harbor remain much as they did in their early days.

San Francisco, California. Among its many attractions are the beautifully painted Victorian homes—"painted ladies"—on the city's hillsides.

Santa Fe, New Mexico. Traditional Southwest building styles using mostly adobe.

Savannah, Georgia. Established in 1710, this gracious Southern city has retained its Colonial charm.

Springfield, Illinois. Lincoln's Home and 27 existing homes in the neighborhood have been maintained.

St. Augustine, Florida. The oldest city in the United States has maintained 31 original buildings.

St. Genevieve, Missouri. This city's French heritage homes are open for viewing.

St. Louis, Missouri. Although most of the cast-iron building façades have been destroyed, many neighborhoods of fine historic houses made of the locally abundant brick are well-maintained.

UNITED STATES (*continued*)

Taos, New Mexico. A Native American Pueblo that retains traditional adobe building style.

Williamsburg, Virginia. Colonial housing has been renovated and reconstructed.

FRANK LLOYD WRIGHT PLACES YOU CAN VISIT

Many volumes have been written about Frank Lloyd Wright's architecture, which totaled 400 structures including windmills, gates, and fountains. His work covers 35 states, with almost 90 percent of the homes still private residences not open to the public. The following are some of Wright's designs that are open to the public, if not all the time, at least for special occasions.

JAPAN

Gakuen School, 1921, 31–34 Nishi, Ikebukuro, 2-Chrome, Tokyo

Imperial Hotel, 1917, Meijimura Park, Inuyama City near Nagoya

UNITED STATES

Arizona

Arizona Biltmore Hotel, 1928, 24th Street at Missouri Avenue, Phoenix

Taliesin West, 1938, 11000 Shea Boulevard, Scottsdale

California

Aline Barnsdall House ("Hollyhock House"), 1920, 4800 Hollywood Boulevard, Los Angeles

Charles Ennis House, 1924, 1607 Glendower Avenue, Los Angeles

Marin County Building, 1957, U.S. 101 at San Pedro Road, San Rafael

Morris Gift Shop, 1948, 140 Maiden Lane, San Francisco

"A doctor can bury his mistakes, but an architect can only advise his clients to plant vines."

—FRANK LLOYD WRIGHT, 1867–1959, American architect

Illinois

Auditorium Building (with Adler and Sullivan), 430 South Michigan Avenue, Chicago (tours)

Charnley House (with Adler and Sullivan), 1891, 1365 Astor Street, Chicago

Dana-Thomas House, 1904, Springfield (tours)

Fabyan House, 1907, Geneva (remodel)

Frank Lloyd Wright Home and Studio, 1889, 951 Chicago Avenue and 428 Forest Avenue, Oak Park (regular tours). An annual tour in May allows visitors to see interiors of other Oak Park and River Forest homes.

Graceland Cemetery, Sullivan Grave, Chicago (cemetery open daily)

Horse Show Association Foundation Fountain, Oak Park

Nathan Moore House, Forest Avenue near Lake Street, Oak Park (tours)

Pettit Memorial Chapel, 1906, Harrison at Webster, Belvidere

Robie House, 1909, 5757 South Woodlawn Avenue, Chicago (tours)

Rookery Building Lobby, 1905, 209 South LaSalle Street, Chicago

Rosehill Cemetery, Catherine Lloyd Wright grave, Chicago (cemetery open daily)

Unity Temple, 1906, 861 Lake Street at Kenilworth Avenue, Oak Park (tours)

Michigan

Gregor S. Afflect House, 1925 North Woodward Avenue, Bloomfield Hills

Meyer May House, 1908, 450 Madison Avenue, SE, Grand Rapids (tours)

Minnesota

> *Fasbender Medical Clinic*, 1957, 801 Pine Street at Highway 55, Hastings
> *Lindholm Service Station*, 1957, 202 Cloquet Avenue, Cloquet

Missouri

> *Russell Kraus House*, 1951, Ballas Road, Kirkwood

Oklahoma

> *Price Tower*, 1952, Dewel Avenue at N.E. 6th Street, Bartlesville (newly
> reopened as a "boutique" hotel)

Wisconsin

> *Albert D. German Warehouse*, 1915, 300 South Church Street, Richland
> Center
> *Annunciation Greek Orthodox Church*, 1956, 9400 West Congress Street,
> Wauwatosa (tours require appropriate dress)
> *Johnson Wax Company Administration Building and Research Tower*,
> 1936, 1525 Howe Street, Racine (tours)
> *Monona Terrace*, 1938, East Martin Luther King Boulevard, Madison
> *Seth Peterson Cottage*, 1958, E. 9982 Ferndell Road, Lake Delton
> (intermittant public tours)
> *Taliesin*, 1911, Route 23, Spring Green (open spring, summer, and fall)
> *Unitarian Meeting House*, 1947, 900 University Bay Drive, Shorewood
> Hills (open for services and tours from May to September)
> *Unity Chapel*, 1886, Cemetery Road, Spring Green (occasional services)
> *Visitors' Center*, 1956, Spring Green (formerly the Riverview Terrace
> Restaurant)

*"Early in life I had to choose between arrogance and
hypocritical humility. I chose honest arrogance and have
seen no occasion to change."*
—FRANK LLOYD WRIGHT, 1867–1959,
American Prairie School architect

LANDSCAPE ARCHITECTS

Gardens, walkways, and parks can define a city. Who could imagine New York without *Central Park*, or Paris without the *Tuilerie Gardens*? This list features some of the world's well-known landscape architects and examples of their work. These people understood that, as Swiss architect Le Corbusier said, "The materials of city planning are sky, space, trees, steel, and cement, in that order and in that hierarchy."

BELGIUM

Wirtz, Jacques, 1925. *Tuilerie Gardens*, Paris

BRAZIL

Burle-Marx, Roberto, 1909–1994. *Ministry of Health and Education*, Rio de Janeiro

ENGLAND

Bridgeman, Charles, d. 1738. *Chicheley Hall, Bower House, Wimbleton House, Warwick Castle, Longleat, Hampton Court*

Brown, Lancelot "Capability," 1716–1783. *Blenheim Palace*, Woodstock

Chambers, Sir William, 1726–1796. *Kew Gardens*, London

Duchène, Achille, 1866–1947. East front gardens of *Blenheim Castle*

Farrand, Beatrix, 1872–1959. *Dartington Hall*, Devonshire

Jekyll, Gertrude, 1843–1932. *Sissinghurst Castle Gardens*, Kent

Jellicoe, Geoffrey, 1900–1996. *Shute House*, Wiltshire; *Sandringham House*, Huntstanton

Kent, William, 1685–1748. *Chiswick House*, London. Kent collaborated on *Chiswick House* with Lord Burlington, particularly integrating the landscape with the house, a revolutionary idea at that time.

Paxton, Sir Joseph, 1801–1865. *Chatsworth: Crystal Palace*, London

Repton, Humphry, 1752–1818. One of the foremost English landscape architects of his generation. His formal treatment of the garden and terraces next to the house, and the invention of the French door were innovations for the time.

FRANCE

Alphand, Jean-Charles-Adolphe, 1817–1891. *Bois de Boulogne,* Paris

André, Edouard François, 1840–1922. *Gardens of Villa Borghese,* Rome

LeNotre, André, 1613–1700. *Vaux-le-Vicompte,* gardens near Fontainebleau

ITALY

Romano, Giulio, 1492–1546. *Palace-garden design, Versailles,* France

MEXICO

Barragan, Luis, 1902–1989. *San Cristobal Estate,* near Mexico City

UNITED STATES

Abbott, Stanley William, 1908–1975. *Blue Ridge Parkway,* Virginia

Bottomly, William Lawrence, 1883–1951. *Williamsburg Restoration,* Virginia

Child, Susan, Mary Miss, Stanton Ekstut (partners). *South Cove, Battery Park,* New York City

Cleveland, Horace William Shafer, 1814–1900. *Jekyll Island Club,* Georgia

Downing, Andrew Jackson, 1815–1852. An American architect, landscape designer, and writer who popularized the idea of landscape gardening.

DuPont, Pierre, 1870–1954. *Longwood Garden,* Pennsylvania

Hall, William Hammond, 1846–1934. *Golden Gate Park,* San Francisco

Halprin, Lawrence, 1916. *McIntyre Watergardens,* Hillsborough, California; *FDR Memorial,* Washington, DC

Jefferson, Thomas, 1743–1826. *University of Virginia* and *Monticello* gardens, Virginia

Jensen, Jens, 1860–1951. *Lincoln Memorial Garden,* Springfield, Illinois

Johnson, Philip, 1906. *Sculpture Garden,* Museum of Modern Art, New York City

Olmsted, Frederick Law, 1822–1903. *Biltmore, Asheville, North Carolina; Central Park,* New York; *Fairmont Park,* Philadelphia

Steele, Fletcher, 1885–1971. *Choate Garden,* Stockbridge, Massachusetts

Verdure, Mordant, 1899–1934. *Barrymore's Summer Castle,* Palm Beach, Florida

ANCIENT GREEK ARCHITECTURE

Many ancient Greek ruins have been restored, but all that remains of others are a few columns; however, often that's enough to give visitors to these sites a sense of the grandeur that was part of this culture. As you will see from this list, lands far beyond modern-day Greece were home to ancient Greeks, including modern-day Turkey and parts of the Middle East. Thus, their architecture can be seen beyond Greece and the Greek Isles.

ATHENS

Erechtheum, 421–405 B.C.

Monument of Lysicrates, c. 334 B.C.

Olympieion, c. 170 B.C.

Parthenon, 447–432 B.C.

Propylaea, 437–432 B.C.

Stadium, begun 331 B.C.

Stoa of Attalos, c. 150 B.C.

Temple of Athena Nike, 427–424 B.C.

Temple of Hephaestus, 449–c. 430 B.C.

Temple of Zeus, A.D. 131–132

Theater of Dionysus, c. 330 B.C.

CORINTH

Temple of Apollo, c. 540 B.C.

Temple of Athena Nike, c. 1st century B.C.

DELOS

Athenian Temple, 425–420 B.C.

Basilica of St. Ciriacus, 3rd to 2nd centuries B.C.

House of Dionysos, 2nd century B.C.

House of the Masks, 2nd century B.C.

Poseidoniastes, 2nd century B.C.

Temple to Apollo, 7th century B.C.

DELPHI

Temple of Apollo, 513–505 B.C.

Theater, 2nd century B.C.

Treasure of the Athenians, c. 500–485 B.C.

Treasury of the Siphnians, c. 530 B.C.

EPIDAURUS

Temple of Aphrodite, 4th to 3rd centuries B.C.

Temple of Apollo, c. 510 B.C.

Temple of Artemis, c. 356 B.C.

Theater, c. 350 B.C.

Tholos (Beehive tomb), c. 350 B.C.

RUINS IN OTHER GREEK CITIES

Lion Gate to the Palace, 1250 B.C., Mycenae

Sanctuary of the Great Gods, 340 B.C., Samothrace

Temple of Aphaia, 490 B.C., Aegina

Temple of Apollo, 5th century B.C., Arkadia

Temple of Artemis, c. 580 B.C., Corfu

Temple of Poseidon, 444–440 B.C., Sounion

Theater, 2nd century B.C., Priene

Treasury of Atreus, c. 1300–1250 B.C., Mycenae

GREEK RUINS IN ITALY

Basilica (Temple of Hera II), 448–430 B.C. (Doric), Paestum

Greek Theater, 2nd century B.C., Pompeii

Greek Theatre, 3rd century B.C., Taormina, Sicily

Greek Theatre, begun 3rd century B.C., Syracuse

Temple of Apollo, c. 565 B.C., Syracuse

Temple of Concord, c. 430 B.C., Agrigento, Sicily

Temple of Demeter, c. 510 B.C., Paestum

Temple of Poseidon, c. 460 B.C., Paestum

Temple of Zeus Olympus, c. 510–409 B.C., Agrigento, Sicily

GREEK RUINS IN LIBYA

Temple of Zeus, 6th century B.C., Cyrene

GREEK RUINS IN TURKEY

Carea Hellenistic Theater, 3rd century B.C., Mysia
Temple of Artemis, c. 350 B.C., Ephesus
Temple of Artemis, c. 334 B.C., Sardis
Temple of Pergamon, c. 180 B.C., Mysia (now in Berlin)

ANCIENT ROMAN ARCHITECTURE

The Romans didn't build an empire by staying at home. They were a people on the move, conquering cultures far and near and making themselves at home in lands in every direction. The evidence of their far-flung empire can be seen in what remains of their architecture in Tunisia, Jordan, France, and Germany, to name just a few places. Excavations continue and are likely to produce new discoveries.

AMPHITHEATERS

Amphitheater, 1st–3rd centuries A.D., Catania, Sicily
Amphitheater, c. 30 B.C., Nimes, France
Amphitheater, 80–70 B.C., Pompeii
Amphitheater, A.D. 50, Orange, France
Amphitheater, A.D. 56, Lepcis, Libya
Amphitheater, 1st to 2nd centuries A.D., Newport, South Wales
Arena, 1st century A.D., Pula, Croatia
Arena, c. 100–50 B.C., Verona, Italy
Colosseum, c. 45 B.C., El Djem, Tunisia
Colosseum, A.D. 80, Rome
Colosseum, before 55 B.C., Arles, France

AQUEDUCTS

Albarregas Aqueduct, 3rd century, Badajoz, Spain
Aqueduct, 122 B.C., Carthage, Tunisia

Aqueduct, 1st century B.C., Merida, Spain

Aqueduct, 1st to 3rd century A.D., Cherchel, Algeria

Aqueduct, c. A.D. 10, Segovia, Spain

Aqueduct, 2nd century A.D., Moria, Lesbos

Las Perreras Aqueduct, 1st or early 2nd century A.D., Tarragona, Spain

Marcian Aqueduct, 144 B.C., near Rome

Pont du Gard, 27 B.C.–A.D. 14, near Nimes, France

TRIUMPHAL ARCHES

Arch of Argentarii, A.D. 204, Rome

Arch of Augustus, 27 B.C., Rimini, Italy

Arch of Augustus, 8 B.C., Susa, Italy

Arch of Augustus, c. 20 B.C., Forum, Rome

Arch of Caracalla, A.D. 217, Meknes, Morocco

Arch of Constantine, A.D. 312–315, Rome

Arch of Galerius, c. A.D. 300, Salonica, Greece

Arch of Hadrian, A.D. 138, Athens

Arch of Janus, A.D. 315, Rome

Arch of Marcus Aurelius, A.D. 163, Oea, Tripoli, Libya

Arch of Septimius Severus, c. A.D. 203, Forum, Rome

Arch of Septimius Severus, c. A.D. 200, Lepcis, Libya

Arch of Septimius Severus, A.D. 235, Dougga, Tunisia

Arch of the Julii, c. 40 B.C., St. Remy, France

Arch of Tiberius, c. A.D. 26, Orange, France

Arch of Trajan, c. A.D. 114, Timgad, Algeria

Arch of Titus, A.D. 81, Rome

Archway, 2nd century A.D., Palmyra, Tadmor, Syria

BASILICAS

Basilica, A.D. 98–117, Cyrene, Libya

Basilica, 2nd century B.C., Tuscany, Italy

Basilica, c. 125 B.C., Pompeii

Basilica, c. A.D. 310, Trier, Germany

Basilica Nova, A.D. 313, Forum, Rome

Basilica of Maxentius and Constantine, c. A.D. 307–312, Forum, Rome

Basilica of Porcia, 184 B.C., Forum, Rome

Basilica Vetus, A.D. 216, Lepcis, Libya

BATHS

Achellian Baths, (no date available), Catania, Sicily

Bath, 1st century, Bath, England

Baths at Trier, c. A.D. 300, Germany

Baths of Caracalla, A.D. 216, Rome

Baths of Diocletian, A.D. 305, Rome (now church of S. Maria degli Angeli)

Baths of Diocletian, c. A.D. 298–306, Split, Croatia

Baths of Titus, c. A.D. 80, Rome

Baths of Trajan, A.D. 109, Rome

Forum Baths, 1st century B.C., Pompeii

Forum Baths, A.D. 160, Ostia, Italy

Hadrianic Baths, A.D. 127, Lepcis, Libya

Harbor Baths, late 2nd century A.D., Ephesus, Turkey

North Baths, 4th century A.D., Timgad, Algeria

Stabian Baths, 2nd century B.C., Pompeii

Winter Baths, 2nd century A.D., Henchir Kasbat, Tunisia

BRIDGES

Alcantara Bridge, A.D. 105–106, River Tagus, Spain

Bridge at Narni, c. 27 B.C., Italy

Bridge at Merida, c. 3rd century A.D., Spain

Pons Aelius, A.D. 135, Rome

Pons Cestius, 46 B.C., Rimini, Italy

Pons Fabricius, 62 B.C., River Tiber, Rome

Ponte Molle, 109 B.C., Rome

Salamanca, c. 1st century A.D., Spain

FORUMS

Forum, 1ˢᵗ century B.C., Annaba, Algeria

Forum, 2ⁿᵈ century A.D., Henchir Kasbat, Tunisia

Forum, c. 1ˢᵗ century B.C., Pompeii

Forum, 2ⁿᵈ century A.D., Dougga, Tunisia

Forum of Augustus, 3–2 B.C., Rome

Forum of Nerva, A.D. 97, Rome

Forum of Trajan, A.D. 113, Rome

Forum of Vespasian, A.D. 71–75, Rome

Forum Romanum, 46 B.C., Rome

Forum Vetus, c. 30–20 B.C., Lepcis, Libya

Hadrian's Forum, A.D. 125–128, Rome

Severan Forum, A.D. 216, Lepcis, Libya

FORTRESSES

Carnuntum, A.D. 73, near Vienna, Austria

Carvoran, c. A.D. 120–132, near Greenhead, England

Chesters Roman Fort, c. A.D. 120–125, near Chollerford, England

Housesteads Roman Fort, 2ⁿᵈ century A.D., near Bardon Mill, England

Vindolanda, c. A.D. 80, near Bardon Mill, England

LIBRARIES

Library, 4ᵗʰ century A.D., Timgad, Algeria

Library of Celsus, A.D. 115, Ephesus, Turkey

MONUMENTS

Ara Pacis, 13–9 B.C., Rome

Column of Marcus Aurelius, A.D. 176–193, Rome

Mausoleaum, 40 B.C., St. Remy, France

Mausoleum of Augustus, c. 25 B.C., Rome

Tomb of Caecilia Metella, c. 20 B.C., Rome

Trajan's Column, A.D. 113, Rome

PALACES

Domitian's Palace, c. A.D. 75, Palatine, Rome
Domus Aurea, 1st century A.D., Rome
Fishbourne, c. A.D. 80, Chichester, England
Palace of Diocletian, c. A.D. 300, Split, Croatia

TEMPLES

Apollo, 431 B.C., Rome
Apollo, 1st century A.D., Pompeii
Artemis, 6th century B.C., Ephesus, Turkey
Artemis, 2nd century A.D., Jerash, Jordan
Bacchus, c. A.D. 150–200, Baalbek, Lebanon
Bel, A.D. 32, Palmyra, Tadmor, Sicily
Capitoline Jupiter, 509 B.C., Rome
Castor and Pollux, 484 B.C., Forum, Rome
Concord, A.D. 10, Rome
Deified Claudius, A.D. 70, Rome
Deified Hadrian, A.D. 145, Rome
Fortuna Virilis, c. 120 B.C., Rome
Hadrian, c. 2nd century A.D., Ephesus, Turkey
Hercules, c. 100 B.C., Latium, Italy
Hercules Victor, c. 120 B.C., Rome
Jupiter, 1st century A.D., Baalbek, Lebanon
Maison Carré, 16 B.C., Nimes, France
Pantheon, c. A.D. 118–128, Rome
Pergamon, 180 B.C., Mysia, Turkey
Portumnus, 31 B.C., Rome
Rome and Augustus, c. 1st century A.D., Lepcis, Libya
Sanctuary of Fortuna Primigenia, 1st century B.C., Praeneste (near Rome)
Septimius Severus, c. 1st century A.D., Djemila, Algeria
The Sybils, early 1st century B.C., Tivoli, Italy
Venus, c. A.D. 118–135, Hadrian's Villa, Tivoli, Italy
Venus, c. A.D. 2nd–3rd century, Baalbek, Lebanon
Venus and Rome, A.D. 123–135, Rome

TEMPLES *(continued)*

Vespasian, c. A.D. 62–79, Pompeii
Vesta (now S. Maria del Sole), c. 27 B.C., Tivoli, Italy
Virile Fortune, c. 100–80 B.C., Rome

THEATERS

Theater, c. 1st century B.C., Annaba, Algeria
Theater, c. 46 B.C., Arles, France
Theater, 8 B.C., Badajoz, Spain
Theater, c. 2nd century B.C., Ephesus, Turkey
Theater, A.D. 1–2, Lepcis, Libya
Theater, 1st century B.C., Lyon, France
Theater, c. 30 B.C., Nimes, France
Theater, 1st century A.D., Orange, France
Theater, 2nd century A.D., Petra, Jordan
Theater, 2nd century A.D., Taormina, Sicily
Theater, c. 100–54 B.C., Veneto, Italy
Theater at Aspendos, A.D. 161–180, Pamphylia, Turkey
Theater at Sabratha, A.D. 180, Tripolis, Libya
Theater at St. Albans, A.D. 43–44, Hertfordshire, England
Theater Marcello, 13–11 B.C., Rome

TOMBS

Catacombs, c. A.D. 100–300, Rome
Mausoleum of Hadrian, A.D. 140, Tivoli, Italy
Pyramid of Caius Cestius, c. 18–12 B.C., Rome
Rock-cut tomb of el-Deir, 2nd century A.D., Petra, Jordan
Tomb of Hunting and Fishing, c. 510–500 B.C., Tarquinia, Italy
Tomb of the Reliefs, 6th–4th centuries B.C., Ceveteri, Italy

TOWN GATEWAYS

Colcester Town Gateway, c. A.D. 120, England
Gate of Augustus, 16 to 15 B.C., Nimes, France
Market Gate, c. A.D. 160, Miletus, Turkey (now in State Museums, Berlin)

Porta Appia, A.D. 275–280, Rome
Porta Augusta, 2nd century B.C., Perugia, Italy
Porta Aurea, c. A.D. 300, Split, Croatia
Porta Borsari, 1st century A.D., Verona, Italy
Porta Maggiore, A.D. 52, Rome
Porta Nigra, c. A.D. 320, Trier, Germany
Porta San Sebastiano, c. 3rd century A.D., Rome
Porta Sanguinaria, 2nd century B.C., Ferentino, Italy
Two Town Gateways, c. 20 B.C., Autun, France

VILLAS

Amor and Psyche, A.D. 4th century, Ostia, Italy
Brading Roman Villa, 3rd century, Brading, England
Diana, 2nd century A.D., Ostia, Italy
Golden House of Nero, c. A.D. 64, Rome
Hadrian's Villa, c. A.D. 125–138, Tivoli, Italy
House of the Faun, 180 B.C., Pompeii
House of the Red Walls, pre A.D. 79, Pompeii
House of the Silver Wedding, 1st century A.D., Pompeii
House of the Surgeon, 3rd century B.C., Pompeii
House of Vettii, A.D. 63–79, Pompeii
Lucretius Fronto, c. A.D. 30, Pompeii
Tiberius' Villa, c. A.D. 27, Capri, Italy
Villa, c. A.D. 200, Tripoli, Lebanon
Villa at Boscoreale, 1st century B.C., near Pompeii
Villa Jovis, A.D. 14–37, Capri, Italy
Villa of the Mysteries, c. 50 B.C., Pompeii

WALLS

Augustan Walls, 6th–3rd centuries B.C., Tarragona, Spain
Aurelian's Wall, c. A.D. 270, Rome
Hadrian's Wall, A.D. 136, England

GREAT PLACES OF WORSHIP

Although some of these structures have been converted to museums and no longer function as places of worship, they still remain buildings that people respectfully visit. Many of these have been carefully preserved, though as religious practices have changed they may have been remodeled. Some Dutch churches, for example, feature stark interiors, as religious icons were carefully removed when Catholicism was no longer the state religion.

Where available, the name of the architect is provided. Because huge religious structures, castles, and palaces sometimes took hundreds of years to complete, many architects were involved. Naturally it was not unusual for an architect to be unable to complete what he had begun.

AUSTRIA

Benedictine Abbey, 1702–1714, Melk, Jakob Prandtauer (1660–1726)

Church of Vierzehnheiligen, 1743–1771, Vienna, Johann Balthasar Neumann (1687–1753)

Karlskirche, 1716–1737, Vienna, Johann Fischer von Erlach (1656–1723)

BELGIUM

Antwerp Cathedral, 1352–1521, Antwerp

BOSNIA-HERZEGOVINA

Byzantine Church, 1318–1321, Gracanica

BRAZIL

Church of Sao Francisco, 1766–1794, Ouro Preto, Antonio Francisco Lisboa (Aleijadinho) (1730–1814)

St. Francis at Pampulha, 1942–1943, near Belo Horizonte, Oscar Niemeier (1902)

CAMBODIA

Angkor Wat Temple-Mountain, 1113–1150, Angkor

CANADA

Cathedral of St. James, 1875–1885, Montreal, Joseph Michaud
    (1822–1902) with Victor Bourgeau (1809–1888)
Notre Dame, 1824–1829, Montreal, James O'Donnel (1774–1830)
St. Joseph Lauzon, 1830–1832, Quebec, Thomas Baillairgé (1791–1859)

CHINA

Big Goose Pagoda, Xian, A.D. 648–704, Ch'ang-an
Fo Kuang Temple Hall, 857, Beijing
Sung Yueh Pagoda, A.D. 523, Mount Sung, Shanghai
Temple of Heaven Group, begun 15th century, Beijing

ENGLAND

All Saints, 1849–1859, London, William Butterfield (1814–1900)
Canterbury Cathedral, 1174, Canterbury, William of Sens (active 1179)
Durham Cathedral, begun 1093, Durham
New St. Paul's, 1675–1712, London, Christopher Wren (1632–1723)
Salisbury Cathedral, 1220–1270, Salisbury
St. Martin's in the Fields, 1726, London, James Gibbs (1662–1754)
St. Pancras Church, 1819–1822, London, Henry W. Inwood (1794–1843)
Stonehenge, c. 1650 B.C., near Salisbury
Winchester Cathedral, c. 1394–1450, Winchester

FRANCE

Abby Church of St. Denis, 1122, St. Denis
Cathedral of St. Etienne, 1067, St. Etienne
Chapel of the Rosary, 1950–1951, Vence, Henri Matisse (1869–1954)
Chartres Cathedral, 1140–1220, Chartres
Church of the Invalides, 1676–1706, Paris, Jules Hardouin-Mansart
    (1646–1708)
Church of the Madeleine, 1806–1843, Paris, Alexander-Pierre Vignon
    (1762–1828)
Mont Saint Michel, 1203–1264, Mont Saint Michel
Notre Dame de Amiens, 1236, Amiens
Notre Dame du Haut Chapel, 1955, Ronchamp, Le Corbusier (Swiss,
    1887–1966)

FRANCE *(continued)*

Notre Dame, 1163–1250, Paris

Panthéon (Ste. Geneviève), 1755–1792, Paris, Jacques Germain Soufflot
    (1713–1780)

Sainte Chappelle, 1243–1248, Paris

St. Sernin Cathedral, 1080–1120, Toulouse

GERMANY

Cathedral, 1248–1322, Cologne

Die Wies Pilgrimage Church, c. 1745, Bavaria, Dominikus Zimmerman
    (1685–1766)

Pilgrimage Church, c. 1960, Neviges, Gottfried Bohm (1920)

Sankt Johannes Nepomuk, 1733–1746, Munich

St. Michael's, 1001, Hildesheim

The Carolingian Palatine Chapel, 792–805, Aachen

GREECE

Altar of Zeus, Pergamon, c. 180 B.C. (now on view in Berlin)

Church of Gorgeopekos, c. 1190–1195, Athens

Church of Our Lady of the Coppersmiths, A.D. 1028, Thessaloniki

Church of the Dormition, c. 1100, Daphni

Church of the Holy Apostles, 1310–1314, Thessaloniki

INDIA

Great Temple Complex, 17th century, Madurai

Jami Masjid, 1424, Ahmadabad, Gujarat

Kailasanatha Temple, c. 757–790, Ellora

Kandariya Mahadeo Temple, c. 1025–1050, Chandella

Kutub Minaret, A.D. 1200, Delhi

Mukteshvara Temple, c. 950, Bhuvaneshvar, Orissa

Shore Temple of the Seven Pagodas, 8th century A.D., Mahabalipuram

Stupa of Sanchi, 1st century A.D., Sanchi

Surya Temple, c. 1240, Konarak, Eastern Ganga

INDONESIA

Stupa at Borobudur, 8th century A.D., Java

IRAN

Blue Mosque, 1467, Tabriz
Great Mosque of Samarra, c. A.D. 850, Samarra
Maliwa (spiral brick minaret), A.D. 847, Samarra
Tarik Khana Mosque, early 8th century A.D., Damghan

IRAQ

White Temple, c. 3000 B.C., Uruk (Warka)
Ziggurat at Ur-Nammu, 2113–2048 B.C., Ur

ISRAEL

Church of the Nativity, A.D. 339, Jerusalem
Church of the Holy Sepulchre, A.D. 335, Jerusalem
Dome of the Rock, 691–692, Jerusalem

ITALY

Basilica of Saint Ambrogio, late 11th and 12th centuries, Milan
Church of S. Sabina, A.D. 422–432, Rome
Church of San Francesco, c. 1450–1461, Rimini, Leon Battista Alberti
    (1404–1472)
Cupola of Santa Maria del Fiore (Cathedral), 1420–1436, Florence,
    Filippo Brunelleschi (1377–1446)
Mausoleum of Galla Placida, c. A.D. 425, Ravenna
Medici Chapel, Church of San Lorenzo, 1524–1534, Florence,
    Michelangelo Buonarroti (1475–1564)
Old St. Peter's Cathedral, A.D. 330, Rome
Pisa Cathedral Complex, Cathedral (1064), (Leaning) Tower (1173–1350),
    and Baptistery (1290), Pisa. Giovanni Pisano (1250–1314) was one of a
    family of builders credited with working on the Cathedral complex and
    especially the *Leaning Tower.*

ITALY *(continued)*

S. Maria Maggiore, c. A.D. 432, Rome

S. Paolo Outside the Walls, begun A.D. 385, Rome

San Apollinare in Classe, A.D. 432–449, Classe (near Ravenna)

San Carlo alle Quattro Fontane, 1665–1667, Rome, Francesco Borromini (1599–1667)

San Lorenzo, 1668–1687, Turin, Guarino Guarini, (1624–1683)

San Vitale, A.D. 526–548, Ravenna

Sant' Agnese, Piazza Navone, 1653–1666, Rome, Francesco Borromini (1599–1667)

Santa Costanza, c. A.D. 350, Rome

Santa Maria delle Grazie, c. 1492, Milan, Donato Bramante (1444–1514)

Sienna Cathedral, 1296, Sienna

St. Mark's Cathedral, c. 1063, Venice

St. Peter's colonnade, 1656–1663, Rome, Gianlorenzo Bernini (1598–1680)

St. Peter's dome, 1546–1564, Rome, Michelangelo Buonarroti (1475–1564)

St. Peter's façade, 1607–1615, Rome, Carlo Maderno (1556–1629)

Tempietto (San Pietro in Montorio), 1502, Rome, Donato Bramante (1444–1514)

The Orthodox Baptistery, c. A.D. 400–450, Rome

JAPAN

Church of the Light, 1987–1989, Osaka, Tadao Ando (1941)
Great Buddha Hall, begun A.D. 738, Nara
Hoodo (Phoenix Hall), 1052, Uji, near Kyoto
Ishiyamadera Temple, 1194, Lake Biwa
Kinkakuji (Golden Pavilion), 1397, Kyoto
Pagoda of the Yakushiji, c. 8th century, Nara
Shrine, A.D. 300 (shrine rebuilt every 20 years since 478), Ise
Temple of Horyu-ji, begun A.D. 607, Nara

JORDAN

El Deir Temple, 2nd century B.C., Petra
Khazna Temple, c. A.D. 120, Petra

LEBANON

Temple of Bacchus, 2nd century A.D., Baalbek

MEXICO

Church of San Francisco, 1521, Tlaxcala
House of the Virgins, c. 530, Chichén-Itza, Yucatan
Metropolitan Cathedral, 1570–c. 1810, Mexico City
Pyramid of the Sun, A.D. 25, Teotihuacan
Temple of Quetzalcoatl, A.D. 770–829, Teotihuacan
Temple of Tlahuizcalpantecuhtli, c. A.D. 1000, Tula

NORWAY

Borgund Church, c. 1150, Borgund

RUSSIA

Basil the Blessed, 1554–1560, Moscow
Cathedral of the Assumption, 12th century, Vladmir
Peter and Paul, 18th century, St. Petersburg

SPAIN

Church of the Sagrada Familia, 1883–1926, Barcelona, Antoni Gaudi
(1852–1926)
Mosque of Cordoba, begun 785, Cordoba
Our Lady of Toledo, begun 1227, Toledo
Sacristy of the Cartuja, 1702–1720, Granada, Francisco Hurtado
Izquierdo (1669–1725)
Santa Maria, 1075–1568, Burgos
Santiago de Compostela, 1060–1130, Compostela

THAILAND

Wat Po (Wat Phra Chetupon), 16th century, Bangkok

TURKEY

Blue Mosque (Sultan Ahmet Mosque), 11th century, Istanbul
Hagia Sophia, 532–537, Istanbul, Isidore of Miletus
(6th century) and Anthemius of Tralles (6th century)
Mosque of Ahmed I, 1609–1616, Istanbul
Mosque of Selim II, 1570–1574, Edirne
Mosque of Sultan Suleyman, 1550–1557, Istanbul
St. Saviour, rebuilt early 14th century, Khora

UKRAINE

St. Sophia, 1037, Kiev, Ukraine

UNITED STATES

Arizona

San Xavier del Bac, 1784–1797, Tucson

Arkansas

Thorncrown Chapel, 1980, Eureka Springs, E. Fay Jones (1921)

California

    Crystal Cathedral, 1980, Garden Grove, Philip Johnson (1906)
    First Baptist Church, 1906, Oakland, Julia Morgan (1872–1957)
    First Church of Christ Scientist, 1909–1911, Berkeley, Bernard Maybeck (1862–1957)
    Garden Grove Community Church, 1962, Garden Grove, Richard Neutra (1892–1970)

District of Columbia

    National Cathedral, 1907, Philip Hubert Frohman (1887–1972)

Maryland

    Baltimore Cathedral, 1804–1821, Baltimore, Benjamin Henry Latrobe (1764–1820)

Massachusetts

    Christ Church, 1759–1761, Cambridge
    Old Ship Meeting House, 1681, Hingham

Missouri

    B'nai Amoona Temple, 1950, St. Louis, Erich Mendelsohn (1887–1953)

New Mexico

    San Esteban, pre-1644, Acoma

New York

    St. Patrick's Cathedral, 1858–1888, New York City, James Renwick (1818–1895)
    Trinity Church, 1839–1846, New York City, Richard Upjohn (1802–1878)

Pennsylvania

    Christ Church, 1727–1754, Philadelphia

Rhode Island

    First Baptist Meeting House, 1774–1775, Providence

South Carolina

    St. Michael's, 1753, Charleston

ASSORTED ARCHITECTURAL ICONS

The following famous structures were built to serve a variety of purposes, ranging from tombs to temples and pyramids to palaces. That they still exist and are treasured and visited by millions of people speaks to the importance of architecture in keeping a culture alive and of the human need to connect with and understand the past.

AFRICA

    Nigerian Railway Corporation Hospital, (date unknown), Lagos, Nigeria, A. Ifeanyi Ekwueme

AUSTRALIA

    Darling Harbor Redevelopment, Sydney, 1988, Philip Cox
    Opera House, 1959–1973, Sydney, Jorn Utzon (1918)

AUSTRIA

    Burgtheater, 1880–1886, Vienna, G. Semper (1803–1879) and Karl von Hasenauer (1833–1894)

CANADA

    American Pavilion (geodesic dome), 1967, Montreal, Buckminster Fuller (1895–1983)

CHINA

    T'ai-ho Tien, Forbidden City, 1406–1420, Beijing

"You have to give this much to the Luftwaffe (German bombers)—when it knocked down our buildings it did not replace them with anything more offensive than rubble. We did that."

—CHARLES, PRINCE OF WALES, English architectural scholar

ENGLAND

Crystal Palace, 1851, (destroyed), London, John Paxton (1801–1865)

St. Katherine's Docks, 1827, London, Thomas Telford (Scottish, 1757–1834)

Travellers' Club, 1829–1831, London, Sir Charles Barry (1795–1860)

EGYPT

Great Sphinx, c. 2530 B.C., Giza

King Zoser's Step Pyramid, c. 2650 B.C., Imhotep, Saqqara

Pyramid of Chefren, 2530 B.C., Giza

Pyramid of Cheops, 2570 B.C., Giza

Pyramid of Mycerinus, 2500 B.C. Giza

Temple of Ramesses II, c. 1257 B.C., Abu Simbel

FINLAND

Finlandia Concert Hall, 1971, Helsinki, Alvar Alto (1898–1976)

FRANCE

Arc de Triomphe de l'Etoile, 1806–1835, Paris, Jean-Francois-Thérèse Chalgrin (1739–1811)

L'Opera, 1861–1875, Paris, Charles Garnier (1829–1898)

Maison Lafitte, 1642–1651, Paris, François Mansart (1598–1666)

Pavilion de Louveciennes and Theater, 1771–1773, Besançon, Claude Nicolas Ledoux (1736–1806)

GERMANY

Ishtar Gate, Babylon, 604–562 B.C., ruin reconstructed at State Museums, Berlin

Schauspielhaus, 1819–1821, Berlin, Karl Friedrich Schinkel (1781–1841)

INDIA

Ajanta Cave #1, late 5th century, Ajanta

Taj Mahal, 1632–1653, Agra

IRAQ

Babylon Ruins, 6th century B.C., near al-Hillah

ITALY

Campidoglio Plaza (Capitoline Hill), 1538–1561, Rome, Michelangelo Buonarroti (1475–1564)

Vittorio Emanuele Monument, 1865–1867, Milan, Giuseppe Mengoni (1829–1877)

JAPAN

Kansai International Airport, 1994, Osaka, Renzo Piano (Italian, 1937)

Kirishimi International Concert Hall, 1994, Kirishimi, Fumihiko Maki (1928)

Olympic Sports Stadium, 1963–1964, Tokyo, Kenzo Tange (1913)

MEXICO

El Castillo, A.D. 800, Chichén Itza, Yucatan

Monte Alban, c. 500 B.C.–A.D. 1469, Oaxaca

Tenochtitlan, begun A.D. 1325, Mexico City

Terraced city, c. A.D. 900, Uxmal

MONACO

Casino, 1878–1881, Monte Carlo, Charles Garnier (1829–1898)

PERU

Machu Picchu Fortress Ruins, c. A.D. 1450, Machu Picchu

PORTUGAL

Sao Victor District Housing, 1974–1977, Porto, Alvaro Siza Vieira (1933)

SPAIN

Puerta del Sol, 1200, Toledo

TURKEY

Binbirdirek Cistern (the Cistern of the Thousand and One Columns), 6th century, Istanbul

UNITED STATES

Iowa

Terrace Hill, 1869, Des Moines, W. W. Boyington (1818–1898)

Massachusetts

Beacon Monument, 1791, Boston, Charles Bulfinch (1763–1844)
Quincy Market, 1825–1826, Boston, Alexander Parris (1780–1852)

Pennsylvania

Carpenters' Hall, 1770–1775, Philadelphia, Robert Smith (c. 1722–1777)
Franklin Institute, 1825–1826, Philadelphia, John Haviland (1792–1852)

Virginia

> *Dulles Airport,* 1962, Chantilly Eero Saarinen (1873–1950) and Cesar
> Pelli (1926)

ZIMBABWE

> *Western Enclosure,* c. A.D. 1000–1500

20ᵀᴴ-CENTURY ARCHITECTURE

Twentieth-century architecture ranged from Art Nouveau and Beaux Arts styles
to the stark simplicity of the "wall of glass" skyscrapers that appeared in major
cities at mid-century. Much architecture of this time reflected the influence of
the Bauhaus school in Weimar, Germany, that emphasized economy of form.
Two oft-quoted phrases that describe this architecture are "less is more" and
"form equals function." Yet there were eccentrics such as Antoni Gaudi of
Barcelona, whose work defies a specific category and whose churches and apartment houses are the antithesis of simplicity and more like sculpture than architecture. In the second half of the 20ᵗʰ century, cities the world over began to
take on a similar appearance, as old city-center buildings gave way to new skyscrapers designed by architects who work internationally. Although architects
generally attempt to retain some of the feel of a country's architecture and to
make new structures at home in it, a skyscraper is inevitably a very tall column
with lots of windows. The architect's "statement" is made in the design of the
lower levels or top of the building and the choice of color and materials. In spite
of the homogeneity of modern architecture and the limitations that come with
building towering structures tens of stories high, office complexes, museums,
university and government buildings, and hotels still offer many opportunities
for architects to give free rein to their imaginations, and many have put the
opportunity to excellent use.

AUSTRALIA

> *Rialto Center,* 1985, Melbourne, Gerard de Preu

AUSTRIA

Attic Conversion (home renovation), 1987–1988, Vienna, Coop
  Himmelbau (1968)
Goldman and Salatsch Building, 1909–1911, Vienna, Adolf Loos
  (1870–1933)

CHINA

Bank of China, 1990, Hong Kong, I. M. Pei (1917) with Henry N. Cobb
  (1926) and James Ingo Freed (1930)
Central Plaza, 1992, Hong Kong, Ng Chun Man & Associates
Jin Mao Bulding, 1998, Shanghai, Louis Skidmore (1897–1962), Nathaniel
  Owings (1903–1984), and John O. Merrill (1896–1975)
Shanghai World Financial Center, 2004, Shanghai, A. Eugene Kohn
  (1930), William Pedersen (1938), and Sheldon Fox (1930), associates

CZECH REPUBLIC

Fred and Ginger Building, Prague, 1994, Frank O. Gehry (1925)
Tugendhat House, 1928–1930, Brno, Ludwig Mies van der Rohe
  (1886–1969)

ENGLAND

Economist Building, 1959–1964, London, Alison Smithson (1928–1993)
  and Peter Smithson (1923–2003)
Lloyd's of London, 1979–1984, London, Richard Rogers (1933)
One Canada Square, 1991, London, Cesar Pelli (1926)
Richmond Riverside Development, 1987, London, Quinlan Terry (1937)
The Ark, 1991, London, Ralph Erskine (1914)

FINLAND

Railroad Station, 1905–1914, Helsinki, Eliel Saarinen (1873–1950)
Sanitorium, 1929–1933, Paimio, Alvar Aalto (1898–1976)

FRANCE

Apartment Building, Rue Franklin, 1903–1904, Paris, Auguste Perret (1874–1954)

Cité de la Musique, 1984–1995, Paris, Christian de Portzamparc (1944)

Congrexpo, 1997, Lille, Rem Koolhaas (1968)

Dirigible Hangars, 1923, Orly, Eugène Freyssinet (1879–1962)

Eiffel Tower, 1899, Paris, Gustave Eiffel (1832–1923)

Grand Palais, 1990–1994, Lille, Rem Koolhaas (1968)

Grande Arche de la Défense, 1981–1989, Paris, Johan Otto von Spreckelsen (1929–1987)

Hotel de Region, 1990, Montpelier, Ricardo Bofil (1939)

Maison de Verre, 1932, Paris, Pierre Chareau (1883–1950) and Bernard Bijvoet (1889–1979)

New Opera House, 1989, Paris, Carlos Ott

Paris Metro Stations, 1898–1904, Paris, Hector Guimard (1867–1942)

Stadium, 1913–1916, Lyon, Tony Garnier (1869–1948)

Unité d'Habitation, 1947–1952, Marseilles, Le Corbusier (1887–1966)

Villa Savoie, 1929–1931, Poissy, LeCorbusier (1887–1966)

GERMANY

A.E.G. Turbine Factory, 1909, Berlin, Peter Behrens (1868–1940)

Bauhaus, 1925–26, Dessau, Walter Gropius (1883–1969)

Bundesbaugellschaft, 1999, Berlin, Norman Foster (1935)

Commerzbank, 1997, Frankfurt, Norman Foster (1935) and Partners

Einstein Tower, 1920–1921, Potsdam, Erich Mendelsohn (1887–1953)

Fagus Factory, 1910–1914, Alfeld-an-der-Leine, Walter Gropius (1883–1969) and Hannes Meyer (1889–1954)

Messeturm, 1991, Frankfurt, C. S. Murphy/Helmut Jahn (1940)

Philharmonie Concert Hall, 1960–1963, Berlin, H. Scharoun (1893–1972)

Reichschancellery, 1933–1938, Berlin, Albert Speer (1905–1981)

INDONESIA

Jakarta Tower, 1996, Jakarta, Peter Pran of NBBJ

ITALY

Brion Tomb, 1978, San Vito d'Altivole, Treviso, Carlo Scarpa (1906–1978)
Malpensa International Airport, 1998, Milan, Ettore Sottsass (1917)
Palazzetto dello Sport, 1956–1957, Rome, Pier Luigi Nervi (1891–1979)
San Cataldo Cemetery, 1980, Modena, Aldo Rossi (1931)
Stadium, 1930–1932, Florence, Pier Luigi Nervi (1891–1979)

JAPAN

Akasaka Prince Hotel, 1983, Tokyo, Kenzo Tange (1913)
Festival Hall, 1961, Kyoto, Kunio Mayekawa (1905–1986)
Kansai International Airport, 1994, Osaka, Renzo Piano (1937)
Kirishimi International Concert Hall, 1994, Kirishimi, Fumihiko Maki
    (1928)
Landmark Tower, 1993, Yokohama, Hugh Stubbins (1912) Associates
Olympia Sports Stadium, 1963–1964, Tokyo, Kenzo Tange (1913)
Readers' Digest Offices, 1949, Tokyo, Antonin Raymond (American,
    1889–1976)
Town Hall, 1919, Hajima, Junzo Sakakura (1904–1969)

MALAYSIA

International Airport, 1992–1998, Kuala Lumpur, Kisho Kurokawa (1934)
Petronas Towers, 1998, Kuala Lumpur, Cesar Pelli (1926)

MOROCCO

Tourist Center and Hotel "Petit Merou," 1968, Cabo Negro, Elie Azagury
    (1918)

NETHERLANDS

Café de Unie, 1925, Rotterdam, J.J.P. Oud (1890–1963)
Central Beheer Office Building, 1968–1972, Apeldoorn, Herman
    Hartzberger (1932)
Diamond Workers' Union Building, 1900, Amsterdam, Hendrik P. Berlage
    (1856–1934)
Kröller-Müller Museum, 1938, Otterlo, Henri van de Velde (1863–1957)

NETHERLANDS *(continued)*

Netherlands Dance Theatre, 1988, The Hague, Rem Koolhaas (1944)
NMB Bank, 1988, Amsterdam, Ton Alberts (1927–1999)
Rietvelt-Schroder House, 1924–25, Utrecht, Gerrit Rietveld (1888–1964)
Shell Building, 1938–1942, The Hague, J.J.P. Oud (1890–1963)

SPAIN

Barcelona Airport, 1992, Barcelona, Ricardo Bofil (1939)
Casa Mila Apartment House, 1905–1907, Barcelona, Antoni Gaudi
   (1852–1926)
German Pavilion, International Exposition, 1929, Barcelona, Mies van der
   Rohe (1886–1969)
Museum of Roman Art, 1980–1985, Mérida, Rafael Moneo (1937)

SWEDEN

The Globe Arena, 1989, Stockholm, Berg Arkitekkontor

SWITZERLAND

Thermal Baths, 1990–1996, Vals, Peter Zumthor (1943)

THAILAND

Baiyoke II Tower, 1998, Bangkok, Plan Architects

UNITED STATES

Arizona

Taliesin West, 1938–1959, Phoenix, Frank Lloyd Wright (1867–1959)

California

Bentham Hall and Tower, 1909, La Jolla, Irving J. Gill (1870–1936)
Los Angeles Central Library, 1926, Los Angeles, Bertram G. Goodhue
   (1869–1924) and Carleton Winslow, Sr. (1876–1946)

District of Columbia

> *Kennedy Center for the Performing Arts,* 1971, Washington, DC, Edward Durrell Stone (1902–1978)

Florida

> *Disney Complex,* 1991–1992, Orlando, Robert A. M. Stern (1939), Arata Isozaki (1931), Frank Gehry (1925), Charles Gwathmey (1938), Robert Siegel (1939), and Michael Graves (1934)
> *Everglades Club,* 1918–1919, Palm Beach, Addison Mizner (1872–1933)
> *Gulfstream Golf Club,* 1923, Palm Beach, Addison Mizner (1872–1933)

Illinois

> *James R. Thompson Center,* 1978–1985, Chicago, Robert Siegel, Helmut Jahn (1940)
> *Tribune Tower,* 1923–1925, Chicago, Raymond Hood (1881–1934) with John Mead Howells (1868–1959)

Iowa

> *Terrace Hill,* 1869, Des Moines, W. W. Boyington (1818–1898)

Kentucky

> *Humana Tower,* 1982–1986, Louisville, Robert Siegel, Michael Graves (1934)

Massachusetts

> *John Hancock Tower,* 1997, Boston, I. M. Pei (1917) and Henry N. Cobb (1926)

New York

> *AOL Time Warner Center,* 2001, New York City, David Childs of SOM (Skidmore, Owings and Merrill)
> *CBS Building,* 1960–1964, New York City, Eero Saarinen (1910–1961)
> *City Corp Center,* 1978, New York City, Hugh Stubbins (1912) Associates

New York (continued)

Condé Nast Building, 1999, New York City, Sheldon Fox (1934) and
Bruce S. Fowle

Lipstick Building, 1986, New York City, Philip Johnson (1906) and John
Burgee (1933)

McGraw-Hill Building, 1931, New York City, Raymond M. Hood
(1881–1934)

Singer Building, 1908, New York City, Ernest Flagg (1857–1947)

Sony Building (formerly *AT & T Corporate Headquarters*), 1979–1984,
New York City, Philip Johnson (1906)

Trump Tower, 1983, New York City, Der Scutt of Swanke Hayden
Connell

World Trade Center, 1972–2001 (destroyed), New York City, Minoru
Yamasaki

Texas

Fountain Place, 1986, Dallas, Henry N. Cobb (1926) of I. M. Pei and
Partners

Virginia

Dulles Airport, 1962, Chantilly, Eero Saarinen (1873–1950) and Cesar
Pelli (1926)

ARCHITECTURE FOR COMMERCE

Somehow one can always tell where the money is when visiting a city! Bank
buildings and world headquarters of international companies make a statement
with the "brand name" architects hired to design them and the quality of the
materials used in their construction. Many cities now require that architects of
such buildings include plazas, green space, public sculpture, and places to sit in
order to make their city-center more people-friendly. Included in this list are
the names of architectural firms or architects who designed these buildings.

CHINA

Citic Center (Bank), 1997, Guangzhou, Dennis Lau and Ng Chun Man
Hong Kong and Shanghai Bank Building, 1979–1986, Hong Kong,
　　Sir Norman Foster (1935)

ENGLAND

Bank of England, c. 1800, London, Sir John Soane (1753–1837)

FRANCE

Médiathèque, 1984–1988, Villeurbane Lyons, Mario Botta (1943)
Satolas TGV Station, 1990–1994, Lyon, Santiago Calatrava (1951)

GERMANY

DG Bank Headquarters, 1993, Frankfurt, Eugene Kohn (1930)

RUSSIA

Electro Stantsiys No. 1 Boiler House, 1926, Moscow, I. V. Zholtovsky
　　(1867–1959)

UNITED STATES

California

First Interstate Bank World Center, 1989, Los Angeles, I. M. Pei (1917),
　　Henry N. Cobb (1926), and James Ingo Freed (1930)
Transamerica Pyramid, 1972, San Francisco, William Pereira (1909–1985)

Georgia

Federal Reserve Bank Headquarters, 1999, Atlanta, Robert A. M. Stern
　　(1939)

Illinois

Auditorium Building (Civic Opera House, Hotel, Office block),
　　1886–1890, Chicago, Dankmar Adler (1844–1900)

Illinois (continued)

> *Ayer Building*, 1900, Chicago, William Holabird (1854–1923) and Kevin Roche (1922)
>
> *Carson Pirie Scott*, 1898–1904, Chicago, Louis Sullivan (1856–1924)
>
> *Home Insurance Building*, 1884–1885, Chicago, William Le Baron Jenney (1832–1907)
>
> *John Hancock Center*, 1970, Chicago, SOM (Louis Skidmore [1897–1962], Nathaniel A. Owings [1903–1984], and John O. Merrill [1896–1975])
>
> *Marshall Field Wholesale Store*, 1887, Chicago, Henry Hobson Richardson (1838–1886)
>
> *Reliance Building*, 1891–1894, Chicago, John Wellborn Root (1850–1891) (Burnham & Root)
>
> *Sears Roebuck Tower*, 1973, Chicago, SOM (Louis Skidmore [1897–1962], Nathaniel A. Owings [1903–1984], and John O. Merrill [1896–1975])

Michigan

> *General Motors Technical Center*, 1948–1952, Warren, Eliel Saarinen (1873–1950) and Eero Saarinen (1910–1961)
>
> *River Rouge Plant* (Ford), 1918–1934, Dearborn, Albert Kahn (1869–1942)

New York City

> *Chrysler Building*, 1928–1930, William Van Alen (1882–1954)
>
> *Empire State Building*, 1932, Richmond Shreve, William Lamb, and Arthur Loomis Harmon
>
> *Flatiron Building*, 1902, Daniel Hudson Burnham (1846–1912)
>
> *Lever House*, 1950–1952, SOM (Louis Skidmore [1897–1962], Nathaniel A. Owings [1903–1984], and John O. Merrill [1896–1975])
>
> *McGraw-Hill Building*, 1931, Raymond Hood (1881–1934)
>
> *MetLife Building* (formerly *Pan Am Building*), 1958–1963, Walter Gropius (1883–1969)
>
> *Rockefeller Center*, 1931–1939, Raymond M. Hood (1881–1934), Wallace K. Harrison (1895–1981) and others
>
> *Seagram Building*, 1954–1958, Ludwig Mies van der Rohe (1886–1969) and Philip Johnson (1906)

Singer Tower, 1907, Ernest Flagg (1857–1947)

T.W.A. Terminal (at Kennedy Airport), 1956–1962, Eero Saarinen (1910–1961)

Union Carbide Building, 1957–1960, SOM (Louis Skidmore [1897–1962], Nathaniel A. Owings [1903–1984], and John O. Merrill [1896–1975])

Woolworth Building, 1910–1913, Cass Gilbert (1859–1934)

Oregon

Portland Public Services Building, 1980, Portland, Michael Graves (1934)

Pennsylvania

Bank of Pennsylvania, 1798–1800, Philadelphia, Benjamin Henry Latrobe (1764–1820)

Philadelphia Savings Fund Society Building, 1931, Philadelphia, George Howe (1886–1955) and Willis Lescaze (1896–1969)

Texas

Pennzoil Place, 1976, Houston, John Burgee (1933) (with Philip Johnson, 1906)

Republic Bank, 1981–1984, Houston, Philip Johnson (1906) and John Burgee (1933)

Wisconsin

Johnson Wax Building, 1936, Racine, Frank Lloyd Wright (1867–1959)

GOVERNMENT BUILDINGS

Government buildings are meant to endure. Very well-known architects are often selected to design such buildings, and the finest materials are used. These buildings are rarely destroyed, but often altered as necessity dictates. The architect's plans generally leave enough space surrounding the original structure to allow for more buildings to be constructed as it is outgrown. Although you may not think of government buildings when you consider great architectural icons you'd like to visit, these are all worth a second thought and a stop on your tour of any of these places.

AFRICA

Regional Tribunal and Palace of Justice, 1964, Mohammedia, Morocco, Jean-François Zevaco (1916)

AUSTRALIA

New Parliamentary Buildings, 1988, Canberra, Romaldo Giurgola (1920) of Michell/Giurgola and Thorp

AUSTRIA

Hofbibliothek, begun 1723, Vienna, Johann Fischer Von Erlach (1656–1723)
Postal Savings Bank Office, 1904–1912, Vienna, Otto Wagner (1841–1918)

BANGLADESH

Parliament Buildings, 1963–1983, Dacca, Louis I. Kahn (1901–1974)

BRAZIL

Brazilian Civic Center, 1955, Brazilia, Oscar Niemeier (1907)
Palace of the National Congress, 1960, Brasilia, Oscar Niemeier (1907)

CANADA

Civic Buildings, 1958–1965, Toronto, Viljo Revell (1910–1964)
Parliamentary Library, 1859–1867, Ottawa, Thomas Fuller (1823–1898) and Chilian Jones

DENMARK

Town Hall, 1939–1942, Sollerod, Arne Jacobsen with Fleming Lassen

ENGLAND

Banqueting House, 1619–1622, London, Inigo Jones (1573–1652)
Houses of Parliament, 1836–c. 1860, London, Sir Charles Barry
  (1795–1860) and A. Welby Pugin (1812–1852)
New Parliament Building, 1997, London, Michael Hopkins
New Zealand Chambers, 1872, London, Richard Norman Shaw
  (1831–1912)
Whitehall, 1862–1873, London, Sir George Gilbert Scott (1811–1878)

FINLAND

Civic Center, 1950–1951, Saynatsalo, Alvar Aalto (1898–1976)

FRANCE

Bibliothèque Nationale de France, 1989–1995, Paris, Dominique Perrault
  (1953)
Bibliothèque Ste. Geneviève, 1838–1850, Paris, H. Labrouste (1801–1875)
Institute de France, begun 1661, Paris, Louis Le Vau (1612–1670) and
  Jules Hardouin-Mansart (1646–1708)
Institute de Monde Arabe, 1983–1987, Paris, Jean Nouvel (1945)
New Opera House, 1989, Paris, Carlos Ott (1946)

GERMANY

Bundesbaugellschaft, 1999, Berlin, Norman Foster (1935)

INDIA

Capitol Buildings, 1951–1957, Chandigarh, LeCorbusier (1887–1966)
United States Embassy, 1957–1959, New Delhi, Edward Stone
  (1902–1978)

IRAN

Legislature Buildings, 1964, Tehran

JAPAN

Civic Center, 1979–1983, Tsukuba, Arata Isozaki (1931)

International Conference Building, 1963–1966, Kyoto, Sachio Otani (1924)

International Conference Building, 1963–1966, Tsukuba, Sachio Otani (1924)

Tokyo City Hall, 1991, Tokyo, Kenzo Tange (1913)

Tsukuba Center Building, 1983, Tokyo, Arata Isozaki (1931)

MEXICO

Central Library, 1953, Mexico City, Juan O'Gorman (1905–1982)

SWEDEN

City Hall, 1909–1923, Stockholm, Ragnar Ostberg (1886–1945)

UNITED STATES

District of Columbia

British Embassy, 1927–1928, Sir Edwin L. Luytens (1869–1944)

Cannon House Office Building, 1908, John M. Carrere (1858–1911) and Thomas Hastings (1860–1929)

State, War and Navy Building, 1888, Alfred B. Mullett (1834–1890)

Treasury Building, 1836–1869, Robert Mills (1781–1855)

United States Capitol, 1855–1864, Thomas Ustick Walter (1804–1887)

Florida

Castillo de San Marcos, 1672–1754, St. Augustine

Illinois

Cahokia Courthouse, 1737, Cahokia

Massachusetts

Boston City Hall, 1964–1969, Boston, Gerhard Kallman (1915), Noel McKinnell (1935), and Edward F. Knowles (1929)

Public Library, 1887–1895, Boston, Charles McKim (1847–1909)

State House, 1795–1798, Boston, Charles Bulfinch (1763–1844)

Missouri

Wainwright Building, 1891, St. Louis, Louis Sullivan (1856–1924)

New Mexico

Governor's Palace, 1609–1614, Santa Fe

New York

Federal Hall, 1788–1789, New York City, Pierre L'Enfant (1754–1825)

United Nations Buildings, 1947–1953, New York City, LeCorbusier (1887–1966)

Pennsylvania

Independence Hall, 1731, Philadelphia, Alexander Hamilton (1755–1804)

U.S. Mint, 1829–1833, Philadelphia, William Strickland (1788–1854)

Tennessee

Tennessee State Capitol, 1845–1859, Nashville, William Strickland (1788–1854)

Virginia

Palace of the Governors, 1706–1720 (redone in 1751), Williamsburg, Henry Cary (b. 1650) was overseer/designer

Virginia State Capitol, 1785–1798, Richmond, Thomas Jefferson (1743–1826)

"No architecture can be truly noble which is not imperfect."

—JOHN RUSKIN, 1819–1900, English art critic

MUSEUM ARCHITECTURE

When you visit any museum, often the museum itself is one of the masterpieces on view. Some are truly distinguishable by their outstanding architecture. Every architect considers it quite a coup to be selected to design a museum. Just as the artwork within was carefully selected either for its cutting-edge aesthetics or for its timelessness, the architect should be one of the greatest "artists" in his or her own field.

The world is experiencing a sudden surge of building new museums and creating additions for existing ones. Practical considerations such as space for display and storage, and educational, restoration, and curatorial needs are primary. In addition, the professionals have recognized that the museum has attracted a new, eager type of visitor. New museum designs are reacting to the needs of today's populace for entertainment, making an "event" of a museum visit. Museums are entering a "golden age." Here are some museums that are internationally recognized for their outstanding design, along with the architects who designed them.

CANADA

> *Canadian Museum of Civilization,* 1989, Quebec, Hull, Douglas Cardinal
> (1934) and Associates
> *National Gallery of Canada,* 1988, Quebec, Moshe Safdie (1938)

ENGLAND

> *British Museum,* 1759, London, Sir Robert Smirke (1781–1867)
> *Museum of Science,* 1855–1858, Oxford, Benjamin Woodward
> (1816–1861)
> *New Tate Gallery at Bankside,* 1998–2000, London, Jacques Herzog
> (1950) and Pierre de Meuron (1950)
> *Sainsbury Center for the Visual Arts,* 1978, Norwich, Norman Foster
> (1935)
> *Soane Museum, Art Gallery,* 1811–1814, Dulwich, Sir John Soane
> (1753–1837)

FINLAND

> *Helsinki Museum of Contemporary Art,* 1998, Helsinki, Steven Holl
> (1947)

FRANCE

Centre Georges Pompidou, 1972–1976, Paris, Richard Rogers (1933) and Renzo Piano (1937)

Entrance Pyramid, Le Grand Louvre, 1989, Paris, I. M. Pei (1917)

Louvre, east front, 1667–1670, Paris, Louis LeVau (1612–1670), Charles Le Brun (1619–1690), and Claude Perrault (1613–1688)

GERMANY

Altes Museum, 1824–1828, Berlin, Karl Friedrich Schinkel (1781–1841)

Contemporary Art Wing, 1986–1996, Hamburg, Oswald Mathias Ungers (1926)

Frieder Burda Collection, 2001, Baden-Baden, Richard Meier (1934)

Goetz Collection, c. 1997, Munich, Jacques Herzog (1950) and Pierre de Meuron (1950)

Museum Abteiberg, 1972–1982, Monchengladbach, Hans Hollein (1934)

Neue Staatsgalerie, 1977–1984, Stuttgart, James Stirling (1926–1994) and Michael Wilford (1938)

The Jewish Museum, 2001, Berlin, Daniel Liebeskind (1947)

Zwinger, 1709, Dresden, Matthaeus Poppelmann (1662–1736)

ITALY

Museo di Castelvecchio, Verona, 1956–1964, Carlo Scarpa (1906–1978)

JAPAN

Hiroshima City Museum of Contemporary Art, 1988, Hiroshima, Kisho Kurokawa (1934)

Imperial Museum, 1938, Tokyo, Hiroshi Watanabe (1905)

Miho Museum, 1999, Shiga, I. M. Pei (1917)

MEXICO

Museo de Arte Moderno, 1964, Mexico City, Pedro Ramirez Vazquez (1919) with Rafael Mijares

Museum of Anthropology, 1964, Mexico City, Rafael Mijares

NETHERLANDS

Gallery of Contemporary Art, 1987–1992, Rotterdam, Rem Koolhaas (1944)

Groningen Museum, 1994, Groningen, Alessandro Mendini (1931)

Kunsthal, 1997, Rotterdam, Rem Koolhaas (1944)

Van Gogh Museum (Wing), 1992, Amsterdam, Kisho Kurokawa (1934)

NORWAY

Archaeological Museum, 1968–1988, Hamar, Sverre Fehn (1924)

SPAIN

Guggenheim Museum, 1999, Bilbao, Frank O. Gehry (1925)

Hospice of San Fernando (Municipal Museum), 1722, Madrid, Pedro de Ribera (c. 1633–1742)

SWITZERLAND

The Olympic Museum, 1995, Lausanne, Pedro Ramirez Vazquez (1919) and Jean-Pierre Cahen

UNITED STATES

California

California Palace of the Legion of Honor, 1916, San Francisco, George A. Applegarth (1875–1972)

Getty Center, 1997, Los Angeles, Richard Meier (1934)

Museum of Contemporary Art, 1986, Los Angeles, Arata Isozaki (1931)

San Francisco Museum of Modern Art, 1995, San Francisco, Mario Botta (1943)

District of Columbia

East Building, National Gallery of Art, 1968–1978, I. M. Pei (1917) and Partners

Hirshhorn Museum, 1973, SOM (Louis Skidmore [1897–1962], Nathaniel Owings [1903–1984], and John O. Merrill [1896–1975])

Renwick Gallery, 1859–1861, James Renwick (1818–1895)

Smithsonian Institution, 1846–1855, James Renwick (1818–1895)

Georgia

High Museum of Art, 1980–1983, Atlanta, Richard Meier (1934)

Minnesota

Milwaukee Art Museum (Wing), 2000, Milwaukee, Santiago Calatrava (1951)

Mississippi

George Ohr Museum (potter), 2001, Biloxi, Frank Gehry (1925)

Missouri

Jefferson Arch, completed 1965, St. Louis, Eero Saarinen (1910–1961)
Kemper Museum of Contemporary Art and Design, 1994, Kansas City, Gunnar Birkerts (1925)
Pulitzer Foundation for the Arts, 2001, St. Louis, Tadao Ando (1941)
St. Louis Art Museum, 1904, St. Louis, Cass Gilbert (1859–1934)

Nevada

Guggenheim Las Vegas, 2001, Las Vegas, Rem Koolhaas (1944)
Hermitage Guggenheim Museum, 2001, Las Vegas, Rem Koolhaas (1944)

New York City

American Folk Art Museum, 2001, Tod Williams (1943), Billie Tsien (1947) and Associates
Frick Gallery, 1914, John M. Carrere (1858–1911) and Thomas Hastings (1860–1929)
Museum of Modern Art Expansion, 2001, Yoshio Taniguchi (1937)
Solomon R. Guggenheim Museum, 1946–1959, Frank Lloyd Wright (1867–1959)
Whitney Museum of American Art, 1963–1966, Marcel Breuer (1902–1981)

Ohio

Wexner Centre for the Visual Arts, 1989, Columbus, Peter Eisenman (1932)

Pennsylvania

> *Pennsylvania Academy of the Fine Arts,* 1871–1876, Philadelphia, Frank
> Furness (1839–1912)

Texas

> *Audrey Jones Beck Building, Museum of Fine Arts,* 2000, Houston, Rafael
> Moneo (1937)
> *Kimbell Art Museum,* 1972, Fort Worth, Louis I. Kahn (1901–1974)

Washington

> *Seattle Art Museum,* c. 1991, Seattle, Robert Venturi (1925) and Denise
> Scott Brown (1931)

FAMOUS UNIVERSITY BUILDINGS

University buildings, like government buildings and museums, are expected to be
representative of the times in which they were built, yet to blend in with the
general color or "feel" of other campus buildings. The "Collegiate Gothic" style
of early university buildings in the eastern and southern United States was reflec-
tive of English universities such as Oxford and Cambridge. Newer campuses,
such as the United States Air Force Academy in Colorado, also have a unified
feeling because most of the buildings were erected within a relatively short time
period. The buildings in this list are a select few that are frequently used as
examples of outstanding university architecture.

AFRICA

> *School of Architecture,* Kumasi University, 1960, Ghana, Charles I.
> Hobbis
> University of Lagos, (date unknown), Lagos, Nigeria, Alan Vaughan-
> Richards (1925–1989)

CANADA

> *University College,* 1856–1858, Toronto, W. C. Cumberland (1821–1881)

ENGLAND

Engineering School, University of Leicester, 1959–1963, Leicester, James Stirling (1926–1994)

Impington Village College, 1936, Impington, Maxwell Fry (1899–1987)

King's College Fellows' Building, 1724–1749, Cambridge, James Gibbs (1662–1754)

SCOTLAND

Glasgow School of Art, 1897–1909, Glasgow, Charles Rennie Macintosh (1868–1928)

UNITED STATES

California

Salk Institute, 1959–1965, La Jolla, Louis I. Kahn (1901–1974)

Colorado

United States Air Force Academy, 1955–1958, Colorado Springs, SOM (Louis Skidmore [1897–1962], Nathaniel Owings [1903–1984], and John O. Merrill [1896–1975])

Connecticut

Yale Center for British Art, 1969–1972, New Haven, Louis I. Kahn (1901–1974)

Massachusetts

Baker House (M.I.T.), 1949, Cambridge, Alvar Aalto (1898–1976)

Kresge Auditorium (M.I.T.), 1955, Cambridge, Eero Saarinen (1901–1961)

Sever Hall (Harvard), 1878–1880, Cambridge, Henry Hobson Richardson (1838–1886)

Michigan

Cranbrook Foundation Buildings, 1926–1943, Bloomfield Hills, Eliel Saarinen (1873–1950)

Michigan (continued)

> *William L. Clements Library*, 1920–1921, Ann Arbor, Albert Kahn
> (1869–1942)

New York

> *New York University*, 1832–1837, New York City, Alexander Jackson Davis
> (1803–1892)

Pennsylvania

> *Richards Medical Research Building*, 1957–1961, Philadelphia, Louis I.
> Kahn (1901–1974)

Virginia

> *College of William and Mary*, 1695–1702, Williamsburg, Christopher
> Wren (1632–1723)
> *Observatory Hill Dining Hall (University of Virginia)*, 1982–1984,
> Charlottesville, Robert Stern (1939)
> *University of Virginia*, 1804–1817, Charlottesville, Thomas Jefferson
> (1743–1826)

SPACES FOR LIVING

For some owners, a dream house is a rambling estate on many acres, replete with guest quarters and riding stables. For others, it's a 100-room estate on a hilltop, and for others, it's a turn-of-the-century Victorian with a well-tended garden. In this list, you'll find homes that fit all three categories and others, as well as those that defy the "dream house" category and edge into fantasy. These homes range from exceedingly small homes such as the Mies Van Der Rohe designed home for Dr. Edith Farnsworth in Plano, Illinois, to rambling American "palaces" such as *Biltmore* in Asheville, North Carolina.

AUSTRIA

> *Steiner House* (Art Deco), 1910, Vienna, Adolf Loos (1870–1933)

BELGIUM

Palais Stoclet (Art Deco), 1905–1911, Brussels, Josef Hoffmann (1870–1956)

Salon, Van Eetvelde House, 1895, Brussels, Victor Horta (1861–1947)

Tassel House (Art Nouveau style), 1892, Brussels, Victor Horta (1861–1947)

CANADA

Habitat (apartments), 1964–1967, Montreal, Moshe Safdie (1938) and Ernest Isbell Barott (1884–1966) with David-Barott-Boulva

ITALY

Casa del Fascio, 1928–1936, Como, Giuseppe Terragni (1904–1933)

Casa Malaparte, 1938–1943, Capri, Adalberto Libera (1903–1963)

JAPAN

Matsumoto Residence, 1980, Wakayama, Tadao Ando (1941)

Rokko Housing, 1983, Kyoto, Tadao Ando (1941)

SPAIN

Casa Batlló, 1905–1907, Barcelona, Antonio Gaudi (1852–1926)

Casa Mila Apartment House, 1905–1907, Barcelona, Antonio Gaudi (1852–1926)

UNITED STATES

Arizona

Taliesin West, 1938–1959, Phoenix, Frank Lloyd Wright (1867–1959)

California

Eames House, 1949, Pacific Palisades, Charles (1907–1978) and Ray (1912–1988) Eames

Gamble House, 1908–1909, Pasadena, Charles Sumner Greene (1868–1957)

California (continued)

H. *Cuthbertson House,* 1902, Pasadena, Charles Sumner Greene (1868–1957) and Henry Mather Greene (1870–1954)

House for Dr. Phillip Lovell, 1927–1929, Los Angeles, Richard Neutra (1892–1970)

La Casa Grande (William Randolph Hearst's opulent home) 1919–1939, San Simeon, Julia Morgan (1872–1957)

Long-Waterman House, 1889, San Diego, B. B. Benson

Lovell Beach House, 1925–1926, Newport Beach, Rudolph Schindler (1887–1953)

Sea Ranch Condominiums, 1965, Gualala, Charles Moore (1925–1993)

Connecticut

Johnson House (Glass House), 1945–1949, New Canaan, Philip Johnson (1906)

Smith House, 1965–1967, Darien, Richard Meier (1934)

Delaware

Winterthur, 1837, Wilmington, Henry Francis DuPont (1880–1969) and Henry Algemon DuPont (1838–1936)

Florida

Vizcaya, 1914–1916, Miami, Francis Burrall Hoffman

Illinois

Dr. Edith Farnsworth House, 1945–1951, Plano, Ludwig Mies van der Rohe (1886–1969)

Frederick C. Robie House, 1908–1909, Chicago, Frank Lloyd Wright (1867–1959)

Lake Shore Apartment Houses, 1949–1951, Chicago, Ludwig Mies van der Rohe (1886–1969)

Twin Towers, Marina City, 1959–1967, Chicago, Bertram Goldberg (1913–1997) and Associates

Winslow House, 1893, River Forest, Frank Lloyd Wright (1867–1959)

Maryland

    Hammond-Harwood House, 1774, Annapolis, William Buckland
    (1734–1774)

Massachusetts

    Hancock House, 1735, Boston, Peter Harrison (1716–1775)
    M. F. Stoughton House, 1882–1883, Cambridge, Henry Hobson
    Richardson (1838–1886)
    Trubek-Wislocki Houses, 1970, Nantucket, Denise Scott Brown (1931)

Mississippi

    Longwood (Octagon House), 1860–1862, Natchez, Orson Squire Fowler
    (1809–1887)

New York

    Villard Houses, 1882–1885, New York City, Stanford White (1853–1906)
    with Charles McKim (1847–1909) and Rutherford Mead (1846–1928)

North Carolina

    Biltmore, 1890–1895, Asheville, Richard Morris Hunt (1827–1895)

"A house is a machine for living."
—BUCKMINSTER FULLER, 1895–1963, American engineer, creator
of the geodesic dome

Pennsylvania

> *Fallingwater, Kaufmann House*, 1936–37, Bear Run, Frank Lloyd Wright
> (1867–1959)
> *Matthew Newkirk House*, 1835, Philadelphia, Thomas U. Walter
> (1804–1887)
> *Vanna Venturi House*, 1963–1965, Chestnut Hill, Robert Venturi (1925)

Rhode Island

> *Griswold House*, 1863, Newport, Richard Morris Hunt (1827–1895)
> *The Breakers*, 1892–1895, Newport, Richard Morris Hunt (1827–1895)
> *William G. Low House*, 1887, Bristol, Charles McKim (1847–1909),
> Rutherford Mead (1846–1928), and Stanford White (1853–1906)

South Carolina

> *Drayton Hall*, 1738–1742, Charleston County, architect unknown

Virginia

> *Governor's Palace*, 1706–1720, Williamsburg, Christopher Wren
> (1632–1723)
> *Monticello*, 1770–1784, and 1796–1806, Charlottesville, Thomas Jefferson
> (1743–1826)

PALACES

While these may vary from relatively modest "palaces" such as the American *White House* to grandiose complexes such as the *Summer Palace* in Beijing, these were considered the finest that could be built in their time in that place. Some, such as the Louvre, were constructed atop ancient castles. Most castles were constructed as strongholds, used for defense in time of attack, whereas a palace was a place for the wealthy or royalty to live and hold court. Perhaps the name "picture palace" came from the luxury and enjoyment that might be found in such a place.

AUSTRIA

Hofburg Palace, begun 1279, Vienna
Hochosterwitz, 1570–1586, Carinthia
Schonbrunn Palace, 1696, Vienna
Schwarzenburg, 1697–1723, Vienna
Upper Belvedere Palace, 1721–1722, Vienna, L. Von Hildebrandt
   (1668–1745)

BRAZIL

Itamarati Palace, 1851–1854, Rio de Janeiro

CHINA

Forbidden City, 1406–1420, Beijing
Summer Palace, 1750 and 1888, Beijing

CROATIA

Diocletian's Palace, A.D. 284–316, Split

CZECH REPUBLIC

Clam-Gallas Palace, 1701, Prague
Vladislav Hall, 1493–1502, Prague

DENMARK

Charlottenborg Palace, 1672–1683, Copenhagen

ENGLAND AND WALES

Blenheim Palace, 1705–1724, Oxfordshire, Sir John Vanbrugh
   (1664–1726)
Buckingham Palace, 1825–1913, London
Chatsworth House, 1686, Derbyshire
Chiswick House, 1724–1729, Middlesex
Easton Neston, 1696–1702, Northhamptonshire

ENGLAND AND WALES *(continued)*

Greenwich Palace, 1616–1635, Kent, Inigo Jones (1573–1652)

Hampton Court Palace, 1514–c. 1700, near London

Holkham Hall, 1734, Norfolk, William Kent (1685–1748) and Lord Burlington (1694–1753)

Kenilworth, 1120, Baddesly Clinton

Royal Crescent, 1767, Bath, John Wood the Elder (1704–1754) and John Wood the Younger (1728–1781)

Royal Pavilion, 1815–1818, Brighton

Sherborne, 1594, Sir Walter Raleigh (1554–1618), Dorset

Somerset House, begun 1776, Brighton, Sir William Chambers (1723–1796)

Strawberry Hill, 1748–1777, Twickenham, Horace Walpole (1717–1797)

Syon House, 1762–1763, Twickenham, Robert Adam (1728–1792)

William Morris home, 1859, Bexley Heath, Phillip Webb (1831–1915)

FRANCE

Azay-le-Rideau, 1518–1527, Indre-et-Loire

Chateau d'Anet, 1541–1563, Eure-et-Loire

Chateau de Blois, 1498–1504, Blois

Chateau de Chambord, 1519–1547, Chambord

Fontainebleau, 1528, near Paris

House in Bordeaux, 1998, Rem Koolhaas (1944)

Louvre, 1667–1670, Paris
Luxembourg Palace, 1614–1624, Paris
Palace of the Popes, 1316–1370, Avignon
Palais Jacques Coeur, 1443–1451, Bourges
Petit Trianon, 1762–1768, Versailles
Vaux-le-Vicomte, 1656–1661, Melun, Seine-et-Marne
Versailles, 1661–1685, Versailles, Louis Le Vau (1612–1670) and Jules
    Hardouin-Mansart (1646–1708)

GERMANY

Aachen, early 9th century, Aachen
Charlottenburg Palace, 1695, Berlin
Der Zwinger, 1711–1722, Dresden
Hohenschwangau, 19th century, Bavaria
Linderhof, 19th century, Bavaria
Nymphenburg Palace, 1664–c. 1728, Munich
Residenz, 1719–1750, Wurzburg, Johann Balthasaar Neumann
    (1687–1753)

GREECE

Palace of King Minos, c. 1500 B.C., Hosios Loukas, Crete

HUNGARY

Esterhazy Palace, 1720, Fertod
Sarospatak, c. 1540–1610, Miskolc

INDIA

Viceroy's Palace, 1920–1931, New Delhi

IRAN

Audience Hall of the Temple, c. 500 B.C., Persepolis, near Shiraz
Darius's Palace, c. 520 B.C., Persepolis

IRAQ

Palace, 849–859, Samarra
Palace, 1764–1778, Ukhaydir

ISRAEL

Palace of Khirbat-al-Mafjar, A.D., 739–744, near Jericho

ITALY

Castello Nuovo, 1260, Naples
Ca'd'Oro, 1422–c. 1440, Venice
Caserta, 1751, near Naples
Doge's Palace, 1309–1340, Venice
Hadrian's Villa, 1st century, B.C., Rome
Palazzo Barberini, 1626, Rome
Palazzo Chiericata, 1550s, Vicenza
Palazzo dei Diamanti, 15th century, Ferrara
Palazzo Ducale, after 1465, Urbino
Palazzo Farnese, begun c. 1519, Rome, Antonio da Sangallo (1485–1546)
Palazzo Medici-Riccardi, 1444, Florence
Palazzo Pitti, 1458–1466, Florence
Palazzo Pubblico, 1298–1348, Siena
Palazzo Rucellai, 1444–1459, Florence, Leon Battista Alberti (1404–1472)
Palazzo Ufizzi, 1560–1580, Florence, Giorgio Vasari (1511–1577)
Palazzo Vecchio, early 14th century, Florence
Royal Hunting Palace, 1719–1733, Stupinigi
Vatican Palace, begun c. 1503, Rome
Villa d'Este, 1550, Tivoli
Villa Farnesina, 1509–1511, Rome
Villa Foscari, c. 1558, Malcontenta
Villa Giulia, 1551–1555, Rome, Giacomo da Vignola (1507–1573)
Villa Lante, 1556–1589, Bagnia
Villa Rotonda, 1567–1570, Vicenza, Andrea Palladio (1508–1580)

JAPAN

Heijou Palace, A.D. 710, Nara
Katsura Palace, c. 1600, Kyoto
Tosanjo Palace, 1043–1166, Kyoto

JORDAN

Umayyad Palace, c. A.D. 743, Mshatta

PORTUGAL

Palacio Nacional de Queluz, 1747–1752, Lisbon, Mateus Vicente de
Oliveira (1710–1786)

SCOTLAND

Holyrood Palace, c. 1128, Edinburgh
Sandringham, 1787–1827, Balmoral

SPAIN

Escorial, begun 1559–1853, Madrid, Juan Bautista da Toledo (d. 1567)
with Juan de Herrera (1530–1597)
Santa Maria de Naranco, 9th century, northern Spain

SWEDEN

Drottningholm Palace, 1662, Stockholm, Nicodemus Tessin II
(1615–1681)

TANZANIA

Husuni Palace, 13th–14th centuries, Kilwa Kisiwani

TURKEY

Topkapi Palace, 15th century, Istanbul

UNITED STATES

The White House, 1792–1829, Washington, DC, James Hoban
(1768–1831)

WALLED CITIES, CASTLES, AND FORTRESSES

Every culture throughout history has taken great pains to fortify itself against and repel invaders. Sometimes what seems like extreme measures were taken. Although they were probably luxurious for their time, castles built in Medieval times were primarily for protection during war, and their architecture reflects that purpose. Castles were often built on a hill with a single approach. If built on flat land, they were typically surrounded by a moat and drawbridge. Many featured an inner courtyard to provide shelter for people and animals during a siege. Provisions, such as food, water, animals, and ammunition, were always on hand. Many castles in England later became fortresses, so cannons and firearms became an essential part of the fortification. The outer walls had crenellation along the top or slits in the walls to allow archers to protect the castle, and high towers or turrets for lookouts to keep watch for enemies. For some cultures, the fear of invaders was so intense that the solution was to build an enclosure around an entire city or country. Castles in this list are in various states of repair. Most may be visited; a few are still private residences.

AFRICA

Great Zimbabwe (ancient stone enclosure), 13th–15th centuries, Zimbabwe

AUSTRIA

Hochosterwitz Castle, 1570–1586, Carinthia

BELGIUM

Gravensteen Castle, 9th century, Ghent

CHINA

Xian City Wall, begun c. 14th century, Xian

CZECH REPUBLIC

Hradcany Castle, 1485–1502, Prague
Hrezda Castle, 1555–1556, Prague

DENMARK

Borreby Castle c. 1550, Zealand

Frederiksborg Castle, 1602–1620, Hillerod

Kronborg Castle, 1574–1585, Elsinore

Rosenborg Castle, 1606–1617, Copenhagen

ENGLAND

Arundel Castle, 11th century, Arundel

Barnard Castle, 14th century, Barnard

Beaumaris Castle, 1283–1323, Anglesey

Berkeley Castle, 1327, Berkeley

Bodiam Castle, 1385, Hawkhurst

Canterbury Castle, c. 12th century, Canterbury

Carisbrooke Castle, 1150–1200, Isle of Wight

Castle Drogo, 1910–1930, Devonshire

Castle Howard, 1699–1712, Yorkshire

Corfe Castle, 1105, Wareham

Deal Castle, c. 1540, Kent

Dover Castle, 1180–1240, Kent

Dunster, 13th century, Somerset

Durham Castle, 1284, Durham

Easton Neston, 1696–1702, Northhamptonshire

Hastings Castle, 1069, Hastings

Hever Castle and Gardens, 13th century, Royal Tunbridge, Wells

Kenilworth Castle, 1120, Baddesly Clinton

Leeds Castle, c. 10th century, Maidstone, Kent

Lincoln Castle, 1068, Lincoln, East Anglia

Niort Castle, 1155, Niort

Norwich Castle, 11th century, Norwich

Penzance Castle, 14th century, Penzance

Portchester Castle, A.D. 400, Portsmouth

Richborough Castle, 4th century, Sandwich

Rochester Castle, 11th–12th centuries, Kent

Sherborne Castle, 1655, Dorset

Sissinghurst Castle, 13th century, near Cranbrook

Stokesay Castle, 1285–1305, Shropshire

ENGLAND *(continued)*

Tattershall Castle, 1436–1446, Lincolnshire
Thornbury Castle, 16th century, Bristol
Tintagel Castle, c. 1150, Tintagel
Tower of London, c. 1077, London
Walmer Castle, c. 1540, Deal
Wardour Castle, 1393, Wiltshire
Warwick Castle, c. 915, Warwickshire
Windsor Castle, 1070, Windsor
York City Walls and Minster, 15th century, York

FRANCE

Chateau D'Angers, 1228, Angers
Chateau de Chinon, begun 10th century, Chinon
Chateau des Ducs de Bretagne, 1466, Nantes
Chateau Gaillard, begun 1196, Les Andeleys
Cité at Carcassonne (walled city), 13th century, Carcassonne
Mont Saint Michel (an island fortress), (1203–1264), Mont Saint Michel

GERMANY

Dinkelsbuhl (walled city), 10th century
Ehrenbreitstein Fortress, 10th century, Koblenz
Heidelberg Castle, 1531–1615, Heidelberg
Kaiserburg Castle, 1050, Nuremberg
Landgrafenschloss, 14th century, Marburg
Marksburg Castle, pre 1400, Braubach
Meissen Castle, 1471–1485, Meissen
Neuschwanstein Castle, begun 1868, Bavaria
Reichenstein Castle, 13th century, Trechtingshausen
Rothenburg ob der Tauber (walled city), c. 1240, Rothenburg
Stahleck Castle, 1135, Bacharach
Stolzenfels Castle, c. 1816–1830, Kapellen
The Wartburg Castle, 1067, Eisenach
Wurtzburg, 8th century, Wurtzburg

IRELAND

Bunratty Castle, 1251, Limerick
Dublin Castle, c. 1300, Dublin
Kilkenny Castle, 1172, Kilkenny

ITALY

Assisi Castle on Rocca Maggiore, 14th century, Assisi
Castel Bari, c. 1220, Bari
Castel Del Monte, c. 1240–1250, Apulia
Castel Nuovo, 13th century, Naples
Castel Sant' Angelo, 11th century, Rome
Castel Ursino, c. 1220, Catania
Castello Sforzesco, 1450–1477, Milan
Trani, c. 1233–1249, Apulia

JAPAN

Himeji Castle, 1601–1614, Himeji
Nijo Castle, 1603, Kyoto

LUXEMBOURG

Luxembourg Castle and Fortifications,
    A.D. 963, Luxembourg City
Vianden, 13th century, Vianden

MEXICO

Teotihuacan, A.D. 300–750,
    near Mexico City

SCOTLAND

Bothwell Castle, 13th century, near Glasgow
Edinburgh Castle, 11th century, Edinburgh
Hume Castle, 13th century, near Kelso
Stirling Castle, 15th and 16th centuries, near Glasgow

SPAIN

Alcazaba, c. 1236–1391, Malaga
Alcazar, c. late 11th century, Segovia
Alhambra, 1234–1492, Granada
Avila Fortifications, c. 1050–1350, Avila
Casa de Pilatos, c. 1510, Seville
Castel Coca, 11th and 12th centuries, near Segovia
Castilo de la Mota, c. 15th century, Medina
Penafiel, 11th–15th centuries, Valadolid
Santa Maria de Naranco, 9th century, northern Spain

SWITZERLAND

Chateau de Chillon, 10th century, Montreux

SYRIA

Citadel, 13th century, Aleppo
Krak des Chevalier (castle/fortress), c. 1100, near Horns, Tripoli
Saladin Castle (Soane Castle), c. 1120, Soane

TURKEY

City Walls of Constantinople, A.D. 5th century, Istanbul

UNITED STATES

Mesa Verde, begun c. 600–1100, Mesa Verde National Park, Colorado

WALES

Caernarvon, c. 1285, Caernarvon
Cardiff, c. 11th century, Cardiff
Conwy Castle, 1283, Conwy
Flint Castle, c. 1275, Flintshire
Harlech Castle, 1286–1290, Gwynedd
Powis Castle, 11th century, Abergavenny

ARCHITECTURAL INFLUENCES OF VARIOUS TIMES AND CULTURES

Often the architecture of a particular time and place has a lot to do with the climate, available building materials, and the cultural norms and tradition of the people who inhabit an area or era. Of course, over the years, styles take on new developments based on trends and availability of new materials. The result is (usually) a building that takes the best of several worlds. A traditional building (such as a "Palladian" home) designed today still has adaptations such as contemporary great rooms, large bathrooms, clerestories, and verandas. Refer to Architectural Terms at the beginning of this chapter for further information.

AFRICAN ARCHITECTURAL CHARACTERISTICS

"Shotgun" house (homes one room wide and several rooms deep). Popularly called this because if a shotgun were fired through the front door, the shot would go straight through and out an open door at the back of the house.

- Double shotgun house (two rooms wide, many rooms deep)
- Camelback shotgun (a shotgun house with a second story added across the back)
- Carved front doors
- Covered front porch
- Gable-roofed house
- Low-relief sculpture designs in adobe
- Square module rooms (10×10 feet or 10×20 feet)
- Veranda
- Wattle and daub construction
- Wide overhanging eaves on hipped roof

ASIAN ARCHITECTURAL CHARACTERISTICS

- Bright colors formerly were only for royalty
- Foot-high barrier at base of entrance doors
- Magnificent tombs for royalty were prepared with grand entrances, such as the life-sized pairs of carved stone animals leading to the Ming tombs
- Pagoda (a temple built of many stories, each smaller than the one below)

ASIAN ARCHITECTURAL CHARACTERISTICS *(continued)*

Rock-cut temples (carved into mountains of stone)

Roofs gently rise to a peak at each corner

Walled square on a north/south axis

EGYPTIAN ARCHITECTURAL CHARACTERISTICS

Capitals based on lotus and papyrus, the symbols of the North and South of Egypt

Engaged columns, not free standing, but attached on one side

Fluted columns (based on original columns created from bundles of reeds)

Frieze

Funerary temple

Hypostyle hall, many columns needed to support a stone roof

Mastaba tombs, step pyramids

Obelisk

Peristyle hall, a many-columned veranda surrounding an open courtyard

Piers

Pilaster

Post and lintel

Pyramid

Rock cut tomb

Sphinx

Thick engraved column

Unified architecture, sculpture, and decorations (all designed at the same time to complement each other in style)

GREEK ARCHITECTURAL CHARACTERISTICS

Acropolis

Bas-relief

Caryatids

Classicism

Columns—Doric, Ionic, Corinthian

Entasis

Frieze

Pediment

Post and lintel

Rectangular temples

Stoa

Theater

Widespread use of marble

ROMAN ARCHITECTURAL INNOVATIONS

Amphitheater
Apartment houses
Aqueduct
Atrium
Barrel vault
Basilica
Bridges
City planning
Coffered ceilings
Coffered dome
Columns with arches

Concrete
Forum
Groin vault
Heated baths
Mosaic
Pilaster
Portico
Rustication
Stadium
Triumphal arch

MEDIEVAL ARCHITECTURAL INNOVATIONS

Baptistery
Basilican plan churches
Battlements
Bay
Blind arcade
Chancel
Corbel table
Groin vaulting
Moats

Monasteries
Pilaster strip
Post and lintel arches
Statue-like columns
String-course
Tall towers
Towers over Narthex
Westwork (Narthex transept)

ROMANESQUE ARCHITECTURAL INNOVATIONS

Apse
Baptistery
Decorated arches
Interior vaults over crossings
Pier buttresses
Rectangular ground plans

Ribbed vaults
Round arches
Thick walls
Tympanum
Variety of columns

RENAISSANCE ARCHITECTURAL INNOVATIONS

Chateaux
Colossal dome
Colossal order (columns that
    extend through two or more
    stories)
Decorative colored marble
    designs
Geometry as basis for
    architecture: circle, square,
    and triangle

Ground-floor arcades
Multi-tiered façades
Neo-Classical revival
Paired columns
Palladian style
Symmetry and balance

BAROQUE ARCHITECTURAL INNOVATIONS

Colonnades
Decorative sculpture, inside and
    out
Elaborate public fountains
Grand scale
Lozenge (diamond-shaped)
    decorations

Mansard roof
Niches
Ostentatious materials
Spherical dome
Undulating façade

19TH-CENTURY ARCHITECTURAL INNOVATIONS

Art Nouveau
Cast-iron building façades
Introduction of elevator
Large exhibition halls and office
buildings
Metal "skeletons" with glass or
concrete walls
Prefabricated structural elements
Skyscraper (1883) (any 5- to 8-
story building was called a
skyscraper)

Structural steel (allowed the first
steel-skeleton skyscraper to be
built in Chicago)
Victorian (included Revivals of
Italianate, Gothic, Greek,
Egyptian, Neo-Baroque and
Neo-Classical)

20TH- AND 21ST-CENTURY ARCHITECTURAL INNOVATIONS

Air conditioning
Austere box-like skyscrapers
Better lighting
Buildings adapted to the site
(such as Frank Lloyd Wright's
Prairie Houses)
Concrete left rough from
pouring forms
Computer-designed architecture
Fireproof buildings and factories
Flat roofs
Geodesic dome
Green architecture (ecologically
and environmentally-friendly
design)
Horizontal and vertical setbacks
of skyscrapers
Industrial materials such as
reinforced concrete, steel, and
large areas of glass

International style: steel and
glass construction
Mobile homes
Monumental public sculpture
outside buildings
Natural materials such as stucco,
rough-cut stone, brick, wood,
marble
Parking garages
Prefabricated structural parts
Pre-stressed and post-stressed
concrete
Renovation of existing structures
Sun-breaks created by set-back
windows

"Architecture should be dedicated to keeping the outside out and the inside in."

—LEONARD BASKIN, 1922–2000,
American sculptor and graphic artist

ARCHITECTURAL CHARACTERISTICS OF HOUSES IN THE UNITED STATES

In countries whose permanent architecture developed relatively late, such as the United States, Canada, and Australia, settlers brought in their customary methods of building, and adapted them to their new environs. Immigrants often sought a climate that resembled that of their homelands, with, for example, Scandinavians seeking Northern regions. The log cabin that was a standard in Scandinavia was easily achieved in these wooded areas; similarly, the adobe building methods of Hispanics easily blended with Native American building traditions in places such as Arizona and New Mexico. As the country grew and basic needs were met, wealthy individuals traveled widely and brought back ideas that they adapted to their own homes.

Listed below are a few houses that typify some of the characteristics listed with them. Obviously many stylistic developments are occurring at the same time, with contemporary buildings sited next to more traditional designs.

NEW ENGLAND COLONIAL ARCHITECTURE, 1600–1750

Ashley House, c. 1733, Deerfield, Massachusetts
Bacon's Castle, c. 1655, Surry County, Virginia
Boardman House, 1686, Saugus, Massachusetts
Elihu Coleman House, 1722, Nantucket Island, Massachusetts
The Sisters' House, 1743, Ephrata, Pennsylvania
Fancy brickwork
Late Medieval features
Lean-to on back (saltbox)
Shingle or clapboard covering
Small-paned lead casement windows
Steep shingled roofs

Symmetrical windows

Tall, grouped central chimneys

Wattle and daub (woven sticks and mud) construction

DUTCH COLONIAL FEATURES, 1600–1750

Jan Ditmar's House, c. 1700, Flatlands, Brooklyn, New York

John Ward House, 1684, Salem, Massachusetts

St. Luke's Church (East End), 1632, Isle of Wight County, Virginia

Von Steuben House, 1739, Hackensack, New Jersey

Brick construction

Gambrel roof

Stepped end or straight-sided gables

SPANISH COLONIAL, 1600–1800

Don Raimundo Arrivas House, 1770–1790, St. Augustine, Florida

Governor's Palace, 1610–1614, Santa Fe, New Mexico

San Estevan, pre-1644, Acoma, New Mexico

San José y San Miguel de Aguayo, 1720–1731, San Antonio, Texas

San Xavier del Bac, 1784–1797, Tucson, Arizona

The Alamo, 1744–1757, San Antonio, Texas

Flat roofs, with timbers or red tile roofs

Ornately decorated entrances

Plain, windowless walls

Rounded adobe shapes

SOUTHERN COLONIAL, 1630–1800

Adam Thoroughgood House, 1636–1640, Princess Anne County, Virginia

Burlington, 18th century, Charles City County, Virginia

Home Place, 1801, Charles Parish, Louisiana

Magnolia Mound, c. 1790, Baton Rouge, Louisiana

Brick construction

End chimneys

Gallery all around house, shaded by hipped roof overhang

One and a half stories

Raised cottage (crawl space underneath)

GEORGIAN, 1698–1720 (GEORGIAN REVIVAL, c. 1800)
(named for three King Georges who ruled from 1714–1820)

Bries House, 1723, East Greenbush, New York

Dalton House, 1775, Newburyport, Massachusetts

Independence Hall, 1731, Philadelphia

Longfellow House, 1759, Cambridge, Massachusetts

Meetinghouse, 1779, Brooklyn, Connecticut

Miles Brewton House, 1765–1769, Charleston, South Carolina

Westover, c. 1730–1734, Charles City, Virginia

Williams House, 1706–1707, Old Deerfield, Massachusetts

Double or two-story portico

Giant pilasters (square columns with Corinthian or Ionic capitals)

Hipped roof with balustrades and dormer windows

Palladian window (curved at top) (late Georgian)

Pediments above windows, first floor

Projecting central pavilion

Quoins (square stones at corners and under windows)

Shutters on windows

Swan's neck pediment above door

Symmetry

JEFFERSONIAN (ROMAN REVIVAL), 1764–1820

Main Hotel Building, 1830s, Old Sweet Springs, West Virginia

Monticello, 1770–1784 and 1796–1806, Charlottesville, Virginia

Morris-Jumel Mansion, 1765, New York City

Mount Vernon, 1775, Mount Vernon, Virginia

Columns with plain capitals

Four-columned Roman portico with pediment

Louvered shutters

Red brick exterior

Roman temple form

Symmetrical façade

Tympanum (half moon shape above doors)

FEDERAL STYLE (NEO-CLASSICISM), 1770–1890

Andrew Ross Tenant Houses, 1810–1811, Washington, DC
Dodge-Shreve House, early 19ᵗʰ century, Salem, Massachusetts
Hunter House, 1748, Newport, Rhode Island
Point of Honor, c. 1815, Lynchburg, Virginia
The Pierce Nichols House, 1782, Salem, Massachusetts (Samuel McIntire)
The White House, 1792–1829, Washington, DC
Doric columns on porches
Entry has sidelights and arched fanlight with tracery
Interior decorative patterns (urns, swags, garlands)
Interior rooms sometimes hexagonal, oval, or round
Low hipped roof with balustrade
Post and beam construction
Simple façades with little exterior decoration
Square or rectangular exterior
Two or three stories high

GREEK REVIVAL, 1820–1860

Andalusia, c. 1797–1834, near Philadelphia
The Governor's Mansion, 1853–1855, Austin, Texas
The Old Patent Office, 1836–1867, Washington, DC
Carved decorative trim
Entablature (architrave, frieze, cornice)
Flat corner pilasters
Fluted Doric and Ionic columns on porches
Low-pitched roof
Pediment-shaped window head
Small windows around door
Wide plain frieze

ITALIANATE, 1830–1880; SIMILAR CHARACTERISTICS TO RENAISSANCE REVIVAL

The Benjamin Harrison House, 1875–1876, Indianapolis, Indiana
Johnson House, 1860, Macon, Georgia
Mercer House, 1860, Savannah, Georgia

ITALIANATE *(continued)*

Morse House, 1863, Portland, Maine
Balcony
Bay windows
Corinthian columns
Low pyramidal roof with wide eaves
Rusticated corner stones (quoins)
Smooth stucco finish
Straight vertical, almost square building
Tall narrow doors
Tall tower or cupola
Windows grouped and with elaborate pediments

GOTHIC REVIVAL, 1830–1860

Bowen House, c. 1845, Woodstock, Connecticut
First Baptist Church, 1884–1886, Lynchburg, Virginia
Lyndhurst, begun 1838, Tarrytown, New York
Wedding Cake House, 1826, Kennebunk, Maine
William J. Rotch House, 1846, New Bedford, Massachusetts
Full-width or one-story porch
Gothic-shaped windows
Stained glass
Steeply pitched roof
Tracery on windows
Turrets, towers, and battlements

VICTORIAN ARCHITECTURE, c. 1840–1904

Because Queen Victoria had such a long reign (1837–1901), many styles fall under this general name. This can include Stick Victorian, Folk Victorian, Carpenter Gothic, Queen Anne, Second Empire, and various exotic revivals. In some cases, several periods were combined in one building, as it suited the architect and/or builder. With few trained architects, pattern books and individual builders adapted and improvised. The general characteristics listed here can be seen in "Victorian" buildings all over the United States.

Longwood (Octagon house), 1862, Natchez, Mississippi

Pratt House, 1847, Baltimore, Maryland

Rosson House, 1895, Phoenix, Arizona

William G. Low House (Shingle style), 1887, Bristol, Rhode Island

Asymmetrical façades

Large windows, some with multiple panes

Circular turrets or towers

Exteriors of shingles, board and batten (wide boards separated by thin
   boards, used vertically), patterned brick, or rusticated stone

Gingerbread millwork added

Large porches with columns

Mixture of styles such as Italianate and Greek

Multicolored walls indoors and out

Octagon-shaped houses (also 6, 10, and 12 sides)

Patterned masonry

Projecting bay windows, often square, one or two story

Rusticated stone

Steep roofs

Wide eave overhangs

EGYPTIAN REVIVAL, 1840–1920

Apthorp House, 1837, New Haven, Connecticut

Cabell House, 1847, Richmond, Virginia

Egyptian Revival Railroad Station, 1922, New Bedford, Massachusetts

Washington Monument, 1848–1884, Washington, DC

Fluted columns

Pylon tower, sloping walls

Smooth exterior finish

Vulture and sun disk symbol

ORIENTAL (AND TURKISH) CHARACTERISTICS, c. 1850–1900

Brewster House, 1849, Rochester, New York

Isaac M. Wise Temple, 1863–1865, Cincinnati, Ohio

Olana, 1874, Church Hill, New York

Front gables

ORIENTAL (AND TURKISH) CHARACTERISTICS *(continued)*

Low pitched roof
Ogee arch (an oval shape with a pointed top)
Onion dome
Second-floor balcony

SECOND EMPIRE, 1855–1885 (FRENCH SECOND EMPIRE: REIGN OF NAPOLEON III)

Captain Edward Penniman House, 1867–1868, Eastham, Massachusetts
Congregational Church, c. 1840, Tallmadge, Ohio
Cornish House, 1886, Omaha, Nebraska
Goyer-Lee House, begun 1843, Memphis, Tennessee
Renwick Gallery, 1859–1861, Washington, DC
Stark House, c. 1820, Louisiana, Missouri
Terrace Hill, 1867–1869, Des Moines, Iowa
Bay windows
Decorative cornices
Front and side pavilions
Mansard roof (boxy roof line) with dormer windows
Paired and triple windows
Paired entry doors
Patterned roof
Quoins (corner stones)
Towers
Veranda-like porches with Classical columns

SWISS CHALET STYLE, c. 1860–1880

Main Lodge, Camp Sagamore, 1896–1897, Sagamore Lake, New York
Miller House, 1875, Chautauqua, New York
Montgomery Place, 1867, Tarrytown, New York
Gingerbread trim on roof
Low pitched roof
Second-floor balcony

QUEEN ANNE, 1870–1910

Col. Walter Gresham House (The Bishop's Palace), 1887–1893, Galveston, Texas
Gray House, 1891, Santa Cruz, California
Long-Waterman House, 1889, San Diego, California
William Watts Sherman House, 1874, Newport, Rhode Island
Corner towers with conical roof
Fish-scale shingles
Patterned masonry
Spindlework
Steep, slate roofs

RICHARDSON ROMANESQUE, 1880–1900

Lionberger House, 1886, Henry Hobson Richardson, St. Louis, Missouri
Riley Row, 1887, St. Paul, Minnesota
Union Station, 1900, Nashville, Tennessee
Asymmetrical façade
Broad hip roof
Deeply recessed windows
Fortress-like designs using stone or brick
Lines of windows
Masonry walls
Round towers, conical roof
Short, squat chimneys

LATE BEAUX-ARTS (NEO-CLASSICISM), 1890–1930

Cannon House Office Building, 1908, Washington, DC
Rosecliff, 1902, Newport, Rhode Island
The Breakers, 1892, Newport, Rhode Island
Classical revival
Colossal columned portico
Few arches
Free-standing statuary
Gigantic paired columns
Mixture of styles: Roman, Renaissance
Pilasters on sides

LATE BEAUX-ARTS *(continued)*

Symmetrical features
Variety of stone finishes

CHICAGO SCHOOL, 1890–1920

The Ayer Building, 1900, Chicago
The Prudential (Guaranty) Building, 1894–1895, Buffalo, New York
The Reliance Building, 1890, Chicago
Combination of linear and geometric forms
Flat roof, decorative cornice at top
Framework allowed to show
Iron and steel structure
Office complexes, 6–20 stories
Pilaster with decorated capital
Use of passenger elevator
Vertical strips of windows

PRAIRIE STYLE, 1905–c. 1915

Amberg House, 1910, Grand Rapids, Michigan
Edward Boynton House, 1907–1908, Rochester, New York
Merchants' National Bank, 1914, Grinnell, Iowa
The Robie House, 1908–1909, Chicago
Brick or stucco combined with wood
Horizontal appearance
Horizontal bands of casement windows
Interior coordinates with exterior
Large, low chimney
Low-pitched roof with wide overhanging eaves
Square porch supports
Terraces and balcony
Windows include stained glass

CRAFTSMAN (BUNGALOW STYLE), 1905–1940

Bentz House, 1906, Pasadena, California
Burgoyne House, 1917, Dallas, Texas

Melville Klauber House, 1908–1909, San Diego, California
The Irwin House, 1906, Pasadena, California
Beamed ceilings
Cobblestone decorations
Combination of materials (wood shingles, stone, brick)
Large porch
Low-pitched gabled roof
One and two stories high
Roof rafters exposed
Small windows flanking chimney
Tapered porch posts to ground level

PUEBLO REVIVAL, 1910–PRESENT

Taos County Courthouse, 1970, Taos, New Mexico
Flat roof, irregular, rounded edges
Roof beams, rough-hewn
Stepped-back roof line

INTERNATIONAL STYLE, 1920–1945

The Farnsworth House, 1949–1951, Plano, Illinois
Lovell Beach House, 1926, Newport Beach, California
Philadelpha Savings Fund Society, 1929–1932, Philadelphia
Seagram Building, 1954–1958, New York City
Asymmetrical façade in homes
Box-like structure
Cantilever
Concrete, glass, and steel
Curtain walls of windows (sheer sheets of windows)
Eaves boxed in or flush with wall
Exposed steel structural elements
Flat rooftops
Little ornamentation
Natural wooden trim
Smooth wall surface

ART DECO, 1925–1940

Butler House, 1937, Des Moines, Iowa

Chrysler Building, 1928–1930, New York City

Commercial Buildings, c. 1930s, Pekin, Illinois

Fox Theater, 1929, St. Louis, Missouri

Knabe Building, 1928, Kansas City, Missouri

Liberty Memorial, 1921–1926, Kansas City, Missouri

Los Angeles Union Station, 1938, Los Angeles

Lovell (Health) House, 1925–1926, Los Angeles

Penobscot Building, 1928, Detroit

Circular patterns used on doors or glass

Concrete, stone, metal

Curved window glass

Decorative colored mirrors

Flat roofs

Glazed ceramic ornamentation

Hard-edged stylized low reliefs

Horizontal bands of windows

Low-relief geometrical designs

Set-back façade (upper stories stepped back from lower stories)

Terra cotta and glass ornamentation

Smooth wall finish

MODERNISM, c. 1935–PRESENT

Garden Grove Community Church (Crystal Cathedral), 1980, Garden
Grove, California

John F. Kennedy Library, 1979, Boston

Johnson Wax Administration Building and Research Tower, 1936–1939, Racine, Wisconsin

Lever House, 1950–1952, New York City

Phillips Exeter Academy Library, 1967–1972, Exeter, New Hampshire

Salk Institute for Biological Studies, 1959–1965, La Jolla, California

A-frames

Aluminum siding

Angular flat-topped buildings

Apartment/condominium living

Box-like buildings with walls of glass set in steel framework

Colonial Revival

Curved glass panels

Homes adapted to site and location

Mobile homes

Pre-cast concrete elements

Ranch house

Revivals: Neo-Classicism, Neo-Colonial, Neo-Victorian, Neo-Tudor, Neo-French

Rhythmical set-backs at regular intervals (required to avoid all blockage of light in a city)

Split level

Stainless steel, glass, concrete

Stretched skin-window walls

Structural elements visible

Vertical, outside supports

LATE 20ᵀᴴ-CENTURY ARCHITECTURE, 1965–PRESENT

Abstract Shingle Style, 1992, Maine Coast

Meridian Condominiums, 1988, San Diego, California

Shingle Style Revival, 1991, New Jersey

State of Illinois Building, 1985, Chicago

Yale University Art & Architecture Building, 1969–1972, New Haven, Connecticut

Classical references on skyscrapers such as base, shaft, capital, entablature or pediment

Decorative elements and color on skyscrapers

Moldings, split pediments, keystones

Revivals in houses: Shingle style, Classical, Federal

LIGHTHOUSES IN THE UNITED STATES

The first lighthouse in the United States was in Boston Harbor and went into operation in 1716, and is the only American lighthouse that still has a keeper. Lighthouses are invariably beautiful (if lonely) locations, and the towers and buildings are picturesque and worth a visit for the view alone. There are hundreds of lighthouses in the United States. This list is a sampling of the better known, along with the dates of their construction. Many have disappeared or been moved to another location.

Alabama

> *Cape Hatteras,* 1873, near Mobile
> *Middle Bay lighthouse,* 1885, Mobile
> *Mobile Point light,* 1831, Fort Morgan near Gulf Shores
> *Sand Island lighthouse,* 1838, near Fort Morgan

Alaska

> *Cape Hinchinbrook lighthouse,* 1912, Prince William Sound
> *Cape St. Elias lighthouse,* 1916, Kayak Island
> *Cape Sarichef lighthouse,* 1904, Unimak Island
> *Cape Spencer lighthouse,* 1925, Juneau
> *Eldred Rock lighthouse,* 1904, Lynn Canal to Haines and Skagway
> *Five Finger light station,* 1902, Frederick Sound
> *Scotch Cap lighthouse,* 1903, Unimak Island
> *Sentinel Island light station,* 1902, Sentinel Island near Skagway

California

> *Alcatraz light station,* 1854, Alcatraz Island
> *Anacapa Island light station,* 1923, off Ventura
> *Battery Point (Old Crescent City) lighthouse,* 1856, Crescent City
> *Cape Mendocino light,* 1868, Cape Mendocino
> *East Brother Island light station,* 1874, Richmond
> *Farallon Islands lighthouse,* c. 1859, west of San Francisco
> *Fort Point lighthouse,* 1853, San Francisco
> *Los Angeles Harbor (San Pedro Harbor) lighthouse,* 1913, Los Angeles

Old Point Loma lighthouse, 1855, San Diego
Piedras Blancas light, 1875, near Monterey
Pigeon Point lighthouse, 1871–1872, San Mateo
Point Arena light, 1870, Point Arena
Point Bonita light, 1855, San Francisco
Point Cabrillo lighthouse, 1909, Mendocino
Point Fermin lighthouse, 1874, San Pedro
Point Loma lighthouse, 1891, San Diego
Point Pinos light station, 1855, Monterey
Point Reyes lighthouse, 1870, Point Reyes
    National Seashore
Point Sur lighthouse, 1889, Big Sur
Point Vincente lighthouse, 1926, Point Vincente
St. George Reef lighthouse, 1856, Crescent City
Santa Barbara lighthouse, 1856, Santa Barbara
Trinidad Head light, 1871, Trinidad

Connecticut

Black Rock Harbor lighthouse, 1809, Fayerweather Island
New Haven Harbor, 1805, Lighthouse Point
New London light, 1760, Thames River
New London Ledge lighthouse, 1909, east side of main channel
Old Lighthouse Museum, 1823, Stonington
Sheffield Island lighthouse, 1868, Norwalk

Delaware

Cape Henlopen lighthouse, 1767, Cape Henlopen
Delaware Breakwater lighthouse, 1885, Cape Henlopen
Liston Range light, 1876–1877, Delaware River, Biddles Corner
Mispillion lighthouse, 1831, Milford

Florida

Amelia Island light station, 1839, Fernandina Beach
Cape Canaveral light, 1848, Cape Kennedy
Cape Florida light, c. 1825, Biscayne Bay

Florida (continued)

Cape St. George lighthouse, 1833, Cape St. George State Park
Cape San Blas lighthouse, 1847, St. Joe
Carysfort Reef lighthouse, 1852, Key Largo
Cedar Keys lighthouse, 1854, Seahorse Key
Crooked River lighthouse, 1895, Carrabelle
Egmont Key lighthouse, 1848, Egmont Key, St. Petersburg
Fort Jefferson lighthouse, 1825, Key West
Fowey Rocks lighthouse, 1878, Cape Florida
Hillsboro Inlet lighthouse, 1907, Pompano Beach
Jupiter Inlet lighthouse, 1860, Jupiter
Key West lighthouse, pre 1825, Key West
Loggerhead Key tower, 1858, Dry Tortugas
Old Pensacola lighthouse, 1825, Santa Rosa Island
Pensacola lighthouse, 1825, Pensacola
Ponce de Leon (Mosquito) lighthouse, 1887, Daytona Beach
Port Boca Grande light station, 1890, Gasparilla Island
Sand Key lighthouse, 1827, near Key West
Sanibel Island lighthouse, 1884, Sanibel Island
St. Augustine lighthouse, 1824, Anastasia Island
St. John's River lighthouse, 1830, Jacksonville
St. Marks (Rear Range) lighthouse, 1831, Newport

Georgia

Cockspur Island lighthouse, 1857, Cockspur Island
Little Cumberland lighthouse, 1838, Little Cumberland Island
St. Simons lighthouse, 1872, St. Simons Island
Tybee Island Museum and lighthouse, 1791, Tybee Island

Hawaii

Diamond Head lighthouse, 1899, Oahu
Kilauea Point lighthouse, 1913, Kilauea, Kauai
Makapuu Point lighthouse, 1909, Makapuu Point, Oahu
Molokai lighthouse, 1909, Kalaupapa National Historic Park

Illinois

> *Chicago Harbor lighthouse*, 1832, Chicago
> *Grosse Point lighthouse*, 1873, Evanston

Indiana

> *Michigan City lighthouse*, 1837, Michigan City
> *Pierhead light*, 1904, Michigan City

Louisiana

> *Chandeleur Island lighthouse*, 1848, Chandeleur Island
> *New Canal lighthouse*, 1838, New Orleans
> *Point au Fer light*, 1827, Eugene Island
> *South Pass tower*, 1831, Mississippi Delta

Maine

> *Baker Island lighthouse*, 1828, Acadia National Park
> *Bass Harbor Head lighthouse*, 1858, Acadia National Park
> *Bear Island lighthouse*, 1839, Acadia National Park
> *Brown's Head lighthouse*, 1832, Vinalhaven Island
> *Burnt Island lighthouse*, 1821, Boothbay Harbor
> *Cape Neddick (Nubble) lighthouse*, 1879, York Beach
> *Doubling Point lights*, 1898, Bath
> *Fort Point lighthouse*, 1836, Fort Point State Park
> *Grindel Point lighthouse*, 1851, Lincolnville Beach
> *Isle au Haut lighthouse*, 1907, Stonington
> *Marshall Point lighthouse*, 1832, Thomaston
> *Monhegan Island light*, 1824, Mohegan Island
> *Owl's Head light*, 1825, Rockland Harbor
> *Permaquid Point lighthouse*, 1827, Damariscotta
> *Perkins Island lighthouse*, 1898, Georgeton
> *Petit Manan lighthouse*, 1817, Jonesport
> *Portland Breakwater lighthouse*, 1855–1875, South Portland
> *Portland Head light*, 1787–1790, Cape Elizabeth
> *Saddleback Ledge lighthouse*, 1839, between Vinalhaven and Isle au Haut

Maine (continued)

Seguin Island lighthouse, 1797, Georgetown
Squirrel Point lighthouse, 1898, Arrowsic Island
Twin light station, 1890s, Matinicus Rock
Two Bush Island light, 1897, Penobscot Bay
Two Lights lighthouse, 1784, Cape Elizabeth, Two Lights State Park
West Quoddy Head light, 1808, Quoddy
Whitehead lighthouse, 1804, East side of Whitehead Island

Maryland

Concord Point lighthouse, 1827, Havre de Grace
Cove Point lighthouse, 1828, Solomons
Craighill Channel Range, 1873, U.S. Coast Guard, Curtis Bay Station
 (near Baltimore)
Drum Point lighthouse, 1833, Calvert Marine Museum, Calvert
Fenwick Island lighthouse, 1859, Route 54 at Maryland border
Fort Washington, c. 1870s, Fort Washington Park
Hooper Strait lighthouse, 1867, Chesapeake Bay Maritime Museum,
 St. Michaels
Piney Point Lookout lighthouse, 1836, St. Clement's Island
Point Lookout, 1830, Point Lookout
Point No Point, 1902, Point No Point, St. Mary's County
Sandy Point Shoal, 1883, Sandy Point State Park, Chesapeake Bay
Seven Foot Knoll light, 1855, moved from Chesapeake Bay to Baltimore
Thomas Point Shoal lighthouse, 1875, Annapolis
Turkey Point lighthouse, 1833, Elk Neck State Park

Massachusetts

Annisquan Harbor lighthouse, 1801, Wigwam Point
Bakers Island lighthouse, 1798, Salem Harbor
Bird Island lighthouse, 1819, Marion
Boston Light Tower, 1783, Little Brewster Island
Brant Point, 1901, Nantucket Island
Butler Flats lighthouse, 1804, New Bedford
Cape Ann Twin lighthouses, 1771, Thacher Island

Cape Cod Highland light, 1859, Truro

Chatham lighthouse, 1808, Chatham

Cleveland Ledge lighthouse, 1943, Bourne (two miles off-shore)

Derby Wharf lighthouse, 1871, Salem

East Chop light station, c. 1924, Martha's Vineyard

Gay Head lighthouse, 1799, Martha's Vineyard, Gay Head

Highlands lighthouse, 1798, Cape Cod

Long Island Head lighthouse, 1820, North end of Long Island

Long Point, 1827, Provincetown

Marblehead Neck lighthouse, 1838, Marblehead

Minots Ledge light, 1850, southeast of Boston

Monomoy lighthouse, 1823, Monomoy Island

Nantucket light, 1784, Great Point, Nantucket Island

Nauset Beach lighthouse, 1877, Nauset Beach, North Eastham

Ned Point lighthouse, 1837, Mattapoisett

Newburyport Harbor lighthouse, 1788, Plum Island

Nobska Point lighthouse, 1829, Woods Hole Harbor

Palmer Island lighthouse, 1849, New Bedford Harbor

Plymouth lighthouse (Gurnet), 1769, Plymouth

Race Point lighthouse, 1816, Cape Cod National Seashore

Sankaty Head light, 1850, Nantucket Island

Scituate lighthouse, 1811, Scituate

Ten Pound Island light, 1821, Gloucester

Three Sisters lights, 1838, Nauset Beach, North Eastham

Michigan

Au Sable (Big Sable) lighthouse, 1874, Ludington

Beaver Island lighthouse, 1852, Beaver Island, near Charlevoix

Big Bay Point lighthouse, 1896, Big Bay Point

Copper Harbor lighthouse, 1849, Keweenaw Peninsula

Detroit River lighthouse, 1885, South Rockwood

Eagle Harbor light station, 1851, Eagle Harbor

Escanaba (Sand Point) lighthouse, 1868, Eagle Harbor

Fort Gratiot lighthouse, 1825, Port Huron

Forty Mile Point lighthouse, 1897, Presque Isle, near Rogers City

Grand Traverse station, 1853, Northport

Michigan (continued)

Holland Harbor South Pierhead lighthouse, 1872, Holland
Huron Island lighthouse, 1868, Skanee
Isle Royale lighthouse, 1875, Menagerie Island
Little Sable lighthouse, 1874, Silver Lake State Park, Hart
Manitou Island lighthouse, 1850, Manitou Island
Marquette Harbor lighthouse, 1853, Marquette
Old Mackinac Point lighthouse, 1892, Mackinaw City
Old Mission Point lighthouse, 1870, Traverse City
Old Presque Isle lighthouse and museum, 1840, Alpena
Passage Island lighthouse, 1882, Passage Island, near Isle Royale
Peninsula Point lighthouse, 1886, Stonington
Point aux Barques lighthouse, 1848, Port Austin
Point Betsie lighthouse, 1858, Frankfort
Point Iroquois lighthouse, 1855, Brimley
Port Sanilac lighthouse, 1886, Port Sanilac
Presque Isle lighthouse, 1871, Presque Isle
Rock Harbor lighthouse, 1855, Isle Royale National Park
Rock of Ages lighthouse, 1908, Isle Royale National Park
Round Island light, 1895, St. Ignace
Seul Choix Point lighthouse, 1892, Seul Choix Point
South Manitou Island lighthouse, 1839, Sleeping Bear Dunes National
    Seashore
Spectacle Reef light, 1874, Lake Michigan
St. Helena Island light tower, 1874, St. Helena Island
St. James (Beaver Island Harbor) lighthouse, 1856, Charlevoix
Sturgeon Point lighthouse, 1870, Alcona
Tawas Point lighthouse, 1870, Alcona
Whitefish Point lighthouse, 1848, Whitefish Point
White River light station museum, c. 1875, Whitehall

Minnesota

Duluth South Breakwater Inner lighthouse, c. 1906, Duluth
Grand Marais lighthouse, 1885, Grand Marais
Split Rock lighthouse, 1910, Two Harbors

Mississippi

  Biloxi light, 1848, Biloxi
  Cat Island light station, 1871, near Gulfport
  Round Island lighthouse, 1833, Pascagoula
  Ship Island light, 1886, Ship Island

New Hampshire

  Isle of Shoals lighthouse, 1821, White Island
  Portsmouth light, 1771, Portsmouth Harbor

New Jersey

  Absecon lighthouse, 1857, Atlantic City
  Ambrose light station, 1823, New York Bay entrance
  Barnegat light, 1835, Barnegat Inlet, north end of Long Beach Island
  Cape May lighthouse, 1823, Cape May
  Finn's Point Rear Range lighthouse, 1877, Supawna Meadows National
    Wildlife Refuge
  Hereford Inlet lighthouse, 1874, North Wildwood
  Navesink (Twin Lights) lighthouses, 1828, Navesink
  Sandy Hook light station, 1764, Sandy Hook
  Sea Girt lighthouse, 1896, Sea Girt

New York

  Barcelona lighthouse, 1829, Barcelona
  Buffalo Breakwater South End lighthouse, 1903, Buffalo
  Buffalo light, 1819, Buffalo
  Cedar Island lighthouse, 1839, Sag Harbor
  Champlain Memorial lighthouse, 1912, Crown Point
  Coney Island lighthouse, 1890, Brooklyn
  Eatons Neck light, 1799, Huntington Bay
  Esopus Meadows lighthouse, 1839, Esopus
  Fire Island light, 1826, Fire Island
  Fort Niagara lighthouse, 1870, Youngstown
  Fort Tompkins light, 1900, Fort Tompkins
  Genesee light, 1822, Rochester

New York (continued)

Hudson City (Hudson-Athens) lighthouse, 1874, between Hudson and Athens

Jeffrey's Hook lighthouse, 1889, New York City

Kingston (Rondout II) lighthouse, 1880, intersection of Rondout Creek and Hudson River

Montauk Point light station, 1797, Montauk, Long Island

Old Stony Point lighthouse, 1825, Stony Point Battlefield Historic Park

Oswego West Pierhead lighthouse, 1822, Oswego

Point Gratiot lighthouse, 1875, Dunkirk

Robbins Reef light, c. 1839, upper New York Harbor

Rock Island lighthouse, 1847, Rock Island

Saugerties lighthouse, 1836, Hudson River and Esopus Creek

Selkirk lighthouse, 1838, Pulaski

Sodus Point lighthouse, 1825, Sodus Point

Staten Island lighthouse, 1912, Staten Island

Tarrytown lighthouse, 1883, North Tarrytown

Thirty Mile Point lighthouse, 1876, Somerset

Tibbits Point lighthouse, 1827, Cape Vincent

North Carolina

Bald Head light station, 1795, Cape Fear

Bodie Island light station, 1847, Bodie Island

Cape Hatteras light station, 1870, Cape Hatteras National Seashore

Cape Lookout lighthouse, 1812, Cape Lookout

Currituck Beach lighthouse, 1875, Outer Banks near Kitty Hawk

Light tower, 1958, Oak Island

Ocracoke lighthouse, 1803, Ocracoke Island

Ohio

Cleveland West Pierhead lighthouse, 1910, Cleveland

Fairport light, 1825, Fairport

Marblehead lighthouse, 1821, Marblehead

Sandusky light, 1821, Sandusky

Toledo Harbor lighthouse, 1904, Toledo

West Sister Island lighthouse, 1848, West Sister Island

Oregon

Cape Arago light station, 1866, Coos Bay
Cape Blanco light, 1870, Cape Blanco
Cape Meares lighthouse, 1881, Tillamook
Heceta Head lighthouse, 1894, Florence
Tillamook Rock light, 1881, Columbia River
Umpqua lighthouse, n.d., Reedsport
Yaquina Bay, 1871, Newport
Yaquina Head lighthouse, 1873, Newport

Pennsylvania

Erie Land lighthouse (Old Presque Isle), 1819, Erie
Presque Isle lighthouse, c. 1870, Erie

Rhode Island

Castle Hill lighthouse, 1890, Newport
Dutch Island lighthouse, 1827, Dutch Island
Ida Lewis Rock (Lime Rock light), pre 1881, Newport
Jamestown (Beavertail light), 1749, Conanicut Island, Narragansett Bay
Newport Harbor lighthouse, 1823, Goat Island
North lighthouse, 1829, New Shoreham, Sandy Point
Point Judith lighthouse, 1810, Point Judith
Prudence Island lighthouse, 1823, Portsmouth
Rose Island light, 1869, Newport
Sakonnet light, 1884, mouth of Sakonnet River
Southeast lighthouse, 1873, Block Island
Warwick lighthouse, 1827, Warwick
Watch Hill lighthouse, 1807, Westerly

South Carolina

Cape Romain light, 1827, Raccoon Key
Charleston light station, 1757, Morris Island
Charleston light station, 1962, Sullivan's Island
Georgetown lighthouse, 1801, North Island, off Georgetown
Harbortown lighthouse, 1970, Hilton Head
Hunting Island lighthouse, 1859, Beaufort

Texas

Aransas Pass light, 1855, Aransas Pass, near Corpus Christi
Galveston Bay light, 1852, Bolivar Point
Lydia Ann lighthouse, 1857, Port Aransas
Matagorda lighthouse, 1852, Matagorda
Point Bolivar lighthouse, 1852, Galveston
Point Isabel lighthouse, 1853, Port Isabel, near Brownsville

Vermont

Colchester Reef lighthouse, 1871, Shelburne Museum

Virginia

Assateague lighthouse, 1833, Chincoteague National Wildlife Refuge
Cape Charles lighthouse, 1828, Smith Island
Cape Henry lighthouse, 1791, Fort Story, Virginia Beach
Jones Point lighthouse, 1855, Alexandria
New Point Comfort lighthouse, 1805, Mobjack Bay, Mathews County
Old Point Comfort lighthouse, 1802, Fort Monroe, Hampton
Screwpile light, 1855, Point of Shoals

Washington

Admiralty Head lighthouse, 1903, Coupeville
Cape Disappointment lighthouse, 1856, Ilwaco
Cape Flattery light station, 1858, Neah Bay
Grays Harbor lighthouse, 1900, Westport
Monots Ledge tower, 1851, Seattle
Mukilteo lighthouse, 1906, Mukilteo
New Dungeness light station, 1857, Straits of Juan de Fuca
North Head Light, 1898, Ilwaco
Point Robinson lighthouse, 1885, Vachon Island
Point Wilson lighthouse, 1879, Townsend
West Point lighthouse, 1881, Seattle

Wisconsin

> *Baileys Harbor Range Lights,* 1870, Baileys Harbor
> *Cana Island lighthouse,* 1870, near Baileys Harbor
> *Chambers Island lighthouse,* 1868, Ephraim
> *Devil's Island lighthouse,* 1891, Devil's Island
> *Eagle Bluff lighthouse,* 1868, Door County
> *La Pointe lighthouse,* 1858, Chequamegon Bay
> *Michigan Island lighthouses,* 1857, Michigan Island
> *North Point lighthouse,* 1855, North Point
> *Pilot Island lighthouse,* 1850, Pilot Island
> *Racine Harbor lighthouse,* 1866, Racine
> *Rawley Point lighthouse,* 1853, Two Rivers
> *Sherwood Point lighthouse,* 1883, Sherwood Point
> *Sturgeon Bay Canal lighthouse,* 1899, Sturgeon Bay
> *Wind Point lighthouse,* 1880, Wind Point

"We shape our buildings; thereafter they shape us."
—SIR WINSTON CHURCHILL, 1960, English statesman and painter

AMERICAN COVERED BRIDGES

Although rare in some parts of the country, many covered bridges in America still exist and are a romantic link to the past. More than 10,000 were built between 1805 and the early 1900s. The bridges were probably originally covered to protect the base structure and to keep the surface dry for crossing. (Because of the privacy afforded, they were sometimes called *kissing bridges.*) Because most are at least 100 years old, they may have had several names. (Former names are listed in parentheses.) Dates of the bridges' construction are given where available.

Alabama

Big Bear Creek Covered Bridge, c. 1850, Allsboro
Buzzard Roost Covered Bridge, c. 1850, Cherokee
Clarkson Covered Bridge, 1904, Clarkson
Coldwater Covered Bridge, c. 1850, Coldwater
Covered Bridge, Manoc
Covered Bridge, pre–Civil War, Eastaboga
Cripple Deer Creek Covered Bridge, 1859, Allsboro
Easley Bridge, 1930s, Oneonta
Horton Mill Covered Bridge, 1934, Gadsden
Lake Lauralee Bridge, Sterrett
Swann Bridge, 1930s, Oneonta

California

Bridge over Sheep Pen Creek, 1970s, Jedediah Smith Redwoods State Park
Bridgeport Covered Bridge, 1861–1862, Bridgeport
Covered Bridge, 1936, Eureka
Knight's Ferry Covered Bridge, 1862, Knight's Ferry

Connecticut

Comstock Bridge, Colchester
Cornwall Bridge, 1837, Cornwall

Delaware

Ashland Covered Bridge, Ashland
Smith's Bridge, 1839, Granogue, Beaver Valley
Wooddale Covered Bridge, Wooddale

Georgia

Auchumpkee Creek Bridge, 1892, Upson County
Big Red Oak Creek Bridge, 1840s, Meriwether County
Callaway Gardens Bridge, 1870, Callaway Gardens

Coheelee Creek Bridge, 1891, Fannie Askew Williams State Park

Concord Bridge (Nickajack Creek), 1872, Cobb County

Covered Bridge, c. 1850, Cobb County, near Atlanta

Cromer's Mill Bridge (Nails Creek), 1906, Cromer's Mill

Elder's Mill Bridge (Rose Creek), Watkinsville

Euharlee Creek Bridge (Lowry), 1886, Euharlee

Howard's Bridge, 1999, Oglethorpe County

Kilgore Mill Covered Bridge, 1874, Winder

Lula Bridge (Blind Susie Bridge), 1910, Lula

Pooles Mill Bridge, 1820s, Forsythe County

Rockdale County Bridge (Haralson Mill Covered Bridge), 1997, Rockdale County

Stone Mountain Bridge (College Avenue, Effie's), 1891, Stone Mountain Park

Stovall Covered Bridge (Helen, Chickamengra Creek, Nacoochee), 1895, White County

Watson Mill Bridge (Carlton Bridge), 1885, Watson Mill State Park

Illinois

Bureau Creek Bridge, Bureau County

Eames Covered Bridge, 1862, near Oquawka

Jack's Mill Covered Bridge, 1845–1846, near Oquawka

Sugar Creek Covered Bridge, 1880, Springfield

Indiana

Adams Mill Covered Bridge, 1871, Cutler

Bean Blossom Bridge, 1838, Brown County State Park, Nashville

Bells Ford Covered Bridge, 1869, Seymour

Brownsville Covered Bridge, 1837–1840, Brownsville

Busching Covered Bridge, 1885, Versailles

Ceylon Covered Bridge, c. 1860, Geneva

Covered Bridge, 1868, Bridgeton, Parke County

Covered Bridge, Cataract Falls State Park

Cumberland Covered Bridge, 1877, Mathews

Darlington Bridge, 1868, Montgomery County

Indiana (continued)

Deer's Mill Covered Bridge, 1878, Alamo
Dunlapsville Covered Bridge, 1870, Dunlapsville
Jackson Covered Bridge, 1861, Bloomingdale
Kennedy Covered Bridge, 1880, near Rushville
Leatherwood Station Covered Bridge, 1899, Montezuma
Mansfield Bridge, 1867, Mansfield
Matthews Covered Bridge, 1876–1877, Marion
Medora Covered Bridge, 1875, Medora
Narrows Covered Bridge, 1882, Turkey Run State Park
Offutt's Ford Bridge, Rush County
Roann Bridge, Wabash County
Symons Creek Bridge, 1831, Straughn
Vermont Covered Bridge, 1874, Kokomo

Iowa

Bridge across North Fork of Skunk River, 1869, Delta
Cedar Covered Bridge, 1883, Madison County
Covered Bridge, 1882, near Carlisle
Cutler-Donahoe Bridge, 1870, Winterset
Hogback Bridge, 1884, Madison County
Holliwell Bridge, 1880, Madison County
Imes Covered Bridge, 1870, St. Charles
McBride Bridge, 1870, Madison County
Roseman Bridge, 1883, Madison County

Kansas

Covered Bridge, c. 1859, near Springdale

Kentucky

Bennett's Mill Bridge, 1855, Ashland
Bridge over Beech Fork River, 1866, Bardstown
Covered Bridge, 1807–1808, Cynthiana
Covered Bridge, 1870, near Butler
Oldtown Bridge, 1880, Ashland

Maine

Babb's Bridge, 1843, South Windham
Bennett Bridge, 1901, near Wilson Mills
Hemlock Bridge, 1857, Fryeburg
Lovejoy Bridge, 1868, South Andover
Lowe's Bridge, 1857, Guilford Village
Porter Bridge, 1876, Porter & Parsonfield
Robyville Bridge, 1876, Corinth
Sunday River Bridge (Artist's Bridge), 1872, Newry
Watson Settlement Bridge, 1911, Littletown

Maryland

Covered Bridge, c. 1858, Jerusalem
Foxcatcher Farms Bridge, Cecil County
Gilpin's Falls Bridge, 1860, Bayview
Jericho Bridge, 1865, near Baltimore
Loy's Station Bridge, 1848–1860, Frederick County
Rocky Ridge Bridge, Hwy. 77 Frederick Road
Roddy Creek Bridge, 1850, near Thurmont
Utica Mill Bridge, 1850, Utica

Massachusetts

Bissell Bridge, 1880, Charlemont
Chicopee Bridge, 1846, Springfield
Covered Bridge, 19th century, Millville
Long Bridge, 1853, Charlemont
Nehemiah Jewett's Bridge, 1818, Pepperell

Michigan

Fallasburg Covered Bridge, Fallasburg

Missouri

Bollinger Mill Covered Bridge and Mill, 1858–1868, Burfordville
Locust Creek Covered Bridge, near Laclede
Noah's Ark Covered Bridge, 1878, near Edgerton

Missouri (continued)

> *Sandy Creek Bridge,* Hillsboro
> *Union Covered Bridge,* near Paris

New Hampshire

> *Albany Bridge,* 1858, White Mountain National Forest
> *Ashuelot Bridge,* 1864, Ashuelot
> *Bridge #37,* c. 1820, Stark Village
> *Cornish-Windsor Bridge,* 1866, Cornish
> *Covered Bridge,* 1850, Orford
> *Covered Bridge,* Hillsborough County
> *The Flume,* 1886, Franconia Notch State Park
> *Haverhill-Bath Covered Bridge,* 1827, Woodsville
> *Honeymoon Bridge #51,* c. 1876, Jackson
> *Passaconway Bridge,* White Mountains
> *Rowell's Bridge,* 1853, West Hopkinton
> *Saco River Bridge,* 1890, Conway
> *Swanzey-Slate Covered Bridge,* Westport
> *Swift River Bridge,* 1870, Conway
> *Swiftwater Bridge,* 1849, Bath
> *Tanner Bridge,* 1936, Enfield
> *Thompson Bridge,* 1832, Swanzey
> *Turner Bridge,* 1936, Enfield

New Jersey

> *Forty-five River,* Fundy National Park, New Brunswick
> *Green Sergeant's Bridge,* 1872, near Sergeantsville
> *Old Covered Bridge and Flood Gates,* 19th century, South Pemberton
> *Scarborough Bridge,* 1959, Cherry Hill

New York

> *Brasher Falls Bridge,* 1861, Brasher Falls
> *Hyde Hall Covered Bridge,* c. 1830, East Springfield
> *Old Blenheim Bridge,* 1855, North Blenheim
> *Perrine's Bridge,* 1850, near Rifton

North Carolina

Reddles River Bridge (Top Hat Bridge), North Wilkesboro

Ohio

Barette's Mill Bridge, 1850, Highland County
Bridge over Little Miami River, 1830, Xenia
Covered Bridge, 1808, Newton Falls
Covered Bridge, 19th century, near Zanesville
Covered Bridge, Buckeye Lake State Park
Covered Bridge, c. 1859, North Lewisburg
Covered Bridge, Clarksville, near Vernon
Ferryboat Bridge, 1858, Newton Falls
John Bright No. 2 Covered Bridge, near Carroll
New Hope Bridge, 1895, Brown County
New London Pike Bridge, 1865, near Hamilton
Olins Bridge, 1873, Ashtabula County

Oregon

Five Bridges, Cottage Grove
Horse Creek Covered Bridge, 1930, near McKenzie Bridge
Jordan Covered Bridge, 1937, near Scio

Pennsylvania

Ackley Bridge, 1832, Green/Washington Counties
Albertus Meyers Bridge, Allentown
Allenwood Covered Bridge, Allenwood
Bartram's Covered Bridge, 1860, near White House
Baumgardener's Covered Bridge, Lancaster County
Beavertown Bridge, Beavertown
Bells Mill Bridge, c. 1850, near West Newton
Bittenbender's Bridge, 1888, Huntington Mills
Bitzer's Mill Bridge, Lancaster County
Bogert Bridge, 1841, Allentown
Bowmansdale Bridge, Cumberland/York Counties
Bridge No. 212, Haupt's Mill

Pennsylvania (continued)

Bridge, 1856, Earlsville

Bucher's Mill Covered Bridge (Cocalico #2 Bridge), Lancaster County

Buck Hill Bridge, Lancaster County

Buttonwood Bridge (Blockhouse), 1898, Buttonwood

Cabin Run, 1871, Smith's Corner

Clark's Ferry Bridge, Clark's Ferry

Cogan House (Buckhorn Bridge), 1877, Lycoming County

Colemanville Covered Bridge (Martic Ford), Lancaster County

Covered Bridge, Chitwood

Creasyville Bridge, 1881, Millville

Davis Bridge, 1875, Catawissa

Detter's Mill Covered Bridge, c. 1815, Detter's Mill

Dr. Kniseley Covered Bridge, Alum Bank

Dreese's Covered Bridge, Beavertown

Dreibelbis Station Bridge, Berks County

East and West Paden Bridges, 1884, Forks

Eberly's Cider Mill (Fiand's Covered Bridge), Lancaster County

Eichelbergers Covered Bridge (Jackson Mill), Lancaster County

Erb's Bridge (Hammer Creek), Lancaster County

Erwinna Covered Bridge, 1871, Erwinna

Esther Furnace Bridge, 1882, Catawissa

Factory Bridge (Horsham Bridge), c. 1800, White Deer Township

Forksville Bridge, 1850, Forksville

Forry's Mill Bridge, Lancaster County

Fowlersville Bridge, 1886, Evansville

Frankenfelt Bridge, Bucks County

Frankenfield Bridge, 1872, Tinicum Township

Gallon House Bridge, Silverton

Geiger Bridge, 1853, Orefield

Glen Hope Bridge, Chester County

Goodpasture Bridge, Vida

Gottlieb Brown, Sam Wagner Bridge, 1881, Potts Grove

Grave Creek, 1920, Josephine County

Griesemer's Mill Bridge, 1832, Spangsville

Grimes Covered Bridge, c. 1888, near Ruff Creek

Gross Covered Bridge, c. 1878, near Beaver Springs

Hall's Sheeder Bridge, Chester County

Harmony Hill Bridge, Chester County

Harrington Covered Bridge, Albion

Harrity Bridge, 1841, Carbon County

Hassenplug Bridge, Mifflenburg

Hayes Clark Bridge, 1882, West Buffalo Township

Heike's Bridge, Adams County

Herr's Covered Bridge, Lancaster County

Hillsgrove Bridge, c. 1850, Hillsgrove

Hollingshead Bridge, 1850, Catawissa

Hubler Bridge, 1850, Lewisburg

Hunsecker's Mill Bridge, 1848, Lancaster County

Jack's Mountain Bridge, Adams County

Johnson Bridge, 1882, Cleveland Township

Johnson's Mill Bridge, 1866, Rapho-Hempfield

Josiah Hess Bridge, 1875, Forks & Jonestown

Jud Christian Bridge, 1876, Millville

Kauffman's Distillery Bridge (Sporting Hill), Lancaster County

Keefer Bridge, 1888, Washingtonville

Kellers Mill Covered Bridge (Guy Bard, Rettew's), Lancaster County

Kennedy Bridge, Chester County

Knapp's Bridge (Brown's Creek, Luther's Mill), 1853, Luther's Mill

Knecht's Bridge (Sleifer's Bridge), 1873, Springtown

Knoebel's Grove Bridge, 1975, Knoebel's Grove

Knox Bridge, Valley Forge

Kramer Bridge, 1881, Rohrsburg

Krickbaum Bridge, 1876, Elysburg

Kuhn's Fording Bridge, 1897, near East Berlin

Kurtz's Mill Bridge (Baer's Mill, Keystone Mill), Lancaster County

Kutz's Mill Bridge, Berks County

L. C. Beavan Old Mill Bridge, 1850, New Milford

Landis Mill Bridge, Lancaster County

Larkin Bridge, Chester County

Lawrence L. Knoebel Bridge, 1875, Columbia/Northumberland
   Counties

Pennsylvania (continued)

    Leaman Rifle Works Bridge, 19th century, Pinetown
    Leaman's Place Covered Bridge (Eshelman's Mill), Lancaster County
    Lime Valley Covered Bridge (Strasburg Bridge), Lancaster County
    Linton Stevens Bridge, Chester County
    Little Gap Bridge, 1880, Little Gap
    Loux Bridge, 1874, Hinkletown
    Luther Mills Bridge, 1853, Luther Mills
    Manassas Guth Bridge, 1858, Orefield
    Mercer's Mill Bridge, 1880, Mercer's Mill
    Millmont Red Bridge, 1855, Union County
    Mood's Bridge, 1874, Pekasie
    Moreland Bridge (Fraser Bridge), 1888, Lairdsville
    Neff's Mill Bridge (Pequea #7), Lancaster County
    Parr's Mill Bridge (Willow Grove Grist Mill), 1865, Catawissa
    Patterson Bridge, 1875, Orangeville/Rohrsburg
    Pine Grove Bridge, Lancaster County
    Pine Valley Covered Bridge (Iron Hill Bridge), 1842, New Britain
        Township
    Pinetown (Bushong's Mill, Nolte's Point Mill), Lancaster County
    Pinetown Covered Bridge (Wegner, Rose Hill), Lancaster County
    Pleasantville Bridge, Berks County
    Pool Forge Bridge, Lancaster County
    Rapp's Dam Bridge, Chester County
    Red Run (Oberholzer's Bridge), Lancaster County
    Rex Bridge, 1858, Orefield
    Richard's Bridge (Reichard), 1852, Elysburg
    Risser's Mill Bridge (Horst's Mill), Lancaster County
    Rudolph and Arthur Bridge, Chester County
    Rupert Bridge, 1847, Bloomsburg & Montour Township
    Sach's Bridge, Adams County
    Sam Eckman Bridge, 1876, Millville
    Sauk's Bridge over Marsh Creek, 1854, Gettysburg
    Schenk Mill Bridge (Big Chickie's #4), Lancaster County

Schlicher Bridge, 1882, Allentown

Schofield Ford Bridge, Bucks County

Sheard's Mill (Thatcher Bridge), 1873, Haycock Township

Shearer's Covered Bridge, Lancaster County

Shoemaker Bridge, 1881, Iola

Short Bridge, 1945, Linn County

Siegrist's Mill Bridge, Lancaster County

Snooks Covered Bridge, Alum Bank

Snyder's Fording Covered Bridge, 1900, Slabtown

Sonestown Bridge, c. 1850, Sonestown

South Perkasie Bridge, 1832, Perkasie

Speakman No. 1, Chester County

Speakman No. 2, Chester County

Stillwater Bridge, 1849, Stillwater

Stoneroads Mill Bridge (George S. Mann Bridge), 1868, near Maple
   Grove

Thomas Mill Covered Bridge, 19th century, Philadelphia (Germantown)

Twining Ford (Schofield Bridge), 1835, Bucks County

Uhlerstown Bridge, 1832, Bucks County

Van Sant Covered Bridge (Beaver Dam Bridge), 1875, Bucks County

Wanich Bridge, 1884, Fernsville & Bloomsburg

Waterford Covered Bridge, 1880–1890, Waterford

Weaver's Mill Bridge (Isaac Shearer's Mill), Lancaster County

Weddle Bridge, Sankey Park, Sweet Home

Wehr Bridge, 1841, Kernsville

Wertz's Bridge, Berks County

White Rock Forge Covered Bridge, Lancaster County

Willow Hill Bridge, Lancaster County

Wilson's Mill Covered Bridge, Avella

Zook's Mill Covered Bridge (Wenger), Lancaster County

Tennessee

   Elizabethton Covered Bridge, 1882, Carter County

Vermont

>*Baltimore Bridge No. 81,* 1870, Springfield
>
>*Bartonsville Bridge,* 1870, Bartonsville
>
>*Battleground Bridge,* 1975, Fayston
>
>*Bests Bridge,* 1890, West Windsor
>
>*Bowers Bridge (Brownsville),* c. 1919, West Windsor
>
>*Braley (Upper Blaisdell or Johnson),* Randolph
>
>*Bridge at the Green,* 1852, Arlington
>
>*Brown Bridge,* 1880, Shrewsbury
>
>*Brown's River Bridge,* 1837–1838, Westford
>
>*Chamberlin (Whitcomb),* 1881, Lyndon
>
>*Chamberlin Bridge,* 1958, Northfield
>
>*Chiselville Bridge,* c. 1870, Sunderland
>
>*Cilley Bridge (Lower),* 1883, Tunbridge
>
>*Coburn (Cemetery),* 1851, East Montpelier
>
>*Colt's Pond Bridge,* 1810, Brookfield
>
>*Columbia Bridge,* 1912, Lemington
>
>*Comstock Bridge,* 1863–1890, Montgomery
>
>*Cooley Bridge,* 1849, Pittsford
>
>*Cornish-Windsor Bridge,* 1866, Windsor
>
>*Creamery Bridge (West Hill, Crystal Springs),* 1863–1890, Montgomery
>
>*Creamery Bridge,* 1879, Brattleboro
>
>*Depot Bridge,* 1840, Pittsford
>
>*Downer's Bridge,* 1840, Weathersfield
>
>*East Fairfield Bridge,* 1965, Fairfield
>
>*Emily's (Stowe Hollow, Gold Brook),* 1844, Stowe
>
>*Fisher Bridge,* 1908, Wolcott
>
>*Flint Bridge,* 1845, Tunbridge
>
>*Fuller Bridge (Black Falls),* 1863–1890, Montgomery
>
>*Gates Farm Bridge (Little),* 1897, Cambridge
>
>*Gibou Road Bridge,* 1863–1890, Montgomery
>
>*Gifford Bridge (C. K. Smith),* 1904, East Randolph
>
>*Giorgetti Bridge,* 1978, Pittsford
>
>*Gorham (Goodnough),* c. 1841, Pittsford
>
>*Green Bank Hollow,* 1886, Arlington
>
>*Green River Bridge,* 1870, Guildford

Hall Berber Perk Bridge (Osgood), 1867, Saxton's River

Halpin Bridge, 1824, Middlebury

Hammond Bridge, c. 1842, Pittsford

Hectorsville Bridge, 1883, Montgomery

Henry Bridge, c. 1840, Bennington

Holmes Creek Bridge (Lakeshore), 1840, Charlotte

Hopkins Bridge, 1863–1890, Enosburg

Howe Bridge, Tunbridge

Hutchins Bridge, 1863–1890, Montgomery

Hyde (Kingsbury), 1904, Randolph

Jaynes (Upper, Codding Hollow), c. 1877, Waterville

Kent's Corner Bridge, 1983, Calais

Kidder Hill Bridge (Kissing Bridge), 1870, Grafton

Kingsley (Mill River), 1870, Clarendon

Larkin Bridge, 1902, Tunbridge

Lincoln Bridge, 1865, Woodstock

Longley Bridge (Harnots, Head), 1863–1890, Montgomery

Lower Bridge, 1881, Coventry

MacMillan Bridge, 1967, Grafton

Maple Street Bridge, 1865, Fairfax

Martins Mill, 1881, Hartland

Middle Bridge, 1969, Woodstock

Mill Bridge (Hayward, Noble), 1883, Tunbridge

Mill Bridge (Junction, Lower), Belvidere

Millers Run (Bradley), 1878, Lyndon

Montgomery Bridge (Lower, Potter), 1887, Waterville

Morgan Bridge (Upper), 1887, Belvidere

Moseley Bridge, 1899, Northfield

Mount Orne Bridge, 1911, Lunenberg

Moxley Bridge (Guy), 1886, Chelsea

New Middle Bridge, 1969, Woodstock

Newell Bridge, Northfield Falls

Orne Bridge (Lord's Creek), 1881 & 1999, Irasburg

Orton Farm, 1890, Marshfield

Paper Mill Bridge, c. 1840, Bennington

Pine Brook Bridge (Wilder), 1872, Waitsfield

Vermont (continued)

Poland Farm Bridge (Junction), 1887, Cambridge

Powerhouse Bridge (School Street), 1870, Johnson

Pulp Mill Bridge, 1808–1820, Middlebury

Queechee Bridge, 1970, Queechee

Quinlan Bridge (Lower), 1849–1850, Charlotte

Randall Bridge (Burrington), 1865, Lyndon

Red Bridge (Sterling), 1896, Morristown

River Road (School, Upper), Troy

Robbins Nest Bridge, 1984, Barre Town

Rutland Railroad Bridge, 1897, Shoreham

Salisbury (Station), 1865, Cornwall

Salmond Bridge, c. 1880, Amsden

Sanborn Bridge (Center), 1969, Lyndon

Sanderson (Lower), 1838, Brandon

Santa's Land Bridge, 1956, Putney

Sayers Bridge, Thetford Center

Schoolhouse Bridge, 1879, Lyndon Corner

Scott Covered Bridge (Grist Mill, Bryant) 1870, West Townshend

Scribner Bridge (Mudget), Johnson

Sequin Bridge, c. 1845, Charlotte

Shelburne Museum Bridge, 1845, Shelburne

Silk (Locust Grove), 1889, Bennington

Slaughterhouse Bridge, Northfield

Smith Bridge, 1973, Brownsville

Spade Farm Bridge, 1824, Ferrisburgh

Station Bridge, Northfield Falls

Taftsville Bridge, 1836, Woodstock

Twigg-Smith Bridge, 1973, West Windsor

Twin Bridge, 1850, Rutland

Union Village Bridge, 1867, Thetford

Upper Blaisdell (Johnson), 1904, East Randolph

Upper Bridge, East Charlotte

Upper Bridge, Northfield Falls

Ventilated Bridge, Lake Sunapee

Victorian Village, 1967, Rockingham
Village (Church Street), c. 1877, Waterville
Village Bridge (Big Eddy), 1833, Waitsfield
Warren Bridge, 1879–1880, Warren
Waterman Bridge (German), 1868, Johnson
West Dummerston Bridge, 1879, Dummerston
White Caps Bridge, 1970, Stowe
Willard Bridge, North Hartland
Williamsville Bridge, 1860, Williamsville
Worralls Bridge, 1868, Bartonsville

Virginia

Covered Bridge, Weston
Humpback Covered Bridge, 1835, Covington
Marysville Covered Bridge, c. 1878, near Gladys
Meems Bottom Bridge, 1892 & 1979, Meems Bottom
Trent's Bridge, c. 1844, near Cumberland

Washington

Gray's River Covered Bridge, 1905, Grays River Valley
Manning Bridge, Manning

West Virginia

Barracksville Covered Bridge, 1853, Barracksville
Herns Mill, Lewisburg
Indian Creek Bridge, Lewisburg
Laurel Creek, Lewisburg
Milton Covered Bridge, 1875–1876, Milton
Philippi Bridge, near Morgantown
Staats Mill Covered Bridge, 1887, near Ripley

Wisconsin

Covered Bridge, 1876, Cedarburg

WORLD-FAMOUS BRIDGES

Whether it's an arch bridge across a river or a suspension bridge to connect countries, whether you're interested in a record-breaking span or a romantic place with a great view, bridges can be potent reminders of human progress. A few bridges have existed for two thousand years, or have been rebuilt in the same location several times over the centuries. Although technological advances have allowed longer and higher suspension bridges to be built, some of the smallest (such as the *Bridge of Sighs*, between two buildings in Venice) sometimes have the greatest appeal. Some bridges are even becoming tourist attractions. Adventure seekers can now climb the *Sydney Harbor Bridge* or bungy-jump from the *Kawarau Bridge* in New Zealand. Tourists who prefer to keep their feet on the ground can find old bridges that have been converted to biking or hiking trails.

AUSTRALIA

Sydney Harbor Bridge, 1932, Australia (If you're feeling adventurous, you can climb this bridge.)

AUSTRIA

Pedestrian Bridge Murau, 1995, Styria (A timber bridge over the river Mur)

Rosenbrucke (Danube Bridge Tulln), 1991, Tulln (A cable-stayed bridge)

Wenner Bridge Murau, 1993, Styria (A timber bridge that crosses the river Mur)

CANADA

Niagara Bridge, 1852–1918, Niagara (This railroad bridge over the Niagara River was one of the first iron suspension bridges.)

Peace Bridge, 1927, United States and Canada, across the Niagara River (Dedicated to 100 years of peaceful sharing of a border.)

Quebec Bridge, 1919, Quebec City (A cantilever bridge considered the Eighth Wonder of the World when it was constructed. Its "sister" bridge was the *Firth of Forth Bridge* in Scotland.)

CHINA

Kap Shui Mun Bridge, 1993–1997, Hong Kong (Links Hong Kong with Lantau Island)

Tsing Ma Bridge, 1997, Hong Kong (The longest double deck [rail and car] bridge in the world, linking Tsing Yi to Ma Wan)

CZECH REPUBLIC

Charles Bridge, 1357, Prague (This beautiful bridge across the Vltava River is lined with statuary.)

DENMARK

Storbaelt, 2001, Denmark (This bridge for cars and trains connects Copenhagen to Malmo, Sweden, and is basically a link from Continental Europe to Scandinavia.)

ENGLAND

The Clifton Suspension Bridge, 1836–1864, Bristol (Crosses the River Avon Gorge)

Gateshead Millennium Bridge, 2000, Tyneside (This bridge between Gateshead and Newcastle was constructed off-site and brought upstream by a floating crane.)

Humber Bridge, 1981, East Yorkshire (When it was built, this was the longest suspension bridge in the world.)

Pulteney Bridge, c. 1774, Bath (One of three bridges in the world that is lined with shops, it was designed by Robert Adam. It is said that later additions *ruined* his design.)

Tower Bridge, 1894, London (River traffic is allowed between the two imposing towers of the bridge by the raising of "bascules" [bridge surfaces] between the towers as needed.)

FRANCE

Pont de Grenelle, 1825–1875 (A small copy of the *Statue of Liberty* by Bartholdi is the distinctive feature of this bridge.)

FRANCE *(continued)*

Le Pont Neuf, 1578–1604, Paris (This famous bridge was "wrapped" by Christo. Legend has it that if you walk for one hour on the bridge you will meet someone you know.)

Le Pont de Normandie, 1997, Le Havre (This bridge goes from Le Havre to Honfleur and is the world's longest cable stay bridge.)

Pont Alexandre III, 1900, Paris (Named for Russian Tsar Alexandre III, its decorations are typical of the end of the 19th century.)

Pont du Gard, late 1st century, Nimes (The Romans built this aqueduct masonry bridge to last.)

IRAN

Pol e Khaju Bridge, 1650, Isfahan (This bridge, built under Shah Abbass, crosses the Zayandeh-Rood River.)

Sio-Seh Pole (Allahverdikhan Bridge—Bridges of 33 arches), 1602, Isfahan (This bridge and the Pol e Khaju bridge face each other when the water level is lowered.)

ITALY

Accademia Bridge, 1854, Venice (This bridge across the Grand Canal to the Accademia was originally built of wood and reinforced with iron. It has been reconstructed to look like the original bridge.)

Bridge of Sighs, 1600, Venice (A short bridge between two buildings, so-called because it was the bridge crossed by prisoners as they went to their executions)

Ponte Sant'Angelo, A.D. 134, Rome (Built by Hadrian as the route to his mausoleum)

Ponte Vecchio, 1345, Florence (The first bridge across the Arno River in this location was built by the Etruscans. The present version originally housed blacksmiths, butchers and tanners, but these merchants, long-gone, have been replaced by goldsmiths and upscale shops.)

Rialto Bridge, 1588, Venice (This was originally a wooden bridge across the Grand Canal. When it was replaced by the existing stone bridge, shops were included.)

JAPAN

Akashi Kaikyo Bridge, 1998, Kobe (Currently holds the title of the world's longest spanning suspension bridge, with towers higher than any in the world, and is the length of four *Brooklyn Bridges* put end to end)

NEW ZEALAND

Kawarau Bridge, Queensland (A 154-foot jump awaits the adventurer who wants to try bungy-jumping from this, the bridge where the "sport" originated.)

SCOTLAND

Firth of Forth Bridge, 1882–1889, Edinburgh (This cantilever railroad bridge is considered one of the most "overbuilt" bridges in the world. The bridge was made extra strong because of the collapse of the *Tay Railroad Bridge* that crossed the Firth of Forth before it, in which 70 lives were lost. In its time it was the longest steel bridge in the world.)

SWITZERLAND

Kapellebrucke Bridge, 1333, Lucerne (This covered bridge, with beautifully painted murals inside, is a pedestrian walkway across Lake Lucerne.)

THAILAND

River Kwai Bridge, 1957, Kanchanaburi, 123 km from Bangkok (The original "Bridge Over the River Kwai" was built by the Japanese during World War II. It was estimated that 100,000 laborers and 16,000 prisoners died during its construction.)

UNITED STATES

Arizona

London Bridge, 1831, London; 1971, Tucson (This bridge was slated for demolition when it was purchased by an American for the Arizona desert, where it now crosses Lake Havasu.)

California

Golden Gate Bridge, 1934, San Francisco (Possibly one of the most famous bridges in the world, this bridge crosses the Golden Gate strait, linking San Francisco with Marin County.)

San Francisco-Oakland Bay Bridge, 1934–1936, San Francisco (Connects San Francisco with Oakland)

Illinois

> *Clark Bridge*, 1995, Alton (This bridge over the Mississippi River links Alton, Illinois, with Missouri. It includes bicycle lanes, as the Great River Road is a popular biking area.)

Michigan

> *Mackinac Island Bridge*, 1954 (Until the bridge was built, the only access to this island was by ferry.)

Missouri

> *Eads Bridge*, 1874, St. Louis (An engineering wonder for its time, this bridge that crosses the Mississippi River was built of stone with wrought iron and steel deck arches.)

New York

> *Brooklyn Bridge*, 1869–1883, New York City (Early in its construction, this bridge was the butt of many jokes that often included the now-familiar line "And if you believe that, I have a bridge I can sell you." It's now one of the most famous bridges in the United States.)
>
> *George Washington Bridge*, 1931, 1946, and 1962, New York City (This bridge opened in 1931, had two lanes added in 1946, and a lower level added in 1962. The two-tier, 14-lane suspension bridge goes across the Hudson River between Fort Lee, New Jersey, and Upper Manhattan.)
>
> *Verrazano Narrows Bridge*, 1964, New York City (Connects Brooklyn to Staten Island across the Verrazano Narrows of the Hudson River)

WALES

> *The Brittania Bridge*, 1838 (This railroad bridge across the Menai Straits connects England to Wales. The bridge was damaged by a fire in 1970, in which the metal was distorted, making the bridge no longer straight enough to carry trains, but it was reopened to traffic in 1980.)

CHAPTER 11

Photography

"Stieglitz with his technique and his whole approach to photography was a master and a great man. I like the idea of wrapping something in light, which he did . . ."
—Consuelo Kanaga, 1894–1978, Group F.64 member

TERMS USED IN PHOTOGRAPHY

Although photography is a relatively new art form (only in existence 175 years or so), almost everyone who has a camera creates images that could be considered art. This list includes photographic terms that you might encounter when purchasing a camera or film, when looking at a photo exhibition in a museum, or when you hear a photograph being described.

Aperture. The opening of a camera lens that is expressed in F. numbers. F.2 is usually the largest opening on a lens, while F.22 (the smallest) might be found on complex cameras. F.64, the smallest opening, is found on professional "view cameras." The smaller the opening, the greater the depth of field will be in focus.

ASA (American Standards Association). A number such as 100, 160, 200, 400 that represents the speed of the film. See also *ISO*.

B (bulb). The shutter-speed dial setting that will hold the aperture open as long as the release is pressed. Used for low light conditions or time exposures.

Bracketing. Taking the same subject several times by doubling and cutting the exposure in half to assure a good print.

Cable release. A flexible cable that attaches to the shutter release to eliminate camera movement upon exposure; includes a locking mechanism that can be turned to hold the aperture open for nighttime exposures.

Camera obscura (literally *dark room*). A box first used by Aristotle (384–322 B.C.) in which images of external objects are received through an opening and projected on a surface, such as glass or paper. Used by such artists as Vermeer, Leonardo da Vinci, and Canaletto.

Carte de visite. Basically the first postcard. These photographs were sometimes mailed to friends.

Cartridge (cassette). The light-tight metal or plastic container in which film is sold.

Cibachrome®. A color reversal process that allows color prints to be made from positive color slides.

Close-up lens. A special lens for bringing small things into focus, allowing extreme detail.

Contact printing. A technique in which negatives are placed on sensitized paper and exposed. Before the enlarger was invented, photographers made prints in this manner by exposing to direct sunlight.

Cyanotype (blueprint). The process developed by Sir John Herschel to make a print from a high contrast negative.

Daguerreotype. A photographic process in which a picture made on a silver surface sensitized with iodine was developed by exposure to mercury vapor. Originated by Louis Daguerre.

Depth-of-field. The degree of sharpness of a photograph in front or in back of the area focused on. The smaller the lens opening, the sharper the depth of field.

Digital camera. A filmless camera that records information on electronic media. Information is then transferred to a computer for storage or manipulation.

Double exposure. Exposing film or paper twice, sometimes with interesting results.

Dye transfer. A color printing method that transfers three separate single-color exposures to a single sheet.

Emulsion. A light-sensitive solution that is transferred to paper or film.

Electronic flash. A flash unit that is synchronized to go off as the lens opens; varying degrees of flash duration and intensity will be used depending on time and distance from the subject.

F.stop (aperture). The size of the lens opening is an F.stop. The smaller the opening, the greater the depth of field will be.

Filters. Small glass circles that are attached to the front of the lens for various purposes: to increase contrast; to use with infrared film; to convert outdoor film for indoor use; or to help eliminate reflections.

Fish-eye lens. An extreme wide-angle lens (180°) that gives a distorted center area.

Fixer (originally called Hypo). This chemical, which is used in the developing process, allows images on film and paper to remain unchanging. Until its discovery, early photographers could create images, but they eventually disappeared.

Grain. Irregular clumps of silver on the photographic image. Higher ISO (or ASA) film gives more grain. A greatly magnified picture will be *grainy*.

High key photo. A photo that consists mainly of light tones.

Highlight. The lightest part of the film (for example, a reflection in the eye of a subject).

Hologram. Three-dimensional image of a subject exposed by two laser light beams and exhibited to show the three-dimensional nature of the photo.

Infrared. Special infrared films are used to record the invisible infrared wavelength (done with a red filter). This results in higher contrasts and causes green foliage to look white.

ISO (International Standards Organization). A term interchangeable with ASA that is a rating of the emulsion speed of the film. (ISO is more commonly used currently.)

Low key photo. A photo that is mostly dark, though it may have some highlights.

Macro lens. A lens for close-up work.

Negative. An image on film from which a paper print is made. The lightest areas on a negative will be the darkest areas on a print.

Panning. Swinging the camera horizontally as the photo is exposed, causing a moving subject to "stop" while blurring the background, emphasizing the subject's motion.

Panoramic camera. A swiveling camera that photographs an area of 150°, and is used for large views or photographs of large groups of people. Many modern still cameras have a "panoramic feature" that enables one to take wide-angle or long horizontal photos. Incidentally, a few photographers still use the old swiveling cameras for such pictures as a school's senior all-class photo.

Photo floods. Light bulbs specially balanced for film, usually used with reflectors on standards.

Photogram. László Moholy-Nagy and Man Ray were masters of this technique, in which objects are placed directly on photo paper that is then exposed to light and developed. The resulting abstract compositions do not require a negative.

Photocollage. A collection of photographs cut and mounted on a support background.

Photomontage. A process in which elements from different photos are combined in the darkroom on one sheet of photographic paper.

Pinhole camera. A pinhole camera can be made in any light, tight box. A pinhole is pricked in a piece of foil that is taped over an opening cut in the side of the box; then a black paper cover is taped so it can be lifted. Sensitized paper is placed opposite the hole in a darkroom. When the pinhole camera is set down and the black paper lifted, the paper is exposed when light enters through the pinhole.

Platinum print. Photo printed on paper that has been sensitized with iron salts and a platinum compound.

Polarizing lens. An adjustable lens that eliminates glare and increases contrast.

Polaroid® Land camera. This camera takes a picture and develops it in less than one minute.

Posterization. A technique used with high contrast film to separate tones.

Reflex camera. Single lens reflex (SLR) or twin lens reflex (TLR). The image is reflected on a ground glass screen through a system of mirrors.

Resin-coated (RC) paper. Printing paper treated with a synthetic resin; prints and dries faster.

Retouching. Applying a dilute color or black to cover flaws.

Salt print. A print made on paper that has been sensitized with ordinary salt, then brushed with silver nitrate, and exposed.

Sensitizing. In the early days of photography, metal, glass, tin, and paper were sensitized (coated) with chemicals just prior to exposing. If you see on a label that something is a "platinum" or "silver" print, it refers to the chemicals used in coating the plate.

Shutter speed. The amount of time a shutter is open. This generally ranges from B (which means the shutter is kept open indefinitely) to $\frac{1}{2000}$ of a second.

Stereograph. A photo taken with a camera with two side-by-side lenses that has a three-dimensional effect when viewed in a stereoscope.

Tintype (ferrotype). A positive photograph made on a sensitized sheet of tin or iron.

Tripod. A three-legged adjustable stand that screws into the bottom of a camera to hold it steady.

View camera (field camera). Term usually applied to a large box camera mounted on a tripod.

Vintage print. A print that was made at approximately the same time as the negative.

Wet collodion. An early process in which the glass plate was sensitized just before exposure (also called wet plate).

Zone system. An exposure system proposed by Ansel Adams and Minor White that assigns numbers to value differences within various areas of a photograph. Zone 0 is a maximum black, Zone X is pure white, Zone I is gray-black, Zone IX is almost white, and so on. Adams later amended this to include 11 zones.

VIDEO DEFINITIONS

Whether you use a video camera to produce artistic short films, or just to photograph important occasions with family and friends, figuring out how to take high quality footage can be frustrating if the instruction manual is full of terms that mean nothing to you. Following are some definitions that you might find useful as you read the operating instructions. Becoming well acquainted with how it works is the first step in producing a video album everyone will enjoy viewing. Some of these terms may also come in handy the next time you read or hear a movie review.

Aperture. The opening on the lens that controls the amount of light passing through.

Available light. Daylight or ordinary indoor light that is not enhanced by additional lighting.

Backlit. A subject is backlit if it is silhouetted against a bright light source such as sunlight, which creates a halo effect. The detail on the backlit subject is likely to be quite dark.

Bust shot. A close-up shot of a person from the chest upward.

Close-up. Any detail or subject that fills the frame.

Depth of field. The amount of the image that is in focus is dependent upon the aperture opening; the smaller the opening, the sharper the image.

Dissolve. A fade-out/fade-in transition from one shot to another, which is more pleasing than an abrupt transition.

Medium shot. If photographing a person, this would be from the waist up.

Panning. To stand in place and move the camera horizontally either to give a panoramic shot or to follow a moving subject.

Soundtrack. The background sound while the video is being shot.

Storyboard. A shot-by-shot plan for shooting videos; opening shots, lighting details, shooting angles.

Tilt. The up and down movement of the camera.

Transition. Making a change of time, location, or subject.

Voice-over. A commentary to accompany the video images, usually added after the shot is made.

White balance. Most cameras adjust internally for differing light conditions, and are in white balance, which means that if a white card is held in front of the lens and the camera adjusts to "see" it as white, then all colors are also automatically correct.

Wide shot. A distance shot. If of a person, this would include the entire figure. Uses a wide-angle lens.

Zoom. Optically bring the subject closer or farther by moving the lens in or out.

"Photography as a fad is well-nigh on its last legs, thanks principally to the bicycle craze."

—ALFRED STIEGLITZ, 1864–1946, American founder of Photo Secession

MUSEUMS WITH OUTSTANDING PHOTOGRAPHY COLLECTIONS

Because photos are made from negatives that allow numerous prints to be created, most museums listed here have vast collections representing a wide spectrum of photographers, and identical prints might be owned by a number of museums. There is never room to display them all at one time and exhibitions of photographs in the collection are frequently rotated. If the negatives are still available, some pictures that were made 75 years ago are still being printed.

AUSTRALIA

Australian Centre for Photography, Sydney
Australian National Gallery, Canberra

AUSTRIA

Osterreichische Fotogalerie im Rupertinum, Salzburg

BELGIUM

Musée de la Photographie à Charleroi, Charleroi
Museum voor Fotografie, Antwerp

BRAZIL

Museu de Arte Contemporanea da Universidade de Sao Paulo

CANADA

National Gallery of Canada, Ottawa
Vancouver Art Gallery, Vancouver

CZECH REPUBLIC

Museum of Decorative Arts, Prague

DENMARK

Museet for Fotokunst. Brandts Klaedefabrik, Odense

ENGLAND

National Museum of Photography, Film and Television, Bradford
National Portrait Gallery, London
Royal Photographic Society, Bath
The British Museum, London
Victoria and Albert Museum, London

FINLAND

The Photographic Museum of Finland, Helsinki

FRANCE

Bibliothèque Nationale, Paris
Centre National de la Photographie, Paris
George Eastman House, International Museum of Photography and Film,
 Paris
Maison Européene de la Photographie, Paris
Musée d'Orsay, Paris
Musée de la Photographie, Mougins
Musée Nicéphore Niépce, Chalon-sur-Saone
Societé Française de Photographie, Paris

GERMANY

Agfa Foto-Historama im Wallraf-Richartz Museum, Cologne
Berlinische Galerie, Museum fur moderne Kunst, Photographie und
 Architektur, Berlin
Museum fur Photographie, Dresden

HUNGARY

Hungarian Museum of Photography, Kecskemét

IRELAND

Gallery of Photography, Dublin

ITALY

Museo Ken Damy, Fotografia Contemporanea, Brescia
Museum of the History of Photography Fratelli Alinari, Florence

JAPAN

Tokyo Metropolitan Museum of Photography, Tokyo

LATVIA

Latvian Museum of Photography, Riga

MEXICO

Centro de la Imagen, Mexico City
Museo de Arte Moderno, Mexico City

NETHERLANDS

Groningen Museum, Groningen
Nederlands Fotoarchief, Rotterdam

SPAIN

Instituto Valenciano de Arte Moderno, Valencia

SWEDEN

Fotografiska Museet I Moderna Museet, Stockholm

SWITZERLAND

Schweizerische Stiftung für die Photographie, Kunsthaus, Zurich

UNITED STATES

Arizona

Center for Creative Photography, Tucson

California

Ansel Adams Center/Friends of Photography, San Francisco
California Museum of Photography, Riverside
J. Paul Getty Museum, Los Angeles
Museum of Contemporary Art, Los Angeles
Museum of Photographic Arts, San Diego
Oakland Museum
San Francisco Museum of Modern Art

Colorado

Denver Art Museum

District of Columbia

> Library of Congress
> National Museum of Natural History
> Smithsonian Institution

Illinois

> Art Institute of Chicago
> Museum of Holography/Chicago
> The Museum of Contemporary Photography, Chicago

Kentucky

> Photographic Archives, Lexington
> Photographic Archives, Louisville

Maryland

> Baltimore Museum of Art

Minnesota

> Walker Art Center, Minneapolis

New Jersey

> Princeton University Museums and Libraries, Princeton

New York

> Brooklyn Museum
> International Center of Photography, New York City
> International Museum of Photography at George Eastman House,
>   Rochester
> Metropolitan Museum of Art, New York City
> Museum of Modern Art, New York City
> The Aperture Foundation/Burden Gallery, New York City
> Whitney Museum of American Art, New York City

Texas

> Museum of Fine Arts, Houston

WHAT MAKES A PHOTO A MASTERPIECE?

What makes one photograph just a mediocre snapshot and another the masterful work of an artist with a keen eye? Of the millions of photographs that have been published, why would some become *icons* of photography? The reasons are many and can include the following.

◈ The subject in the photograph is unique and makes you come back again and again as you notice something new. This might be called "the *aha*! factor."

◈ Put simply, the photograph is beautiful. Everything in it works together perfectly.

◈ It contains a strong focal point.

◈ Extraneous detail is eliminated. Every single element in the picture is important to the whole.

◈ It projects a mood: serenity, tragedy, menace, joy.

◈ It has flawless printing: no stains, scratches, or white spots that indicate a dirty negative.

◈ It has a "magic moment." French photographer Henri Cartier-Bresson felt that if he waited until the perfect time to snap the picture, he would capture his "decisive moment."

FORMAL ANALYSIS OF A PHOTO

Although a great photographer, like a great painter, may have a "gift" for this art form, it takes more than a gift to produce a masterpiece. A true photographic artist also has knowledge of the elements and principles that must be at work and in balance to produce a photograph that speaks to those who view it.

ART ELEMENTS USED IN PHOTOGRAPHY

Formal analysis of a photograph according to the elements and principles used to analyze art may help you realize what it is about a photo that makes it a masterpiece. Analyze one photo. Try to figure out the meaning, why the artist took the photo the way it was taken, what the dominant element is, whether it makes you *feel* anything. Or compare two photos and note the similarities and differences. (Look at edges, use of space, subject, and mood.) Specific elements you should pay particular attention to when examining a photograph include the following:

- ◇ *Lines.* What kinds of lines are there in the photo? Thick, thin, curved, interrupted, or parallel lines? The eye may be led toward the center of interest through converging lines.

- ◇ What about *line direction?* Diagonal lines give a photo an energetic feel. Horizontal lines sometimes create a restful feeling.

- ◇ *Space.* Is there a center of interest? Does space isolate one dominant subject? Does the subject fill the space? Do you feel there is too much space?

- ◇ *Shape.* Is there more than one major shape? Is the negative shape (the area around the main subject) interesting?

- ◇ *Texture.* Texture is "implied" in a photograph by its appearance. If we see weathered wood, for example, we will know how it would feel to the touch. A baby's skin shows its softness by the texture seen in a photo. How has the photographer used texture? Can you see it? Would you consider it the dominant element? Would the photo be better if there were more textures?

- ◇ *Color.* If the photograph is in color, look at the subject and decide if the color adds to the idea or detracts from it. Most contemporary photographers use color film to great effect through the use of color filters, taking advantage of atmospheric light, and being aware of the drama of color.

- ◇ *Value.* Difference in values is one of the major tools of the photographer. A black and white photograph should have a pure black, a pure white, and several tones (eight) in between.

ART PRINCIPLES USED IN PHOTOGRAPHY

Art principles are the practical application of the art elements. Perhaps more in photography than in some of the other art forms, the principles of repetition, contrast, balance, variety, rhythm, emphasis, and unity define the photograph.

- ◇ *Repetition.* The apparently inadvertent repetition of an element such as shape or color is what makes many classical photographs so dynamic. For example, a photo may feature repetition of circles (shape) or certain colors.

◇ *Contrast.* There are many kinds of contrasts: figure/ground, old/young, rough/smooth, shiny/dull, dark/light, and so on. The conscious use of contrast may be the dominant factor in a photo.

◇ *Emphasis.* Has the artist decided on a focal point or center of interest? Discover what it is by closing your eyes, then opening them and making note of the first thing you see. It may be the lightest or darkest area, or the most complex.

◇ *Variety.* Are there varieties of lines, shapes, or values? Are there varieties of texture?

◇ *Rhythm.* Some photos show rhythm through a use of undulating lines and repetition of forms that lead the eye through the photograph.

◇ *Balance.* Does the photo show symmetrical or asymmetrical balance? Does it look lopsided, or is a dominant subject balanced by one or more smaller shapes?

◇ *Unity.* Do all the parts of the composition work together to make a pleasing overall design?

COLLECTING PHOTOGRAPHS

Like most people, you undoubtedly have a collection of photographs, with most of them in photo albums, some framed, and perhaps others stored away in a box. But what about collecting artistic photographs? How would you know which ones to choose, how to display them thematically and so they complement one another? The first criterion in choosing photographic art, of course, is to find what you like.

This quotation from photo collector and dealer Lee Witkin may be helpful to you as you begin your collection.

"I have always used two criteria in my collecting: first, the image must produce a strong emotional feeling in me; and second, there must be a high quality to the photographic print itself."

In addition, the following tips should also prove helpful.

◇ If you are just beginning, you need to educate yourself by reading and visiting museums and galleries. Don't hesitate to ask questions of dealers and other collectors.

◇ If you are an Internet user, give yourself a treat by simply typing in the name of a photographer from the lists in this section and find the innumerable sites devoted to contemporary and historical photography.

◇ Make your purchases at galleries, special photo/print/works-on-paper fairs, flea markets, secondhand stores, and Internet photography sites (galleries, photographers' home pages).

◇ Some collectors focus on one aspect of photography such as a particular time period, style, the human figure. You may find it helpful to narrow your focus at first.

◇ Look for a print that is in pristine condition without nicks, smudges, scratches, bends, or uneven edges or irregularities in printing.

◇ Consider the sharpness or lack of focus of a print. Romantic photos, such as those by the early English photographer Julia Margaret Cameron, had a "soft focus" while the F.64 group (so-called because of their insistence on using the smallest possible lens opening) specialized in the greatest possible clarity. The size of the camera affects the sharpness of the print. View cameras (the negative is 4 × 5 to 8 × 10 inches) give a much sharper print than a 35mm camera. After looking for a time, you may decide that the sharpness of the print is not as important to you as some other quality.

◇ Find out the age of a print. If it's a *modern* print (from the original negative, but printed much later), it will not have the same value as a *vintage* print (printed at approximately the same time as the negative).

◇ If possible, find out how many prints were made from one negative. Usually the value goes down as the number of prints goes up. There are exceptions, of course, such as Edward Weston's *Peppers* and Ansel Adams's *Moonrise Over Hernandez,* which are not apparently affected by the number of reprints, simply because they are "icons" of photography.

◇ Consider buying a less-well-known print from a well-known photographer.

◇ Look for an original signature or stamp, which may be found on the back or on the mount of a print.

◇ A small border is normally found on a print that allows it to be matted. Some photos were "bleed mounted" (the mountboard and the photo were trimmed at the same time to remove a border). If the photo is in good condition, this should not be a factor.

TYPES OF PHOTOGRAPHY

Although the idea of taking two or three rolls of pictures during a week-long vacation is commonplace now, at one time photography was reserved for important purposes, and certainly not available to the masses. Over the approximately 175 years of photographic history, photographers have found various applications for their work. Many of the most enduring and memorable photos were created for a practical purpose such as these listed here.

- *Photojournalism:* Records of wars, famines, floods, and the happy and sad photographs that illustrate newspapers, magazines, and books
- *Studio photography:* Weddings, graduation portraits, and family pictures
- *Commercial photography:* Fashion illustration, architecture, medical illustration, food, sports, editorial illustration
- *Travel and regional photography:* Landscape; people and customs in their own countries and abroad
- *Pictorialism:* A unique vision of the world created by artists with a camera
- *Artistic photography:* For use in an "environmental sculpture," silk-screen printing, interpretation in a painting

FRAMING AND CARING FOR PHOTOGRAPHS

Whether it's your favorite photograph of a recent trip abroad, a sepia-toned print of your great grandmother, or a black and white print by Ansel Adams you just purchased at a gallery, proper care of your photographs can help you preserve them for generations. In addition, choosing the right frame and mat can truly accentuate the beauty of a photo.

FRAMING PHOTOGRAPHS

- Use UV Plexiglas in place of glass to protect from sunlight and avoid scratching the photo if it should fall.
- Use only archival (rag-based and acid-free) mats.
- For black and white photographs, use only black, white, or gray mats.
- For old (toned) photos, use an antique white mat similar to the lightest color of the photo.

◇ For a color photo, a mat of a neutral color is ideal, but a colored liner (small border) that complements the photo may be used inside the neutral mat.

CARING FOR PHOTOGRAPHS

◇ Keep photos away from direct sunlight. If you display photos in an area that gets too much direct sunlight, change the photos frequently to avoid damaging them. Advice from a museum professional is that works on paper be displayed no more than 50 percent of the time.

◇ Ideally, photos not on display should be stored in an enameled metal box or an archival cardboard box. Prints may be kept in transparent uncoated polyethylene print files. Several companies exist that provide archival albums, mats, frames, storage, and preservation materials. Ask at your local framer or dealer for more information.

◇ Handle photos by the edges to avoid breaking the corner (older photos become brittle) or getting oils from hands on the photo that might ultimately cause damage.

TIMELINE: EVENTS IN PHOTOGRAPHY

384–322 B.C.	Aristotle first used a *camera obscura.*
1560–1600s	Renaissance artists used the camera obscura as an aid in drawing. Long before the advent of the modern camera, this device was used by such artists as Vermeer, Leonardo da Vinci, and Canaletto as an aid to composition.
1725	Johann Heinrich Schulze discovered that some silver compounds were light-sensitive.
1802	Contact images on paper. Anything that blocks light, placed on a photo-sensitized surface (metal, stone, cloth, paper) will cause a photographic image. Thomas Wedgwood and Sir Humphry Davy first used this process. A photographic negative, which has a range of values from black to clear, held "in contact" with a sensitized surface and exposed to light, produces a photographic print.

1816	First negative printed on stone by Joseph Nicéphore Niépce.
1819	Hypo-fixer, a chemical that made photo images permanent, was discovered by Sir John Frederick Herschel.
1826	First photograph taken and developed on polished pewter by Joseph Nicéphore Niépce.
1833	Paper negative developed by William Henry Fox Talbot.
1837	Sensitized paper exposed in the camera by Hippolyte Bayard.
1839	Daguerreotype invented by Louis Daguerre. Daguerre's one-of-a-kind images, made on a polished silvered metal plate, have a positive/negative appearance, depending on the angle of view. To protect the delicate surface, these are normally displayed in a case.
1839	First experiments in color photography.
1840	Lens suitable for portraiture invented by Josepf Max Petzval.
1840	First portrait studio opened in New York by Alexander Wolcott.
1841	Exposure on paper from a negative—known as Calotype or Talbotype—developed by William Henry Fox Talbot.
1842	Cyanotype (blueprint) perfected by Sir John Frederick Herschel.
1845	Daguerreotype camera invented.
1851	Collodion wet-plate process; glass was sensitized immediately before exposure: Frederick Scott Archer.
1853	Tintype process originated by Adolphe-Alexandre Martin.
1853	Sliding-box folding camera for 8 x 10-inch plates developed.
1853	Binocular camera built by John Benjamin Dancer.
1857	Enlarger (magic lantern or sun-enlarger); made it possible to project a small negative image onto paper and make a larger positive print. A mirror reflected sun rays for enlarging.
1859	Wide-angle lens is used in photography.
1860	View/field camera invented. This much larger camera allowed the print to be of the same size as the camera. It opened the possibilities of taking the camera out of the studio and onto a battlefield (after a battle) and for landscape photography.

1860–1865	Mathew Brady used photography to document the Civil War.
1861	Stereoscope invented for use with stereographs.
1861	Variable aperture used by William England to make differences in the sharpness of the print. A small aperture opening gives a sharper picture than a large lens opening. In portraits, for example, a large lens opening gives a softer appearance, while a small lens opening might be preferred for landscape.
1867	Timothy O'Sullivan and William H. Jackson photographed the American West.
1871	Dry plate negatives perfected by Richard Leach Maddox.
1872	First celluloid film (thermoplastic) developed by The Reverend Hannibal Goodwin allows a flexible backing for sensitized plates.
1875	Panoramic camera. The panoramic camera was most used at this time for taking photos of large groups of people. It would "scan" the group from one end to the other. The panoramic camera as used today gives a wider than normal view of the subject.
1878	Motion sequence photographs of horses taken by Eadweard Muybridge. He was considered the "father of the motion picture."
1879	Photogravure process (photo image with the quality of a lithograph) invented, enabling the use of halftone images in newspapers.
1880–1908	Photography used to document social issues. Lewis Hine (social-realist photographer) documents child labor in factories.
1881	Halftone system of preparing photographs for printing perfected by Frederic Ives.
1882	Orthochromatic plates (enabling high contrast) are manufactured.
1883	Negatives are exposed on celluloid rather than glass.
1885	Eadweard Muybridge's motion sequence photographs of humans.
1885	Coated printing paper developed by George Eastman.
1887	Shutter with diaphragm and blades designed by Edward Bausch.
1887	Celluloid roll film developed by Hannibal Goodwin enabled

loading the camera with multiple exposures rather than the cumbersome single plates that had to be individually loaded.

1888	Kodak box camera (contained 100 exposures) invented by George Eastman.
1890	Folding box field camera developed. This enabled photographers to take pictures away from the studio more easily.
1890	The kinetoscope invented by Thomas Edison and William Dickson, a forerunner of the motion picture.
1890	Spy cameras (concealed in a tie, cane, top hat, beauty case, book) become popular.
1891	Daylight-loading roll film introduced by Kodak.
1891	First telephoto lens invented by Thomas Rudolf Dallmeyer.
1895	Kodak Bulls Eye No. 2, a box camera with a red window in the back. It was used for roll film or a single plate.
1896	X-ray photography discovered by Wilhelm Konrad Roentgen.
1898	Jumelle Stereo Camera introduced high-speed photography.
1900	Mammoth Camera introduced. So called because it was 1,400 pounds, 20 ft long when extended, and needed 15 men to operate.
1900	Halftone reproductions of photographs now commonplace in magazines, books, and newspapers.
1900–1935	Kodak Brownie Series Cameras make photography available to the masses.
1902	Photo Secession movement. Alfred Stieglitz, the founder, proposed that photography be recognized as an independent art form.
1903	Folding bellows camera introduced. Its collapsible accordion-folded leather bellows extended when the camera was opened, giving extraordinary sharpness to photographs.
1905	Color separation camera (Lancaster of London).
1905	Picture postcards become popular.
1912	Speed Graphic camera introduced. This camera was the precursor of the era of modern photography. It was smaller than a field camera and produced high quality photographs. It was also known as a "Press Camera" after World War II.

1912	Motorized movie camera instead of hand-cranked introduced.
1920s	Advertising photography widely used.
1920s–present	The photojournalistic style in photography that began in the 1920s, telling a story in photographs, and the photo-essay, are art forms that continue in popularity.
1922	First 3-D movie shown in theaters.
1925	Leica I, Model A. The 35mm camera introduced, designed by Oskar Barnack and Ernst Leitz.
1925	Flashbulbs invented.
1927	Zeiss Ikon 35mm camera. This German-made camera was considered one of the classics for photographers and collectors.
1928	Twin-lens reflex (TLR) Rolieflex camera manufactured.
1932–c.1936	Group F.64 photographers exhibited their work together.
1933–1940	Farm Security Administration photographs (FSA) taken by Dorothea Lange, Ben Shahn, Walker Evans, among others, who were hired by the U.S. Government to photograph Depression conditions.
1935	Portable electronic flash introduced.
1935	Kodachrome color transparency film for color slides was perfected. The color dyes are added in the processing, with the colors therefore being permanent, while other transparency films may fade over time.
1937	First 35mm single-lens-reflex (SLR) camera, the Exacta, introduced.
1938	Xerography invented by Chester Carlson.
1938	Strobe light (stroboscope) invented by Harold Edgerton. Edgerton's study of whirling motors by using intermittent flash was the beginning of high-speed photography, allowing, for example, photographs of a bullet that was shot through an apple and the splash of a drop of milk. Edgerton revolutionized sports, underwater, and wildlife photography.
1941	Kodacolor (print) film for color negatives and positive prints.
1941–1945	World War II documented in photographs by Robert Capa, W. Eugene Smith, Carl Mydans, Margaret Bourke-White, Gordon Parks.
1942	Ektachrome positive reversal color film (for slides) introduced.

1947	Ektacolor (print) film for color negatives introduced.
1947	Hologram invented by Dennis Gabor.
1948	Polaroid Land Camera invented by Dr. Edwin Land.
1950s	Photo silk screens done by Andy Warhol and Robert Rauschenberg, among others.
1950s	Advent of television in the home.
1960s	Photo realism in painting. Artists used their photographs as the basis for painting in extreme detail what the camera sees. Well-known artists of this genre are Chuck Close, Audrey Flack, Richard Estes.
1963	Kodak Instamatic introduced.
1963	Polaroid instant color camera available.
1966	First photograph of Earth from the moon.
1978	Auto focus camera introduced by Konica.
1980s	Video camcorders introduced.
1980s	Photo Collage. Multiple photos of the same subject were combined by artist David Hockney to make a large pictorial composition.
1982	Film on disc cassette (video cassette) introduced by Kodak.
1985	Digital cameras available to the public.
1987	Single-use (disposable) camera introduced by Kodak.
1990s	Computer enhancement of regular photographs introduced.
1995	Full-length feature film available on a CD-ROM disk.
1996	Kodak Advantix system introduced.
1996–present	Digital camera. Filmless technology records images electronically, allows images to be stored on CD-ROM, and transfers directly from the camera to a personal computer or printer.

"I can't recreate my feelings about how I happened to do this or that, because a lot of my stuff was done without any motivation more than just what I call having a good time and fooling around."

—IMOGEN CUNNINGHAM, 1883–1976, Group F.64 photographer

ARTISTS AND PHOTOGRAPHY

Although we think of photography as a relatively new art form, it has been around long enough to profoundly influence great numbers of painters. At the end of the 19th century, artists often made use of photographic images. Many modern painters (such as Robert Rauschenberg) use actual photographic images on canvas, while contemporary artists incorporate still and video images in a variety of ways. Painters (Andy Warhol, for example) occasionally "appropriated" into their compositions photographs taken by other photographers. Featured in this list are established artists who, while not photographers *per se,* have made photography an integral part of their work.

BELGIUM

Ensor, James, 1860–1949
Magritte, René, 1898–1967

ENGLAND

Bacon, Francis, 1909–1992
Barlett, William, 1809–1854
Goldsworthy, Andy, 1956
Hamilton, Richard, 1922
Hockney, David, 1937
Kitaj, R. B., 1932
Millet, Sir John E., 1829–1896

FRANCE

Cézanne, Paul, 1839–1906
Corot, Jean Baptiste Camille, 1796–1875
Courbet, Gustave, 1819–1877
Daumier, Honoré, 1808–1879
Dégas, Edgar, 1834–1917
Delacroix, Eugène, 1798–1863
Delaunay, Robert, 1885–1941
Derain, André, 1880–1954

FRANCE *(continued)*

Duchamp-Villon, Raymond, 1876–1918
Fantin-Latour, Henri, 1836–1904
Gauguin, Paul, 1848–1903
Hausmann, Raoul, 1886–1971
Manet, Edouard, 1832–1883
Matisse, Henri, 1869–1954
Mucha, Alphonse Marie, 1860–1939
Picasso, Pablo, 1881–1973
Rouault, Georges, 1871–1958
Toulouse-Lautrec, Henri de, 1864–1901
Vallotton, Felix, 1865–1925
Villon, Jacques, 1875–1963

GERMANY

Anschutz, Ottomar, 1846–1907
Becher, Bernhard, 1931
Becker, Hilla, 1934
Ernst, Max, 1891–1976
Grosz, George, 1893–1959
Hoch, Hannah, 1889–1978

ITALY

Balla, Giacomo, 1874–1958

MEXICO

Rivera, Diego, 1886–1957

NETHERLANDS

Citroen, Paul, 1896–1983
Dibbets, Jan, 1941
Vermeer, Jan, 1632–1675 (used
the camera obscura as an aid
for painting)

NORWAY

Munch, Edvard, 1863–1944

RUSSIA

Rodchenko, Alexander,
1891–1956

SCOTLAND

Adamson, Robert, 1821–1848
Hill, David Octavius, 1802–1870

SPAIN

Dali, Salvador, 1904–1988
Picasso, Pablo, 1881–1973

UNITED STATES

Artschwager, Richard, 1924
Baldessari, John, 1931
Bayer, Herbert, 1900–1986
Bearden, Romare, 1914–1988

UNITED STATES (continued)

Christo (Javacheff), 1935
Church, Frederic, 1826–1900
Close, Chuck, 1940
Cornell, Joseph, 1903–1972
de Kooning, Elaine, 1920–1989
Dine, Jim, 1935
Eakins, Thomas, 1844–1916
Estes, Richard, 1932
Flack, Audrey, 1931
Gorky, Arshile, 1904–1948
Groover, Jan, 1943
Hartley, Marsden, 1877–1943
Homer, Winslow, 1836–1910
Kasten, Barbara, 1936
Kepes, Gyorgy, 1906–2002, born
Hungary
Kruger, Barbara, 1945
Lichtenstein, Roy, 1923–1997
Man Ray, 1890–1976
Marsh, Reginald, 1898–1954
Moholy-Nagy, László, 1895–1946
Peto, John F., 1854–1907
Rauschenberg, Robert, 1925
Rivers, Larry, 1923–2002
Ruscha, Edward, 1937
Samaras, Lucas, 1936
Sargent, John Singer, 1856–1925
Shahn, Ben, 1898–1969
Sheeler, Charles, 1883–1965
Sully, Thomas, 1783–1872
Tchelitchew, Pavel, 1898–1957
Warhol, Andy, 1930–1987
Wesselman, Tom, 1931

"In photography, visual organization can stem only from a developed instinct."

—HENRI CARTIER-BRESSON, 1908, French photographer, on the "decisive moment" at which to take a photograph

SPECIFIC PHOTOGRAPHIC GROUPS

These photographers became associated with others of the same era who either used a similar method or worked for the same employer.

PHOTO SECESSION, 1905–1917

Alfred Stieglitz was the founder of the Little Galleries of the Photo Secession, called Gallery 291. The Photo Secession movement was a rebellion against the pictorial photography that had dominated the field prior to the 20th century. The artists and photographers who exhibited in the Gallery led the way into Modernism in the United States. In addition to the photographers listed here, Stieglitz introduced the work of Modernist painters Georgia O'Keeffe, John Marin, Marsden Hartley, Arthur Dove, and others.

Brigman, Anne, 1869–1950
Day, F. Holland, 1864–1933
Frank, Eugene, 1845–1914
Kasebier, Gertrude, 1852–1934
Keiley, Joseph, 1869–1914
Mather, Margrethe, 1885–1952

Steichen, Edward 1879–1973
Stieglitz, Alfred, 1864–1946
Struss, Carl, 1886–1981
Ulmann, Doris, 1884–1934
Weston, Edward, 1886–1958
White, Clarence, 1871–1925

FARM SECURITY ADMINISTRATION PHOTOGRAPHERS, 1935–c. 1941

During the Depression, the Farm Security Administration (FSA), administered by Roy Stryker, sought to document, through photography, the lives of the American poor—migrant workers, the homeless (some displaced by dust storms in the Midwest), and the unemployed. It was hoped that bringing the seriousness of their situation to the attention of the rest of the nation could result in an improvement in their lives. The Library of Congress Archives has 250,000 negatives made during this time. The FSA employed the following photographers for the task.

Bubley, Esther, 1921–1998
Carter, Paul, 1903–1938
Charlotte Brooks, 1918
Collier, John, Jr., 1913–1992
Collins, Marjorie, 1912–1985
Delano, Jack, 1914–1997
Dick, Sheldon 1906–1950
Evans, Walker, 1903–1975
Jung, Theodor, 1906
Lange, Dorothea, 1895–1965
Lee, Russell, 1903–1986

Locke, Edwin
Mydans, Carl, 1907
Parks, Gordon, Sr., 1912
Rosskam, Edwin, 1903
Rothstein, Arthur, 1915–1985
Shahn, Ben, 1898–1969
Siegel, Arthur, 1913–1978
Stryker, Roy, 1893–1975
Vachon, John, 1914–1975
Wolcott, Marion Post,
1910–1990

GROUP F.64 PHOTOGRAPHERS, 1932–c. 1936

This group of photographers felt that everything in their work should be of the highest possible clarity, which was achieved by use of the smallest lens opening, at the time, F.64 on the view camera. Most of them went on to become well-known photographers. The most famous of the group was Ansel Adams, who specialized in black and white photographs of the California landscape.

Adams, Ansel, 1902–1984
Cunningham, Imogen,
1883–1976
Edwards, John Paul, 1883–1958
Noskowiak, Sonya, 1900–1975
Swift, Henry, 1891–1960
Van Dyke, Willard, 1906–1986
Weston, Edward, 1886–1958

Photographers Who Later Exhibited with F.64

Holder, Preston, 1907
Kanaga, Consuela, 1894–1978
Lavenson (Wahrhaftig), Alma,
1897–1989
Weston, Brett, 1911–1993

"The name (F.64) has come to describe a certain kind of photography characterized by great depth of field, sharp focus, and images that were usually uninfluenced by painting."
—WILLARD VAN DYKE, 1906–1986, member of Group F.64

25 FAMOUS CONTEMPORARY PHOTOGRAPHERS

These artists are among the hundreds who are recognized (at least in their own countries) as outstanding contemporary photographers. Their work is in galleries, books, fashion and news magazines, museums, and private collections.

1. **Close, Chuck, United States**

   Close is an artist/photographer whose sole subject is oversized faces of himself or people he knows. His photo-realist paintings are always based on photos he has taken, although he uses many different media besides paint to interpret the photos, including fingerprints and handmade paper.

   Big Self-Portrait, 1968, Walker Art Center, Minneapolis, Minnesota
   Fanny, Fingerpainting, 1985, National Gallery of Art, Washington, DC
   Phil, 1969, The Whitney Museum of American Art, New York City

2. **Dijkstra, Rineke, Netherlands**

   Dijkstra's series of pictures of isolated figures on a beach are portraits of people at their most vulnerable. His subjects are rarely posed.

   Beach Portrait Series, 1992, Museum of Modern Art, New York City
   Hilton Head Island, 1993, Galerie Paul Andriesse, Amsterdam

3. **Eggleston, William, United States**

   Eggleston chose to print in color his ordinary photos of people, places, and objects in the South. Although most viewers consider his photos "fine snapshots," a closer look reveals a true artistic eye.

   Yellow Flowers, Hillside, 1974, The Oakland Museum, Oakland, California
   Tallahatchie County, Mississippi, 1972, Museum of Modern Art, New York City
   Plains, Georgia, 1976, Museum of Modern Art, New York City

4. **Gilbert and George (Gilbert Proesch, George Passmore), England**

   These creative artists work together on their wall-sized (mostly) black and white photographic compositions, which usually feature themselves, dressed in suits. Their work is a commentary on English life as they see it.

   The Decorators, 1978, Morton G. Neumann Family Collection
   Thumbing, 1991, Collection of the artist

5. **Goldin, Nan, United States**

Nan Goldin does some fashion photography, but using nontypical models such as family and friends. Her unconventional life has led her to subjects such as human sexuality, drug use, and the "human condition" as she sees it. She has taught at Harvard and has curated many exhibitions.

Misty and Jimmy Paulette in a Taxi, NYC, 1991, multiple edition

6. **Groover, Jan, United States**

Groover takes available-light photographs of whatever is happening in a place that appeals to her, such as highways and urban landscapes. Flowers (taken in close-ups) are another of her subjects.

Tybee Forks and Starts K, 1978, Collection of the artist
Untitled (still life), 1988, Robert Miller Gallery, New York City
Untitled (trucks on a highway), 1975, Museum of Modern Art,
  New York City

7. **Hockney, David, England**

Hockney, who lives in California, uses photography as a tool, sometimes making montages of photographs, other times documenting life on the West Coast, with its swimming pools, highways, and affluence.

Herrenhausen-Hanover, 1976, Collection of Paul F. Walter, New York
Pearblossom Hwy., 11–18 April 1986, #2, 1986, Collection of the artist
My Mother, Bolton Abbey, Yorkshire, 1982, Collection of the artist

8. **Iturbide, Graciela, Mexico**

Iturbide worked with Manual Alvarez Bravo, and shows the same interest in photographing Mexican culture with all its diversity. Her photos of festivities, political events, and the everyday life of Mexican women are seen in her 1989 book *Juchitan de las Mujeres.*

Our Lady of the Iguanas, 1979, Parrish Art Museum, Southampton,
  New York
Mujer angel, Desierto de Sonora, 1979, Center for Creative
  Photography, University of Arizona

9. **Kruger, Barbara, United States**

Kruger was a design editor at *Mademoiselle* before she began her satirical black and white photographs combined with red lettering. Her collage-style commentaries are on the subject of love and the role of women in society.

Untitled (You Get Away with Murder), 1987, Hallmark Photographic
  Collection, Kansas City, Missouri
Untitled (Use Only as Directed), 1988, St. Louis Art Museum
Untitled (We Are Not What We Seem), 1988, Private collection

10. Leibovitz, Annie, United States

Leibovitz began as a *Rolling Stone* magazine photographer, specializing in
celebrity portraits.
  John Lennon and Yoko Ono, December 8, 1980, 1981, *Rolling Stone*
    cover
  Mick Jagger, 1977, *Rolling Stone* 10th Anniversary Issue
  The Blues Brothers, 1979, *Rolling Stone* cover, February

11. Mark, Mary Ellen, United States

Mark photographs ordinary people, some over a period of many
years, because she considers them "more deserving to be photographed."
Among others, her 12 books include documentary photographs of Mother
Teresa's Missions of Charity, circuses in India, the mentally ill, and brothels
in Calcutta.
  Street Child, Trabzon, Turkey, 1965, Collection of the artist

12. Meyerowitz, Joel, United States

Meyerowitz specialized in Cape Cod landscapes in color, frequently taken to
capture the magic light of dusk or dawn. He also published a book of photographs of the St. Louis Arch taken from every conceivable angle.
  Provincetown Porch, 1977, Collection of the artist
  Bay Sky Series, Provincetown, 1977, Hallmark Photographic
    Collection, Kansas City, Missouri

13. Michaels, Duane, United States

Michaels's attempts to show the unseen or hidden idea with his photography.
He was greatly influenced by Surrealist René Magritte.
  Giorgio de Chirico at Home Near the Spanish Steps, 1972, Collection
    of the artist
  I Build a Pyramid, 1978, Collection of the artist
  Magritte Front and Back, 1965, Hallmark Photographic Collection,
    Kansas City, Missouri

14. **Morimura, Yasumasa, Japan**

   Morimura's huge photographs of himself dressed as a reincarnation of a famous painting or personage are unique and demonstrate enormous talent and wit.

   > *Doublannage'* (Dancer I), (Nijinsky), 1989, Yoshiko Isshiki, Tokyo
   >
   > *Mother (Judith II)*, 1991, Coleccòn Fundaciòn Familia Peter Norton

15. **Muniz, Vic, Brazil**

   Muniz photographs the lives of ordinary people and objects. However, he is also known for his unconventional "chocolate series" (large Cibachrome prints that have been partially covered with chocolate).

   > *The Sugar Children*, 1996, Galerie Carmargo Vilaça, Sao Paulo
   >
   > *Charlton Heston, Pictures of Chocolate*, 1999, Ikon Ltd. Gallery, Santa Monica, California

16. **Newton, Helmut, Germany**

   Prior to becoming one of the world's leading fashion photographers, Newton specialized in dispassionate photos of nudes and women. Although he no longer photographs the nudes for which he became famous, he continues photographing a variety of themes.

   > *They Are Coming*, 1981, Collection of the artist
   >
   > *Woman Examining Man*, Saint Tropez, 1975

17. **Ruff, Thomas, Germany**

   Ruff has several subjects and is noted for his giant portraits and architectural photography. His abstract night scenes are especially dramatic.

   > *Night 19 III*, 1995, Collection of the artist
   >
   > *Portrait*, 1987, Royal Photographic Society, Bath, England

18. **Salgado, Sebastiao, Brazil**

   Salgado photographs the human condition. His subjects have included gold mining in Brazil, famine in Ethiopia, and the lives of refugees.

   > *Serra Pelada Goldmine, Para, Brazil*, 1986, Collection of the artist
   >
   > *Refugee, Former Yugoslavia*, 1994, Collection of the artist and Network photos

19. **Samaras, Lucas, United States, b. Greece**

Samaras used himself as his subject in his Polaroid prints, sometimes altering the perception with lights, makeup, and costume, but at other times altering the print itself as an abstraction.

> *Figure,* 1978 (Polaroid Print with Ink), Hallmark Photographic
> Collection, Kansas City, Missouri
> *Sittings,* c. 1979, Denver Art Museum, Colorado

20. **Sherman, Cindy, United States**

Sherman's subject is herself, sometimes grotesquely made up, usually unrecognizable. Her large color photographs are in collections around the world.

> *Untitled Film Still #16,* 1978, Hallmark Photographic Collection,
> Kansas City, Missouri
> *Untitled,* 1981, Museum of Modern Art, New York City
> *Untitled Film Still #56,* 1980, The Art Institute of Chicago

21. **Skoglund, Sandy, United States**

Skoglund is a sculptor/photographer who places bizarre objects in an environment, carefully controlling the color, then records them through photography.

> *Fox Games,* 1989, Hallmark Photographic Collection, Kansas City,
> Missouri
> *Radioactive Cats,* 1980, St. Louis Art Museum
> *Walking on Eggshells,* 1996–1997, Collection of the artist

22. **Uelsman, Jerry N., United States**

Uelsman specializes in darkroom manipulation, using several negatives on the same black and white image. He coined the phrase "post-visualization" to describe this process.

> *Untitled* (decaying house with ancient sculpture head), 1964,
> Museum of Modern Art, New York City
> *Untitled* (office interior with a "cloud" ceiling), 1976, Metropolitan
> Museum of Art, New York City
> *Small Woods Where I Met Myself,* 1967, Hallmark Photographic
> Collection, Kansas City, Missouri

23. **Wall, Jeff, Canada**

Wall hires actors and actresses to stage photographs sometimes based on works of art. His large works are sometimes displayed in the format of a lighted box covered with a photo transparency, which gives the work the slick look of an advertisement rather than a work of art.

> *The Destroyed Room,* 1978, National Gallery of Canada, Ottawa
> *A Sudden Gust of Wind (after Hokusai),* 1993, Tate Gallery, London
> *The Stumbling Block,* 1991, Ydessa Hendeles Art Foundation,
> Toronto

24. **Wegman, William, United States**

Wegman's witty photographs of his weimaraner dogs in human activities or attire have been used in advertising, books, greeting cards, and television spots.

> *Ray-O-Vac,* 1973, Museum of Modern Art, New York City
> *Red/Grey-Grey/Red,* 1982, Museum of Modern Art, New York City
> *Cinderella,* 1994, Edition of 120

25. **Witkin, Joel Peter, United States**

Witkin's subject matter is the dark side of life: dead people, body parts (which he photographs at a morgue), or people with deformities. He sometimes arranges his subjects to mimic famous artwork or historical and mythological symbols. The result often resembles a vintage photograph.

> *Leda and the Swan,* 1986, Pace Wildenstein MacGill, New York

75 MASTER PHOTOGRAPHERS

These photographers' works will be found in most major museum collections, books about photography, and exhibitions that cover the history of photography. They were pioneers and innovators whose work continues to be relevant and appealing.

1. **Abbott, Bérénice, 1898–1991, United States**

Abbott, who had studied in Europe with Parisian photographer Eugene Atget, primarily created urban portraits of New York City.

> *El at Columbus and Broadway, New York City,* 1935–1939, Art
> Institute of Chicago

Newsstand, 32nd Street and 3rd Avenue, Manhattan, 1935, Hallmark
Photographic Collection, Kansas City, Missouri

Zito's Bakery, Bleecker Street, New York, c. 1937, Museum of
Modern Art, New York City

2. Adams, Ansel, 1902–1984, United States

Possibly the best known of American photographers, Adams photographed
majestic landscapes, impeccably exposed and printed.

Clearing Winter Storm, Yosemite National Park, California, 1944,
Center for Creative Photography, University of Arizona, Tucson

Moonrise Over Hernandez, 1941, Collection of the Ansel Adams Trust

Winter Sunrise, Sierra Nevada, from Lone Pine, California, 1944,
Center for Creative Photography, University of Arizona, Tucson

3. Adams, Robert, 1937, United States

Adams's special interest was examining the effect of population growth upon
the landscape. Images of suburban housing tracts, a shopping mall, and a
drive-in theater are revealed in his cold, hard light.

Outdoor Theater and Cheyenne Mountain, 1968, Castelli Graphics,
New York City

4. Annan, Thomas, 1829–1887, England

Annan began as a copper engraver, later becoming a successful commercial
photographer. The works for which he is best known are his social-
realist documentary photos of the dark streets and mean living conditions in
Glasgow.

Close No. 31, Salt Mkt., c. 1868, St. Louis Art Museum

The Old Closes and Streets of Glasgow series, 1900, University of
Maryland Collection

5. Arbus, Diane, 1923–1971, United States

Arbus's photographs were often sensitive, intimate portraits of "outsiders" of
society, such as developmentally disabled people en route to a costume party.

Identical Twins, Cathleen and Colleen, 1967, Roselle, New Jersey,
Metropolitan Museum of Art, New York City

Untitled (People in Masks), 1970–1971, Museum of Modern Art,
New York City

Xmas Tree in a Living Room, Levittown, NY, 1963, Center for
Creative Photography, University of Arizona, Tucson

6. **Atget, Eugene, 1856–1927, France**

Atget photographed his surroundings and the people in them. His photographs are simple, beautifully designed recordings of a time in the past.

> *Boulevard de Strasbourg,* c. 1910, International Museum of
> Photography at George Eastman House, Rochester, New York
> *Notre Dame,* 1925, Museum of Modern Art, New York City
> *Ragpicker,* 1899–1900, Museum of Modern Art, New York City

7. **Avedon, Richard, 1923, United States**

Avedon, a fashion photographer and portrait artist, compels the viewer to look at his insightful portraits. He managed to perfectly "capture" the personality of a sitter, as illustrated in his photo of the malevolent glare of carnival artist Juan Patricio Lobato.

> *Dovina with Elephants,* Paris, 1955, Hallmark Photographic
> Collection, Kansas City, Missouri
> *Juan Patricio Lobato, Carney, Rocky Ford, Colorado, 8/25/80,* 1980,
> Collection of the artist
> *Oscar Levant, Pianist, Beverly Hills, California, 4/12/72,* 1972,
> Hallmark Photographic Collection, Kansas City, Missouri

8. **Beaton, Cecil, 1904–1980, England**

A fashion photographer, Beaton also specialized in theatrical design. He applied this early training to advantage with his use of dramatic lighting and props in fashion photographs for *Vogue* and *Harpers' Bazaar.* He was the official photographer for the British Royal Family.

> *Audrey Hepburn,* 1954, Staley Wise Gallery, London
> *Self Portrait as King George V,* Staley Wise Gallery, London

9. **Becher, Bernhard, 1931, and Hilla Becher, 1934, Germany**

These two artists work collaboratively mostly on industrial and architectural images that are grouped together on one background to show similarity of structures.

> *Typology of Water Towers,* 1972, The Eli and Edythe L. Broad
> Collection, Santa Monica, California
> *Anonymous Sculpture (Water Towers),* 1970, Museum of Modern
> Art, New York City

10. **Bourke-White, Margaret, 1904–1971, United States**

Bourke-White began her career photographing industrial and architectural subjects. She later became a regular staff member of both *Fortune* and *Life* magazines. Her simple style of photography and use of light gave a poster-like effect. During World War II, her photos from the front brought her national recognition.

> *The Kremlin, Moscow,* Night Bombing by the Germans, 1941,
> Hallmark Photographic Collection, Kansas City, Missouri
> *At the Time of the Flood,* 1937, Museum of Modern Art, New York
> City

11. **Brady, Mathew, c. 1823–1896, United States**

Brady is best known for his portraits of President Lincoln and documentation of the American Civil War. He did not actually take all the photos that are credited to him, but had several photographers working for him.

> *Abraham Lincoln,* 1864, National Archives, Washington, DC
> *Portrait,* c. 1860, Museum of Modern Art, New York City
> *Thomas Cole,* c. 1845, National Portrait Gallery, Smithsonian
> Institution, Washington, DC

12. **Brandt, Bill, 1904–1983, England**

Brandt recorded the restricted life of England's working class prior to World War II. He later concentrated on portraits and landscapes, frequently incorporating Surrealistic experimentation.

> *At Charlie Brown's,* London, c. 1936, Museum of Modern Art,
> New York City
> *Portrait of a Young Girl, Eaton Place,* London, 1955, Museum of
> Modern Art, New York City

13. **Brassai (Gyula Halasz), 1899–1984, France**

When he moved to Paris from Transylvania, Brassai fell in love with Paris nightlife. His portraits of artists and writers were distinguished by his use of artificial light. He loved strolling the city streets and taking pictures in half-light.

> *Bijou of Montmarte,* 1933, Museum of Modern Art, New York City

14. **Bravo, Manuel Alvarez, 1902–2002, Mexico**

Recording the daily lives of Mexican people, using light to its best advantage, his black and white photos (frequently sepia toned) were studies in contrast.

How Small the World Is, 1942, Center for Creative Photography, University of Arizona, Tucson

Sparrow, Of Course (Skylight), 1938, International Museum of Photography at George Eastman House, Rochester, New York

15. **Callahan, Harry, 1912–1999, United States**

Callahan's sense of design was the basis of his many black and white photographs of city streets, nudes, patterns, and deliberate double exposures.

Chicago, c. 1950, Art Institute of Chicago

Detroit Street Scene, 1943, Art Institute of Chicago

Telephone Wires, c. 1968, Center for Creative Photography, University of Arizona, Tucson

16. **Cameron, Julia Margaret, 1815–1879, England**

Cameron staged her photos, often using people dressed in costume, to resemble the soft, romantic paintings popular in the mid-1800s.

Alice Liddell as Pomona, 1872, Metropolitan Museum of Art, New York City

Call, I Follow; I Follow, Let Me Die, c. 1867, Royal Photographic Society, Bath, England

The Astronomer: Sir John Herschel, 1867, Royal Photographic Society, London

17. **Capa, Robert (Andre Friedmann), 1913–1954, United States**

Capa was a *Life* magazine staff member, noted for his coverage of the Spanish Civil War and World War II. He landed with the Allied troops on D-Day.

Naples, 1943, Art Institute of Chicago

Soldier at the Moment of Death, Spanish Civil War, 1936, International Center of Photography, New York City

18. **Caponigro, Paul, 1932, United States**

Caponigro photographed megaliths of the British Isles and other ancient monuments while funded by a Guggenheim grant. He studied under Minor White and Alfred W. Richter.

Avebury Stone Circle, Avebury, Wiltshire, England, 1967, Museum of
Modern Art, New York City

Fungus, Ipswich, Massachusetts, 1962, International Museum of
Photography at George Eastman House, Rochester, New York

Kilclooney, 1967, International Museum of Photography at George
Eastman House, Rochester, New York

Stonehenge, 1967, International Museum of Photography at George
Eastman House, Rochester, New York

19. Cartier-Bresson, Henri, 1908, France

Cartier-Bresson would wait for what he called "The Decisive Moment" to
take a photo, selecting a place to photograph, then waiting for something to
happen in that space.

Behind the Gare Saint-Lazare, Paris, 1932, St. Louis Art Museum

Seville, Spain, 1933, J. Paul Getty Museum, Los Angeles

Siphnos, Greece, 1961, Museum of Modern Art, New York City

20. Coburn, Alvin Langdon, 1882–1966, England

Coburn specialized in city scenes and portraits of artists and writers. He
invented a kaleidoscopic mirror attachment for his camera that gave abstract
effects to images, which he called "vortographs."

Williamsburg Bridge, 1909, University of Texas, Austin

Vortograph, 1917, Art Institute of Chicago

21. Cunningham, Imogen, 1883–1976, United States

Cunningham specialized in scenes of the city, taken with a view camera. A
member of Group F.64, her lovely photos of calla lilies and other flowers
were known for their remarkable clarity.

The Unmade Bed, 1957, The Imogen Cunningham Trust, Berkeley,
California

Two Callas, 1929, The Imogen Cunningham Trust, Berkeley,
California

Water Hyacinth, c. 1928, St. Louis Art Museum

22. Curtis, Edward Sheriff, 1868–1952, United States

By the time Curtis began an earnest attempt to record Native American life
in his 20-volume publication, *The North American Indian,* few Indians were
wearing traditional dress. He staged some of his portraits, persuading his

subjects to change to infrequently worn ceremonial dress. He also documented an Alaskan expedition.

> *Waiting in the Forest—Cheyenne,* 1911, Metropolitan Museum of Art, New York City
>
> *Wishnam Fisherman,* 1909, Hallmark Photographic Collection, Kansas City, Missouri

23. Daguerre, Louis Jacques Mande, 1787–1851, France

Daguerre developed the process of sensitizing a metal plate and exposing it to create a one-of-a-kind photo. The daguerreotype bears his name.

> *Collection of Shells and Miscellany,* 1839, Conservatoire Nationale des Arts et Metiers, Paris
>
> *Premiere Epreuve fait par Daguerre devant ses Colleagues des Beaux-Arts,* 1839, Musée National des Techniques du CNAM, Paris
>
> *A Portrait of Charles L. Smith,* 1843, International Museum of Photography at George Eastman House, Rochester, New York

24. DeCarava, Roy, 1919, United States

DeCarava's photographs of Harlem and New York City followed his dictum "It must be good to look at." A painter and printmaker before becoming a photographer, he was the first black artist to ever win a Guggenheim fellowship. He became a mainstream photographer with his photos of famous jazz artists and the African American experience.

> *Coltrane No. 24,* 1963, Hallmark Photographic Collection, Kansas City, Missouri
>
> *Dancers, New York,* 1956, St. Louis Art Museum

25. Doisneau, Robert, 1912–1994, France

Doisneau photographed Parisian street-life during the mid-1950s. Artists such as Picasso, Braque, and Leger were also common subjects of his work. He was always on the lookout for "the oddities of life."

> *M. et Mme Garfino, Vagabonds,* 1951, Bibliothèque Nationale, Paris
>
> *Fox Terrier on the Pont des Arts,* 1953, The Witkin Gallery, Inc., New York City

26. **Eakins, Thomas, 1844–1916, United States**

Eakins, a professor at the Philadelphia Academy of Art, used photography as an aid in his paintings as early as 1880. His stop-action photos of horses pulling a carriage or an oarsman in a scull on the river were frequently the basis of his paintings. He was responsible for bringing Eadweard Muybridge to the University of Pennsylvania to demonstrate his "figure-in-motion" photography.

Female Nude from the Back, c. 1880, Metropolitan Museum of Art, New York City

Nude Broad Jumping, 1884–1885, The Library Company of Philadelphia

27. **Edgerton, Harold, 1903–1990, United States**

Edgerton's high-speed photos of such things as a bird's wing stopped in flight, a milk drop just as it splashes, or a bullet as it emerges after being shot through an apple demonstrate his creative ability at its best. Known as the inventor of the strobe flash, a deep-sea camera, and the underwater flash, his technical ability is legendary.

Milk Drop Coronet, 1936, Hallmark Photographic Collection, Kansas City, Missouri

28. **Evans, Frederick, 1853–1943, England**

Evans is known for the beautiful lighting of his architectural studies and interiors, and for portraits of literary figures.

York Minster: Into the North Transept, 1902, Museum of Fine Arts, Boston

The Sea of Steps, Wells Cathedral, 1903, Museum of Modern Art, New York City

29. **Evans, Walker, 1903–1975, United States**

Evans worked during the 1930s depression for the WPA-FSA. He photographed signs and billboards, often making ironic connections between out-of-work people posed next to signs of affluence.

Circus Poster, 1936, Metropolitan Museum of Art, New York City

View of Railroad Station, Edwards, Mississippi, 1936, San Francisco Museum of Modern Art

30. **Fox Talbot, William Henry, 1800–1877, England**

A pioneer in photography, Talbot was best known for developing the Calotype (sometimes called the Talbotype).

Courtyard Scene, c. 1844, National Museum of American History, Washington, DC

The Game Keeper, c. 1843, National Museum of American History, Washington, DC

Trafalgar Square, 1845, Nelson Column Under Construction, New York Public Library

31. **Frank, Robert, 1924, United States, b. Switzerland**

Frank worked as a commercial photographer for a time, then did a photo essay, *The Americans,* under a Guggenheim grant. Since 1960 he has spent most of his career working as a filmmaker.

Chicago, 1956, St. Louis Art Museum

Parade, Hoboken, New Jersey, 1955, Museum of Modern Art, New York City

US 285, New Mexico, c. 1956, Museum of Modern Art, New York City

32. **Friedlander, Lee, 1934, United States**

Friedlander sometimes photographs monuments. Many books of his work have been published, allowing him artistic freedom to take photographs that would express his view of the world. Not all photographers have enjoyed this independence because of the need to earn a living through studio or journalistic photography.

Colorado, 1967, Museum of Modern Art, New York City

Galax, Virginia, 1962, Museum of Modern Art, New York City

Gettysburg, 1974, Hallmark Photographic Collection, Kansas City, Missouri

33. **Frith, Francis, 1822–1898, England**

Frith brought faraway places to people through his many travel pictures.

Colossal Sculptures at Philae (Egypt), 1860, New York Public Library, New York City

The Great Pyramid at Giza, From the Plain, 1859, Library of Congress, Washington, DC

Fallen Colossus, c. 1858, Janet Lehr, Inc., New York

34. **Gardner, Alexander, 1821-1882, United States, b. Scotland**

Gardner was a contemporary of Abe Lincoln. His *Gardner's Photographic Sketch Book of the War*, published in 1866, documented some of the locales of battle and some photos taken by him during the Civil War.

> *Abraham Lincoln*, 1865, National Portrait Gallery, Smithsonian Institution, Washington, DC
>
> *Home of a Rebel Sharpshooter*, Gettysburg, 1863, Library of Congress, Washington, DC

35. **Gilpin, Laura, 1891-1979, United States**

Gilpin recorded the life of the Native American in her book *The Enduring Navajo*. At age 81 she took photographs of Canyon de Chelly from the ground and air.

> *Bryce Canyon #2*, 1930, Hallmark Photographic Collection, Kansas City, Missouri
>
> *Scissors, String and Two Books*, 1930, Amon Carter Museum, Fort Worth, Texas
>
> *Sunburst, the Castillo, Chichen Itza*, 1932, Amon Carter Museum, Fort Worth, Texas

36. **Herschel, Sir John Frederick, 1792-1871, England**

An astronomer by profession, Herschel became an early pioneer of photography through his association with Henry Fox Talbot and Daguerre. He is credited with inventing Hypo (the chemical "fixer" that allowed previous "fleeting" images to become permanent and unfading).

> *Latticed Window of Laycock Abbey*, 1835, Science Museum of London

37. **Hill, David Octavius, 1802-1870, Scotland, and Robert Adamson, 1821-1848, Scotland**

This photographic duo became known for portraiture of Scottish clerics and artists as well as cityscapes and architectural studies.

> *Highland Guard*, c. 1844–1845, Royal Photographic Society, Bath, England
>
> *John Henning and Female Audience*, c. 1844, Royal Photographic Society, Bath, England

38. **Hine, Lewis Wickes, 1874–1940, United States**

Hine's documentary photos of child-labor abuses led to labor reform for workers. He also photographed Ellis Island immigrants prior to World War I.

Fresh Air for the Baby, Italian Quarter, New York City, 1910, New York Public Library

Powerhouse Mechanic, c. 1925, Hallmark Photographic Collection, Kansas City, Missouri

Bowery Mission Bread Line, 1906, Museum of Modern Art, New York City

39. **Kasebier, Gertrude, 1852–1934, United States**

Kasebier was a portrait photographer and founding member of the Photo Secession. She was considered one of the leading portrait photographers in the United States.

Portrait of a Woman, c. 1900, International Museum of Photography at George Eastman House, Rochester, New York

Portrait of Auguste Rodin, 1906, Art Museum, Princeton University, Princeton, New Jersey

The Heritage of Motherhood, c. 1905, International Museum of Photography at George Eastman House, Rochester, New York

40. **Kertész, André, 1894–1985, United States, b. Hungary**

Kértesz demonstrated an outstanding sense of design in simple things such as a vase of flowers or a woman on a couch.

Chairs, The Medici Fountain, 1926, Museum of Fine Arts, Houston

Chez Mondrian, 1926, Art Institute of Chicago

Satiric Dancer, 1926, St. Louis Art Museum

41. **Koudelka, Josef, 1938, Czech Republic**

Koudelka photographed radical poverty in his homeland of Czechoslovakia (Czech Republic) and in Spain. His documentary photography book, *Gypsies,* was published in 1975.

Velka Lomnica, Czechoslovakia, 1966, Museum of Modern Art, New York City

Jarabina, 1963, Collection of the artist

42. **Lange, Dorothea, 1895–1965, United States**

During the Great Depression, she photographed migrant workers in California for the Works Progress Administration (WPA/FSA).

Funeral Cortege, The End of an Era in a Small Valley Town,
California, 1938, Oakland Museum, California
Migrant Mother, Nipomo, California, 1936, Oakland Museum,
California
Three Families, Fourteen Children, 1938, St. Louis Art Museum

43. **Lartigue, Jacques-Henri, 1894–1986, France**

Lartigue received his first camera at age 7, and quickly turned his keen eye to photography of French Society at the races, the beach at Deauville, and strolling in the park.

Gerard Willemetz and Dani, 1926, Association des Amis de J. H.
Lartigue, Paris
Grand Prix of the Automobile Club of France, 1912, Museum of
Modern Art, New York City
Paris, Avenue des Acacias, 1912, Museum of Modern Art,
New York City

44. **Levitt, Helen, 1918, United States**

Levitt's documentary photographs of New York City children in the slums are compared to those of Cartier-Bresson because they capture the "decisive moment." She was one of a number of "street photographers" who believed that a photographer must record what he or she sees—no more, no less.

New York, c. 1942, Museum of Modern Art, New York City

45. **Man Ray (Emmanuel Rudnitsky), 1890–1976, United States**

Man Ray mostly made "Rayographs." These were his version of the photogram, a contact print created with abstract shapes He was also well known for his solarized photographs that were exposed during the developing stage, creating a positive/negative effect, or a halo around the subject. His quirky view of life caused him to become a major figure in Dada and Surrealism. For example, one of his artworks is a photograph of an eye mounted on the hand of a metronome.

Gala Dali Looking at "The Birth of Liquid Desires," 1935, Boston
Museum of Fine Arts

Portrait of Jean Cocteau, 1922, J. Paul Getty Museum, Los Angeles

Rayogram, 1923, Museum of Modern Art, New York City

46. Mapplethorpe, Robert, 1946–1989, United States

Mapplethorpe beautifully photographed flowers and other serene subjects, but became a controversial figure through his later graphic exploration of human sexuality.

Ken Moody, 1983, Hallmark Photographic Collection, Kansas City, Missouri

Tulips, 1977, Museum of Modern Art, New York City

Thomas in a Circle, 1987, Estate of the artist

47. Model, Lisette, 1906–1985, United States

Model's unglamorous photographs of Americans on the beach reflected themes she had begun in Europe titled *Boredom, Greed, Self-satisfaction.* She portrayed ordinary people in ordinary situations.

Coney Island Bather, New York, 1940, © The Lisette Model Foundation

Promenade des Anglais, Nice, 1934, Hallmark Photographic Collection, Kansas City, Missouri

48. Moholy-Nagy, László, 1895–1946, United States

Moholy-Nagy was a founder of the American Bauhaus, especially known for his photograms and his photos taken from unusual viewpoints, such as looking straight down from the top of a building.

Abstraction (photogram), 1925, St. Louis Art Museum

Berlin Radio Tower, c. 1928, Art Institute of Chicago

Oskar Schlemmer, Ascona, 1926, Art Institute of Chicago

49. Morgan, Barbara, 1900–1992, United States

Morgan is primarily known for her photographs of dancer Martha Graham's professional life. She also specialized in children's portraiture and photomontages of New York City.

Letter to the World (Kick), 1994, Museum of Modern Art, New York City

50. **Muybridge, Eadweard, 1830–1904, United States**

Muybridge took 20,000 negatives of humans and animals to demonstrate the process of motion. For example, he arranged cameras all around a track to be tripped as a horse went by to show how at times all four legs were in the air. His photos of humans in motion have been considered the forerunner of the motion picture. He also photographed the Modoc Indian War and Western landscapes in Yosemite, California.

> *Athletes and Classical Groupings,* 1879, Stanford University Museum
>   of Art, Stanford, California
> *Daisy Jumping a Hurdle,* c. 1885, George Eastman House, Rochester,
>   New York
> *Nude Men, Motion Study,* 1877, Museum of Modern Art,
>   New York City

51. **Nadar (Gaspard-Félix Tournachon), 1820–1910, France**

Nadar was the "Annie Liebovitz" of Paris, able to bring character to life in his portraiture of famous people. He was the first to take photographs of Paris from a balloon. He also descended into the sewers and catacombs of Paris to take photos there by carbon arc lights.

> *Auguste Vacquerie,* 1855, The J. Paul Getty Museum, Los Angeles,
>   California
> *Sarah Bernhardt,* 1859, International Museum of Photography at
>   George Eastman House, Rochester, New York

52. **Newman, Arnold, 1918, United States**

Newman became known for his photographs of famous artists and musicians in their natural environment. One of his most famous photographs is Stravinsky at his piano. He also did industrial photography and abstractions.

> *Georgia O'Keeffe, Ghost Ranch, New Mexico,* 1968, © Arnold
>   Newman
> *Igor Stravinsky,* 1946, Collection of the artist

53. **Niépce, Joseph Nicéphore, 1765–1833, France**

In France, Niépce is credited with being the father of photography because he created the earliest surviving permanent (non-fading) photograph (of a view from a window). The lens of the camera was open for 8 hours for this exposure. He collaborated for a short time with Louis Daguerre.

> *View from His Window at La Gras,* 1827, University of Texas, Austin

54. **O'Sullivan, Timothy H., c. 1840–1882, United States**

O'Sullivan documented the Civil War. After the war he traveled throughout the West, documenting parts of the North American landscape that had not been seen before by most of the world.

> *Ancient Ruins in Canyon de Chelle, N.M.*, 1873, New York Public Library
>
> *Black Canyon, Colorado River, From Camp 8, Looking Above*, 1871, J. Paul Getty Museum, Los Angeles
>
> *Sand Dunes, Carson Desert*, 1867, National Archives, Washington DC

55. **Outerbridge, Paul, Jr., 1896–1958, United States**

While some of Outerbridge's work was straight commercial and editorial photography, he became associated with nudes and Surrealism. His photographs of ordinary objects became abstractions.

> *Cheese and Crackers*, 1922, Metropolitan Museum of Art, New York City

56. **Penn, Irving, 1917, United States**

Penn is known for his studio work of still lifes, portraiture, and monumental nudes that appeared to fill the picture plane. His illustrations were sometimes used in *Vogue* magazine. He also did documentary studies of Peru, New Guinea, and Morocco.

> *Duke Ellington, New York*, May 19, 1948, Hallmark Photographic Collection, Kansas City, Missouri
>
> *Woman with Umbrella, New York*, 1950, Hallmark Photographic Collection, Kansas City, Missouri

57. **Porter, Eliot, 1901–1990, United States**

Porter did documentary photos of Glen Canyon just before it was inundated by a dam built on the Colorado River. He specialized in photographs of nature, specifically in the Southwest, and won a Guggenheim fellowship to photograph birds.

> *Dark Canyon, Glen Canyon*, 1965, Art Institute of Chicago
>
> *Pool in a Brook, Pond Brook, Near Whiteface, New Hampshire*, October 1953, Metropolitan Museum of Art, New York City
>
> *Red Ossier*, 1945, Museum of Modern Art, New York City

58. **Riis, Jacob, 1849–1914, United States**

Riis, who began his career as a police reporter, became one of the earliest proponents of social reform through his photography. He admits that his photographic technique never became very good, but his nighttime flash photographs of the "underbelly" of New York City were effectively used in his lectures and one of his published books, *How the Other Half Lives.*

> *In the Home of an Italian Rag-Picker, Jersey Street,* c. 1888, Museum of the City of New York

59. **Rodchenko, Alexander, 1891–1956, Russia**

Rodchenko's photomontage compositions were used to help further the cause of a Socialist society. His abstract work, with its unusual camera angles, resembled that of László Moholy-Nagy.

> *Assembling for a Demonstration,* 1928, Museum of Modern Art, New York City

60. **Sander, August, 1876–1964, Germany**

Sander specialized in formal, documentary portraits demonstrating German genetic traits and occupations. His work was published in a book called *People of the Twentieth Century.*

> *Circus Artists,* 1930, Collection of John Dunivent
> *Group of Children, Westerwald,* 1920, J. Paul Getty Museum, Los Angeles
> *Police Officer,* 1925, Museum of Modern Art, New York City

61. **Sheeler, Charles, 1883–1965, United States**

One of the "Immaculates"—a group of photographers whose photos rarely included human beings, and whose rather sterile images were of mechanization and industry—Sheeler used the stark contrasts in his photographs as inspiration for his paintings.

> *Self-Portrait at Easel,* 1931–1932, Art Institute of Chicago
> *Stairwell,* 1914, Museum of Modern Art, New York City
> *Wheels,* 1939, Museum of Fine Arts, Boston

62. **Siskind, Aaron, 1903–1991, United States**

Although he began as a documentary photographer in the Great Depression, Siskind eventually became interested in photos of ordinary subjects (such as a flat rock or a wall with peeling posters) that became abstractions of reality.

> *Savoy Ballroom, New York,* 1936, George Eastman House, Rochester, New York
>
> *Pleasures and Terrors of Levitation 99,* 1961, Hallmark Photographic Collection, Kansas City, Missouri

63. Sleet, Moneta, 1926–1996, United States

Moneta Sleet's career primarily involved photographing famous African American entertainers and statesmen such as Haile Selassie, emperor of Ethiopia. He won a Pulitzer Prize in photography for his 1968 photograph of Coretta Scott King at Dr. King's funeral and took numerous photographs of Martin Luther King's family and his crusade against racism.

> *Billie Holiday,* 1956, *Ebony* magazine, September, 1956
>
> *Rosa Parks—Montgomery, Alabama,* 1956, *Ebony* magazine, July, 1956
>
> *Story Hour, St. Louis, Missouri,* 1991, St. Louis Art Museum

64. Smith, W. Eugene, 1918–1978, United States

War correspondent and *Life* photographer Smith's photo essays show his involvement with his subjects. One such example was his coverage of the Japanese village of Minamata, whose inhabitants suffered from mercury poisoning.

> *Tomoko in the Bath,* Museum of Fine Arts, Boston
>
> *Waiting for Survivors of the Andrea Doria Sinking,* 1956, Hallmark Photographic Collection, Kansas City, Missouri
>
> *Untitled* (Three soldiers with the Spanish Guardia Civil), 1950, Center for Creative Photography, University of Arizona, Tucson

65. Steichen, Edward, 1879–1973, United States

A member of the Photo Secession movement, Steichen is best known for his portraits. He believed that the personality of the photographer should not overshadow the reality of the subject.

> *Flatiron Building,* 1904, Metropolitan Museum of Art, New York City
>
> *Rodin—The Thinker,* 1902, Museum of Modern Art, New York City
>
> *Wind Fire: Therese Duncan on the Acropolis,* 1921, International Museum of Photography at George Eastman House, Rochester, New York

66. **Stieglitz, Alfred, 1864–1946, United States**

Stieglitz is considered the father of American Photography because of his work with *Aperture* magazine and his founding of the Little Galleries of the Photo Secession. He was married to artist Georgia O'Keeffe.

> *Hands, Georgia O'Keeffe,* 1920, Metropolitan Museum of Art, New York City
> *Flatiron,* 1902, National Gallery of Art, Washington, DC
> *Music: A Sequence of Ten Cloud Photographs, No. 1,* 1922, National Gallery of Art, Washington, DC

67. **Strand, Paul, 1890–1976, United States**

Strand was both an artist and a documentary photographer. His photography was sometimes quite abstract.

> *Chair Abstract, Twin Lakes, Connecticut,* 1916, San Francisco Museum of Modern Art
> *The Family, Luzzara, Italy,* 1953, Hallmark Photographic Collection, Kansas City, Missouri
> *Photograph, New York (Blind Woman),* 1916, Metropolitan Museum of Art, New York City

68. **Sudek, Josef, 1896–1976, Czech Republic**

During the Nazi occupation of his country, Sudek was restricted to his house and garden. His subject matter became the intimacy of small spaces, which continued to be a familiar theme in his work throughout his career.

> *Chair in Janacek's House,* 1972, J. Paul Getty Museum, Malibu, California

69. **Van Der Zee, James, 1886–1983, United States**

Van Der Zee photographed social events such as weddings, funerals, and graduations in Harlem where he lived for most of his career. His life's work inspired a James Van Der Zee Institute, sponsored by the Metropolitan Museum of Art in New York City.

> *Couple in Raccoon Coats,* c. 1929, Art Institute of Chicago

70. **Warhol, Andy, 1928–1987, United States**

Warhol popularized the use of photo silk screen, with his subjects ranging from film and political figures to starkly realistic electric chairs.

> *Lana Turner,* 1976–1987, Hallmark Photographic Collection, Kansas City, Missouri

Marilyn Monroe, 1967, Museum of Modern Art, New York City

Elvis, 1963, Australian National Gallery, Canberra

71. Watkins, Carleton E., 1829–1916, United States

Watkins documented the opening of the West. He was a photographic pioneer, taking his darkroom with him to expose and develop on site.

Mirror View, El Capitan, No. 38, c. 1866, New York Public Library

Mirror View, Yosemite Valley, c. 1866, Art Institute of Chicago

Yosemite Falls, c. 1878–1881, St. Louis Art Museum

72. Weegee (Arthur Fellig), 1899–1968, United States, b. Hungary

Weegee could be considered the stereotype of a tough city news photographer. He kept his radio turned to police calls, and usually made it to a crime scene with the police. His photos of expressions on the faces of onlookers sometimes told the story. New York City was his beat.

Hedda Hopper, 1953, Collection of John Coplans, New York City

The Critic, 1943, Hallmark Photographic Collection, Kansas City, Missouri

73. Weston, Edward, 1886–1958, United States

Weston was a member of Group F.64. His photography included vegetables, nudes, and sometimes vegetables that looked like nudes. His stark desert scenes and beach pictures demonstrated his mastery of design.

Dry Salt Pool, Point Lobos, 1939, Art Museum, Princeton University, Princeton, New Jersey

Nude, 1936, International Museum of Photography at George Eastman House, Rochester, New York

Pepper, 1930, Los Angeles County Museum of Art

Shell, 1927, Center for Creative Photography, University of Arizona, Tucson

74. White, Minor, 1908–1976, United States

Before becoming a photographer, White was a poet. He did documentary projects such as the iron-front buildings and waterfront areas of the West Coast, progressing from buildings to landscapes—to close-ups. His work reflected his commitment to the Asian Zen philosophy.

Pacific, Devil's Slide, California, 1947, Museum of Modern Art, New York City

Ritual Branch, 1958, The Art Museum, Princeton University, Princeton, New Jersey

Surf Vertical, San Mateo County, California, 1947, Art Institute of Chicago

75. Winogrand, Garry, 1928–1984, United States

A photojournalist, Winogrand worked exclusively with a 35mm camera, and was considered a street photographer "par excellence."

Circle Line Ferry, New York, 1971, Museum of Modern Art, New York City

Los Angeles, 1964, Museum of Modern Art, New York City

Utah, 1964, Center for Creative Photography, University of Arizona, Tucson

200 MORE NOTABLE PHOTOGRAPHERS

These photographers are among the thousands whose works have had an impact in the world of photography. Their work may be found in books, exhibitions, and photographic references. They are listed by the country where they spent most of their photographic careers.

BRAZIL

1. Muniz, Vik, 1961

CANADA

2. Karsh, Yousuf, 1908–2002
3. Rubenstein, Meridel, 1948

CZECH REPUBLIC

4. Drahos, Tom, 1947
5. Drtikol, Frantisek, 1878–1961
6. Hablik, Wenzel August, 1881–1934

ENGLAND

7. Arbuthnot, Malcolm, 1874–1968
8. Archer, Frederick Scott, 1813–1857
9. Armstrong-Jones, Anthony (Lord Snowdon), 1930
10. Beato, Felice, active c. 1850–1903
11. Bedford, Francis, 1816–1894
12. Burgin, Victor, 1941
13. Burrows, Larry, 1926–1971
14. Carroll, Lewis (Charles Lutwidge Dodgson), 1832–1898

ENGLAND *(continued)*

15. Clifford, Charles, 1800–1863
16. Collins, Hannah, 1956
17. Currey, Francis Edmund, 1814–1896
18. Delamotte, Phillip Henry, 1820–1889
19. Emerson, Peter Henry, 1856–1936
20. Fenton, Roger, 1819–1869
21. Filmer, Lady, c. 1840–1903
22. Fuss, Adam, 1961
23. Gabor, Dennis, 1900–1979
24. Galton, Francis, 1822–1911
25. Grace, John G., 1809–1889
26. Howlett, Robert, 1831–1858
27. Macpherson, Robert, 1811–1872
28. Maingot, Rosalind, 1891–1957
29. Man, Felix (Hans Baumann), 1893–1985
30. Price, William Lake, c. 1810–1896
31. Rejlander, Oscar Gustave, 1813–1875
32. Robinson, Henry Peach, 1830–1901
33. Sutcliffe, Frank Meadow, 1853–1941
34. Whistler, John, 1836–1897
35. Wilson, George Washington, 1823–1893

FRANCE

36. Aubry, Charles Hippolyte, 1811–1877
37. Baldus, Edouard Denis, 1815–1882
38. Bayard, Hippolyte, 1801–1877
39. Boubat, Edouard, 1923–1999
40. Braun, Adolphe, 1811–1877
41. Bustamante, Jean Marc, 1952
42. Cadmus, Paul, 1904–1999
43. Cahun, Claude, 1894–1954
44. Calle, Sophie, 1953
45. Carjat, Etienne, 1828–1906
46. Charbonnier, Jean-Philippe, 1921
47. Demachy, Robert, 1859–1937
48. Disderi, André A. E., 1819–1889
49. Ducamp, Maxime, 1822–1894
50. Famin, C., active 1860s–1870s
51. Faucon, Bernard, 1950
52. Fernique, Albert, active c. 1870–1904
53. Hauron, Louis Ducos, 1837–1920
54. Le Gray, Gustave, 1820–1882
55. Le Secq, Henri, 1818–1882
56. Marey, Etienne-Jules, 1830–1904
57. Marr, Dora, 1907–1997

FRANCE *(continued)*

58. Martin, Adolphe Alexandre, 1824–1886
59. Mieusement, Robert, active c. 1875
60. Negre, Charles, 1820–1880
61. Niépce, Joseph Nicéphore, 1765–1833
62. Robert, Louis, 1810–1882
63. Salzmann, Auguste, 1842–1872
64. Sieff, Jeanloup, 1933–2000
65. Vallou de Villeneuve, Julien, 1795–1866

GERMANY

66. Anschutz, Ottomar, 1846–1907
67. Auerbach, Ellen, 1906
68. Becher, Bernhard, 1931
69. Becher, Hilla Wobeser, 1934
70. Bing, Ilse, 1899–1998
71. Bischof, Werner, 1916–1954
72. Blossfeldt, Karl, 1865–1932
73. De Meyer, Baron Adolf, 1868–1946
74. Hausmann, Raoul, 1886–1971
75. Henri, Florence, 1893–1982
76. Kiefer, Anselm, 1945
77. Kuhn, Heinrich, 1866–1944
78. List, Herbert, 1903–1975

GERMANY *(continued)*

79. Peterhans, Walter, 1897–1960
80. Prinz, Bernhard, 1953
81. Renger-Patzsch, Albert, 1897–1966
82. Salomon, Dr. Erich, 1886–1944
83. Schwitters, Kurt, 1887–1948
84. Sieverding, Katherina, 1944
85. Steinert, Otto, 1915–1978
86. Struth, Thomas, 1954
87. Trockel, Rosemarie, 1952

ITALY

88. Alinari, Leopoldo, 1832–1865
89. Gioli, Paolo, 1942
90. Modotti, Tina, 1896–1942

JAPAN

91. Akiyama, Ryoji, 1942
92. Araki, Nobuyoshi, 1940
93. Fukuhara, Shinzo, 1883–1948
94. Hanawa, Gingo, 1957
95. Hosoe, Eikoh, 1933
96. Ishimoto, Yasuhiro, 1921
97. Nojima, Yasuzo, 1889–1964
98. Sugimoto, Hiroshi, 1948

MEXICO

99. Yampolsky, Marians, 1925

NETHERLANDS

100. Boonstra, Rommert, 1942
101. Dibbets, Jan, 1941
102. Evers, Winfred, 1954
103. Hocks, Teun, 1947
104. Oorthuys, Cas, 1908–1975
105. Sixma, Tjarda, 1962
106. Zwerver, Ton, 1951

NEW ZEALAND

107. Geddes, Anne
108. Webb, Boyd, 1947

POLAND

109. Vishniac, Roman, 1897–1990
110. Witkiewicz, Stanislaw Ignacy, 1855–1939

RUSSIA

111. Baltermants, Dmitry, 1912–1991
112. Khaldei, Yevgeny, 1917
113. Kozyrev, Yuri
114. Lissitzky, El, 1890–1941

SCOTLAND

115. Annan, James Craig, 1864–1946
116. Colvin, Calum, 1961

SWITZERLAND

117. Bischof, Werner, 1916–1954
118. Fischli, Peter, 1952
119. Schulthess, Emil, 1913–1996
120. Weiss, David, 1946

UNITED STATES

121. Acconci, Vito, 1940
122. Anderson, Paul L., 1880–1956
123. Anthony, Edward, 1818–1888
124. Antin, Eleanor, 1935
125. Arnold, Charles Dudley, 1844–1917
126. Arnold, Eve, 1913
127. Austen, E. Alice, 1866–1952
128. Baldessari, John, 1931
129. Baltz, Lewis, 1945
130. Barney, Tina, 1945
131. Barrow, Thomas F., 1938
132. Bayer, Herbert, 1900–1986
133. Bearden, Romare, 1914–1988
134. Brigman, Anne, 1869–1950
135. Bruguiere, Francis Joseph, 1879–1945
136. Bullock, Wynn, 1902–1975
137. Campus, Peter, 1937
138. Casebere, James, 1953
139. Christenberry, William, 1936
140. Coplans, John, 1920

UNITED STATES *(continued)*

141. Cornell, Joseph, 1903–1972
142. Cosindas, Marie, 1925
143. Dater, Judy, 1941
144. Davidson, Bruce, 1933
145. Davis, Lynn, 1944
146. Eastman, Michael, 1947
147. Eisenstaedt, Alfred, 1898–1995
148. Erwitt, Elliott, 1928
149. Eugene, Frank, 1895–1936
150. Falkenstein, Claire, 1908–1997
151. Feininger, Andreas, 1906–1999
152. Frank, Robert, 1924
153. Genthe, Arnold, 1869–1942
154. Gowin, Emmet, 1941
155. Haas, Ernst, 1921–1986
156. Heinecken, Robert, 1931
157. Hoyningen-Huene, George, 1900–1968
158. Jackson, William Henry, 1843–1942
159. Jacobi, Lotte, 1896–1990
160. Kanaga, Consuela, 1894–1978
161. Kasten, Barbara, 1936
162. Kepes, Gyorgy, 1906–2001
163. Klein, William, 1928
164. Klett, Mark, 1952
165. Koons, Jeff, 1955
166. Krims, Les, 1942

167. Lanker, Brian, 1947
168. Laughlin, Clarence John, 1905–1985
169. Lavenson, Alma, 1897–1989
170. Levine, Sherrie, 1947
171. Liberman, Alexander, 1912–1999
172. Lynes, George Platt, 1907–1955
173. Lyon, Danny, 1942
174. Mann, Sally, 1951
175. Matta-Clark, Gordon, 1943–1978
176. Metzker, Ray, 1931
177. Moon, Karl E., 1878–1948
178. Newhall, Beaumont, 1908–1993
179. Nixon, Nicholas, 1947
180. Parker, Olivia, 1941
181. Parks, Gordon, 1912
182. Ritts, Herb, 1952–2003
183. Rosenblum, Walter, 1919
184. Rothstein, Arthur, 1915–1985
185. Ruscha, Edward, 1937
186. Serrano, Andres, 1950
187. Shahn, Ben, 1898–1969
188. Shore, Stephen, 1947
189. Slavin, Neal, 1941
190. Starn, Doug and Mike (twins), 1961
191. Ulmann, Doris, 1884–1934

UNITED STATES *(continued)*

192. Van Dyke, Willard, 1906–1986

193. Vroman, Adam Clark, 1856–1916

194. Weems, Carrie Mae, 1950

195. Weston, Brett, 1911–1993

196. Weston, Cole, 1919

197. White, Clarence H., 1871–1925

198. Wilke, Hannah, 1940–1993

199. Wojnaronicz, David, 1955–1992

200. Wolcott, Marion Post, 1910–1990

"Photography is not about the thing photographed. It is how that thing looks that is photographed."

—GARRY WINOGRAND, 1928–1984, American photographer

DIGITAL ARTISTS

Digital photography is still such a new art form, and has so much potential, that artists are pioneering ways to use it in their artwork. Applications include animation, commercial art, Web pages, and "art for art's sake." Of course, because of the ease of combining words with visual images, a primary use for the medium is advertising. Web sites, interactive video, and computer games all take advantage of the potential for digital art.

Computer animation, another digital art form, has been done for twenty years or more, but has become increasingly sophisticated. With computer animation, animated films can be brought to life in a relatively short time period (especially when compared with the years it used to take to produce a film such as *Snow White* or *Beauty and the Beast*).

Art galleries are now showing national and international digital artists in their exhibitions. As with any new medium, artists are pushing the boundaries. Sometimes they produce the artwork, then change it by transferring it to the computer. Or they produce the work on the computer, then translate it into another medium such as sculpture. Sculptor Robert Lazzarini distorts ordinary objects (a telephone or skull) on the computer, then translates the distortions back into the original materials (cast bone, plastic, and so on). This new technology is similar to the early days of photography, when artists and photographers were experimenting and almost daily making new discoveries.

In this relatively new field, a few names begin to emerge from the pack. The work of the following artists may be seen in galleries, on Web sites, and in books.

CANADA

Wall, Jeff

ENGLAND

Cohen, Harold
Hamilton, Richard
Hockney, David

UNITED STATES

Acconci, Vito
Blake, Jeremy
Haacke, Hans
Hébert, Jean-Pierre
Kosuth, Joseph
Lazzarini, Robert

UNITED STATES *(continued)*

Molnar, Vera
Napier, Mark
Noll, Michael
Pfeiffer, Paul
Ritchie, Matthew
Schwartz, Lillian
Simon, John F., Jr.
Spalter, Ann Morgan
Steinkamp, Jennifer
Sze, Sarah
Truckenbrod, Joan
Vanderbeek, Stan
Weintraub, Annette
Wright, Michael

"Stieglitz would never say that certain objects of the world were more or less beautiful than others—telegraph poles, for instance, compared with oak trees. He would accept them for what they are, and use the most appropriate object to express his thoughts and convey his vision."
—ANSEL ADAMS, 1902–1984, landscape photographer and member of the Farm Security Administration (FSA) photographers

Index